DERIC McKAMEY's
2008
Minor League Baseball Analyst

Shandler Enterprises LLC
Roanoke, VA

Shandler Enterprises LLC
P.O. Box 20303
Roanoke, VA 24018

Offices	540-772-6315
Fax	540-772-1969
Customer service	800-422-7820

E-mail	info@baseballhq.com
Internet	http://www.baseballhq.com/books/mlba.shtml

Deric McKamey's Minor League Baseball Analyst is intended for entertainment purposes only. Neither the author nor publisher assume any liability beyond the purchase price for any reason.

Cover design by Jon Resh@Go-Undaunted.com
Cover photograph by Ron Shandler

ISBN 978-1-891566-72-1
Printed in the United States of America

ACKNOWLEDGMENTS

Authoring the third edition of this prospect book has been an honor and would not be possible without the support of the following people:

My wife, Leeanna, and daughters, Megan, Kristen, and Shannon. You continue to sacrifice a lot to allow me to indulge in something I love and have patiently let me squeeze in a couple of minor league games during our family vacations.

My parents, John and Louise McKamey, who brought me into this world, introduced me to baseball, and raised me to respect people and always strive to do my best.

Ron Shandler, for giving my first analysis job and the opportunity to author this book. You have been both a boss and friend to me the past twelve years, and I am proud to be associated with you and your excellent work.

Terry Linhart, for partnering with me twelve years ago and getting me into this mess. None of this would have been possible without you and I value your friendship tremendously.

David Rawnsley, for your friendship and your knowledge of baseball that you imparted to me. A lot of what I do comes from your comprehension and blending of both scouting and statistical analysis.

Rob Gordon, for compiling and generating the statistics in the book and being a valuable member of the minor league department at Baseball HQ.

No prospect analysis would be possible by anyone without the fine work of *Baseball America*. Minor league baseball is more accessible and a better game through their outstanding coverage.

I have never viewed fellow prospect analysts as competitors, but as friends who continually push me to do better. Jim Callis, Jeremy Deloney, David Cameron and John Sickels have a great deal of baseball knowledge, and I enjoy sharing information with all of them.

There are hundreds of people in the game of baseball who have shared their thoughts with me on scouting, player development, and coaching, knowingly and unknowingly, and I have valued each and every one of them over the years. My sincerest thanks go to Jeff Luhnow, Jim Martz, Brian Hopkins, Brian Graham, Spin Williams, Mark Shapiro, Ross Atkins, Dan O'Brien, Gene Bennett, Jerry Narron, Dave Miley, Bob Boone, Ron Oester, Jack Billingham, Joe Nuxhall, Donnie Scott, Sixto Lezcano, Bobby Valentine, Mike Davis, Craig Colbert, Wally Joyner, Jerry Reuss, Charlie Poe, Joe Pittman, Keith Law, Greg Hunter, and Marc Gustafson.

The Major League Scouting Bureau, including Don Pries, Frank Marcos, and Jim Elliott, for allowing me to attend the Scout Development Program. I have a better understanding of hitting/pitching mechanics and the evaluation of amateur players after going through your program.

I have been fortunate to work with and associate with some excellent baseball writers and industry people over the years. Thank you to Jeff Barton, John Burnson, Doug Dennis, Jeff Erickson, Jason Gray, Vince Koza, Gene McCaffrey, Steve Moyer, Mat Olkin, Nate Ravitz, Joe Sheehan, Scott Smith, Todd Walker, Brian Walton and Rick Wilton.

CONTENTS

INTRODUCTION and METHODS

This year, I did something I have not done in awhile; I read and studied subject matter that was not related to baseball or The Bible. Now, before everyone assumes that I'm a non-intellectual type or am narrowly focused, the honest reason is that I haven't taken the time to delve into other subjects. My latest readings have centered on understanding personality and how it relates to others.

Learning about the traits and tendencies (or makeup, if you will) that make me who I am has always intrigued me. Most people, to themselves, believe they are entirely normal and what they believe is right, and in most cases, that may be so. However, the things we say, the body language we give off, or our reactions, may not always be interpreted the way we want, and thus, it is very important to be able to understand others and to adapt in some cases if we want things to go smoothly.

You may be asking yourself, "How does reading books on makeup, molding personality, and understanding people have anything to do with baseball?" Plenty.

Though minor league baseball players aren't in the spotlight like their Major League counterparts, we do view them on an elevated status. Oftentimes, we forget that they are people too, and young, impressionable people at that. All of these players have shown above average baseball ability at some point, otherwise, they wouldn't have been drafted and/or signed in the first place. These players gained attention through their physical skills and/or performance, which are things that scouts can quantify.

But what about things that are difficult to quantify, such as instincts, intelligence, confidence, work habits, and the ability to adapt? In some cases, a scout can gauge some of these traits if they have seen the player a number of times or have talked to enough people that have, but you never really know until these players are put in the very situations in which they are expected to succeed.

Most, if not all, baseball players were the best players on their high school or college teams and are used to performing well. In the minor leagues, they are placed in organizations with players who are just as good, if not better, than they are. How do they deal with the increased competition? How do they handle adversity, whether it be performance or environment related? How do they cope when they aren't promoted on their timetable?

The prevalence of high school showcases and travel baseball has lessened the anxiety associated with increased competition, but it is the issues that aren't under a player's control (performance and organizational handling) that usually causes the most stress. While we hear about the extreme cases of players who react violently when faced with adversity, like Elijah Dukes and Delmon Young, there are an equal number of players who handle situations differently, perhaps wilting under pressure quietly and never living up to their potential.

Many teams give each amateur player a psychological test prior to the Draft. This can provide some of the answers that I have been reading in the personality books. Some clubs also employ psychologists to help players deal with their various issues.

The aforementioned traits are extremely important for success on the baseball diamond, and most of the better players have most, if not all, of these traits. But a player still has to have the physical skills to succeed. A player cannot will himself to a .300 batting average just because he has excellent instincts and works hard. A pitcher won't win 20 games solely because he is confident and can out-think hitters.

Still, the makeup of the player may often determine how his skills develop. Confidence is especially important and one that I look for constantly during games. You can tell by the movement of a foot or the hips if a hitter shows fear at the plate. A pitcher may be reluctant to pitch inside, showing a lack of confidence in his pitches and/or command. On the flip side, players that have above average instincts will have their tools play up, just because they may play a little harder or smarter than their competition.

Makeup is also important in regard to opportunities. Players with marginal physical skills, but a tireless work ethic and instincts that are off-the-chart will often get an extra opportunity or become the player that an organization likes to hang on to. If I were a player development director, I would love to have my minor league fillers be those types whose work ethic and attitude rubs off on the other players.

Though we may not be able to easily quantify makeup, we can observe those types of traits in players. There are attributes that can be measured objectively and that's what this book is about. The rankings and comments are certainly subjective, but the statistics are factual and much of the scouting information is quantifiable. It is this subjectivity that makes this book unique and hopefully, paints an accurate picture of each player.

METHODS

The analysis contained in this book is a blend of traditional scouting and statistical analysis. As in any line of work, to be successful, an individual should have knowledge of all pertinent information available to them. That is the way I have tried to approach the analysis of minor league players; to know as much about scouting techniques and statistical analysis as I possibly can.

When I first started analyzing minor leaguers, I leaned more to the statistical analysis side. I was a season ticket holder for the Fort Wayne Wizards and would travel to Indianapolis for Triple-A games, but the majority of my rankings were based on stats and formulas that I trusted.

Working for Baseball HQ the past 13 years, I've had the privilege of having media access to both Major and minor league games, spring training, and the Arizona Fall League. I have never been shy about approaching general managers, scouts, player development personnel, managers, coaches, and players, trying to tap into their knowledge and perspectives about baseball. All have imparted their wisdom to me and each trip to the ballpark is counted as a learning experience. Gradually, as I have gained more knowledge and understanding about the game, I have gravitated towards the scouting side of analysis.

I was very fortunate to be able to expand on this knowledge by attending the Major League Scouting Bureau's Scout Development Program in 2002, through the generosity of the Scouting Bureau and *Street & Smith's* publications, which I have provided minor league coverage for the past five years. The information attained while attending the program, especially in the breakdown of hitting and pitching mechanics and judging body types, provides the backbone of the knowledge that I use today.

What I believe separates me from other analysts is the depth of analysis. It doesn't take a brain surgeon to deduce that a pitcher with a 1.2-1 strikeout-to-walk ratio has below average command, but I want to know *why*. Does he fail to repeat his delivery, does he nibble at the strike zone, or is he just plain wild?

Similarly, a hitter may have a propensity to strike out. Does he have a long swing, possess a slow trigger, fail to recognize pitches, or show fear at the plate? In both cases, the stats will reveal the weaknesses, but the weaknesses can also be backed up through visualization (scouting).

Nothing is as important as seeing the player. I try to get to as many minor league games as possible and make annual trips to spring training in Florida and the Arizona Fall League, but I do not get to see every player. That is impossible for one person. Some analysts will admit to seeing virtually no games, while others will claim to see hundreds. Seeing a great volume of games might be nice, but if you don't know how to properly analyze what you see, it will not do you any good.

Minor league analysts judge players in a variety of ways. I prefer the combination method of scouting and statistical analysis. Here is a breakdown of how I evaluate players:

Body types

Before evaluating a hitter or pitcher's tools, I like to note their body type and athletic ability, targeting athletes who possess the abilities of strength, speed, and agility. I believe that players who are athletic and demonstrate good mechanics usually turn out to be better players and have a better chance to improve. Strength is such a big part of today's game and it is important to establish which players possess it and which players project to have it through physical maturity. Some players are not athletic and are not projectable, but can still play the game. Being athletic in and of itself does not make one a better baseball player, but it gives a player a better chance to succeed.

Hitting

Hitting is the most important skill for a position player, as that usually determines if they make it to the Majors or not. Strength is the most important ingredient to hitting and allows the hitter to generate bat speed and drive the baseball. Most good hitters will demonstrate balance, a quick and timely trigger, hands going back before going forward, a short stride, proper extension as they make contact, and proper weight transfer.

Three other factors are common to good hitters; bat plane, confidence, and plate discipline. The plane of the bat through the strike zone determines the trajectory of the baseball. Most hitters possess a slight uppercut, but there are those who have extreme uppercuts or chop at the baseball. Confidence plays a bigger role than most would think. Good hitters want to be at the plate and attack the baseball with controlled aggression. Hitters who show fear by stepping "into the bucket" or who flinch will face an uphill battle in trying to hit. Plate discipline involves discerning balls and strikes, recognizing pitches, and knowing which pitches to swing at. How a hitter judges the strike zone can be visualized during his at-bats and can be measured statistically by his batting eye and OBP.

The two biggest ingredients for a hitter to generate offense is the ability to get on base and hit for power. On-base percentage correlates well with runs scored and is a function of a hitter's ability to make contact and draw walks. Measuring power statistically has its plusses and minuses, but I like to use a combination of slugging percentage, isolated power, and extra-base hit rate. I also like to look at the basic stats, such as HR and doubles, noting that a young hitter with some body projection may be able to turn some of those doubles into HR as he matures. As with any stat, one must pay attention to the age of the player, level of competition, and ballpark factors.

Speed

Speed is an important aspect of baseball on both offense and defense. The stolen base can be a weapon offensively, but is a generally overrated statistic. Base-stealers need to run in the right situations and need to be successful two-thirds of the time to have value. Possessing the speed to beat out infield singles and take the extra base may be of greater importance. Speed in and of itself doesn't guarantee a good baserunner. Baserunning is very instinctual, with the better players knowing when to run and having the proper technique to round the bases. The speed rating in this book factors speed, instincts, and aggressiveness.

Defensively, raw speed is mostly reserved for outfielders, giving them the ability to range after fly balls. Agility and first-step quickness are more important attributes to defenders, allowing them to reach batted balls quickly. I believe that defensive speed is more effectively judged by observing players on a daily basis.

Fielding

Fielding can sometimes carry a player to the Major Leagues. For middle infielders, I look for agility, quickness, arm strength, soft/quick hands, and instincts. Fielders with soft hands usually give the impression that the baseball disappears into the glove. Possessing hard hands may be a detriment, but is a correctable flaw. Positioning and turning the double play are traits that usually come with experience. Corner infielders should exhibit arm strength, soft hands, and first-step quickness.

Outfielders need to show agility, quickness, speed, and arm strength. Having quickness and speed alone do not give the outfielder range, as they must also take the proper angles and routes. Demonstrating good arm strength is a plus, but accuracy and throwing to the proper base/cut-off man is important as well. I do not always get a chance to look at a fielder during game conditions, so paying close attention to pre-game infield/outfield practice is imperative.

The catching position is the most difficult position to play. A good catcher should possess arm strength, agility, receiving skills, and durability. Good arm strength is beneficial in halting the running game, but equally important is the glove-to-hand transfer and proper footwork. Agility and receiving skills are also important in the development of a good catcher. You want a catcher who moves well behind the plate, can get out and field the bunt, and block the plate. Being a good receiver entails having soft hands with a knack for framing pitches. Game calling and leadership skills come with experience and are usually measured at the upper levels of the minors.

There are several available defensive metrics such as Range Factor, Win Shares, and Ultimate Zone Rating, which have their usefulness, but each has its limitations.

Pitching

Pitching comes down to velocity, movement, deception, and command, but to evaluate pitching correctly, it must be broken down into its component parts. Arm action is the first thing I look for. The better the arm action, the livelier the arm, and hence more velocity and movement a pitcher will have. Pitchers like Roy Oswalt and Erik Bedard have impressive arm action. The ball appears to explode out of their hands, though their arm action is very fluid and quiet. Pitchers that demonstrate effort to their deliveries can become problematic. While these pitchers can still throw hard, it is difficult for them to maintain their velocity at higher pitch counts and leaves them susceptible to injury.

Velocity is related to the pitcher's arm strength, ability to generate leverage through proper mechanics, and hand speed. The ability of a pitcher to hold velocity throughout the game is important for starting pitchers. Scouts are usually equipped with a radar gun to measure velocity, but in lieu of not having a radar gun velocity and movement can be noted by how often pitches miss hitters' bats, the number of broken bats, how often a hitter is fooled, and/or the number of groundballs.

While the velocity of a fastball is its primary component, movement also plays an important role in its overall quality. Pitchers like Derek Lowe and Brandon Webb possess average fastball velocity, but with the tremendous movement that they get on their sinker, the final fastball grade would be well above average. The velocity component is weighed more heavily at the amateur level.

Deception can come in the form of hiding the baseball, preventing the hitter from seeing the release too soon, and by repeating the delivery on all of the pitches, keeping hitters off balance. Repeating a delivery not only creates deception, but is very integral to a pitcher's command. Pitchers will not only want to repeat their arm action, but will want to show the same arm slot for every pitch. Athletic types are better equipped to repeat their deliveries more consistently and make mechanical adjustments than non-athletic pitchers. Pedro Martinez and Greg Maddux are masters at repeating their delivery, which is one of the major reasons for their success.

The pitch common to all pitchers is the fastball. Pitchers possess one or both types of fastballs, a four-seam, which appears to maintain its plane through the strike zone, and a two-seam, which has sinking action. Four-seam fastballs are generally thrown harder and are common to most power pitchers. Fastballs that possess horizontal movement will behave in one of three different ways; boring (into the batter hard), tailing (into the batter slightly), and cutting

(away from the batter).

Some pitchers throw a cut fastball, which is accomplished by the pitcher cutting off his extension out front and/or applying different finger pressures. They may also throw a split-fingered fastball (forkball), which is thrown with the fingers spread apart against the seams, and demonstrates violent downward movement.

The curveball and slider are the two most common breaking pitches. Curveballs should have a tight rotation, breaking late in a vertical direction, and are more effective from high arm angles. The curveball will appear to spin on a single point as it arrives to the plate. The slider is held with two fingers on the narrow part of the seams. It should have tight rotation as well and make a sharp, horizontal break. On its way to the plate, a slider will appear to be spinning with a small round circle in the middle.

A slurve is a less effective breaking pitch, having a slower rotation and appearing to be more flat. A lack of arm speed is usually the culprit. Some pitchers will vary their curveball grip and throw a knuckle-curve, bit is a little more difficult to command.

Most successful starting pitchers will also possess an off-speed pitch. Change-ups can take the form of a circle-change, straight-change, or palmball. To be effective, they need to be 8-10 MPH slower than the fastball and be thrown with the same arm speed. Trick pitches like a knuckle-curve or screwball can serve as breaking or off-speed pitches, and though they often show good movement, they are much tougher to control.

Measuring pitching statistically can be more complicated than measuring offense and goes beyond the traditional ERA. While important, ERA can be affected by external factors such as team defense and the bullpen. To evaluate pitching, I like to use numbers that are situation independent like strikeouts per game (K/9 or DOM), walks per game (BB/9 or CTL), home runs per game (HR/9), and strikeout-to-walk ratio (K/BB or CMD); all of which remain under the control of the pitcher.

Individually, these statistics can accent what we know about the pitcher from a scouting perspective. Strikeouts per game, along with hits per game (H/9) and a pitcher's opposition batting average (oppBA), measure a pitcher's stuff and his ability to miss bats. Home runs per game, along with a pitcher's groundball/flyball ratio can show a pitcher's ability to keep the ball down and prevent extra-base hits. Walks per game and strikeout-to-walk ratio can show the pitcher's ability to throw strikes.

ERA is still a valuable tool, but it must be looked at within the context of a pitcher's peripheral skills and with a ballpark adjustment. I like to look at a newer statistic called expected ERA (xERA) which represents the expected ERA of a pitcher based on the distribution of strikeouts, walks, hits, and home runs allowed (see glossary). xERA should mirror ERA, but variances exist and can be accounted for by examining additional statistics.

Final note

The rankings in this book are the creation of the minor league department at Baseball HQ. While several baseball personnel contributed player information to the book, no opinions were solicited or received in comparing players.

ESSAYS

The rebound from a poor season

by Jeremy Deloney

It isn't surprising to see prospects that have stellar campaigns appear on pre-season Top 100 lists for the following season. After all, most top prospects churn out high-caliber statistics at each level of the minors. But should one poor season derail that player's potential? Does a misstep on the path to the Majors reduce that player to a non-prospect?

There are a number of reasons why prospects have seasons that fail to match previous successful seasons. Injuries could strike or perhaps expectations were much too high. Maybe that player just couldn't find his groove. Or, possibly previous success was the outlier. Whatever the explanation, every year there are players who either drop down on Top 100 lists or fall out altogether. Let's examine ten such prospects that had disappointing 2007 seasons and determine whether they should still be considered among the elite in the minors.

Daniel Bard (RHP, BOS) was the Red Sox' first round selection in the 2006 draft out of North Carolina. He didn't pitch in organized ball in 2006, but expectations were high entering 2007. He began the season in Baseball HQ's Top 100 list (#91) and started his campaign in the High-A California League, an aggressive assignment. After five horrendous starts, Bard was demoted to the Low-A South Atlantic League where he continued to experience command problems.

For the season, he was 3-7 with a 7.08 ERA, 9.4 Ctl and 5.6 Dom. He can run his explosive fastball into the high 90s and he complements it with a hard curveball and slider that can wipe out hitters. At times, he can be unhittable. Unfortunately he couldn't find the plate. Bard, 22, is tall and athletic (6'4"/185#) and has the talent to rebound quickly. He pitched in the bullpen in the Hawaiian Winter League, but still had command issues. With a more consistent delivery and arm slot, Bard could still become a top-notch pitcher. The likelihood of that has diminished, but the talent is still there.

Command and control problems also haunted 20 year-old **Brandon Erbe** (RHP, BAL). The 6'4" 180 pounder was coming off a highly successful 2006 season when he was virtually untouchable in Low A. That success didn't carry over to 2007. Erbe struggled all season long and posted a 6.26 ERA at High-A Frederick. He walked too many hitters (4.7 Ctl) and was forced to use his fastball too often as he was consistently behind in the count. Much like Bard, Erbe has a plus fastball and a hard breaking ball with late bite. Also like Bard, he may move to the bullpen if he can't find more consistency or a dependable off-speed pitch.

As a flyball pitcher, Erbe will need to maintain a high Dom in order to succeed. His delivery can get out of whack, especially when he overthrows. On the bright side, he's still very young and has the projectable body and athleticism to regain his prospect status. Though he may not be found on Top 100 lists entering 2008 (he was #62 on

HQ's 2007 list), Erbe still has significant upside due to his arm and his youth.

There aren't many prospects with the athleticism of 22 year-old **Dexter Fowler** (OF, COL). At 6'4"/175 lb, he offers outstanding baseball instincts in addition to his power potential, plus speed and defensive tools. The switch-hitter, #86 on the 2007 Top 100 list, got off to a slow start, but was batting .273/.397/.367 at High-A Modesto before he broke his hand in June. Fowler's power hasn't developed as quickly as hoped and he's hitting an inordinate amount of groundballs as he's learning his swing. He's also been sidetracked by injuries.

There are a lot of things to like about Fowler, however. His batting skills should continue to improve – he has excellent bat speed to go along with a mature hitting approach. He gets on base consistently and isn't afraid to work the count. He also has above average defensive skills, including a strong arm and good range. Fowler returned from his hand injury to play in the Arizona Fall League and he should be at full strength to begin 2008. He's likely to begin 2008 back in the California League, but he's one to keep an eye on.

It isn't often you'll see #1 overall draft picks fall out of the spotlight, but **Luke Hochevar** (RHP, KC) has gained some detractors after a so-so 2007 season. The 24 year-old was #31 on HQ's Top 100 entering 2007 and he began the season in Double-A. He proved to be hittable (4.69 ERA in 16 starts), but was nevertheless promoted to Triple-A where he posted a 5.12 ERA in 10 starts. He finished the season in the Majors.

Hochevar has the talent to become a #2 or #3 starter in the big leagues. He has a plethora of above average offerings and the ability to dominate while also keeping the ball on the ground. Hochevar also throws consistent strikes and can use any pitch in any count. He ran into trouble in 2007 when he started to nibble at the corners. Once he trusts his stuff and polishes his overall game, he could become one of the AL's top starters. Hochevar will still show up on Top 100 lists, but without as much fanfare as his first full-season of pro ball in 2007. He has a chance to begin 2008 in the Royals starting rotation.

After a surprising 2006 campaign in which he hit .371/.467/.484 in Rookie ball, 20 year-old **Cedric Hunter** (OF, SD) failed to live up to lofty expectations in 2007. He hit .282/.344/.373 in the Low-A Midwest League, but looked very raw at times. Ranked #93 prior to the 2007 season, Hunter was one of the youngest players in the league and he got better as the season progressed.

He should continue to hit for a high BA because of his good plate discipline and smooth stroke. Whether his bat speed translates to power is yet to be seen. The left-handed hitting Hunter was mature enough to hit .340/.394/.447 against lefties in 2007 and should continue to get better as he becomes more polished. He has the speed to steal bases, but his techniques must improve. He also could become a stellar defender, but poor routes have hampered him thus far. Hunter's upside may not be as high as previously thought, but he still has a chance to become a starting centerfielder down the line. Perhaps previous expectations were just a tad too high.

Falling victim to the curse of Pirates first round picks was 22 year-old **Brad Lincoln** (RHP, PIT). After an outstanding collegiate career at the University of Houston, Pittsburgh selected him with the fourth overall pick in 2006. Unfortunately, he underwent Tommy John surgery in April 2007 and didn't pitch all season. He was ranked #52 in 2007; not pitching in 2007 and starting 2008 late will probably keep him off most Top 100 lists. But that doesn't mean he's not a top prospect.

Armed with a fastball that reaches 96 MPH and a sinking two-seamer, Lincoln has the ability to pound the strike zone. He's an aggressive pitcher with a hard curveball that notches strikeouts. However, he's experienced some trouble commanding his change-up and a long layoff won't help in that regard. In addition, he's only 5'11" and that could lead to durability issues. Though he may not pitch until mid 2008, many eyes will be on Lincoln as he attempts to reach the Majors quickly. He has the athleticism and pitch mix to do so.

Jeff Niemann (RHP, TAM) could begin 2008 at the tail-end of the Devil Rays starting rotation, but the 6'9" 260 pounder has lost some of his luster. He was 12-6 with a 3.98 ERA, 3.2 Ctl and 8.5 Dom at Triple-A in 2007. Those, of course, aren't bad numbers, but when one is the fourth overall draft pick from '04, more is expected. It was thought that he would have already made his Major League debut, but Niemann has encountered bouts of shoulder soreness in each of the past three seasons. He started only eight games in 2005 and 14 games in 2006. He was #43 in HQ's Top 100 entering 2007 despite his ailments.

Niemann has a solid repertoire consisting of an 88-96 MPH fastball, knuckle-curve, slider and circle-change. He uses his size to pitch on a downhill plane and generally has good command and control – career 3.4 Ctl and 9.4 Dom. He has struggled against left-handed hitters and stamina issues will always be a concern. When healthy, Niemann is a top prospect. Considering the stable of young arms the Devil Rays have acquired or developed, he may begin 2008 back in Triple-A. But, he should debut sometime in 2008 – unless injuries reoccur.

Similar to Hunter, 20 year-old **Chris Parmelee** (OF, MIN) was one of the youngest players in the Low-A Midwest League. He was considered to be one of the top pure hitters in baseball entering 2007 (ranked #84 overall on HQ's list), but failed to deliver on his vast potential. He continued to showcase his power potential, but not much else in 2007. For the season, Parmelee hit .239/.313/.414 with 23 doubles and 15 HR. His all-or-nothing approach made him easy to pitch to and his long swing resulted in loads of strikeouts. The left-handed hitter only hit .198 against lefties, but was able to slug .463 against righties.

Parmelee played mostly RF in 2007, though some consider 1B his best long-term position because of the lack of agility. It's possible that his prospect status could return with a strong 2008. Despite the numbers, Parmelee does know the strike zone and has good baseball acumen. With the dearth of position player prospects in the Minnesota organization, the Twins could aggressively push him. Don't count him out just yet.

After beginning 2007 at #54 on HQ's Top 100 list, **Donald Veal** (LHP, CHC) had possibly the most disappointing season of any prospect in 2007. He was 8-10 with a 4.97 ERA in Double-A and had erratic control (5.0 Ctl). While somewhat unhittable in previous seasons, Veal couldn't find consistent mechanics or the plate. As he was constantly behind in the count, he was forced to rely on his 87-93 mph fastball and allowed the opposition to pounce.

With a projectable frame and excellent pure stuff, Veal still has significant upside. He has shown dominance at times and has a delivery that can be deceptive. Though he was surprisingly effective against right-handed hitters (.248/.346/.366), lefties carved him up (.326/.425/.432). He must develop a change-up to complement his fastball/curveball combination. At 23 years-old, there's still time for Veal to recover from his poor 2007 season. His walks decreased and strikeouts rose as 2007 progressed. However, the command issues need to be honed in order for the Cubs to count on him in the future.

Due to shoulder tendinitis that forced him to the sidelines in July, 21 year-old **Travis Wood** (LHP, CIN) has mostly been forgotten in an improving Reds farm system. He was #96 on the HQ Top 100 list in 2007. At High-A Sarasota, Wood went 3-2 with a 4.86 ERA in 12 starts while posting a 5.2 Ctl and 10.5 Dom. At 6'0"/165 lb, the former second rounder in 2005 isn't a flamethrower – he sits between 87-92 MPH – but he has the organization's best changeup and a quick, projectable arm.

He has the potential to become more than a crafty lefthander. He can register strikeouts by effectively mixing his pitches and he can spot his fastball well. Unless he smoothes out his delivery, Wood could have durability problems in the future. He doesn't project to a high Dom pitcher in the Majors, but he has the skill set to succeed. He may begin 2008 back in Sarasota, but could quickly jump back into top prospect lists with a positive season.

Regardless of the type of season a minor league prospect has, each player progresses at a different rate. Some players will encounter little resistance in their path to the Majors, whereas others will stumble and find the road not so smooth. It is relatively easy to predict success for a player who has cruised through the minor leagues effortlessly. However, it is also too early to count out a former top prospect after one poor season, especially when that player has an excellent pedigree and is still young compared to the rest of their league.

2007 Arizona Fall League — Top 20

1. Evan Longoria (3B, TAM) played the first half of the AFL season before leaving to join Team USA, but was the best player in the league, hitting .308/.378/.585 with four homers. His power is his greatest offensive asset, but may need to improve his plate discipline (0.29 Eye) to keep his BA consistent. He plays a solid defensive 3B with soft hands and a strong throwing arm.

2. Cameron Maybin (CF, FLA): The projectable athlete received minimal at-bats while nursing a left shoulder strain and only hit .219/.286/.438 with a 0.60 Eye. To take greater advantage of his bat speed and power potential, he was working on developing more of an uppercut to his swing and increasing trajectory to his hits. Defensively, he can handle CF with range and arm strength.

3. Andrew McCutchen (CF, PIT): The league's most exciting player, exhibiting plus speed and the ability to get on base (.381 OBP). He hit .286 with eight steals and showed improved strike zone judgment (1.17 Eye), but still struggles versus RH pitching. He chases everything down in CF and though his arm strength is average, he is highly accurate. He will need a half season in Triple-A.

4. Travis Snider (RF, TOR) displayed the most bat speed in the league and excelled despite having just low Class-A experience. Hit .316/.404/.541 with four HR and a 0.52 Eye, while being excellent in the clutch. His speed and defense are below average, but he does have good arm strength in the corner outfield.

5. Adam Miller (RHP, CLE): The highest profile arm in the AFL, featuring two plus pitches (89-94 MPH fastball and 84-87 MPH slider) and projectable size. His 9.00 ERA was slightly misleading as he posted solid base skills (3.7 Cmd and 7.6 K/9) and was working on his change-up. He will need to prove that he can stay healthy (elbow/finger), but has all the ingredients to dominate.

6. Reid Brignac (SS, TAM): No player struggled more in the AFL, as he hit .177/.218/.248 with a miserable 0.19 Eye. To his defense, the Rays had him work on making contact and using the whole field, and he batted in an uncustomary leadoff position. An athletic, bigger-type SS, he showed improved arm strength, and though he is naturally low-key, he needs to play with a bit more fire.

7. Jordan Schafer (CF, ATL) showed fluid hitting mechanics, moderate power, and above average speed, and could be the type that can hit about anywhere in the lineup. He hit .324/.395/.429 with ten steals and a 0.48 Eye, while hitting pitchers from both sides. His defense in CF is stellar, featuring plus arm strength and outstanding range.

8. Elvis Andrus (SS, TEX): The league's youngest player and one who took on a leadership role for his team. Blessed with outstanding defensive tools, he is capable of making any type of play. Offensively, he makes solid contact and utilizes his plus speed on the bases. He hit .353/.411/.471 with a 0.50 Eye and should be ready to tackle Double-A in 2008.

9. Taylor Teagarden (C, TEX): One of the better all-around catchers in the minors, he showed no ill effects from elbow surgery that forced him to DH for much of 2007. His offense blossomed during the season and carried

it over to the AFL, where he hit .271/.345/.479 with three homers and a 0.33 Eye.

10. Matt Antonelli (2B, SD): The top 2B in the minors, he continued to show impressive strike zone judgment (1.11 Eye), but it failed to translate into production, as he hit just .214/.333/.268. His gap power was non-existent, but he did make solid contact and use the whole field. Scouts were impressed with his defense, where he showed better footwork and good arm strength.

11. Matt LaPorta (LF, MIL): The lone offensive player from the 2007 Draft, he generates plus power from his bat speed and natural strength, tying for the league lead with six HR. He hit .241/.351/.500 with 0.61 Eye and is making adjustments in LF where he shows below average range and average arm strength.

12. Anthony Swarzak (RHP, MIN) needed to regain the innings he lost after a 50-game suspension for testing positive for a banned substance during the season. He notched a 2.05 ERA and showed excellent command (3.0 Cmd) featuring an 87-93 MPH fastball and three solid comps. His strikeout rate (4.9 K/9) declined, but he did a much better job of pitching to contact.

13. Jeff Clement (C, SEA): The Mariners sent him to the AFL to work on his defense, where he shows a lack of agility and receiving skills. Offense makes up the majority of his value and he hit .269/.367/.481 with three homers. He is a disciplined hitter with power to all fields and the ability to hit for BA, but his mediocre defense may keep him in the minors a bit longer.

14. Max Scherzer (RHP, ARI): Arizona's top pick in 2006, he didn't sign until June and thus missed valuable innings during the season. He is equipped with two and four-seam fastballs that range between 88-95 MPH and a nasty slider. Pitching in relief, he posted a 2.13 ERA with impressive base skills (3.6 Cmd and 12.8 K/9), and with the effort to his delivery, he may end up in the bullpen.

15. Jed Lowrie (SS/2B/3B, BOS): A fundamentally sound infielder who did everything except hit (.163/.236/.245). He makes solid contact and exercises patience (0.71 Eye), but his power is more of the doubles variety. Defensively, he makes plays at both middle infield spots, and even played some 3B to increase his versatility and to possibly get him ready for a utility role in Boston.

16. Nolan Reimold (LF, BAL): The strong-framed outfielder led the AFL with 23 RBI and tied for the league lead with six homers, but struggled overall, hitting .245/.331/.453 with a 0.33 Eye. He torches LH pitching and can hit the ball hard to all parts of the field. His defense is solid in both corner outfield positions where he shows solid arm strength and average range.

17. Matt Harrison (LHP, TEX) dismissed any concerns over the shoulder soreness that kept him out most of August, hitting 92 MPH with his four-seam fastball and tossing 27 innings. His change-up was one of the best in the league and he demonstrated pinpoint command (2.7 Cmd). His five wins led the league and he posted a 2.00 ERA while striking out 6.3 per game.

18. Ryan Sweeney (RF, CHW): A strong, athletic outfielder who makes solid contact and discerns balls and strikes (0.50 Eye), he hit .286 with a .347 OBP, but hitting for power has proved elusive (.345 SLG) for someone with his bat speed and size. He is a natural for RF with a strong arm and average range, but at some point, he's going to have to break out offensively.

19. Joe Savery (LHP, PHI): One of three pitchers from the 2007 Draft to pitch in the AFL, his base skills (0.5 Cmd, 7.1 BB/9, and 3.2 K/9) certainly weren't indicative of his 0.64 ERA. He did pitch out of trouble on several occasions by inducing groundball outs with his 86-92 MPH sinker and kept hitter off-balance by mixing his curveball and change-up, which prevented hits.

20. Jake Arrieta (RHP, BAL): The most dominating performance in the AFL, he tossed 16 scoreless IP and only gave up eight hits. His base skills (2.3 Cmd, 9.0 K/9) were solid, overpowering hitters with an 87-94 MPH fastball, slider, and splitter. Hi strong frame allows him to maintain velocity, but needs to repeat his ¾ drop-and-drive delivery.

TOP PERFORMANCES

Juan Miranda (1B, NYY): The Cuban has good bat speed and a disciplined approach. He launched five homers and hit .295/.423/.551 with a 0.89 Eye. He can murder LH pitching and will draw walks, but does tend to strike out. His defense is below average due to a lack of agility and he lacks speed on the bases.

Chris Coghlan (2B, FLA) got off to a very hot start, before settling at .329/.407/.425. His usage of the whole field, inside-out swing and plate discipline (1.25 Eye) should allow him to hit for BA, and he hits for power and steals bases above what his tools would indicate. His defense at 2B is improving after moving over from 3B, as he shows solid-average arm strength and range.

Eugenio Velez's (2B/CF, SF) athleticism and knack for making things happen endeared him to scouts and could put him in a utility role. He hit .303/.361/.461 with a line-drive stroke and his plus speed netted him 14 steals. He doesn't draw many walks, which limits his OBP, and is barely average defensively at 2B and CF. He fractured his right wrist during the last week.

Corey Wimberly (2B, COL): A short, stocky athlete, he finished with a flourish to lead the AFL with a .407 BA. He makes solid contact, judges the strike zone (1.00 Eye), and draws walks, giving him a solid OBP (.462) and allowing him to utilize his plus speed (two triples and seven steals). He ranges well and has soft, quick hands, but his arm strength is only adequate for 2B.

Sergio Santos (3B/SS, TOR): One of the more consistent hitters from start to finish, he has always been able to show moderate power, but lacked plate discipline and possessed a long swing. He hit .319/.337/.585 with five homers, but isn't very patient (0.20 Eye) and struggles against good pitching. He split his time between 3B and SS, which may suit him in a utility role.

Scott Sizemore (SS/2B, DET): A smaller-type athlete that gets the most out of his tools, he displayed solid defense at both middle infield positions, with soft hands and arm strength. Despite average speed, he led the AFL with four triples, while hitting .356/.416/.578 with a 0.71 Eye. He hits for BA and is a solid situational hitter, but may lack the secondary skills to be an everyday regular.

Sam Fuld (CF, CHC): The AFL MVP led the league with a .492 OBP, .626 SLG, 43 hits, 11 doubles, and 67 total bases, while hitting .402 with ten steals and a 1.13 Eye. A small, muscular athlete with speed and plenty of hustle, he makes exceptional contact and even showed some pop in his bat. His range and solid-average arm strength allow him to play all three outfield positions.

Brett Gardner (CF, NYY): A solid, leadoff-type hitter with bat-handling ability and plus speed. He led the AFL with 27 runs scored and 16 steals while hitting .343 with a .433 OBP and a 1.00 Eye. His inside-out swing is conducive to making contact and will use the whole field, but has no power whatsoever. Defensively, he shows plus range and fringe-average arm strength in CF.

Nate Schierholtz (RF, SF) ended the 2007 season as the Giants' RF and solidified his spot by hitting .348/.363/.596 with four homers. It is hard to imagine him sustaining a .300+ BA with his poor batting eye (0.08 Eye), but made a commitment to make better contact without sacrificing power. A former infielder, he still needs to take better routes in the outfield, but does have solid arm strength.

Caleb Stewart (RF, NYM) tied for the league lead with six homers while hitting .318/.400/.773. A strong player with bat speed and an aggressive approach, there are holes in his swing that make him susceptible to good pitching. He is a below average runner and defender.

Nick Blackburn (RHP, MIN) toyed with AFL hitters with his plus command (10.0 Cmd) and ability to subtract from his 88-93 MPH fastball with a cutter and change. He notched a 1.64 ERA and 8.2 K/9, while leading starting pitchers with a 0.68 WHIP. His inability to miss bats and spin the baseball limits his upside, but could see action as a fifth starter/middle reliever.

Sean Gallagher (RHP, CHC) succeeds by mixing three pitches with excellent command (3.3 Cmd) and being deceptive with his repeatable delivery. He establishes his 87-93 MPH fastball early and can get strikeouts with his curveball. He notched a 1.13 ERA and continues to miss bats (7.3 K/9).

Bob McCrory (RHP, BAL): Armed with the best fastball in the league, he dominated hitters with velocity (91-98 MPH) and a nasty slider that he throws off the plate. He led the AFL with five saves, while notching a 1.50 ERA and 8.3 K/9, and showed better command (2.8 Cmd) than he did in the regular season. His max-effort delivery is concerning and has had prior elbow surgery.

David Purcey (LHP, TOR): The former #1 pick (2004) hasn't had much to get excited about lately, but pitched extremely well, with a 1.23 ERA, a 2.8 Cmd, and 10.2 K/9. His minor league season was interrupted by an elbow strain and only pitched 62 innings. He hides the ball well which enhances the look of his 89-93 MPH fastball and showed better command of his curveball.

Sergio Romo (RHP, SF): A short, strong-armed reliever with excellent arm action, he led minor league relievers in strikeout rate and was just as dominant in the AFL (10.3 K/9). Not blessed with great velocity (86-91 MPH), but keeps ball low with his sinker and uses curveball for strikeouts. His command was solid (4.0 Cmd) and notched a 0.64 ERA while holding down a setup role.

BATTERS

POSITIONS: Up to three positions are listed for each batter and represent those for which he appeared (in order) the most games at in 2007. Positions are shown with their numeric designation (2=CA, 3=1B, 7=LF, 0=DH, etc.)

BATS: Shows which side of the plate he bats from — right (R), left (L) or switch-hitter (S).

AGE: Player's age, as of April 1, 2008.

DRAFTED: The year, round, and school that the player performed at as an amateur if drafted, or where the player was signed from, if a free agent.

EXP MLB DEBUT: The year a player is expected to debut in the Major Leagues.

PROJ ROLE: The role that the batter is expected to have for the majority of his Major League career, not necessarily his greatest upside.

SKILLS: Each skill a player possesses is graded and designated with a "+",indicating the quality of the skills, taking into context the batter's age and level played. An average skill will receive three "+" marks.

- **PWR:** Measures the player's ability to drive the ball and hit for power.
- **BAVG:** Measures the player's ability to hit for batting average and judge the strike zone.
- **SPD:** Measures the player's raw speed and baserunning ability.
- **DEF:** Measures the player's overall defense, which includes arm strength, arm accuracy, range, agility, hands, and defensive instincts.

PLAYER STAT LINES: Players receive statistics for the last five teams that they played for (if applicable), including the Major Leagues.

TEAM DESIGNATIONS: Each team that the player performed for during a given year is included. "JPN" means Japan, "MEX" means Mexico, "KOR" means Korea, "TWN" means Taiwan, "CUB" means Cuba and "IND" means independent league.

LEVEL DESIGNATIONS: The level for each team a player performed is included. "AAA" means Triple-A, "AA" means Double-A, "A+" means high Class-A, "A-" means low Class-A, and "Rk" means rookie level.

SABERMETRIC CATEGORIES: Descriptions of all the sabermetric categories appear in the glossary. The decimal point has been suppressed on several categories to conserve space.

CAPSULE COMMENTARIES: For each player, a brief analysis of their skills/statistics, and their future potential is provided.

ELIGIBILITY: Eligibility for inclusion is the standard for which Major League Baseball adheres to; 130 at-bats or 45 days on the 25-man roster, not including the month of September.

POTENTIAL RATINGS

The Potential Ratings are a two-part system in which a player is assigned a number rating based on his upside potential (1-10) and a letter rating based on the probability of reaching that potential (A-E).

Potential

10: Hall of Famer	5: MLB reserve
9: Elite player	4: Top minor leaguer
8: Solid regular	3: Averge minor leaguer
7: Average regular	2: Minor league reserve
6: Platoon player	1: Minor league roster filler

Probability Rating

A: 90% probability of reaching potential
B: 70% probability of reaching potential
C: 50% probability of reaching potential
D: 30% probability of reaching potential
E: 10% probability of reaching potential

SKILLS

Scouts usually grade a player's skills on the 20-80 scale, and while most of the grades are subjective, there are grades that can be given to represent a certain hitting statistic or running speed. These are indicated on the chart below.

Scout Grade	HR	BattAvg	Speed (L)	Speed (R)
80	39+	.320+	3.9	4.0
70	32-38	.300-.319	4.0	4.1
60	25-31	.286-.299	4.1	4.2
50 (avg)	17-24	.270-.285	4.2	4.3
40	11-16	.250-.269	4.3	4.4
30	6-10	.220-.249	4.4	4.5
20	0-5	.219-	4.5	4.6

CATCHER POP TIMES

Catchers are timed (in seconds) from the moment the pitch reaches the catcher's mitt until the time that the middle infielder receives the baseball at second base. This number will assist both teams in assessing whether a baserunner should steal second base or not.

1.85	+
1.95	MLB average
2.05	-

Adams,Ryan — 4 — Baltimore

EXP MLB DEBUT: 2010 **POTENTIAL:** Reserve 2B/3B **7D**

Bats R Age 21
2006 (2) HS (LA)

Pwr	++		
BAvg	+++		
Spd	++++		
Def	++		

Year	Lev	Team	AB	R	H	HR	RBI	Avg	OB	Slg	OPS	bb%	ct%	Eye	SB	CS	X/H%	Iso	RC/G
2006	Rk	Bluefield	133	24	34	2	7	256	349	376	725	13	76	0.59	2	2	32	120	4.74
2006	A-	Aberdeen	20	2	6	1	5	300	417	600	1017	17	65	0.57	0	0	67	300	9.61
2007	A-	Aberdeen	246	29	58	3	22	236	288	329	617	7	74	0.29	8	3	26	93	3.01

Athletic infielder who is moving down defensive spectrum due to below average range and arm. Inside-out swing and flat bat prevent him from hitting with power and lacks the plate discipline to draw walls, undercutting OBP. Has chance as utility player, but must improve offense.

Ahrens,Kevin — 56 — Toronto

EXP MLB DEBUT: 2011 **POTENTIAL:** Starting 3B **9E**

Bats B Age 19
2007 (1-C) HS (TX)

Pwr	++++		
BAvg	+++		
4.30 Spd	++		
Def	+++		

Year	Lev	Team	AB	R	H	HR	RBI	Avg	OB	Slg	OPS	bb%	ct%	Eye	SB	CS	X/H%	Iso	RC/G
2007	Rk	GCL Blue Jays	165	19	38	3	21	230	332	321	653	13	72	0.53	3	0	24	91	3.70

Excellent bat speed didn't produce expected offense, but swing is long and did have to learn to hit with wood. Power will come, but may not be a great BA hitter. Possesses plus arm strength and soft hands while playing both SS and 3B, but average range makes 3B the long-term fit.

Allen,Brandon — 3 — Chicago (A)

EXP MLB DEBUT: 2010 **POTENTIAL:** Platoon 1B **7E**

Bats L Age 22
2004 (5) HS (TX)

Pwr	++++		
BAvg	++		
4.40 Spd	++		
Def	+++		

Year	Lev	Team	AB	R	H	HR	RBI	Avg	OB	Slg	OPS	bb%	ct%	Eye	SB	CS	X/H%	Iso	RC/G
2004	Rk	Bristol	185	17	38	3	23	205	269	314	582	8	68	0.27	2	3	34	108	2.56
2005	Rk	Great Falls	231	41	61	11	42	264	354	472	825	12	70	0.46	7	5	39	208	6.05
2006	A-	Kannapolis	395	36	84	15	71	213	254	382	636	5	68	0.17	6	4	42	170	3.15
2007	A-	Kannapolis	516	84	146	18	93	283	333	483	816	7	76	0.31	7	4	42	200	5.60

Possesses bat speed and power potential, but poor pitch recognition and contact ability limits power and BA. Plate discipline regressed and doesn't hit LH pitching, so may be relegated to a platoon role. Solid defensively, being able to scoop low throws and displaying good arm strength.

Almanzar,Michael — 6 — Boston

EXP MLB DEBUT: 2012 **POTENTIAL:** Starting 3B **9E**

Bats R Age 17
2007 FA (DR)

Pwr	++++		
BAvg	+++		
Spd	++++		
Def	++		

Year	Lev	Team	AB	R	H	HR	RBI	Avg	OB	Slg	OPS	bb%	ct%	Eye	SB	CS	X/H%	Iso	RC/G
2007																			

Tall/athletic infielder who possesses top-of-the-line bat speed and power potential. Makes hard contact and should hit for BA despite aggressive approach and lack of discipline. Arm strength is playable at SS, but lacks range and possesses stiff hands, so may switch to 3B as he matures.

Almonte,Denny — 8 — Seattle

EXP MLB DEBUT: 2011 **POTENTIAL:** Starting CF **8E**

Bats B Age 19
2007 (2) HS (FL)

Pwr	++++		
BAvg	++		
Spd	++++		
Def	+++		

Year	Lev	Team	AB	R	H	HR	RBI	Avg	OB	Slg	OPS	bb%	ct%	Eye	SB	CS	X/H%	Iso	RC/G
2007	Rk	AZL Mariners	56	11	9	0	5	161	242	232	474	10	54	0.23	3	0	33	71	1.17
2007	A-	Everett	20	0	2	0	1	100	143	100	243	5	45	0.09	1	0	0	0	-3.45

Lean/athletic outfielder with speed and power potential bases on moderate bat speed and body projection. Plate discipline and slow trigger will suppress BA and hits better from LH side. Arm strength and range provide him with above average defense.

Anderson,Bryan — 2 — St. Louis

EXP MLB DEBUT: 2009 **POTENTIAL:** Starting CA **8B**

Bats L Age 21
2005 (4) HS (CA)

Pwr	+		
BAvg	++++		
Spd	+		
Def	++		

Year	Lev	Team	AB	R	H	HR	RBI	Avg	OB	Slg	OPS	bb%	ct%	Eye	SB	CS	X/H%	Iso	RC/G
2005	Rk	Johnson City	154	28	51	6	36	331	391	513	904	9	81	0.52	6	1	29	182	6.63
2006	A-	Quad Cities	381	50	115	3	51	302	371	417	788	10	83	0.64	2	6	30	115	5.46
2007	AA	Springfield	389	51	116	6	53	298	352	388	740	8	80	0.42	0	1	19	90	4.60

Solid hitter with moderate bat speed that produces doubles power and BA. Strike zone judgment declined slightly, but was making two-classification jump. Defense still lags offense, as he possesses arm strength and a quick release (1.95), but lacks receiving skills and agility.

Anderson,Josh — 8 — Atlanta

EXP MLB DEBUT: 2007 **POTENTIAL:** Platoon CF **7B**

Bats L Age 25
2003 (4) E Kentucky

Pwr	+		
BAvg	+++		
4.00 Spd	+++		
Def	+++		

Year	Lev	Team	AB	R	H	HR	RBI	Avg	OB	Slg	OPS	bb%	ct%	Eye	SB	CS	X/H%	Iso	RC/G
2004	A+	Salem	280	45	75	2	21	268	320	379	679	4	81	0.25	31	4	28	111	3.79
2005	AA	Corpus Christi	524	67	148	1	26	282	320	355	675	5	85	0.36	50	19	16	73	3.82
2006	AA	Corpus Christi	560	83	173	3	50	309	341	384	725	5	87	0.37	43	13	18	75	4.35
2007	AAA	Round Rock	513	84	140	2	43	273	316	341	657	6	85	0.43	40	8	18	68	3.63
2007	MLB	Houston	67	10	24	0	11	358	403	403	806	7	91	0.83	1	1	13	45	5.47

Slash-and-run type hitter who has proved track record for BA and is disruptive on bases with his plus speed. Lacks power, but can drive the gaps with regularity. Arm strength and range play well in CF and may run into playing time if he can continue to get on-base.

Anderson,Lars — 3 — Boston

EXP MLB DEBUT: 2010 **POTENTIAL:** Starting 1B **9D**

Bats L Age 20
2006 (18) HS (CA)

Pwr	++++		
BAvg	+++		
4.30 Spd	++		
Def	+++		

Year	Lev	Team	AB	R	H	HR	RBI	Avg	OB	Slg	OPS	bb%	ct%	Eye	SB	CS	X/H%	Iso	RC/G
2007	A+	Lancaster	35	13	12	1	9	343	500	486	986	24	74	1.22	0	0	25	143	8.87
2007	AA	Greenville	458	69	132	10	69	288	384	443	827	13	76	0.63	2	4	36	155	6.15

A Draft steal in 2006, he has the makings of a top run producer that exhibits above average power to all fields. Excellent plate discipline and bat control for age/level and cut-down on strikeouts. Has the defensive tools to be average at 1B, but his fair speed will decline as he adds muscle.

Andino,Robert — 6 — Florida

EXP MLB DEBUT: 2005 **POTENTIAL:** Reserve SS/2B **6A**

Bats R Age 24
2002 (2) HS (FL)

Pwr	+		
BAvg	++		
4.30 Spd	++		
Def	++++		

Year	Lev	Team	AB	R	H	HR	RBI	Avg	OB	Slg	OPS	bb%	ct%	Eye	SB	CS	X/H%	Iso	RC/G
2005	AA	Carolina	516	63	139	5	48	269	318	357	675	7	78	0.33	22	7	25	87	3.78
2006	AAA	Albuquerque	497	70	127	8	46	256	302	364	666	6	80	0.33	13	11	25	109	3.64
2006	MLB	Florida	24	0	4	0	2	167	200	208	408	4	75	0.17	1	0	25	42	0.19
2007	AAA	Albuquerque	598	85	166	13	50	278	323	428	751	6	78	0.31	21	13	31	151	4.72
2007	MLB	Florida	13	0	5	0	0	385	385	462	846	0	85	0.00	1	0	20	77	5.41

Athletic infielder with strong defensive skills, he turned-in best offensive season-to-date. Hitting for BA has never been a problem with solid contact ability, but added muscle produced more power and was utilized his speed on the bases. Possesses arm strength and soft hands.

Andrus,Elvis — 6 — Texas

EXP MLB DEBUT: 2009 **POTENTIAL:** Starting SS **9C**

Bats R Age 19
2004 FA (Venezuela)

Pwr	++		
BAvg	++++		
4.00 Spd	++++		
Def	+++++		

Year	Lev	Team	AB	R	H	HR	RBI	Avg	OB	Slg	OPS	bb%	ct%	Eye	SB	CS	X/H%	Iso	RC/G
2005	Rk	GCL Braves	166	26	49	1	20	295	368	398	765	10	83	0.68	7	4	20	102	5.09
2005	Rk	Danville	18	3	5	0	1	278	409	333	742	18	78	1.00	1	0	20	56	5.32
2006	A-	Rome	438	67	116	3	50	265	321	361	681	8	79	0.40	23	15	28	96	3.97
2007	A+	MB/Bak	495	78	127	5	49	257	330	343	673	10	78	0.50	40	15	24	87	3.93

One of the younger regulars in high Class-A, but offense was slightly disappointing. Makes contact and steals bases with his plus speed, but low loft and a flat bat plane kept power low despite good bat speed. Defense may be best in all of the minors with his plus range and arm strength.

Angelini,Carmine — 6 — New York (A)

EXP MLB DEBUT: 2011 **POTENTIAL:** Starting SS **9E**

Bats R Age 19
2007 (10) HS (LA)

Pwr	+++		
BAvg	++++		
Spd	++++		
Def	+++		

Year	Lev	Team	AB	R	H	HR	RBI	Avg	OB	Slg	OPS	bb%	ct%	Eye	SB	CS	X/H%	Iso	RC/G
2007	Rk	GCL Yankees	1	0	0	0	0	0	0	0	0	0	0	0.00	0	0	0	0	0.00

Top football recruit in Texas, but was lured away with high signing bonus. Athletic with plenty of strength, he could post excellent power numbers with his bat speed and contact ability. Plus arm strength and adequate range plays at SS, but will need to show better groundball reads.

Angle, Matt — 8 — Baltimore

EXP MLB DEBUT: 2010 POTENTIAL: Reserve CF/RF **7E**

Bats L Age 22
2007 (7) Ohio St

Pwr	+	
BAvg	+++	
Spd	++++	
Def	+++	

Year	Lev	Team	AB	R	H	HR	RBI	Avg	OB	Slg	OPS	bb%	ct%	Eye	SB	CS	X/H%	Iso	RC/G
2007	A-	Aberdeen	236	60	71	0	14	301	417	352	769	17	83	1.18	34	4	11	51	5.61

Light-framed athlete with leadoff hitter skills. Quick bat, contact ability, and use of whole field gives him solid BA and draws plenty of walks to improve OBP. Above average runner with solid instincts that produce steals. Arm strength and range can play in either CF or RF.

Antonelli, Matt — 4 — San Diego

EXP MLB DEBUT: 2008 POTENTIAL: Starting 2B **8B**

Bats R Age 23
2006 (1) Wake Forest

Pwr	+++	
BAvg	++++	
4.20 Spd	++++	
Def	+++	

Year	Lev	Team	AB	R	H	HR	RBI	Avg	OB	Slg	OPS	bb%	ct%	Eye	SB	CS	X/H%	Iso	RC/G
2006	A-	Eugene	189	38	54	0	22	286	426	360	785	20	84	1.48	9	1	24	74	6.03
2006	A-	Ft. Wayne	16	3	2	0	0	125	222	313	535	11	63	0.33	0	0	100	188	2.31
2007	A+	Lk Elsinore	347	89	109	14	54	314	405	499	904	13	83	0.91	18	6	29	184	6.88
2007	AA	San Antonio	187	34	55	7	24	294	392	476	868	14	81	0.83	10	3	35	182	6.51

Advanced hitter with plate discipline and ability to hit for BA. Unlikely to improve HR output with his bat plane, but has strength to drive gaps. Above average speed and instincts should provide SB. Made defensive transition to 2B where his soft hands and arm strength are assets.

Arencibia, JP — 23 — Toronto

EXP MLB DEBUT: 2009 POTENTIAL: Starting CA **8D**

Bats R Age 22
2007 (1) Tennessee

Pwr	++++	
BAvg	+++	
Spd	+	
Def	++	

Year	Lev	Team	AB	R	H	HR	RBI	Avg	OB	Slg	OPS	bb%	ct%	Eye	SB	CS	X/H%	Iso	RC/G
2007	A-	Auburn	228	31	58	3	25	254	309	377	686	6	75	0.25	0	0	36	123	4.23

Possessing bat speed and a balanced swing, his power should come easy, but poor pitch recognition and tendency to pull baseball could suppress BA. Agile with good arm strength, he doesn't receive the ball well and has a slow release which could limit innings behind the dish.

Arias, Joaquin — 6 — Texas

EXP MLB DEBUT: 2006 POTENTIAL: Platoon SS/2B **7C**

Bats R Age 23
2001 FA (Venezuela)

Pwr	+	
BAvg	+++	
4.10 Spd	++++	
Def	++++	

Year	Lev	Team	AB	R	H	HR	RBI	Avg	OB	Slg	OPS	bb%	ct%	Eye	SB	CS	X/H%	Iso	RC/G
2005	AA	Frisco	499	65	157	5	56	315	337	423	760	3	91	0.37	20	10	23	108	4.72
2006	AAA	Oklahoma	493	56	132	4	49	268	295	361	656	4	87	0.30	26	10	21	93	3.53
2006	MLB	Texas	11	4	6	0	1	545	583	636	1220	8	100		0	1	17	91	9.96
2007	Rk	AZL Rangers	7	1	2	0	1	286	286	429	714	0	71	0.00	0	1	50	143	4.24
2007	AAA	Oklahoma	11	3	2	0	1	182	182	182	364	0	82	0.00	1	0	0	0	-0.33

Wiry athlete with plus speed and defense, possessing both arm strength and range that are well above average. Makes contact and can bunt, but offense is limited due to a lack of power and ability to draw walks. Missed most of 2007 with shoulder surgery, but will be 100% in spring training.

Ashley, Nevin — 2 — Tampa Bay

EXP MLB DEBUT: 2009 POTENTIAL: Reserve CA **7D**

Bats R Age 23
2006 (6) Indiana St

Pwr	++	
BAvg	+++	
Spd	+++	
Def	+++	

Year	Lev	Team	AB	R	H	HR	RBI	Avg	OB	Slg	OPS	bb%	ct%	Eye	SB	CS	X/H%	Iso	RC/G
2006	Rk	Princeton	153	25	51	4	28	333	414	477	891	12	74	0.53	7	3	25	144	6.93
2007	A-	Columbus	429	76	120	12	60	280	354	431	785	10	79	0.53	20	8	28	152	5.32

Athletic catcher with well-rounded offensive skills. Drives the gaps with moderate power and provides solid OBP with ability to walk and make contact. Runs well for a catcher and can steal bases. Receiving skills need lots of work, though he does throw well and works hard.

Ash, Johnathan — 4 — Houston

EXP MLB DEBUT: 2008 POTENTIAL: Reserve 2B **7D**

Bats L Age 25
2004 (11) Stanford

Pwr	+	
BAvg	++++	
4.15 Spd	++++	
Def	++	

Year	Lev	Team	AB	R	H	HR	RBI	Avg	OB	Slg	OPS	bb%	ct%	Eye	SB	CS	X/H%	Iso	RC/G
2004	A-	Tri City	239	50	71	2	25	297	364	377	740	9	93	1.56	5	4	17	79	4.99
2005	A-	Lexington	256	44	82	8	38	320	360	436	795	9	92	1.25	3	7	31	116	5.40
2005	A+	Salem	225	32	72	1	25	320	381	473	853	6	93	0.93	3	5	26	152	6.07
2006	AA	Corpus Christi	392	39	124	1	28	314	355	403	758	6	91	0.67	5	8	23	89	4.93
2007	AA	Corpus Christi	280	33	84	3	33	300	374	404	778	8	94	1.53	2	3	25	104	4.77

Small/compact athlete who is an extreme contact hitter that uses the whole field. Hits for BA and has a discerning eye at the plate, but lacks power. Possesses above average speed that may lessen after knee surgery in August. Makes plays at 2B with range, soft hands, and average arm.

Aubrey, Michael — 3 — Cleveland

EXP MLB DEBUT: 2008 POTENTIAL: Platoon 1B **7C**

Bats L Age 26
2003 (1) Tulane

Pwr	+++	
BAvg	++++	
Spd	+	
Def	+++++	

Year	Lev	Team	AB	R	H	HR	RBI	Avg	OB	Slg	OPS	bb%	ct%	Eye	SB	CS	X/H%	Iso	RC/G
2005	AA	Akron	106	17	30	4	20	283	327	462	790	6	83	0.39	1	0	33	179	5.08
2006	A+	Kinston	28	7	8	2	10	286	412	607	1019	18	82	1.20	0	0	63	321	8.50
2006	AA	Akron	26	3	7	1	2	269	321	462	783	7	85	0.50	0	0	43	192	5.08
2007	A+	Kinston	50	15	20	5	11	400	464	800	1264	11	86	0.86	0	0	50	400	10.72
2007	AA	Akron	206	22	51	7	34	248	282	403	685	5	83	0.29	0	0	35	155	3.74

Pure hitter with fluid hitting mechanics and bat speed that produces gap power and BA. Judges strike zone and will use entire field, but unlikely to produce HR power. Plus defender at 1B with soft hands, agility, and arm strength. Chronic back problems continue to cost him at-bats.

Aviles, Mike — 654 — Kansas City

EXP MLB DEBUT: 2008 POTENTIAL: Reserve SS/3B **6A**

Bats R Age 27
2003 (7) Concordia

Pwr	+++	
BAvg	+++	
4.30 Spd	+++	
Def	+++	

Year	Lev	Team	AB	R	H	HR	RBI	Avg	OB	Slg	OPS	bb%	ct%	Eye	SB	CS	X/H%	Iso	RC/G
2003	Rk	AZL Royals	212	51	77	6	39	363	400	585	985	6	87	0.46	11	5	39	222	7.43
2004	A+	Wilmington	463	66	139	6	69	300	355	443	797	8	88	0.68	2	5	36	143	5.45
2005	AA	Wichita	521	79	146	14	80	280	339	447	767	5	88	0.47	11	6	36	167	4.87
2006	AAA	Omaha	469	52	124	8	47	264	306	373	679	6	90	0.58	14	5	26	109	3.94
2007	AAA	Omaha	538	78	159	17	77	296	333	463	796	5	89	0.51	5	5	31	167	5.15

Wiry athlete with moderate bat speed and contact ability that provides doubles power and BA. Aggressive approach doesn't give him many walks or strikeouts. Versatile on defense, capable of playing three infield positions, possessing soft hands, range, and average arm strength.

Baez, Edgardo — 8 — Washington

EXP MLB DEBUT: 2009 POTENTIAL: Platoon RF/LF **7D**

Bats R Age 23
2000 FA (Venezuela)

Pwr	+++	
BAvg	++	
4.40 Spd	++	
Def	+++	

Year	Lev	Team	AB	R	H	HR	RBI	Avg	OB	Slg	OPS	bb%	ct%	Eye	SB	CS	X/H%	Iso	RC/G
2004	A-	Savannah	191	16	34	5	29	178	252	309	561	9	71	0.34	1	0	44	131	2.24
2005	A-	Savannah	447	62	110	11	64	246	329	394	722	11	71	0.43	11	4	35	148	4.63
2006	A-	Savannah	355	46	99	6	44	279	335	403	738	8	77	0.38	3	2	30	124	4.64
2006	A+	Potomac	68	4	7	2	3	103	197	221	418	11	62	0.31	0	0	57	118	-0.10
2007	A+	Potomac	270	37	75	10	50	278	369	437	806	13	73	0.53	10	7	29	159	5.74

Athletic outfielder began to show a mature approach to hitting, driving ball more consistently and improving walk rate, but lost at-bats to injury. Steals bases through instincts as his speed is below average. Possesses average arm strength and range.

Baez, Pedro — 5 — Los Angeles (N)

EXP MLB DEBUT: 2012 POTENTIAL: Starting 3B **9E**

Bats R Age 19
2007 FA (DR)

Pwr	++++	
BAvg	+++	
4.35 Spd	++	
Def	++++	

Year	Lev	Team	AB	R	H	HR	RBI	Avg	OB	Slg	OPS	bb%	ct%	Eye	SB	CS	X/H%	Iso	RC/G
2007	Rk	GCL Dodgers	201	35	55	3	39	274	330	408	738	8	80	0.43	3	1	35	134	4.68

Maturely built youngster with bat speed and strong wrists that makes him capable of plus power. Lacks pitch recognition, so BA may fluctuate in lower minors. Below average runner and has to watch body. Possesses plus arm strength and soft hands in providing above average defense.

Baisley, Jeff — 5 — Oakland

EXP MLB DEBUT: 2009 POTENTIAL: Platoon 3B **6B**

Bats R Age 25
2005 (12) South Florida

Pwr	+++	
BAvg	+++	
Spd	++	
Def	++++	

Year	Lev	Team	AB	R	H	HR	RBI	Avg	OB	Slg	OPS	bb%	ct%	Eye	SB	CS	X/H%	Iso	RC/G
2005	A-	Vancouver	218	28	55	6	38	252	335	413	748	11	88	1.00	3	5	40	161	5.00
2006	A-	Kane Co	465	86	139	22	110	299	381	520	902	12	82	0.72	5	1	42	222	6.78
2007	AA	Midland	404	60	104	11	46	257	307	408	716	7	79	0.35	4	1	35	151	4.25

Skipped to Double-A after winning MWL MVP, he was able to maintain power and overall offensive level. Possesses fluid hitting mechanics and makes contact, but uses too much of the middle to hit for power. First-step quickness and arm strength make him a solid defender.

BATTERS

Balentien,Wladimir | 9 | Seattle
EXP MLB DEBUT: 2007 | POTENTIAL: Starting RF/LF | 8B

Bats R Age 23	Year	Lev	Team	AB	R	H	HR	RBI	Avg	OB	Slg	OPS	bb%	ct%	Eye	SB	CS	X/H%	Iso	RC/G
2000 FA (Curacao)	2004	A-	Wisconsin	260	39	72	15	46	277	309	519	828	4	70	0.16	10	2	42	242	5.69
Pwr ++++	2005	A+	Inland Emp	492	76	143	25	93	291	335	553	888	6	67	0.21	9	2	50	262	6.92
BAvg ++	2006	AA	San Antonio	444	76	102	22	82	230	335	435	769	14	68	0.50	14	7	45	205	5.31
4.30 Spd +++	2007	AAA	Tacoma	477	77	139	24	84	291	363	509	873	10	78	0.51	15	4	37	218	6.35
Def ++	2007	MLB	Seattle	3	1	2	1	4	667	667	2000	2667	0	100		0	0	100	1333	22.65

Aggressive hitter who improved approach and cut-down swing enabling him to hit for BA. Possesses light-tower power with bat speed/whip and made it more game-usable by being more selective. Runs well for size and has the tools to be above average in RF with arm strength and range.

Barney,Darwin | 6 | Chicago (N)
EXP MLB DEBUT: 2009 | POTENTIAL: Starting SS | 7C

Bats R Age 22	Year	Lev	Team	AB	R	H	HR	RBI	Avg	OB	Slg	OPS	bb%	ct%	Eye	SB	CS	X/H%	Iso	RC/G
2007 (4) Oregon St																				
Pwr +																				
BAvg +++																				
4.25 Spd ++++	2007	Rk	AZL Cubs	18	6	8	0	2	444	545	611	1157	18	100		0	0	38	167	10.37
Def ++++	2007	A-	Peoria	176	27	48	2	21	273	316	392	708	6	88	0.50	5	2	29	119	4.28

High-energy athlete who plays the game right, playing better than the sum of his tools. Makes excellent contact with a line-drive stroke and draws walks, giving him a solid OBP. Aggressiveness is a plus on the bases and is a solid defender with arm strength and impressive range.

Barton,Brian | 8 | St. Louis
EXP MLB DEBUT: 2008 | POTENTIAL: Starting RF | 8C

Bats R Age 26	Year	Lev	Team	AB	R	H	HR	RBI	Avg	OB	Slg	OPS	bb%	ct%	Eye	SB	CS	X/H%	Iso	RC/G
2004 NDFA Miami-FL	2005	A+	Kinston	223	42	61	3	32	274	370	435	805	13	74	0.60	13	8	39	161	5.95
Pwr +++	2006	A+	Kinston	295	56	90	12	56	305	386	502	888	12	72	0.47	24	3	34	197	6.89
BAvg ++++	2006	AA	Akron	151	32	53	6	26	351	402	503	906	8	83	0.50	15	5	21	152	6.51
Spd ++++	2007	AA	Akron	389	56	122	9	59	314	379	440	819	10	75	0.41	20	9	24	126	5.78
Def +++	2007	AAA	Buffalo	87	9	23	1	7	264	319	333	652	7	79	0.39	1	1	17	69	3.50

Plus athlete with contact ability, moderate power, and speed. Power decreased and strikeout rate increased at upper levels, but was able to maintain BA. Aggressive on bases and chooses situation to steal. Arm strength and range are above average and can play all three outfield spots.

Barton,Daric | 35 | Oakland
EXP MLB DEBUT: 2007 | POTENTIAL: Starting 1B | 8A

Bats L Age 22	Year	Lev	Team	AB	R	H	HR	RBI	Avg	OB	Slg	OPS	bb%	ct%	Eye	SB	CS	X/H%	Iso	RC/G
2003 (1) HS (FL)	2005	AA	Midland	212	38	67	5	37	316	413	491	904	14	86	1.17	1	1	39	175	7.06
Pwr +++	2006	Rk	AZL Athletics	5	1	1	0	2	200	200	400	600	0	100		0	0	100	200	3.41
BAvg +++++	2006	AAA	Sacramento	147	25	38	2	22	259	391	395	786	18	82	1.23	1	0	32	136	5.87
4.50 Spd +	2007	AAA	Sacramento	516	84	151	9	70	293	386	438	824	13	87	1.13	3	4	34	145	6.07
Def ++	2007	MLB	Oakland	72	16	25	4	8	347	427	639	1066	12	85	0.91	1	0	52	292	8.76

Strong/stocky hitter with bat speed and plate discipline that promotes a line-drive stroke and a high BA. Hits produce too much topspin and prefers the middle of field, which will keep HR power in the low teens. Possesses soft hands and low agility in becoming an average defender.

Bates,Aaron | 3 | Boston
EXP MLB DEBUT: 2009 | POTENTIAL: Platoon 1B | 7C

Bats R Age 24	Year	Lev	Team	AB	R	H	HR	RBI	Avg	OB	Slg	OPS	bb%	ct%	Eye	SB	CS	X/H%	Iso	RC/G
2006 (3) North Carolina																				
Pwr +++	2006	A-	Lowell	100	17	36	3	14	360	413	530	943	8	79	0.43	2	1	31	170	7.19
BAvg +++	2006	AA	Greenville	150	13	41	4	16	273	351	400	751	11	83	0.69	0	0	27	127	4.90
Spd ++	2007	A+	Lancaster	373	89	124	24	88	332	437	592	1029	16	78	0.83	0	1	38	260	8.64
Def +++	2007	AA	Portland	91	16	18	4	13	198	324	429	753	16	68	0.59	0	0	72	231	5.24

Tall/strong hitter with solid approach and bat speed. Centers baseball well, allowing him to hit for BA, though power was byproduct of home environment. Strikes out in droves, but will draw walks, leading CAL in OBP. Average defensively at 1B, featuring soft hands and arm strength.

Bell,Bubba | 8 | Boston
EXP MLB DEBUT: 2009 | POTENTIAL: Platoon CF/LF | 7D

Bats L Age 25	Year	Lev	Team	AB	R	H	HR	RBI	Avg	OB	Slg	OPS	bb%	ct%	Eye	SB	CS	X/H%	Iso	RC/G
2005 (39) Nicholls St	2006	A-	Lowell	91	22	39	2	13	429	500	637	1137	13	86	1.00	2	3	33	209	9.78
Pwr ++++	2006	A+	Wilmington	60	8	17	1	9	283	368	433	801	12	88	1.14	2	0	35	150	5.75
BAvg +++	2006	AA	Greenville	208	29	49	3	28	236	323	327	650	11	86	0.90	4	6	24	91	3.86
4.20 Spd +++	2007	A+	Lancaster	322	95	119	22	83	370	451	665	1116	13	88	1.23	10	4	42	295	9.22
Def +++	2007	AA	Portland	147	23	39	4	22	265	329	408	737	9	88	0.82	4	0	28	143	4.73

Bat speed generates power to all fields and plate discipline helped him lead CAL in BA and SLG, but strong start was diluted due to his home ballpark. Numbers came back to earth in Double-A, which is true level of ability. Average defender in CF with average arm and sufficient range.

Bell,Josh | 5 | Los Angeles (N)
EXP MLB DEBUT: 2010 | POTENTIAL: Platoon LF/1B | 8D

Bats B Age 21	Year	Lev	Team	AB	R	H	HR	RBI	Avg	OB	Slg	OPS	bb%	ct%	Eye	SB	CS	X/H%	Iso	RC/G
2005 (4) HS (FL)																				
Pwr ++++	2005	Rk	GCL Dodgers	157	26	50	1	21	318	395	395	790	11	79	0.61	5	2	18	76	5.53
BAvg ++	2006	Rk	Ogden	250	45	77	12	53	308	366	544	910	8	71	0.32	4	0	42	236	7.07
Spd ++	2007	A-	Great Lakes	398	65	115	15	62	289	352	470	822	9	73	0.36	5	1	34	181	5.81
Def ++	2007	A+	Inland Emp	75	4	13	2	9	173	205	307	512	4	75	0.16	0	0	38	133	1.45

All-or-nothing swing and bat speed gives him unlimited power potential and hits well from both sides of the plate. Poor contact rate suppresses BA and can be exploited by good pitching. Possesses plus arm strength, but led MWL with 35 errors due to inaccurate throws and poor agility.

Beltre,Engel | 9 | Texas
EXP MLB DEBUT: 2012 | POTENTIAL: Starting RF | 9E

Bats L Age 18	Year	Lev	Team	AB	R	H	HR	RBI	Avg	OB	Slg	OPS	bb%	ct%	Eye	SB	CS	X/H%	Iso	RC/G
2006 FA (DR)																				
Pwr ++++																				
BAvg +++																				
Spd ++++	2007	Rk	AZL/GCL	209	39	52	9	28	249	314	474	788	9	69	0.31	9	5	42	225	5.50
Def ++++	2007	A-	Spokane	38	3	8	0	1	211	250	211	461	5	74	0.20	2	1	0	0	0.77

Athletic outfielder with bat speed that generates power to all fields and plus speed to make him a threat on the bases. Aggressive hitter who can hit for BA despite marginal plate discipline. Demonstrates above average arm strength and range with RF a likely destination.

Benson,Joe | 8 | Minnesota
EXP MLB DEBUT: 2010 | POTENTIAL: Starting RF | 7C

Bats R Age 20	Year	Lev	Team	AB	R	H	HR	RBI	Avg	OB	Slg	OPS	bb%	ct%	Eye	SB	CS	X/H%	Iso	RC/G
2006 (2) HS (IL)																				
Pwr ++++																				
BAvg ++	2006	Rk	GCL Twins	196	30	51	5	28	260	332	444	776	10	79	0.51	9	10	41	184	5.25
4.10 Spd ++++	2006	A-	Beloit	19	2	5	0	1	263	263	263	526	0	68	0.00	0	0	0	0	1.36
Def +++	2007	A-	Beloit	432	73	110	5	38	255	331	368	699	10	71	0.40	18	16	28	113	4.34

Muscular athlete blessed with plus speed and power potential, but poor strike zone judgment and low contact rate kept power down. Mediocre BA wasn't too much of a surprise for age/level, but his bat speed should produce more power. Possesses the range and arm strength to play CF.

Bernadina,Rogearvin | 8 | Washington
EXP MLB DEBUT: 2008 | POTENTIAL: Platoon CF/LF | 7D

Bats L Age 24	Year	Lev	Team	AB	R	H	HR	RBI	Avg	OB	Slg	OPS	bb%	ct%	Eye	SB	CS	X/H%	Iso	RC/G
2001 FA (Holland)	2004	A-	Savannah	450	67	108	7	68	240	329	371	701	12	75	0.53	24	2	35	131	4.39
Pwr +++	2005	A-	Savannah	417	64	97	12	54	233	350	369	719	15	78	0.82	35	8	31	137	4.69
BAvg +++	2006	A+	Potomac	434	60	117	6	42	270	353	369	722	11	77	0.57	27	11	24	99	4.62
Spd ++++	2007	AA	Harrisburg	371	58	100	6	36	270	337	369	707	9	78	0.48	40	13	23	100	4.29
Def +++	2007	AAA	Columbus	42	6	7	0	1	167	314	238	552	18	74	0.82	0	1	43	71	2.62

Solid athlete who has forsaken power to focus on BA/OBP and to take advantage of his plus speed and instincts. Possesses moderate power to pull field, but prefers middle of field. Arm strength and range play well in CF, but needs to take better routes to flyballs.

Bianchi,Jeff | 6 | Kansas City
EXP MLB DEBUT: 2009 | POTENTIAL: Starting 2B | 7C

Bats R Age 21	Year	Lev	Team	AB	R	H	HR	RBI	Avg	OB	Slg	OPS	bb%	ct%	Eye	SB	CS	X/H%	Iso	RC/G
2005 (2) HS (PA)																				
Pwr ++																				
BAvg ++++	2005	Rk	AZL Royals	98	29	40	6	30	408	491	745	1236	14	78	0.73	5	2	43	337	11.42
4.10 Spd ++++	2006	Rk	AZL Royals	42	13	18	2	6	429	529	667	1196	18	93	3.00	1	1	33	238	10.50
Def +++	2007	A-	Burlington	368	43	91	2	36	247	295	315	610	6	80	0.35	15	4	23	68	3.00

Coming off a shoulder injury, his offense didn't meet expectations as he struggled with plate discipline and ability to drive ball. Makes good contact with short stroke, but to utilize plus speed, he needs to improve walk rate. Ranges well at SS, but arm strength is slightly below average.

Bixler,Brian

6 | **Pittsburgh** | EXP MLB DEBUT: 2007 | POTENTIAL: Starting SS | **7C**

Bats R Age 25
2004 (2) E Michigan
Pwr +
BAvg + + +
4.10 Spd + + +
Def + + + +

Year	Lev	Team	AB	R	H	HR	RBI	Avg	OB	Slg	OPS	bb%	ct%	Eye	SB	CS	X/H%	Iso	RC/G
2004	A-	Williamsport	228	40	63	0	21	276	321	342	663	6	78	0.29	14	5	17	66	3.65
2005	A-	Hickory	502	74	141	9	50	281	331	388	720	7	73	0.28	21	10	24	108	4.37
2006	A+	Lynchburg	267	46	81	5	33	303	384	434	819	12	78	0.60	18	7	28	131	5.88
2006	AA	Altoona	226	36	68	3	19	301	347	407	754	7	75	0.28	6	2	25	106	4.82
2007	AAA	Indianapolis	475	77	130	5	51	274	348	396	744	10	72	0.41	28	4	29	122	4.97

Small/wiry infielder with excellent contact ability and plus speed, he led the IL in triples. Medium bat speed will preclude him from hitting for power and needs to draw more walks. Makes plays defensively with soft/quick hands, range, and average arm strength. Instincts are off the chart.

Blanco,Gregor

8 | **Atlanta** | EXP MLB DEBUT: 2007 | POTENTIAL: Reserve LF/CF | **6B**

Bats L Age 24
2000 FA (Venezuela)
Pwr +
BAvg + + +
Spd + + + +
Def + + +

Year	Lev	Team	AB	R	H	HR	RBI	Avg	OB	Slg	OPS	bb%	ct%	Eye	SB	CS	X/H%	Iso	RC/G
2004	A+	Myrtle Beach	436	73	116	8	41	266	337	401	739	10	74	0.41	25	9	29	135	4.80
2005	AA	Mississippi	401	64	101	6	37	252	367	384	751	15	69	0.59	28	12	29	132	5.35
2006	AA	Mississippi	251	45	72	0	9	287	391	375	766	15	77	0.75	18	6	26	88	5.48
2006	AAA	Richmond	270	43	78	0	18	289	402	341	743	16	80	0.96	14	9	17	52	5.21
2007	AAA	Richmond	464	81	131	3	35	282	368	362	730	12	82	0.74	23	18	20	80	4.82

Leadoff-type hitter with BA ability, plate discipline, and plus speed, which helped him lead IL in runs scored. Good situational hitter and can bunt, but lacks power due to light frame. Possesses excellent range and average arm strength in CF, and could be solid fourth outfielder.

Blanks,Kyle

3 | **San Diego** | EXP MLB DEBUT: 2009 | POTENTIAL: Starting 1B | **9D**

Bats R Age 21
2004 (42) Yavapai CC
Pwr + + + +
BAvg + +
Spd + +
Def + + +

Year	Lev	Team	AB	R	H	HR	RBI	Avg	OB	Slg	OPS	bb%	ct%	Eye	SB	CS	X/H%	Iso	RC/G
2005	Rk	AZL Padres	164	33	49	7	30	299	392	500	892	13	70	0.51	3	1	37	201	7.09
2006	A-	Ft. Wayne	308	41	90	10	52	292	366	455	821	10	74	0.46	2	0	33	162	5.84
2007	A+	Lk Elsinore	465	94	140	24	100	301	361	540	901	9	79	0.45	11	2	42	239	6.62

Tall/strong hitter with bat speed and power to all fields, he led CAL with 100 RBI. Shortened his lengthy swing, which cut-down strikeouts and improved BA. Runs well for size with long strides and has good instincts. Possesses solid defense at 1B with soft hands and agility.

Boesch,Brennan

73 | **Detroit** | EXP MLB DEBUT: 2009 | POTENTIAL: Platoon RF/LF | **7C**

Bats L Age 23
2006 (3) California
Pwr + + +
BAvg + +
4.15 Spd + + + +
Def + + +

Year	Lev	Team	AB	R	H	HR	RBI	Avg	OB	Slg	OPS	bb%	ct%	Eye	SB	CS	X/H%	Iso	RC/G
2006	A-	Oneonta	292	27	85	5	54	291	339	435	774	7	86	0.50	3	4	31	144	5.06
2007	A-	W. Michigan	513	52	137	10	86	267	299	378	677	4	84	0.28	15	4	24	111	3.68

Wiry strong athlete with good secondary skills and hitting mechanics, but a poor contact rate and strike zone judgment will leave BA wanting. Utilizes speed well on bases. Arm strength and range are solid in corner outfield, but may not have enough bat to be a starter at the MLB level.

Boeve,Adam

9 | **Pittsburgh** | EXP MLB DEBUT: 2008 | POTENTIAL: Platoon LF/RF | **6C**

Bats R Age 27
2003 (12) Iowa
Pwr + + +
BAvg + + +
4.25 Spd + + +
Def +

Year	Lev	Team	AB	R	H	HR	RBI	Avg	OB	Slg	OPS	bb%	ct%	Eye	SB	CS	X/H%	Iso	RC/G
2005	AA	Altoona	160	24	46	5	23	288	374	450	824	12	66	0.41	5	2	33	163	6.30
2006	AA	Altoona	138	26	46	3	24	333	410	478	889	12	75	0.51	3	2	26	145	6.88
2006	AAA	Indianapolis	316	32	85	6	37	269	328	389	718	8	74	0.35	24	5	31	120	4.40
2007	AA	Altoona	330	55	89	17	53	270	366	479	845	13	70	0.50	17	5	37	209	6.34
2007	AAA	Indianapolis	83	13	23	4	6	277	381	458	839	14	72	0.61	6	3	26	181	6.22

Muscular athlete with solid secondary skills. Moderate bat speed provides gap power and is the type that both walks and strikes-out which keeps BA at average level. Runs bases well with average speed. Arm strength and range are average, but needs to track flyballs better.

Boggs,Brandon

8 | **Texas** | EXP MLB DEBUT: 2008 | POTENTIAL: Reserve CF/LF | **7C**

Bats B Age 25
2004 (4) Georgia Tech
Pwr + + +
BAvg + + +
4.20 Spd + + + +
Def + + +

Year	Lev	Team	AB	R	H	HR	RBI	Avg	OB	Slg	OPS	bb%	ct%	Eye	SB	CS	X/H%	Iso	RC/G
2004	A-	Spokane	149	27	35	3	19	235	360	369	729	16	71	0.67	6	2	40	134	4.96
2005	A-	Clinton	309	54	76	13	51	246	351	437	788	14	78	0.72	14	6	41	191	5.48
2006	A+	Bakersfield	284	48	74	8	37	261	352	444	796	12	78	0.63	13	4	43	183	5.63
2007	A+	Bakersfield	92	17	23	4	17	250	349	500	849	13	70	0.50	5	1	61	250	6.58
2007	AA	Frisco	354	69	94	19	55	266	387	508	895	17	71	0.68	10	4	47	243	7.20

Athletic outfielder with solid secondary skills in being able to hit for power, draw walks, and steal bases. Bat speed gives him power to all fields and can hit from both sides of plate. Possesses arm strength and range that plays at all three outfield positions.

Bonifacio,Emilio

4 | **Arizona** | EXP MLB DEBUT: 2008 | POTENTIAL: Starting 2B | **7C**

Bats B Age 23
2002 FA (DR)
Pwr + +
BAvg + + +
3.80 Spd + + + + +
Def + + +

Year	Lev	Team	AB	R	H	HR	RBI	Avg	OB	Slg	OPS	bb%	ct%	Eye	SB	CS	X/H%	Iso	RC/G
2004	A-	South Bend	411	59	107	1	37	260	303	319	621	6	70	0.20	40	10	15	58	3.05
2005	A-	South Bend	522	81	141	1	44	270	341	330	670	10	83	0.62	55	17	16	59	3.98
2006	A+	Lancaster	546	117	175	7	50	321	372	449	821	8	81	0.43	58	14	28	128	5.69
2007	AA	Mobile	551	84	157	2	40	285	331	352	683	6	81	0.36	41	13	18	67	3.91
2007	MLB	Arizona	23	2	5	0	2	217	333	261	594	15	87	1.33	0	1	20	43	3.49

Small/athletic infielder with plus speed which helped him lead SL in SB. Slaps baseball to all fields and is an excellent bunter, but needs to make better contact and draw more walks. Ranges well in all directions, possesses soft/quick hands, and turns a solid double-play.

Boone,James

8 | **Pittsburgh** | EXP MLB DEBUT: 2009 | POTENTIAL: Platoon CF/RF | **7C**

Bats B Age 25
2005 (3) Missouri
Pwr + + +
BAvg + +
4.20 Spd + + + +
Def + + +

Year	Lev	Team	AB	R	H	HR	RBI	Avg	OB	Slg	OPS	bb%	ct%	Eye	SB	CS	X/H%	Iso	RC/G
2005	A-	Williamsport	278	44	81	8	42	291	330	450	780	5	69	0.19	8	4	30	158	5.22
2006	A-	Hickory	99	11	19	0	3	192	286	222	508	12	70	0.43	3	0	16	30	1.64
2007	A-	Hickory	107	18	35	4	17	327	374	495	869	7	81	0.40	0	2	29	168	6.07
2007	A+	Lynchburg	192	31	49	6	34	255	316	411	727	8	82	0.49	8	4	37	156	4.46

Athletic switch-hitter got off to a hot start after missing most of 2006 with foot and shoulder surgery. Produces moderate power from both sides, but poor contact rate and plate discipline may suppress BA at upper levels. Possesses arm strength and average range in CF.

Borbon,Julio

8 | **Texas** | EXP MLB DEBUT: 2009 | POTENTIAL: Starting CF | **8C**

Bats L Age 22
2007 (1-S) Tennessee
Pwr +
BAvg + + +
4.00 Spd + + + +
Def + + + +

Year	Lev	Team	AB	R	H	HR	RBI	Avg	OB	Slg	OPS	bb%	ct%	Eye	SB	CS	X/H%	Iso	RC/G
2007	Rk	AZL Rangers	8	0	2	0	0	250	333	375	708	11	88	1.00	0	1	50	125	4.74
2007	A-	Spokane	29	1	5	0	2	172	226	172	398	6	90	0.67	3	1	0	0	0.87

Ability to hit for BA and plus speed should make him a dynamic leadoff hitter, but possesses a miserable walk rate and lacks power. Exhibits plus range in CF and makes-up for a below average arm by being highly accurate. Speed was limited by a broken right ankle suffered in college.

Bourjos,Peter

8 | **Los Angeles (A)** | EXP MLB DEBUT: 2010 | POTENTIAL: Starting CF | **8D**

Bats R Age 21
2005 (10) HS (AZ)
Pwr + + +
BAvg + +
4.05 Spd + + + +
Def + + +

Year	Lev	Team	AB	R	H	HR	RBI	Avg	OB	Slg	OPS	bb%	ct%	Eye	SB	CS	X/H%	Iso	RC/G
2006	Rk	Orem	250	42	73	5	28	292	349	472	821	8	73	0.33	13	5	38	180	5.92
2007	Rk	AZL Angels	16	3	5	0	2	313	353	438	790	6	88	0.50	0	0	20	125	5.32
2007	A-	Cedar Rapids	237	37	65	5	29	274	331	426	757	8	78	0.38	19	9	31	152	4.90

Plus athlete missed part of season with ruptured ring finger ligament. Possesses bat speed that should produce moderate power as he matures. Legitimate threat on bases, but has to make better contact and draw more walks. Plus range and average arm strength make him solid outfielder.

Bourquin,Ronnie

5 | **Detroit** | EXP MLB DEBUT: 2009 | POTENTIAL: Platoon 3B/1B | **7D**

Bats L Age 23
2006 (2) Ohio St
Pwr + + +
BAvg + + +
Spd + +
Def + +

Year	Lev	Team	AB	R	H	HR	RBI	Avg	OB	Slg	OPS	bb%	ct%	Eye	SB	CS	X/H%	Iso	RC/G
2006	A-	Oneonta	252	37	67	2	24	266	379	349	728	15	82	1.00	3	4	24	83	4.99
2007	A-	Oneonta	194	31	63	2	28	325	418	454	871	14	82	0.89	2	2	29	129	6.72
2007	A+	Lakeland	78	9	15	0	3	192	315	218	533	15	68	0.56	1	0	13	26	2.07

Considered an overdraft, but had a solid season offensively, hitting for BA and drawing walks. Has bat speed to hit for power, but hasn't adjusted to wood and lacks trajectory to hits. Defense is average at best as he makes poor groundball reads and doesn't have much range.

Bowker,John — 9 — San Francisco

EXP MLB DEBUT: 2008 | POTENTIAL: Platoon LF/RF | 7C

Bats L | Age 24
2004 (3) Long Beach St
Pwr ++++
BAvg +++
Spd ++
Def ++

Year	Lev	Team	AB	R	H	HR	RBI	Avg	OB	Slg	OPS	bb%	ct%	Eye	SB	CS	X/H%	Iso	RC/G
2004	A-	Salem-Keizer	127	23	41	4	16	323	363	520	883	6	80	0.32	1	0	37	197	6.30
2005	A+	San Jose	464	66	124	13	67	267	320	414	734	7	77	0.33	3	7	33	147	4.50
2006	A+	San Jose	462	61	131	7	66	284	337	424	761	7	78	0.37	6	3	34	141	4.96
2006	AAA	Fresno	4	0	2	0	0	500	500	500	1000	0	100		0	0	0	0	6.83
2007	AA	Connecticut	522	79	160	22	90	307	357	523	880	7	80	0.40	3	7	39	216	6.29

Tweener outfielder with quick hands and extension that allows him to stay on baseball and hit for BA. Produces moderate power to pull field and could help fortune with improve plate discipline. Ranges well in outfield, but possesses slightly below average arm strength.

Brantley,Michael — 73 — Milwaukee

EXP MLB DEBUT: 2009 | POTENTIAL: Platoon LF/CF | 7C

Bats L | Age 21
2005 (7) HS (FL)
Pwr +
BAvg +++
Spd ++++
Def +++

Year	Lev	Team	AB	R	H	HR	RBI	Avg	OB	Slg	OPS	bb%	ct%	Eye	SB	CS	X/H%	Iso	RC/G
2005	Rk	AZL Brewers	173	34	60	0	19	347	421	376	796	11	92	1.69	14	5	7	29	5.70
2005	Rk	Helena	34	8	11	0	3	324	425	382	807	15	88	1.50	2	0	18	59	6.06
2006	A-	W. Virginia	360	47	108	0	42	300	401	339	740	14	86	1.20	24	7	11	39	5.17
2007	A-	W. Virginia	218	41	73	2	32	335	418	440	858	12	90	1.41	18	6	25	106	6.46
2007	AA	Huntsville	187	28	47	0	21	251	352	294	646	13	87	1.16	18	3	15	43	4.01

Athletic outfielder possesses best plate discipline in system, allowing him to hit for BA. Tore-up SAL and skipped a level where he was overmatched. Lacks power, but plus speed allows him to be a threat on the bases. Poor throwing arm limits him to LF, but does have excellent range.

Brewer,Brent — 6 — Milwaukee

EXP MLB DEBUT: 2010 | POTENTIAL: Starting SS/CF | 8D

Bats R | Age 20
2006 (2) HS (GA)
Pwr +++
BAvg +++
4.20 Spd ++++
Def +++

Year	Lev	Team	AB	R	H	HR	RBI	Avg	OB	Slg	OPS	bb%	ct%	Eye	SB	CS	X/H%	Iso	RC/G
2006	Rk	AZL Brewers	182	25	48	3	22	264	323	396	719	8	71	0.30	10	0	25	132	4.52
2007	A-	W. Virginia	518	86	130	11	49	251	312	390	702	8	67	0.27	42	7	33	139	4.35

Athletic infielder with excellent secondary offensive skills. Drives ball with lock-and-load swing, but most of hits are to pull field. Runs bases aggressively and is an efficient base-stealer. Struggles to read hops and rushes throws, but has a solid arm and ranges well in all directions.

Brignac,Reid — 6 — Tampa Bay

EXP MLB DEBUT: 2008 | POTENTIAL: Starting SS | 9C

Bats L | Age 22
2004 (2) HS (LA)
Pwr ++++
BAvg +++
4.10 Spd ++++
Def +++

Year	Lev	Team	AB	R	H	HR	RBI	Avg	OB	Slg	OPS	bb%	ct%	Eye	SB	CS	X/H%	Iso	RC/G
2004	Rk	Princeton	97	16	35	1	25	361	415	474	889	8	90	0.90	2	1	20	113	6.52
2005	A-	SW Michigan	512	77	135	15	61	264	317	416	733	7	74	0.31	5	5	34	152	4.52
2006	A+	Visalia	411	82	135	21	84	328	381	560	941	8	80	0.43	11	6	37	231	7.02
2006	AA	Montgomery	110	18	33	3	16	300	342	473	815	6	72	0.23	3	0	33	173	5.68
2007	AA	Montgomery	527	91	137	17	81	260	330	433	763	9	82	0.59	15	5	38	173	4.99

Wiry athlete didn't match his 2006 numbers in the CAL, but did improve his walk rate and X/H%, while leading SL in runs scored. BA will always fluctuate with his lengthy swing, but will hit for moderate power. Has the range and arm to stay at SS, but needs cleaner footwork.

Brown,Corey — 9 — Oakland

EXP MLB DEBUT: 2010 | POTENTIAL: Starting CF/RF | 9D

Bats L | Age 22
2007 (1-S) Oklahoma St
Pwr ++++
BAvg ++
4.15 Spd ++++
Def +++

Year	Lev	Team	AB	R	H	HR	RBI	Avg	OB	Slg	OPS	bb%	ct%	Eye	SB	CS	X/H%	Iso	RC/G
2007	A-	Vancouver	213	31	57	11	48	268	376	545	921	15	64	0.48	5	3	58	277	8.06

Plus athlete with excellent power potential based on bat speed and fluid stroke. Likely to struggle with BA due to contact issues and struggles versus LH pitching, but will draw walks and utilize his speed. Possesses the arm strength and range to play anywhere in the outfield.

Brown,Dominic — 9 — Philadelphia

EXP MLB DEBUT: 2011 | POTENTIAL: Starting RF | 9E

Bats L | Age 20
2006 (20) HS (GA)
Pwr ++++
BAvg +++
Spd ++++
Def ++

Year	Lev	Team	AB	R	H	HR	RBI	Avg	OB	Slg	OPS	bb%	ct%	Eye	SB	CS	X/H%	Iso	RC/G
2006	Rk	GCL Phillies	117	13	25	1	7	214	287	265	552	9	74	0.40	13	3	16	51	2.21
2007	A-	Williamsport	285	43	84	3	32	295	356	400	756	9	83	0.55	14	7	23	105	4.94
2007	A+	Clearwater	9	2	4	1	7	444	545	889	1434	18	100		0	0	50	444	12.69

Plus athlete with strength and speed, his potential is enormous. Bat speed produces power and will draw walks, but swing is lengthy and struggles with breaking stuff. Arm strength and range are solid for RF, but needs to take better routes which will come with experience.

Brown,Dusty — 2 — Boston

EXP MLB DEBUT: 2008 | POTENTIAL: Reserve CA | 6B

Bats R | Age 25
2000 (35) HS (AZ)
Pwr ++
BAvg ++
Spd +
Def ++++

Year	Lev	Team	AB	R	H	HR	RBI	Avg	OB	Slg	OPS	bb%	ct%	Eye	SB	CS	X/H%	Iso	RC/G
2005	Rk	GCL Red Sox	18	3	4	0	3	222	364	278	540	18	89	2.00	0	0	25	56	2.88
2005	A+	Wilmington	219	32	56	8	36	256	348	420	768	12	76	0.60	1	1	36	164	4.89
2006	AA	Portland	296	32	66	5	40	224	284	332	616	8	78	0.37	2	2	33	108	3.77
2007	AA	Portland	254	43	68	9	43	268	344	453	797	10	75	0.44	0	0	40	185	5.22
2007	AAA	Pawtucket	27	1	5	0	3	185	241	259	500	7	63	0.20	0	0	40	74	2.02

Athletic catcher with excellent receiving skills and can shut-down running game with a quick release and average arm strength. Uses the whole field with line-drive power and though he doesn't judge the strike zone well, he does make in-bat adjustments that improve opportunities.

Brown,Jordan — 37 — Cleveland

EXP MLB DEBUT: 2008 | POTENTIAL: Reserve LF/1B | 7C

Bats L | Age 24
2004 (5) Arizona
Pwr +++
BAvg ++++
Spd ++
Def ++

Year	Lev	Team	AB	R	H	HR	RBI	Avg	OB	Slg	OPS	bb%	ct%	Eye	SB	CS	X/H%	Iso	RC/G
2005	A-	Mahoning Val	75	15	19	3	7	253	282	387	669	4	91	0.43	2	1	21	133	3.58
2006	A+	Kinston	473	71	137	15	88	290	359	474	832	10	88	0.86	4	0	36	184	5.89
2007	AA	Akron	483	85	161	11	76	333	410	484	895	12	88	1.13	11	2	30	151	6.75

Strong/stocky hitter was league MVP last two seasons (EL and CAR). Centers ball well, shows moderate power to all fields, and judges strike zone, but lacks the over-the-fence power desired for a MLB corner. Runs bases well despite below average speed and defense is much better at 1B.

Brown,Matt — 574 — Los Angeles (A)

EXP MLB DEBUT: 2007 | POTENTIAL: Reserve 3B/2B | 6B

Bats R | Age 25
2001 (10) HS (MD)
Pwr ++
BAvg +++
4.40 Spd ++
Def +++

Year	Lev	Team	AB	R	H	HR	RBI	Avg	OB	Slg	OPS	bb%	ct%	Eye	SB	CS	X/H%	Iso	RC/G
2004	A-	Cedar Rapids	437	67	102	23	82	233	287	455	743	7	71	0.26	6	6	46	222	4.60
2005	A+	Rancho Cuc	488	68	128	12	65	262	318	432	751	8	74	0.32	4	5	43	170	4.85
2006	AA	Arkansas	515	77	149	19	79	289	349	491	840	8	79	0.44	7	6	42	202	5.91
2007	AAA	Salt Lake	391	69	108	19	60	276	351	509	860	10	73	0.42	5	9	47	233	6.38
2007	MLB	Los Angeles (A)	5	0	0	0	0	0	286	0	286	29	80	2.00	1	0	0	0	0.00

Versatile infielder who can play three positions with soft hands and average arm strength. Lacks speed and first-step quickness. Produces doubles power and draw walks, but a long swing, poor contact rate, and tendency to pull baseball drives-down BA.

Bruce,Jay — 8 — Cincinnati

EXP MLB DEBUT: 2008 | POTENTIAL: Starting RF | 10C

Bats L | Age 21
2005 (1) HS (TX)
Pwr ++++
BAvg ++++
4.25 Spd +++
Def ++++

Year	Lev	Team	AB	R	H	HR	RBI	Avg	OB	Slg	OPS	bb%	ct%	Eye	SB	CS	X/H%	Iso	RC/G
2005	Rk	GCL Reds	122	29	33	5	25	270	331	500	831	8	75	0.35	4	6	48	230	5.90
2006	A-	Dayton	444	69	129	16	80	291	355	516	870	9	76	0.42	19	9	49	225	6.45
2007	A+	Sarasota	268	49	87	11	49	325	380	586	966	8	75	0.36	4	4	49	261	7.73
2007	AA	Chattanooga	66	10	22	4	15	333	405	652	1057	11	70	0.40	2	1	55	318	9.41
2007	AAA	Louisville	187	28	57	11	25	305	356	567	923	7	74	0.31	2	2	44	262	6.97

Top player in the minors with an impact bat that produces power and BA. Plus bat speed is basis of power and uses whole field. An above average runner for now, though is unlikely to steal bases. Defensive tools profile better in RF, but plays a solid CF and is ready for Majors.

Burgess,Michael — 9 — Washington

EXP MLB DEBUT: 2012 | POTENTIAL: Starting RF | 9E

Bats L | Age 19
2007 (1-S) HS (FL)
Pwr ++++
BAvg +++
4.35 Spd ++
Def +++

Year	Lev	Team	AB	R	H	HR	RBI	Avg	OB	Slg	OPS	bb%	ct%	Eye	SB	CS	X/H%	Iso	RC/G
2007	Rk	GCL Nationals	128	22	43	8	32	336	444	617	1062	16	71	0.68	1	2	40	281	9.57
2007	A-	Vermont	70	10	20	3	10	286	375	457	832	13	67	0.43	1	1	25	171	6.28

Muscular athlete with plus bat speed and advanced approach which let him lead GCL in OBP and SLG. Takes ball out to all parts of the park and contact problems in high school were non-existent. Arm strength is excellent, but fringe-average speed and range makes RF a better fit.

Burke,Kyler — 9 — Chicago (N)

EXP MLB DEBUT: 2010 **POTENTIAL:** Starting LF/RF **8E**

Bats L Age 20
2006 (1-S) HS (TN)
- Pwr + + + +
- BAvg + +
- Spd + + + (4.20)
- Def + + +

Year	Lev	Team	AB	R	H	HR	RBI	Avg	OB	Slg	OPS	bb%	ct%	Eye	SB	CS	X/H%	Iso	RC/G
2006	Rk	AZL Padres	163	24	34	1	15	209	317	294	612	14	66	0.46	1	3	24	86	3.26
2007	A-	Boise	224	35	57	10	41	254	327	446	773	10	72	0.38	1	3	39	192	5.14
2007	A-	Ft. Wayne	213	24	45	1	21	211	297	268	565	11	66	0.36	3	1	20	56	2.42

Bat speed and natural strength propel power to all fields, though he lost some BA by lunging at pitches, being over-aggressive, and showing mediocre plate discipline. Possesses an outstanding throwing arm, but average speed and inexperience gives him marginal range.

Burriss,Emmanuel — 6 — San Francisco

EXP MLB DEBUT: 2009 **POTENTIAL:** Starting 2B **7C**

Bats B Age 23
2006 (1-S) Kent St
- Pwr +
- BAvg + + +
- Spd + + + + + (3.95)
- Def + + +

Year	Lev	Team	AB	R	H	HR	RBI	Avg	OB	Slg	OPS	bb%	ct%	Eye	SB	CS	X/H%	Iso	RC/G
2006	Rk	Salem-Keizer	254	50	78	1	27	307	374	366	740	10	91	1.23	35	11	14	59	4.95
2007	A-	Augusta	365	64	117	0	38	321	369	381	750	7	87	0.57	51	15	15	60	4.82
2007	A+	San Jose	139	23	23	0	8	165	232	180	412	8	86	0.60	17	3	9	14	0.88

Plus athlete with blazing speed, he was overmatched in an aggressive promotion to the CAL, but hit more comfortably in the SAL. Hits for BA using slap-type approach and by bunting, and will draw walks, but lacks power. May not have arm strength for SS, but has good range and soft hands.

Buscher,Brian — 5 — Minnesota

EXP MLB DEBUT: 2007 **POTENTIAL:** Platoon 3B **6B**

Bats L Age 27
2003 (3) South Carolina
- Pwr + + +
- BAvg + + +
- Spd + +
- Def + + +

Year	Lev	Team	AB	R	H	HR	RBI	Avg	OB	Slg	OPS	bb%	ct%	Eye	SB	CS	X/H%	Iso	RC/G
2005	A+	San Jose	206	37	58	5	29	282	365	422	787	12	77	0.57	0	2	31	141	5.45
2005	AA	Norwich	215	19	49	1	23	228	294	288	582	9	83	0.56	5	3	20	60	2.84
2007	AA	New Britain	247	37	76	7	37	308	385	478	863	11	88	1.03	2	2	36	170	6.34
2007	AAA	Rochester	132	21	41	7	22	311	372	523	895	9	92	1.18	1	0	34	212	6.43
2007	MLB	Minnesota	82	8	20	2	10	244	326	329	655	11	80	0.63	1	0	15	85	3.65

Strong/muscular player with solid hitting skills, featuring BA ability through good plate discipline, use of the whole field, and ability to make contact. Power is more of the doubles variety, but will turn on a mistake. Arm strength and soft hands provide average defense.

Cain,Lorenzo — 9 — Milwaukee

EXP MLB DEBUT: 2009 **POTENTIAL:** Starting RF **7C**

Bats R Age 22
2004 (17) Tallahassee C
- Pwr + +
- BAvg + + +
- Spd + + + +
- Def + + +

Year	Lev	Team	AB	R	H	HR	RBI	Avg	OB	Slg	OPS	bb%	ct%	Eye	SB	CS	X/H%	Iso	RC/G
2005	Rk	AZL Brewers	205	45	73	5	37	356	413	566	979	9	84	0.63	12	3	38	210	7.66
2005	Rk	Helena	24	4	5	0	1	208	240	208	448	4	75	0.17	0	0	0	0	0.61
2006	A-	W. Virginia	527	91	161	6	60	306	374	423	798	10	80	0.56	33	11	29	118	5.55
2007	A+	Brevard Co	482	67	133	2	44	276	328	344	672	7	80	0.38	24	9	20	68	3.80

Athletic with plus speed, he suffered a decline in both strike zone judgment and power which casts doubt on his offensive ceiling. Maintained BA, but walk rate/OBP dropped, limiting his running. Displays range and solid average arm strength in both RF and CF.

Campbell,Eric — 5 — Atlanta

EXP MLB DEBUT: 2009 **POTENTIAL:** Starting 3B **8D**

Bats R Age 22
2004 (2) HS (IN)
- Pwr + + + +
- BAvg + +
- Spd + + + (4.30)
- Def + +

Year	Lev	Team	AB	R	H	HR	RBI	Avg	OB	Slg	OPS	bb%	ct%	Eye	SB	CS	X/H%	Iso	RC/G
2004	Rk	GCL Braves	211	30	53	7	29	251	301	384	685	7	78	0.32	3	1	26	133	3.76
2004	A-	Rome	22	0	3	0	1	136	208	136	345	8	68	0.29	0	0	0	0	-0.93
2005	Rk	Danville	262	77	82	18	64	313	379	634	1013	10	76	0.44	15	4	56	321	8.24
2006	A-	Rome	449	83	132	22	77	294	328	514	843	5	85	0.34	18	4	39	220	5.59
2007	A+	Myrtle Beach	298	47	66	14	49	221	305	406	711	11	84	0.75	6	3	41	185	4.36

Disappointing season after solid 2006. Bat speed and strong frame produces above average power and improved walk rate, but struggled with contact. In his defense, he battled thumb/shoulder injuries during season. Defense remains mediocre and work ethic is questionable.

Canham,Mitch — 2 — San Diego

EXP MLB DEBUT: 2009 **POTENTIAL:** Platoon CA **7C**

Bats L Age 23
2007 (1-S) Oregon St
- Pwr + +
- BAvg + + +
- Spd + + + (4.20)
- Def + + +

Year	Lev	Team	AB	R	H	HR	RBI	Avg	OB	Slg	OPS	bb%	ct%	Eye	SB	CS	X/H%	Iso	RC/G
2007	A-	Eugene	116	20	34	2	18	293	354	397	751	9	70	0.31	5	2	21	103	4.96
2007	A+	Lk Elsinore	7	0	0	0	1	0	0	0	0	0	71	0.00	0	0	0	0	0.00

Athletic catcher with contact ability and moderate power, he drives the gaps consistently and will turn on inside pitches. Runs well for a catcher and will pick spots to steal. Possesses average arm strength and a quick release, netting a 31% CS%, but needs work on his receiving skills.

Cannon,Chip — 3 — Toronto

EXP MLB DEBUT: 2007 **POTENTIAL:** Platoon 1B/DH **6B**

Bats L Age 26
2004 (8) The Citadel
- Pwr + + + +
- BAvg + +
- Spd +
- Def +

Year	Lev	Team	AB	R	H	HR	RBI	Avg	OB	Slg	OPS	bb%	ct%	Eye	SB	CS	X/H%	Iso	RC/G
2005	A-	Lansing	168	22	45	11	36	268	346	542	887	11	72	0.43	0	0	49	274	6.71
2005	A+	Dunedin	112	28	43	14	39	384	461	830	1291	13	71	0.50	0	1	47	446	12.22
2005	AA	New Hamp	170	15	42	7	23	247	289	459	748	6	66	0.17	2	0	50	212	4.92
2006	AA	New Hamp	474	78	118	27	69	249	322	475	797	10	67	0.32	0	2	44	226	5.61
2007	AA	New Hamp	394	57	95	17	53	241	333	434	767	12	61	0.35	1	0	43	193	5.67

All or nothing swinger with excellent power. Poor pitch recognition and a long swing prevent him from hitting for BA and is essentially a mistake hitter. Clubbed feet make him a liability on the bases and due to his poor agility and stiff hands, is a below average fielder.

Cardenas,Adrian — 4 — Philadelphia

EXP MLB DEBUT: 2010 **POTENTIAL:** Starting 2B **8C**

Bats L Age 20
2006 (1-S) HS (FL)
- Pwr + + +
- BAvg + + +
- Spd + + + (4.30)
- Def + + +

Year	Lev	Team	AB	R	H	HR	RBI	Avg	OB	Slg	OPS	bb%	ct%	Eye	SB	CS	X/H%	Iso	RC/G
2006	Rk	GCL Phillies	154	22	49	2	21	318	386	442	828	10	82	0.61	13	3	22	123	5.90
2007	A-	Lakewood	499	70	147	9	79	295	355	417	772	9	84	0.59	19	7	28	122	5.10

Offensive-minded second sacker with wiry strength and ability to center baseball. Hitting for BA should pose no problem and power should increase. Runs bases exceptionally well despite below average speed. Adapting well to 2B showing soft hands and adequate arm strength.

Carp,Mike — 3 — New York (N)

EXP MLB DEBUT: 2008 **POTENTIAL:** Platoon 1B **7C**

Bats L Age 21
2004 (9) HS (CA)
- Pwr + + + +
- BAvg + +
- Spd + +
- Def + + +

Year	Lev	Team	AB	R	H	HR	RBI	Avg	OB	Slg	OPS	bb%	ct%	Eye	SB	CS	X/H%	Iso	RC/G
2004	Rk	GCL Mets	191	30	51	4	26	267	343	393	735	10	73	0.43	2	1	31	126	4.75
2005	A-	Hagerstown	313	49	78	19	63	249	325	476	801	10	69	0.36	2	2	41	227	5.53
2006	A+	St. Lucie	490	69	140	17	87	286	353	447	800	9	78	0.48	2	1	31	161	5.42
2007	A+	St. Lucie	4	0	1	0	0	250	250	250	500	0	100	0.00	0	0	0	0	2.09
2007	AA	Binghamton	359	55	90	11	48	251	324	387	711	10	79	0.52	2	1	30	136	4.31

Power hitter with moderate bat speed and natural strength, but makes poor contact rendering power useless in games. Tried to focus more on contact, but needs more controlled aggression. Fields position well with soft hands, but lacks agility. Broken finger in May cost him several at-bats.

Carrasco,Felix — 5 — San Diego

EXP MLB DEBUT: 2010 **POTENTIAL:** Starting 3B **8E**

Bats B Age 21
2006 FA (DR)
- Pwr + + + +
- BAvg + + +
- Spd + +
- Def + +

Year	Lev	Team	AB	R	H	HR	RBI	Avg	OB	Slg	OPS	bb%	ct%	Eye	SB	CS	X/H%	Iso	RC/G
2006	Rk	AZL Padres	172	32	47	4	37	273	339	424	763	9	72	0.35	2	0	36	151	5.11
2007	Rk	AZL Padres	52	5	15	0	6	288	393	327	720	15	69	0.56	0	2	7	38	4.87
2007	A-	Eugene	49	5	9	0	4	184	245	245	490	8	51	0.17	1	2	22	61	1.57

Strong/athletic player with bat speed and power potential. Mediocre contact rate and plate discipline will keep BA suppressed until he makes adjustments. Possesses plus arm strength and first-step quickness at 3B, but stiff hands and poor groundball reads means more work defensively.

Carroll,Brett — 9 — Florida

EXP MLB DEBUT: 2007 **POTENTIAL:** Platoon RF/LF **6C**

Bats R Age 25
2004 (10) Mid Tenn St
- Pwr + + + +
- BAvg + +
- Spd + +
- Def + + + +

Year	Lev	Team	AB	R	H	HR	RBI	Avg	OB	Slg	OPS	bb%	ct%	Eye	SB	CS	X/H%	Iso	RC/G
2006	AA	Carolina	250	29	58	9	30	232	284	424	708	7	75	0.29	4	1	47	192	4.16
2006	AAA	Albuquerque	216	31	52	8	30	241	299	417	716	8	78	0.38	9	3	40	176	4.26
2007	AA	Carolina	100	9	27	3	12	270	348	490	838	11	80	0.60	0	2	59	220	6.10
2007	AAA	Albuquerque	318	60	100	19	70	314	351	597	949	5	78	0.26	0	4	46	283	7.04
2007	MLB	Florida	49	10	9	0	2	184	231	204	435	6	69	0.20	0	0	11	20	0.38

Muscular athlete with bat speed and power, but is mostly a guess-hitter and struggles to make contact, limiting BA/OBP. Has one minors' strongest arms, but poor speed/range limits him to an outfield corner. Success versus LH pitching makes him a perfect platoon option.

Carter,Chris V — 53 — Oakland

EXP MLB DEBUT: 2010 | POTENTIAL: Starting 1B | 8D

Bats R Age 21
2005 (15) HS (NV)
Pwr ++++
BAvg ++
Spd ++
Def +

Year	Lev	Team	AB	R	H	HR	RBI	Avg	OB	Slg	OPS	bb%	ct%	Eye	SB	CS	X/H%	Iso	RC/G
2005	Rk	Bristol	233	33	66	10	37	283	332	485	817	7	73	0.27	2	1	41	202	5.63
2006	Rk	Great Falls	251	37	75	15	59	299	382	570	952	12	72	0.49	4	4	49	271	7.73
2006	A-	Kannapolis	46	4	6	1	5	130	216	261	477	10	63	0.29	0	0	67	130	0.98
2007	A-	Kannapolis	467	84	136	25	93	291	383	522	905	13	76	0.60	3	2	40	231	7.08

One of the better, pure hitters in the minors, possessing power, contact ability, and plate discipline. Bat speed is solid and seems to hit the ball hard each time. Arm strength solid enough for 3B and LF, but lack of agility/range and stiff hands will make 1B his permanent home.

Carter,Chris W — 73 — Boston

EXP MLB DEBUT: 2008 | POTENTIAL: Platoon LF/1B | 8C

Bats L Age 25
2004 (17) Stanford
Pwr ++++
BAvg +++
Spd ++
Def +

Year	Lev	Team	AB	R	H	HR	RBI	Avg	OB	Slg	OPS	bb%	ct%	Eye	SB	CS	X/H%	Iso	RC/G
2004	A-	Yakima	256	47	86	15	63	336	437	578	1015	15	87	1.35	2	3	36	242	8.24
2005	A+	Lancaster	412	71	122	21	85	296	367	522	889	10	84	0.70	0	0	40	226	6.46
2005	AA	Tennessee	128	21	38	10	30	297	388	563	950	13	91	1.73	0	3	37	266	7.19
2006	AAA	Tucson	509	87	153	19	97	301	394	483	877	13	86	1.13	10	4	34	183	6.58
2007	AAA	Tuc/Paw	550	80	174	19	88	316	377	504	880	9	86	0.72	2	0	36	187	6.60

Showed no ill effects from right hamate surgery over off-season, possessing one of the better bats in Triple-A. Bat speed and plate discipline allow him to hit for both power and BA. Bat must play big for a role in the Majors, as his speed and defensive skills are well below average.

Carvajal,Yefri — 8 — San Diego

EXP MLB DEBUT: 2011 | POTENTIAL: Platoon LF/RF | 8E

Bats R Age 19
2005 FA (DR)
Pwr ++++
BAvg ++
4.30 Spd +++
Def +++

Year	Lev	Team	AB	R	H	HR	RBI	Avg	OB	Slg	OPS	bb%	ct%	Eye	SB	CS	X/H%	Iso	RC/G
2006	Rk	AZL Padres	75	14	19	2	9	253	282	373	655	4	79	0.19	2	0	26	120	3.29
2007	Rk	AZL Padres	100	27	34	1	22	340	400	500	900	9	78	0.45	5	0	41	160	6.91
2007	A-	Eugene	122	15	32	2	19	262	291	369	660	4	68	0.13	2	0	25	107	3.52

Strong/physical athlete with upside and was named MVP of Padres' instructional league. Possesses bat speed and pole-to-pole power, but needs better contact rate and plate discipline or power will go south with BA. Played mostly CF, but has just average speed and arm strength.

Casto,Kory — 573 — Washington

EXP MLB DEBUT: 2007 | POTENTIAL: Reserve LF/3B | 6A

Bats L Age 26
2003 (3) Portland
Pwr +++
BAvg ++
Spd ++
Def +++

Year	Lev	Team	AB	R	H	HR	RBI	Avg	OB	Slg	OPS	bb%	ct%	Eye	SB	CS	X/H%	Iso	RC/G
2004	A	Savannah	483	67	138	16	88	286	329	474	803	6	86	0.44	1	2	40	188	5.29
2005	A+	Potomac	500	86	145	22	90	290	392	510	902	14	80	0.86	6	3	43	220	6.98
2006	AA	Harrisburg	490	84	133	20	80	271	375	467	842	14	79	0.78	6	5	38	196	6.22
2007	AAA	Columbus	411	56	101	11	55	246	333	384	718	12	74	0.51	4	4	33	139	4.52
2007	MLB	Washington	54	1	7	0	3	130	161	167	327	4	69	0.12	0	0	29	37	-1.19

Aggressive hitter with compact swing, his BA/OBP tumbled trying to hit for power by uppercutting. Exercises patience at the plate, but tends to wait too long, putting him behind in the count. Possesses a strong arm, but is a below average fielder and WAS is using him at multiple positions.

Castro,Jose — 6 — Cincinnati

EXP MLB DEBUT: 2009 | POTENTIAL: Reserve SS/2B | 7D

Bats B Age 21
2005 (32) Miami-Dade C
Pwr +
BAvg +++
Spd ++++
Def ++++

Year	Lev	Team	AB	R	H	HR	RBI	Avg	OB	Slg	OPS	bb%	ct%	Eye	SB	CS	X/H%	Iso	RC/G
2005	Rk	GCL Mets	116	15	34	1	10	293	328	379	707	5	92	0.67	2	0	18	86	4.29
2005	Rk	Kingsport	14	1	4	0	1	286	375	286	661	13	93	2.00	0	1	0	0	4.29
2006	A-	Hagerstown	433	38	94	0	38	217	250	245	495	4	88	0.36	6	4	13	28	1.75
2007	A+	St. Lucie	308	47	98	2	25	318	342	383	725	3	93	0.52	7	10	15	65	4.36
2007	AA	Chattanooga	54	5	15	0	1	278	304	352	655	4	85	0.25	1	0	20	74	3.51

Short/athletic infielder with a strong defensive reputation, possessing plus range and arm strength. Offense improved as he made better contact and utilized his speed. Marginal bat speed lowers power and over-aggressiveness keeps walk rate low.

Cervelli,Francisco — 2 — New York (A)

EXP MLB DEBUT: 2009 | POTENTIAL: Platoon CA | 7D

Bats B Age 22
2003 FA (Venezuela)
Pwr ++
BAvg +++
Spd ++
Def ++++

Year	Lev	Team	AB	R	H	HR	RBI	Avg	OB	Slg	OPS	bb%	ct%	Eye	SB	CS	X/H%	Iso	RC/G
2005	Rk	GCL Yankees	58	10	11	1	9	190	288	276	564	12	78	0.62	1	0	27	86	2.54
2006	A-	Staten Island	137	22	41	2	18	299	360	416	776	9	78	0.43	0	0	29	117	5.18
2007	A+	Tampa	290	34	81	2	32	279	359	397	755	11	80	0.61	4	3	35	117	5.13

Athletic catcher converted from an infielder in 2006 and already possesses MLB defensive skills. Shows solid arm strength and receiving skills that belie experience level. Makes contact and uses whole field which should provide BA, but lacks secondary skills of power and OBP.

Chalk,Brad — 8 — San Diego

EXP MLB DEBUT: 2009 | POTENTIAL: Platoon CF/LF | 7D

Bats L Age 22
2007 (2) Clemson
Pwr +
BAvg ++++
3.95 Spd ++++
Def +++

Year	Lev	Team	AB	R	H	HR	RBI	Avg	OB	Slg	OPS	bb%	ct%	Eye	SB	CS	X/H%	Iso	RC/G
2007	Rk	AZL Padres	44	11	16	0	7	364	440	477	917	12	86	1.00	3	2	31	114	7.19
2007	A-	Eugene	83	14	19	0	6	229	312	301	613	11	73	0.45	0	2	21	72	3.21

Small/athletic outfielder with plus speed, ability to make contact, and plate discipline which should ensure strong BA/OBP. Slap-type approach and lack of bat speed make power non-existent, but has potential to hit leadoff. Ranges well in CF, but has below average arm strength.

Chapman,Stephen — 73 — Milwaukee

EXP MLB DEBUT: 2010 | POTENTIAL: Platoon LF/1B | 8E

Bats L Age 22
2004 (6) HS (FL)
Pwr +++
BAvg +++
4.20 Spd +++
Def ++

Year	Lev	Team	AB	R	H	HR	RBI	Avg	OB	Slg	OPS	bb%	ct%	Eye	SB	CS	X/H%	Iso	RC/G
2004	Rk	AZL Brewers	192	33	44	4	18	229	292	401	693	8	74	0.34	4	3	41	172	4.16
2005	Rk	Helena	167	25	45	6	25	269	348	443	791	11	77	0.53	10	3	36	174	5.39
2006	Rk	Helena	276	50	85	6	40	308	374	496	870	10	77	0.46	20	6	38	188	6.52
2006	A	W. Virginia	17	3	3	0	0	176	222	176	399	6	65	0.17	0	1	0	0	-0.32
2007	A	W. Virginia	455	77	119	24	89	262	316	501	817	7	70	0.26	12	3	46	240	5.73

Projectable power hitter with moderate bat speed, but could struggle to hit for BA due to poor contact ability and a platoon differential. Steals occasional base with average speed. Defense is questionable with below average arm strength and marginal range, and may move to 1B.

Chavez,Angel — 546 — New York (A)

EXP MLB DEBUT: 2005 | POTENTIAL: Reserve 3B/2B | 6B

Bats R Age 26
1998 FA (Panama)
Pwr +
BAvg ++
Spd ++++
Def ++++

Year	Lev	Team	AB	R	H	HR	RBI	Avg	OB	Slg	OPS	bb%	ct%	Eye	SB	CS	X/H%	Iso	RC/G
2005	AAA	Fresno	334	46	94	11	64	281	316	449	765	5	82	0.29	5	1	33	168	4.73
2005	MLB	San Francisco	19	1	5	0	1	263	263	316	579	0	84	0.00	0	0	20	53	2.34
2006	AA	Bowie/Read	254	0	65	5	33	256	303	366	669	6	81	0.35	7	3	26	110	3.65
2006	AAA	Scranton/WB	210	27	58	6	28	276	318	476	795	6	80	0.32	6	0	50	200	5.25
2007	AAA	Scranton/WB	430	62	125	11	66	291	333	433	765	6	81	0.34	6	3	30	142	4.81

Strong defensive player with plus arm strength, range, and the ability to play three infield positions. Offense began to show life, hitting for modest power. BA was solid, but with poor plate discipline it will always fluctuate. Despite good speed, he doesn't run much.

Chavez,Yohermyn — 7 — Toronto

EXP MLB DEBUT: 2011 | POTENTIAL: Starting LF/RF | 8D

Bats R Age 19
2004 FA (Venezuela)
Pwr ++++
BAvg ++
4.30 Spd +++
Def +++

Year	Lev	Team	AB	R	H	HR	RBI	Avg	OB	Slg	OPS	bb%	ct%	Eye	SB	CS	X/H%	Iso	RC/G
2006	Rk	Pulaski	105	19	29	0	18	276	333	362	695	8	78	0.39	1	2	31	86	4.20
2007	Rk	GCL Blue Jays	176	29	53	6	21	301	372	494	867	10	72	0.40	7	2	38	193	6.60

Strong/athletic outfielder known for his bat speed and power, but managed a solid BA/OBP by improving strike zone judgment and becoming less pull-conscious. Will draw walks and utilized average speed well. Below average range and adequate arm strength may only play in LF.

Chen,Yung-Chi — 4 — Seattle

EXP MLB DEBUT: 2008 | POTENTIAL: Reserve 2B/3B | 6B

Bats R Age 24
2003 FA (Taiwan)
Pwr ++
BAvg +++
4.30 Spd +++
Def ++++

Year	Lev	Team	AB	R	H	HR	RBI	Avg	OB	Slg	OPS	bb%	ct%	Eye	SB	CS	X/H%	Iso	RC/G
2005	A	Wisconsin	503	77	147	7	80	292	341	416	756	7	85	0.49	15	6	28	123	5.04
2006	Rk	AZL Mariners	11	1	3	0	2	273	333	545	879	8	100		0	0	67	273	6.86
2006	A+	Inland Emp	278	49	95	5	48	342	390	478	868	7	86	0.55	21	7	26	137	6.17
2006	AA	San Antonio	149	22	44	3	22	295	371	443	814	11	85	0.78	5	3	32	148	5.77
2007	AAA	Tacoma	15	2	5	0	3	333	294	467	667	0	80	0.00	1	1	40	134	4.14

Small/athletic infielder with good contact skills and BA ability, missed most of 2007 with a dislocated shoulder. Lacks bat speed to hit for power and despite average speed, is not a factor on the bases. Solid defender with range, soft/quick hands, and a strong DP turn.

Chiang,Chih-Hsien — 4 — Boston

EXP MLB DEBUT: 2010 | POTENTIAL: Starting 2B | 7E

Bats L Age 20 — 2005 FA (Taiwan)

- Pwr +
- BAvg +++
- 4.20 Spd +++
- Def +++

Year	Lev	Team	AB	R	H	HR	RBI	Avg	OB	Slg	OPS	bb%	ct%	Eye	SB	CS	X/H%	Iso	RC/G
2006	Rk	GCL Red Sox	122	12	35	1	12	287	310	410	719	3	91	0.36	2	0	31	123	4.33
2006	A-	Lowell	36	6	10	1	8	278	316	528	844	5	75	0.22	1	0	40	250	6.07
2007	AA	Greenville	355	35	93	5	41	262	305	392	697	6	77	0.27	1	1	37	130	4.05

Pure hitter with contact ability and line-drive stroke from gap-to-gap. Improving plate discipline could enhance OBP and power might improve with physical maturity. Defense may only be average at best with average arm strength and range, and stiff hands.

Ciriaco,Pedro — 6 — Arizona

EXP MLB DEBUT: 2009 | POTENTIAL: Reserve SS/2B | 7E

Bats R Age 22 — 2003 FA (DR)

- Pwr +
- BAvg +++
- 4.00 Spd +++++
- Def ++++

Year	Lev	Team	AB	R	H	HR	RBI	Avg	OB	Slg	OPS	bb%	ct%	Eye	SB	CS	X/H%	Iso	RC/G
2006	Rk	Missoula	254	28	61	2	31	240	261	331	591	3	80	0.14	7	2	25	91	2.58
2006	A-	South Bend	550	77	145	2	32	264	304	320	624	5	83	0.33	19	8	15	56	3.15
2007	A+	Visalia	463	61	116	3	39	251	282	322	603	4	83	0.25	20	11	19	71	2.98

Athletic with plus speed and plus defense that should get him to Majors as utility infielder. Arm strength is average, but range is outstanding and makes every conceivable play. Makes contact and has hit for BA before, but lacks power and plate discipline.

Clemens,Koby — 5 — Houston

EXP MLB DEBUT: 2010 | POTENTIAL: Platoon 3B/1B | 7E

Bats R Age 21 — 2005 (8) HS (TX)

- Pwr ++++
- BAvg ++
- Spd ++
- Def +++

Year	Lev	Team	AB	R	H	HR	RBI	Avg	OB	Slg	OPS	bb%	ct%	Eye	SB	CS	X/H%	Iso	RC/G
2005	Rk	Greenville	111	14	33	4	17	297	395	477	873	14	77	0.69	4	0	36	180	6.67
2005	A-	Tri City	32	3	9	0	6	281	361	438	799	11	84	0.80	1	0	33	156	5.80
2006	A-	Lexington	306	40	70	5	39	229	302	346	648	9	78	0.48	2	1	36	118	3.58
2007	A-	Lexington	413	65	104	15	56	252	337	412	749	11	73	0.47	8	2	35	160	4.89

Muscular hitter with bat speed and power potential from LF to RC, but needs work on pitch recognition in order to hit for BA. Plus arm strength is only above average defensive tool, as he lacks first-step quickness, footwork, and playable hands.

Clement,Jeff — 2 — Seattle

EXP MLB DEBUT: 2007 | POTENTIAL: Starting CA | 9C

Bats L Age 24 — 2005 (1) USC

- Pwr ++++
- BAvg +++
- 4.60 Spd +
- Def ++

Year	Lev	Team	AB	R	H	HR	RBI	Avg	OB	Slg	OPS	bb%	ct%	Eye	SB	CS	X/H%	Iso	RC/G
2005	A	Wisconsin	113	17	36	6	20	319	384	522	906	10	78	0.48	1	2	31	204	6.69
2006	AA	San Antonio	59	7	17	2	10	288	364	525	889	11	86	0.88	0	0	53	237	6.66
2006	AAA	Tacoma	245	23	63	4	32	257	303	347	650	6	78	0.30	0	2	22	90	3.38
2007	AAA	Tacoma	455	76	125	20	80	275	360	497	857	12	81	0.69	0	0	46	222	6.27
2007	MLB	Seattle	16	4	6	2	3	375	474	813	1286	16	81	1.00	0	0	50	438	11.46

Offensive-minded catcher possessing bat speed and strong wrists which gives him power to all fields. Improved plate discipline and shortened swing, leading to better BA/OBP. Receives ball well, but arm strength is average at best and has a slow release (2.1), resulting in a 27% CS%.

Clevenger,Steven — 32 — Chicago (N)

EXP MLB DEBUT: 2009 | POTENTIAL: Reserve 1B/CA | 8E

Bats L Age 22 — 2006 (7) Chipola JC

- Pwr ++
- BAvg ++++
- Spd ++
- Def +

Year	Lev	Team	AB	R	H	HR	RBI	Avg	OB	Slg	OPS	bb%	ct%	Eye	SB	CS	X/H%	Iso	RC/G
2006	A-	Boise	220	35	62	2	21	286	363	359	722	11	87	0.93	5	2	17	73	3.88
2007	A-	Boise	83	10	31	0	18	346	470	605	1075	5	93	0.67	0	0	29	259	9.04
2007	A+	Daytona	164	21	53	2	24	323	368	421	789	7	97	2.60	0	0	21	98	4.98

Strong/athletic player with advanced hitting approach, featuring excellent plate discipline and hand/eye coordination. Lacks power due to flat bat plane, but drives gaps and hits for BA. Needs catching experience, where his arm and receiving skills are fringe-average.

Clevlen,Brent — 9 — Detroit

EXP MLB DEBUT: 2006 | POTENTIAL: Platoon RF | 6B

Bats R Age 24 — 2002 (2) HS (TX)

- Pwr ++++
- BAvg ++
- 4.30 Spd +++
- Def +++

Year	Lev	Team	AB	R	H	HR	RBI	Avg	OB	Slg	OPS	bb%	ct%	Eye	SB	CS	X/H%	Iso	RC/G
2006	AA	Erie	392	47	90	11	45	230	311	357	668	11	65	0.34	6	2	31	128	3.87
2006	MLB	Detroit	39	9	11	3	6	282	317	641	958	5	62	0.13	0	0	55	359	8.46
2007	Rk	GCL Tigers	48	10	15	2	8	313	353	458	811	6	83	0.38	1	0	20	146	5.21
2007	AAA	Toledo	322	33	71	7	36	220	305	360	665	11	65	0.35	4	4	37	140	3.94
2007	MLB	Detroit	10	2	1	0	0	100	100	100	200	0	30	0.00	0	0	0	0	-3.60

On-again/off-again offense was in a down year in 2007. Possesses power to all fields with bat speed, but can be overly aggressive and lacks pitch recognition, so won't hit for BA. Features strong arm in RF with average range. Missed two months with broken right finger.

Coghlan,Chris — 5 — Florida

EXP MLB DEBUT: 2009 | POTENTIAL: Starting 2B | 8C

Bats L Age 23 — 2006 (1-S) Mississippi

- Pwr +++
- BAvg ++++
- 4.20 Spd +++
- Def +++

Year	Lev	Team	AB	R	H	HR	RBI	Avg	OB	Slg	OPS	bb%	ct%	Eye	SB	CS	X/H%	Iso	RC/G
2006	Rk	GCL Marlins	7	2	2	0	3	286	286	286	571	0	86	0.00	0	0	0	0	2.18
2006	A-	Jamestown	94	14	28	0	12	298	383	372	756	12	90	1.44	5	2	21	74	5.34
2007	A-	Greensboro	305	60	99	10	64	325	415	534	949	13	86	1.09	19	4	40	210	7.52
2007	A+	Jupiter	130	17	26	2	18	200	283	331	614	10	85	0.79	5	1	38	131	3.41

Plays above average tools. Makes solid contact with inside-out swing and judges strike zone resulting in improved power and high BA/OBP. Steals bases through instincts and average speed. Switched to 2B from 3B where he can be an average defender who makes plays.

Collins,Joel — 2 — Toronto

EXP MLB DEBUT: 2011 | POTENTIAL: Reserve CA | 7D

Bats R Age 22 — 2007 (10) So Alabama

- Pwr ++++
- BAvg ++
- Spd +
- Def ++++

Year	Lev	Team	AB	R	H	HR	RBI	Avg	OB	Slg	OPS	bb%	ct%	Eye	SB	CS	X/H%	Iso	RC/G
2007	Rk	GCL Blue Jays	70	13	18	7	16	257	342	614	956	11	76	0.53	0	0	61	357	7.32
2007	A+	Dunedin	1	0	0	0	1	0	500	0	500	50	100		0	0	0	0	0.00

Strong defensive catcher who stalls running game and handles pitchers. Arm strength and receiving skills may get him to Majors alone. Showed impressive power with wood featruing moderate bat speed and power to pull field. Will need continuance of offense at upper levels.

Colvin,Tyler — 8 — Chicago (N)

EXP MLB DEBUT: 2008 | POTENTIAL: Starting RF | 8B

Bats L Age 22 — 2006 (1) Clemson

- Pwr +++
- BAvg +++
- 4.20 Spd +++
- Def +++

Year	Lev	Team	AB	R	H	HR	RBI	Avg	OB	Slg	OPS	bb%	ct%	Eye	SB	CS	X/H%	Iso	RC/G
2006	A-	Boise	265	50	71	11	53	268	312	483	795	6	79	0.31	12	5	41	215	5.19
2007	A+	Daytona	245	38	75	7	50	306	333	514	848	4	81	0.21	10	4	45	208	5.78
2007	AA	Tennessee	247	34	72	9	31	291	306	462	767	2	78	0.09	7	1	31	170	4.57

Tall/athletic outfielder who plays with intensity and maximizes skills. Drives ball to all parts of the field with moderate power, and though his aggressiveness doesn't help his patience, he can hit for BA. Has played mostly CF, but arm strength and range are better suited for corners.

Conger,Hank — 2 — Los Angeles (A)

EXP MLB DEBUT: 2010 | POTENTIAL: Starting CA | 9D

Bats B Age 20 — 2006 (1-C) HS (CA)

- Pwr ++++
- BAvg ++++
- Spd +
- Def ++

Year	Lev	Team	AB	R	H	HR	RBI	Avg	OB	Slg	OPS	bb%	ct%	Eye	SB	CS	X/H%	Iso	RC/G
2006	Rk	AZL Angels	68	10	21	1	10	309	373	500	873	9	84	0.64	1	0	33	191	6.50
2007	Rk	AZL Angels	15	2	4	0	3	267	267	333	600	0	80	0.00	0	0	25	67	2.54
2007	A-	Cedar Rapids	290	33	84	11	48	290	338	472	810	7	83	0.44	9	4	37	183	5.36

Strong/stocky receiver with bat speed and uppercut swing, resulting in plus power potential from both sides. Should hit for better BA once he learns pitch recognition. Arm strength, release (1.9), and receiving skills are fine, but lacks agility and ability to stop running game (21% CS%).

Corley,Brad — 7 — Pittsburgh

EXP MLB DEBUT: 2009 | POTENTIAL: Platoon LF/RF | 7D

Bats R Age 24 — 2005 (2) Mississippi St

- Pwr ++++
- BAvg ++
- Spd ++
- Def ++

Year	Lev	Team	AB	R	H	HR	RBI	Avg	OB	Slg	OPS	bb%	ct%	Eye	SB	CS	X/H%	Iso	RC/G
2005	A-	Williamsport	265	29	74	4	35	279	320	408	728	6	79	0.29	3	7	27	128	4.42
2006	A-	Hickory	534	87	150	16	99	281	304	438	743	3	80	0.17	9	3	33	157	4.37
2007	A+	Lynchburg	485	73	138	14	89	285	305	462	766	3	80	0.14	3	2	39	177	4.68
2007	AA	Altoona	39	3	10	0	4	256	256	308	564	0	85	0.00	1	0	20	51	2.18

Physical strength and bat speed provides power and led CAR in RBI, but his all-or-nothing approach and futility versus breaking pitches will keep BA suppressed. Added weight reduces speed and range, but does possess a strong arm in LF.

Costanzo, Mike — 5 — Baltimore

EXP MLB DEBUT: 2008 | POTENTIAL: Starting 3B | 8D

Bats L | Age 24
2005 (2) Coast Carolina

Pwr ++++
BAvg ++
Spd ++
Def ++

Year	Lev	Team	AB	R	H	HR	RBI	Avg	OB	Slg	OPS	bb%	ct%	Eye	SB	CS	X/H%	Iso	RC/G
2005	A-	Batavia	281	47	77	11	50	274	354	473	828	11	68	0.39	0	1	40	199	6.19
2006	A+	Clearwater	504	72	130	14	81	258	353	411	764	13	74	0.56	3	2	37	153	5.22
2007	AA	Reading	508	92	137	27	86	270	364	490	854	13	69	0.48	2	0	42	220	6.50

Power hitter with good bat speed, he finally produced offensively. Exercised more patience and took loop out of swing, but still needs to make better contact, stay off front foot, and hit against LH pitching. Displays plus arm strength at 3B, but poor footwork and stiff hands caused 34 errors.

Cousins, Scott — 9 — Florida

EXP MLB DEBUT: 2010 | POTENTIAL: Platoon RF/LF | 7D

Bats L | Age 23
2006 (3) San Francisco

Pwr ++++
BAvg ++
Spd ++
Def +++

Year	Lev	Team	AB	R	H	HR	RBI	Avg	OB	Slg	OPS	bb%	ct%	Eye	SB	CS	X/H%	Iso	RC/G
2006	A-	Jamestown	90	11	19	1	6	211	245	256	500	4	81	0.24	3	1	11	44	1.47
2007	A-	Greensboro	421	69	123	18	74	292	351	480	831	8	78	0.41	16	7	35	188	5.71

Two-way player in college, but power bat graded-out better than his pitching. Bat speed propels baseball to all parts of the field, though his contact rate could hinder his BA at upper levels. Possesses a strong arm in RF, but range and proper route taking are lacking.

Cozart, Zach — 6 — Cincinnati

EXP MLB DEBUT: 2009 | POTENTIAL: Starting SS | 7D

Bats R | Age 22
2007 (2) Mississippi

Pwr +
BAvg ++
4.35 Spd ++
Def +++++

Year	Lev	Team	AB	R	H	HR	RBI	Avg	OB	Slg	OPS	bb%	ct%	Eye	SB	CS	X/H%	Iso	RC/G
2007	A-	Dayton	184	28	44	2	18	239	288	332	620	6	80	0.31	3	1	25	93	3.88

Athletic middle infielder with excellent defensive reputation, featuring plus arm strength and soft/quick hands. Makes solid contact with inside-out swing and is patient enough to draw walks. Power will be limited and his below average speed makes him a non-threat on the bases.

Crabbe, Callix — 47 — San Diego

EXP MLB DEBUT: 2008 | POTENTIAL: Reserve 2B/LF | 6C

Bats B | Age 25
2002 (12) Manatee CC

Pwr ++
BAvg +++
Spd ++++
Def +++

Year	Lev	Team	AB	R	H	HR	RBI	Avg	OB	Slg	OPS	bb%	ct%	Eye	SB	CS	X/H%	Iso	RC/G
2003	A-	Beloit	465	79	121	1	46	260	355	346	701	13	89	1.31	25	9	26	86	4.71
2004	A+	High Desert	540	89	157	7	61	291	361	419	779	10	88	0.92	34	11	28	128	5.37
2005	AA	Huntsville	387	42	94	1	33	243	352	310	662	14	83	1.00	18	6	21	67	4.16
2006	AA	Huntsville	472	59	126	5	46	267	363	345	708	13	87	1.15	32	13	20	78	4.68
2007	AAA	Nashville	457	84	131	9	38	287	378	435	813	13	85	0.96	17	14	31	149	5.89

Over-achiever with plus speed, plate discipline, and contact skills that result in solid BA/OBP and stolen bases. Power is limited to doubles and can be pitched inside. Provides versatility by playing 2B and two outfield positions, and possesses average arm strength and range.

Craig, Allen — 53 — St. Louis

EXP MLB DEBUT: 2009 | POTENTIAL: Reserve 3B/1B | 7C

Bats R | Age 23
2006 (8) California

Pwr ++++
BAvg +++
Spd +
Def ++

Year	Lev	Team	AB	R	H	HR	RBI	Avg	OB	Slg	OPS	bb%	ct%	Eye	SB	CS	X/H%	Iso	RC/G
2006	A-	State College	175	21	45	4	29	257	309	400	709	7	84	0.46	0	0	38	143	4.24
2007	A+	Palm Beach	423	77	132	21	77	312	365	530	894	8	81	0.44	8	3	36	217	6.40
2007	AA	Springfield	24	5	7	3	3	292	320	750	1070	4	75	0.17	0	0	71	458	8.41

Breakout season with ability to hit for power with moderate bat speed and aggressive swing. Uses whole field to hit, but poor contact rate and plate discipline will keep BA suppressed. Arm strength is only defensive tool as his hands, footwork, and range are all below average.

Craig, Casey — 8 — Seattle

EXP MLB DEBUT: 2009 | POTENTIAL: Platoon RF/LF | 7D

Bats L | Age 23
2003 (21) HS (CA)

Pwr +++
BAvg +++
4.35 Spd ++
Def +++

Year	Lev	Team	AB	R	H	HR	RBI	Avg	OB	Slg	OPS	bb%	ct%	Eye	SB	CS	X/H%	Iso	RC/G
2005	A-	Everett	241	53	67	6	28	278	336	423	759	8	76	0.37	18	4	28	145	4.90
2006	A-	Wisconsin	220	32	57	5	35	259	326	414	740	9	79	0.47	14	4	37	155	4.74
2006	A+	Inland Emp	245	28	72	9	41	294	352	457	809	8	80	0.44	3	8	26	163	5.44
2007	A+	High Desert	378	83	115	11	49	304	388	474	862	12	82	0.78	20	4	33	169	6.38
2007	AA	West Tenn	97	10	21	0	7	216	315	289	604	13	76	0.61	3	2	24	72	3.21

Athletic player with solid secondary skills. Bat speed and contact ability allows him to hit for BA and moderate power, and adds dimension of drawing walks and stealing bases. Possesses range in outfield, but below average arm strength limits value and makes his bat have to play up.

Crowe, Trevor — 8 — Cleveland

EXP MLB DEBUT: 2008 | POTENTIAL: Platoon LF/CF | 7C

Bats B | Age 24
2005 (1) Arizona

Pwr ++
BAvg ++++
4.20 Spd ++++
Def +++

Year	Lev	Team	AB	R	H	HR	RBI	Avg	OB	Slg	OPS	bb%	ct%	Eye	SB	CS	X/H%	Iso	RC/G
2005	A	Lake County	178	46	18	0	23	101	184	169	352	9	86	0.72	7	5	56	67	0.37
2006	A-	Lake County	5	0	0	0	0	0	0	0	0	0	80	0.00	0	0	0	0	0.00
2006	A+	Kinston	218	72	52	4	31	239	376	381	757	18	80	1.09	29	6	40	142	5.44
2006	AA	Akron	154	36	20	1	13	130	351	530	451	11	84	0.83	16	6	50	91	1.51
2007	AA	Akron	518	134	87	5	50	168	257	263	519	11	86	0.87	28	9	40	95	2.36

Short/compact athlete with above average speed and OBP. Power hasn't materialized due to moderate bat speed and hitting gap-to-gap. Possesses a fluid swing, which should keep BA and improved walk rate. Ranges well in CF, but a below average arm may put him in LF.

Cruz, Arnoldi — 5 — St. Louis

EXP MLB DEBUT: 2010 | POTENTIAL: Platoon 3B | 7D

Bats R | Age 21
2005 (26) Oklaw-Wisc

Pwr +++
BAvg +++
Spd ++
Def ++

Year	Lev	Team	AB	R	H	HR	RBI	Avg	OB	Slg	OPS	bb%	ct%	Eye	SB	CS	X/H%	Iso	RC/G
2007	Rk	AZL Cardinals	32	8	12	0	4	375	394	531	925	3	78	0.14	1	0	42	156	6.91
2007	Rk	Johnson City	25	2	7	2	2	280	333	600	933	7	92	1.00	1	0	57	320	6.68
2007	A-	Batavia	16	2	6	0	4	375	375	438	813	0	69	0.00	0	0	17	63	5.48
2007	A-	Quad Cities	195	26	55	5	34	282	340	421	760	8	87	0.68	3	1	29	138	4.92

Offensive-minded infielder with moderate bat speed and contact ability, which allows him to hit for power and BA. Will draw walks, but needs better pitch recognition. Defensively, he possesses arm strength and agility, but stiff hands and poor groundball reads limits value.

Culberson, Charles — 6 — San Francisco

EXP MLB DEBUT: 2011 | POTENTIAL: Starting SS | 8E

Bats R | Age 19
2007 (1-S) HS (GA)

Pwr +++
BAvg +++
Spd ++++
Def +++

Year	Lev	Team	AB	R	H	HR	RBI	Avg	OB	Slg	OPS	bb%	ct%	Eye	SB	CS	X/H%	Iso	RC/G
2007	Rk	AZL Giants	161	32	46	1	16	286	374	416	790	11	76	0.50	19	1	30	130	5.04

Athletic with excellent instincts that allow tools to play up. Bat speed and aggressive approach produces moderate power, but lacks plate discipline which will make BA inconsistent. Possesses arm strength and range, but has stiff hands and needs better groundball reads.

Cumberland, Drew — 6 — San Diego

EXP MLB DEBUT: 2012 | POTENTIAL: Starting SS | 8D

Bats L | Age 19
2007 (1-S) HS (FL)

Pwr +
BAvg +++
4.00 Spd ++++
Def ++++

Year	Lev	Team	AB	R	H	HR	RBI	Avg	OB	Slg	OPS	bb%	ct%	Eye	SB	CS	X/H%	Iso	RC/G
2007	Rk	AZL Padres	84	16	26	0	7	310	363	357	720	8	88	0.70	6	1	12	48	4.53
2007	A-	Eugene	18	6	6	0	0	333	400	389	789	10	89	1.00	0	0	17	56	5.50

Athletic infielder with plus speed, his defense is solid. Range, soft hands, and quick release compensate for average arm strength, allowing him to make all types of plays. Offense will be centered around BA, OBP, and baserunning, as power will be limited to doubles.

Cumberland, Shaun — 9 — Cincinnati

EXP MLB DEBUT: 2009 | POTENTIAL: Platoon RF/LF | 7D

Bats L | Age 23
2003 (10) HS (FL)

Pwr ++++
BAvg +
4.20 Spd +++
Def +++

Year	Lev	Team	AB	R	H	HR	RBI	Avg	OB	Slg	OPS	bb%	ct%	Eye	SB	CS	X/H%	Iso	RC/G
2003	Rk	Princeton	218	28	55	1	32	252	312	362	675	8	81	0.46	13	3	31	110	3.97
2004	A-	Hudson Val	164	25	54	1	11	329	371	439	810	6	86	0.48	9	1	22	110	5.48
2005	A-	SW Michigan	436	62	117	13	69	268	326	422	748	8	77	0.37	23	8	32	154	4.70
2006	A+	Visalia	520	86	134	16	100	258	313	396	709	7	74	0.32	29	9	28	138	4.17
2007	AA	Mont/Chat	467	22	121	7	51	259	312	362	674	7	81	0.40	4	9	26	103	3.80

Strong wrists and bat speed should provide power, but struggled to drive ball in 2007. Plate discipline and contact rate are below average, which keeps BA suppressed. Average speed makes playing CF a push, but has enough arm strength for RF, assuming bat plays up.

Cunningham, Aaron — 8 — Oakland
EXP MLB DEBUT: 2009 | **POTENTIAL:** Platoon CF/LF | **8C**

Bats R | Age 22 | 2005 (6) Everett CC | Pwr +++ | BAvg ++++ | Spd +++ | Def +++ | 4.30

Year	Lev	Team	AB	R	H	HR	RBI	Avg	OB	Slg	OPS	bb%	ct%	Eye	SB	CS	X/H%	Iso	RC/G
2005	Rk	Bristol	222	41	70	5	25	315	361	446	807	7	80	0.36	6	5	24	131	5.39
2005	A-	Kannapolis	26	7	3	0	2	115	207	115	322	10	73	0.43	1	0	0	0	-0.93
2006	A-	Kannapolis	340	58	103	11	41	303	366	494	860	9	79	0.47	19	10	39	191	6.23
2007	A+	W-S/Vis	375	76	118	11	57	315	379	501	881	9	83	0.63	27	11	35	187	6.45
2007	AA	Mobile	118	25	34	5	20	288	354	534	888	9	77	0.44	1	3	47	246	6.64

Strong/athletic outfielder with excellent secondary skills. Bat speed and plate coverage give him moderate power and BA ability, and is a proficient basestealer with average speed. Aggressive defender who tracks ball well and displays a solid-average throwing arm.

Curtis, Colin — 8 — New York (A)
EXP MLB DEBUT: 2009 | **POTENTIAL:** Starting CF | **7D**

Bats L | Age 23 | 2006 (4) Arizona St | Pwr + | BAvg ++++ | Spd ++++ | Def +++ | 4.10

Year	Lev	Team	AB	R	H	HR	RBI	Avg	OB	Slg	OPS	bb%	ct%	Eye	SB	CS	X/H%	Iso	RC/G
2006	Rk	GCL Yankees	9	3	4	1	4	444	500	1000	1500	10	100		1	0	75	556	12.74
2006	A-	Staten Island	159	25	48	1	18	302	351	403	753	7	88	0.63	4	5	25	101	4.89
2007	A+	Tampa	245	37	73	5	26	298	372	412	785	11	82	0.67	4	4	22	114	5.34
2007	AA	Trenton	240	32	58	3	15	242	292	329	621	7	80	0.36	1	1	24	88	3.11

Athletic outfielder with bat control and contact ability which should ensure strong BA. Judges strike zone and runs bases well with good speed, but power will be below average. Displays solid range and average arm strength, with bat determining his eventual playing time.

D'Alessio, Andy — 3 — San Francisco
EXP MLB DEBUT: 2010 | **POTENTIAL:** Platoon 1B | **7C**

Bats L | Age 23 | 2007 (19) Clemson | Pwr ++++ | BAvg ++ | Spd + | Def +

Year	Lev	Team	AB	R	H	HR	RBI	Avg	OB	Slg	OPS	bb%	ct%	Eye	SB	CS	X/H%	Iso	RC/G
2007	Rk	AZL Giants	186	41	57	14	51	306	377	624	1000	10	77	0.49	0	2	53	317	7.96
2007	A-	Salem-Keizer	18	8	10	2	8	556	600	1222	1822	10	83	0.67	0	0	70	667	17.84

Possessor of enormous strength and bat speed which produces light-tower power to all fields. Feasted on low level pitching, but BA will suffer with promotion due to poor contact ability and a long swing. Lacks speed/agility and features stiff hands, making him below average defensively.

D'Antona, Jamie — 235 — Arizona
EXP MLB DEBUT: 2007 | **POTENTIAL:** Reserve CA/1B | **7C**

Bats R | Age 26 | 2003 (2) Wake Forest | Pwr ++++ | BAvg ++ | Spd ++ | Def ++

Year	Lev	Team	AB	R	H	HR	RBI	Avg	OB	Slg	OPS	bb%	ct%	Eye	SB	CS	X/H%	Iso	RC/G
2004	A+	Lancaster	273	45	86	13	57	315	353	531	884	6	87	0.44	2	3	37	216	6.10
2004	AA	El Paso	71	2	15	0	7	211	233	282	515	3	77	0.13	0	0	27	70	1.62
2005	AA	Tennessee	410	58	102	9	49	249	322	385	707	10	84	0.66	5	6	35	137	4.38
2006	AA	Tennessee	462	72	144	17	68	312	384	487	871	10	81	0.61	2	1	33	175	6.34
2007	AAA	Tucson	483	79	149	13	86	308	361	499	860	8	88	0.70	3	2	41	190	6.11

Improved approach and hitting mechanics allows bats to stay in zone, increasing BA opportunities. Power is to pull field and drives doubles to opposite field. Improved receiving skills behind plate and also sports plus arm strength, but defense is average at best at all three positions.

D'Arnaud, Travis — 2 — Philadelphia
EXP MLB DEBUT: 2012 | **POTENTIAL:** Starting CA | **7E**

Bats R | Age 19 | 2007 (1-S) HS (CA) | Pwr +++ | BAvg ++ | Spd + | Def ++++

Year	Lev	Team	AB	R	H	HR	RBI	Avg	OB	Slg	OPS	bb%	ct%	Eye	SB	CS	X/H%	Iso	RC/G
2007	Rk	GCL Phillies	141	18	34	4	20	241	262	348	610	3	84	0.17	4	2	21	106	2.71

Defense-oriented catcher with a strong/accurate arm that is enhanced by a quick release (1.9). Receives ball well, but doesn't have a lot of agility. Moderate bat speed will allow him to run into a few HR, but struggles to make contact and judge balls and strikes, limiting BA/OBP.

Daeges, Zach — 735 — Boston
EXP MLB DEBUT: 2009 | **POTENTIAL:** Platoon LF/1B | **7C**

Bats L | Age 24 | 2006 (6) Creighton | Pwr ++++ | BAvg +++ | Spd ++ | Def +

Year	Lev	Team	AB	R	H	HR	RBI	Avg	OB	Slg	OPS	bb%	ct%	Eye	SB	CS	X/H%	Iso	RC/G
2006	A-	Lowell	198	24	57	4	32	288	395	409	804	15	80	0.88	3	1	26	121	5.85
2007	A+	Lancaster	515	124	170	21	113	330	422	579	1001	14	81	0.85	4	1	48	249	8.24

Tall/strong hitter led minors in doubles, extra-base hits, and runs scored, but was the benefactor of a hitter-friendly home park. Selectivity gave him good pitches to hit and has the bat speed to catch-up to pitches. TJS surgery weakened arm strength and has below average range.

Daniel, Mike — 9 — Washington
EXP MLB DEBUT: 2009 | **POTENTIAL:** Reserve RF/CF | **6C**

Bats L | Age 23 | 2005 (7) North Carolina | Pwr +++ | BAvg ++ | Spd ++++ | Def +++

Year	Lev	Team	AB	R	H	HR	RBI	Avg	OB	Slg	OPS	bb%	ct%	Eye	SB	CS	X/H%	Iso	RC/G
2005	A-	Vermont	235	41	61	3	25	260	341	357	698	11	73	0.45	6	7	21	98	4.31
2006	A-	Vermont	181	29	55	3	18	304	360	431	791	8	71	0.31	13	4	25	127	5.51
2006	A-	Savannah	181	20	35	4	16	193	298	298	596	13	71	0.52	8	4	29	105	2.87
2007	A+	Hagerstown	207	38	60	7	37	290	350	473	823	8	76	0.38	9	5	38	184	5.75
2007	A+	Potomac	280	37	83	4	41	296	362	446	809	9	78	0.47	16	6	35	150	5.71

Fluid athlete with average offensive tools that will slot him as a fourth outfielder. Possesses moderate power, but can get pull-conscious and lacks plate discipline which lowers BA. Arm strength and range play up at all three outfield positions. Can have a career as reserve outfielder.

Davis, Blake — 6 — Baltimore
EXP MLB DEBUT: 2008 | **POTENTIAL:** Reserve SS/2B | **7C**

Bats L | Age 24 | 2006 (4) Cal St Fulleton | Pwr + | BAvg +++ | Spd ++++ | Def +++ | 4.10

Year	Lev	Team	AB	R	H	HR	RBI	Avg	OB	Slg	OPS	bb%	ct%	Eye	SB	CS	X/H%	Iso	RC/G
			194	29	51	3	19	263	313	351	663	7	86	0.50	8	2	20	88	3.70
2007	A+	Frederick	357	49	104	4	28	291	355	409	764	9	80	0.49	11	13	30	118	5.07
2007	AA	Bowie	115	12	24	0	10	209	266	270	536	7	78	0.36	1	1	29	61	2.11

Over-achiever whose season didn't deviate from projection. Hits for BA, is a good situational hitter, and runs the bases instinctively with average speed. Doesn't drive ball with authority and uses opposite field. Range and hands play at SS, but lack of arm strength is a problem in the hole.

Davis, Chris — 5 — Texas
EXP MLB DEBUT: 2009 | **POTENTIAL:** Starting 1B/LF | **8C**

Bats L | Age 22 | 2006 (5) Navarro College | Pwr +++++ | BAvg ++ | Spd + | Def +

Year	Lev	Team	AB	R	H	HR	RBI	Avg	OB	Slg	OPS	bb%	ct%	Eye	SB	CS	X/H%	Iso	RC/G
2006	A-	Spokane	253	38	70	15	42	277	337	534	871	8	74	0.35	2	3	49	257	6.31
2007	A+	Bakersfield	386	69	115	24	93	298	336	573	908	5	68	0.18	3	3	48	275	7.03
2007	AA	Frisco	109	21	32	12	25	294	369	688	1057	11	75	0.48	0	0	59	394	8.61

Power hitter possessing bat speed and strong wrists and was able to maintain high BA despite long swing and poor plate discipline. While he does possess arm strength, he wasn't fooling anyone at 3B, making 34 errors and displaying stiff hands and low mobility. Bat can play at 1B.

De la Cruz, Luis — 2 — St. Louis
EXP MLB DEBUT: 2012 | **POTENTIAL:** Starting CA | **8E**

Bats R | Age 28 | 2006 FA (DR) | Pwr +++ | BAvg +++ | Spd ++ | Def ++++

Year	Lev	Team	AB	R	H	HR	RBI	Avg	OB	Slg	OPS	bb%	ct%	Eye	SB	CS	X/H%	Iso	RC/G
2007	Rk	AZL Cardinals	96	10	27	0	9	281	330	385	716	7	83	0.44	3	3	30	104	4.45

Strong/projectable catcher with plus arm strength and receiving skills which helped him lead GCL with a 51% CS%. Bat speed produces moderate power and can hit for BA, but may need to tighten-up strike zone. Experience in game calling and hitting repetitions could elevate game.

DeJesus, Ivan — 6 — Los Angeles (N)
EXP MLB DEBUT: 2009 | **POTENTIAL:** Reserve SS/2B | **7C**

Bats R | Age 21 | 2005 (2) HS (PR) | Pwr + | BAvg +++ | Spd +++ | Def ++++ | 4.30

Year	Lev	Team	AB	R	H	HR	RBI	Avg	OB	Slg	OPS	bb%	ct%	Eye	SB	CS	X/H%	Iso	RC/G
2005	Rk	GCL Dodgers	121	18	41	0	11	339	389	380	769	8	82	0.45	8	2	12	41	5.02
2005	Rk	Ogden	72	4	15	0	3	208	269	222	491	8	75	0.33	3	3	7	14	1.37
2006	A-	Columbus	483	65	134	1	44	277	361	327	688	12	82	0.74	15	5	15	50	4.28
2007	A+	Inland Emp	428	69	123	4	52	287	371	381	752	12	85	0.89	11	6	24	93	5.11

Premium defender with soft/quick hands and range, but positions self well to compensate for average arm strength. Offense is based around BA where he features a short/compact swing and likes to use opposite field. Lacks secondary skills with little power and average speed.

Delaney, Jason — 37 — Pittsburgh

EXP MLB DEBUT: 2009 | POTENTIAL: Platoon LF/1B | **7C**

Bats R | Age 25
2005 (12) Boston College

		Year	Lev	Team	AB	R	H	HR	RBI	Avg	OB	Slg	OPS	bb%	ct%	Eye	SB	CS	X/H%	Iso	RC/G
Pwr	++++	2005	A-	Williamsport	197	19	42	0	13	213	282	254	536	9	83	0.58	2	2	19	41	2.32
BAvg	+++	2006	A-	Hickory	456	64	137	9	75	300	377	432	809	11	83	0.71	5	5	28	132	5.69
Spd	++	2007	A+	Lynchburg	250	39	85	9	44	340	427	536	963	13	79	0.73	2	1	33	196	7.76
Def	++	2007	AA	Altoona	223	25	59	7	35	265	372	404	775	15	77	0.73	0	0	29	139	5.38

Strong hitter with moderate bat speed and plate discipline that provides above average power and on-base ability. BA should remain stable unless given a steady dose of breaking pitches. Possesses arm strength in corner outfield, but poor range makes him a better fit at 1B.

DeLeon, Kelvin — 9 — New York (A)

EXP MLB DEBUT: 2012 | POTENTIAL: Starting RF | **9E**

Bats L | Age 17
2007 FA (DR)

		Year	Lev	Team	AB	R	H	HR	RBI	Avg	OB	Slg	OPS	bb%	ct%	Eye	SB	CS	X/H%	Iso	RC/G
Pwr	++++																				
BAvg	+++																				
4.20 Spd	+++																				
Def	+++	2007																			

Wiry athlete who was one of the top international signs. Uses whole field and possesses good bat speed which makes power projectable, but lunges at pitches and needs better plate discipline. Average speed puts his range in the corner outfield, but does display a strong throwing arm.

Denker, Travis — 45 — San Francisco

EXP MLB DEBUT: 2009 | POTENTIAL: Reserve 2B/3B | **7D**

Bats R | Age 22
2003 (21) HS (CA)

		Year	Lev	Team	AB	R	H	HR	RBI	Avg	OB	Slg	OPS	bb%	ct%	Eye	SB	CS	X/H%	Iso	RC/G
Pwr	+++	2005	A-	Columbus	358	65	111	21	68	310	419	556	975	16	78	0.86	2	5	41	246	7.95
		2005	A+	Vero Beach	108	14	20	2	9	185	285	269	553	12	76	0.58	1	2	25	83	2.34
BAvg	+++	2006	A-	Columbus	250	47	67	11	45	268	419	452	871	21	85	1.76	2	1	34	184	6.90
4.30 Spd	+++	2006	A+	Vero Beach	191	24	42	5	25	220	307	330	637	11	81	0.67	0	2	26	110	3.48
Def	+	2007	A+	IE/SJ	427	130	128	11	66	300	380	461	841	11	84	0.82	9	2	34	162	6.10

Athletic infielder resurrected prospect status with improved offense, but was helped by home conditions. Plate discipline improved, allowing him to make better contact and drive ball. Split time between 2B and 3B, but defense is poor with stiff hands and mediocre range.

Dent, Ryan — 46 — Boston

EXP MLB DEBUT: 2011 | POTENTIAL: Starting 2B | **8E**

Bats R | Age 19
2007 (1-S) HS (CA)

		Year	Lev	Team	AB	R	H	HR	RBI	Avg	OB	Slg	OPS	bb%	ct%	Eye	SB	CS	X/H%	Iso	RC/G
Pwr	++																				
BAvg	++++																				
4.10 Spd	++++	2007	Rk	GCL Red Sox	35	7	13	1	2	371	450	600	1050	13	86	1.00	4	3	31	229	8.72
Def	+++	2007	A-	Lowell	45	5	8	0	3	178	196	200	396	2	71	0.08	4	1	13	22	-0.24

Instinctual player with plus speed, plate discipline, bat control, and BA ability, which should allow him to hit at the top of the order. Possesses soft/quick hands and excellent range, but his arm strength is below average and has already begun to see action at 2B.

Descalso, Dan — 5 — St. Louis

EXP MLB DEBUT: 2010 | POTENTIAL: Starting 3B | **7D**

Bats L | Age 21
2007 (3) UC Davis

		Year	Lev	Team	AB	R	H	HR	RBI	Avg	OB	Slg	OPS	bb%	ct%	Eye	SB	CS	X/H%	Iso	RC/G
Pwr	++++																				
BAvg	+++																				
Spd	++																				
Def	+++	2007	A-	Batavia	250	29	67	0	31	268	346	336	682	9	85	0.70	12	3	18	68	3.77

Advanced college hitter with bat speed and strike zone judgment which provides BA and moderate power. Hits pitching from both sides and will use whole field. First-step quickness and arm strength are fine for 3B, but stiff hands makes his defense play average.

Desme, Grant — 9 — Oakland

EXP MLB DEBUT: 2009 | POTENTIAL: Starting RF/CF | **8D**

Bats R | Age 22
2007 (2-C) Cal Poly

		Year	Lev	Team	AB	R	H	HR	RBI	Avg	OB	Slg	OPS	bb%	ct%	Eye	SB	CS	X/H%	Iso	RC/G
Pwr	++++																				
BAvg	++																				
4.30 Spd	+++																				
Def	+++	2007	A-	Vancouver	46	6	12	1	6	261	358	391	749	12	54	0.29	2	2	33	130	4.88

Strong hitter that plays above tools and possesses solid bat speed that projects power. Mediocre plate discipline, a long swing, and contact rate could suppress BA. Runs bases well with average speed and though he has the arm for CF, his range may push him to a corner.

Desmond, Ian — 6 — Washington

EXP MLB DEBUT: 2009 | POTENTIAL: Reserve SS/3B | **7D**

Bats R | Age 22
2004 (3) HS (FL)

		Year	Lev	Team	AB	R	H	HR	RBI	Avg	OB	Slg	OPS	bb%	ct%	Eye	SB	CS	X/H%	Iso	RC/G
		2005	A-	Savannah	296	37	73	4	23	247	278	334	613	4	80	0.22	20	6	22	88	2.86
Pwr	+++	2005	A+	Potomac	219	37	56	3	15	256	321	384	704	9	76	0.40	13	6	34	128	4.31
BAvg	+	2006	A+	Potomac	365	50	89	9	45	244	299	384	683	7	78	0.37	14	8	35	140	3.88
4.40 Spd	++	2006	AA	Harrisburg	125	9	23	0	3	184	221	232	453	5	70	0.16	4	1	22	48	0.68
Def	+++++	2007	A+	Potomac	458	69	121	13	45	264	346	432	778	11	78	0.58	27	11	39	168	5.30

Plus athlete with fluid movements is one of the top defenders in the minors. Possesses plus arm strength, plus hands, and range in all directions. Produces loft with moderate bat speed, but struggles with breaking pitches and contact rate, giving him a below average BA.

DeWitt, Blake — 5 — Los Angeles (N)

EXP MLB DEBUT: 2009 | POTENTIAL: Starting 3B | **8D**

Bats R | Age 22
2004 (1-C) HS (MO)

		Year	Lev	Team	AB	R	H	HR	RBI	Avg	OB	Slg	OPS	bb%	ct%	Eye	SB	CS	X/H%	Iso	RC/G
Pwr	++++	2005	A-	Columbus	481	61	136	11	65	283	330	428	758	7	84	0.43	0	1	33	146	4.81
		2006	A+	Vero Beach	425	61	114	18	61	268	338	442	781	10	81	0.57	8	5	32	174	5.12
BAvg	+++	2006	A+	Jacksonville	104	6	19	1	6	183	241	221	462	7	80	0.38	0	1	18	38	1.10
Spd	++	2007	A+	Inland Emp	339	48	101	8	46	298	337	466	803	6	88	0.48	2	3	39	168	5.31
Def	+++	2007	AA	Jacksonville	178	20	50	6	20	281	308	466	774	4	85	0.27	0	1	40	185	4.80

Bat speed and quick wrists provide power and can make contact, but his aggressive approach doesn't help OBP. Knows how to judge strike zone, but needs improved pitch recognition. Returned to 3B which suits defense better, but needs to read hops better and improve arm accuracy.

Diaz, Kelvin — 5 — Cleveland

EXP MLB DEBUT: 2011 | POTENTIAL: Starting 3B | **9E**

Bats R | Age 20
2006 FA (DR)

		Year	Lev	Team	AB	R	H	HR	RBI	Avg	OB	Slg	OPS	bb%	ct%	Eye	SB	CS	X/H%	Iso	RC/G
Pwr	++++																				
BAvg	++++																				
Spd	++																				
Def	+++	2007																			

Missed 2007 season with visa problems in the Dominican. Bat speed and plate discipline should deliver power and is a proven contact hitter who can hit for BA. Lacks speed and range, but has good arm strength and playable hands, making him average defensively.

Diaz, Robinson — 2 — Toronto

EXP MLB DEBUT: 2008 | POTENTIAL: Reserve CA | **6A**

Bats R | Age 24
2000 FA (DR)

		Year	Lev	Team	AB	R	H	HR	RBI	Avg	OB	Slg	OPS	bb%	ct%	Eye	SB	CS	X/H%	Iso	RC/G
		2004	A-	Charleston	407	62	117	2	42	287	332	361	693	6	92	0.87	10	4	21	74	4.24
Pwr	+	2005	A+	Dunedin	388	47	114	1	65	294	320	376	696	4	93	0.54	5	2	21	82	4.14
BAvg	+++	2006	A+	Dunedin	418	59	128	3	44	306	338	383	721	5	91	0.54	8	1	20	77	4.37
4.35 Spd	++	2007	AA	New Hamp	301	33	95	3	30	316	344	409	753	4	95	0.69	5	0	22	93	4.51
Def	++++	2007	AAA	Syracuse	65	4	22	1	10	338	358	431	789	2	91	0.17	0	0	18	93	4.84

Athletic catcher with BA and contact ability. Doesn't walk or display power, making BA his only offensive asset. Improved defense, showing better receiving skills and 32% CS%. Arm strength and release time (2.0) are average. Missed last month with hamate surgery.

Dickerson, Chris — 9 — Cincinnati

EXP MLB DEBUT: 2008 | POTENTIAL: Reserve RF/LF | **7D**

Bats L | Age 26
2003 (16) Nevada

		Year	Lev	Team	AB	R	H	HR	RBI	Avg	OB	Slg	OPS	bb%	ct%	Eye	SB	CS	X/H%	Iso	RC/G
		2004	A-	Dayton	314	50	95	4	34	303	400	408	808	14	71	0.55	27	14	23	105	6.05
Pwr	+++	2005	A+	Sarasota	436	68	103	11	43	236	319	383	702	11	72	0.43	19	3	34	147	4.33
BAvg	+	2006	AA	Chattanooga	389	65	94	12	48	242	350	424	774	14	67	0.50	21	6	43	183	5.64
4.00 Spd	++++	2007	AA	Chattanooga	114	11	31	1	11	272	314	351	665	6	73	0.23	7	2	19	79	3.61
Def	+++	2007	AAA	Louisville	354	58	92	13	44	260	355	435	790	13	63	0.40	23	5	33	175	5.95

Strong/athletic outfielder with excellent speed and ability to draw walks. Medium bat speed doesn't produce power, makes poor contact, and struggles versus LH pitching, causing low BA. Plays all three outfield positions with above average arm strength and range.

Dickerson, Joe — 8 — Kansas City

EXP MLB DEBUT: 2010 | POTENTIAL: Starting CF | **8E**

Bats L Age 21
2005 (4) HS (CA)

	Pwr	+++
	BAvg	+++
	Spd	++++
	Def	+++

Year	Lev	Team	AB	R	H	HR	RBI	Avg	OB	Slg	OPS	bb%	ct%	Eye	SB	CS	X/H%	Iso	RC/G
2005	Rk	AZL Royals	214	27	63	4	40	294	373	491	864	11	79	0.59	9	12	40	196	6.55
2006	Rk	Idaho Falls	243	36	68	7	37	280	332	449	781	7	86	0.56	9	8	35	169	5.12
2007	A-	Burlington	419	50	121	3	43	289	348	375	723	8	82	0.50	26	13	23	86	4.51

Athletic player with plus speed and the BA ability to project him as a future leadoff hitters. Makes hard contact and draws the occasional walk, but despite good bat speed, his power will be limited. Runs bases aggressively and has the arm strength and range to play a quality CF.

Dominguez, Matt — 5 — Florida

EXP MLB DEBUT: 2011 | POTENTIAL: Starting 3B | **9E**

Bats R Age 18
2007 (1) HS (CA)

	Pwr	++++
	BAvg	++++
4.30	Spd	+++
	Def	+++++

Year	Lev	Team	AB	R	H	HR	RBI	Avg	OB	Slg	OPS	bb%	ct%	Eye	SB	CS	X/H%	Iso	RC/G
2007	Rk	GCL Marlins	20	0	2	0	2	100	143	100	243	5	90	0.50	0	0	0	0	-0.88
2007	A-	Jamestown	37	3	7	1	4	189	211	324	535	3	68	0.08	0	0	43	135	1.65

Strong athletic hitter with the bat speed and plate discipline to hit for both power and BA. Needs to shorten his swing, but that's correctable. An average runner, but is instinctive and aggressive on the bases. Outstanding defensively, with plus arm, first-step quickness, and soft hands.

Donaldson, Josh — 2 — Chicago (N)

EXP MLB DEBUT: 2010 | POTENTIAL: Starting CA | **8D**

Bats R Age 22
2007 (1-S) Auburn

	Pwr	+++
	BAvg	++++
	Spd	+
	Def	+++

Year	Lev	Team	AB	R	H	HR	RBI	Avg	OB	Slg	OPS	bb%	ct%	Eye	SB	CS	X/H%	Iso	RC/G
2007	Rk	AZL Cubs	11	1	2	0	0	182	308	364	671	15	64	0.50	0	1	100	182	4.52
2007	A-	Boise	162	37	56	9	35	346	467	605	1072	19	79	1.09	6	2	39	259	9.42

Offensive-minded receiver with bat speed and contact ability, giving him power and BA ability. Judges strike zone well and led NWL in OBP. Quick release (1.95) allowed him to nail 40% of attempted runners, but arm strength is average and needs better receiving skills.

Donald, Jason — 6 — Philadelphia

EXP MLB DEBUT: 2009 | POTENTIAL: Platoon SS/2B | **7C**

Bats R Age 23
2006 (3) Arizona

	Pwr	+
	BAvg	+++
4.30	Spd	+++
	Def	+++

Year	Lev	Team	AB	R	H	HR	RBI	Avg	OB	Slg	OPS	bb%	ct%	Eye	SB	CS	X/H%	Iso	RC/G
2006	A-	Batavia	213	33	55	1	24	258	331	357	687	10	80	0.55	11	1	31	99	4.20
2007	A-	Lakewood	197	41	61	4	30	310	398	447	845	13	80	0.74	2	5	26	137	6.27
2007	A+	Clearwater	293	48	88	8	41	300	375	491	866	11	76	0.50	3	2	40	191	6.52

Overachiever provided solid season offensively by improving pitch recognition and contact ability, leaving him with a solid BA. Supplied moderate power, but will be limited to mostly doubles at upper levels. Possesses arm strength and soft hands, but range could be a push for SS.

Doolittle, Sean — 3 — Oakland

EXP MLB DEBUT: 2010 | POTENTIAL: Starting 1B | **8C**

Bats L Age 21
2007 (1-S) Virginia

	Pwr	+++
	BAvg	++++
	Spd	+++
	Def	++++

Year	Lev	Team	AB	R	H	HR	RBI	Avg	OB	Slg	OPS	bb%	ct%	Eye	SB	CS	X/H%	Iso	RC/G
2007	A-	Vancouver	46	6	13	0	4	283	400	348	748	16	78	0.90	0	0	23	65	5.31
2007	A-	Kane Co	193	23	45	4	29	233	318	347	665	11	79	0.60	1	0	31	114	3.85

Two-way collegian showed more potential with the bat possessing bat speed and plate discipline which should help BA. Power has been mainly doubles, but adjusted hitting mechanics and turns on pitches better. Above average defender with soft hands and excellent arm strength.

Dorn, Daniel — 7 — Cincinnati

EXP MLB DEBUT: 2009 | POTENTIAL: Platoon LF/CF | **7C**

Bats L Age 23
2006 (32) Cal St Fullerto

	Pwr	+
	BAvg	++++
4.20	Spd	+++
	Def	+++

Year	Lev	Team	AB	R	H	HR	RBI	Avg	OB	Slg	OPS	bb%	ct%	Eye	SB	CS	X/H%	Iso	RC/G
2006	Rk	Billings	206	48	73	8	40	354	457	573	1030	15	83	1.00	3	0	30	218	9.12
2007	A+	Sarasota	338	49	95	12	66	281	359	456	815	9	80	0.46	3	1	36	175	6.07
2007	AA	Chattanooga	90	20	28	8	21	311	422	667	1089	14	74	0.65	1	0	54	356	9.81

Athletic outfielder with contact ability, fluid swing, and strike zone judgment, which will allow him to hit for BA. Power is average and body isn't always balanced at the plate. Runs the bases intelligently and has good range, but a shoulder injury in 2005 has left him with a below average arm.

Drennen, John — 8 — Cleveland

EXP MLB DEBUT: 2010 | POTENTIAL: Starting LF | **9E**

Bats L Age 21
2005 (1-S) HS (CA)

	Pwr	++++
	BAvg	++
4.30	Spd	+++
	Def	+++

Year	Lev	Team	AB	R	H	HR	RBI	Avg	OB	Slg	OPS	bb%	ct%	Eye	SB	CS	X/H%	Iso	RC/G
2005	Rk	Burlington	168	24	40	8	29	238	312	435	746	10	78	0.49	6	3	40	196	4.69
2006	A-	Lake County	240	33	76	6	30	317	395	467	862	11	78	0.60	6	6	28	150	6.40
2006	A+	Kinston	113	15	27	0	8	239	312	327	639	10	81	0.57	2	1	30	88	3.64
2007	A+	Kinston	496	72	126	13	77	254	326	391	717	10	79	0.51	6	6	32	137	4.42

Patient hitter with excellent bat speed and power potential, but got into some bad habits and became too pull-conscious, driving down offense. Providing more lift to hits, and tightening strike zone could do wonders. Possesses below average arm and range which will limit him to LF.

Duarte, Jose — 8 — Kansas City

EXP MLB DEBUT: 2009 | POTENTIAL: Starting CF/LF | **7D**

Bats R Age 23
2004 FA (Venezuela)

	Pwr	++
	BAvg	+++
	Spd	++++
	Def	+++

Year	Lev	Team	AB	R	H	HR	RBI	Avg	OB	Slg	OPS	bb%	ct%	Eye	SB	CS	X/H%	Iso	RC/G
2005	Rk	AZL Royals	178	33	55	3	36	309	394	466	860	12	82	0.78	11	7	29	157	6.48
2006	A-	Burlington	465	65	122	1	37	262	334	338	672	10	79	0.51	30	9	24	75	3.96
2007	A+	Wilmington	493	82	143	1	42	290	353	369	722	9	84	0.62	34	13	22	79	4.61

Ability to make contact, draw walks, and utilize plus speed on bases make him a solid leadoff candidate. Strike zone judgment improved and is making harder contact as he has gotten stronger. Possesses excellent range and average arm strength in CF.

Duncan, Eric — 35 — New York (A)

EXP MLB DEBUT: 2007 | POTENTIAL: Platoon 1B/3B | **7C**

Bats L Age 23
2003 (1) HS (NJ)

	Pwr	+++
	BAvg	++
4.20	Spd	+++
	Def	++

Year	Lev	Team	AB	R	H	HR	RBI	Avg	OB	Slg	OPS	bb%	ct%	Eye	SB	CS	X/H%	Iso	RC/G
2004	A+	Tampa	173	23	44	4	26	254	368	462	830	15	73	0.66	0	2	59	208	6.41
2005	AA	Trenton	451	60	106	19	61	235	324	408	732	12	70	0.43	9	3	35	173	4.67
2006	AA	Trenton	206	32	51	10	29	248	349	485	834	13	82	0.84	0	0	53	238	6.05
2006	AAA	Columbus	110	7	23	0	6	209	269	255	523	8	78	0.38	0	1	17	45	1.93
2007	AAA	Scranton/WB	411	46	99	11	61	241	320	389	710	10	80	0.59	2	2	38	148	4.39

Free-swinger with power potential, moderate bat speed, and ability to draw walks, but collapses backside which hinders contact rate and struggles versus breaking pitches. Has seen little action at 3B past two years due to stiff hands, but has arm strength and can play 1B well.

Duncan, Shelley — 73 — New York (A)

EXP MLB DEBUT: 2007 | POTENTIAL: Platoon LF/1B | **7C**

Bats R Age 28
2001 (2) Arizona

	Pwr	++++
	BAvg	++
	Spd	+
	Def	+

Year	Lev	Team	AB	R	H	HR	RBI	Avg	OB	Slg	OPS	bb%	ct%	Eye	SB	CS	X/H%	Iso	RC/G
2005	AA	Trenton	537	86	129	19	78	240	312	490	802	11	72	0.45	6	3	50	250	5.39
2006	AA	Trenton	351	47	90	19	61	256	322	487	809	9	78	0.44	3	1	48	231	5.45
2006	AAA	Columbus	43	1	8	1	4	186	271	279	550	10	77	0.50	0	0	25	93	2.22
2007	AA	Scranton/WB	336	58	99	19	61	295	380	577	957	9	78	0.44	3	1	44	282	7.44
2007	AAA	New York (A)	74	16	19	7	17	257	329	554	883	12	76	0.40	0	0	42	297	6.57

Tall/strong hitter with plus raw power and bat speed who tightened-up strike zone and made better contact. He still struggles against good breaking pitches with his long swing and can get pull conscious. Defensively, he's a liability in either LF or 1B, but bat can play in platoon role.

Durango, Luis — 8 — San Diego

EXP MLB DEBUT: 2010 | POTENTIAL: Platoon CF | **7D**

Bats B Age 21
2003 FA (DR)

	Pwr	+
	BAvg	++++
3.80	Spd	+++++
	Def	++

Year	Lev	Team	AB	R	H	HR	RBI	Avg	OB	Slg	OPS	bb%	ct%	Eye	SB	CS	X/H%	Iso	RC/G
2006	Rk	AZL Padres	143	35	54	0	14	378	464	448	911	14	89	1.44	17	6	11	70	7.20
2007	A-	Eugene	300	60	110	2	32	367	422	460	882	9	89	0.91	17	10	15	93	6.46

Thin/athletic outfielder with plus speed led league in BA for second consecutive year. Solid plate discipline, contact ability, and use of whole field keeps BA consistent, though his lack of strength will prevent power. Has range for CF, but effectiveness is limited by a below average throwing arm.

Duran, German — 4 — Texas

EXP MLB DEBUT: 2008 | POTENTIAL: Starting 2B | 7B

Bats R | Age 23 | 2005 (6) Weatherford JC
Pwr +++ | BAvg +++ | Spd ++++ | Def +++ | 4.25

Year	Lev	Team	AB	R	H	HR	RBI	Avg	OB	Slg	OPS	bb%	ct%	Eye	SB	CS	X/H%	Iso	RC/G
2005	A-	Spokane	252	36	66	4	33	262	311	393	704	7	78	0.32	6	4	35	131	4.17
2006	A+	Bakersfield	457	81	130	13	72	284	335	446	782	7	81	0.39	15	9	35	162	5.10
2007	AA	Frisco	480	81	144	22	84	300	346	525	871	7	84	0.44	11	2	41	225	6.07

Went from organizational player to prospect with offensive outburst. Hitting from a crouch, he makes excellent contact and began turning on pitches, improving power. Marginal plate discipline hinders BA. Runs bases aggressively and is an average defender at 2B after moving from SS.

Easley, Ed — 2 — Arizona

EXP MLB DEBUT: 2009 | POTENTIAL: Starting CA | 7C

Bats R | Age 22 | 2007 (1-S) Mississippi St
Pwr +++ | BAvg +++ | Spd + | Def +++

Year	Lev	Team	AB	R	H	HR	RBI	Avg	OB	Slg	OPS	bb%	ct%	Eye	SB	CS	X/H%	Iso	RC/G
2007	A-	Yakima	124	21	31	6	20	250	301	419	720	7	76	0.30	1	0	26	169	4.15

Solid, all-around catcher, he squares up to the ball well, hitting for BA and driving pitches from LF to RC. Will need to improve plate discipline and counter-adjust to pitchers. Possesses arm strength, agility, and receiving skills behind the plate and can be an everyday catcher.

Edwards, Jon — 9 — St. Louis

EXP MLB DEBUT: 2010 | POTENTIAL: Starting RF | 8D

Bats R | Age 20 | 2006 (14) HS (TX)
Pwr ++++ | BAvg ++ | Spd +++ | Def +++ | 4.25

Year	Lev	Team	AB	R	H	HR	RBI	Avg	OB	Slg	OPS	bb%	ct%	Eye	SB	CS	X/H%	Iso	RC/G
2006	Rk	Johnson City	154	23	41	4	27	266	351	461	812	11	79	0.61	0	0	51	195	5.82
2007	Rk	Johnson City	188	27	46	7	33	245	345	431	776	13	64	0.41	0	3	43	186	5.04
2007	A-	Batavia	33	1	13	1	7	394	429	606	1035	6	79	0.29	0	0	38	212	8.80

Strong framed outfielder with bat speed and power potential. Patient enough to draw walks, but a long swing and failure to hit breaking pitches will keep BA/OBP low. Possesses one of the better outfield arms in the system, but doesn't track flyballs well and has below average range.

Eiland, Eric — 8 — Toronto

EXP MLB DEBUT: 2011 | POTENTIAL: Starting CF | 8D

Bats L | Age 19 | 2007 (2-C) HS (TX)
Pwr +++ | BAvg +++ | Spd +++++ | Def +++ | 3.95

Year	Lev	Team	AB	R	H	HR	RBI	Avg	OB	Slg	OPS	bb%	ct%	Eye	SB	CS	X/H%	Iso	RC/G
2007	Rk	GCL Blue Jays	176	22	38	1	14	216	303	284	587	11	65	0.35	16	1	24	68	2.79

Excellent athlete who was drafted for his power/speed combination, but found hitting difficult with wood. Bat speed should produce power, but will need to address plate discipline, over-aggressiveness, and tendency to pull ball. Possesses range, but arm strength is below average.

Einertson, Mitch — 8 — Houston

EXP MLB DEBUT: 2009 | POTENTIAL: Platoon LF/RF | 7C

Bats R | Age 22 | 2004 (5) HS (CA)
Pwr +++ | BAvg ++ | Spd +++ | Def ++ | 4.35

Year	Lev	Team	AB	R	H	HR	RBI	Avg	OB	Slg	OPS	bb%	ct%	Eye	SB	CS	X/H%	Iso	RC/G
2004	Rk	Greeneville	227	53	70	24	67	308	394	692	1085	12	69	0.46	4	4	56	383	9.58
2004	A-	Tri City	7	1	1	1	1	143	143	571	714	0	71	0.00	1	0	100	429	3.48
2005	A-	Lexington	355	52	83	7	45	234	332	352	684	13	72	0.53	5	4	33	118	4.15
2006	A-	Lexington	425	51	90	12	61	212	265	360	625	7	82	0.40	6	2	42	148	3.17
2007	A+	Salem	446	68	136	11	87	305	356	482	838	7	83	0.47	5	4	40	177	5.83

CAR MVP, showing a consistent bat all season. Produces moderate power and BA ability with moderate bat speed, but plate discipline is lacking. Average range and below average arm strength will only work in LF and doesn't have the offensive capacity to play there in the Majors.

Ellsbury, Jacoby — 8 — Boston

EXP MLB DEBUT: 2007 | POTENTIAL: Starting CF | 9C

Bats L | Age 24 | 2005 (1) Oregon St
Pwr ++ | BAvg ++++ | Spd +++++ | Def ++++ | 4.00

Year	Lev	Team	AB	R	H	HR	RBI	Avg	OB	Slg	OPS	bb%	ct%	Eye	SB	CS	X/H%	Iso	RC/G
2006	A+	Wilmington	244	35	72	4	32	295	361	414	775	9	89	0.89	25	9	22	119	5.24
2006	AA	Portland	198	29	61	3	19	308	383	434	817	11	87	0.96	16	8	26	126	5.84
2007	AA	Portland	73	16	33	0	13	452	494	644	1138	8	90	0.86	8	1	36	192	9.38
2007	AAA	Pawtucket	363	66	108	2	28	298	354	380	735	8	87	0.68	33	6	19	83	4.72
2007	MLB	Boston	116	20	41	3	18	353	395	509	904	6	87	0.53	9	0	27	155	6.46

Plus athlete with excellent leadoff skills in his ability to make contact, get on base, and utilize plus speed. Likes to slap baseball to opposite field, but showed that he can turn on pitches for modest power. Plus range in CF with arm strength that is below average, yet accurate.

Engel, Reid — 9 — Boston

EXP MLB DEBUT: 2010 | POTENTIAL: Platoon RF | 7D

Bats L | Age 21 | 2005 (5) HS (CO)
Pwr + | BAvg ++++ | Spd ++ | Def +++

Year	Lev	Team	AB	R	H	HR	RBI	Avg	OB	Slg	OPS	bb%	ct%	Eye	SB	CS	X/H%	Iso	RC/G
2005	Rk	GCL Red Sox	103	9	24	2	8	233	307	330	637	10	65	0.31	2	2	21	97	3.41
2006	Rk	GCL Red Sox	20	2	4	0	0	200	304	300	604	13	75	0.60	1	0	25	100	3.26
2006	A-	Lowell	231	20	58	4	26	251	282	355	637	4	79	0.21	4	2	24	104	3.14
2007	AA	Greenville	411	60	120	9	49	292	352	436	787	8	81	0.49	13	4	29	144	5.28

Athletic outfielder exhibits strong plate discipline and contact ability, accounting for a solid BA. Runs bases well with above average speed and hasn't displayed anything more than gap power. Defense in corner outfield is above average with solid-average range and arm strength.

Englund, Stephen — 8 — Washington

EXP MLB DEBUT: 2010 | POTENTIAL: Platoon CF/LF | 8E

Bats R | Age 20 | 2006 (2-C) HS (WA)
Pwr ++++ | BAvg ++ | Spd ++++ | Def +++

Year	Lev	Team	AB	R	H	HR	RBI	Avg	OB	Slg	OPS	bb%	ct%	Eye	SB	CS	X/H%	Iso	RC/G
2006	Rk	GCL Nationals	115	16	21	1	12	183	288	235	523	13	64	0.41	5	1	19	52	1.75
2007	Rk	GCL Nationals	79	18	20	0	2	253	449	291	740	26	70	1.17	13	4	15	38	5.59
2007	A-	Vermont	59	10	13	1	7	220	313	339	652	12	63	0.36	0	3	38	119	3.86

Plus athlete and is purely projection at this stage, possessing bat speed and power potential. Over-aggressiveness hinders walk rate and ability to hit good pitches, and misses time with a fractured left thumb. Features above average speed and defensive tools, but needs repetitions.

Errecart, Chris — 3 — Milwaukee

EXP MLB DEBUT: 2009 | POTENTIAL: Platoon 1B/LF | 7D

Bats B | Age 23 | 2006 (5) California
Pwr ++++ | BAvg ++ | Spd ++ | Def +++

Year	Lev	Team	AB	R	H	HR	RBI	Avg	OB	Slg	OPS	bb%	ct%	Eye	SB	CS	X/H%	Iso	RC/G
2006	Rk	Helena	271	49	86	13	61	317	375	520	895	8	79	0.45	5	3	34	203	6.49
2007	A+	Brevard Co	424	63	111	10	55	262	315	392	707	7	79	0.36	1	3	31	130	4.16

Bat speed and propensity to pull ball gives him excellent power to leftfield, but marginal plate discipline and contact rate may preclude him hitting for BA and making power game-usable. Despite strong throwing arm, Milwaukee moved him to 1B where his defense is average.

Escobar, Alcides — 6 — Milwaukee

EXP MLB DEBUT: 2009 | POTENTIAL: Starting SS | 7C

Bats R | Age 19 | 2003 FA (Venezuela)
Pwr + | BAvg +++ | Spd ++++ | Def ++++ | 4.15

Year	Lev	Team	AB	R	H	HR	RBI	Avg	OB	Slg	OPS	bb%	ct%	Eye	SB	CS	X/H%	Iso	RC/G
2004	Rk	Helena	231	38	65	2	24	281	339	342	681	8	81	0.45	20	9	15	61	3.91
2005	A-	W. Virginia	520	80	141	2	36	271	298	362	660	4	83	0.22	30	13	25	90	3.53
2006	A+	Brevard Co	348	47	90	2	33	259	297	307	604	5	84	0.34	28	8	13	49	2.90
2007	A+	Brevard Co	268	37	87	0	25	325	342	377	719	3	87	0.20	18	10	13	52	4.13
2007	AA	Huntsville	226	27	64	1	28	283	316	354	670	5	84	0.31	4	3	16	71	3.69

Thin/athletic infielder displays sporadic offense, but hit consistently for BA all season. Medium bat speed will limit power, but could improve production with an increased walk rate. Plus defender featuring arm strength and range that are well above average.

Evans, Nick — 3 — New York (N)

EXP MLB DEBUT: 2009 | POTENTIAL: Platoon 1B | 7C

Bats R | Age 22 | 2004 (5) HS (AZ)
Pwr +++ | BAvg +++ | Spd + | Def ++

Year	Lev	Team	AB	R	H	HR	RBI	Avg	OB	Slg	OPS	bb%	ct%	Eye	SB	CS	X/H%	Iso	RC/G
2004	Rk	GCL Mets	182	36	47	7	27	258	311	462	773	7	72	0.27	3	2	43	203	5.11
2005	Rk	Kingsport	64	11	22	6	22	344	382	734	1117	6	73	0.24	1	0	59	391	9.43
2005	A-	Brooklyn	226	30	57	6	33	252	305	407	712	7	85	0.50	0	1	35	155	4.29
2006	A-	Hagerstown	512	55	131	15	68	256	315	424	739	8	80	0.44	2	0	40	168	4.62
2007	A+	St. Lucie	378	65	108	15	54	286	374	476	850	12	83	0.83	3	0	38	190	6.18

Minor league slugger with above average power and plate discipline, though power is more physical strength than bat speed. BA could dwindle at higher levels with poor contact rate. Below average runner and defender, but has ability to bring defense to average level.

Evans,Terry — 9 — Los Angeles (A)

EXP MLB DEBUT: 2007 | POTENTIAL: Platoon RF/LF | 8C

Bats R Age 26
2001 (47) Mid Georgia J(
Pwr ++++
BAvg ++
4.30 Spd +++
Def +++

Year	Lev	Team	AB	R	H	HR	RBI	Avg	OB	Slg	OPS	bb%	ct%	Eye	SB	CS	X/H%	Iso	RC/G
2005	A+	Palm Beach	385	34	85	8	47	221	275	330	605	7	71	0.26	12	6	29	109	2.80
2006	A+	Palm Beach	238	43	74	15	45	311	364	550	915	8	79	0.40	20	1	35	239	6.63
2006	AA	Spr/Ark	262	96	81	18	42	309	360	580	941	7	71	0.28	16	7	41	271	7.31
2007	AAA	Salt Lake	475	70	150	15	75	316	351	512	863	5	75	0.22	24	9	39	196	6.16
2007	MLB	Los Angeles (A)	11	3	1	1	2	91	231	364	594	15	64	0.50	0	0	100	273	2.35

Tall/strong outfielder proved 2006 breakout was no fluke. Generates power to all fields and was able to maintain BA despite a long swing and trouble with breaking pitches. Runs bases well despite average speed and plays a solid RF, featuring above average arm strength and range.

Fairley,Wendell — 8 — San Francisco

EXP MLB DEBUT: 2012 | POTENTIAL: Starting CF | 8E

Bats L Age 20
2007 (1-C) HS (MS)
Pwr +++
BAvg +++
Spd ++++
Def +++

Year	Lev	Team	AB	R	H	HR	RBI	Avg	OB	Slg	OPS	bb%	ct%	Eye	SB	CS	X/H%	Iso	RC/G
2007																			

Plus athlete with exceptional speed and offensive potential. Possesses bat speed and plate discipline which should allow for moderate power and BA. Stolen base totals should improve with experience in reading pitchers' moves. Features plus range in CF with average arm strength.

Falu,Irving — 64 — Kansas City

EXP MLB DEBUT: 2008 | POTENTIAL: Reserve 2B/SS | 6C

Bats B Age 25
2003 (21) Indian Hills CC
Pwr +
BAvg ++
Spd ++++
Def +++

Year	Lev	Team	AB	R	H	HR	RBI	Avg	OB	Slg	OPS	bb%	ct%	Eye	SB	CS	X/H%	Iso	RC/G
2004	Rk	AZL Royals	223	33	61	1	15	274	349	350	699	10	91	1.37	23	10	20	76	4.59
2005	A-	Burlington	445	71	113	1	28	254	344	328	672	12	91	1.56	34	15	23	74	4.41
2005	AA	Wichita	17	1	4	0	2	235	278	294	572	6	100		0	0	25	59	3.30
2006	A+	High Desert	531	87	160	3	49	301	350	388	738	7	91	0.87	31	11	21	87	4.77
2007	AA	Wichita	476	46	115	1	28	242	294	298	592	7	91	0.80	15	9	17	57	3.14

Short/athletic infielder with contact skills and plus speed. Walk rate decreased and has no power to speak of, so offensive value lies entirely with BA. Provides plus range and soft/quick hands at both middle infield positions, but arm strength is better suited for 2B.

Fernandez-Oliva,Carlos — 8 — Boston

EXP MLB DEBUT: 2010 | POTENTIAL: Starting RF | 9E

Bats R Age 21
2004 FA (Venezuela)
Pwr ++++
BAvg +++
4.20 Spd ++++
Def ++++

Year	Lev	Team	AB	R	H	HR	RBI	Avg	OB	Slg	OPS	bb%	ct%	Eye	SB	CS	X/H%	Iso	RC/G
2006	Rk	GCL Red Sox	155	32	46	3	23	297	374	452	825	11	83	0.73	9	5	35	155	5.93
2007	A-	Lowell	267	35	82	2	42	307	369	401	769	9	85	0.65	6	3	24	94	5.14
2007	AA	Greenville	167	24	39	0	16	234	293	269	562	8	74	0.32	2	1	15	36	2.32

Projectable athlete who can impact game with power and speed, while taking a mature approach to hitting. Struggles against breaking pitches, but knows the strike zone well enough to draw walks. Arm strength and range play in CF, but may move to RF as he matures physically.

Fiorentino,Jeff — 7 — Baltimore

EXP MLB DEBUT: 2005 | POTENTIAL: Platoon LF/RF | 7C

Bats L Age 25
2004 (3) Florida Atlantic
Pwr +++
BAvg +++
4.25 Spd +++
Def +++

Year	Lev	Team	AB	R	H	HR	RBI	Avg	OB	Slg	OPS	bb%	ct%	Eye	SB	CS	X/H%	Iso	RC/G
2005	A+	Frederick	413	70	118	22	66	286	340	508	849	8	78	0.38	12	6	37	223	5.86
2005	MLB	Baltimore	44	7	11	1	5	250	283	364	646	4	77	0.20	1	0	27	114	3.22
2006	AA	Bowie	385	63	106	13	62	275	363	413	776	12	85	0.91	9	3	25	138	5.26
2006	MLB	Baltimore	39	8	10	0	7	256	370	308	677	15	92	2.33	1	0	20	51	4.70
2007	AA	Bowie	436	68	123	15	65	282	348	445	793	9	80	0.49	8	4	30	163	5.31

Prospect status gradually declining as OBP and power output are not adequate for a corner outfielder. Wiry strong and generates good bat speed, but saw a regression in plate discipline. Runs well underway, but defensive skills are average at best, further damaging his playing time.

Flores,Josh — 8 — Houston

EXP MLB DEBUT: 2009 | POTENTIAL: Platoon LF/CF | 7D

Bats R Age 22
2005 (4) Triton College
Pwr ++
BAvg +++
3.90 Spd +++++
Def +++

Year	Lev	Team	AB	R	H	HR	RBI	Avg	OB	Slg	OPS	bb%	ct%	Eye	SB	CS	X/H%	Iso	RC/G
2005	Rk	Greeneville	248	49	83	8	25	335	375	520	895	6	77	0.28	20	6	30	185	6.52
2005	A-	Lexington	18	1	5	0	1	278	316	389	705	5	78	0.25	4	0	40	111	4.22
2006	A-	Lexington	475	81	120	11	35	253	301	371	672	6	77	0.31	28	6	27	118	3.66
2007	A+	Salem	246	49	80	5	30	325	383	500	883	9	81	0.49	25	5	34	175	6.52
2007	AA	Corpus Christi	192	29	42	2	12	219	286	323	609	9	79	0.45	14	0	31	104	3.09

Plus speed makes him a threat on the bases and provides him with outstanding range in CF. Short/compact stroke allows him to hit for BA, but power has declined and doesn't draw walks. Possesses below average arm strength, but shows accuracy.

Florimon,Pedro — 6 — Baltimore

EXP MLB DEBUT: 2010 | POTENTIAL: Starting SS | 8E

Bats B Age 21
2004 FA (DR)
Pwr ++
BAvg +++
Spd ++++
Def +++

Year	Lev	Team	AB	R	H	HR	RBI	Avg	OB	Slg	OPS	bb%	ct%	Eye	SB	CS	X/H%	Iso	RC/G
2006	Rk	Bluefield	120	23	40	1	8	333	459	425	884	19	76	0.97	7	6	20	92	7.27
2006	A-	Aberdeen	105	13	26	0	5	248	331	305	635	11	75	0.50	0	0	19	57	3.51
2007	A-	Delmarva	371	50	73	4	34	197	253	272	525	7	71	0.26	16	6	26	75	1.73

Tall/athletic SS lost all semblance of plate discipline and struggled to hit. Lacks balance and bat speed, so power is unlikely, but has shown contact ability in past. Plus speed makes him a SB threat. Range and arm strength are defensive assets, but needs to cut-down errors.

Flowers,Tyler — 32 — Atlanta

EXP MLB DEBUT: 2010 | POTENTIAL: Starting CA | 8D

Bats R Age 22
2005 (33) Chipola JC
Pwr ++++
BAvg +++
Spd +
Def +++

Year	Lev	Team	AB	R	H	HR	RBI	Avg	OB	Slg	OPS	bb%	ct%	Eye	SB	CS	X/H%	Iso	RC/G
2006	Rk	Danville	129	24	36	5	16	279	359	465	824	11	77	0.53	0	0	39	186	5.84
2007	A-	Rome	389	65	116	12	70	298	377	488	865	11	81	0.66	3	4	41	190	6.40

Tall/strong player with excellent bat speed and plate discipline that produced above average power and BA. Played predominantly at 1B due to off-season knee surgery, but has the arm strength and receiving skills to be an above average defender behind the plate.

Fontaine,Chase — 465 — Atlanta

EXP MLB DEBUT: 2009 | POTENTIAL: Reserve 2B/SS | 7D

Bats L Age 22
2006 (2) Daytona CC
Pwr +++
BAvg +++
4.30 Spd ++
Def +++

Year	Lev	Team	AB	R	H	HR	RBI	Avg	OB	Slg	OPS	bb%	ct%	Eye	SB	CS	X/H%	Iso	RC/G
2006	Rk	Danville	199	42	60	4	26	302	411	417	828	16	77	0.82	4	2	25	116	6.21
2007	A-	Rome	313	60	90	3	26	288	399	399	798	16	76	0.77	10	9	26	112	5.92
2007	A+	Myrtle Beach	78	6	16	0	7	205	279	256	535	9	67	0.31	1	0	25	51	1.97

Pure hitting athlete with solid contact ability and plate discipline, which should keep BA respectable. Didn't hit for power despite bat speed, and average speed won't be much of a factor on the bases. Arm strength and range work at 2B, which is where his offensive level works best.

Ford,Darren — 8 — Milwaukee

EXP MLB DEBUT: 2010 | POTENTIAL: Starting CF | 7C

Bats R Age 22
2004 (18) Chipola JC
Pwr ++
BAvg +++
4.00 Spd +++++
Def +++

Year	Lev	Team	AB	R	H	HR	RBI	Avg	OB	Slg	OPS	bb%	ct%	Eye	SB	CS	X/H%	Iso	RC/G
2005	Rk	Helena	236	57	64	1	24	271	361	326	687	12	70	0.47	18	4	13	55	4.24
2006	A-	W. Virginia	491	93	139	7	54	283	356	387	743	10	73	0.42	64	15	24	104	4.89
2007	A-	W. Virginia	224	48	75	5	33	335	397	504	901	9	75	0.41	31	10	32	170	6.95
2007	A+	Brevard Co	273	46	63	4	27	231	318	308	626	11	75	0.52	36	6	19	77	3.29

Explosive athlete with plus speed who unnerves pitchers on the bases and makes consistent contact. Doesn't strike-out or walk much, and lacks power. Ranges well in outfield with closing speed, but arm strength is below average. Primary need is to get on-base.

Ford,Shelby — 4 — Pittsburgh

EXP MLB DEBUT: 2009 | POTENTIAL: Reserve 2B/SS | 7C

Bats B Age 23
2006 (3) Oklahoma St
Pwr ++
BAvg +++
Spd ++++
Def +++

Year	Lev	Team	AB	R	H	HR	RBI	Avg	OB	Slg	OPS	bb%	ct%	Eye	SB	CS	X/H%	Iso	RC/G
2006	A-	Williamsport	25	3	10	0	2	400	464	520	984	11	88	1.00	1	0	30	120	7.86
2006	A-	Hickory	223	43	60	6	27	269	312	448	761	6	77	0.27	4	3	42	179	4.85
2007	A+	Lynchburg	360	64	101	5	55	281	343	433	776	9	81	0.50	14	0	38	153	5.24

Athletic infielder with promising offensive skills. Possesses sufficient bat speed to hit for power, and improved plate discipline/contact ability, giving him a chance to hit for BA. Steals bases with good speed. Arm strength plays at 2B, but lacks range and smooth double-play turn.

Fowler,Dexter — 8 — Colorado

EXP MLB DEBUT: 2009 | POTENTIAL: Starting CF | 9D

Plus athlete with power and speed, he has ability to impact games. Bat speed is better from natural RH side and improved his strike zone judgment, but BA will hinge on contact ability and length of swing. Possesses plus arm strength and range in CF, but needs to take better routes.

Bats B | Age 22
2004 (14) HS (FL)

		Year	Lev	Team	AB	R	H	HR	RBI	Avg	OB	Slg	OPS	bb%	ct%	Eye	SB	CS	X/H%	Iso	RC/G
Pwr	++++																				
BAvg	++	2005	Rk	Casper	220	43	60	4	23	273	352	409	761	11	67	0.37	18	6	30	136	5.38
4.00 Spd	+++++	2006	A-	Asheville	405	92	118	8	46	291	359	457	816	10	80	0.54	42	23	38	165	5.76
Def	++++	2007	A+	Modesto	245	43	67	2	23	273	384	367	751	15	74	0.69	20	11	21	94	5.27

Fox,Jake — 732 — Chicago (N)

EXP MLB DEBUT: 2008 | POTENTIAL: Reserve LF/CA | 6C

Short/stocky player with moderate power and BA ability. Compact swing enhances contact rate, but doesn't have much plate discipline. Played sparingly at catcher, playing mostly 1B and LF. Arm strength remains solid, but is incredibly slow, making him a defensive liability.

Bats R | Age 25
2003 (3) Michigan

		Year	Lev	Team	AB	R	H	HR	RBI	Avg	OB	Slg	OPS	bb%	ct%	Eye	SB	CS	X/H%	Iso	RC/G
		2006	A+	Daytona	249	46	78	16	61	313	380	574	955	10	80	0.55	4	1	41	261	7.24
Pwr	+++	2006	AA	West Tenn	193	20	52	5	25	269	302	435	737	4	77	0.20	0	0	42	166	4.45
BAvg	++	2007	AA	Tennessee	359	60	102	18	60	284	316	504	821	5	80	0.24	6	2	41	220	5.33
4.70 Spd	+	2007	AAA	Iowa	100	18	28	6	19	280	314	530	844	5	77	0.22	2	0	46	250	5.67
Def	++	2007	MLB	Chicago (N)	14	3	2	0	1	143	200	286	486	7	86	0.50	0	0	100	143	1.91

Francisco,Ben — 8 — Cleveland

EXP MLB DEBUT: 2007 | POTENTIAL: Reserve LF/CF | 6A

Led IL in BA by being more selective and making better contact, and slightly improved secondary skills. Unlikely to be a corner outfield starter due to modest power and low walk rate, but runs well and can handle platoon role. Range and arm strength play at any outfield position.

Bats R | Age 26
2002 (5) UCLA

		Year	Lev	Team	AB	R	H	HR	RBI	Avg	OB	Slg	OPS	bb%	ct%	Eye	SB	CS	X/H%	Iso	RC/G
		2005	AA	Akron	323	45	99	7	46	307	354	474	828	7	82	0.41	15	4	33	167	5.71
Pwr	++	2005	AAA	Buffalo	16	4	8	0	3	500	529	563	1092	6	81	0.33	1	0	13	63	8.82
BAvg	+++	2006	AAA	Buffalo	515	80	143	17	59	278	336	454	790	8	86	0.63	25	5	37	177	5.25
4.30 Spd	+++	2007	AAA	Buffalo	377	60	120	12	51	318	378	496	874	9	82	0.55	22	8	34	178	6.30
Def	+++	2007	MLB	Cleveland	62	10	17	3	12	274	308	500	808	5	69	0.16	0	2	47	226	5.52

Francisco,Juan — 5 — Cincinnati

EXP MLB DEBUT: 2010 | POTENTIAL: Starting 3B | 8D

All-or-nothing swinger with bat speed and power, he led MWL in HR. Most of power is to pull field, but swing isn't balanced, makes poor contact, and is susceptible to low/outside pitches. Runs well for size, but lacks first-step quickness and footwork at 3B which negates arm strength.

Bats L | Age 20
2004 FA (DR)

		Year	Lev	Team	AB	R	H	HR	RBI	Avg	OB	Slg	OPS	bb%	ct%	Eye	SB	CS	X/H%	Iso	RC/G
Pwr	++++																				
BAvg	++	2006	Rk	Billings	36	6	12	0	2	333	333	417	750	0	78	0.00	2	1	25	83	4.39
4.50 Spd	++	2006	Rk	GCL Reds	182	24	51	3	30	280	303	407	710	3	81	0.17	2	0	33	126	4.03
Def	+++	2007	A-	Dayton	534	69	143	25	90	268	298	463	761	4	70	0.14	12	6	35	195	4.76

Frazier,Todd — 6 — Cincinnati

EXP MLB DEBUT: 2009 | POTENTIAL: Starting 3B/RF | 8C

Oversized infielder with bat speed and power potential, and proved he can hit with wood. Scouts point to a long swing as a reason for him not hitting for BA, but is selective and makes solid contact. Has arm strength and soft hands, but below average range may push him off of SS.

Bats R | Age 22
2007 (1-S) Rutgers

		Year	Lev	Team	AB	R	H	HR	RBI	Avg	OB	Slg	OPS	bb%	ct%	Eye	SB	CS	X/H%	Iso	RC/G
Pwr	++++																				
BAvg	++																				
4.40 Spd	++	2007	Rk	Billings	160	29	51	5	25	319	388	513	900	10	86	0.82	3	3	31	194	6.71
Def	+++	2007	A-	Dayton	22	4	7	2	5	318	375	727	1102	8	82	0.50	0	0	71	409	8.92

Freeman,Freddie — 35 — Atlanta

EXP MLB DEBUT: 2012 | POTENTIAL: Starting 1B | 8E

Natural strength, bat speed, and uppercut swing provide power potential, and poor plate discipline and upright stance negatively affects contact/BA ability. Lacks speed and agility, which coupled with his stiff hands, makes him below average defensively.

Bats L | Age 18
2007 (2) HS (CA)

		Year	Lev	Team	AB	R	H	HR	RBI	Avg	OB	Slg	OPS	bb%	ct%	Eye	SB	CS	X/H%	Iso	RC/G
Pwr	++++																				
BAvg	++																				
Spd	+																				
Def	++	2007	Rk	GCL Braves	224	24	60	6	30	268	290	379	670	3	85	0.21	1	2	22	112	3.47

Freese,David — 5 — St. Louis

EXP MLB DEBUT: 2009 | POTENTIAL: Platoon 3B/1B | 7C

Strong hitter with moderate bat speed that produces moderate power. Improved plate discipline and contact rate which allowed him to hit for BA. Lacks speed and agility, but does have solid arm strength and playable hands at 3B. Played both 1B and catcher in instructional league.

Bats R | Age 25
2006 (9) So Alabama

		Year	Lev	Team	AB	R	H	HR	RBI	Avg	OB	Slg	OPS	bb%	ct%	Eye	SB	CS	X/H%	Iso	RC/G
Pwr	+++																				
BAvg	+++	2006	A-	Eugene	58	19	22	5	26	379	446	776	1222	11	79	0.58	0	0	59	397	10.73
Spd	++	2006	A-	Ft. Wayne	204	27	61	8	43	299	364	500	864	9	78	0.48	1	1	38	201	6.26
Def	+++	2007	A+	Lk Elsinore	503	104	152	17	96	302	386	489	875	12	80	0.70	6	1	36	187	6.55

Friday,Brian — 6 — Pittsburgh

EXP MLB DEBUT: 2010 | POTENTIAL: Reserve SS/2B | 7D

Athletic player with bat handling skills and plus speed. Makes contact, but lacks power due to a flat bat and medium bat speed. Has a tendency to both strike-out and draw walks. Defensive tools grade average to above, but lacks consistency and concentration, culminating in errors.

Bats R | Age 22
2007 (3) Rice

		Year	Lev	Team	AB	R	H	HR	RBI	Avg	OB	Slg	OPS	bb%	ct%	Eye	SB	CS	X/H%	Iso	RC/G
Pwr	+																				
BAvg	+++																				
Spd	++++																				
Def	+++	2007	A-	State College	156	31	46	2	13	295	337	410	748	6	79	0.30	6	4	28	115	4.68

Fuenmayor,Balbino — 5 — Toronto

EXP MLB DEBUT: 2011 | POTENTIAL: Starting 3B | 8E

Bat speed and athleticism didn't translate into performance, as he struggled with plate discipline, breaking pitches, and contact rate. Possesses arm strength and soft hands at 3B, but already shown a lack of agility and speed. Talent is here, but could be fairly one-dimensional.

Bats R | Age 18
2006 FA (Venezuela)

		Year	Lev	Team	AB	R	H	HR	RBI	Avg	OB	Slg	OPS	bb%	ct%	Eye	SB	CS	X/H%	Iso	RC/G
Pwr	+++																				
BAvg	++																				
Spd	++																				
Def	+++	2007	Rk	GCL Blue Jays	178	13	31	1	12	174	226	242	468	6	62	0.18	0	0	26	67	0.83

Fukodome,Kosuke — 9 — Chicago (N)

EXP MLB DEBUT: 2008 | POTENTIAL: Starting RF | 8A

Missed most of 2007 due to elbow surgery. Drives ball to all fields, makes outstanding contact, and runs bases with good speed. Draws plenty of walks and gets on-base, but will also strike-out. Possesses plus arm strength and solid range in RF.

Bats L | Age 31
2007 FA (Japan)

		Year	Lev	Team	AB	R	H	HR	RBI	Avg	OB	Slg	OPS	bb%	ct%	Eye	SB	CS	X/H%	Iso	RC/G
		2003	Int	Chunichi	528	107	165	34	96	313	401	604	1005	13	78	0.66	10	5	45	292	8.21
Pwr	+++	2004	Int	Chunichi	350	61	97	23	81	277	364	569	933	12	73	0.52	8	3	51	291	7.37
BAvg	++++	2005	Int	Chunichi	515	102	169	28	103	328	431	590	1021	15	75	0.73	13	5	48	262	8.74
Spd	++++	2006	Int	Chunichi	496	117	174	31	104	351	437	653	1090	13	81	0.81	11	2	48	302	9.22
Def	++++	2007	Int	Chunichi	269	64	79	13	48	294	438	520	958	20	75	1.05	5	2	44	227	8.14

Fuld,Sam — 8 — Chicago (N)

EXP MLB DEBUT: 2008 | POTENTIAL: Reserve CF/LF | 6B

High energy athlete with BA ability, above average speed, and ability to turn on inside pitches. Never gives-up at-bats and will use the whole field. Possesses excellent instincts and plays aggressively. Demonstrates plus range in CF and has an average arm with plenty of accuracy.

Bats L | Age 26
2004 (10) Stanford

		Year	Lev	Team	AB	R	H	HR	RBI	Avg	OB	Slg	OPS	bb%	ct%	Eye	SB	CS	X/H%	Iso	RC/G
		2005	A-	Peoria	443	82	133	5	37	300	371	433	805	10	90	1.14	18	11	32	133	5.73
Pwr	++	2006	A+	Daytona	354	63	106	4	40	299	371	421	791	10	85	0.74	22	3	27	121	5.50
BAvg	++++	2007	AA	Tennessee	335	56	97	2	27	290	367	388	755	11	89	1.08	10	3	28	99	5.19
Spd	++++	2007	AAA	Iowa	52	13	14	1	2	269	377	442	819	15	90	1.80	2	0	43	173	6.20
Def	+++	2007	MLB	Chicago (N)	6	3	0	0	0	0	333	0	333	33	50	1.00	0	0	0	0	0.00

Gaetti, Joe — 9 — Colorado

Bats R **Age** 26 2003 (12) N Carolina St
EXP MLB DEBUT: 2008 POTENTIAL: Reserve LF/RF **6C**

		Pwr	+++
		BAvg	++
4.35		Spd	++
		Def	++

Year	Lev	Team	AB	R	H	HR	RBI	Avg	OB	Slg	OPS	bb%	ct%	Eye	SB	CS	X/H%	Iso	RC/G
2004	A-	Asheville	370	62	95	16	55	257	353	457	810	13	71	0.51	16	6	43	200	5.85
2005	A+	Modesto	395	90	131	21	87	332	409	605	1014	12	71	0.46	5	7	44	273	8.72
2006	AA	Tulsa	392	68	116	16	62	296	358	497	856	9	75	0.38	5	2	37	202	6.20
2007	AA	Tulsa	177	24	41	8	28	232	313	429	743	11	71	0.40	2	1	46	198	4.79
2007	AAA	Colo Springs	244	40	66	11	32	270	333	504	837	9	64	0.26	3	4	45	234	6.53

Strong/stocky outfielder generates power with bat speed and uppercut swing. Swings at a lot of bad pitches and isn't very patient which decreases BA/OBP, but is adept at making contact. Possesses average arm strength in corner outfield, but lacks range due to below average speed.

Gallagher, Austin — 5 — Los Angeles (N)

Bats L **Age** 19 2007 (3) HS (PA)
EXP MLB DEBUT: 2011 POTENTIAL: Starting 3B **8D**

		Pwr	++++
		BAvg	+++
		Spd	++
		Def	++

Year	Lev	Team	AB	R	H	HR	RBI	Avg	OB	Slg	OPS	bb%	ct%	Eye	SB	CS	X/H%	Iso	RC/G
2007	Rk	Ogden	197	28	56	4	17	284	347	401	748	9	83	0.58	1	1	27	117	4.80

Tall/projectable hitter with bat speed and plate discipline that should make him an above average hitter for power and BA. Swing can get long, but has ability to adjust. Arm strength and soft hands play at 3B, but lacks first-step quickness which will only worsen with maturity.

Gamel, Matt — 5 — Milwaukee

Bats L **Age** 22 2005 (4) Chipola JC
EXP MLB DEBUT: 2009 POTENTIAL: Starting 3B **7C**

		Pwr	++++
		BAvg	+++
		Spd	++
		Def	++

Year	Lev	Team	AB	R	H	HR	RBI	Avg	OB	Slg	OPS	bb%	ct%	Eye	SB	CS	X/H%	Iso	RC/G
2005	Rk	Helena	199	34	65	5	37	327	365	497	862	6	75	0.24	7	4	34	171	6.18
2005	A-	W. Virginia	23	2	4	1	1	174	321	304	626	18	61	0.56	0	0	25	130	3.24
2006	A-	W. Virginia	493	65	141	17	88	288	359	469	825	10	84	0.64	9	2	35	181	5.74
2007	A+	Brevard Co	466	78	140	9	60	300	378	472	850	11	79	0.59	14	7	39	172	6.01

Improved hitting approach, focusing more on contact and using whole field, kept BA up. Power is more of a doubles variety, but has the bat speed to increase HR output. Arm strength is solid, but lack of first-step quickness and stiff hands accounted for 53 errors.

Garabedian, Alex — 2 — Los Angeles (N)

Bats R **Age** 22 2007 (8) Charleston
EXP MLB DEBUT: 2009 POTENTIAL: Platoon CA **7D**

		Pwr	+++
		BAvg	+++
		Spd	+
		Def	++++

Year	Lev	Team	AB	R	H	HR	RBI	Avg	OB	Slg	OPS	bb%	ct%	Eye	SB	CS	X/H%	Iso	RC/G
2007	Rk	Ogden	186	26	47	4	21	253	332	371	703	11	78	0.55	0	1	30	118	4.29

Plus defensive catcher with arm strength and quick release that negates running game, and excellent receiving skills. Moderate bat speed produces moderate power and judges strike zone well, but doesn't make consistent contact or run well, which will hamper BA.

Garcia, Emmanuel — 46 — New York (N)

Bats L **Age** 22 2004 NDFA (Canada)
EXP MLB DEBUT: 2010 POTENTIAL: Reserve 2B/SS **7D**

		Pwr	+
		BAvg	+++
		Spd	+++
		Def	++

Year	Lev	Team	AB	R	H	HR	RBI	Avg	OB	Slg	OPS	bb%	ct%	Eye	SB	CS	X/H%	Iso	RC/G
2005	Rk	GCL Mets	186	43	63	2	30	339	406	409	814	10	81	0.58	17	1	14	70	5.69
2005	A+	St. Lucie	9	1	2	0	0	222	222	333	556	0	78	0.00	0	0	50	111	2.08
2006	Rk	Kingsport	206	35	60	3	26	291	373	379	752	12	80	0.66	19	6	17	87	5.00
2006	A-	Brooklyn	50	7	12	0	3	240	309	240	549	9	74	0.38	3	0	0	0	2.14
2007	A+	St. Lucie	488	65	125	0	31	256	341	301	642	11	79	0.61	34	13	14	45	3.66

Plus athlete with disruptive speed and bat handling ability. Possesses very little strength and bat speed, so won't hit for power, but can make contact and draw walks. Defensively, his arm strength is slightly below average and made 36 errors, but compensates with outstanding range.

Gardner, Brett — 8 — New York (A)

Bats L **Age** 24 2005 (3) Charleston
EXP MLB DEBUT: 2008 POTENTIAL: Platoon CF/LF **7B**

		Pwr	+
		BAvg	+++
3.90		Spd	+++++
		Def	+++

Year	Lev	Team	AB	R	H	HR	RBI	Avg	OB	Slg	OPS	bb%	ct%	Eye	SB	CS	X/H%	Iso	RC/G
2005	A-	Staten Island	282	62	80	5	32	284	371	376	747	12	83	0.80	19	3	19	92	4.96
2006	A+	Tampa	224	46	72	0	21	321	431	420	850	16	79	0.90	28	7	24	98	6.69
2006	AA	Trenton	217	41	59	0	13	272	352	318	670	11	82	0.69	28	5	12	46	4.04
2007	AA	Trenton	203	43	61	0	17	300	398	419	817	14	84	1.03	18	4	31	118	6.14
2007	AAA	Scranton/WB	181	37	47	1	9	260	337	331	668	10	76	0.49	21	3	17	72	3.90

Leadoff type hitter with contact ability, plate discipline, and plus speed, but got off to slow start with a broken hand. Inside-out swing and focus on hitting ball on ground doesn't leave him much power, but knows limitations. Features plus range and fringe-average arm strength in CF.

Getz, Chris — 4 — Chicago (A)

Bats L **Age** 24 2005 (4) Michigan
EXP MLB DEBUT: 2008 POTENTIAL: Reserve 2B **6A**

		Pwr	+
		BAvg	+++
4.15		Spd	++++
		Def	+++

Year	Lev	Team	AB	R	H	HR	RBI	Avg	OB	Slg	OPS	bb%	ct%	Eye	SB	CS	X/H%	Iso	RC/G
2005	Rk	Great Falls	24	3	8	0	4	333	360	375	735	4	92	0.50	2	1	13	42	4.49
2005	A-	Kannapolis	214	38	65	1	28	304	402	397	799	14	95	3.50	11	4	25	93	6.06
2006	AA	Birmingham	508	67	130	2	36	256	325	321	646	9	91	1.11	18	6	18	65	3.89
2007	AA	Birmingham	278	40	83	3	29	299	379	381	760	11	89	1.20	13	7	18	83	5.23

Missed half of season after fouling ball off leg. Extreme contact hitter who sprays ball to all fields, has impressive plate discipline, and runs bases aggressively. Bat speed and swing plane isn't conducive to power. Solid defender with soft/quick hands, range, and average arm strength.

Giarratano, Tony — 6 — Detroit

Bats R **Age** 25 2003 (4) Tulane
EXP MLB DEBUT: 2005 POTENTIAL: Starting SS **7C**

		Pwr	++
		BAvg	+++
		Spd	++++
		Def	++++

Year	Lev	Team	AB	R	H	HR	RBI	Avg	OB	Slg	OPS	bb%	ct%	Eye	SB	CS	X/H%	Iso	RC/G
2003	A-	Oneonta	189	31	62	3	27	328	368	476	844	6	88	0.55	9	4	29	148	5.84
2004	A-	W. Michigan	165	20	47	1	13	285	379	352	730	13	87	1.14	11	3	17	67	4.97
2004	A+	Lakeland	202	30	76	5	25	376	422	505	927	7	81	0.42	14	8	21	129	6.84
2005	AA	Erie	346	40	92	4	32	266	328	373	701	8	78	0.43	12	5	30	107	4.26
2006	AA	Erie	269	35	76	0	19	283	337	390	727	8	83	0.49	16	4	32	108	4.64

Missed most of last two years with right knee and shoulder surgeries. Fundamentally sound player with speed and defensive ability, highlighted by soft hands and arm strength. Offensively, he hits for BA in situations, but medium bat speed leaves him with little power.

Gillespie, Cole — 7 — Milwaukee

Bats R **Age** 23 2006 (3) Oregon St
EXP MLB DEBUT: 2009 POTENTIAL: Starting LF **7C**

		Pwr	+++
		BAvg	+++
4.25		Spd	++++
		Def	+++

Year	Lev	Team	AB	R	H	HR	RBI	Avg	OB	Slg	OPS	bb%	ct%	Eye	SB	CS	X/H%	Iso	RC/G
2006	Rk	Helena	186	49	64	8	31	344	463	548	1011	18	82	1.21	18	4	33	204	8.56
2007	A+	Brevard Co	438	75	117	12	62	267	371	420	791	14	78	0.76	16	8	34	153	5.61

Plays above tools, capitalizing on solid plate discipline to maintain BA and moderate power. Speed is slightly above average and picks spots to steal. Played LF exclusively in 2007, showing solid range and a below average arm, but has experience at both corner infield spots.

Gilmore, Jon — 5 — Atlanta

Bats R **Age** 19 2007 (1-S) HS (IA)
EXP MLB DEBUT: 2012 POTENTIAL: Starting 3B **8D**

		Pwr	+++
		BAvg	+++
4.35		Spd	++
		Def	+++

Year	Lev	Team	AB	R	H	HR	RBI	Avg	OB	Slg	OPS	bb%	ct%	Eye	SB	CS	X/H%	Iso	RC/G
2007	Rk	GCL Braves	162	11	46	1	29	284	301	346	647	2	83	0.14	0	0	15	62	3.21

Proven hitter with wood, he generates moderate power with bat speed and a short stroke. Maintained BA with aggressive approach, but lacks plate discipline. Moved from 2B to 3B where his arm is more of an asset and his lack of range and stiff hands less of an issue.

Gil, Jerry — 68 — Cincinnati

Bats R **Age** 25 1999 FA (DR)
EXP MLB DEBUT: 2007 POTENTIAL: Reserve SS/CF **6B**

		Pwr	++
		BAvg	++
4.10		Spd	++++
		Def	+++

Year	Lev	Team	AB	R	H	HR	RBI	Avg	OB	Slg	OPS	bb%	ct%	Eye	SB	CS	X/H%	Iso	RC/G
2004	MLB	Arizona	86	3	15	0	8	174	174	221	395	0	62	0.00	2	0	20	47	-0.41
2005	AA	Tennessee	199	28	51	10	29	256	285	472	757	4	74	0.15	10	7	39	216	4.60
2006	AA	Tennessee	446	71	117	26	85	262	291	520	811	4	75	0.16	6	6	49	258	5.28
2006	AAA	Tucson	47	6	6	1	3	128	128	213	340	0	68	0.00	1	0	33	85	-1.23
2007	MLB	Cincinnati	0	0	0	0	0	0	0	0	0	0	0	0.00	0	0	0	0	0.00

Athlete with plus speed, who missed most of 2007 due to TJS. Ability to drive baseball has improved through added strength, but lacks the contact ability and plate discipline to hit for BA. Features plus arm strength and range, but hands are stiff and is error-prone at SS.

Gindl,Caleb — 9 — Milwaukee

EXP MLB DEBUT: 2012 | POTENTIAL: Platoon LF/RF | 8E

Bats L Age 19
2007 (5) HS (FL)
Pwr +++
BAvg ++++
Spd ++++
Def ++

Year	Lev	Team	AB	R	H	HR	RBI	Avg	OB	Slg	OPS	bb%	ct%	Eye	SB	CS	X/H%	Iso	RC/G
2007	Rk	Helena	207	40	77	5	42	372	427	580	1007	9	82	0.53	4	4	39	208	8.06

Short/stocky athlete with ability to make hard contact and judge strike zone, which gives him solid BA/OBP and moderate power. Above average speed hasn't translated to steals or range in outfield. Possesses strong throwing arm and has work ethic to improve defensively.

Goedert,Jared — 54 — Cleveland

EXP MLB DEBUT: 2009 | POTENTIAL: Platoon 3B/2B | 8D

Bats R Age 23
2006 (9) Kansas St
Pwr +++
BAvg ++++
Spd ++
Def +

Year	Lev	Team	AB	R	H	HR	RBI	Avg	OB	Slg	OPS	bb%	ct%	Eye	SB	CS	X/H%	Iso	RC/G
2006	A-	Mahoning Val	238	31	64	3	26	269	323	382	705	7	88	0.68	1	0	30	113	4.35
2007	A-	Lake County	165	44	60	16	51	364	475	715	1190	18	82	1.21	0	1	43	352	10.44
2007	A+	Kinston	125	23	32	4	23	256	372	424	796	16	80	0.92	1	0	41	168	5.73

Advanced hitter with outstanding plate discipline, BA ability, and moderate power. Uses whole field and centers ball well. Numbers fell-off at high Class-A, but was battling shoulder inflammation. Below average defender with stiff hands and average arm, and is better suited for 3B.

Gold,Nate — 3 — Texas

EXP MLB DEBUT: 2008 | POTENTIAL: Reserve 1B | 6C

Bats R Age 28
2002 (10) Gonzaga
Pwr ++++
BAvg ++
Spd ++
Def +++

Year	Lev	Team	AB	R	H	HR	RBI	Avg	OB	Slg	OPS	bb%	ct%	Eye	SB	CS	X/H%	Iso	RC/G
2004	A+	Stockton	500	85	121	20	94	242	329	434	763	12	72	0.46	5	0	45	192	5.13
2005	A+	Bakersfield	381	63	107	21	69	281	352	528	880	10	83	0.65	2	2	47	247	6.35
2005	AA	Frisco	79	9	18	0	11	228	256	266	522	4	80	0.19	0	0	17	38	1.74
2006	AA	Frisco	452	74	132	34	103	292	369	582	951	11	81	0.65	3	4	47	290	7.18
2007	AAA	Oklahoma	469	74	137	26	103	292	348	516	864	8	78	0.38	0	0	38	224	6.06

Muscular build and moderate bat speed produces above average power. Plate discipline improved slightly, but a long swing ties him up against good pitching. Below average speed makes him a liability on the bases, but does play a solid defensive 1B.

Golson,Greg — 8 — Philadelphia

EXP MLB DEBUT: 2008 | POTENTIAL: Platoon CF | 8D

Bats R Age 22
2004 (1) HS (TX)
Pwr +++
BAvg +++
4.10 Spd ++++
Def ++++

Year	Lev	Team	AB	R	H	HR	RBI	Avg	OB	Slg	OPS	bb%	ct%	Eye	SB	CS	X/H%	Iso	RC/G
2005	A-	Lakewood	375	51	99	4	27	264	312	389	701	6	72	0.25	25	9	31	125	4.23
2006	A-	Lakewood	388	56	85	7	31	219	256	332	588	5	72	0.18	23	7	31	113	2.50
2006	A+	Clearwater	159	31	42	6	17	264	312	472	783	6	67	0.21	7	3	45	208	5.47
2007	A+	Clearwater	418	66	119	12	52	285	319	450	769	5	70	0.17	25	8	35	165	5.01
2007	AA	Reading	153	20	37	3	16	242	252	359	611	1	68	0.04	5	0	27	118	2.71

Plus athlete with above average speed and emerging bat, he is beginning to live-up to Draft status. Displayed moderate power and solid BA, but whether he can maintain this level with his poor plate discipline is the big question. Excellent defender in CF with plus arm strength and range.

Gomez,Hector — 65 — Colorado

EXP MLB DEBUT: 2011 | POTENTIAL: Starting SS | 7C

Bats R Age 20
2005 FA (DR)
Pwr +
BAvg +++
Spd ++++
Def +++

Year	Lev	Team	AB	R	H	HR	RBI	Avg	OB	Slg	OPS	bb%	ct%	Eye	SB	CS	X/H%	Iso	RC/G
2006	Rk	Casper	202	24	66	5	35	327	362	485	847	5	87	0.42	5	3	27	158	5.74
2006	A-	Tri-City	45	4	11	0	6	244	244	311	556	0	69	0.00	0	1	27	67	1.95
2007	A-	Asheville	534	89	142	11	61	266	304	421	725	5	78	0.24	20	10	37	155	4.36

Excellent athlete with superior defensive skills and an emerging offense. Supplies plus range and a strong infield arm with the bulk of his 39 errors coming on plays others wouldn't get to. Speed is best asset and makes good contact, but poor plate discipline will hinder both BA and power.

Gonzalez,Alberto — 6 — New York (A)

EXP MLB DEBUT: 2007 | POTENTIAL: Reserve SS | 7C

Bats R Age 25
2003 FA (Venezuela)
Pwr +
BAvg +++
Spd ++++
Def +++++

Year	Lev	Team	AB	R	H	HR	RBI	Avg	OB	Slg	OPS	bb%	ct%	Eye	SB	CS	X/H%	Iso	RC/G
2006	AA	Tennessee	434	67	125	6	50	288	344	389	733	8	90	0.88	5	1	23	101	4.71
2006	AAA	Tucson	15	2	2	0	1	133	188	133	321	6	93	1.00	0	0	0	0	0.29
2007	AA	Trenton	109	18	36	0	16	330	387	440	827	8	87	0.71	1	1	31	110	5.88
2007	AAA	Scranton/WB	384	44	95	1	35	247	292	362	654	6	87	0.49	11	5	34	115	3.74
2007	MLB	New York (A)	14	3	1	0	1	71	133	71	205	7	93	1.00	0	1	0	0	-0.95

Defensive standout with plus range, quick hands, and enough arm strength to play a major league SS. Improved walk rate and plate discipline, which coupled with his contact ability, gave him a respectable OBP. Lacks power and will need to make better use of his above average speed.

Gonzalez,Carlos — 9 — Oakland

EXP MLB DEBUT: 2008 | POTENTIAL: Starting RF | 9C

Bats L Age 22
2002 FA (Venezuela)
Pwr ++++
BAvg +++
4.40 Spd ++
Def ++++

Year	Lev	Team	AB	R	H	HR	RBI	Avg	OB	Slg	OPS	bb%	ct%	Eye	SB	CS	X/H%	Iso	RC/G
2005	A-	South Bend	515	91	158	18	92	307	366	489	855	9	83	0.56	7	3	33	183	6.04
2006	A+	Lancaster	404	82	121	21	93	300	348	562	910	7	74	0.29	15	8	50	262	6.84
2006	AA	Tennessee	61	11	13	2	5	213	294	410	704	10	80	0.58	1	0	62	197	4.34
2007	AA	Mobile	458	63	131	16	75	286	333	476	809	7	78	0.31	9	5	40	190	5.43
2007	AAA	Tucson	42	9	13	1	11	310	396	500	896	13	86	1.00	1	0	46	190	6.88

Bat speed and wiry strength propel ball and though his HR total decline, his XBH/H was up. Mediocre plate discipline and struggles versus LH pitching will always cause fluctuation with BA. Plus arm strength and range make him a strong defender in RF.

Gonzalez,Esmailyn — 6 — Washington

EXP MLB DEBUT: 2011 | POTENTIAL: Starting SS | 8D

Bats B Age 18
2006 FA (DR)
Pwr ++
BAvg ++++
4.20 Spd +++
Def +++

Year	Lev	Team	AB	R	H	HR	RBI	Avg	OB	Slg	OPS	bb%	ct%	Eye	SB	CS	X/H%	Iso	RC/G
2007	Rk	GCL Nationals	106	13	26	0	11	245	360	311	671	15	83	1.06	4	2	19	66	4.34

Athletic infielder with bat control from both sides and plate discipline which gave him a solid OBP in debut. Squares baseball well and uses whole field, with power and baserunning instincts developing later. Arm strength and soft hands offset average range.

Gorneault,Nick — 8 — Texas

EXP MLB DEBUT: 2007 | POTENTIAL: Reserve LF/RF | 6B

Bats R Age 29
2001 (19) Umass
Pwr ++++
BAvg +++
4.35 Spd ++
Def ++

Year	Lev	Team	AB	R	H	HR	RBI	Avg	OB	Slg	OPS	bb%	ct%	Eye	SB	CS	X/H%	Iso	RC/G
2004	AA	Arkansas	496	91	139	21	81	280	340	480	820	8	74	0.35	7	5	38	200	5.69
2005	AAA	Salt Lake	488	106	143	26	108	293	368	551	919	11	76	0.49	7	6	44	258	7.09
2006	AAA	Salt Lake	407	66	115	15	78	283	344	499	843	9	74	0.36	5	4	43	216	6.10
2007	AAA	Salt Lake	471	82	123	19	59	261	342	437	780	11	77	0.54	17	8	36	176	5.22
2007	MLB	Los Angeles (A)	4	1	0	0	0	0	200	0	200	20	75	1.00	0	0	0	0	0.00

Strong outfielder with solid, all-around skills. Possesses bat speed with ability to hit for power and is selective enough to fashion a decent OBP. Runs bases well despite below average speed. Defense is limited to outfield corners with average arm strength and mediocre range.

Granadillo,Tony — 45 — Boston

EXP MLB DEBUT: 2009 | POTENTIAL: Reserve 2B/3B | 7C

Bats B Age 23
2001 FA (Venezuela)
Pwr +++
BAvg ++
4.20 Spd +++
Def +++

Year	Lev	Team	AB	R	H	HR	RBI	Avg	OB	Slg	OPS	bb%	ct%	Eye	SB	CS	X/H%	Iso	RC/G
2005	Rk	GCL Red Sox	52	9	14	1	9	269	397	385	781	17	81	1.10	0	1	29	115	5.70
2005	AA	Greenville	234	43	68	5	31	291	364	427	791	10	78	0.52	2	0	28	137	5.45
2006	AA	Greenville	421	70	118	13	67	280	347	451	798	9	81	0.52	3	0	37	171	5.42
2007	A+	Lancaster	445	104	145	8	63	326	399	492	891	11	85	0.83	2	0	35	166	6.73
2007	AA	Portland	27	4	9	0	4	333	400	444	844	10	89	1.00	0	1	33	111	6.21

Offensive minded infielder with solid hitting skills and ability to play above tools. Possesses doubles power with moderate bat speed , makes exceptional contact, and is patient at the plate. Lacks the range to play 2B well, but has soft hands and solid-average arm strength.

Greene,Tyler — 6 — St. Louis

EXP MLB DEBUT: 2008 | POTENTIAL: Reserve SS | 7C

Bats R Age 24
2005 (1) Georgia Tech
Pwr +++
BAvg ++
4.20 Spd ++++
Def +++

Year	Lev	Team	AB	R	H	HR	RBI	Avg	OB	Slg	OPS	bb%	ct%	Eye	SB	CS	X/H%	Iso	RC/G
2005	A-	New Jersey	138	28	36	1	18	261	333	370	703	10	73	0.41	13	1	36	109	4.39
2005	A+	Palm Beach	85	17	23	2	5	271	311	388	699	6	67	0.18	6	0	26	118	4.13
2006	A-	Quad Cities	223	42	64	15	47	287	346	552	897	8	71	0.31	11	0	41	265	6.75
2006	A+	Palm Beach	268	38	60	5	19	224	300	325	624	10	66	0.32	22	3	27	101	3.21
2007	AA	Springfield	221	41	54	8	25	244	295	448	743	7	72	0.26	10	2	50	204	4.71

Missed second half with dislocated knee cap which required surgery. Bat speed should provide moderate power, but struggles to make contact and is overly aggressive, which suppresses BA/OBP. Defense remains solid with arm strength, soft hands, and range.

Green,Taylor — 5 — Milwaukee
EXP MLB DEBUT: 2009 | POTENTIAL: Reserve 3B/1B | 8D

Bats L Age 21
2005 (26) Cypress JC
Pwr ++++
BAvg ++
4.40 Spd ++
Def ++

Year	Lev	Team	AB	R	H	HR	RBI	Avg	OB	Slg	OPS	bb%	ct%	Eye	SB	CS	X/H%	Iso	RC/G
2006	Rk	Helena	221	36	51	1	23	231	320	308	628	12	84	0.83	0	1	27	77	3.62
2007	A-	W. Virginia	397	68	130	14	86	327	404	516	920	11	84	0.78	0	5	35	189	7.01

Stocky infielder with offensive promise, possessing moderate bat speed and plate discipline. Swings aggressively, so will strike-out, but should hit for BA and drill 20+ HR. Adjusting to 3B after playing middle infield in college, showing strong arm, but lacks range and proper footwork.

Guzman,Freddy — 8 — Detroit
EXP MLB DEBUT: 2004 | POTENTIAL: Reserve CF/LF | 6B

Bats B Age 27
2000 FA (DR)
Pwr +
BAvg +++
3.90 Spd +++++
Def ++++

Year	Lev	Team	AB	R	H	HR	RBI	Avg	OB	Slg	OPS	bb%	ct%	Eye	SB	CS	X/H%	Iso	RC/G
2005																			
2006	AAA	Port/OCI	376	90	105	3	28	279	364	367	731	12	85	0.91	42	12	22	88	4.87
2006	MLB	Texas	7	1	2	0	0	286	375	286	661	13	86	1.00	0	0	0	0	4.04
2007	AAA	Oklahoma	535	92	144	4	34	269	345	363	708	10	84	0.70	56	14	24	93	4.49
2007	MLB	Texas	6	2	1	1	1	167	167	667	833	0	67	0.00	0	1	100	500	5.27

Plus speed and aggressive instincts helped him lead PCL in steals. Sprays ball to all fields and draws walks which promotes OBP, but has zero power. Possesses plus range in CF, but arm strength has declined following surgical repair of his elbow.

Guzman,Javier — 647 — Pittsburgh
EXP MLB DEBUT: 2007 | POTENTIAL: Reserve SS/2B | 6C

Bats B Age 24
2001 FA (DR)
Pwr +
BAvg ++
Spd ++++
Def ++++

Year	Lev	Team	AB	R	H	HR	RBI	Avg	OB	Slg	OPS	bb%	ct%	Eye	SB	CS	X/H%	Iso	RC/G
2005	A+	Lynchburg	256	40	83	5	35	324	373	488	861	7	84	0.49	13	5	30	164	6.13
2005	AA	Altoona	263	27	62	3	24	236	264	312	576	4	83	0.22	8	5	21	76	2.43
2006	AA	Altoona	485	57	130	7	40	268	304	379	683	5	87	0.39	12	8	27	111	3.89
2007	Rk	GCL Pirates	21	2	2	0	1	95	95	143	238	0	86	0.00	0	0	50	48	-1.40
2007	AA	Altoona	171	19	53	2	25	310	330	421	751	3	88	0.25	7	0	28	111	4.54

Athletic with wiry strength, his below average offense will result in him being turned into a utility player. Makes fair contact, but lacks power and won't draw walks. Defensively, he has plus arm strength and soft hands, and is capable of playing both middle infield positions.

Guzman,Jesus — 457 — Seattle
EXP MLB DEBUT: 2009 | POTENTIAL: Reserve 3B/2B | 6C

Bats R Age 24
2001 FA (Venezuela)
Pwr +++
BAvg +++
4.40 Spd ++
Def +

Year	Lev	Team	AB	R	H	HR	RBI	Avg	OB	Slg	OPS	bb%	ct%	Eye	SB	CS	X/H%	Iso	RC/G
2004	A+	Inland Emp	442	80	137	6	71	310	389	443	832	11	76	0.54	9	8	32	133	6.14
2005	AA	San Antonio	453	61	117	9	53	258	325	393	718	9	78	0.45	6	11	30	135	4.45
2006	AA	San Antonio	407	57	105	9	55	258	333	383	717	10	82	0.62	7	3	29	125	4.48
2007	A+	High Desert	518	102	156	25	112	301	363	539	901	9	84	0.59	3	3	44	237	6.58

Demoted to high Class-A to work on defense at 2B and versatility, so offensive outburst must be taken into context. Drove ball better and hit for BA with added strength and improved contact rate. Arm strength plays anywhere, but range works better at his natural 3B.

Guzman,Joel — 53 — Tampa Bay
EXP MLB DEBUT: 2006 | POTENTIAL: Starting 1B/3B | 8D

Bats R Age 23
2001 FA (DR)
Pwr ++++
BAvg ++
4.40 Spd ++
Def +++

Year	Lev	Team	AB	R	H	HR	RBI	Avg	OB	Slg	OPS	bb%	ct%	Eye	SB	CS	X/H%	Iso	RC/G
2006	AAA	Las Vegas	317	44	94	11	55	297	350	461	810	8	77	0.36	8	5	30	164	5.46
2006	MLB	Los Angeles (N)	19	2	4	0	3	211	318	211	529	14	89	1.50	0	0	0	0	2.73
2006	A+	Durham	88	7	17	4	9	193	228	386	615	4	74	0.17	0	0	53	193	2.75
2007	AAA	Durham	414	44	100	16	64	242	281	408	690	5	72	0.20	9	2	35	167	3.81
2007	MLB	Tampa Bay	37	5	9	0	4	243	282	378	660	5	73	0.20	0	0	33	135	3.73

Bat speed and power predominates his game, but poor plate discipline and a long swing limits BA/OBP. Breaking pitches tie him up easily and his speed is becoming a non-factor. With his agility and arm strength, he has become a solid defensive option at both infield and outfield corners.

Haerther,Cody — 9 — St. Louis
EXP MLB DEBUT: 2008 | POTENTIAL: Reserve RF/LF | 6B

Bats L Age 24
2002 (6) HS (CA)
Pwr ++
BAvg +++
4.20 Spd +++
Def ++

Year	Lev	Team	AB	R	H	HR	RBI	Avg	OB	Slg	OPS	bb%	ct%	Eye	SB	CS	X/H%	Iso	RC/G
2005	A+	Palm Beach	173	29	55	8	30	318	379	584	963	9	82	0.55	8	3	42	266	7.42
2005	AA	Springfield	208	30	62	10	37	298	327	500	827	4	79	0.20	0	1	34	202	5.39
2006	AA	Springfield	411	56	113	11	51	275	335	436	770	8	86	0.63	3	3	36	161	5.06
2007	Rk	AZL Cardinals	12	1	4	0	1	333	385	583	968	8	92	1.00	0	0	50	250	7.62
2007	AA	Springfield	142	22	41	5	28	289	361	486	847	10	78	0.52	0	0	44	197	6.11

Missed most of 2007 with hamate bone surgery. Moderate bat speed and inside-out swing allows him to hit for BA, but power is of the doubles variety and adds nothing with his average speed. A former infielder, he doesn't take good routes in the outfield, but has playable arm strength.

Hallberg,Mark — 6 — Arizona
EXP MLB DEBUT: 2010 | POTENTIAL: Reserve 2B/SS | 7E

Bats R Age 22
2007 (9) Florida St
Pwr +
BAvg ++++
4.30 Spd +++
Def ++

Year	Lev	Team	AB	R	H	HR	RBI	Avg	OB	Slg	OPS	bb%	ct%	Eye	SB	CS	X/H%	Iso	RC/G
2007	A-	Yakima	233	44	73	6	32	313	384	464	848	9	91	1.05	12	1	50	151	6.09

Athletic/fundamentally sound player hit well in debut, but was old for level. BA should remain strong with contact ability and plate discipline, and can drive gaps for doubles. Possesses speed and baserunning instincts, though defense is marginal due to stiff hands and average arm strength.

Halman,Greg — 8 — Seattle
EXP MLB DEBUT: 2010 | POTENTIAL: Starting RF/CF | 9E

Bats R Age 20
2003 FA Netherlands
Pwr ++++
BAvg ++
Spd ++++
Def +++

Year	Lev	Team	AB	R	H	HR	RBI	Avg	OB	Slg	OPS	bb%	ct%	Eye	SB	CS	X/H%	Iso	RC/G
2005	Rk	AZL Mariners	89	17	23	3	11	258	333	449	783	10	79	0.53	1	3	35	191	5.30
2006	A-	Everett	116	19	30	5	16	259	277	509	786	3	72	0.09	10	4	50	250	5.11
2007	A-	Everett	238	37	73	16	37	307	371	597	968	8	64	0.25	16	8	49	290	7.89
2007	A-	Wisconsin	187	26	34	4	15	182	234	273	507	4	59	0.10	15	7	26	91	2.55

Raw athlete with excellent power/speed combination, leading NWL in SLG. Bat speed and strength produces tape-measure shots, but has poor pitch recognition and swings too wildly to hit for BA. Runs bases with long strides and has the arm strength and range to play CF.

Hamilton,Mark — 3 — St. Louis
EXP MLB DEBUT: 2009 | POTENTIAL: Starting 1B | 8D

Bats L Age 23
2006 (2-S) Tulane
Pwr ++++
BAvg +++
4.50 Spd +
Def ++

Year	Lev	Team	AB	R	H	HR	RBI	Avg	OB	Slg	OPS	bb%	ct%	Eye	SB	CS	X/H%	Iso	RC/G
2006	A-	State College	106	18	28	8	24	264	345	538	882	11	77	0.54	1	1	43	274	6.38
2006	A-	Quad Cities	142	16	36	3	24	254	303	373	676	7	77	0.31	0	0	31	120	3.74
2007	A+	Palm Beach	221	31	64	13	49	290	349	520	869	8	78	0.42	1	0	39	231	6.12
2007	AA	Springfield	248	32	62	6	41	250	316	383	699	9	78	0.44	1	1	34	133	4.15

Power hitter with natural strength and plus bat speed, giving him pole-to-pole power. Judges strike zone, but struggles with breaking pitches and a long swing hurts contact/BA ability. Below average speed and agility, and struggles defensively with stiff hands and low arm strength.

Hankerd,Cyle — 7 — Arizona
EXP MLB DEBUT: 2009 | POTENTIAL: Starting LF | 8D

Bats R Age 23
2006 (3) USC
Pwr +++
BAvg ++++
4.30 Spd +++
Def ++

Year	Lev	Team	AB	R	H	HR	RBI	Avg	OB	Slg	OPS	bb%	ct%	Eye	SB	CS	X/H%	Iso	RC/G
2006	A-	Yakima	216	24	83	4	38	384	419	519	938	6	75	0.24	0	0	25	134	7.16
2006	A+	Lancaster	65	15	24	8	23	369	438	800	1238	11	86	0.89	0	0	50	431	10.27
2007	A+	Visalia	386	55	110	8	54	285	344	422	767	8	84	0.58	2	3	33	137	5.03

Bat speed is best asset, but power is limited with a flat bat plane and battled wrist problems. Makes solid contact and will draw walks, which enhances OBP. Arm strength and range are below average which limits him to LF. Bat will be ticket to Majors, so has to improve power.

Harbin,Taylor — 46 — Arizona
EXP MLB DEBUT: 2010 | POTENTIAL: Starting 2B | 7D

Bats R Age 22
2007 (8) Clemson
Pwr +++
BAvg +++
4.30 Spd +++
Def +++

Year	Lev	Team	AB	R	H	HR	RBI	Avg	OB	Slg	OPS	bb%	ct%	Eye	SB	CS	X/H%	Iso	RC/G
2007	Rk	Missoula	243	42	67	10	42	276	331	477	808	8	84	0.53	5	4	40	202	5.40
2007	A-	South Bend	14	2	3	0	1	214	214	286	500	0	86	0.00	0	0	33	71	1.55

Hard-nosed player with above average power for middle infielder. Exhibits good bat speed and contact ability, with just enough plate discipline to hit for BA consistently. Soft/quick hands highlight defensive skills, with his average range and arm strength suiting 2B better than SS.

BATTERS

Harman,Brad

4 | Philadelphia | EXP MLB DEBUT: 2009 | POTENTIAL: Reserve 2B | 6C

Bats R Age 22	Year	Lev	Team	AB	R	H	HR	RBI	Avg	OB	Slg	OPS	bb%	ct%	Eye	SB	CS	X/H%	Iso	RC/G
2004 FA (Australia)																				
Pwr +++	2004	Rk	GCL Phillies	183	23	42	2	19	230	273	317	590	6	78	0.27	2	1	29	87	2.64
BAvg ++	2005	A-	Lakewood	419	63	127	11	58	303	371	442	812	10	79	0.51	5	11	28	138	5.62
4.30 Spd +++	2006	A+	Clearwater	423	59	102	2	24	241	318	305	623	10	76	0.47	6	2	22	64	3.29
Def ++	2007	A+	Clearwater	448	63	126	13	62	281	341	449	790	8	77	0.38	1	1	35	167	5.11

Athletic player produces doubles power from moderate bat speed and hit for BA despite aggressive approach. Pitches with a wrinkle tend to neutralize him and doesn't run much with his average speed. Below average defender with stiff hands and average arm strength.

Harper,Brett

3 | New York (N) | EXP MLB DEBUT: 2008 | POTENTIAL: Reserve 1B | 6B

Bats L Age 26	Year	Lev	Team	AB	R	H	HR	RBI	Avg	OB	Slg	OPS	bb%	ct%	Eye	SB	CS	X/H%	Iso	RC/G
2000 (45) HS (AZ)	2004	AA	Binghamton	174	24	43	7	26	247	303	437	740	7	66	0.23	0	0	44	190	4.85
Pwr ++++	2005	A+	St. Lucie	239	35	67	20	60	280	338	586	924	8	73	0.33	0	1	48	305	6.91
BAvg ++	2005	AA	Binghamton	227	37	62	16	42	273	348	533	881	10	63	0.31	0	0	44	260	7.14
Spd +	2006	AA	Binghamton	65	8	22	0	8	338	403	446	849	10	71	0.37	1	0	32	108	6.56
Def +	2007	AA	Binghamton	476	69	141	24	88	296	343	500	843	7	75	0.29	2	0	35	204	5.81

Muscular hitter recovered well from labrum surgery, showing solid offensive level. Possesses strong bat speed and power to all fields, and although he is aggressive and will strike-out, he has maintained a respectable BA. Defense is well below average and is a liability on the bases.

Harvey,Ryan

9 | Chicago (N) | EXP MLB DEBUT: 2009 | POTENTIAL: Platoon RF | 7E

Bats R Age 23	Year	Lev	Team	AB	R	H	HR	RBI	Avg	OB	Slg	OPS	bb%	ct%	Eye	SB	CS	X/H%	Iso	RC/G
2003 (1) HS (FL)	2004	A-	Boise	231	42	61	14	43	264	323	481	803	8	66	0.26	2	2	36	216	5.61
Pwr ++++	2005	A-	Peoria	467	71	120	24	100	257	293	484	777	5	71	0.18	8	4	47	227	5.03
BAvg +	2006	A+	Daytona	475	64	118	20	84	248	286	432	718	5	74	0.20	7	0	39	183	4.14
Spd ++	2007	Rk	AZL Cubs	17	1	2	0	1	118	167	118	284	6	59	0.14	0	0	0	0	-2.32
Def +++	2007	A+	Daytona	224	30	55	11	35	246	268	446	715	3	76	0.13	0	1	40	201	3.95

Strong/athletic hitter with plus bat speed, but poor pitch recognition and a long swing prevent power from being game usable. Possesses plus arm strength in RF and adequate range, but was hampered through much of 2007 with a nagging leg injury. May shift to the mound in 2008.

Hatch,Anthony

54 | Toronto | EXP MLB DEBUT: 2009 | POTENTIAL: Platoon 3B/2B | 7D

Bats R Age 24	Year	Lev	Team	AB	R	H	HR	RBI	Avg	OB	Slg	OPS	bb%	ct%	Eye	SB	CS	X/H%	Iso	RC/G
2005 (13) Nicolls St																				
Pwr ++	2005	Rk	Pulaski	128	16	35	5	26	273	321	508	829	7	77	0.30	0	1	51	234	5.76
BAvg ++++	2006	A-	Lansing	239	46	75	9	37	314	401	548	950	13	85	0.95	5	1	47	234	7.49
4.20 Spd +++	2006	A+	Dunedin	8	3	4	0	2	500	600	750	1350	20	100		0	0	50	250	12.64
Def +++	2007	A+	Dunedin	481	67	120	15	53	249	296	418	714	6	82	0.37	5	4	38	168	4.22

Athletic infielder lost offensive edge in a tough FSL, but was coming off bi-lateral wrist surgeries. Makes good contact and should hit for BA, but power will be limited due to topspin placed on his hits. Versatile defender with average skills, which appear to work better at 3B and 2B.

Haydel,Lee

8 | Milwaukee | EXP MLB DEBUT: 2011 | POTENTIAL: Starting CF | 7D

Bats L Age 20	Year	Lev	Team	AB	R	H	HR	RBI	Avg	OB	Slg	OPS	bb%	ct%	Eye	SB	CS	X/H%	Iso	RC/G
2006 (19) Delgado CC																				
Pwr ++																				
BAvg ++++																				
3.90 Spd +++++																				
Def +++	2007	Rk	Helena	254	42	70	0	20	276	308	362	670	5	83	0.27	12	5	24	87	3.73

Draft-and-follow hit an outstanding .421 in junior college, but struggled with plate discipline in professional debut. Drives ball to gaps on occasion, but offensive strength lies with his plus speed and contact ability. Possesses excellent range in CF with average arm strength.

Hayes,Brett

2 | Florida | EXP MLB DEBUT: 2009 | POTENTIAL: Platoon CA | 6C

Bats R Age 24	Year	Lev	Team	AB	R	H	HR	RBI	Avg	OB	Slg	OPS	bb%	ct%	Eye	SB	CS	X/H%	Iso	RC/G
2005 (2-S) Nevada	2005	Rk	GCL Marlins	12	2	5	0	2	417	417	500	917	0	83	0.00	0	1	20	83	6.24
Pwr ++	2005	A-	Jamestown	117	11	28	1	12	239	310	333	643	9	82	0.57	3	3	29	94	3.62
BAvg +++	2006	A-	Greensboro	278	39	69	9	39	248	319	399	718	9	78	0.48	4	3	33	151	4.39
Spd +	2007	A+	Jupiter	65	10	22	1	11	338	419	462	880	12	85	0.90	2	3	23	123	6.65
Def ++++	2007	AA	Carolina	273	22	64	3	31	234	282	326	608	6	81	0.35	2	0	30	92	2.97

Athletic catcher with arm strength, a quick release (1.9), and receiving skills, but only threw-out 21% of attempted runners. Offensively, he has hit for BA on occasion, but lacks power and ability to walk. Defense, work ethic, and makeup will give him opportunities as a reserve catcher.

Headley,Chase

5 | San Diego | EXP MLB DEBUT: 2007 | POTENTIAL: Starting 3B | 8B

Bats B Age 24	Year	Lev	Team	AB	R	H	HR	RBI	Avg	OB	Slg	OPS	bb%	ct%	Eye	SB	CS	X/H%	Iso	RC/G
2005 (2-C) Tennessee	2005	A-	Eugene	220	29	59	6	33	268	366	441	807	13	78	0.71	1	1	39	173	5.82
Pwr +++	2005	A-	Ft. Wayne	15	2	3	0	1	200	250	200	450	6	73	0.25	0	0	0	0	0.67
BAvg ++++	2006	A+	Lk Elsinore	483	79	141	12	73	292	387	435	822	13	80	0.78	4	5	32	143	5.98
Spd ++	2007	AA	San Antonio	433	82	143	20	78	330	428	580	1008	15	74	0.65	1	0	44	249	8.66
Def ++	2007	MLB	San Diego	18	1	4	0	0	222	300	278	578	10	78	0.50	0	0	25	56	2.75

MVP of TL leading league in all three percentage categories. Possesses moderate bat speed, plate coverage, and plate discipline which provides BA and moderate power. Defense is average at best with average arm strength, but possesses agility and soft hands.

Head,Stephen

3 | Cleveland | EXP MLB DEBUT: 2009 | POTENTIAL: Platoon 1B | 7D

Bats L Age 24	Year	Lev	Team	AB	R	H	HR	RBI	Avg	OB	Slg	OPS	bb%	ct%	Eye	SB	CS	X/H%	Iso	RC/G
2005 (2) Mississippi St	2005	A-	Mahoning Val	37	11	16	6	14	432	533	1027	1560	18	86	1.60	0	0	63	595	14.47
Pwr ++++	2005	A+	Kinston	203	31	58	4	36	286	313	419	732	4	84	0.24	4	0	33	133	4.32
BAvg +++	2006	A+	Kinston	477	65	112	14	73	235	311	377	689	10	84	0.72	2	1	36	143	4.14
Spd +	2007	A+	Kinston	387	73	97	13	61	251	321	426	747	9	82	0.56	5	0	43	176	4.79
Def +++	2007	AA	Akron	98	13	27	3	18	276	330	459	789	8	82	0.44	1	0	44	184	5.23

Strong hands and bat speed generate moderate power, but tends to pull-off pitches, won't go the other way, and is a mistake hitter. Draws walks, but contact rate is too low to project BA. Above average fielder at 1B with soft hands and agility, and will be given reps in LF over off-season.

Heether,Adam

5 | Milwaukee | EXP MLB DEBUT: 2008 | POTENTIAL: Reserve 3B/1B | 6B

Bats R Age 26	Year	Lev	Team	AB	R	H	HR	RBI	Avg	OB	Slg	OPS	bb%	ct%	Eye	SB	CS	X/H%	Iso	RC/G
2003 (11) Long Beach S	2005	A+	Brevard Co	338	48	103	6	54	305	368	450	818	9	86	0.71	3	1	34	145	5.73
Pwr +++	2005	AA	Huntsville	51	11	16	0	9	314	340	412	751	4	84	0.25	2	1	31	98	4.66
BAvg +	2006	A+	Brevard Co	166	20	36	3	16	217	319	331	651	13	78	0.68	0	0	36	114	3.76
Spd ++	2006	AA	Huntsville	244	21	52	1	18	213	289	250	539	10	79	0.51	1	1	13	37	2.20
Def +++	2007	AA	Huntsville	432	60	129	9	62	299	373	447	819	11	79	0.57	2	6	32	148	5.83

Strong/advanced hitter with bat speed and power to pull field. Improved plate discipline and contact rate which increased BA. Lacks agility on defense and is a below average runner, but has soft hands and a strong arm, making him an average defender at the hot corner.

Henry,Justin

47 | Detroit | EXP MLB DEBUT: 2010 | POTENTIAL: Reserve 2B/LF | 7D

Bats L Age 23	Year	Lev	Team	AB	R	H	HR	RBI	Avg	OB	Slg	OPS	bb%	ct%	Eye	SB	CS	X/H%	Iso	RC/G
2007 (9) Mississippi																				
Pwr +																				
BAvg +++																				
Spd ++++																				
Def ++	2007	A-	Oneonta	250	49	85	1	31	340	417	412	829	12	91	1.50	14	7	16	72	6.10

Plus athlete with leadoff-hitter ability. Possesses plus speed, and his inside-out swing, use of the whole field, and plate discipline provides a solid BA/OBP. Medium bat speed prevents power. Played 2B with range and average arm strength, but stiff hands may mean shift to OF.

Henry,Sean

8 | Cincinnati | EXP MLB DEBUT: 2009 | POTENTIAL: Reserve CF/RF | 7C

Bats R Age 22	Year	Lev	Team	AB	R	H	HR	RBI	Avg	OB	Slg	OPS	bb%	ct%	Eye	SB	CS	X/H%	Iso	RC/G
2004 (20) Diablo Valley C	2005	Rk	Kingsport	149	24	38	5	31	255	351	416	767	13	71	0.51	15	1	34	161	5.27
Pwr ++	2006	Rk	Kingsport	149	28	41	4	27	275	365	463	828	12	81	0.72	23	3	44	188	6.04
BAvg +++	2006	A-	Hagerstown	67	7	17	3	14	254	286	463	748	4	76	0.19	6	3	47	209	4.50
4.20 Spd ++++	2007	A+	St. Lucie	450	59	132	11	57	293	354	456	809	9	84	0.58	18	11	33	162	5.55
Def +++	2007	AA	Chattanooga	58	9	14	1	2	241	313	345	657	9	81	0.55	1	1	29	103	3.71

Athletic player with solid secondary skills. Drives ball with good bat speed, can hit for BA due to contact ability and plate discipline, and runs bases with above average speed. A former SS, he has adapted well to the outfield, showing solid-average arm strength and range.

Henson,Tyler — 65 — Baltimore

EXP MLB DEBUT: 2010 | POTENTIAL: Starting 3B | 7E

Bats R Age 20
2006 (5) HS (OK)

Skill	Rating	Year	Lev	Team	AB	R	H	HR	RBI	Avg	OB	Slg	OPS	bb%	ct%	Eye	SB	CS	X/H%	Iso	RC/G
Pwr	++++																				
BAvg	++	2006	Rk	Bluefield	148	21	34	0	13	230	313	291	604	11	67	0.37	1	1	21	61	3.06
Spd	++++	2007	A-	Aberdeen	256	44	74	5	31	289	345	449	795	8	73	0.32	20	2	36	160	5.51
Def	++	2007	A+	Frederick	17	0	1	0	1	59	111	59	170	6	53	0.13	0	0	0	0	-4.61

Wiry athlete with blossoming offense featuring moderate power and speed on the bases. Lacks plate discipline which will hurt BA as he gets promoted, and needs to make better contact. Arm strength and soft hands play at SS, but fringe-average range could push him to 3B.

Hernandez,Anderson — 64 — New York (N)

EXP MLB DEBUT: 2005 | POTENTIAL: Starting SS/2B | 6B

Bats B Age 25
2001 FA (DR)

Skill	Rating	Year	Lev	Team	AB	R	H	HR	RBI	Avg	OB	Slg	OPS	bb%	ct%	Eye	SB	CS	X/H%	Iso	RC/G
		2006	A+	St. Lucie	9	0	1	0	0	111	111	111	222	0	89	0.00	0	0	0	0	-1.44
Pwr	+	2006	AAA	Norfolk	414	44	103	0	23	249	285	295	580	5	83	0.30	15	5	15	46	2.61
BAvg	+++	2006	MLB	New York (N)	66	4	10	1	3	152	164	242	407	1	82	0.08	0	0	30	91	0.31
4.10 Spd	++++	2007	AAA	N. Orleans	554	84	167	5	42	301	338	397	736	5	85	0.38	16	9	23	96	4.50
Def	++++	2007	MLB	New York (N)	3	1	1	0	0	333	333	333	667	0	67	0.00	0	0	0	0	3.37

Regained batting stroke after battling injuries, though offense will be predicated on BA as he lacks power and walks very little. Aggressive and efficient runner who will steal bases. Defense remains best attribute where he shows range and arm strength at both middle infield positions.

Hernandez,Diory — 64 — Atlanta

EXP MLB DEBUT: 2009 | POTENTIAL: Reserve SS | 7C

Bats R Age 24
2002 FA (DR)

Skill	Rating	Year	Lev	Team	AB	R	H	HR	RBI	Avg	OB	Slg	OPS	bb%	ct%	Eye	SB	CS	X/H%	Iso	RC/G
		2005	A+	Myrtle Beach	265	30	67	5	30	253	300	374	674	6	80	0.34	5	5	31	121	3.74
Pwr	++	2006	Rk	GCL Braves	7	0	1	0	0	143	143	143	286	0	57	0.00	0	0	0	0	-2.36
BAvg	+++	2006	A+	Myrtle Beach	286	37	68	6	47	238	285	336	621	6	82	0.37	9	1	24	98	3.07
Spd	++++	2007	A+	Myrtle Beach	64	9	20	0	9	313	333	500	833	3	83	0.18	2	2	50	188	5.75
Def	+++	2007	AA	Mississippi	433	50	133	7	59	307	351	418	769	6	84	0.43	22	20	25	111	4.91

Athletic infielder with plus speed and strong defense, featuring excellent range and soft hands. Makes solid contact and has enough bat speed to produce doubles power. BA will fluctuate with plate discipline and needs to show better instincts in the field and on the bases.

Hernandez,Francisco — 2 — Chicago (A)

EXP MLB DEBUT: 2009 | POTENTIAL: Starting CA | 7D

Bats B Age 22
2002 FA (DR)

Skill	Rating	Year	Lev	Team	AB	R	H	HR	RBI	Avg	OB	Slg	OPS	bb%	ct%	Eye	SB	CS	X/H%	Iso	RC/G
		2004	Rk	Bristol	181	32	59	5	30	326	371	492	863	7	82	0.41	0	0	32	166	6.05
Pwr	++	2005	Rk	Great Falls	212	37	74	6	34	349	403	524	926	8	88	0.76	0	1	34	175	6.85
BAvg	+++	2005	A-	Kannapolis	153	15	34	3	18	222	283	314	597	8	81	0.45	0	0	24	92	2.84
Spd	++	2006	A-	Kannapolis	316	29	78	6	34	247	296	361	657	7	90	0.71	3	1	29	114	3.76
Def	++++	2007	A-	Kannapolis	271	42	75	4	36	277	359	413	773	11	89	1.21	0	1	37	137	5.42

Short/athletic catcher with excellent hitting skills that starts with plus plate discipline. Compact swing and contact ability allow him to hit for BA, but power will be sparse. Possesses agility and solid-average arm strength, but needs to improve receiving skills and caught stealing rate (29%).

Hernandez,Gorkys — 8 — Atlanta

EXP MLB DEBUT: 2010 | POTENTIAL: Starting CF | 9C

Bats R Age 20
2005 FA (DR)

Skill	Rating	Year	Lev	Team	AB	R	H	HR	RBI	Avg	OB	Slg	OPS	bb%	ct%	Eye	SB	CS	X/H%	Iso	RC/G
Pwr	+++																				
BAvg	++++																				
4.05 Spd	++++	2006	Rk	GCL Tigers	205	41	67	5	24	327	358	463	822	5	87	0.37	20	4	24	137	5.38
Def	+++	2007	A-	W. Michigan	481	84	141	4	50	293	342	391	733	7	86	0.52	54	11	24	98	4.60

Athlete with plus speed and advanced hitting skills, making him a leadoff candidate. Puts ball in-play and draws walks, which enhances BA. Power will be of the gap variety and led MWL in steals with improved SB efficiency. Arm strength and range are above average in CF.

Hernandez,Luis — 6 — Baltimore

EXP MLB DEBUT: 2007 | POTENTIAL: Reserve SS | 6C

Bats B Age 23
2000 FA (Venezuela)

Skill	Rating	Year	Lev	Team	AB	R	H	HR	RBI	Avg	OB	Slg	OPS	bb%	ct%	Eye	SB	CS	X/H%	Iso	RC/G
		2006	AA	Mississippi	380	39	102	1	29	268	305	329	634	5	88	0.43	4	4	17	61	3.38
Pwr	+	2006	AAA	Richmond	73	3	14	1	5	192	192	288	479	0	89	0.00	0	1	36	96	1.40
BAvg	++	2007	AA	Bowie	364	42	88	0	37	242	277	316	593	5	86	0.36	6	5	24	74	2.91
4.25 Spd	++++	2007	AAA	Norfolk	33	4	9	0	3	273	273	273	545	0	85	0.00	0	0	0	0	1.87
Def	++++	2007	MLB	Baltimore	69	5	20	1	7	290	300	362	662	1	86	0.10	2	2	15	72	3.32

Plus defender possessing arm strength, range, and soft/quick hands, making routine and spectacular play. Offense is limited as he lacks power and ability to draw walks, but hits in situations and bunts. Speed has diminished since early days and is a non-factor on the bases.

Herren,KC — 9 — Texas

EXP MLB DEBUT: 2009 | POTENTIAL: Platoon RF/LF | 7D

Bats L Age 22
2004 (2) HS (WA)

Skill	Rating	Year	Lev	Team	AB	R	H	HR	RBI	Avg	OB	Slg	OPS	bb%	ct%	Eye	SB	CS	X/H%	Iso	RC/G
		2004	Rk	AZL Rangers	185	32	55	0	21	297	378	389	767	11	71	0.44	7	6	27	92	5.46
Pwr	++++	2005	A-	Spokane	216	22	57	4	27	264	348	417	765	11	71	0.44	6	4	39	153	5.34
BAvg	++	2006	A-	Clinton	303	24	67	2	21	268	333	429	762	11	73	0.44	3	6	30	73	5.07
4.40 Spd	++	2006	A-	Spokane	112	15	39	3	13	221	304	294	598	9	72	0.35	4	2	22	161	2.93
Def	++	2007	A-	Clinton	453	68	125	6	49	276	364	435	799	12	82	0.76	12	10	38	159	5.51

Strong/athletic player whose skills and production make him a tweener. Produces moderate power and can hit for BA if he can stay back, exercise patience, and shrink platoon split. Possesses fringe-average range and arm strength, but needs work in taking proper routes.

Herrera,Javier — 9 — Oakland

EXP MLB DEBUT: 2009 | POTENTIAL: Starting CF/RF | 8D

Bats R Age 23
2001 FA (Venezuela)

Skill	Rating	Year	Lev	Team	AB	R	H	HR	RBI	Avg	OB	Slg	OPS	bb%	ct%	Eye	SB	CS	X/H%	Iso	RC/G
		2004	A-	Vancouver	263	50	87	12	47	331	387	555	942	8	78	0.41	23	1	36	224	7.19
Pwr	++++	2005	A-	Kane Co	360	70	99	13	62	275	359	444	803	12	69	0.43	26	5	33	169	5.78
BAvg	+++	2005	AAA	Sacramento	12	5	5	1	3	417	462	750	1212	8	92	1.00	1	0	40	333	9.69
Spd	++++	2007	A+	Stockton	252	45	69	9	39	274	325	448	773	7	76	0.32	11	7	38	175	4.98
Def	+++	2007	AA	Midland	71	13	18	3	13	254	293	451	744	5	82	0.31	1	0	44	197	4.48

Plus athlete who was limited by a strained hamstring and lingering effects from being out all of 2006 with elbow surgery. Possesses power and speed that can impact game, but must improve strike zone judgment and make better contact. Range and arm strength are solid in CF.

Herrera,Jonathan — 6 — Colorado

EXP MLB DEBUT: 2009 | POTENTIAL: Reserve SS/2B | 7C

Bats B Age 23
2002 FA (DR)

Skill	Rating	Year	Lev	Team	AB	R	H	HR	RBI	Avg	OB	Slg	OPS	bb%	ct%	Eye	SB	CS	X/H%	Iso	RC/G
		2004	A-	Asheville	380	71	106	6	35	279	389	335	724	6	79	0.33	21	12	18	111	4.01
Pwr	++	2005	A-	Asheville	87	17	27	0	5	310	368	333	701	8	87	0.73	6	6	7	23	4.32
BAvg	+++	2005	A+	Modesto	310	48	80	2	30	258	309	332	642	7	83	0.44	9	4	19	74	3.46
Spd	++++	2006	A+	Modesto	487	87	152	7	77	310	383	427	811	11	86	0.87	34	15	23	117	5.73
Def	++++	2007	AA	Tulsa	509	65	131	3	40	257	315	338	653	7	87	0.53	18	12	24	81	3.33

Small/athletic infielder with plus speed and ability to draw walks. Short/compact stroke is conducive for BA, but lacks the bat speed and strength to hit for power. Defense is outstanding, possessing arm strength, soft/quick hands, and range that are all above average.

Heyward,Jason — 9 — Atlanta

EXP MLB DEBUT: 2011 | POTENTIAL: Starting RF | 9D

Bats L Age 18
2007 (1) HS (GA)

Skill	Rating	Year	Lev	Team	AB	R	H	HR	RBI	Avg	OB	Slg	OPS	bb%	ct%	Eye	SB	CS	X/H%	Iso	RC/G
Pwr	++++																				
BAvg	++++																				
4.30 Spd	++	2007	Rk	Danville	16	3	5	0	1	313	353	375	728	6	69	0.20	0	0	20	63	4.63
Def	+++	2007	Rk	GCL Braves	27	1	8	1	5	296	345	556	900	7	85	0.50	1	1	63	259	6.56

Tall/athletic hitter with plus bat speed and power, but will also hit for BA, displaying contact ability and plate discipline. Drives ball to all fields and isn't afraid to shorten-up when behind. Runs well for size and is an average defender in the outfield with good arm strength and average range.

Hickman,Thomas — 8 — Florida

EXP MLB DEBUT: 2010 | POTENTIAL: Platoon RF/LF | 8E

Bats L Age 24
2006 (2) HS (GA)

Skill	Rating	Year	Lev	Team	AB	R	H	HR	RBI	Avg	OB	Slg	OPS	bb%	ct%	Eye	SB	CS	X/H%	Iso	RC/G
Pwr	+++																				
BAvg	+++																				
4.20 Spd	+++	2006	Rk	GCL Marlins	175	28	46	2	20	263	371	411	782	15	75	0.70	4	5	39	149	5.70
Def	+++	2007	A-	Jamestown	164	15	30	1	17	183	268	256	524	10	62	0.30	3	0	30	73	1.81

Athletic outfielder with fluid swing, bat speed, and plate discipline, he is expected to hit for more power as he fills-out his frame. Hits for BA and draws walks, but isn't a factor on the bases with his average speed. Arm strength is above average, but limited range will place him in the corners.

BATTERS

Hicks,Brandon — 6 — Atlanta
EXP MLB DEBUT: 2010 | POTENTIAL: Starting SS | 7C

Bats R Age 22
2007 (3) Texas A&M
Pwr ++ | BAvg +++ | Spd ++++ | Def +++

Year	Lev	Team	AB	R	H	HR	RBI	Avg	OB	Slg	OPS	bb%	ct%	Eye	SB	CS	X/H%	Iso	RC/G
2007	Rk	Danville	58	14	13	3	13	224	357	466	823	17	69	0.67	1	2	54	241	6.24
2007	A-	Rome	128	26	40	4	15	313	432	492	924	17	80	1.04	5	3	38	180	7.52

Athletic infielder plays above tools and is always in the middle of things. Noted for his strong defense where his arm and soft hands stand-out, but offensive production was a mild surprise. Contact ability and plate discipline should ensure solid BA/OBP, but drives ball and utilizes speed.

Hilligoss,Mitch — 7 — New York (A)
EXP MLB DEBUT: 2010 | POTENTIAL: Platoon LF/RF | 7D

Bats L Age 23
2006 (7) Purdue
Pwr ++ | BAvg ++++ | 4.15 Spd ++++ | Def ++

Year	Lev	Team	AB	R	H	HR	RBI	Avg	OB	Slg	OPS	bb%	ct%	Eye	SB	CS	X/H%	Iso	RC/G
2006	A-	Staten Island	269	40	80	2	37	297	355	361	716	8	83	0.51	12	2	15	63	4.38
2007	A-	Charleston	520	83	161	4	53	310	351	415	766	6	88	0.51	35	7	27	106	4.95

Athletic outfielder with pure hitting skills, fashioning a 38-game hitting streak. Possesses fluid hitting mechanics, contact ability, and plate discipline, but is short on power. A collegiate infielder, he has transitioned well to LF, showing average range and arm strength.

Hodges,Wes — 5 — Cleveland
EXP MLB DEBUT: 2009 | POTENTIAL: Starting 3B | 8D

Bats R Age 23
2006 (2-C) Georgia Tech
Pwr ++++ | BAvg ++ | Spd ++ | Def +++

Year	Lev	Team	AB	R	H	HR	RBI	Avg	OB	Slg	OPS	bb%	ct%	Eye	SB	CS	X/H%	Iso	RC/G
2007	A+	Kinston	393	60	113	15	71	288	359	473	833	10	77	0.49	0	0	35	186	5.90

Strong player with bat speed who improved power by altering swing and incorporating lower half. Mediocre plate discipline will keep BA suppressed and adds nothing with his speed. Defense is average due to low agility, but has arm strength. Missed time with foot and hamstring injuries.

Hoffmann,Jamie — 8 — Los Angeles (N)
EXP MLB DEBUT: 2009 | POTENTIAL: Platoon CF/RF | 7D

Bats R Age 23
2003 NDFA HS (MN)
Pwr ++ | BAvg +++ | Spd ++++ | Def +++

Year	Lev	Team	AB	R	H	HR	RBI	Avg	OB	Slg	OPS	bb%	ct%	Eye	SB	CS	X/H%	Iso	RC/G
2005	A-	Columbus	321	53	99	1	24	308	383	414	797	11	77	0.53	10	4	23	106	5.29
2005	A+	Vero Beach	166	26	40	1	10	241	287	319	606	6	94	0.22	3	1	23	78	3.77
2006	A+	Vero Beach	433	50	110	5	30	254	311	326	637	7	74	0.37	15	11	19	72	4.02
2006	AAA	Las Vegas	10	0	3	0	0	300	417	300	717	9	70	0.33	1	0	0	0	4.34
2007	A+	Inl Empire	433	67	134	9	81	309	378	455	833	10	84	0.67	19	7	28	146	5.88

Athletic outfielder that combines strength and speed well. Hits for BA despite an unorthodox swing, but his stroke limits his power, even though he has sufficient bat speed and strong wrists. Above average arm strength led to 17 assists and has enough range to play CF.

Hoffpauir,Jarrett — 4 — St. Louis
EXP MLB DEBUT: 2008 | POTENTIAL: Reserve 2B | 6C

Bats R Age 25
2004 (6) So Mississippi
Pwr ++ | BAvg +++ | Spd ++++ | Def +++

Year	Lev	Team	AB	R	H	HR	RBI	Avg	OB	Slg	OPS	bb%	ct%	Eye	SB	CS	X/H%	Iso	RC/G
2005	A-	Quad Cities	227	27	71	2	28	313	371	419	789	8	94	1.50	5	1	27	106	5.49
2005	A+	Palm Beach	226	23	58	0	19	257	349	310	659	12	88	1.23	11	5	19	53	4.17
2006	AA	Springfield	392	54	97	7	46	247	339	355	693	12	90	1.32	6	6	28	107	4.50
2007	AA	Springfield	203	23	70	7	33	345	419	527	946	11	91	1.44	3	1	33	182	7.27
2007	AAA	Memphis	190	27	57	4	24	300	393	416	808	13	89	1.38	2	3	25	116	5.86

Diminutive infielder with small-ball skills, possessing speed, contact ability, and plate discipline from a low crouch setup. Typically draws more walks than strikeouts, but doesn't have much power. Can only play 2B due to poor arm strength, but has soft/quick hands and good range.

Holliman,Michael — 64 — Detroit
EXP MLB DEBUT: 2008 | POTENTIAL: Reserve SS/3B | 7C

Bats B Age 26
2005 (16) Oral Roberts
Pwr +++ | BAvg +++ | 4.20 Spd +++ | Def +++

Year	Lev	Team	AB	R	H	HR	RBI	Avg	OB	Slg	OPS	bb%	ct%	Eye	SB	CS	X/H%	Iso	RC/G
2005	A-	Oneonta	256	66	71	13	53	277	391	559	950	16	70	0.63	8	3	51	281	8.09
2006	A-	W. Michigan	449	69	124	15	54	278	384	501	885	15	72	0.62	19	5	46	223	7.09
2007	AA	Erie	471	91	133	14	76	282	371	478	849	12	74	0.53	17	6	42	195	5.97
2007	AAA	Toledo	19	2	4	0	2	211	250	368	618	5	79	0.25	0	0	50	158	3.99

Athletic middle infielder noted more for his defense, but provided offensive value while skipping a level. Moderate bat speed and plate discipline allows him to hit for moderate power, but struggles to make contact. Runs bases well and defense is highlighted by soft hands and good range.

Horton,Josh — 6 — Oakland
EXP MLB DEBUT: 2009 | POTENTIAL: Platoon SS | 7C

Bats L Age 22
2007 (2) North Carolina
Pwr ++ | BAvg ++++ | 4.20 Spd +++ | Def +++

Year	Lev	Team	AB	R	H	HR	RBI	Avg	OB	Slg	OPS	bb%	ct%	Eye	SB	CS	X/H%	Iso	RC/G
2007	A-	Vancouver	41	7	11	1	6	268	388	390	778	16	83	1.14	1	1	27	122	5.58
2007	A-	Kane Co	122	28	34	1	15	279	413	352	766	19	78	1.04	3	1	21	74	5.60

Overachiever with athleticism and plus instincts who does the little things necessary to win. Makes solid contact, uses the whole field, and is patient enough to draw walks. Aggressive runner who will pick spots to run. Defensive tools are average and likely ends-up in a utility role.

Horwitz,Brian — 73 — San Francisco
EXP MLB DEBUT: 2008 | POTENTIAL: Reserve LF/1B | 6C

Bats R Age 25
2004 NDFA California
Pwr + | BAvg ++++ | 4.40 Spd ++ | Def ++

Year	Lev	Team	AB	R	H	HR	RBI	Avg	OB	Slg	OPS	bb%	ct%	Eye	SB	CS	X/H%	Iso	RC/G
2006	A+	San Jose	207	26	67	2	31	324	409	425	834	13	89	1.30	0	2	22	101	6.19
2006	AA	Connecticut	269	23	77	2	29	286	360	349	709	10	87	0.89	3	3	16	63	4.53
2006	AAA	Fresno	16	1	2	0	1	125	222	188	410	11	88	1.00	0	0	50	63	1.21
2007	AA	Connecticut	136	17	42	2	10	309	369	390	759	9	93	1.30	2	1	17	81	5.07
2007	AAA	Fresno	264	32	86	1	21	326	375	432	807	7	92	0.95	2	0	28	106	5.60

Athletic outfielder whose value is tied to BA where he makes outstanding contact and is patient at the plate. Medium bat speed and a flat bat minimize power and possesses below average speed. Range and arm strength are average in the outfield and has experience at 1B.

House,J.R. — 23 — Baltimore
EXP MLB DEBUT: 2006 | POTENTIAL: Reserve 1B/CA | 6B

Bats R Age 28
1999 (5) HS (FL)
Pwr +++ | BAvg +++ | Spd ++ | Def +

Year	Lev	Team	AB	R	H	HR	RBI	Avg	OB	Slg	OPS	bb%	ct%	Eye	SB	CS	X/H%	Iso	RC/G
2004	AAA	Nashville	309	38	89	15	49	288	337	508	845	7	77	0.32	1	1	42	220	5.86
2004	MLB	Pittsburgh	9	1	1	0	0	111	111	222	333	0	78	0.00	0	0	100	111	-0.63
2006	AA	Corpus Christi	378	58	123	10	69	325	377	475	852	8	88	0.73	2	2	28	151	5.97
2006	AAA	Round Rock	114	25	47	5	36	412	455	675	1131	7	87	0.60	0	0	43	263	9.14
2007	AAA	Norfolk	419	52	125	11	66	124	206	289	494	9	86	0.73	1	5	36	165	1.95

Strong athlete continues to improve offensively, taking a mature approach and utilizing his bat speed. Produces power from gap-to-gap and makes solid contact, giving him a strong BA. HR power not sufficient for 1B or OF and doesn't have the arm or receiving skills to catch everyday.

Huber,Justin — 37 — Kansas City
EXP MLB DEBUT: 2005 | POTENTIAL: Platoon 1B/LF | 7C

Bats R Age 25
2000 FA (Australia)
Pwr ++++ | BAvg ++ | 4.50 Spd + | Def +++

Year	Lev	Team	AB	R	H	HR	RBI	Avg	OB	Slg	OPS	bb%	ct%	Eye	SB	CS	X/H%	Iso	RC/G
2006	AAA	Omaha	352	47	98	15	44	278	352	480	832	10	73	0.43	2	2	40	202	5.98
2006	MLB	Kansas City	10	1	2	0	1	200	273	300	573	9	60	0.25	1	0	50	100	2.76
2007	Rk	AZL Royals	25	4	9	2	7	360	407	760	1167	7	84	0.50	0	0	67	400	9.61
2007	AAA	Omaha	286	39	79	18	68	276	324	517	841	7	83	0.42	1	0	41	241	5.59
2007	MLB	Kansas City	10	2	1	0	0	100	100	100	200	0	80	0.00	0	0	0	0	-2.36

Left for dead at Triple-A and may be better off in another organization. Solid contact hitter with moderate power and improving pitch recognition. Can play both 1B and LF, but is no better than average at either position. At-bats were limited to an early hamstring injury.

Huffman,Chad — 7 — San Diego
EXP MLB DEBUT: 2009 | POTENTIAL: Starting LF | 8C

Bats R Age 23
2006 (2) TCU
Pwr +++ | BAvg ++++ | Spd ++++ | Def ++

Year	Lev	Team	AB	R	H	HR	RBI	Avg	OB	Slg	OPS	bb%	ct%	Eye	SB	CS	X/H%	Iso	RC/G
2006	A-	Eugene	198	41	68	9	40	343	417	576	993	11	83	0.74	2	3	40	232	7.87
2006	A-	Ft. Wayne	14	2	3	0	0	214	313	357	670	13	86	1.00	0	1	33	143	4.35
2007	A+	Lk Elsinore	316	63	97	15	76	307	388	522	910	12	82	0.75	0	1	37	215	6.86
2007	AA	San Antonio	167	28	45	7	28	269	354	431	786	12	74	0.50	0	0	27	162	5.34

Strong offensive player with the bat speed to hit for power and ability to draw walks, enhancing OBP. Long swing could affect BA at upper levels and doesn't utilize his above average speed. Below average arm strength and poor route taking will limit him to LF defensively.

Hundley,Nick

2 | **San Diego** | EXP MLB DEBUT: 2008 | POTENTIAL: Platoon CA | **7C**

Bats R Age 24 — 2005 (2-C) Arizona

Pwr +++ | BAvg + | Spd + | Def ++++

Year	Lev	Team	AB	R	H	HR	RBI	Avg	OB	Slg	OPS	bb%	ct%	Eye	SB	CS	X/H%	Iso	RC/G
2005	A-	Eugene	148	30	37	7	22	250	387	453	839	18	76	0.94	1	0	41	203	6.35
2005	A-	Ft. Wayne	36	2	8	0	5	222	300	278	578	10	75	0.44	0	0	25	56	2.69
2006	A-	Ft. Wayne	215	29	59	8	44	274	350	474	824	10	79	0.56	1	1	46	200	5.82
2006	A+	Lk Elsinore	176	18	49	3	23	278	352	403	755	10	75	0.45	1	1	33	125	5.03
2007	AA	San Antonio	373	55	92	20	72	247	323	475	797	10	80	0.57	0	2	48	228	5.35

Athletic catcher who took advantage of a hitter-friendly league, improving power output. BAPIP was low, so underachieved with BA. Threw-out 36% of attempted runners with a quick release and arm strength, and adds solid receiving and game-calling skills.

Hunter,Cedric

8 | **San Diego** | EXP MLB DEBUT: 2010 | POTENTIAL: Starting CF | **8C**

Bats L Age 20 — 2006 (3) HS (GA)

Pwr +++ | BAvg +++ | 4.15 Spd ++++ | Def +++

Year	Lev	Team	AB	R	H	HR	RBI	Avg	OB	Slg	OPS	bb%	ct%	Eye	SB	CS	X/H%	Iso	RC/G
2006	Rk	AZL Padres	213	46	79	1	44	371	470	484	954	16	90	1.82	17	5	23	113	7.85
2006	A-	Eugene	15	0	4	0	0	267	313	267	579	6	80	0.33	0	1	0	0	2.52
2007	A-	Ft. Wayne	496	53	140	7	58	282	344	373	717	9	84	0.60	8	9	21	91	4.45
2007	AAA	Portland	4	1	2	1	3	500	600	1250	1850	20	75	1.00	0	0	50	750	19.22

Raw athlete with good hitting skills, showing a patient approach which gives him good pitches to hit. Hitting for BA shouldn't pose a problem and power should improve with physical maturity. Lack of experience shows in baserunning and taking proper routes in the outfield.

Hu,Chin-Lung

6 | **Los Angeles (N)** | EXP MLB DEBUT: 2007 | POTENTIAL: Starting SS | **8B**

Bats R Age 24 — 2003 FA (Taiwan)

Pwr ++ | BAvg +++ | 4.15 Spd ++++ | Def +++++

Year	Lev	Team	AB	R	H	HR	RBI	Avg	OB	Slg	OPS	bb%	ct%	Eye	SB	CS	X/H%	Iso	RC/G
2005	A+	Vero Beach	470	80	147	8	56	313	339	430	769	4	91	0.48	23	6	26	117	4.84
2006	AA	Jacksonville	488	71	125	5	37	256	324	338	662	9	87	0.78	11	5	22	82	3.92
2007	AA	Jacksonville	325	56	107	6	34	329	379	508	887	7	90	0.79	12	4	38	178	6.44
2007	AAA	Las Vegas	192	33	61	8	28	318	338	505	844	3	91	0.33	3	4	31	188	5.48
2007	MLB	Los Angeles (N)	29	5	7	2	5	241	241	517	759	0	72	0.00	0	0	43	276	4.42

Short athlete with plus defensive skills, and improved offense by adding muscle. Exhibits plus range and solid-average arm strength, making all the plays at SS. Compact swing and use of opposite field is conducive to BA and began turning on inside pitches, improving power output.

Iorg,Cale

6 | **Detroit** | EXP MLB DEBUT: 2010 | POTENTIAL: Starting SS | **8D**

Bats R Age 22 — 2007 (6) Alabama

Pwr +++ | BAvg +++ | Spd ++++ | Def ++++

Year	Lev	Team	AB	R	H	HR	RBI	Avg	OB	Slg	OPS	bb%	ct%	Eye	SB	CS	X/H%	Iso	RC/G
2007	A+	Lakeland	18	0	5	0	5	278	316	389	705	5	72	0.20	0	0	40	111	4.29

Athletic infielder who hasn't played in two years, following a Mormon mission. Makes solid contact and can drive the gaps for doubles, but hasn't shown much plate discipline, which could affect BA. Possesses smooth infield actions and utilizes speed on defense and bases.

Iorg,Eli

9 | **Houston** | EXP MLB DEBUT: 2009 | POTENTIAL: Platoon RF/CF | **7C**

Bats R Age 25 — 2005 (1-S) Tennessee

Pwr +++ | BAvg +++ | 4.25 Spd +++ | Def +++

Year	Lev	Team	AB	R	H	HR	RBI	Avg	OB	Slg	OPS	bb%	ct%	Eye	SB	CS	X/H%	Iso	RC/G
2005	Rk	Greeneville	138	36	46	7	34	333	374	565	939	6	80	0.33	12	3	35	232	6.89
2006	A-	Lexington	469	68	120	15	85	256	305	437	742	7	75	0.28	42	6	43	181	4.63
2007	A+	Salem	162	35	48	5	24	296	352	512	865	8	78	0.39	14	2	44	216	6.30

Strong/athletic outfielder missed most of the season with elbow surgery. Drives ball to gaps with moderate power and steals bases, but unlikely to sustain BA due to marginal plate discipline. Features a strong throwing arm and has enough range to man the outfield corners.

Iribarren,Hernan

4 | **Milwaukee** | EXP MLB DEBUT: 2008 | POTENTIAL: Starting 2B | **7C**

Bats L Age 23 — 2002 FA (Venezuela)

Pwr + | BAvg ++++ | 4.10 Spd ++++ | Def ++

Year	Lev	Team	AB	R	H	HR	RBI	Avg	OB	Slg	OPS	bb%	ct%	Eye	SB	CS	X/H%	Iso	RC/G
2004	Rk	AZL Brewers	189	40	83	4	36	439	490	630	1120	9	88	0.83	15	7	23	190	9.21
2004	A-	Beloit	67	12	25	1	10	373	417	657	1073	7	76	0.31	1	0	48	284	9.29
2005	A-	W. Virginia	486	72	141	4	48	290	358	379	736	9	80	0.52	38	15	19	88	4.73
2006	A+	Brevard Co	398	50	127	2	50	319	380	384	764	9	86	0.70	19	15	14	65	5.07
2007	AA	Huntsville	479	72	147	4	53	307	365	430	795	8	77	0.40	18	16	27	123	5.50

Small/athletic player with "little ball" skills who keeps having to prove himself. Makes contact and bunts well, but could enhance OBP if he walked more and chased less breaking pitches. Aggressive base-thief, but needs better SB%. Makes plays defensively, with soft hands and range.

Ishikawa,Travis

3 | **San Francisco** | EXP MLB DEBUT: 2006 | POTENTIAL: Platoon 1B | **6B**

Bats L Age 24 — 2002 (21) HS (WA)

Pwr +++ | BAvg ++ | 4.40 Spd ++ | Def ++++

Year	Lev	Team	AB	R	H	HR	RBI	Avg	OB	Slg	OPS	bb%	ct%	Eye	SB	CS	X/H%	Iso	RC/G
2005	A+	San Jose	432	87	122	22	79	282	382	532	915	14	70	0.54	1	4	47	250	7.46
2006	AA	Connecticut	298	33	69	10	42	232	312	403	715	11	70	0.40	0	0	39	171	4.47
2006	MLB	San Francisco	24	1	7	0	4	292	320	500	820	4	75	0.17	0	0	57	208	5.88
2007	A+	San Jose	198	35	53	13	34	268	332	551	882	9	61	0.24	0	0	55	283	7.42
2007	AA	Connecticut	173	17	37	3	17	214	284	295	579	9	72	0.35	0	0	19	81	2.50

Athletic player whose bat didn't produce, even with demotion. Uses middle of field to line doubles with a fluid swing and bat speed, but doesn't turn on pitches and poor plate discipline suppresses BA. Above average defender with fluid actions, but mobility was limited by a knee injury.

Ivany,Devin

2 | **Washington** | EXP MLB DEBUT: 2007 | POTENTIAL: Reserve CA | **5B**

Bats R Age 25 — 2004 (6) So Florida

Pwr +++ | BAvg ++ | Spd ++ | Def ++++

Year	Lev	Team	AB	R	H	HR	RBI	Avg	OB	Slg	OPS	bb%	ct%	Eye	SB	CS	X/H%	Iso	RC/G
2006	A+	Potomac	442	60	114	6	53	258	298	353	651	5	86	0.39	12	3	24	95	3.50
2007	Rk	GCL Nationals	3	0	1	0	2	333	500	333	833	25	33	0.50	0	0	0	0	13.10
2007	A-	Hagerstown	12	1	2	0	0	167	333	250	583	20	92	3.00	1	0	50	83	3.92
2007	A+	Potomac	131	18	36	5	19	275	312	427	739	5	80	0.27	4	2	28	153	4.35
2007	AA	Harrisburg	73	8	13	0	7	178	250	233	483	9	71	0.33	1	1	31	55	1.27

Athletic catcher with solid defensive skills. Quick release and clean footwork compensate for below average arm strength, and receives ball well. Offensively, he can crush mistakes with moderate power, but lacks the contact ability and plate discipline to hit for BA.

Jackson,Austin

8 | **New York (A)** | EXP MLB DEBUT: 2010 | POTENTIAL: Starting CF | **9C**

Bats R Age 21 — 2005 (8) HS (TX)

Pwr +++ | BAvg +++ | 4.20 Spd ++++ | Def +++

Year	Lev	Team	AB	R	H	HR	RBI	Avg	OB	Slg	OPS	bb%	ct%	Eye	SB	CS	X/H%	Iso	RC/G
2005	Rk	GCL Yankees	148	32	45	0	14	304	380	405	785	11	82	0.69	11	2	29	101	5.52
2006	A-	Charleston	535	90	138	4	47	258	333	344	677	10	72	0.39	36	11	24	86	4.01
2007	A-	Charleston	235	33	61	3	25	260	328	374	703	9	75	0.41	19	6	33	115	4.30
2007	A+	Tampa	258	53	89	10	34	345	396	566	962	8	81	0.46	13	5	35	221	7.35

Plus athlete improved plate discipline which subsequently increased OBP and power production. Above average speed allows him to steal bases and shows good instincts. Has the defensive tools (range/arm strength) to play CF, but may have to move to RF as he gets bigger.

Jackson,Justin

6 | **Toronto** | EXP MLB DEBUT: 2012 | POTENTIAL: Starting SS | **8E**

Bats R Age 19 — 2007 (1-S) HS (NC)

Pwr + | BAvg ++++ | Spd ++++ | Def ++++

Year	Lev	Team	AB	R	H	HR	RBI	Avg	OB	Slg	OPS	bb%	ct%	Eye	SB	CS	X/H%	Iso	RC/G
2007	Rk	GCL Blue Jays	166	20	31	2	13	187	274	241	515	11	73	0.45	7	4	13	54	1.72

One of the better athletes in the 2007 Draft, but as scouts projected, his bat would be a question mark. Makes good contact and runs the bases with abandon, but lacks power and the ability to draw walks. Defensively, he makes all the plays with above average range and arm strength.

Janish,Paul

64 | **Cincinnati** | EXP MLB DEBUT: 2008 | POTENTIAL: Reserve SS/2B | **6B**

Bats R Age 25 — 2004 (6) Rice

Pwr + | BAvg +++ | 4.40 Spd ++ | Def ++++

Year	Lev	Team	AB	R	H	HR	RBI	Avg	OB	Slg	OPS	bb%	ct%	Eye	SB	CS	X/H%	Iso	RC/G
2006	A-	Dayton	98	19	39	5	18	398	438	612	1050	7	90	0.70	0	0	28	214	7.97
2006	A+	Sarasota	336	53	93	9	55	277	350	420	770	10	88	0.95	8	2	30	143	5.19
2006	AA	Chattanooga	15	1	4	0	2	267	313	333	646	6	67	0.20	0	0	25	67	3.54
2007	AA	Chattanooga	324	46	79	1	20	244	345	330	675	13	83	0.93	10	3	30	86	4.30
2007	AAA	Louisville	199	20	44	3	19	221	272	317	589	7	84	0.45	2	0	27	95	2.82

Fundamentally sound player regressed offensively, especially in driving the ball, but is a good situational hitter who draws walks. Steals and takes extra bases despite below average speed. Makes routine plays in middle infield, featuring soft hands, range, and average arm.

Jaramillo,Jason — 2 — Philadelphia — EXP MLB DEBUT: 2008 — POTENTIAL: Reserve CA — 6C

Bats B Age 25	Year	Lev	Team	AB	R	H	HR	RBI	Avg	OB	Slg	OPS	bb%	ct%	Eye	SB	CS	X/H%	Iso	RC/G
2004 (2) Oklahoma St	2004	A-	Batavia	112	11	25	1	14	223	298	295	593	10	76	0.44	0	1	24	71	2.84
Pwr ++	2005	A-	Lakewood	448	46	136	8	63	304	366	438	803	9	84	0.61	2	3	29	134	5.52
BAvg ++	2006	AA	Reading	322	35	80	6	39	248	316	388	705	9	83	0.57	0	1	40	140	4.34
4.60 Spd +	2006	AAA	Scranton/WB	6	0	1	0	1	167	167	167	333	0	83	0.00	0	0	0	0	-0.59
Def ++++	2007	AAA	Ottawa	435	52	118	6	56	271	346	361	707	10	82	0.63	0	1	19	90	4.39

Strong defensive catcher nailed 31% of attempted runners with his quick release (1.9) and agility. Arm strength is average, but improved receiving and game-calling skills. Makes contact and draws walks, but possesses little power and doesn't have enough offense to be a MLB starter.

Jaso,John — 32 — Tampa Bay — EXP MLB DEBUT: 2008 — POTENTIAL: Platoon 1B/CA — 7C

Bats L Age 24	Year	Lev	Team	AB	R	H	HR	RBI	Avg	OB	Slg	OPS	bb%	ct%	Eye	SB	CS	X/H%	Iso	RC/G
2003 (12) Southwestern	2003	A-	Hudson Val	154	20	34	2	20	221	330	305	635	14	83	0.96	2	0	26	84	3.74
Pwr ++++	2004	A-	Hudson Val	199	34	60	2	35	302	371	437	808	10	84	0.69	1	0	35	136	5.71
BAvg +++	2005	A-	SW Michigan	332	61	102	14	50	307	385	515	900	11	84	0.79	3	1	39	208	6.72
Spd +	2006	A+	Visalia	367	58	113	10	56	308	360	452	813	8	87	0.63	1	2	29	144	5.48
Def ++	2007	AA	Montgomery	380	62	120	12	71	316	408	484	892	13	87	1.20	2	2	32	168	6.80

Offensive-minded receiver with solid plate discipline and above average power. Shows power to all fields and makes enough contact to hit for BA. Despite questionable arm strength and receiving skills, he nailed 35% of attempted runners with his quick release and footwork.

Jay, Jon — 7 — St. Louis — EXP MLB DEBUT: 2009 — POTENTIAL: Platoon LF/CF — 7C

Bats L Age 23	Year	Lev	Team	AB	R	H	HR	RBI	Avg	OB	Slg	OPS	bb%	ct%	Eye	SB	CS	X/H%	Iso	RC/G
2006 (2) Miami-FL																				
Pwr ++	2006	A-	Quad Cities	234	42	80	3	46	342	412	462	874	11	88	1.04	9	4	24	120	6.49
BAvg ++++	2007	Rk	GCL Cardinals	2	0	1	0	0	500	500	500	1000	0	50	0.00	0	0	0	0	18.22
Spd ++++	2007	A+	Palm Beach	126	19	36	2	10	286	321	397	718	4	80	0.20	5	2	28	111	4.55
Def +++	2007	AA	Springfield	102	17	24	2	11	235	333	373	706	10	81	0.58	4	1	33	137	3.69

Excellent athlete with speed, bat handing skills, and ability to draw walks. Flat bat and moderate bat speed limits power, but uses whole field and knows limitations. Ranges well in outfield, but has little arm strength. Missed part of season with a shoulder injury.

Jennings,Desmond — 8 — Tampa Bay — EXP MLB DEBUT: 2010 — POTENTIAL: Starting CF — 8B

Bats R Age 21	Year	Lev	Team	AB	R	H	HR	RBI	Avg	OB	Slg	OPS	bb%	ct%	Eye	SB	CS	X/H%	Iso	RC/G
2006 (10) Itawamba JC																				
Pwr ++																				
BAvg ++++																				
4.05 Spd ++++	2006	Rk	Princeton	213	48	59	4	20	277	345	390	734	9	82	0.56	32	5	25	113	4.66
Def ++++	2007	A-	Columbus	387	75	122	9	37	315	387	465	852	10	86	0.85	45	15	29	150	6.17

Outstanding athlete with plus speed and the ability to get on base, making him an excellent leadoff option. Demonstrated moderate power and does have good bat speed, but his home ballpark attenuated home runs. Above average defender in CF with plus range and average arm strength.

Jeroloman,Brian — 2 — Toronto — EXP MLB DEBUT: 2009 — POTENTIAL: Reserve CA — 6C

Bats R Age 23	Year	Lev	Team	AB	R	H	HR	RBI	Avg	OB	Slg	OPS	bb%	ct%	Eye	SB	CS	X/H%	Iso	RC/G
2006 (6) Florida																				
Pwr +++																				
BAvg +																				
Spd ++	2006	A-	Auburn	141	27	34	0	21	241	359	326	686	16	73	0.68	0	0	32	85	4.44
Def ++++	2007	A+	Dunedin	290	32	75	3	39	259	427	338	765	23	80	1.49	0	0	23	79	5.79

Defensive-oriented catcher with receiving skills, agility, and a quick release (1.9), but arm strength came-up short, resulting in a 28% CS%. Offense is centered on walk rate and ability to pull mistake pitches, as he struggles to make contact, especially against breaking pitches away.

Jimerson,Charlton — 8 — Seattle — EXP MLB DEBUT: 2005 — POTENTIAL: Reserve CF/LF — 7D

Bats R Age 28	Year	Lev	Team	AB	R	H	HR	RBI	Avg	OB	Slg	OPS	bb%	ct%	Eye	SB	CS	X/H%	Iso	RC/G
2001 (5) Miami-FL	2006	AAA	Round Rock	470	56	116	18	45	247	282	445	727	5	61	0.13	28	8	44	198	4.87
Pwr +++	2006	MLB	Houston	6	2	2	1	1	333	333	833	1167	0	50	0.00	2	0	50	500	13.66
BAvg +	2007	AA	West Tenn	322	54	89	23	73	276	336	565	901	8	64	0.25	30	9	49	289	7.35
Spd ++++	2007	AAA	Tacoma	65	7	20	2	7	308	357	492	849	7	66	0.23	5	1	35	185	6.54
Def +++	2007	MLB	Seattle	2	5	2	1	1	1000	1000	2500	3500	0	100		2	0	50	1500	29.61

Plus athlete with 30/30 potential, but poor plate discipline, a long swing, and propensity to pull baseball lowers BA and makes power non-usable. Stolen base proficiency has improved and shows better overall instincts. Features superior range in outfield with average arm strength.

Johnson,Cody — 7 — Atlanta — EXP MLB DEBUT: 2010 — POTENTIAL: Starting LF/1B — 8D

Bats L Age 19	Year	Lev	Team	AB	R	H	HR	RBI	Avg	OB	Slg	OPS	bb%	ct%	Eye	SB	CS	X/H%	Iso	RC/G
2006 (1) HS (FL)																				
Pwr ++++																				
BAvg ++																				
4.30 Spd ++	2006	Rk	GCL Braves	114	13	21	1	16	184	262	281	543	10	57	0.24	1	0	38	96	2.23
Def +	2007	Rk	Danville	243	51	74	17	57	305	372	630	1001	10	70	0.36	7	0	54	325	8.42

Rebounded from wretched 2006 by leading APPY in HR/SLG. Strong wrists and bat speed give him above average power to all fields and was able to maintain BA despite a long swing and poor plate discipline. Below average defender in LF with poor range, but does possess arm strength.

Johnson,Elliot — 4 — Tampa Bay — EXP MLB DEBUT: 2008 — POTENTIAL: Reserve 2B — 6B

Bats B Age 24	Year	Lev	Team	AB	R	H	HR	RBI	Avg	OB	Slg	OPS	bb%	ct%	Eye	SB	CS	X/H%	Iso	RC/G
2002 NDFA HS (AZ)	2004	A	Charleston	503	92	132	6	41	262	334	370	704	10	82	0.59	43	15	27	107	4.36
Pwr ++	2005	A+	Visalia	227	42	62	8	33	273	343	449	792	10	78	0.49	28	5	34	176	5.34
BAvg +++	2005	AA	Montgomery	264	31	69	3	21	261	296	375	671	5	74	0.19	15	5	26	114	3.67
4.00 Spd ++++	2006	AA	Montgomery	445	62	121	13	43	272	322	440	763	7	75	0.29	15	15	34	169	4.92
Def +++	2007	AAA	Durham	463	56	96	11	45	207	275	341	616	8	70	0.31	16	6	35	134	3.03

Wiry athlete with plus speed and offensive upside. Struggled to hit for first time in career, as he lost some plate discipline and was over-anxious. Makes contact, hits the occasional HR, and steals bases. Defense at 2B is average at best with playable range and a fringe-average arm.

Johnson,Rob — 2 — Seattle — EXP MLB DEBUT: 2007 — POTENTIAL: Reserve CA — 6B

Bats R Age 24	Year	Lev	Team	AB	R	H	HR	RBI	Avg	OB	Slg	OPS	bb%	ct%	Eye	SB	CS	X/H%	Iso	RC/G
2004 (4) Houston	2005	A-	Wisconsin	305	41	83	9	51	272	317	430	746	6	90	0.65	10	3	35	157	4.69
Pwr +++	2005	A+	Inland Emp	70	15	22	2	12	314	400	443	843	13	80	0.71	2	0	23	129	6.13
BAvg ++	2006	AAA	Tacoma	337	28	78	4	33	231	260	318	578	4	78	0.18	14	7	22	86	2.38
Spd +	2007	AAA	Tacoma	422	57	113	6	40	268	330	372	702	8	85	0.63	7	7	28	104	4.29
Def ++++	2007	MLB	Seattle	3	1	1	0	0	333	333	333	667	0	100		1	0	0	0	3.67

Defensive-minded catcher with excellent receiving skills and a quick release that compensates for average arm strength. Runs well and will steal occasional bases. Moderate bat speed produces gap power, but struggles to make contact and doesn't judge strike zone, lowering BA.

Johnston,Seth — 64 — San Diego — EXP MLB DEBUT: 2009 — POTENTIAL: Reserve 2B/SS — 7C

Bats R Age 25	Year	Lev	Team	AB	R	H	HR	RBI	Avg	OB	Slg	OPS	bb%	ct%	Eye	SB	CS	X/H%	Iso	RC/G
2005 (5) Texas																				
Pwr +++	2005	A-	Eugene	170	15	43	2	23	253	306	347	653	7	76	0.32	2	4	26	94	3.51
BAvg +++	2006	Rk	AZL Padres	10	1	1	0	0	100	100	100	200	0	60	0.00	0	0	0	0	-3.65
4.30 Spd +++	2006	A-	Ft. Wayne	459	72	126	10	58	275	322	410	731	7	83	0.40	3	1	33	135	4.47
Def +++	2007	A+	Lk Elsinore	363	56	106	8	51	292	356	433	788	9	77	0.44	1	2	29	140	5.34

Athletic infielder with excellent instincts and secondary skills that work in utility role. Produces moderate power and BA ability with solid bat speed and contact ability. Speed is slightly below average, but runs bases aggressively. Possesses range and average arm in middle infield.

Jones,Brandon — 7 — Atlanta — EXP MLB DEBUT: 2008 — POTENTIAL: Starting LF — 8B

Bats L Age 24	Year	Lev	Team	AB	R	H	HR	RBI	Avg	OB	Slg	OPS	bb%	ct%	Eye	SB	CS	X/H%	Iso	RC/G
2004 (24) Tallahassee C	2006	A+	Myrtle Beach	226	27	58	7	35	257	331	420	751	10	78	0.51	11	6	34	164	4.86
Pwr ++++	2006	AA	Mississippi	176	18	48	7	24	273	330	477	807	8	78	0.39	4	2	40	205	5.45
BAvg +++	2007	AA	Mississippi	365	58	107	15	74	293	369	507	876	11	77	0.52	12	7	39	214	6.53
4.20 Spd +++	2007	AAA	Richmond	170	26	51	4	26	300	364	453	817	9	79	0.47	5	0	33	153	5.69
Def +++	2007	MLB	Atlanta	19	0	3	0	4	158	158	211	368	0	58	0.00	0	0	33	53	-0.82

Complete player with projectable power and BA ability. Covers plate well, swings hard, and improved plate discipline led to breakout season. Steals bases through instincts, as his speed is average. Needs to take better outfield routes, but has sufficient range and average arm strength.

Jones, Travis — 4 — Atlanta

Bats R　Age 22
2007 (7) South Carolina

EXP MLB DEBUT: 2010　POTENTIAL: Starting 2B　7D

Pwr +
BAvg ++++
Spd ++++
Def +++

Year	Lev	Team	AB	R	H	HR	RBI	Avg	OB	Slg	OPS	bb%	ct%	Eye	SB	CS	X/H%	Iso	RC/G
2007	Rk	Danville	48	9	13	2	7	271	352	438	789	11	81	0.67	1	1	31	167	5.31
2007	A-	Rome	164	34	42	10	27	256	384	482	866	17	78	0.94	6	4	38	226	6.53

Short/athletic infielder possesses excellent contact ability and plate discipline that should provide a high BA. Bat speed isn't conducive to power and doesn't steal bases despite above average speed. Makes plays defensively, with outstanding range and soft/quick hands.

Joyce, Matt — 8 — Detroit

Bats L　Age 23
2005 (7) Fla Southern

EXP MLB DEBUT: 2008　POTENTIAL: Reserve CF/RF　6B

Pwr +++
BAvg +++
4.20 Spd +++
Def ++++

Year	Lev	Team	AB	R	H	HR	RBI	Avg	OB	Slg	OPS	bb%	ct%	Eye	SB	CS	X/H%	Iso	RC/G
2005	A-	Oneonta	245	51	81	4	45	331	404	453	857	11	88	1.03	9	5	22	122	6.29
2006	A-	W. Michigan	465	75	120	11	86	258	338	415	753	11	85	0.80	5	4	38	157	5.03
2007	AA	Erie	456	61	117	17	70	257	331	454	785	10	72	0.40	4	6	45	197	5.41

Strong/athletic outfielder produces moderate power with good bat speed, but was helped by his home environment. BA will always be low with a poor contact rate and tendency to be pull-conscious. Above average defender in CF with impressive range and a strong throwing arm.

Kaaihue, Kala — 3 — Atlanta

Bats R　Age 23
2003 (22) So Mountain C

EXP MLB DEBUT: 2009　POTENTIAL: Reserve 1B　7C

Pwr ++++
BAvg ++
Spd +
Def +++

Year	Lev	Team	AB	R	H	HR	RBI	Avg	OB	Slg	OPS	bb%	ct%	Eye	SB	CS	X/H%	Iso	RC/G
2005	Rk	Danville	16	4	7	2	3	438	438	1000	1438	0	69	0.00	0	0	71	563	14.11
2006	Rk	Rome	228	44	75	15	49	329	454	614	1068	19	71	0.79	3	0	44	285	9.74
2006	A+	Myrtle Beach	185	34	41	13	29	222	324	476	800	13	74	0.58	0	1	51	254	5.46
2007	A+	Myrtle Beach	309	57	92	22	61	298	401	583	983	15	70	0.58	2	0	47	285	8.31
2007	AA	Mississippi	118	14	15	0	8	127	202	186	388	9	57	0.22	0	0	40	59	-0.44

Strong/muscular frame is behind power as his bat speed is moderate and possesses a slow trigger. BA could suffer at upper levels by facing pitchers with better command and breaking pitches. Lacks speed and agility, making him a clogger on the bases and a below average defender.

Kalish, Ryan — 8 — Boston

Bats L　Age 20
2006 (9) HS (NJ)

EXP MLB DEBUT: 2010　POTENTIAL: Starting CF　9D

Pwr ++
BAvg ++++
Spd ++++
Def +++

Year	Lev	Team	AB	R	H	HR	RBI	Avg	OB	Slg	OPS	bb%	ct%	Eye	SB	CS	X/H%	Iso	RC/G
2006	Rk	GCL Red Sox	20	6	6	1	2	300	333	550	883	5	90	0.50	0	0	50	250	6.08
2006	A-	Lowell	35	8	7	0	4	200	243	257	500	5	60	0.14	2	0	14	57	1.40
2007	A-	Lowell	87	27	32	3	13	368	466	540	1006	16	86	1.33	18	3	25	172	8.28

Exceptional athlete with plus speed and a projectable bat, he has good barrel awareness and plate discipline which should keep BA high. Bat speed is good enough to project power and should improve with physical maturity. Features excellent range and arm strength in CF.

Katin, Brendan — 9 — Milwaukee

Bats R　Age 25
2005 (23) Miami-FL

EXP MLB DEBUT: 2008　POTENTIAL: Platoon RF/LF　7D

Pwr +++
BAvg ++
4.60 Spd +
Def +++

Year	Lev	Team	AB	R	H	HR	RBI	Avg	OB	Slg	OPS	bb%	ct%	Eye	SB	CS	X/H%	Iso	RC/G
2005	Rk	Helena	114	30	44	8	26	386	466	649	1115	13	78	0.68	3	1	32	263	9.53
2005	A-	W. Virginia	84	7	17	1	5	202	272	250	522	9	65	0.28	0	0	12	48	1.60
2006	A+	Brevard Co	450	64	130	13	75	289	339	464	803	7	75	0.30	4	6	38	176	5.47
2006	AA	Huntsville	58	11	13	4	8	224	237	466	703	2	81	0.09	0	0	46	241	3.62
2007	AA	Huntsville	450	72	116	24	94	258	320	471	791	8	64	0.25	3	2	41	213	5.66

Strong/muscular player with raw power and a quick bat, leading SL in HR and RBI. Aggressive approach reduces patience and increases strikeouts, which keeps BA low. Arm strength is very good in RF, but his speed and ragne are well below average.

Keel, Jared — 53 — Pittsburgh

Bats R　Age 23
2006 (31) Troy St

EXP MLB DEBUT: 2009　POTENTIAL: Reserve 3B/1B　7D

Pwr +++
BAvg +++
Spd ++
Def ++

Year	Lev	Team	AB	R	H	HR	RBI	Avg	OB	Slg	OPS	bb%	ct%	Eye	SB	CS	X/H%	Iso	RC/G
2006	Rk	GCL Pirates	74	15	32	2	13	432	481	622	1103	9	86	0.70	5	1	28	189	8.96
2006	A-	Williamsport	140	19	35	3	11	250	323	400	723	10	79	0.50	2	3	40	150	4.56
2007	A-	Hickory	326	63	85	17	56	261	369	494	863	15	76	0.71	5	2	48	233	6.51

Strong hitter with moderate bat speed and power to all fields. Plate discipline appears solid, but is the type that walks and strikes-out. Bat may have to carry him, as he is a below average defender with stiff hands and poor first-step quickness, but does have good arm strength.

Kelly, Paul — 6 — Minnesota

Bats R　Age 21
2005 (2) HS (TX)

EXP MLB DEBUT: 2010　POTENTIAL: Platoon SS　7D

Pwr ++
BAvg +++
4.25 Spd ++++
Def ++++

Year	Lev	Team	AB	R	H	HR	RBI	Avg	OB	Slg	OPS	bb%	ct%	Eye	SB	CS	X/H%	Iso	RC/G
2005	Rk	GCL Twins	137	16	38	2	20	277	344	365	709	9	74	0.39	3	5	21	88	4.33
2005	A-	Beloit	16	2	5	1	4	313	389	625	1014	11	81	0.67	0	0	60	313	8.14
2006	A-	Beloit	378	58	106	3	48	280	337	384	720	8	84	0.53	5	5	27	103	4.50
2007	Rk	GCL Twins	5	0	1	0	1	200	200	200	400	0	80	0.00	0	0	0	0	0.01

Athletic infielder missed 2007 season with knee surgery. Solid situational hitter with bat control, contact ability, and plate discipline. Lacks bat speed to hit for power, but adds element of speed. Possesses plus arm strength and soft hands, but range is fringe-average.

King, Stephen — 65 — Washington

Bats R　Age 20
2006 (3) HS (FL)

EXP MLB DEBUT: 2010　POTENTIAL: Reserve 2B/3B　7D

Pwr ++
BAvg +++
Spd ++++
Def +++

Year	Lev	Team	AB	R	H	HR	RBI	Avg	OB	Slg	OPS	bb%	ct%	Eye	SB	CS	X/H%	Iso	RC/G
2007	Rk	GCL Nationals	161	20	40	9	30	248	301	466	766	7	71	0.26	1	2	40	217	4.89
2007	A-	Vermont	24	3	8	0	2	333	360	417	777	4	71	0.14	0	0	25	83	5.18
2007	A-	Hagerstown	128	16	23	2	9	180	255	258	513	9	60	0.25	5	4	26	78	1.52

Athletic infielder with solid defense and an emerging bat. More of a BA/doubles hitter as he hasn't matured physically and lacks plate discipline. Runs bases aggressively with above average speed. Plays both middle infield spots with arm strength and range, but possesses stiff hands.

Koshansky, Joe — 3 — Colorado

Bats L　Age 26
2004 (6) Virginia

EXP MLB DEBUT: 2007　POTENTIAL: Platoon 1B　7C

Pwr ++++
BAvg ++
Spd +
Def ++

Year	Lev	Team	AB	R	H	HR	RBI	Avg	OB	Slg	OPS	bb%	ct%	Eye	SB	CS	X/H%	Iso	RC/G
2005	A-	Asheville	453	92	132	36	103	291	366	603	968	10	73	0.43	6	6	52	311	7.69
2005	AA	Tulsa	45	5	12	2	12	267	298	467	765	4	67	0.13	0	0	42	200	5.01
2006	AA	Tulsa	500	84	142	31	109	284	365	526	891	11	73	0.48	3	2	42	242	6.72
2007	AAA	Colo Springs	498	79	147	21	99	295	379	490	869	12	74	0.52	4	3	36	195	6.52
2007	MLB	Colorado	12	0	1	0	2	83	214	167	381	14	58	0.40	0	0	100	83	-0.53

Plus bat speed and strong hands give him solid power to all fields. Plate discipline continues to improve which may give him a chance to hit for BA. LH pitchers and breaking pitches still give him fits. Below average defender with low agility and stiff hands, so bat has to carry him.

Kottaras, George — 2 — Boston

Bats L　Age 25
2002 (20) Connors St JC

EXP MLB DEBUT: 2008　POTENTIAL: Reserve CA　6B

Pwr ++
BAvg ++
4.50 Spd +
Def ++

Year	Lev	Team	AB	R	H	HR	RBI	Avg	OB	Slg	OPS	bb%	ct%	Eye	SB	CS	X/H%	Iso	RC/G
2005	A+	Lk Elsinore	337	54	102	9	50	303	393	469	862	13	82	0.83	2	1	37	166	6.45
2005	AA	Mobile	101	16	29	2	15	287	400	416	816	16	77	0.83	0	0	31	129	6.08
2006	AA	Mobile	256	40	71	8	33	277	395	453	849	16	73	0.74	0	1	39	176	6.57
2006	AAA	Portland	119	14	25	2	17	210	282	361	644	9	75	0.40	0	0	52	151	3.54
2007	AAA	Pawtucket	294	32	71	9	39	241	316	408	724	10	76	0.45	1	1	44	167	4.53

Athletic receiver regressed offensively as he appeared more aggressive and didn't get his normal pitches to hit. Hitting for power is unlikely, but good contact rate should supply BA. Defense is questionable with average arm strength, poor receiving skills, and a 20% CS%.

Kozma, Peter — 6 — St. Louis

Bats R　Age 20
2007 (1) HS (OK)

EXP MLB DEBUT: 2011　POTENTIAL: Starting SS　8C

Pwr ++
BAvg ++++
4.10 Spd ++++
Def ++++

Year	Lev	Team	AB	R	H	HR	RBI	Avg	OB	Slg	OPS	bb%	ct%	Eye	SB	CS	X/H%	Iso	RC/G
2007	Rk	AZL Cardinals	13	4	2	0	0	154	267	154	708	13	85	1.00	0	0	0	0	0.00
2007	Rk	Johnson City	106	16	28	2	9	264	350	396	746	10	80	0.57	3	2	36	132	4.88
2007	A-	Batavia	27	1	4	0	2	148	179	222	401	4	74	0.14	1	1	25	74	0.24

Athletic SS with above average defense, possessing a strong infield arm and range in all directions. Contact hitter with enough bat speed to project moderate power and is patient enough to draw walks. Instincts and aggressiveness allow his tools to play up and does what it takes to win.

Kreuzer, Josh — 3 — Toronto

Bats R Age 25
2002 (16) West Valley
EXP MLB DEBUT: 2009 POTENTIAL: Platoon 1B **7D**

	Pwr	++++
	BAvg	++
	Spd	+
	Def	++

Year	Lev	Team	AB	R	H	HR	RBI	Avg	OB	Slg	OPS	bb%	ct%	Eye	SB	CS	X/H%	Iso	RC/G
2003	A-	Spokane	199	35	45	6	40	226	325	357	681	13	82	0.83	1	0	31	131	4.13
2004	A-	Clinton	360	46	96	10	65	267	361	461	822	13	76	0.62	2	0	49	194	6.04
2005	A+	Bakersfield	400	63	104	11	74	260	341	410	751	11	78	0.55	3	2	36	150	4.92
2006	A+	Dunedin	187	30	48	7	31	257	332	465	797	10	75	0.46	1	0	52	209	5.52
2007	A+	Dunedin	404	92	125	20	71	309	401	542	943	13	80	0.76	1	2	43	233	7.42

Power hitter with breakout season, leading FSL in OBP and SLG. Possesses strong hands and moderate bat speed which gives him power, but is also very selective and doesn't strike-out much. Bat makes-up majority of value as he has no speed and is a defensive liability at 1B.

Kroeger, Josh — 9 — Chicago (N)

Bats L Age 25
2000 (4) HS (CA)
EXP MLB DEBUT: 2008 POTENTIAL: Reserve LF/RF **6C**

	Pwr	+++
	BAvg	++
4.25	Spd	+++
	Def	+++

Year	Lev	Team	AB	R	H	HR	RBI	Avg	OB	Slg	OPS	bb%	ct%	Eye	SB	CS	X/H%	Iso	RC/G
2004	MLB	Arizona	54	5	9	0	2	167	182	222	404	2	61	0.05	0	1	33	56	-0.22
2005	AAA	Tucson	472	73	123	14	62	261	313	422	735	7	77	0.33	17	4	37	161	4.51
2006	AAA	Scranton/WB	441	41	102	9	41	231	269	370	639	5	76	0.22	6	3	38	138	3.23
2007	AA	Tennessee	225	40	86	11	50	382	448	609	1057	11	84	0.77	8	3	31	227	8.52
2007	AAA	Iowa	175	27	46	10	31	263	342	474	816	11	78	0.55	0	1	37	211	5.57

Athletic player with secondary skills that could play as a reserve outfielder. Sprays ball to all fields with moderate power, but contact rate and aggressiveness keeps BA low. Runs bases well despite average speed and plays all three outfield spots with solid arm strength and range.

Kulbacki, Kellen — 9 — San Diego

Bats L Age 22
2007 (1-S) James Madis
EXP MLB DEBUT: 2009 POTENTIAL: Starting LF **8C**

	Pwr	++++
	BAvg	+++
4.25	Spd	++
	Def	++

Year	Lev	Team	AB	R	H	HR	RBI	Avg	OB	Slg	OPS	bb%	ct%	Eye	SB	CS	X/H%	Iso	RC/G
2007	A-	Eugene	226	33	68	8	39	301	375	491	867	11	75	0.48	1	1	35	190	6.46

Possesses top-of-the-line bat speed and power. Contact ability and plate discipline should allow him to hit for BA if he can stay focused. Speed is below average, but runs bases instinctively. Played mostly RF, but may not have the range or arm strength to play that position at the MLB level.

Lambin, Chase — 64 — Florida

Bats B Age 28
2002 (34) Lou-Lafayette
EXP MLB DEBUT: 2008 POTENTIAL: Reserve 2B/3B **6B**

	Pwr	+++
	BAvg	+++
4.30	Spd	+++
	Def	+++

Year	Lev	Team	AB	R	H	HR	RBI	Avg	OB	Slg	OPS	bb%	ct%	Eye	SB	CS	X/H%	Iso	RC/G
2005	AA	Binghamton	181	26	60	14	29	331	398	657	1055	10	79	0.53	2	0	52	326	8.55
2005	AAA	Norfolk	211	35	61	10	34	289	351	526	877	9	78	0.43	2	3	46	237	6.38
2006	AAA	Binghamton	133	29	37	7	20	278	373	534	906	13	74	0.57	2	1	54	256	7.12
2006	AAA	Norfolk	270	28	60	2	31	222	314	300	614	12	79	0.64	3	3	23	78	3.30
2007	AA	Carolina	434	64	123	15	59	283	351	486	837	9	74	0.41	3	6	42	203	6.05

Athletic infielder with defensive versatility and offensive potential. Aggressive/hard-swinging approach allows him to hit for moderate power, but will strike-out which depresses BA. Played mostly SS, showing range and soft hands, but can play up to five positions with average arm strength.

Lambo, Andrew — 93 — Los Angeles (N)

Bats L Age 19
2007 (4) HS (CA)
EXP MLB DEBUT: 2012 POTENTIAL: Starting RF/1B **9E**

	Pwr	++++
	BAvg	++++
4.40	Spd	++
	Def	++

Year	Lev	Team	AB	R	H	HR	RBI	Avg	OB	Slg	OPS	bb%	ct%	Eye	SB	CS	X/H%	Iso	RC/G
2007	Rk	GCL Dodgers	181	38	62	5	32	343	433	519	953	14	81	0.85	1	2	34	177	7.66

Strong hitter with bat speed, fluid swing, plate discipline, and ability to use whole field giving him unlimited offensive potential. Hits pitchers from opposite side and stays inside ball. Average defensively at 1B, but being used in corner outfield where he will need to show better range.

LaPorta, Matt — 7 — Milwaukee

Bats R Age 23
2007 (1) Florida
EXP MLB DEBUT: 2008 POTENTIAL: Starting LF/1B **9C**

	Pwr	++++
	BAvg	+++
4.45	Spd	+
	Def	+

Year	Lev	Team	AB	R	H	HR	RBI	Avg	OB	Slg	OPS	bb%	ct%	Eye	SB	CS	X/H%	Iso	RC/G
2007	Rk	Helena	27	4	7	2	4	259	286	519	804	4	70	0.13	0	0	43	259	5.18
2007	A-	W. Virginia	88	18	28	10	27	318	368	750	1118	7	75	0.32	0	1	64	432	9.29

Possesses incredible power with bat speed and strong wrists, but enhances power with excellent plate discipline. Led NCAA in SLG and OPS, and was SEC Player of the Year. MIL moved him from 1B to LF where he stands as a liability with below average range and arm strength.

Larish, Jeff — 3 — Detroit

Bats L Age 25
2005 (5) Arizona St
EXP MLB DEBUT: 2008 POTENTIAL: Platoon LF/1B **7C**

	Pwr	++++
	BAvg	++
4.60	Spd	+
	Def	+++

Year	Lev	Team	AB	R	H	HR	RBI	Avg	OB	Slg	OPS	bb%	ct%	Eye	SB	CS	X/H%	Iso	RC/G
2005	Rk	GCL Tigers	18	1	4	0	4	222	364	278	641	18	72	0.80	0	1	25	56	3.87
2005	A-	Oneonta	64	16	19	6	13	297	416	625	1041	17	91	2.17	0	0	47	328	8.42
2006	A+	Lakeland	457	76	118	18	65	258	371	460	831	15	78	0.81	9	7	46	201	6.15
2007	AA	Erie	454	71	121	28	101	267	384	515	900	16	76	0.81	6	2	45	249	6.99

Led EL in HR and RBI, showing improved bat speed and plate discipline. Made mechanical adjustments, bringing balance to swing, but focused too much on pulling baseball and struggled to reach outside pitches, which kept BA low. Solid defender, exhibiting soft hands and arm strength.

LaRoche, Andy — 57 — Los Angeles (N)

Bats R Age 24
2003 (39) Grayson Co C
EXP MLB DEBUT: 2007 POTENTIAL: Starting 3B **9C**

	Pwr	++++
	BAvg	+++
	Spd	++
	Def	+++

Year	Lev	Team	AB	R	H	HR	RBI	Avg	OB	Slg	OPS	bb%	ct%	Eye	SB	CS	X/H%	Iso	RC/G
2005	AA	Jacksonville	227	41	62	9	43	273	363	445	808	12	76	0.59	2	2	34	172	5.67
2006	AA	Jacksonville	230	42	71	9	46	309	413	483	896	15	86	1.28	6	3	31	174	6.90
2006	AAA	Las Vegas	202	35	65	10	35	322	396	550	946	11	84	0.78	3	2	38	228	7.22
2007	AAA	Las Vegas	265	55	82	18	48	309	398	589	987	13	84	0.93	2	2	45	279	7.74
2007	MLB	Los Angeles (N)	93	16	21	1	10	226	363	312	675	18	74	0.83	2	1	29	86	4.27

Pure hitter with bat speed and plate discipline, allowing him to hit for BA and power. Much of power is to pull field and will leak slightly forward, but has ability to go with the pitch. 3B defense improved with arm strength and soft/quick hands, and added to versatility by playing LF.

Lemon, Marcus — 6 — Texas

Bats L Age 20
2006 (3) HS (FL)
EXP MLB DEBUT: 2010 POTENTIAL: Starting 2B **7D**

	Pwr	++
	BAvg	++++
4.35	Spd	++
	Def	+++

Year	Lev	Team	AB	R	H	HR	RBI	Avg	OB	Slg	OPS	bb%	ct%	Eye	SB	CS	X/H%	Iso	RC/G
2006	Rk	AZL Rangers	84	16	26	0	9	310	420	405	825	16	88	1.60	11	2	23	95	6.37
2007	A-	Clinton	459	62	120	3	38	261	342	364	706	11	78	0.56	12	14	29	102	4.46

Strong/athletic player with BA/OBP ability due to contact and walk rate. Lack of strength and a flat bat plane give him below average power. Runs bases aggressively, but needs better proficiency. Possesses soft hands, but arm strength and range are not ideal for SS.

Lewis, Ozzie — 9 — Minnesota

Bats R Age 22
2007 (21) Fresno St
EXP MLB DEBUT: 2011 POTENTIAL: Platoon LF/RF **7C**

	Pwr	+++
	BAvg	++++
4.30	Spd	+++
	Def	+++

Year	Lev	Team	AB	R	H	HR	RBI	Avg	OB	Slg	OPS	bb%	ct%	Eye	SB	CS	X/H%	Iso	RC/G
2007	Rk	Elizabethton	235	46	76	9	50	323	374	523	897	7	78	0.37	3	1	37	200	6.58

MVP of APPY possessing power to all fields with moderate bat speed and aggressive approach. BA stayed high despite poor plate discipline and though he has college experience, his skills are raw. Possesses average range and arm strength, so is relegated to the corners.

Liddi, Alex — 5 — Seattle

Bats R Age 19
2005 FA (Italy)
EXP MLB DEBUT: 2010 POTENTIAL: Starting 3B **7D**

	Pwr	++++
	BAvg	++
	Spd	++
	Def	++++

Year	Lev	Team	AB	R	H	HR	RBI	Avg	OB	Slg	OPS	bb%	ct%	Eye	SB	CS	X/H%	Iso	RC/G
2006	Rk	AZL Mariners	182	31	57	3	25	313	356	500	856	6	74	0.25	9	2	39	187	6.31
2006	A-	Wisconsin	38	4	7	0	2	184	205	211	416	3	79	0.13	0	1	14	26	0.34
2007	A-	Wisconsin	400	41	96	8	52	240	303	385	688	8	69	0.29	5	4	41	145	4.11

Tall/projectable athlete with moderate bat speed that produces gap power now, but could provide HR power later. Plate discipline is weak, so may not hit for BA. Defensively, he possesses plus arm strength and soft hands, with enough range to be above average.

Lillibridge,Brent — 6 — Atlanta

EXP MLB DEBUT: 2008 | POTENTIAL: Starting SS | 8B

Bats R Age 24	Year	Lev	Team	AB	R	H	HR	RBI	Avg	OB	Slg	OPS	bb%	ct%	Eye	SB	CS	X/H%	Iso	RC/G
2005 (4) Washington	2005	A-	Williamsport	169	19	41	4	18	243	301	432	732	8	79	0.40	10	3	49	189	4.62
Pwr ++	2006	A-	Hickory	274	59	82	11	43	299	409	522	931	16	78	0.84	28	8	41	223	7.53
BAvg +++	2006	A+	Lynchburg	201	47	62	2	28	308	414	418	831	15	79	0.84	24	5	24	109	6.31
4.15 Spd ++++	2007	AA	Mississippi	204	31	56	3	17	275	339	387	727	9	71	0.33	14	7	25	113	4.65
Def ++++	2007	AAA	Richmond	321	47	92	10	41	287	328	436	765	6	82	0.34	28	5	28	150	4.76

Wiry athlete with secondary skill set, he makes solid contact and has driven ball better with physical maturity. Plate discipline regressed, which affected OBP more than BA. All of defensive tools are above average and makes both the routine and spectacular play.

Lin,Che-Hsuan — 8 — Boston

EXP MLB DEBUT: 2011 | POTENTIAL: Starting CF | 8D

Bats R Age 19	Year	Lev	Team	AB	R	H	HR	RBI	Avg	OB	Slg	OPS	bb%	ct%	Eye	SB	CS	X/H%	Iso	RC/G
2007 FA (Taiwan)																				
Pwr +++																				
BAvg +++																				
Spd ++++	2007	Rk	GCL Red Sox	175	33	46	4	22	263	328	457	785	9	76	0.40	14	3	43	194	5.41
Def +++	2007	A-	Lowell	43	7	7	0	3	163	250	209	459	10	77	0.50	3	2	29	47	1.18

Projectable athlete with fluid hitting mechanics, which coupled with his use of the whole field, gives him solid BA ability. Drives ball well for size, but can get pull-conscious and needs more patience. Arm strength and range play well in CF and has value as a baserunner with his speed.

Lisson,Mario — 5 — Kansas City

EXP MLB DEBUT: 2009 | POTENTIAL: Starting 3B | 7D

Bats R Age 24	Year	Lev	Team	AB	R	H	HR	RBI	Avg	OB	Slg	OPS	bb%	ct%	Eye	SB	CS	X/H%	Iso	RC/G
2002 FA (Venezuela)																				
Pwr ++++	2004	Rk	Idaho Falls	256	60	74	8	49	289	393	438	831	15	68	0.54	15	6	27	148	6.40
BAvg ++	2005	A-	Burlington	260	57	65	6	36	250	377	408	785	17	74	0.78	23	4	38	158	5.75
4.25 Spd +++	2006	A-	Burlington	463	67	121	13	72	261	353	419	773	12	76	0.61	41	11	37	158	5.30
Def +++	2007	A+	Wilmington	463	72	132	8	61	285	343	408	751	8	80	0.44	23	9	29	123	4.82

Athletic player with secondary skills, providing BA, doubles power, and ability to draw walks. Possesses above average speed and picks spots to steal. Defensively he has a strong infield arm and soft hands, but lacks first-step quickness in being average at 3B.

Lis,Erik — 73 — Minnesota

EXP MLB DEBUT: 2009 | POTENTIAL: Reserve 1B/LF | 7D

Bats R Age 24	Year	Lev	Team	AB	R	H	HR	RBI	Avg	OB	Slg	OPS	bb%	ct%	Eye	SB	CS	X/H%	Iso	RC/G
2005 (9) Evansville																				
Pwr +++																				
BAvg +++	2005	Rk	Elizabethton	168	29	53	10	41	315	350	577	928	5	79	0.26	0	0	43	262	6.69
Spd ++	2006	A-	Beloit	411	69	134	16	70	326	400	547	948	11	80	0.61	4	3	42	221	7.42
Def +	2007	A+	Fort Myers	492	58	135	18	97	274	330	470	800	8	78	0.38	3	1	41	195	5.37

Strong/stocky hitter with moderate power and ability to make hard contact, which helped him lead FSL in RBI. Aggressive approach and high strikeout rate suppresses BA and has little speed on bases. Played both LF and 1B with below average range and arm strength.

Loadenthal,Carl — 8 — Atlanta

EXP MLB DEBUT: 2008 | POTENTIAL: Reserve CF/LF | 6C

Bats L Age 26	Year	Lev	Team	AB	R	H	HR	RBI	Avg	OB	Slg	OPS	bb%	ct%	Eye	SB	CS	X/H%	Iso	RC/G
2003 NDFA Rider	2005	A-	Rome	210	35	55	1	23	262	349	348	696	12	87	1.00	17	4	27	86	4.52
Pwr +	2005	A+	Myrtle Beach	230	47	65	5	20	283	340	439	779	8	80	0.43	17	6	34	157	5.18
BAvg +++	2006	A+	Myrtle Beach	365	64	118	7	48	323	422	427	849	15	82	0.93	24	10	19	104	6.37
Spd ++++	2006	AA	Mississippi	48	7	8	1	4	167	259	271	530	11	90	1.20	5	0	38	104	2.58
Def +++	2007	AA	Mississippi	476	72	143	0	31	300	381	357	738	12	83	0.78	40	18	15	57	4.93

Plus speed, solid contact rate, and ability to draw walks gives him upside offensively. Struggles to hit for power and against LH pitching. Plays all three outfield positions with solid range, but below average arm strength. Hitting from LH side, speed, and defense could play as an outfield reserve.

Longoria,Evan — 5 — Tampa Bay

EXP MLB DEBUT: 2008 | POTENTIAL: Starting 3B | 9A

Bats R Age 22	Year	Lev	Team	AB	R	H	HR	RBI	Avg	OB	Slg	OPS	bb%	ct%	Eye	SB	CS	X/H%	Iso	RC/G
2006 (1) Long Beach St	2006	A-	Hudson Val	33	5	14	4	11	424	500	879	1379	13	85	1.00	1	0	43	455	12.22
Pwr ++++	2006	A+	Visalia	110	22	36	8	28	327	398	618	1017	11	83	0.68	1	1	44	291	7.96
BAvg ++++	2006	AA	Montgomery	105	14	28	6	19	267	274	486	759	1	81	0.05	2	1	39	219	4.30
4.30 Spd +++	2007	AA	Montgomery	381	78	117	21	76	307	389	528	916	12	79	0.63	4	0	36	220	6.94
Def ++++	2007	AAA	Durham	104	19	28	5	19	269	397	490	887	17	72	0.76	0	0	46	221	7.10

SL MVP, leading league in SLG and hit for consistent power all season due to his bat speed and plate discipline. Breaking pitches give him trouble and tends to lunge, but should still hit for BA. Solid defender, showing arm strength, soft hands, and average range.

Lopez,Pedro — 64 — Toronto

EXP MLB DEBUT: 2005 | POTENTIAL: Reserve SS/2B | 6B

Bats R Age 24	Year	Lev	Team	AB	R	H	HR	RBI	Avg	OB	Slg	OPS	bb%	ct%	Eye	SB	CS	X/H%	Iso	RC/G
2000 FA (DR)	2005	AAA	Charlotte	188	14	38	3	17	202	231	282	513	4	87	0.29	1	1	24	80	1.85
Pwr ++	2006	AA	Birmingham	259	30	83	5	34	320	360	452	812	6	88	0.50	3	6	27	131	5.40
BAvg ++	2006	AAA	Charlotte	208	32	57	5	24	274	311	404	714	5	87	0.39	4	0	30	130	4.19
Spd ++++	2007	AAA	Char/Lou	285	40	81	3	28	284	348	368	717	9	87	0.74	4	3	21	84	4.52
Def ++++	2007	MLB	Cincinnati	45	1	8	0	0	178	196	222	418	2	78	0.10	0	0	25	44	0.34

Athletic infielder with excellent defense, featuring arm strength and range. Makes contact with short stroke, runs well, and can bunt, but has little power and doesn't draw enough walks. Ability to play both middle infield positions gives him value in a utility role.

Lowrie,Jed — 64 — Boston

EXP MLB DEBUT: 2008 | POTENTIAL: Starting SS/3B | 8B

Bats B Age 24	Year	Lev	Team	AB	R	H	HR	RBI	Avg	OB	Slg	OPS	bb%	ct%	Eye	SB	CS	X/H%	Iso	RC/G
2005 (1-S) Stanford																				
Pwr ++	2005	A-	Lowell	201	36	66	4	32	328	426	448	873	14	85	1.13	7	5	24	119	6.68
BAvg ++++	2006	A+	Wilmington	374	43	98	3	50	262	355	374	729	13	83	0.83	2	2	31	112	4.90
4.30 Spd +++	2007	AA	Portland	337	61	100	8	49	297	410	501	912	16	83	1.12	5	3	46	205	7.35
Def +++	2007	AAA	Pawtucket	160	21	48	5	21	300	349	506	855	7	79	0.36	0	1	46	206	6.07

Fundamentally sound player rebounded from an injury plagued 2006, showing excellent contact ability, moderate power, and plate discipline. Average speed limits stolen bases, but runs aggressively. Makes plays defensively with soft hands and quick release, but arm is average.

Lubanski,Chris — 8 — Kansas City

EXP MLB DEBUT: 2008 | POTENTIAL: Platoon LF/CF | 7C

Bats L Age 23	Year	Lev	Team	AB	R	H	HR	RBI	Avg	OB	Slg	OPS	bb%	ct%	Eye	SB	CS	X/H%	Iso	RC/G
2003 (1) HS (PA)	2004	A-	Burlington	439	2	121	9	48	276	338	419	757	9	77	0.41	16	11	31	144	4.93
Pwr +++	2005	A+	High Desert	531	91	160	28	116	301	348	554	902	7	75	0.29	14	1	45	252	6.64
BAvg ++	2006	AA	Wichita	524	93	148	15	71	282	369	475	844	12	79	0.64	11	7	41	193	6.24
4.10 Spd ++++	2007	AA	Wichita	241	33	71	9	34	295	368	490	858	10	82	0.65	3	5	37	195	6.19
Def +++	2007	AAA	Omaha	168	20	35	6	22	208	277	363	640	9	71	0.33	0	3	37	155	3.29

Shows glimpses of potential, but offense is inconsistent and may not be enough to be outfield starter in Majors. Drives ball to all fields and makes good contact, but trigger is slow, doesn't hit LH pitching, and batting eye fluctuates. Ranges well in outfield, but arm strength is below average.

Lucroy,Jon — 2 — Milwaukee

EXP MLB DEBUT: 2010 | POTENTIAL: Platoon CA | 7C

Bats R Age 22	Year	Lev	Team	AB	R	H	HR	RBI	Avg	OB	Slg	OPS	bb%	ct%	Eye	SB	CS	X/H%	Iso	RC/G
2007 (3) Lou-Lafayette																				
Pwr ++++																				
BAvg ++																				
Spd +																				
Def +++	2007	Rk	Helena	234	35	80	4	39	342	383	487	870	6	84	0.43	0	3	30	145	7.44

Offensive-minded catcher with bat speed and fluid hitting mechanics that produces both power and BA. Receives ball well, halts running game (43% CS%), and takes charge on field, but tends to overthrow to make-up for his below average arm, causing his throws to tail, and lacks agility.

Mach,Tyler — 4 — Philadelphia

EXP MLB DEBUT: 2010 | POTENTIAL: Reserve 2B/3B | 7D

Bats R Age 23	Year	Lev	Team	AB	R	H	HR	RBI	Avg	OB	Slg	OPS	bb%	ct%	Eye	SB	CS	X/H%	Iso	RC/G
2007 (4) Oklahoma St																				
Pwr ++																				
BAvg ++++																				
4.30 Spd +++																				
Def ++	2007	A-	Williamsport	247	33	71	5	38	287	343	441	785	8	87	0.64	1	2	37	154	5.26

Athletic infielder with moderate bat speed and ability to make hard contact, giving him BA ability and moderate power despite lowly plate discipline. Defense at 2B is below average, where he has stiff hands, fringe-average arm strength, and mediocre range.

Macri,Matt — 54 — Minnesota

EXP MLB DEBUT: 2008 | **POTENTIAL:** Reserve 3B/2B | **6C**

Bats R Age 26	Year	Lev	Team	AB	R	H	HR	RBI	Avg	OB	Slg	OPS	bb%	ct%	Eye	SB	CS	X/H%	Iso	RC/G
2004 (5) Notre Dame	2005	A+	Modesto	244	40	69	7	34	283	368	443	811	12	73	0.49	6	1	35	160	5.86
Pwr +++	2005	AA	Tulsa	3	1	0	0	0	0	250	0	250	25	100		0	0	0	0	0.00
BAvg +++	2006	AA	Tulsa	289	35	67	8	35	232	286	370	656	7	77	0.33	2	4	33	138	3.49
4.40 Spd ++	2007	AA	Tulsa	275	46	82	11	33	298	346	502	848	7	79	0.34	4	4	41	204	5.88
Def ++	2007	AAA	CS/Roch	56	6	16	4	10	286	322	554	876	5	77	0.23	1	0	44	268	6.01

Well-proportioned athlete with ability to make contact, but lacks power due to poor plate discipline, a lack of balance, and tendency to pull baseball. Missed at-bats early due to a hamstring strain. Range is lacking at 2B, but possesses soft hands and good arm strength that plays at 3B.

Maier,Mitch — 8 — Kansas City

EXP MLB DEBUT: 2006 | **POTENTIAL:** Platoon LF/CF | **6B**

Bats L Age 25	Year	Lev	Team	AB	R	H	HR	RBI	Avg	OB	Slg	OPS	bb%	ct%	Eye	SB	CS	X/H%	Iso	RC/G
2003 (1) Toledo	2005	A+	High Desert	211	42	71	8	32	336	372	583	955	5	80	0.28	6	1	49	246	7.21
Pwr ++	2005	AA	Wichita	322	55	82	7	49	255	288	416	704	4	85	0.32	10	3	40	161	4.10
BAvg ++++	2006	AA	Wichita	543	95	166	14	92	306	354	473	828	7	82	0.43	13	12	34	168	5.67
4.30 Spd +++	2006	MLB	Kansas City	13	3	2	0	0	154	267	154	421	13	69	0.50	0	0	0	0	0.34
Def ++	2007	AAA	Omaha	544	75	152	14	62	279	321	428	749	6	84	0.37	7	2	32	149	4.62

Average tools across board, but maximizes ability. Lacks bat speed, but drives pitches he can handle and has maintained consistent BA. Steals bases with good instincts as he possesses average speed. Arm strength and range will play at both corner infield and outfield positions.

Majewski,Val — 93 — Baltimore

EXP MLB DEBUT: 2004 | **POTENTIAL:** Platoon RF/1B | **7D**

Bats R Age 27	Year	Lev	Team	AB	R	H	HR	RBI	Avg	OB	Slg	OPS	bb%	ct%	Eye	SB	CS	X/H%	Iso	RC/G
2002 (3) Rutgers	2004	AA	Bowie	433	71	133	15	80	307	356	490	846	7	84	0.49	14	4	33	182	5.83
Pwr +++	2004	MLB	Baltimore	13	3	2	0	1	154	154	231	385	0	92	0.00	0	0	50	77	0.65
BAvg +++	2006	AAA	Ottawa	323	44	84	4	39	260	336	381	717	10	78	0.51	7	8	30	121	4.55
Spd ++	2007	AA	Bowie	332	49	98	3	42	295	355	410	765	9	80	0.48	6	4	30	114	5.07
Def +++	2007	AAA	Norfolk	124	16	26	2	11	210	305	323	628	12	76	0.57	7	1	35	113	3.40

Athletic outfielder who has had tough time staying healthy and hasn't regained hitting stroke, especially his power. Possesses fluid hitting mechanics and can hit for BA, but doesn't get lift to hits. Shoulder surgery has decreased arm strength, but does have solid range in corner outfield.

Maldonado,Brahiam — 9 — New York (N)

EXP MLB DEBUT: 2010 | **POTENTIAL:** Platoon RF/LF | **7D**

Bats R Age 22	Year	Lev	Team	AB	R	H	HR	RBI	Avg	OB	Slg	OPS	bb%	ct%	Eye	SB	CS	X/H%	Iso	RC/G
2004 (10) HS (PR)	2004	Rk	GCL Mets	151	21	28	1	12	185	272	238	510	9	68	0.31	8	2	24	53	1.04
Pwr +++	2005	Rk	GCL Mets	117	23	30	1	21	256	355	359	714	13	69	0.47	8	1	30	103	4.89
BAvg +++	2005	A+	St. Lucie	16	4	5	0	3	313	421	375	796	11	63	0.33	0	0	25	63	5.75
4.30 Spd +++	2006	Rk	Kingsport	185	29	52	7	35	281	363	530	913	11	74	0.47	5	2	41	249	7.70
Def +++	2007	A-	Savannah	306	40	95	10	39	310	349	500	849	6	74	0.24	11	4	36	190	6.89

Strong athlete with solid secondary skills, but lacks contact ability and plate discipline, which could suppress offense at upper levels. Possesses good bat speed, but power is limited to pull field. Arm strength is a plus in corner outfield where he shows average range.

Mangini,Matt — 5 — Seattle

EXP MLB DEBUT: 2009 | **POTENTIAL:** Platoon 3B/1B | **8D**

Bats L Age 22	Year	Lev	Team	AB	R	H	HR	RBI	Avg	OB	Slg	OPS	bb%	ct%	Eye	SB	CS	X/H%	Iso	RC/G
2007 (1-S) Oklahoma St																				
Pwr +++																				
BAvg +++	2007	Rk	AZL Mariners	6	0	0	0	0	0	250	0	250	25	83	2.00	0	0		0	
Spd ++	2007	A-	Everett	79	12	23	2	9	291	391	418	809	14	77	0.72	3	0	26	127	5.84
Def ++	2007	A+	High Desert	62	7	14	2	8	226	294	403	697	9	66	0.29	1	0	36	177	4.30

Solid hitter with ability to hit for power with natural strength, bat speed, and fluid hitting mechanics. Uses entire field, but power hasn't manifested itself due to poor contact and a widened stance. Possesses arm strength, but is a below average fielder with stiff hands and poor agility.

Manriquez,Salomon — 2 — Texas

EXP MLB DEBUT: 2008 | **POTENTIAL:** Reserve CA | **7D**

Bats R Age 25	Year	Lev	Team	AB	R	H	HR	RBI	Avg	OB	Slg	OPS	bb%	ct%	Eye	SB	CS	X/H%	Iso	RC/G
2000 FA (Venezuela)	2004	A+	Brevard Co	52	5	13	1	2	250	264	404	668	2	73	0.07	0	0	46	154	3.52
Pwr +++	2004	AA	Harrisburg	27	2	4	1	2	148	148	296	444	0	85	0.00	0	0	50	148	0.75
BAvg +++	2005	A+	Potomac	443	64	127	15	68	287	332	479	810	6	81	0.35	0	0	42	192	5.41
Spd +	2006	AA	Harrisburg	339	39	87	10	45	257	321	398	719	9	75	0.37	0	0	32	142	4.37
Def +++	2007	AA	Frisco	247	34	68	16	53	275	342	518	860	9	77	0.45	0	1	41	243	6.05

Short/stocky catcher with bat speed who makes hard contact that enables him to hit for power. Poor plate discipline will cause BA to fluctuate. Lacks agility and receiving skills, but arm strength allows him to compensate for those shortcomings and can be average defensively.

Manzella,Tommy — 6 — Houston

EXP MLB DEBUT: 2008 | **POTENTIAL:** Reserve SS/2B | **6B**

Bats R Age 25	Year	Lev	Team	AB	R	H	HR	RBI	Avg	OB	Slg	OPS	bb%	ct%	Eye	SB	CS	X/H%	Iso	RC/G
2005 (3) Tulane																				
Pwr ++	2005	A-	Tri City	220	24	51	0	18	232	262	295	557	4	82	0.23	5	3	20	64	2.30
BAvg +++	2006	A-	Lexington	338	50	93	7	43	275	340	408	748	9	76	0.41	16	8	32	133	4.82
4.30 Spd +++	2007	A+	Salem	223	28	53	0	24	238	298	296	593	8	87	0.63	5	2	25	58	3.09
Def +++	2007	AA	Corpus Christi	228	35	66	1	15	289	344	382	726	8	82	0.48	10	2	24	92	4.55

Athletic middle infielder with average tools, but intelligence and aggressiveness let his tools play up. Offensively, he makes good contact, draws walks, and steals bases, but severely lacks power. Range is just average at SS, but has soft/quick hands and playable arm strength.

Marrero,Chris — 7 — Washington

EXP MLB DEBUT: 2010 | **POTENTIAL:** Starting 1B | **9C**

Bats R Age 19	Year	Lev	Team	AB	R	H	HR	RBI	Avg	OB	Slg	OPS	bb%	ct%	Eye	SB	CS	X/H%	Iso	RC/G
2006 (1) HS (FL)																				
Pwr ++++																				
BAvg +++	2006	Rk	GCL Nationals	81	10	25	0	16	309	371	420	791	9	77	0.42	0	0	36	111	5.54
4.40 Spd ++	2007	A-	Hagerstown	222	31	65	14	53	293	337	545	882	6	82	0.36	0	4	43	252	7.22
Def +++	2007	A+	Potomac	255	40	66	9	35	259	338	431	769	11	75	0.51	0	0	35	173	4.11

Strong/athletic hitter was impressive with his bat speed and ability to handle good pitching at his age. Drives ball hard to all fields, and though he is aggressive and doesn't walk, his BA should be fine. Shows arm strength in corner outfield, but range is limited and will be moved to 1B.

Marson,Lou — 2 — Philadelphia

EXP MLB DEBUT: 2010 | **POTENTIAL:** Starting CA | **7C**

Bats R Age 21	Year	Lev	Team	AB	R	H	HR	RBI	Avg	OB	Slg	OPS	bb%	ct%	Eye	SB	CS	X/H%	Iso	RC/G
2004 (4) HS (AZ)																				
Pwr +++	2004	Rk	GCL Phillies	113	18	29	4	8	257	333	389	722	10	84	0.72	4	0	36	133	3.81
BAvg ++	2005	A-	Batavia	220	25	45	5	25	245	329	391	720	11	76	0.52	0	1	33	145	3.88
Spd +	2006	A	Lakewood	350	44	85	4	39	243	343	351	694	12	77	0.60	4	0	24	109	3.39
Def ++++	2007	A+	Clearwater	393	68	113	7	63	288	373	407	780	12	80	0.65	3	1	28	120	4.50

Solid, all-around catcher with offensive upside. Drives ball hard to all fields and exercises patience, but a long swing will keep BA low. Arm strength helped him nail 37% of attempted runners, receives ball well, and works well with pitchers.

Martinez-Esteve,Eddy — 7 — San Francisco

EXP MLB DEBUT: 2008 | **POTENTIAL:** Starting LF | **8D**

Bats R Age 24	Year	Lev	Team	AB	R	H	HR	RBI	Avg	OB	Slg	OPS	bb%	ct%	Eye	SB	CS	X/H%	Iso	RC/G
2004 (2) Florida St	2005	A+	San Jose	479	89	150	17	94	313	421	524	945	16	83	1.09	4	2	43	211	7.63
Pwr +++	2006	AA	Connecticut	92	8	25	2	11	272	337	446	782	9	85	0.64	0	0	48	174	5.30
BAvg ++++	2007	Rk	AZL Giants	42	2	13	0	3	310	463	333	796	21	79	1.22	0	0	7	24	5.15
4.60 Spd +	2007	AA	Connecticut	134	10	32	1	10	239	306	291	597	8	75	0.36	2	1	13	52	1.98
Def +	2007	A+	San Jose	82	5	17	0	8	207	286	268	554	10	84	0.69	0	0	29	61	1.70

Reshaped body and lost weight, but still couldn't stay healthy (shoulder). Pure hitter with bat speed, BA ability, and moderate power, but doesn't use whole field like he should. Speed is well below average and defense is still a liability in LF with his poor range and arm strength.

Martinez,Fernando — 8 — New York (N)

EXP MLB DEBUT: 2009 | **POTENTIAL:** Starting RF | **9C**

Bats L Age 19	Year	Lev	Team	AB	R	H	HR	RBI	Avg	OB	Slg	OPS	bb%	ct%	Eye	SB	CS	X/H%	Iso	RC/G
2005 FA (DR)	2006	Rk	GCL Mets	4	1	1	0	0	250	250	250	500	0	75	0.00	0	0	0	0	1.07
Pwr ++++	2006	A-	Hagerstown	195	24	64	5	28	333	382	505	887	7	81	0.39	7	4	33	168	6.56
BAvg +++	2006	A+	St. Lucie	119	18	23	5	11	193	232	387	619	5	80	0.25	1	1	48	193	2.91
4.30 Spd ++	2007	Rk	GCL Mets	9	1	1	0	1	111	200	333	533	10	33	0.17	0	0	100	222	5.82
Def +++	2007	AA	Binghamton	236	32	64	4	21	271	328	377	705	8	78	0.39	3	4	25	106	4.19

Promising hitter with moderate power and BA ability who has hit at each level despite being incredibly young. Spread stance limits leg drive and doesn't have good plate discipline, but makes contact. Range and arm strength may not play up in CF. Missed second half with a right hand injury.

Martinez, Jose — 46 — St. Louis

EXP MLB DEBUT: 2009 | POTENTIAL: Reserve 2B/SS | 7C

Bats R | Age 22 | 2004 FA (Venezuela)

	Year	Lev	Team	AB	R	H	HR	RBI	Avg	OB	Slg	OPS	bb%	ct%	Eye	SB	CS	X/H%	Iso	RC/G
Pwr ++	2005	Rk	Johnson City	150	28	45	6	31	300	382	500	882	12	90	1.33	9	2	36	200	6.56
BAvg +++	2006	A-	Quad Cities	326	47	88	8	36	270	308	417	725	5	92	0.69	7	7	34	147	4.47
Spd ++++	2007	A+	Palm Beach	226	22	56	2	19	248	280	323	603	4	91	0.50	4	4	21	75	3.07
Def ++++	2007	AA	Springfield	250	37	75	10	46	300	337	472	809	5	90	0.58	0	0	31	172	5.26

Athletic middle infielder with blossoming offense. Contact ability and plate discipline have always been strong, but hit for more power after adding muscle to slight frame. Possesses speed, but doesn't have the instincts to steal bases. Defensive skills profile better at 2B.

Martinez, Jose — 9 — Chicago (A)

EXP MLB DEBUT: 2012 | POTENTIAL: Starting RF | 9E

Bats R | Age 19 | 2006 FA (Venezuela)

	Year	Lev	Team	AB	R	H	HR	RBI	Avg	OB	Slg	OPS	bb%	ct%	Eye	SB	CS	X/H%	Iso	RC/G
Pwr ++++																				
BAvg +++																				
Spd ++++																				
Def +++	2007	Rk	Bristol	245	34	69	7	37	282	341	437	778	8	78	0.42	12	2	30	155	5.11

Tall/athletic outfielder with power/speed potential, but is raw in abilities. Bat speed generates power to all fields and centers ball well, but will need to tighten strike zone. Arm strength and range are best suited for RF and should be above average when he learns to take better routes.

Martinez, Mario — 56 — Seattle

EXP MLB DEBUT: 2011 | POTENTIAL: Starting 3B | 8D

Bats R | Age 18 | 2006 FA (DR)

	Year	Lev	Team	AB	R	H	HR	RBI	Avg	OB	Slg	OPS	bb%	ct%	Eye	SB	CS	X/H%	Iso	RC/G
Pwr ++++																				
BAvg +++																				
4.40 Spd ++																				
Def +++	2007	Rk	AZL Mariners	196	36	55	1	26	281	302	352	654	3	84	0.19	3	2	20	71	3.39

Dominican athlete offensive potential at a premium position. Moderate bat speed produces power to all field and hit for BA by making solid contact. Plate discipline is lacking and will chase pitches. Arm strength and soft hands are fine at SS, but range is low and may move to 3B.

Martin, Dustin — 8 — Minnesota

EXP MLB DEBUT: 2009 | POTENTIAL: Reserve CF/LF | 6C

Bats L | Age 24 | 2006 (26) Sam Houston

	Year	Lev	Team	AB	R	H	HR	RBI	Avg	OB	Slg	OPS	bb%	ct%	Eye	SB	CS	X/H%	Iso	RC/G
Pwr +++																				
BAvg ++	2006	A-	Brooklyn	253	22	79	2	35	312	376	451	827	9	80	0.52	7	5	30	138	5.94
4.15 Spd ++++	2007	Rk	GCL Mets	4	1	2	0	0	500	500	500	1000	0	100		0	0	0	0	6.83
Def +++	2007	A+	SL/FM	482	46	139	8	71	288	359	425	784	10	76	0.45	16	7	32	137	5.41

Solid athlete who plays above average tools with hustle and instincts, but projects to a reserve. Moderate bat speed produces doubles and will draw walks, but hasn't hit for BA consistently. Arm strength and range are slightly above average and can play all three outfield positions.

Mather, Joe — 39 — St. Louis

EXP MLB DEBUT: 2008 | POTENTIAL: Platoon 1B/LF | 7C

Bats R | Age 25 | 2000 (3) HS (AZ)

	Year	Lev	Team	AB	R	H	HR	RBI	Avg	OB	Slg	OPS	bb%	ct%	Eye	SB	CS	X/H%	Iso	RC/G
	2005	A-	Quad Cities	209	30	46	9	33	220	288	440	728	9	77	0.41	0	0	57	220	4.50
Pwr ++++	2005	A+	Palm Beach	200	31	55	8	27	275	316	475	791	6	81	0.31	4	0	40	200	5.09
BAvg ++	2006	A+	Palm Beach	442	64	119	16	74	269	324	457	781	8	79	0.40	8	0	42	188	5.10
Spd ++	2007	AA	Springfield	234	48	71	18	46	303	380	607	987	11	86	0.91	4	0	49	303	7.55
Def ++	2007	AAA	Memphis	253	32	61	13	31	241	304	443	747	8	80	0.45	6	0	39	202	4.60

Reshaped body, providing more flexibility, and retooled swing allowing him to make better contact. Bat speed generates power to all fields and improved plate discipline helping him get better pitches to hit. Defense is below average at 1B and LF with below average arm and range.

Mattair, Travis — 5 — Philadelphia

EXP MLB DEBUT: 2010 | POTENTIAL: Starting 3B | 9E

Bats R | Age 19 | 2007 (2) HS (WA)

	Year	Lev	Team	AB	R	H	HR	RBI	Avg	OB	Slg	OPS	bb%	ct%	Eye	SB	CS	X/H%	Iso	RC/G
Pwr ++++																				
BAvg +++																				
4.30 Spd +++																				
Def ++	2007	Rk	GCL Phillies	200	19	47	3	21	235	278	340	618	6	71	0.21	3	1	30	105	2.97

Combines athleticism and strength, with the bat speed that could produce an impact bat. Centers ball well and drives ball to all parts of the field, but lacks plate discipline. Arm strength and hands play at SS, but his size and average speed makes his range more suitable for 3B.

Mattingly, Preston — 46 — Los Angeles (N)

EXP MLB DEBUT: 2010 | POTENTIAL: Starting 2B | 8E

Bats R | Age 20 | 2006 (1-S) HS (IN)

	Year	Lev	Team	AB	R	H	HR	RBI	Avg	OB	Slg	OPS	bb%	ct%	Eye	SB	CS	X/H%	Iso	RC/G
Pwr +++																				
BAvg +++																				
Spd ++++	2006	Rk	GCL Dodgers	186	22	54	1	29	290	323	403	726	5	79	0.23	12	3	30	113	4.39
Def ++	2007	A-	Great Lakes	404	42	85	3	40	210	251	297	548	5	71	0.18	11	3	26	87	2.03

Athletic with good bat speed, but displayed poor plate discipline which depressed both power and BA. Line-drive stroke allows him to use whole field and runs bases well with above average speed. Moved from SS to 2B where his below average arm and range are better suited.

Maxwell, Justin — 8 — Washington

EXP MLB DEBUT: 2007 | POTENTIAL: Starting CF/RF | 8C

Bats R | Age 24 | 2005 (4) Maryland

	Year	Lev	Team	AB	R	H	HR	RBI	Avg	OB	Slg	OPS	bb%	ct%	Eye	SB	CS	X/H%	Iso	RC/G
	2006	A-	Vermont	271	36	73	4	33	269	336	376	712	9	77	0.44	20	5	25	107	4.37
Pwr ++++	2006	A-	Savannah	58	8	10	1	7	172	273	328	600	12	60	0.35	1	0	50	155	3.15
BAvg ++	2007	A-	Hagerstown	209	51	63	14	40	301	379	579	958	11	73	0.46	14	3	44	278	7.66
4.35 Spd +++	2007	A+	Potomac	228	35	60	13	45	263	333	491	825	10	71	0.37	21	5	43	228	5.81
Def +++	2007	MLB	Washington	26	5	7	2	5	269	296	500	796	4	69	0.13	0	0	29	231	5.03

Power/speed prospect with ability to impact game in several ways. Provides pull power, but lacks balance and can swing defensively. BA will be determined by strike zone judgment and ability to hit good pitches. Arm strength is solid and has good closing speed/range in CF.

Mayberry, John — 9 — Texas

EXP MLB DEBUT: 2008 | POTENTIAL: Starting RF/LF | 8D

Bats R | Age 24 | 2005 (1) Stanford

	Year	Lev	Team	AB	R	H	HR	RBI	Avg	OB	Slg	OPS	bb%	ct%	Eye	SB	CS	X/H%	Iso	RC/G
Pwr ++++	2005	A-	Spokane	265	51	67	11	26	253	320	438	757	9	73	0.37	7	3	40	185	4.88
BAvg ++	2006	A-	Clinton	459	77	123	21	77	268	351	479	831	11	75	0.50	8	3	41	211	5.97
4.30 Spd +++	2007	A+	Bakersfield	244	47	56	16	45	230	309	496	805	10	74	0.44	9	1	57	266	5.48
Def +++	2007	AA	Frisco	245	35	59	14	38	241	298	453	751	8	75	0.32	7	1	41	212	4.61

Combines height, strength, and athleticism, and began to tap into his power showing bat speed and improved contact. A hitch and length to his swing may keep BA low, but has enough secondary skills. Arm strength is solid, but doesn't take good routes in corner outfield.

Maybin, Cameron — 8 — Florida

EXP MLB DEBUT: 2007 | POTENTIAL: Starting CF | 9B

Bats R | Age 21 | 2005 (1) HS (NC)

	Year	Lev	Team	AB	R	H	HR	RBI	Avg	OB	Slg	OPS	bb%	ct%	Eye	SB	CS	X/H%	Iso	RC/G
	2006	A-	W. Michigan	380	58	115	9	66	303	382	458	840	11	70	0.43	27	7	30	155	6.40
Pwr ++++	2007	Rk	GCL Tigers	7	1	4	0	1	571	667	571	1238	22	71	1.00	0	0	0	0	12.85
BAvg ++++	2007	A+	Lakeland	296	58	90	10	44	304	392	486	879	13	72	0.52	25	6	32	182	6.86
4.05 Spd ++++	2007	AA	Erie	20	9	8	4	8	400	538	1050	1588	23	70	1.00	0	0	63	650	16.89
Def ++++	2007	MLB	Detroit	49	8	7	1	2	143	192	265	458	6	57	0.14	5	0	57	122	0.66

Prime athlete with power, speed, and defense. Power could be limited due to high G/F ratio, long swing, and propensity to hit off front foot, but makes solid contact. Arm strength and range are sufficient for CF. Missed two months with partially dislocated shoulder.

Mayora, Daniel — 4 — Colorado

EXP MLB DEBUT: 2009 | POTENTIAL: Starting 2B | 7D

Bats R | Age 22 | 2003 FA (DR)

	Year	Lev	Team	AB	R	H	HR	RBI	Avg	OB	Slg	OPS	bb%	ct%	Eye	SB	CS	X/H%	Iso	RC/G
Pwr +++																				
BAvg +++	2005	Rk	Casper	151	20	40	1	14	265	306	377	684	6	76	0.25	4	3	35	113	3.92
Spd ++++	2006	A-	Tri-City	276	40	84	5	30	304	358	442	800	8	75	0.33	8	4	31	138	5.50
Def +++	2007	A-	Asheville	516	88	160	14	78	310	361	477	838	7	76	0.33	26	9	36	167	5.91

Athletic middle infielder with offensive outburst that was ballpark-tinged, but does have underlying skills. Makes solid contact and can drive ball for doubles, and possesses speed on the bases. Moved from SS to 2B where his average range and arm strength are less of a burden.

BATTERS

May,Lucas | 2 | Los Angeles (N) | EXP MLB DEBUT: 2009 | POTENTIAL: Reserve CA | 7D

Bats R Age 23	Year	Lev	Team	AB	R	H	HR	RBI	Avg	OB	Slg	OPS	bb%	ct%	Eye	SB	CS	X/H%	Iso	RC/G
2003 (8) HS (MO)	2003	Rk	GCL Dodgers	159	19	40	0	10	252	331	302	633	11	76	0.50	11	1	20	50	3.47
Pwr ++++	2004	Rk	Ogden	147	25	42	5	30	286	323	449	772	5	75	0.22	4	3	29	163	4.88
BAvg ++	2005	A-	Columbus	385	46	88	9	53	229	259	345	605	4	76	0.17	5	2	28	117	2.67
Spd ++	2006	A-	Columbus	450	76	123	18	82	273	326	493	819	7	71	0.27	14	2	44	220	5.80
Def ++	2007	A+	Inland Emp	507	81	130	25	89	256	306	465	771	7	79	0.34	5	7	41	209	4.84

Athletic receiver with excellent power using an aggressive swing and moderate bat speed. Struggles to make contact and strikes-out plenty, thus will never hit for a high BA. Possesses arm strength and agility behind the plate, but needs better receiving skills and quicker release.

McAnulty,Paul | 753 | San Diego | EXP MLB DEBUT: 2005 | POTENTIAL: Reserve 1B/LF | 6A

Bats L Age 27	Year	Lev	Team	AB	R	H	HR	RBI	Avg	OB	Slg	OPS	bb%	ct%	Eye	SB	CS	X/H%	Iso	RC/G
2002 (12) Long Beach St	2006	AAA	Portland	478	76	148	19	79	310	389	521	910	11	83	0.78	1	2	39	211	6.89
Pwr +++	2006	MLB	San Diego	13	3	3	1	3	231	333	538	872	13	69	0.50	0	0	67	308	6.67
BAvg +++	2007	Rk	AZL Padres	15	2	6	0	4	400	471	467	937	12	87	1.00	0	0	17	67	7.33
4.60 Spd +	2007	AAA	Portland	233	25	61	4	31	262	344	373	717	11	80	0.62	0	2	28	112	4.54
Def ++	2007	MLB	San Diego	40	5	8	1	5	200	256	300	556	7	75	0.30	0	0	25	100	2.10

Pure hitter with BA ability and power to gaps. Centers ball well and is patient enough to draw walks. Speed is well below average, but shows instincts on bases. Has proved versatile on defense, playing four corner positions, but is below average lacking arm strength and range.

McBride,Matt | 2 | Cleveland | EXP MLB DEBUT: 2009 | POTENTIAL: Platoon CA | 7C

Bats R Age 23	Year	Lev	Team	AB	R	H	HR	RBI	Avg	OB	Slg	OPS	bb%	ct%	Eye	SB	CS	X/H%	Iso	RC/G
2006 (2-S) HS (PA)																				
Pwr +++																				
BAvg +++	2006	A-	Mahoning Val	184	24	50	4	32	272	330	402	732	8	88	0.73	5	2	32	130	4.64
Spd ++	2007	A-	Lake County	421	66	119	8	66	283	342	432	774	8	87	0.70	1	0	38	150	5.18
Def ++	2007	AA	Akron	7	2	4	0	0	571	571	857	1429	0	100		0	0	50	286	11.44

Offensive-oriented catcher with contact ability, moderate power, and plate discipline. Developed into a tough out with runners in scoring position. Receives ball well and is agile, but rates below average defensively due to poor footwork and fringe-average arm strength.

McCutchen,Andrew | 8 | Pittsburgh | EXP MLB DEBUT: 2008 | POTENTIAL: Starting CF | 9C

Bats R Age 21	Year	Lev	Team	AB	R	H	HR	RBI	Avg	OB	Slg	OPS	bb%	ct%	Eye	SB	CS	X/H%	Iso	RC/G
2005 (1) HS (FL)	2005	Rk	GCL Pirates	158	36	47	2	30	297	406	430	837	16	85	1.21	13	1	30	133	6.39
Pwr +++	2006	A-	Hickory	453	77	131	14	62	289	349	444	793	8	80	0.47	22	7	29	155	5.29
BAvg ++++	2006	AA	Altoona	78	12	24	3	12	308	372	474	846	9	74	0.40	1	1	29	167	6.07
4.05 Spd +++++	2007	AA	Altoona	446	70	115	10	48	258	324	383	708	9	81	0.53	17	1	29	126	4.30
Def ++++	2007	AAA	Indianapolis	67	7	21	1	5	313	352	418	770	6	84	0.36	4	3	24	104	4.88

Wiry strong athlete with blazing speed, he shows the bat speed and plate discipline to hit for BA and moderate power. Overmatched against upper level pitchers, but adjusted late. Defense is exceptionally strong with plus range and average arm strength in CF.

McKenry,Mike | 2 | Colorado | EXP MLB DEBUT: 2010 | POTENTIAL: Platoon CA | 7D

Bats R Age 23	Year	Lev	Team	AB	R	H	HR	RBI	Avg	OB	Slg	OPS	bb%	ct%	Eye	SB	CS	X/H%	Iso	RC/G
2006 (7) Tennessee St																				
Pwr ++++																				
BAvg +++																				
Spd +	2006	A-	Tri-City	245	28	53	4	23	216	303	339	642	8	80	0.45	3	3	40	122	3.72
Def ++++	2007	A-	Asheville	408	79	117	22	90	287	392	539	931	14	79	0.79	8	9	50	252	7.55

Strong/agile catcher with excellent defense, featuring arm strength, receiving skills, and a quick release, that helped him nail 34% of attempted runners. Power enhanced by friendly home confines, but has solid bat speed and strike zone judgment, which gives him value offensively.

Melillo,Kevin | 4 | Oakland | EXP MLB DEBUT: 2007 | POTENTIAL: Reserve 2B/3B | 6B

Bats L Age 26	Year	Lev	Team	AB	R	H	HR	RBI	Avg	OB	Slg	OPS	bb%	ct%	Eye	SB	CS	X/H%	Iso	RC/G
2004 (5) So Carolina	2005	A+	Stockton	90	21	36	9	23	400	471	800	1271	12	80	0.67	2	0	47	400	11.24
Pwr ++	2005	AA	Midland	131	33	37	7	34	282	352	519	871	10	82	0.61	9	2	46	237	6.23
BAvg +++	2006	AA	Midland	501	73	140	12	73	279	366	425	791	12	80	0.69	14	7	33	146	5.51
4.25 Spd +++	2007	AAA	Sacramento	382	63	100	10	55	262	353	442	796	12	74	0.54	8	7	43	181	5.70
Def ++	2007	MLB	Oakland	0	0	0	0	0	0	1000	0	1000	100	0	0.00	0	0	0	0	0.00

Scrappy player with average tools and athleticism. Thrives on making contact and being patient, but has enough power to crush a mistake. Struggles against LH pitching and is susceptible to good breaking pitches. Makes plays defensively, but tools are fringe-average at best.

Mesoraco,Devin | 2 | Cincinnati | EXP MLB DEBUT: 2012 | POTENTIAL: Starting CA | 8D

Bats R Age 20	Year	Lev	Team	AB	R	H	HR	RBI	Avg	OB	Slg	OPS	bb%	ct%	Eye	SB	CS	X/H%	Iso	RC/G
2007 (1) HS (PA)																				
Pwr ++++																				
BAvg ++																				
4.30 Spd ++																				
Def ++++	2007	Rk	GCL Reds	137	16	30	1	8	219	296	270	566	10	81	0.58	2	0	17	51	2.61

Top rated high school catcher with strong defensive skills including arm strength, receiving skills, and ability to halt running game (35% CS%). Very athletic, he runs well and is agile behind plate. Bat speed provides moderate power from LF to RC, but will need to make better contact.

Middlebrooks,Will | 5 | Boston | EXP MLB DEBUT: 2011 | POTENTIAL: Starting 3B | 8D

Bats R Age 19	Year	Lev	Team	AB	R	H	HR	RBI	Avg	OB	Slg	OPS	bb%	ct%	Eye	SB	CS	X/H%	Iso	RC/G
2007 (5) HS (TX)																				
Pwr ++++																				
BAvg +++																				
4.30 Spd +++																				
Def +++	2007																			

Draftable as a two-way player, but bat was too much to ignore with solid bat speed and power. Contact rate and plate discipline need work and may suppress BA. Fringe-average speed and range will decline with maturity, but can play a solid 3B with soft hands and arm strength.

Miller,Jai | 8 | Florida | EXP MLB DEBUT: 2008 | POTENTIAL: Reserve CF/LF | 7D

Bats R Age 23	Year	Lev	Team	AB	R	H	HR	RBI	Avg	OB	Slg	OPS	bb%	ct%	Eye	SB	CS	X/H%	Iso	RC/G
2003 (5) HS (AL)	2003	A-	Jamestown	43	5	10	0	6	233	283	302	585	7	65	0.20	1	1	30	70	2.68
Pwr +++	2004	A-	Greensboro	390	51	80	12	49	205	265	351	617	8	58	0.20	11	4	38	146	3.27
BAvg ++	2005	A-	Greensboro	415	69	86	13	34	207	303	345	648	12	67	0.41	16	11	34	137	3.56
4.05 Spd ++++	2006	AAA	Albuquerque	346	40	72	0	24	208	299	266	565	12	67	0.39	24	10	25	58	2.50
Def +++	2007	AA	Carolina	406	54	106	14	58	261	349	438	788	12	69	0.43	12	5	40	177	5.63

Tall/athletic player with plus speed improved approach, taking more walks and getting better pitches to hit. Produces moderate power, but high strikeout rate will keep BA suppressed. Above average arm strength and range make him solid defensively at all three outfield spots.

Mills,Beau | 53 | Cleveland | EXP MLB DEBUT: 2009 | POTENTIAL: Starting 3B/1B | 9D

Bats L Age 21	Year	Lev	Team	AB	R	H	HR	RBI	Avg	OB	Slg	OPS	bb%	ct%	Eye	SB	CS	X/H%	Iso	RC/G
2007 (1) Lewis & Clark																				
Pwr ++++																				
BAvg +++	2007	A-	Mahoning Val	28	5	5	0	1	179	258	250	508	10	75	0.43	0	0	40	71	1.78
Spd ++	2007	A-	Lake County	177	32	48	5	36	271	325	435	760	7	79	0.37	0	0	38	164	4.85
Def +	2007	A+	Kinston	40	7	11	1	5	275	341	500	841	9	80	0.50	0	0	64	225	6.10

Pure hitter with bat speed, strong hands, and short swing provides above average power and BA ability. Plate discipline could be better, but Cleveland doesn't want to suppress aggressiveness. Possesses arm strength, but poor first-step quickness and stiff hands makes defense a problem.

Milons,Jereme | 8 | Arizona | EXP MLB DEBUT: 2009 | POTENTIAL: Platoon RF/LF | 8E

Bats R Age 25	Year	Lev	Team	AB	R	H	HR	RBI	Avg	OB	Slg	OPS	bb%	ct%	Eye	SB	CS	X/H%	Iso	RC/G
2001 (21) HS (MS)	2004	A	Col/SB	465	71	124	10	54	267	311	391	703	6	77	0.28	26	9	25	125	4.06
Pwr +++	2004	A+	Vero Beach	39	5	8	0	2	205	262	231	493	7	77	0.33	4	0	13	26	1.44
BAvg +++	2005	A-	South Bend	491	81	130	10	66	265	310	415	725	6	77	0.28	11	6	35	151	4.41
4.10 Spd ++++	2006	A+	Lancaster	386	56	116	11	54	301	351	446	797	7	75	0.32	13	5	24	145	5.32
Def ++++	2007	A+	Visalia	309	39	95	4	46	307	344	417	761	5	77	0.24	17	9	25	110	4.80

Solid athlete with above average speed and power, but poor contact rate, tendency to pull-off baseball, and mediocre plate discipline diminishes power and OBP which doesn't allow him to use his legs. Arm strength and range are above average and can play all three outfield positions.

Miranda, Juan — 3 — New York (A)

Bats L | Age 25 — 2006 FA (Cuba)
EXP MLB DEBUT: 2010 | POTENTIAL: Platoon 1B | 7C

Pwr	++++
BAvg	+++
Spd	+
Def	++

Year	Lev	Team	AB	R	H	HR	RBI	Avg	OB	Slg	OPS	bb%	ct%	Eye	SB	CS	X/H%	Iso	RC/G
2007	A+	Tampa	250	35	66	9	50	264	341	464	805	10	76	0.48	1	0	44	200	5.62
2007	AA	Trenton	196	29	52	7	46	265	342	480	822	11	77	0.50	0	1	50	214	5.87

Cuban slugger with solid bat speed and power to all parts of the field. BA isn't a strong suit and will strike-out, but is selective enough to get good pitches to hit. Below average runner and adds nothing defensively with stiff hands and mediocre range.

Miranda, Sergio — 6 — Chicago (A)

Bats B | Age 21 — 2007 (13) Virginia Comm
EXP MLB DEBUT: 2009 | POTENTIAL: Reserve SS | 7D

Pwr	++
BAvg	+++
4.20 Spd	+++
Def	+++

Year	Lev	Team	AB	R	H	HR	RBI	Avg	OB	Slg	OPS	bb%	ct%	Eye	SB	CS	X/H%	Iso	RC/G
2007	Rk	Great Falls	28	2	13	0	1	464	516	643	1159	10	86	0.75	1	2	31	179	9.94
2007	A-	Kannapolis	238	45	67	1	30	282	378	349	727	13	89	1.37	5	3	18	67	5.01

Fundamentally sound college infielder with BA ability and solid plate discipline. Lacks power, but hits well in situations and has the speed to steal bases. Arm strength and range are above average and makes the plays he gets to. Defense should allow him to fill utility role.

Mitchell, Jermaine — 8 — Oakland

Bats L | Age 23 — 2006 (5) UNC Greensbo
EXP MLB DEBUT: 2009 | POTENTIAL: Platoon CF | 8C

Pwr	++
BAvg	+++
4.10 Spd	++++
Def	+++

Year	Lev	Team	AB	R	H	HR	RBI	Avg	OB	Slg	OPS	bb%	ct%	Eye	SB	CS	X/H%	Iso	RC/G
2006	A-	Vancouver	138	23	50	3	23	362	450	507	957	14	80	0.81	14	6	24	145	7.74
2007	A-	Kane Co	431	79	124	8	58	288	392	413	805	15	73	0.64	24	8	27	125	5.94

Leadoff type hitter with on-base ability and plus speed. Started to show some power after adding some muscle, but is content with driving gaps, making contact, and drawing walks. Possesses outstanding range in CF and makes up for a below average arm by being accurate and quick.

Mitchell, Lee — 5 — Florida

Bats R | Age 26 — 2003 (6) Georgia
EXP MLB DEBUT: 2008 | POTENTIAL: Reserve 3B/1B | 6B

Pwr	+++
BAvg	+++
Spd	++
Def	+++

Year	Lev	Team	AB	R	H	HR	RBI	Avg	OB	Slg	OPS	bb%	ct%	Eye	SB	CS	X/H%	Iso	RC/G
2003	A-	Greensboro	79	7	18	2	7	228	282	354	637	7	78	0.35	1	1	33	127	3.25
2004	A+	Jupiter	426	49	92	12	58	216	274	362	635	7	68	0.25	1	2	35	146	3.26
2005	A+	Jupiter	468	65	106	14	60	226	303	378	681	10	70	0.36	4	1	40	152	3.97
2006	AA	Carolina	461	56	117	11	57	254	321	410	731	9	70	0.33	2	6	42	156	4.73
2007	AA	Carolina	451	73	127	20	73	282	380	488	868	14	66	0.47	2	1	40	206	6.99

Strong wrists and moderate bat speed was behind his best offensive output of career, though was old for level of play. Draws walks, but strikes-out too much which lowers BA. Defense at 3B is playable with average arm strength, but lacks first-step quickness.

Montero, Jesus — 23 — New York (A)

Bats R | Age 19 — 2006 FA (Venezuela)
EXP MLB DEBUT: 2011 | POTENTIAL: Starting 1B | 9D

Pwr	+++++
BAvg	++++
Spd	+
Def	+

Year	Lev	Team	AB	R	H	HR	RBI	Avg	OB	Slg	OPS	bb%	ct%	Eye	SB	CS	X/H%	Iso	RC/G
2007	Rk	GCL Yankees	107	13	30	3	19	280	353	421	774	10	83	0.67	0	0	30	140	5.15

Strong/muscular hitter with excellent bat speed and power, and enough plate discipline to hit for BA. Poor agility and receiving skills overshadow strong arm and may not be able to stay behind the plate, but bat will play at 1B. A right ankle sprain cost him the first part of season.

Moore, Adam — 2 — Seattle

Bats R | Age 24 — 2006 (6) NW Texas CC
EXP MLB DEBUT: 2009 | POTENTIAL: Platoon CA | 7D

Pwr	+++
BAvg	+++
Spd	+
Def	++

Year	Lev	Team	AB	R	H	HR	RBI	Avg	OB	Slg	OPS	bb%	ct%	Eye	SB	CS	X/H%	Iso	RC/G
2006	A-	Everett	63	8	20	0	9	317	338	460	799	3	84	0.20	0	0	45	143	5.24
2006	A-	Wisconsin	165	21	44	7	24	267	324	430	754	8	77	0.37	0	0	30	164	4.69
2007	A+	High Desert	433	74	133	22	102	307	367	543	910	9	81	0.49	1	0	41	236	6.69

Strong catcher with offensive upside and improving defense. Took advantage of his hitter-friendly environment by driving ball for power and hitting for BA with his good bat speed. Arm strength and receiving skills are solid, but needs cleaner footwork and agility.

Moore, Scott — 537 — Baltimore

Bats L | Age 24 — 2001 (1) HS (CA)
EXP MLB DEBUT: 2006 | POTENTIAL: Platoon 3B/1B | 6A

Pwr	+++
BAvg	++
Spd	++
Def	+++

Year	Lev	Team	AB	R	H	HR	RBI	Avg	OB	Slg	OPS	bb%	ct%	Eye	SB	CS	X/H%	Iso	RC/G
2006	AA	West Tenn	463	52	128	22	75	276	353	479	833	11	73	0.44	12	7	39	203	5.98
2006	AAA	Iowa	4	1	1	0	0	250	250	500	750	0	75	0.00	0	0	100	250	4.87
2006	MLB	Chicago (N)	38	6	10	2	5	263	300	474	774	5	74	0.20	0	0	40	211	4.84
2007	AAA	Iowa	321	61	85	19	69	265	360	526	887	13	69	0.48	4	3	49	262	7.01
2007	MLB	Bal/Chi (N)	52	2	12	1	11	231	245	327	572	2	67	0.06	0	1	25	96	2.14

Sustained power with bat speed and proper hitting mechanics, and OBP with improved plate discipline. A former SS, he has adapted well to both infield and outfield corners, showing arm strength and soft hands. Defensive versatility and hitting from LH side should provide opportunities.

Morales, Angel — 8 — Minnesota

Bats R | Age 18 — 2007 (3) HS (PR)
EXP MLB DEBUT: 2012 | POTENTIAL: Starting RF | 8E

Pwr	++++
BAvg	++
4.25 Spd	+++
Def	+++

Year	Lev	Team	AB	R	H	HR	RBI	Avg	OB	Slg	OPS	bb%	ct%	Eye	SB	CS	X/H%	Iso	RC/G
2007	Rk	GCL Twins	121	18	31	2	15	256	323	405	728	9	64	0.27	11	5	35	149	5.01

Top amateur in Puerto Rico possesses bat speed and power potential. Upper body swing, lack of extension, and mediocre plate discipline could cripple BA/OBP. Possesses good speed, but physical maturity will decrease steals and force him to RF where he displays a strong arm.

Morales, Jose — 2 — Minnesota

Bats B | Age 25 — 2001 (3) HS (PR)
EXP MLB DEBUT: 2007 | POTENTIAL: Platoon CA | 6B

Pwr	++
BAvg	+++
Spd	+
Def	+++

Year	Lev	Team	AB	R	H	HR	RBI	Avg	OB	Slg	OPS	bb%	ct%	Eye	SB	CS	X/H%	Iso	RC/G
2005	AA	New Britain	20	1	5	0	0	250	286	300	586	5	85	0.33	0	0	20	50	2.74
2006	AA	New Britain	251	23	54	3	27	215	270	319	589	7	78	0.34	2	1	35	104	2.72
2006	AAA	Rochester	7	0	1	0	0	143	143	143	286	0	100	0.00	0	0	0	0	0.05
2007	AAA	Rochester	376	42	117	2	37	311	362	394	761	7	88	0.68	1	4	24	88	4.99
2007	MLB	Minnesota	3	1	3	0	0	1000	1000	1333	2333	0	100	0.00	0	0	33	333	20.12

Strong/medium-built catcher with good catch-and-throw skills and ability to halt running game. Hits for BA showing contact ability from both sides, but doesn't walk or have much power. Sprained ankle in debut with Minnesota, but has chance at a reserve role to back-up Joe Mauer in 2007.

Moran, Javon — 8 — Philadelphia

Bats R | Age 25 — 2003 (5) Auburn
EXP MLB DEBUT: 2008 | POTENTIAL: Reserve CF/LF | 6C

Pwr	+
BAvg	+++
4.10 Spd	++++
Def	+++

Year	Lev	Team	AB	R	H	HR	RBI	Avg	OB	Slg	OPS	bb%	ct%	Eye	SB	CS	X/H%	Iso	RC/G
2006	AA	Chattanooga	250	34	79	1	12	316	345	396	741	4	90	0.42	16	7	19	80	4.56
2007	Rk	GCL Phillies	3	1	0	0	0	0	400	0	400	40	100	0.00	1	0	0	0	0.00
2007	A+	Clearwater	13	3	2	0	0	154	267	154	421	13	54	0.33	1	0	0	0	-0.05
2007	AA	Reading	255	52	76	2	19	298	381	384	765	12	85	0.89	24	12	21	86	5.27
2007	AAA	Ottawa	170	26	41	0	3	241	287	318	605	6	75	0.26	5	2	24	76	2.91

Incredibly fast athlete and is beginning to grasp offensive limits with focus on making contact and getting on-base. Hits pitchers from both sides equally well and is a good bunter. Range is excellent in CF and makes-up for a poor throwing arm by getting to ball quickly.

Morgan, Nyjer — 8 — Pittsburgh

Bats L | Age 27 — 2002 (33) Walla Walla C
EXP MLB DEBUT: 2007 | POTENTIAL: Reserve CF/LF | 6B

Pwr	+
BAvg	+++
Spd	+++++
Def	+++

Year	Lev	Team	AB	R	H	HR	RBI	Avg	OB	Slg	OPS	bb%	ct%	Eye	SB	CS	X/H%	Iso	RC/G
2006	AA	Lynchburg	228	43	70	0	22	307	363	364	727	8	82	0.50	35	11	14	57	4.57
2006	AA	Altoona	219	39	67	1	10	306	350	393	743	6	88	0.54	21	11	18	87	4.71
2007	Rk	GCL Pirates	13	3	4	1	1	308	400	538	938	13	77	0.67	0	0	25	231	7.17
2007	AAA	Indianapolis	164	30	50	0	10	305	363	354	717	8	83	0.54	26	7	12	49	4.46
2007	MLB	Pittsburgh	107	15	32	1	7	299	353	430	783	8	82	0.47	7	3	25	131	5.27

Athletic outfielder with plus speed, contact/bunting ability, and ability to draw walks, giving him an outside chance to be a leadoff hitter. Lacks power, is old for level, and missed at-bats with a torn thumb ligament. Chases flyballs well to gaps, though his arm strength is below average.

Morrison,Logan — 3 — Florida

EXP MLB DEBUT: 2010 | POTENTIAL: Platoon 1B | **8E**

Bats L Age 20	Year	Lev	Team	AB	R	H	HR	RBI	Avg	OB	Slg	OPS	bb%	ct%	Eye	SB	CS	X/H%	Iso	RC/G
2005 (22) HS (FL)																				
Pwr ++++																				
BAvg +++	2006	Rk	GCL Marlins	89	10	24	1	7	270	343	348	692	10	87	0.83	1	0	21	79	4.29
Spd +	2006	A-	Jamestown	74	6	15	1	11	203	306	284	590	13	77	0.65	0	0	27	81	2.93
Def ++	2007	A-	Greensboro	453	71	121	24	86	267	337	483	821	10	79	0.50	2	2	40	216	5.61

Strong wrists and natural strength give him excellent power to pull field. Patient enough to draw walks and may be able to hit for BA, but struggles against LH pitching and breaking balls. Speed and defense is below average, but has the work ethic to bring his defense to average.

Morton,Colt — 2 — San Diego

EXP MLB DEBUT: 2007 | POTENTIAL: Platoon CA/1B | **7C**

Bats R Age 26	Year	Lev	Team	AB	R	H	HR	RBI	Avg	OB	Slg	OPS	bb%	ct%	Eye	SB	CS	X/H%	Iso	RC/G
2003 (3) No Carolina St	2006	AA	Mobile	139	15	37	6	21	266	320	468	788	7	68	0.25	0	0	43	201	5.41
Pwr ++++	2007	Rk	AZL Padres	31	9	9	0	8	290	389	419	808	14	65	0.45	0	0	44	129	6.53
BAvg +	2007	A+	Lk Elsinore	24	5	12	3	8	500	571	1167	1738	14	88	1.33	0	0	83	667	16.60
4.50 Spd ++	2007	AA	San Antonio	94	17	25	6	19	266	367	489	856	14	64	0.44	0	0	36	223	6.76
Def ++	2007	MLB	San Diego	1	0	0	0	0	0	0	0	0	0	100	0.00	0	0	0	0	0.00

Tall/muscular catcher with bat speed and raw power who is making it more game-usable. Swing can get lengthy and struggles with breaking pitches which will hinder BA. Long actions and marginal receiving skills negate arm strength and agility, but could form platoon combination.

Moses,Matt — 5 — Minnesota

EXP MLB DEBUT: 2008 | POTENTIAL: Platoon 3B | **7E**

Bats L Age 23	Year	Lev	Team	AB	R	H	HR	RBI	Avg	OB	Slg	OPS	bb%	ct%	Eye	SB	CS	X/H%	Iso	RC/G
2003 (1) HS (VA)	2005	A+	Fort Myers	265	37	81	7	42	306	372	453	825	10	78	0.47	13	4	30	147	5.81
Pwr +++	2005	AA	New Britain	186	25	39	6	30	210	265	366	631	7	73	0.27	3	2	41	156	3.12
BAvg +++	2006	AA	New Britain	474	47	118	15	72	249	301	386	687	7	76	0.31	2	2	28	137	3.82
4.35 Spd ++	2007	AA	New Britain	262	30	69	4	44	263	308	401	709	6	81	0.33	7	0	41	137	4.23
Def ++	2007	AAA	Rochester	174	15	39	2	18	224	242	305	546	2	76	0.10	5	3	26	80	1.87

Short/muscular hitter missed part of 2007 with a disc injury at the neck level. Drives ball to gaps with bat speed and strong wrists, but lacks BA ability with poor pitch recognition and struggles versus LH pitching. Average defender with soft hands and average arm strength.

Moss,Brandon — 9 — Boston

EXP MLB DEBUT: 2007 | POTENTIAL: Platoon LF/RF | **7B**

Bats L Age 24	Year	Lev	Team	AB	R	H	HR	RBI	Avg	OB	Slg	OPS	bb%	ct%	Eye	SB	CS	X/H%	Iso	RC/G
2002 (8) HS (GA)	2004	A-	Augusta	433	66	147	13	101	339	403	515	918	10	83	0.61	19	8	30	176	6.90
Pwr +++	2005	AA	Portland	503	87	135	16	61	268	338	441	779	10	74	0.41	6	3	38	173	5.27
BAvg +++	2006	AA	Portland	508	76	145	12	83	285	356	439	795	10	79	0.52	8	5	35	154	5.48
4.30 Spd +++	2007	AAA	Pawtucket	493	66	139	16	78	282	361	471	832	11	70	0.41	3	5	42	189	6.22
Def +++	2007	MLB	Boston	25	6	7	0	1	280	379	440	819	14	76	0.67	0	0	43	160	6.28

Muscular athlete improved approach and began using whole field which kept BA high without sacrificing power. Struggles against LH pitching which may reduce him to a platoon role. Arm strength plays at any outfield spot, but needs to take better routes. Will play some 1B during winter.

Mount,Ryan — 46 — Los Angeles (A)

EXP MLB DEBUT: 2010 | POTENTIAL: Reserve 2B/SS | **7D**

Bats L Age 21	Year	Lev	Team	AB	R	H	HR	RBI	Avg	OB	Slg	OPS	bb%	ct%	Eye	SB	CS	X/H%	Iso	RC/G
2005 (2) HS (CA)																				
Pwr ++	2005	Rk	AZL Angels	102	15	22	1	17	216	328	333	661	14	70	0.55	4	1	41	118	4.00
BAvg +++	2006	Rk	Orem	277	54	79	9	39	285	367	448	815	12	76	0.54	10	3	32	162	5.79
Spd ++++	2007	Rk	AZL Angels	12	0	4	0	0	333	385	333	718	8	92	1.00	0	0	0	0	4.52
Def ++++	2007	A-	Cedar Rapids	303	47	76	7	36	251	316	376	693	9	77	0.41	19	6	28	125	4.06

Wiry athlete with plus speed that impacts game, but hasn't produced offensively. Makes good contact, but medium bat speed prevents hitting for power and doesn't draw enough walks. Possesses arm strength and range that plays at both middle infield spots.

Moustakas,Mike — 6 — Kansas City

EXP MLB DEBUT: 2010 | POTENTIAL: Starting SS | **9D**

Bats L Age 19	Year	Lev	Team	AB	R	H	HR	RBI	Avg	OB	Slg	OPS	bb%	ct%	Eye	SB	CS	X/H%	Iso	RC/G
2007 (1) HS (CA)																				
Pwr ++++																				
BAvg ++++																				
Spd ++																				
Def ++	2007	Rk	Idaho Falls	41	6	12	0	10	293	293	439	732	0	100		4	8	42	146	4.56

Aggressive hitter with excellent bat speed, strong hands, and plus power potential. Makes hard contact, but has to do better against breaking pitches and draw more walks. Possesses plus arm strength, but below average speed hinders range. KC seems content on leaving him at SS.

Mulhern,Ryan — 3 — Cleveland

EXP MLB DEBUT: 2008 | POTENTIAL: Reserve 1B | **6C**

Bats R Age 27	Year	Lev	Team	AB	R	H	HR	RBI	Avg	OB	Slg	OPS	bb%	ct%	Eye	SB	CS	X/H%	Iso	RC/G
2003 (11) South Alabam	2004	A-	Lake Cty	372	48	95	7	42	255	314	392	707	8	77	0.37	3	2	38	137	4.26
Pwr ++++	2005	A+	Kinston	159	32	51	17	48	321	393	711	1104	11	69	0.38	2	2	55	390	9.83
BAvg ++	2005	AA	Akron	244	40	76	15	46	311	382	594	977	10	74	0.44	4	2	47	283	7.89
Spd +	2006	AA	Akron	452	65	121	15	69	268	327	438	765	8	73	0.33	1	0	36	170	5.02
Def ++	2007	AAA	Buffalo	476	67	138	16	76	290	350	475	825	8	72	0.30	1	3	39	185	5.84

Strong/muscular hitter with bat speed and ability to hammer LH pitching. Plate discipline has disintegrated at upper levels and swings aggressively during entire at-bat, lowing BA and OBP. Below average speed and stiff hands give him little value outside of his bat.

Murphy,Dan — 5 — New York (N)

EXP MLB DEBUT: 2009 | POTENTIAL: Platoon 3B/1B | **8E**

Bats L Age 23	Year	Lev	Team	AB	R	H	HR	RBI	Avg	OB	Slg	OPS	bb%	ct%	Eye	SB	CS	X/H%	Iso	RC/G
2006 (13) Jacksonville																				
Pwr +++	2006	Rk	GCL Mets	18	2	1	0	0	56	227	56	283	18	83	1.33	0	0	0	0	1.01
BAvg ++++	2006	Rk	Kingsport	33	2	9	2	7	273	351	455	806	11	97	4.00	0	0	22	182	5.33
Spd ++	2006	Rk	Brooklyn	29	2	7	0	3	241	324	276	600	12	90	1.33	0	0	14	34	3.22
Def +	2007	A+	St. Lucie	502	68	143	11	78	285	338	430	768	8	88	0.69	6	3	34	145	5.00

Combination of plate discipline, moderate bat speed, and short path to baseball gives him BA ability and moderate power. Uses whole field and will shorten-up with two strikes. Possesses arm strength at 3B, but lacks first-step quickness and playable hands which attributed to 35 errors.

Murphy,David — 8 — Texas

EXP MLB DEBUT: 2006 | POTENTIAL: Platoon CF/RF | **7B**

Bats L Age 26	Year	Lev	Team	AB	R	H	HR	RBI	Avg	OB	Slg	OPS	bb%	ct%	Eye	SB	CS	X/H%	Iso	RC/G
2003 (1) Baylor	2006	AA	Portland	172	22	47	3	25	273	317	436	753	6	83	0.38	4	2	45	163	4.79
Pwr +++	2006	AAA	Pawtucket	318	45	85	8	44	267	358	447	805	12	83	0.85	3	3	42	179	5.75
BAvg ++	2006	MLB	Boston	22	4	5	1	2	227	346	409	755	15	82	1.00	0	0	40	182	5.11
4.15 Spd +++	2007	AAA	Paw/OC	407	50	114	9	47	280	346	420	766	9	83	0.58	8	2	30	140	5.05
Def ++++	2007	MLB	Boston/Texas	105	17	36	2	14	343	384	552	936	6	81	0.35	0	0	44	210	7.10

Athletic outfielder acquitted himself well in Sept trial. Uses whole field, can hit for BA, and drove ball more consistently. Runs bases aggressively and will steal on occasion. Defensively, he has no flaws, possessing excellent range and arm strength in all three outfield positions.

Myers,D'Arby — 8 — Philadelphia

EXP MLB DEBUT: 2011 | POTENTIAL: Platoon CF/LF | **7E**

Bats R Age 19	Year	Lev	Team	AB	R	H	HR	RBI	Avg	OB	Slg	OPS	bb%	ct%	Eye	SB	CS	X/H%	Iso	RC/G
2006 (14) HS (CA)																				
Pwr ++																				
BAvg ++																				
4.00 Spd +++++	2006	Rk	GCL Phillies	128	20	40	2	13	313	348	430	778	5	75	0.22	11	4	25	117	5.04
Def +++	2007	A-	Williamsport	179	28	43	1	17	240	284	296	580	6	81	0.32	11	6	19	56	2.59

Fastest player in organization and can be very disruptive, but needs to find a way to get to first base. Has some juice in his bat with moderate bat speed, but struggles to make contact, swing is long, and rarely walks. Possesses plus range in CF, but arm strength is slightly below average.

Natale,Jeff — 34 — Boston

EXP MLB DEBUT: 2008 | POTENTIAL: Reserve 2B/1B | **6C**

Bats R Age 25	Year	Lev	Team	AB	R	H	HR	RBI	Avg	OB	Slg	OPS	bb%	ct%	Eye	SB	CS	X/H%	Iso	RC/G
2005 (32) Trinity	2005	A-	Lowell	41	9	20	0	9	488	523	610	1132	7	93	1.00	2	0	25	122	9.08
Pwr ++	2005	AA	Greenville	160	35	54	2	35	338	436	544	980	15	91	2.00	1	0	46	206	8.13
BAvg ++++	2006	A+	Wilmington	273	46	75	7	46	275	409	399	808	19	80	1.15	1	0	27	125	6.05
4.30 Spd +++	2006	AA	Greenville	175	38	59	10	41	337	463	566	1029	19	89	2.05	2	1	34	229	8.64
Def ++	2007	AA	Portland	404	66	109	5	64	270	400	381	782	18	91	2.44	5	3	31	111	5.98

Exceptional plate discipline drives BA/OBP and his contact ability makes him a solid situational hitter. Lacks secondary skills of power and speed which limits overall offense. Stiff hands and below average arm strength make him a defensive liability and split time between 1B and 2B.

Navarro, Oswaldo — 64 — Seattle

EXP MLB DEBUT: 2006 | POTENTIAL: Reserve SS/2B | 6C
Bats R | Age 23 | 2001 FA (Venezuela)

Ratings	
Pwr	+
BAvg	++
Spd	++++
Def	++++

Year	Lev	Team	AB	R	H	HR	RBI	Avg	OB	Slg	OPS	bb%	ct%	Eye	SB	CS	X/H%	Iso	RC/G
2005	A-	Wisconsin	450	57	121	9	69	269	327	393	721	8	87	0.65	11	7	31	124	4.49
2006	AA	San Antonio	266	27	71	1	24	267	361	335	695	13	79	0.68	7	6	21	68	4.40
2006	AAA	Tacoma	183	15	45	2	21	246	317	328	645	9	82	0.58	1	2	24	82	3.59
2006	MLB	Seattle	3	0	2	0	0	667	667	667	1333	0	67	0.00	0	0	0	0	12.86
2007	AAA	Tacoma	446	51	111	4	45	249	301	323	623	7	81	0.38	4	3	23	74	3.17

Plus defender at both middle infield positions with quick hands, plus range, and average arm strength. Offense is severely limited as he lacks power and plate discipline, making his BA the only positive marker. Despite good speed, he isn't much of a threat on the bases.

Navarro, Reynaldo — 6 — Arizona

EXP MLB DEBUT: 2012 | POTENTIAL: Starting SS | 8E
Bats B | Age 18 | 2007 (3) HS (PR)

Ratings	
Pwr	+++
BAvg	+++
Spd (3.90)	+++++
Def	++

Year	Lev	Team	AB	R	H	HR	RBI	Avg	OB	Slg	OPS	bb%	ct%	Eye	SB	CS	X/H%	Iso	RC/G
2007	Rk	Missoula	212	21	53	1	17	250	271	283	554	3	81	0.15	6	3	9	33	2.04

Light-framed athlete with plus speed, he hits for BA and moderate power with good bat speed and a short swing path. Plate discipline is a problem and lacks instincts. Possesses plus range at SS, but stiff hands and a tendency to rush throws cost him 28 errors defensively.

Navarro, Yamaico — 65 — Boston

EXP MLB DEBUT: 2011 | POTENTIAL: Starting SS | 9E
Bats R | Age 19 | 2006 FA (DR)

Ratings	
Pwr	+++
BAvg	++++
Spd (4.25)	++++
Def	+++

Year	Lev	Team	AB	R	H	HR	RBI	Avg	OB	Slg	OPS	bb%	ct%	Eye	SB	CS	X/H%	Iso	RC/G
2007	A-	Lowell	225	36	65	5	37	289	352	409	761	9	77	0.42	12	6	25	120	4.95

High-energy infielder with offensive potential based on moderate bat speed and ability to draw walks. Struck-out close to 25% of the time and has to tone-down aggressiveness. Shows above average speed on the bases and is an average defender with arm strength and range.

Neal, Thomas — 9 — San Francisco

EXP MLB DEBUT: 2010 | POTENTIAL: Starting RF | 8E
Bats R | Age 20 | 2005 (36) Riverside CC

Ratings	
Pwr	++++
BAvg	+++
Spd	++
Def	+++

Year	Lev	Team	AB	R	H	HR	RBI	Avg	OB	Slg	OPS	bb%	ct%	Eye	SB	CS	X/H%	Iso	RC/G
2006	A-	Salem-Keizer	176	26	44	4	20	250	279	375	654	4	75	0.16	1	3	27	125	3.31
2007	Rk	AZL Giants	39	7	12	1	4	308	386	462	848	11	82	0.71	0	0	33	154	6.18

Strong/muscular player missed most of 2007 season with right shoulder surgery. Possesses excellent bat speed and power, but can hit for BA despite below average plate discipline. Forced to DH for most of 2007, but has the arm strength and enough range to play a solid RF.

Nelson, Chris — 6 — Colorado

EXP MLB DEBUT: 2009 | POTENTIAL: Starting SS | 9D
Bats R | Age 22 | 2004 (1) HS (GA)

Ratings	
Pwr	+++
BAvg	++++
Spd (4.05)	+++++
Def	+++

Year	Lev	Team	AB	R	H	HR	RBI	Avg	OB	Slg	OPS	bb%	ct%	Eye	SB	CS	X/H%	Iso	RC/G
2004	Rk	Casper	147	36	51	4	20	347	432	510	942	12	71	0.48	6	5	25	163	7.98
2005	A-	Asheville	315	51	76	3	38	241	297	330	627	7	72	0.28	7	4	25	89	3.19
2006	A-	Asheville	466	69	121	11	76	260	307	416	724	6	78	0.32	14	2	41	157	4.38
2007	A+	Modesto	529	97	153	19	99	289	358	503	861	9	83	0.60	27	5	38	214	6.44

Plus athlete put himself back on prospect map. Bat speed, lower hand position, and improved plate discipline gave him solid power and BA ability. Utilizes plus speed to steal bases. Possesses plus arm strength, soft hands, and range, though a lack of concentration resulted in 31 errors.

Nix, Jayson — 4 — Colorado

EXP MLB DEBUT: 2008 | POTENTIAL: Platoon 2B | 7C
Bats R | Age 25 | 2001 (1-S) HS (TX)

Ratings	
Pwr	+++
BAvg	++
Spd (4.30)	+++
Def	+++

Year	Lev	Team	AB	R	H	HR	RBI	Avg	OB	Slg	OPS	bb%	ct%	Eye	SB	CS	X/H%	Iso	RC/G
2003	A+	Visalia	562	107	158	21	86	281	344	475	819	9	77	0.41	24	8	42	194	5.69
2004	AA	Tulsa	456	58	97	14	58	213	276	346	623	8	78	0.40	14	3	33	134	3.08
2005	AA	Tulsa	501	68	118	11	47	236	277	355	633	5	82	0.32	10	6	32	120	3.19
2006	AAA	Colo Springs	358	39	90	2	26	251	313	313	626	8	83	0.52	15	3	19	61	3.33
2007	AAA	Colo Springs	439	80	128	11	58	292	338	451	789	7	82	0.39	24	8	36	159	5.18

Strong/muscular infielder improved all facets of game and was MVP of World Cup. Raising hands and shortening stride allowed him to make better contact and drive ball better. Arm strength, soft hands, and better positioning elevated defense to above average.

Noonan, Nick — 46 — San Francisco

EXP MLB DEBUT: 2011 | POTENTIAL: Starting 2B | 9E
Bats L | Age 19 | 2007 (1-S) HS (CA)

Ratings	
Pwr	+++
BAvg	++++
Spd (4.15)	++++
Def	++

Year	Lev	Team	AB	R	H	HR	RBI	Avg	OB	Slg	OPS	bb%	ct%	Eye	SB	CS	X/H%	Iso	RC/G
2007	Rk	AZL Giants	206	33	65	3	40	316	353	451	805	6	90	0.60	18	3	28	136	5.37

Offensive-oriented infielder who uses whole field to hit for BA and moderate power. Judges strike zone well, giving him good pitches to hit. Speed is above average and is instinctive on bases. Arm strength and range are fringe-average for SS and will move strictly to 2B eventually.

Nunez, Eduardo — 6 — New York (A)

EXP MLB DEBUT: 2009 | POTENTIAL: Reserve SS/2B | 7D
Bats B | Age 21 | 2004 FA (DR)

Ratings	
Pwr	++
BAvg	++
Spd	++++
Def	++++

Year	Lev	Team	AB	R	H	HR	RBI	Avg	OB	Slg	OPS	bb%	ct%	Eye	SB	CS	X/H%	Iso	RC/G
2005	A-	Staten Island	281	37	88	3	46	313	359	427	786	7	85	0.47	6	3	23	114	5.19
2006	A-	Charleston	339	35	78	2	39	230	279	298	577	6	86	0.48	14	5	21	68	2.75
2006	A+	Tampa	147	17	27	4	26	184	226	340	566	5	81	0.29	6	1	44	156	2.38
2007	A-	Charleston	328	36	78	1	28	238	292	290	581	7	87	0.60	20	8	17	52	2.89
2007	A+	Tampa	123	16	35	1	13	285	323	350	673	5	85	0.39	9	0	17	65	3.74

Wiry strong athlete with plus defense, featuring plus arm strength and range. Proficient base-thief with his solid speed, but struggles to get on-base with a questionable walk rate. Has enough bat speed to project moderate power, but has yet to display it in game action.

Oeder, Ross — 46 — St. Louis

EXP MLB DEBUT: 2010 | POTENTIAL: Reserve 2B/SS | 6C
Bats R | Age 23 | 2007 (28) Wright St

Ratings	
Pwr	+
BAvg	+++
Spd (4.20)	++++
Def	+++

Year	Lev	Team	AB	R	H	HR	RBI	Avg	OB	Slg	OPS	bb%	ct%	Eye	SB	CS	X/H%	Iso	RC/G
2007	A-	Batavia	148	18	40	0	8	270	321	304	625	7	77	0.32	7	2	13	34	3.14

Short/athletic infielder with plus instincts that allow him to play above tools. Makes excellent contact to all fields and run bases with abandon, but doesn't hit for power and will need to improve walk rate. Soft/quick hands and range play well in middle infield with enough arm for SS.

Oeltjen, Trent — 7 — Minnesota

EXP MLB DEBUT: 2008 | POTENTIAL: Reserve LF/RF | 6B
Bats L | Age 25 | 2001 FA (Australia)

Ratings	
Pwr	++
BAvg	+++
Spd (4.05)	++++
Def	+++

Year	Lev	Team	AB	R	H	HR	RBI	Avg	OB	Slg	OPS	bb%	ct%	Eye	SB	CS	X/H%	Iso	RC/G
2003	A-	Quad Cities	466	73	139	4	44	298	350	384	734	7	88	0.65	29	14	17	86	4.65
2004	A+	Fort Myers	324	45	90	2	28	278	316	352	668	5	81	0.30	25	8	17	74	3.64
2005	A+	Fort Myers	341	44	98	4	43	287	338	396	734	7	77	0.34	21	9	26	109	4.57
2006	AA	New Britain	400	61	120	3	44	300	358	413	770	8	86	0.62	23	11	24	113	5.15
2007	AAA	Rochester	244	33	58	2	23	238	268	340	608	4	82	0.23	14	7	28	102	2.90

Athletic outfielder with above average speed and instincts. Struggled with plate discipline and was more aggressive which cut-into BA, with power being non-existent. Possesses range at all three outfield spots, but prior elbow surgery leaves him with below average arm strength.

Orr, Kyle — 3 — Los Angeles (N)

EXP MLB DEBUT: 2011 | POTENTIAL: Starting 1B/RF | 9E
Bats L | Age 19 | 2006 (4) HS (Canada)

Ratings	
Pwr	++++
BAvg	+++
Spd	++
Def	+++

Year	Lev	Team	AB	R	H	HR	RBI	Avg	OB	Slg	OPS	bb%	ct%	Eye	SB	CS	X/H%	Iso	RC/G
2007	Rk	GCL Dodgers	158	25	36	3	19	228	311	329	640	11	70	0.40	1	1	28	101	3.43

Tall/strapping hitter who generates tremendous power with plus bat speed and extension. Judges strike zone, but pitchers got underneath his long arms, decreasing BA. Possesses agility and soft hands at 1B, but has enough arm and range to play corner outfield.

BATTERS

Ortiz,Adrian — 8 — Kansas City

EXP MLB DEBUT: 2010 | POTENTIAL: Platoon CF/LF | 7E

Bats L Age 21 | 2007 (5) Pepperdine | Pwr + | BAvg +++ | 3.90 Spd +++++ | Def ++++

Year	Lev	Team	AB	R	H	HR	RBI	Avg	OB	Slg	OPS	bb%	ct%	Eye	SB	CS	X/H%	Iso	RC/G
2007	Rk	Idaho Falls	264	44	86	0	24	326	348	367	715	3	86	0.25	17	7	12	42	4.12

Solid athlete with plus speed, his offense centers around his BA and ability to steal bases. Medium bat speed prevents him from hitting for power, but is patient enough to draw walks. Possesses excellent range in CF, but arm strength is below average which could be a problem.

Ortiz,Jamie — 3 — Los Angeles (N)

EXP MLB DEBUT: 2012 | POTENTIAL: Starting 1B | 8E

Bats R Age 19 | 2006 (7) HS (PR) | Pwr ++++ | BAvg ++ | Spd + | Def ++

Year	Lev	Team	AB	R	H	HR	RBI	Avg	OB	Slg	OPS	bb%	ct%	Eye	SB	CS	X/H%	Iso	RC/G
2006	Rk	GCL Dodgers	181	21	42	2	22	232	310	304	614	9	75	0.40	1	2	19	72	2.88
2007	Rk	Ogden	226	30	62	11	35	274	333	473	806	5	73	0.21	0	0	35	199	5.70

Tall power hitter with bat speed and strong wrists. Tends to be pull-conscious, overly aggressive, and doesn't hit LH pitching, which dampens BA. Adds little in the way of speed and agility, but can be an average defender with soft hands and average arm strength.

Owings,Jon Mark — 9 — Atlanta

EXP MLB DEBUT: 2010 | POTENTIAL: Platoon RF/LF | 7E

Bats R Age 23 | 2004 (17) HS (GA) | Pwr ++++ | BAvg ++ | 4.30 Spd +++ | Def +++

Year	Lev	Team	AB	R	H	HR	RBI	Avg	OB	Slg	OPS	bb%	ct%	Eye	SB	CS	X/H%	Iso	RC/G
2005	Rk	Danville	116	27	34	12	31	293	328	707	1035	5	73	0.19	1	2	65	414	8.25
2006	Rk	Danville	162	28	46	8	29	284	337	519	856	7	80	0.41	2	1	46	235	5.97
2006	Rk	GCL Braves	38	5	14	0	6	368	455	474	928	14	84	1.00	2	0	29	105	7.45
2006	A-	Rome	24	2	4	1	2	167	200	333	533	4	75	0.17	0	0	50	167	1.66
2007	A-	Rome	403	62	103	16	51	256	314	432	745	8	77	0.36	10	7	36	176	4.62

Strong/athletic outfielder with solid bat speed and power potential, but lacks the contact ability and plate discipline to make it game-usable. Hitting for BA will be an afterthought and has a platoon differential. Possesses arm strength and average range in corners.

Palmisano,Lou — 2 — Milwaukee

EXP MLB DEBUT: 2009 | POTENTIAL: Platoon CA | 7C

Bats R Age 25 | 2003 (3) Broward CC | Pwr +++ | BAvg ++ | Spd + | Def ++

Year	Lev	Team	AB	R	H	HR	RBI	Avg	OB	Slg	OPS	bb%	ct%	Eye	SB	CS	X/H%	Iso	RC/G
2003	Rk	Helena	174	32	68	6	43	391	448	592	1040	9	83	0.62	13	2	31	201	8.33
2004	A-	Beloit	409	59	120	7	65	293	361	413	774	10	77	0.46	3	2	27	120	5.19
2005	A+	Brevard Co	432	47	110	5	49	255	309	359	668	7	85	0.52	3	1	25	104	3.84
2006	AA	Huntsville	332	39	80	4	37	241	337	334	671	13	80	0.74	2	0	28	93	4.07
2007	AA	Huntsville	351	49	90	11	63	256	360	419	779	14	77	0.71	8	2	38	162	5.43

Shortened swing and laid-off high fastballs, which gave him better contact ability and power. Bat speed remains strong and improved plate discipline. Arm strength and receiving skills are solid, but doesn't show much agility behind the plate and release is slow (2.05).

Parmalee,Chris — 93 — Minnesota

EXP MLB DEBUT: 2010 | POTENTIAL: Starting RF | 8D

Bats L Age 20 | 2006 (1) HS (CA) | Pwr ++++ | BAvg +++ | Spd ++ | Def ++

Year	Lev	Team	AB	R	H	HR	RBI	Avg	OB	Slg	OPS	bb%	ct%	Eye	SB	CS	X/H%	Iso	RC/G
2006	Rk	GCL Twins	154	29	43	8	32	279	373	532	905	13	69	0.49	3	3	44	253	7.31
2006	A-	Beloit	22	2	5	0	2	227	370	273	643	19	59	0.56	0	2	20	45	4.01
2007	A-	Beloit	447	56	107	15	70	239	313	414	727	9	69	0.34	8	4	40	174	4.81

Struggled in full-season league, failing to hit for BA due to mediocre plate discipline, contact rate, and a long swing. Possesses excellent bat speed and hit for power, but will have to make adjustments. Adapting well to RF where he displays good arm strength and average range.

Parraz,Jordan — 9 — Houston

EXP MLB DEBUT: 2009 | POTENTIAL: Starting RF | 8C

Bats L Age 23 | 2004 (3) So Nevada CC | Pwr ++++ | BAvg +++ | 4.30 Spd +++ | Def +++

Year	Lev	Team	AB	R	H	HR	RBI	Avg	OB	Slg	OPS	bb%	ct%	Eye	SB	CS	X/H%	Iso	RC/G
2004	Rk	Greeneville	180	35	44	4	21	244	333	400	733	12	76	0.55	8	5	34	156	4.81
2005	A-	Tri City	282	31	73	5	35	259	289	365	654	4	84	0.26	17	3	25	106	3.41
2006	A-	Tri City	253	46	85	6	38	336	413	494	907	12	83	0.75	22	3	31	158	6.92
2007	A-	Lexington	462	69	130	14	76	281	348	446	794	9	81	0.53	33	10	35	165	5.36

Tall/athletic outfielder adjusted to full-season baseball, showing solid secondary skills. Makes contact and drives ball from RF to LC and is a good runner underway, giving him SB capability. Features plus arm strength and above average range, and fits the perfect RF profile.

Parra,Gerardo — 8 — Arizona

EXP MLB DEBUT: 2010 | POTENTIAL: Starting CF | 8C

Bats L Age 20 | 2004 FA (Venezuela) | Pwr ++ | BAvg +++ | 4.20 Spd ++++ | Def ++++

Year	Lev	Team	AB	R	H	HR	RBI	Avg	OB	Slg	OPS	bb%	ct%	Eye	SB	CS	X/H%	Iso	RC/G
2006	Rk	Missoula	265	43	86	4	43	325	385	464	849	9	89	0.87	23	8	29	140	6.10
2006	Rk	Missoula	45	43	11	0	8	244	306	289	595	8	93	1.33	1	0	18	44	3.37
2007	A-	South Bend	444	64	142	6	57	320	363	435	798	6	89	0.59	24	8	25	115	5.30
2007	A+	Visalia	102	11	29	2	14	284	311	382	694	4	83	0.24	2	3	17	98	3.81

Athletic outfielder led MWL in BA with quick stroke and a bat that stays in the strike zone a long time. Power is of gap variety and could improve as he gets stronger. Intelligent baserunner with fringe-average speed. Possesses plus arm strength and solid range, playing both RF and CF.

Pascucci,Val — 3 — Philadelphia

EXP MLB DEBUT: 2004 | POTENTIAL: Platoon 1B | 6B

Bats R Age 29 | 1999 (15) Oklahoma | Pwr ++++ | BAvg ++ | Spd + | Def +

Year	Lev	Team	AB	R	H	HR	RBI	Avg	OB	Slg	OPS	bb%	ct%	Eye	SB	CS	X/H%	Iso	RC/G
2003	AAA	Edmonton	459	80	129	15	85	281	411	447	857	18	71	0.77	3	2	35	166	6.81
2004	AAA	Edmonton	392	83	117	25	92	298	415	577	991	17	76	0.82	9	2	50	278	8.30
2004	MLB	Montreal	62	6	11	2	6	177	292	290	582	14	65	0.45	1	0	27	113	2.55
2007	AAA	Albuquerque	447	93	127	34	98	284	377	577	955	13	72	0.54	9	1	49	293	7.66

Combines bat speed and plus strength to generate power to all fields, and led PCL in HR. Will draw walks, but will strike-out in droves and can be gotten out by good pitching or anything with a wrinkle. Defense is well below average and is a clogger on bases.

Patterson,Eric — 47 — Chicago (N)

EXP MLB DEBUT: 2007 | POTENTIAL: Starting 2B | 8C

Bats L Age 25 | 2004 (8) Georgia Tech | Pwr ++ | BAvg +++ | 4.05 Spd ++++ | Def +++

Year	Lev	Team	AB	R	H	HR	RBI	Avg	OB	Slg	OPS	bb%	ct%	Eye	SB	CS	X/H%	Iso	RC/G
2005	A-	Peoria	432	90	144	13	71	333	406	535	941	11	78	0.56	40	11	35	201	7.43
2006	AA	West Tenn	441	66	116	8	47	263	333	408	741	9	80	0.52	37	12	34	145	4.80
2006	AAA	Iowa	67	14	23	2	11	343	397	478	875	8	87	0.67	8	0	17	134	6.19
2007	AAA	Iowa	516	94	153	14	65	297	363	455	819	9	84	0.64	24	9	31	159	5.69
2007	MLB	Chicago (N)	8	0	2	0	0	250	250	375	625	0	63	0.00	0	0	50	125	3.32

Continued offensive excellence, but ran into roadblocks for playing time. Plus speed is best asset, but hits for BA, drills mistake pitches, and draws walks. Plus range and soft hands highlight defensive skills and has average arm strength. CHC played him in CF/LF to improve versatility.

Patterson,Ryan — 8 — Toronto

EXP MLB DEBUT: 2008 | POTENTIAL: Platoon RF/LF | 7C

Bats R Age 25 | 2005 (4) Louisiana St | Pwr ++++ | BAvg ++ | 4.35 Spd ++ | Def +++

Year	Lev	Team	AB	R	H	HR	RBI	Avg	OB	Slg	OPS	bb%	ct%	Eye	SB	CS	X/H%	Iso	RC/G
2005	A-	Auburn	274	52	93	13	65	339	386	595	981	7	81	0.40	5	2	43	255	7.53
2006	A+	Dunedin	353	66	101	19	68	286	326	516	842	6	83	0.34	2	4	43	229	5.61
2006	AA	New Hamp	183	19	48	6	20	262	311	448	759	7	73	0.27	2	0	44	186	4.89
2007	A+	Dunedin	21	1	4	0	1	190	261	286	547	9	86	0.67	0	0	50	95	2.63
2007	AA	New Hamp	446	53	119	18	68	267	303	448	751	5	77	0.23	1	4	38	182	4.54

Bat speed and aggressiveness make him a constant threat for power. Sacrificed plate discipline with negative results to BA and OBP. Torches LH pitching and has a knack for driving-in runs. Defensively, his skills are average at best, which makes it necessary for his bat to play up.

Paul,Xavier — 8 — Los Angeles (N)

EXP MLB DEBUT: 2008 | POTENTIAL: Reserve LF/RF | 6B

Bats L Age 23 | 2003 (4) HS (LA) | Pwr +++ | BAvg ++ | 4.10 Spd +++ | Def +++

Year	Lev	Team	AB	R	H	HR	RBI	Avg	OB	Slg	OPS	bb%	ct%	Eye	SB	CS	X/H%	Iso	RC/G
2003	Rk	Ogden	264	60	81	7	47	307	386	489	875	11	78	0.59	11	4	35	182	6.61
2004	A	Columbus	465	69	122	9	72	262	342	402	744	11	73	0.44	10	7	34	140	4.94
2005	A+	Vero Beach	288	42	71	7	41	247	322	392	714	10	72	0.40	1	5	35	146	4.47
2006	A+	Vero Beach	470	62	134	13	49	285	339	430	768	7	76	0.33	23	15	29	145	4.97
2007	AA	Jacksonville	422	64	123	11	50	291	364	429	793	10	73	0.43	17	9	28	137	5.49

Athletic outfielder with solid secondary skills, but lacks bat to be a MLB starter. Drives ball hard to gaps and can hit for BA, but high strikeout rate limits power. Runs bases well with above average speed. Possesses strong throwing arm, but marginal range limits him to corners.

Payne, Danny — 8 — San Diego

Bats L — **Age** 22 — 2007 (1-S) Georgia Tech
EXP MLB DEBUT: 2009 — POTENTIAL: Reserve CF/LF — **7C**

Pwr +
BAvg +++
Spd ++++
Def +++

Year	Lev	Team	AB	R	H	HR	RBI	Avg	OB	Slg	OPS	bb%	ct%	Eye	SB	CS	X/H%	Iso	RC/G
2007	A-	Eugene	183	35	51	0	21	279	441	355	796	22	71	1.00	17	3	22	77	6.33
2007	A	Ft. Wayne	7	2	0	0	1	0	222	0	222	22	14	0.33	0	0	0	0	0.00

Short/athletic outfielder with excellent speed and aggressive style of play. Hits for BA and will draw walks, but lacks power due to slight frame. Arm strength and range fit well in CF. Bat may not make him an everyday regular, but could have value as platoon or fourth outfielder.

Pearce, Steven — 39 — Pittsburgh

Bats R — **Age** 25 — 2005 (8) So Carolina
EXP MLB DEBUT: 2008 — POTENTIAL: Starting RF/1B — **8B**

Pwr ++++
BAvg +++
Spd ++
Def ++

Year	Lev	Team	AB	R	H	HR	RBI	Avg	OB	Slg	OPS	bb%	ct%	Eye	SB	CS	X/H%	Iso	RC/G
2006	A+	Lynchburg	328	48	87	14	60	365	334	482	816	9	80	0.52	7	5	48	216	5.62
2007	A+	Lynchburg	75	19	26	11	24	347	412	867	1279	10	83	0.62	2	0	62	520	10.21
2007	AA	Altoona	290	57	97	14	72	334	400	586	986	10	84	0.73	7	2	44	252	8.66
2007	AAA	Indianapolis	122	18	39	6	17	320	366	557	923	5	90	0.50	5	0	41	238	8.35
2007	MLB	Pittsburgh	68	13	20	0	6	294	342	397	779	10	83	0.42	2	1	30	103	5.41

Strong hands, bat speed, and plate discipline propelled him into one of the better power displays in the minors. Can struggle with pitch recognition, but was able to maintain high BA by cutting-down swing. Moved from 1B to RF where his range and arm strength are below average.

Pedroza, Jamie — 6 — Los Angeles (N)

Bats B — **Age** 21 — 2007 (9) UC Riverside
EXP MLB DEBUT: 2010 — POTENTIAL: Starting SS — **7C**

Pwr +++
BAvg +++
Spd ++++
Def +++

Year	Lev	Team	AB	R	H	HR	RBI	Avg	OB	Slg	OPS	bb%	ct%	Eye	SB	CS	X/H%	Iso	RC/G
2007	Rk	Ogden	211	33	76	8	40	360	413	569	982	6	79	0.32	4	4	36	209	8.44
2007	A+	Inland Emp	12	1	3	0	1	250	400	250	650	20	83	1.50	1	1	0	0	3.37

Strong hands, bat speed, and plate discipline propelled him into one of the better power displays in the minors. Can struggle with pitch recognition, but was able to maintain high BA by cutting-down swing. Moved from 1B to RF where his range and arm strength are below average.

Pedroza, Sergio — 72 — Tampa Bay

Bats L — **Age** 24 — 2005 (3) Cal St Fullerton
EXP MLB DEBUT: 2009 — POTENTIAL: Platoon RF/LF — **7B**

Pwr ++++
BAvg +++
Spd ++
Def ++

Year	Lev	Team	AB	R	H	HR	RBI	Avg	OB	Slg	OPS	bb%	ct%	Eye	SB	CS	X/H%	Iso	RC/G
2005	Rk	Ogden	46	13	23	4	18	500	558	783	1340	12	83	0.75	4	0	22	283	11.83
2005	A	Columbus	179	31	37	12	30	207	272	480	752	8	68	0.28	0	0	65	274	4.85
2006	A	Columbus	317	61	89	14	75	281	415	562	977	19	71	0.80	2	6	52	281	8.39
2006	A+	VB/Vis	138	30	37	7	18	268	392	514	906	17	68	0.64	0	2	51	246	7.55
2007	A+	Vero Beach	399	59	114	22	70	286	355	539	894	10	76	0.45	1	2	46	253	6.66

Pure hitter with power and OBP, topping a .900 OPS for second straight year. Drives ball to all fields, but struggles against LH pitching and strikes-out. Began season as a part-time catcher, but struggled with receiving skills and was returned to LF where his arm strength remains an asset.

Pellot, Hector — 4 — New York (N)

Bats R — **Age** 21 — 2005 (4) HS (PR)
EXP MLB DEBUT: 2010 — POTENTIAL: Starting 2B — **7D**

Pwr +
BAvg +++
Spd ++++ (4.10)
Def ++++

Year	Lev	Team	AB	R	H	HR	RBI	Avg	OB	Slg	OPS	bb%	ct%	Eye	SB	CS	X/H%	Iso	RC/G
2006	A	Hagerstown	359	30	68	2	16	189	273	259	532	10	74	0.43	5	5	29	70	2.02
2007	A	Savannah	431	52	118	7	34	274	331	381	712	8	76	0.36	33	17	25	107	4.29
2007	A+	St. Lucie	23	3	7	1	3	304	407	522	929	15	87	1.33	2	1	29	217	7.29

Live-bodied athlete with plus speed and improving offense. Uses whole field with line-drive stroke, and since he has below average power, drawing walks will be imperative. Aggressive baserunner and makes plays defensively with arm strength, range, and soft/quick hands.

Pena, Francisco — 2 — New York (N)

Bats R — **Age** 18 — 2006 FA (DR)
EXP MLB DEBUT: 2011 — POTENTIAL: Platoon CA — **7E**

Pwr ++++
BAvg ++
Spd + (4.70)
Def ++

Year	Lev	Team	AB	R	H	HR	RBI	Avg	OB	Slg	OPS	bb%	ct%	Eye	SB	CS	X/H%	Iso	RC/G
2007	A	Savannah	367	26	77	5	30	210	258	283	542	6	79	0.32	1	1	22	74	2.05

Large-framed receiver with bat speed and power potential, but poor plate discipline and contact rate prevent it from being game-usable. Arm strength and receiving skills are solid, but is very immobile, lacked motivation, and had just a 23% CS%.

Pennington, Cliff — 6 — Oakland

Bats B — **Age** 24 — 2005 (1) Texas A&M
EXP MLB DEBUT: 2008 — POTENTIAL: Platoon 2B/SS — **7B**

Pwr ++
BAvg +++
Spd ++++ (4.20)
Def ++++

Year	Lev	Team	AB	R	H	HR	RBI	Avg	OB	Slg	OPS	bb%	ct%	Eye	SB	CS	X/H%	Iso	RC/G
2005	A	Kane Co	290	49	80	3	29	276	362	359	720	12	84	0.83	25	6	23	83	4.69
2006	Rk	AZL Athletics	28	3	13	0	6	464	531	643	1174	13	93	2.00	0	0	31	179	10.13
2006	A+	Stockton	177	36	37	2	21	209	303	282	586	12	80	0.69	7	1	24	73	2.94
2007	A+	Stockton	286	50	73	6	36	255	353	399	751	13	81	0.80	9	2	36	143	5.10
2007	AA	Midland	271	41	68	2	21	251	343	336	679	12	87	1.09	8	2	25	85	4.34

Offense returned after a horrible 2006 season which was marred by a hamstring injury. Makes contact and draws walks, so will have a solid OBP, but lacks bat speed to hit for power. Very athletic with above average speed, his defense is very good with excellent range and arm strength.

Pequero, Carlos — 9 — Seattle

Bats L — **Age** 21 — 2005 FA (DR)
EXP MLB DEBUT: 2010 — POTENTIAL: Starting RF — **8E**

Pwr ++++
BAvg ++
Spd +++ (4.20)
Def +++

Year	Lev	Team	AB	R	H	HR	RBI	Avg	OB	Slg	OPS	bb%	ct%	Eye	SB	CS	X/H%	Iso	RC/G
2007																			

Tall/athletic outfielder with bat speed and power potential, but a long swing and marginal plate discipline depress overall offense. Arm strength and average range are well-suited for RF. With his speed and body life likely to decline, his power will have to come through.

Perez, Eduardo — 35 — Los Angeles (N)

Bats B — **Age** 23 — 2002 FA (Venezuela)
EXP MLB DEBUT: 2010 — POTENTIAL: Starting 1B/3B — **7D**

Pwr +++
BAvg +++
Spd +++ (4.30)
Def ++

Year	Lev	Team	AB	R	H	HR	RBI	Avg	OB	Slg	OPS	bb%	ct%	Eye	SB	CS	X/H%	Iso	RC/G
2005	Rk	GCL Dodgers	179	35	63	6	37	352	393	553	946	6	85	0.46	4	0	37	201	6.96
2005	A	Columbus	33	0	7	0	4	212	235	273	508	3	70	0.10	0	0	29	61	1.40
2006	Rk	Ogden	106	13	27	0	13	255	378	292	670	17	80	1.00	0	0	15	38	4.30
2006	A	Columbus	185	24	46	4	28	249	325	395	720	10	79	0.55	3	1	39	146	4.54
2007	A	Great Lakes	447	56	139	14	60	311	360	459	818	7	80	0.37	8	5	26	148	5.50

Wiry athlete with power potential based on bat speed and contact ability. Patient enough to wait on pitch, but swings aggressively on any count, increasing strikeouts. Below average defender at 3B with stiff hands and marginal mobility, but has good arm strength and can play 1B.

Perez, Fernando — 8 — Tampa Bay

Bats B — **Age** 25 — 2004 (7) Columbia
EXP MLB DEBUT: 2009 — POTENTIAL: Reserve CF/LF — **7C**

Pwr +
BAvg +++
Spd +++++ (3.95)
Def +++

Year	Lev	Team	AB	R	H	HR	RBI	Avg	OB	Slg	OPS	bb%	ct%	Eye	SB	CS	X/H%	Iso	RC/G
2004	A-	Hudson Val	267	46	62	2	20	232	310	322	632	10	74	0.43	24	4	24	90	3.40
2005	A	SW Michigan	522	93	151	6	48	289	360	406	766	10	85	0.73	57	17	24	117	5.18
2006	A+	Visalia	547	123	166	4	56	303	390	393	783	12	76	0.58	33	16	19	90	5.55
2007	AA	Montgomery	393	84	121	8	33	308	420	481	901	16	74	0.73	32	18	35	173	7.41

Fastest player in organization and is quietly improving hitting skills, giving him outside chance of being a leadoff hitter in the Majors. Makes contact with slap-type approach and will draw walks, but has zero power. Flashes incredible range in CF, but has a below average throwing arm.

Perez, Yohannis — 6 — Milwaukee

Bats R — **Age** 25 — 2006 FA (Cuba)
EXP MLB DEBUT: 2008 — POTENTIAL: Platoon SS/2B — **7B**

Pwr +
BAvg ++++
Spd ++++ (4.05)
Def ++++

Year	Lev	Team	AB	R	H	HR	RBI	Avg	OB	Slg	OPS	bb%	ct%	Eye	SB	CS	X/H%	Iso	RC/G
2007	A+	Brevard Co	223	26	64	1	33	287	329	341	670	6	85	0.41	6	2	14	54	3.74
2007	AA	Huntsville	190	19	37	0	16	195	257	237	494	8	71	0.29	2	3	16	42	1.36

Wiry-strong athlete with plus speed and excellent defense. Arm strength, range, and hands are rate above average and can make every conceivable play. Solid bat speed doesn't yield power, but makes good contact in hitting for BA. Will need to improve patience to improve offense.

Peterson, Brock — 3 — Minnesota

EXP MLB DEBUT: 2008 | POTENTIAL: Platoon 1B | 7D

Bats R · Age 24 · 2002 (49) HS (WA)

- Pwr ++++
- BAvg ++
- Spd +
- Def ++

Year	Lev	Team	AB	R	H	HR	RBI	Avg	OB	Slg	OPS	bb%	ct%	Eye	SB	CS	X/H%	Iso	RC/G
2003	Rk	Elizabethton	207	53	60	9	31	290	385	473	858	13	77	0.67	5	1	32	184	6.37
2004	A-	Quad Cities	454	66	115	7	65	253	335	346	681	11	77	0.54	5	4	24	93	4.04
2005	A+	Fort Myers	424	49	106	12	60	250	323	401	724	10	76	0.45	1	2	35	151	4.52
2006	A+	Fort Myers	447	65	130	21	76	291	349	494	843	8	79	0.43	6	6	35	204	5.84
2007	AA	New Britain	389	67	111	15	64	285	358	476	834	10	77	0.49	1	0	36	190	5.93

Bat speed generates power to all fields and OBP plays up with decent walk rate. Will struggle to hit for BA with mediocre contact rate and doesn't hit breaking pitches from RH batters well. Agility on defense is below average, but has soft hands and arm strength.

Peterson, Bryan — 8 — Florida

EXP MLB DEBUT: 2010 | POTENTIAL: Platoon CF/RF | 7D

Bats R · Age 22 · 2007 (4) UC Irvine

- Pwr +++
- BAvg ++
- Spd ++++
- Def ++++

Year	Lev	Team	AB	R	H	HR	RBI	Avg	OB	Slg	OPS	bb%	ct%	Eye	SB	CS	X/H%	Iso	RC/G
2007	A-	Jamestown	216	27	54	5	24	250	318	389	707	8	75	0.34	11	2	35	139	4.22

Experienced collegiate with slightly above average skills across the board. Drives ball to gaps with moderate power and can steal bases with good speed, but poor plate discipline makes hitting for BA unlikely. Solid defensive outfielder with arm strength and ability to track flyballs.

Petit, Gregorio — 64 — Oakland

EXP MLB DEBUT: 2008 | POTENTIAL: Reserve SS/2B | 7C

Bats R · Age · 2001 FA (Venezuela)

- Pwr ++
- BAvg ++
- Spd ++++
- Def ++++

Year	Lev	Team	AB	R	H	HR	RBI	Avg	OB	Slg	OPS	bb%	ct%	Eye	SB	CS	X/H%	Iso	RC/G
2004	A-	Vancouver	254	34	65	4	35	256	310	354	665	7	74	0.30	3	3	23	98	3.64
2005	A-	Kane Co	287	55	83	9	33	289	348	446	794	8	85	0.59	8	2	28	157	5.29
2006	A+	Stockton	519	71	133	8	63	256	307	378	685	7	82	0.40	22	13	30	121	3.95
2007	AA	Midland	268	33	82	4	31	306	365	403	768	9	84	0.57	9	3	22	97	5.03
2007	AAA	Sacramento	235	20	65	2	28	277	323	353	676	6	80	0.33	1	2	22	77	3.78

Light-framed athlete with solid defensive skills and above average speed. Features plus range, quick/soft hands, and average arm strength from both middle infield positions. Offense is limited to hitting for BA, which he can do with his quick stroke, but could benefit by drawing more walks.

Pettit, Chris — 8 — Los Angeles (A)

EXP MLB DEBUT: 2009 | POTENTIAL: Platoon LF/RF | 8C

Bats R · Age 23 · 2006 (19) Loyola Marym

- Pwr +++
- BAvg +++
- 4.25 Spd +++
- Def +++

Year	Lev	Team	AB	R	H	HR	RBI	Avg	OB	Slg	OPS	bb%	ct%	Eye	SB	CS	X/H%	Iso	RC/G
2006	Rk	Orem	225	41	76	7	54	338	418	569	987	12	79	0.66	5	1	46	231	8.10
2007	A-	Cedar Rapids	228	47	79	9	41	346	406	579	985	9	82	0.56	17	4	43	232	7.71
2007	A+	Rancho Cuc	265	54	82	9	54	309	392	502	894	12	82	0.75	13	3	38	192	6.76

Fundamentally sound player with slightly above average tools. Drives ball to gaps and will use whole field, which should keep BA high. Aggressiveness should net steals and extra bases. Outfield defense is questionable and will play both corner infield positions in instructional league.

Phillips, PJ — 6 — Los Angeles (A)

EXP MLB DEBUT: 2010 | POTENTIAL: Platoon 3B/SS | 8D

Bats R · Age 21 · 2005 (2) HS (GA)

- Pwr +++
- BAvg +++
- 4.30 Spd +++
- Def +++

Year	Lev	Team	AB	R	H	HR	RBI	Avg	OB	Slg	OPS	bb%	ct%	Eye	SB	CS	X/H%	Iso	RC/G
2007	A-	Cedar Rapids	436	67	107	13	37	245	283	397	680	3	65	0.10	34	4	30	151	3.81

Strong athlete with the bat speed to hit for power and excellent baserunning instincts, but his over-aggressiveness and poor plate discipline will keep BA/OBP below average. Arm strength and soft/quick hands will play at SS, but may move to 3B where range is more suitable.

Place, Jason — 8 — Boston

EXP MLB DEBUT: 2010 | POTENTIAL: Starting RF | 9E

Bats R · Age 20 · 2006 (1) HS (SC)

- Pwr ++++
- BAvg +++
- 4.30 Spd +++
- Def +++

Year	Lev	Team	AB	R	H	HR	RBI	Avg	OB	Slg	OPS	bb%	ct%	Eye	SB	CS	X/H%	Iso	RC/G
2006	Rk	GCL Red Sox	112	14	33	4	21	295	388	446	834	13	70	0.50	3	3	24	152	6.26
2007	AA	Greenville	459	60	98	12	55	214	294	359	653	10	65	0.33	9	8	40	146	3.70

Athletic outfielder had a disappointing season after a solid debut in 2006. Possesses short stroke and bat speed, but can be pull-conscious, contains a slight hitch, and struggles to make contact which doomed BA. Arm strength and range are well-suited for RF.

Plouffe, Trevor — 6 — Minnesota

EXP MLB DEBUT: 2009 | POTENTIAL: Starting SS | 7C

Bats R · Age 22 · 2004 (1) HS (CA)

- Pwr ++
- BAvg +++
- Spd ++++
- Def ++++

Year	Lev	Team	AB	R	H	HR	RBI	Avg	OB	Slg	OPS	bb%	ct%	Eye	SB	CS	X/H%	Iso	RC/G
2004	Rk	Elzbton	237	29	67	4	28	283	336	380	716	7	86	0.56	2	1	19	97	4.36
2005	A-	Beloit	466	58	104	13	60	223	298	345	644	10	83	0.64	8	4	30	122	3.54
2006	A+	Fort Myers	455	60	111	4	45	244	329	345	674	11	80	0.62	8	5	31	101	4.08
2007	AA	New Britain	497	75	136	9	50	274	325	410	736	7	82	0.43	12	7	35	137	4.59

Wiry athlete made offensive surge showing gap power and utilization of speed. Pitch recognition and a long swing may always keep BA suppressed. On the flip side, his defense, usually regarded as a strength with his plus arm, regressed significantly, showing stiff hands and low range.

Pope, Kieron — 9 — Baltimore

EXP MLB DEBUT: 2011 | POTENTIAL: Platoon RF/LF | 8E

Bats R · Age 21 · 2005 (4) HS (GA)

- Pwr ++++
- BAvg +
- 4.25 Spd +++
- Def ++

Year	Lev	Team	AB	R	H	HR	RBI	Avg	OB	Slg	OPS	bb%	ct%	Eye	SB	CS	X/H%	Iso	RC/G
2005	Rk	Bluefield	149	23	34	5	22	228	268	362	630	5	58	0.13	5	0	26	134	3.37
2006	Rk	Bluefield	135	20	46	5	29	341	386	585	971	7	73	0.28	4	3	48	244	7.82
2006	Rk	Aberdeen	75	9	8	0	7	107	130	107	237	3	56	0.06	1	0	0	0	-3.23
2007	Rk	Bluefield	66	4	13	0	5	197	284	227	511	7	67	0.23	0	1	15	30	-1.32

Projectable power hitter with bat speed and strength, but struggled with injuries. Poor strike zone judgment and contact ability may keep power from being game-usable and will likely always struggle to hit for BA. Range and arm strength are average at best and is limited to LF.

Pope, Van — 5 — Atlanta

EXP MLB DEBUT: 2009 | POTENTIAL: Starting 3B | 8D

Bats R · Age 24 · 2004 (5) Meridian JC

- Pwr ++++
- BAvg ++
- Spd ++
- Def ++++

Year	Lev	Team	AB	R	H	HR	RBI	Avg	OB	Slg	OPS	bb%	ct%	Eye	SB	CS	X/H%	Iso	RC/G
2004	Rk	Danville	233	39	63	5	39	270	303	429	732	5	81	0.25	5	1	40	159	4.40
2005	A-	Rome	386	48	107	6	60	277	348	422	770	10	82	0.60	0	1	35	145	5.21
2005	A+	Myrtle Beach	84	7	14	1	5	167	247	214	462	10	75	0.43	0	0	14	48	1.00
2006	A+	Myrtle Beach	467	78	123	15	74	263	345	426	771	11	80	0.63	7	4	37	163	5.16
2007	AA	Mississippi	421	48	94	6	43	223	284	340	624	8	82	0.47	10	5	35	116	3.28

Muscular infielder experienced a decline in plate discipline, which lowered BA and power. Swings aggressively early in count and bat speed produces above average power to all parts of the field. Possesses plus arm strength and first-step quickness at 3B.

Powell, Landon — 2 — Oakland

EXP MLB DEBUT: 2008 | POTENTIAL: Platoon CA | 7C

Bats B · Age 26 · 2004 (1) So Carolina

- Pwr ++++
- BAvg ++
- Spd +
- Def ++

Year	Lev	Team	AB	R	H	HR	RBI	Avg	OB	Slg	OPS	bb%	ct%	Eye	SB	CS	X/H%	Iso	RC/G
2004	A-	Vancouver	135	24	32	3	19	237	360	363	723	16	84	1.18	0	0	31	126	4.93
2006	A+	Stockton	326	44	86	15	47	264	350	439	788	12	76	0.56	0	0	31	175	5.32
2006	AA	Midland	41	4	11	1	4	268	318	341	660	7	71	0.25	0	0	9	73	3.43
2007	AA	Midland	219	46	64	11	39	292	392	502	894	14	82	0.90	1	0	34	210	6.78
2007	AAA	Sacramento	17	3	5	3	3	294	294	824	1118	0	76	0.00	0	0	60	529	8.33

Strong/muscular catcher missed half of 2007 with a second ACL injury. Power is above average and will judge strike zone, but a long swing prevents a consistent BA. Shows a strong arm and quick release, but carries too much weight, costing him agility and making him susceptible to injury.

Prado, Martin — 456 — Atlanta

EXP MLB DEBUT: 2007 | POTENTIAL: Reserve 2B/3B | 6B

Bats R · Age 24 · 2001 FA (Venezuela)

- Pwr +
- BAvg +++
- Spd ++++
- Def +++

Year	Lev	Team	AB	R	H	HR	RBI	Avg	OB	Slg	OPS	bb%	ct%	Eye	SB	CS	X/H%	Iso	RC/G
2006	AA	Mississippi	176	17	49	1	15	278	332	352	684	7	80	0.40	3	2	18	74	3.96
2006	AAA	Richmond	241	30	68	2	23	282	316	365	681	5	88	0.43	2	2	22	83	3.89
2006	MLB	Atlanta	42	3	11	1	9	262	340	405	745	11	83	0.71	0	0	27	143	4.89
2007	AAA	Richmond	395	61	125	4	41	316	371	420	791	8	90	0.83	5	4	24	104	5.37
2007	MLB	Atlanta	59	5	17	0	2	288	323	339	662	5	90	0.50	0	0	18	51	3.73

Athletic infielder with good contact skills and ability to walk, giving him a respectable OBP. Drives ball well enough to amass doubles, but doesn't utilize speed on bases. Arm strength and soft hands play anywhere in infield, but range limits him at SS.

Pridie,Jason

8 | **Minnesota** | EXP MLB DEBUT: 2008 | POTENTIAL: Reserve CF/LF | **6A**

Bats L Age 24
2002 (2) HS (AZ)
Pwr ++
BAvg +++
4.00 Spd ++++
Def ++++

Year	Lev	Team	AB	R	H	HR	RBI	Avg	OB	Slg	OPS	bb%	ct%	Eye	SB	CS	X/H%	Iso	RC/G
2004	A-	Charleston	515	103	142	17	86	276	324	470	794	7	78	0.32	17	6	39	194	5.27
2005	AA	Montgomery	94	15	20	3	8	213	275	394	668	8	69	0.28	5	1	45	181	3.77
2006	AA	Montgomery	460	39	106	5	34	230	279	304	583	6	80	0.33	15	5	19	74	2.61
2007	AA	Montgomery	279	42	81	4	27	290	324	441	765	5	84	0.31	14	7	33	151	4.86
2007	AAA	Durham	245	47	78	10	39	318	375	539	913	8	81	0.47	12	3	38	220	6.77

Athletic outfielder with plus speed who resurrected career with comeback season. Drives ball well for size with good bat speed and aggressive approach, but BA is very inconsistent and doesn't recognize pitches well. Above average defender with solid arm strength and range.

Putnam,Danny

7 | **Oakland** | EXP MLB DEBUT: 2007 | POTENTIAL: Platoon LF/1B | **7C**

Bats L Age 25
2004 (1-S) Stanford
Pwr +++
BAvg +++
4.50 Spd +
Def ++

Year	Lev	Team	AB	R	H	HR	RBI	Avg	OB	Slg	OPS	bb%	ct%	Eye	SB	CS	X/H%	Iso	RC/G
2007	Rk	AZL Athletics	19	2	6	1	1	316	381	474	855	10	84	0.67	0	0	17	158	5.89
2007	A+	Stockton	14	3	4	1	5	286	286	571	857	0	100		0	0	50	286	5.47
2007	AA	Midland	52	9	17	2	15	327	386	615	1001	9	92	1.25	1	2	59	288	7.81
2007	AAA	Sacramento	171	14	37	1	17	216	287	310	597	9	76	0.41	2	2	35	94	2.94
2007	MLB	Oakland	28	3	6	1	2	214	290	321	612	10	61	0.27	0	0	17	107	2.96

Pure hitter with a compact swing and plate discipline that produces BA, but has yet to hit for power despite bat speed. Struggles against LH pitching so will be relegated to a platoon role. Below average range and arm strength give him low defensive markers in LF.

Ramirez,Alexei

648 | **Chicago (A)** | EXP MLB DEBUT: 2008 | POTENTIAL: Starting SS/CF | **8C**

Bats R Age 26
2007 FA (Cuba)
Pwr +++
BAvg ++++
Spd ++++
Def +++

Year	Lev	Team	AB	R	H	HR	RBI	Avg	OB	Slg	OPS	bb%	ct%	Eye	SB	CS	X/H%	Iso	RC/G
2007																			

Wiry athlete with above average speed and BA ability, he led the Cuban League with 20 HR prior to his defection. Drives ball hard to all parts of the field and is very aggressive. Defensively, he can play three positions in the middle adequately, showing solid arm strength and range.

Ramirez,Maximiliano

2 | **Texas** | EXP MLB DEBUT: 2009 | POTENTIAL: Platoon CA/1B | **8D**

Bats R Age 23
2002 FA (Venezuela)
Pwr ++++
BAvg ++++
Spd +
Def +

Year	Lev	Team	AB	R	H	HR	RBI	Avg	OB	Slg	OPS	bb%	ct%	Eye	SB	CS	X/H%	Iso	RC/G
2004	Rk	GCL Braves	204	20	56	8	35	275	336	480	817	9	75	0.38	1	0	45	206	5.67
2005	Rk	Danville	239	45	83	8	47	347	422	527	949	11	83	0.76	1	2	33	180	7.38
2006	A-	Rome/LC	362	38	108	13	60	298	420	472	892	17	75	0.84	2	0	33	174	7.14
2007	A+	Kin/Bak	391	62	119	16	82	304	415	504	919	16	74	0.73	2	0	39	199	7.46

Strong/athletic receiver with excellent hitting skills, showing ability to hit for power and BA while judging the strike zone. Possesses slow feet which hinders footwork and causes slow release time (2.1). Arm strength is average and definitely needs better receiving skills.

Ramirez,Ronald

6 | **Houston** | EXP MLB DEBUT: 2009 | POTENTIAL: Platoon SS/2B | **7D**

Bats R Age 22
2003 FA (Venezuela)
Pwr +
BAvg +++
4.30 Spd +++
Def +++

Year	Lev	Team	AB	R	H	HR	RBI	Avg	OB	Slg	OPS	bb%	ct%	Eye	SB	CS	X/H%	Iso	RC/G
2006	Rk	Greeneville	222	19	66	3	33	297	328	441	769	4	79	0.22	5	3	36	144	4.89
2006	A-	Lexington	10	0	2	0	0	200	200	200	400	0	80	0.00	0	0	0	0	-0.49
2007	A-	Lexington	70	10	22	0	8	314	342	400	742	4	70	0.14	1	2	27	86	4.75
2007	A-	Tri-City	7	0	1	0	2	143	143	286	429	0	57	0.00	0	0	100	143	0.48

Wiry athlete with BA ability despite low contact rate. Lacks bat speed and strength to hit for power, but hits well in situations and runs bases well despite average speed. Ranges well in all directions, but arm strength is fringy for SS. Missed most of 2007 with a dislocated shoulder.

Ramirez,Wilken

9 | **Detroit** | EXP MLB DEBUT: 2010 | POTENTIAL: Platoon RF/LF | **7E**

Bats R Age 22
2003 FA (DR)
Pwr ++++
BAvg ++
4.30 Spd +++
Def ++

Year	Lev	Team	AB	R	H	HR	RBI	Avg	OB	Slg	OPS	bb%	ct%	Eye	SB	CS	X/H%	Iso	RC/G
2005	A-	W. Michigan	493	129	69	16	65	140	197	288	485	7	71	0.24	21	8	57	148	1.08
2006	A+	Lakeland	249	55	31	8	32	124	158	289	447	4	72	0.14	8	2	68	165	0.56
2007	AA	Erie	121	26	15	2	14	124	178	215	393	6	69	0.21	6	2	40	91	-0.24
2007	A+	Lakeland	331	88	49	10	41	148	197	284	481	6	72	0.22	28	6	43	136	1.02
2003	Rk	GCL Tigers	200	55	34	5	35	170	221	345	566	6	75	0.25	6	1	53	175	2.35

Projectable athlete with excellent bat speed, hip rotation, and power potential, but poor plate discipline prevents power from being game-usable. Speed is asset on bases and has adjusted well to RF where he shows average arm strength, but will need to take better routes.

Rasmus,Colby

8 | **St. Louis** | EXP MLB DEBUT: 2008 | POTENTIAL: Starting CF | **9B**

Bats L Age 21
2005 (1-C) HS (AL)
Pwr ++++
BAvg ++++
4.05 Spd ++++
Def ++++

Year	Lev	Team	AB	R	H	HR	RBI	Avg	OB	Slg	OPS	bb%	ct%	Eye	SB	CS	X/H%	Iso	RC/G
2005	Rk	Johnson City	216	47	64	7	27	296	359	514	873	9	66	0.29	13	3	44	218	7.01
2006	A-	Quad Cities	303	49	94	11	49	310	370	512	882	9	82	0.53	17	5	38	201	6.41
2006	A+	Palm Beach	192	22	49	5	35	255	347	406	753	12	82	0.77	10	3	29	151	5.06
2007	AA	Springfield	472	93	130	29	72	275	369	551	920	13	77	0.65	18	3	53	275	7.12

Smooth swinging hitter with bat speed and plate discipline. Led TL in HR and runs scored, and with his speed, is capable of hitting anywhere in lineup. Arm strength and range are outstanding in CF and has been able to meet every aggressive challenge STL has thrown at him.

Raynor,John

7 | **Florida** | EXP MLB DEBUT: 2009 | POTENTIAL: Reserve LF/CF | **6C**

Bats R Age 24
2006 (9) UNC Wilmingto
Pwr +
BAvg +++
Spd ++++
Def +++

Year	Lev	Team	AB	R	H	HR	RBI	Avg	OB	Slg	OPS	bb%	ct%	Eye	SB	CS	X/H%	Iso	RC/G
2006	A-	Jamestown	199	36	57	4	21	286	343	427	770	8	74	0.33	21	2	28	141	5.10
2007	A-	Greensboro	445	110	148	13	57	333	419	519	938	13	78	0.67	54	8	33	187	7.50

Plus speed and being older than his competition earned him the SAL MVP, leading league in runs scored and finishing second in SB. Draws walks and has enough bat speed to hit for moderate power, but won't hit for BA. Poor arm strength limits him to LF.

Reddick,Josh

9 | **Boston** | EXP MLB DEBUT: 2010 | POTENTIAL: Platoon RF/LF | **7C**

Bats L Age 21
2006 (17) Middle Georgi
Pwr +++
BAvg +++
4.30 Spd +++
Def +++

Year	Lev	Team	AB	R	H	HR	RBI	Avg	OB	Slg	OPS	bb%	ct%	Eye	SB	CS	X/H%	Iso	RC/G
2007	AA	Greenville	369	60	113	18	72	306	352	531	883	7	86	0.51	8	5	36	225	6.17
2007	AA	Portland	1	0	0	0	0	0	0	0	0	0	100	0.00	0	0	0	0	0.00

Athletic outfielder showed moderate bat speed and contact ability, while hitting well against pitchers from both sides. Walk rate needs to improve and makes the most of his average speed. Arm strength and range are sufficient for RF, which is where he'll end up long-term.

Reimold,Nolan

9 | **Baltimore** | EXP MLB DEBUT: 2008 | POTENTIAL: Starting RF/LF | **8C**

Bats R Age 24
2005 (2) Bowling Green
Pwr ++++
BAvg +++
4.30 Spd +++
Def +++

Year	Lev	Team	AB	R	H	HR	RBI	Avg	OB	Slg	OPS	bb%	ct%	Eye	SB	CS	X/H%	Iso	RC/G
2005	A-	Aberdeen	180	33	53	9	30	294	392	550	942	14	76	0.66	2	0	49	256	7.60
2005	A+	Frederick	83	17	22	6	11	265	358	554	912	13	67	0.44	3	0	55	289	7.36
2006	A+	Frederick	415	73	106	19	75	255	371	455	826	15	74	0.71	14	8	42	200	6.09
2007	Rk	GCL Orioles	30	4	7	0	8	233	361	433	794	17	87	1.50	0	0	71	200	6.16
2007	AA	Bowie	186	30	57	11	34	306	365	565	929	8	75	0.36	2	3	46	258	7.07

Strong/athletic corner outfielder who missed first part of season with a strained oblique. Power limited to pull field, but can sustain solid OBP with ability to draw walks and can punish LH pitching. Defensively, he has plenty of arm strength and range to be above average in RF.

Revere,Ben

8 | **Minnesota** | EXP MLB DEBUT: 2011 | POTENTIAL: Starting CF | **8C**

Bats L Age 20
2007 (1) HS (KY)
Pwr +
BAvg ++++
3.90 Spd +++++
Def +++

Year	Lev	Team	AB	R	H	HR	RBI	Avg	OB	Slg	OPS	bb%	ct%	Eye	SB	CS	X/H%	Iso	RC/G
2007	Rk	GCL Twins	191	46	62	0	29	325	368	461	828	6	90	0.65	21	9	26	136	5.81

Small with incredible speed, he projects as a leadoff hitter with his ability to make contact, draw walks, and steal bases. Utilized a compact swing and favors the opposite field, while leading GCL in runs scored and triples. Work ethic drew raves and can play a solid CF with plus range.

BATTERS

Richardson,Antoan | 8 | San Francisco

EXP MLB DEBUT: 2009 | POTENTIAL: Reserve CF/LF | 7D

Bats B Age 24
2005 (35) Vanderbilt
Pwr +
BAvg +++
4.00 Spd +++++
Def +++

Year	Lev	Team	AB	R	H	HR	RBI	Avg	OB	Slg	OPS	bb%	ct%	Eye	SB	CS	X/H%	Iso	RC/G
2005	Rk	AZL Giants	193	45	62	1	10	321	447	378	825	19	78	1.02	40	6	11	57	6.41
2006	A-	Augusta	419	78	121	2	28	289	371	363	734	12	83	0.75	65	9	19	74	4.86
2007	A+	San Jose	384	85	107	2	29	279	386	362	748	15	76	0.71	43	11	20	83	5.21

Athlete with plus speed that makes him a threat on the bases and gives him range in outfield. Makes contact, stays balanced at the plate, and draws walks which enhances OBP, but lacks power in his swing. Weak throwing arm limits value in CF, but has tools that will play in Majors.

Riggans,Shawn | 2 | Tampa Bay

EXP MLB DEBUT: 2006 | POTENTIAL: Reserve CA | 6B

Bats R Age 27
2000 (24) Indian River C
Pwr +++
BAvg ++
4.60 Spd +
Def +++

Year	Lev	Team	AB	R	H	HR	RBI	Avg	OB	Slg	OPS	bb%	ct%	Eye	SB	CS	X/H%	Iso	RC/G
2006	AAA	Durham	417	43	122	11	54	293	336	444	779	6	79	0.31	2	2	32	151	5.02
2006	MLB	Tampa Bay	29	3	5	0	1	172	273	207	480	12	76	0.57	0	0	20	34	1.46
2007	A+	Vero Beach	30	3	9	0	5	300	323	367	689	3	83	0.20	0	0	22	67	3.83
2007	AAA	Durham	121	10	34	4	16	281	304	471	775	3	75	0.13	0	3	41	190	4.88
2007	MLB	Tampa Bay	10	1	1	0	2	100	100	100	200	0	90	0.00	0	0	0	0	-1.59

Defensive-oriented catcher with good catch-and-throw skills, nailing 33% of attempted runners. Offense centers around moderate power as he turns-on mistakes, but lacks plate discipline and contact ability which drives-down BA. Defense should earn him backup role.

Rivero,Carlos | 6 | Cleveland

EXP MLB DEBUT: 2010 | POTENTIAL: Starting SS | 8E

Bats R Age 20
2005 FA (DR)
Pwr ++++
BAvg ++
4.40 Spd ++
Def +++

Year	Lev	Team	AB	R	H	HR	RBI	Avg	OB	Slg	OPS	bb%	ct%	Eye	SB	CS	X/H%	Iso	RC/G
2006	Rk	Burlington	66	3	14	1	7	212	268	303	571	7	83	0.45	0	1	29	91	2.59
2006	Rk	GCL Indians	134	17	38	2	22	284	333	373	706	7	85	0.50	0	0	21	90	4.21
2007	A-	Lake County	436	59	114	7	62	261	333	369	703	10	81	0.56	1	2	29	108	4.30

Tall/rangy middle infielder with offensive upside based on bat speed and strike zone judgment. Power should come with maturity, but may always struggle with BA. Improved his defense and possesses a plus arm and soft hands, but may outgrow SS and his range is just average.

Rizzo,Anthony | 3 | Boston

EXP MLB DEBUT: 2011 | POTENTIAL: Starting 1B | 8E

Bats L Age 19
2007 (6) HS (FL)
Pwr ++++
BAvg +++
Spd +
Def ++

Year	Lev	Team	AB	R	H	HR	RBI	Avg	OB	Slg	OPS	bb%	ct%	Eye	SB	CS	X/H%	Iso	RC/G
2007	Rk	GCL Red Sox	21	6	6	1	3	286	318	429	747	5	90	0.50	0	0	17	143	4.42

Strong/projectable power hitter with excellent bat speed and advanced approach that should allow him to hit for BA as well. May need to shorten swing as he can get tied-up inside. Adds little in the way of speed or defensive ability, but has the aptitude to improve on defense.

Roberts,Brandon | 8 | Minnesota

EXP MLB DEBUT: 2008 | POTENTIAL: Reserve CF/LF | 6C

Bats L Age 23
2005 (7) Cal Poly
Pwr +
BAvg +++
4.00 Spd ++++
Def ++++

Year	Lev	Team	AB	R	H	HR	RBI	Avg	OB	Slg	OPS	bb%	ct%	Eye	SB	CS	X/H%	Iso	RC/G
2004	Rk	Billings	32	3	7	0	4	219	375	281	656	20	53	0.53	1	1	29	63	4.59
2004	Rk	GCL Reds	123	11	27	1	8	220	324	276	600	13	76	0.63	3	1	19	57	3.08
2005	Rk	Billings	274	50	87	4	36	318	372	438	810	8	84	0.55	32	7	22	120	5.55
2006	A+	Sar/FM	532	80	156	4	49	293	338	355	693	6	85	0.44	49	14	15	62	4.03
2007	AA	New Britain	369	50	108	3	39	293	349	374	723	8	85	0.57	14	7	19	81	4.51

Plus speed and contact ability gives him chance to hit for BA, but witnessed a decrease in plate discipline which affected OBP. Possesses some life in his bat, but has yet to translate into power. Exceptional range in CF is off-set by below average arm strength.

Robinson,Derrick | 8 | Kansas City

EXP MLB DEBUT: 2010 | POTENTIAL: Reserve CF/LF | 6C

Bats B Age 20
2006 (4) HS (FL)
Pwr +
BAvg +++
3.90 Spd +++++
Def +++

Year	Lev	Team	AB	R	H	HR	RBI	Avg	OB	Slg	OPS	bb%	ct%	Eye	SB	CS	X/H%	Iso	RC/G
2006	Rk	AZL Royals	176	25	40	1	24	227	320	313	633	12	69	0.44	20	14	25	85	3.50
2007	A-	Burlington	407	42	99	2	26	243	298	300	598	7	75	0.32	34	7	16	57	2.79
2007	A+	Wilmington	13	1	5	0	0	385	429	462	890	7	100	0.00	1	0	20	77	6.57

Pure athlete and fastest player in system, his value is based on his stolen bases and range in CF. Takes a slap approach at the plate and is a good bunter. Lacks power or the ability to draw walks, which damages OBP. Arm strength is below average, but grades higher with good accuracy.

Robnett,Richie | 8 | Oakland

EXP MLB DEBUT: 2008 | POTENTIAL: Platoon CF/LF | 7B

Bats L Age 24
2004 (1) Fresno St
Pwr +++
BAvg +++
4.20 Spd +++
Def +++

Year	Lev	Team	AB	R	H	HR	RBI	Avg	OB	Slg	OPS	bb%	ct%	Eye	SB	CS	X/H%	Iso	RC/G
2006	A+	Stockton	267	46	70	11	38	262	348	431	778	12	73	0.48	4	3	30	169	5.28
2006	AA	Midland	14	5	5	1	2	357	500	643	1143	22	71	1.00	0	0	40	286	10.95
2006	AAA	Sacramento	11	0	1	0	0	91	91	182	273	0	73	0.00	0	0	100	91	-1.69
2007	AA	Midland	490	73	131	18	74	267	315	465	780	6	73	0.26	4	3	45	198	5.14
2007	AAA	Sacramento	33	6	5	0	1	152	243	152	395	11	52	0.25	0	0	0	0	-0.51

Athletic outfielder with bat speed and fluid hitting mechanics which produces power, but poor plate discipline and a long swing suppresses BA. Legs haven't been 100% for two years, so doesn't run much despite fair speed. Ranges well in all directions and possesses average arm strength.

Rodriguez,Josh | 64 | Cleveland

EXP MLB DEBUT: 2009 | POTENTIAL: Starting SS/2B | 7C

Bats R Age 23
2006 (2-C) Rice
Pwr +++
BAvg +++
4.40 Spd ++
Def +++

Year	Lev	Team	AB	R	H	HR	RBI	Avg	OB	Slg	OPS	bb%	ct%	Eye	SB	CS	X/H%	Iso	RC/G
2006	A-	Mahoning Val	157	26	42	4	24	268	327	465	792	8	79	0.42	2	0	45	197	5.40
2007	A+	Kinston	493	84	129	20	82	262	351	460	812	12	81	0.72	21	8	38	199	5.71

Overachiever with average tools and excellent secondary numbers, he led CAR in runs scored. Judges strike zone, makes contact, and added power to resume. Runs bases well despite average speed and hasn't let his average range deter him at SS where he features a strong arm.

Rodriguez,Sean | 68 | Los Angeles (A)

EXP MLB DEBUT: 2008 | POTENTIAL: Starting SS/2B | 8C

Bats R Age 23
2003 (3) HS (FL)
Pwr ++++
BAvg +++
4.30 Spd +++
Def ++++

Year	Lev	Team	AB	R	H	HR	RBI	Avg	OB	Slg	OPS	bb%	ct%	Eye	SB	CS	X/H%	Iso	RC/G
2005	A-	Cedar Rapids	448	86	112	14	45	250	361	422	783	15	81	0.92	27	11	41	172	5.55
2006	A+	Rancho Cuc	455	78	136	24	77	299	365	543	907	9	73	0.38	16	3	43	244	6.96
2006	AA	Arkansas	65	16	23	5	9	354	447	662	1109	14	72	0.61	0	3	43	308	9.94
2006	AAA	Salt Lake	2	0	0	0	0	0	0	0	0	0	0	0.00	0	0	0	0	0.00
2007	AA	Arkansas	508	84	129	17	73	254	326	423	749	10	74	0.41	15	8	39	169	4.84

Loaded with secondary skills, but hitting for BA will be very inconsistent. Drives ball hard to all fields with moderate power and steals bases through instincts and aggressiveness. Arm strength is solid for SS, but stiff hands and average range will push him to either CF or 2B.

Rogowski,Casey | 3 | Oakland

EXP MLB DEBUT: 2007 | POTENTIAL: Platoon 1B/LF | 6C

Bats L Age 27
1999 (13) HS (MI)
Pwr +++
BAvg +++
4.25 Spd +++
Def +

Year	Lev	Team	AB	R	H	HR	RBI	Avg	OB	Slg	OPS	bb%	ct%	Eye	SB	CS	X/H%	Iso	RC/G
2003	A+	Win-Sal	357	46	88	7	38	246	344	367	711	13	80	0.73	18	4	32	120	4.55
2004	A+	Win-Sal	465	88	133	18	90	286	403	471	874	16	80	0.97	16	9	36	185	6.74
2005	AA	Birmingham	505	83	148	9	78	293	366	444	809	10	78	0.52	20	12	35	150	5.74
2006	AAA	Charlotte	459	69	125	13	76	272	348	436	783	10	79	0.55	26	9	38	163	5.32
2007	AAA	Charlotte	453	62	111	14	54	245	335	400	734	12	76	0.56	17	5	38	155	4.73

Solid Triple-A performer with solid secondary skills. Produces gap power with moderate bat speed, draws walks, and steals bases despite below average speed. Strikes-out too much will keeps BA low. Excellent defender at 1B, but is stretched in LF with poor arm strength.

Romak,Jamie | 9 | Pittsburgh

EXP MLB DEBUT: 2009 | POTENTIAL: Platoon RF/LF | 7C

Bats R Age 22
2003 (4) HS (Canada)
Pwr ++++
BAvg ++
4.45 Spd ++
Def +++

Year	Lev	Team	AB	R	H	HR	RBI	Avg	OB	Slg	OPS	bb%	ct%	Eye	SB	CS	X/H%	Iso	RC/G
2004	Rk	Danville	158	25	30	5	22	190	256	329	585	8	65	0.25	1	1	37	139	2.53
2005	Rk	Danville	124	25	34	7	27	274	348	540	888	10	69	0.37	2	1	53	266	6.92
2006	A-	Rome	347	55	86	16	68	248	357	473	830	15	71	0.58	3	1	51	225	6.22
2007	A-	Hickory	69	16	19	5	15	275	359	551	910	12	65	0.38	0	2	47	275	7.42
2007	A+	Lynchburg	294	49	74	15	45	252	370	483	853	16	69	0.61	2	2	50	231	6.62

Strong/athletic hitter with excellent bat speed and power to all fields. High strikeout rate and aggressive approach limits BA, but plate discipline improved during season. Lacks speed and range to hits over his head, but his strong arm makes him adequate in corner outfield.

Romero,Alex — 9 — Arizona

EXP MLB DEBUT: 2008 | POTENTIAL: Reserve LF/CF | **6C**

Bats B Age 24	Year	Lev	Team	AB	R	H	HR	RBI	Avg	OB	Slg	OPS	bb%	ct%	Eye	SB	CS	X/H%	Iso	RC/G
2000 FA (Venezuela)	2004	A+	Fort Myers	380	59	111	6	42	292	380	405	785	12	88	1.15	6	4	26	113	5.56
Pwr +++	2005	AA	New Britain	509	65	153	15	77	301	347	458	805	7	86	0.52	12	11	31	157	5.32
BAvg +++	2006	AA	New Britain	167	29	47	5	16	281	378	461	839	13	89	1.37	15	7	38	180	6.23
Spd ++++	2006	AAA	Rochester	236	20	59	0	26	250	295	301	596	6	91	0.68	6	2	17	51	3.13
Def ++	2007	AAA	Tucson	535	82	166	5	66	310	355	421	775	6	90	0.70	12	10	26	110	5.12

Athletic outfielder with fluid hitting mechanics and plate discipline who has hit for BA at every level. HR power has dwindled with each promotion, but can drive gaps for doubles and will draw walks. Not an instinctive player, and possesses a below average arm in being confined to LF.

Romero,Deibinson — 5 — Minnesota

EXP MLB DEBUT: 2011 | POTENTIAL: Starting 3B | **8E**

Bats R Age 21	Year	Lev	Team	AB	R	H	HR	RBI	Avg	OB	Slg	OPS	bb%	ct%	Eye	SB	CS	X/H%	Iso	RC/G
2006 FA (DR)																				
Pwr ++++																				
BAvg +++	2006	Rk	GCL Twins	176	37	55	4	38	313	360	460	820	7	79	0.35	6	3	29	148	5.60
Spd +	2007	Rk	Elizabethton	247	60	78	9	52	316	399	506	905	12	81	0.72	9	3	35	190	6.89
Def ++	2007	A-	Beloit	10	2	3	0	3	300	364	400	764	9	60	0.25	0	0	33	100	5.92

Strong/well-proportioned hitter with impressive debut, showing power to all fields and a mature approach that produces a solid BA/OBP. Only negative to game is lack of speed and agility, but is a solid defender at 3B, possessing arm strength and playable hands.

Romine,Andrew — 6 — Los Angeles (A)

EXP MLB DEBUT: 2009 | POTENTIAL: Reserve SS | **7D**

Bats B Age 22	Year	Lev	Team	AB	R	H	HR	RBI	Avg	OB	Slg	OPS	bb%	ct%	Eye	SB	CS	X/H%	Iso	RC/G
2007 (5) Arizona St																				
Pwr +																				
BAvg ++																				
4.15 Spd ++++																				
Def +++++	2007	Rk	Orem	231	38	66	5	35	286	332	429	761	6	84	0.42	12	4	26	143	4.83

Heady-type athlete who maximizes tools. Outstanding defender, possessing plus range, arm strength, and soft/quick hands. Contact ability and inside-out swing is conducive to BA, but will need to draw more walks as power is unlikely. Hits better from LH side due to more repetitions.

Romine,Austin — 2 — New York (A)

EXP MLB DEBUT: 2012 | POTENTIAL: Starting CA | **7E**

Bats R Age 19	Year	Lev	Team	AB	R	H	HR	RBI	Avg	OB	Slg	OPS	bb%	ct%	Eye	SB	CS	X/H%	Iso	RC/G
2007 (2) HS (CA)																				
Pwr +++																				
BAvg ++																				
Spd ++																				
Def ++++	2007	Rk	GCL Yankees	2	2	1	0	1	500	667	1000	1667	33	50	1.00	0	0	100	500	27.45

Top rated defensive catcher amongst high school catchers, he possesses plus arm strength and solid receiving skills in being able to shut-down running game. Moderate bat speed generated gap power, but hasn't shown much plate discipline which could curtail BA.

Rottino,Vinny — 273 — Milwaukee

EXP MLB DEBUT: 2007 | POTENTIAL: Reserve CA/1B | **6C**

Bats R Age 28	Year	Lev	Team	AB	R	H	HR	RBI	Avg	OB	Slg	OPS	bb%	ct%	Eye	SB	CS	X/H%	Iso	RC/G
2003 UDFA Wis-LaCross	2005	AA	Nashville	29	4	10	1	2	345	406	483	889	9	79	0.50	0	1	20	138	6.48
Pwr +++	2006	AAA	Nashville	398	55	125	7	42	314	377	440	816	9	82	0.55	12	7	27	126	5.68
BAvg ++	2006	MLB	Milwaukee	14	1	3	0	1	214	267	286	552	7	86	0.50	1	0	33	71	2.54
Spd ++	2007	AAA	Nashville	377	59	109	12	53	289	363	446	809	9	85	0.64	15	9	29	157	5.98
Def +++	2007	MLB	Milwaukee	9	0	2	0	3	222	222	333	555	9	85	0.64	15	9	50	111	2.66

Strong/muscular player with defensive versatility and secondary skills. Plays all four corner positions in addition to catcher, but arm strength is only defensive skill. Drives ball to all fields with moderate power and runs bases instinctively despite below average speed.

Rowell,Billy — 5 — Baltimore

EXP MLB DEBUT: 2010 | POTENTIAL: Starting RF | **9C**

Bats L Age 19	Year	Lev	Team	AB	R	H	HR	RBI	Avg	OB	Slg	OPS	bb%	ct%	Eye	SB	CS	X/H%	Iso	RC/G
2006 (1) HS (NJ)																				
Pwr ++++																				
BAvg ++++	2006	Rk	Bluefield	152	38	50	2	26	329	424	507	930	14	69	0.53	3	0	40	178	8.04
4.20 Spd +++	2006	A-	Aberdeen	43	8	14	1	6	326	383	488	871	9	72	0.33	0	0	36	163	6.60
Def +	2007	A-	Delmarva	352	47	96	9	57	273	335	426	771	8	70	0.30	3	2	34	153	4.85

Tall/projectable hitter with impressive bat speed and power. BA may be limited due to poor pitch recognition and tendency to lunge. Long defensive actions, coupled with stiff hands may preclude a shift to RF where arm strength would be an asset. Strained oblique limited action in first half.

Royster,Ryan — 7 — Tampa Bay

EXP MLB DEBUT: 2010 | POTENTIAL: Platoon LF/RF | **8D**

Bats R Age 21	Year	Lev	Team	AB	R	H	HR	RBI	Avg	OB	Slg	OPS	bb%	ct%	Eye	SB	CS	X/H%	Iso	RC/G
2004 (6) HS (OR)																				
Pwr ++++	2004	Rk	Princeton	176	25	48	5	26	273	293	438	730	3	73	0.11	3	3	35	165	4.31
BAvg ++	2005	Rk	Princeton	187	30	46	12	37	246	295	481	776	7	74	0.27	6	0	43	235	4.87
Spd ++	2006	A-	Hudson Val	231	20	57	8	29	247	275	424	699	4	72	0.14	6	2	42	177	3.94
Def ++	2007	A-	Columbus	474	90	156	30	98	329	376	601	978	7	74	0.30	17	5	42	272	7.64

Power hitter with strong hands, ability to center baseball, and controlled aggressiveness. Led SAL in HR, SLG, and extra-base hits, but an excessive strikeout rate tempers BA. Runs bases well despite below average speed and adds little defensively as he is limited to LF.

Ruggiano,Justin — 8 — Tampa Bay

EXP MLB DEBUT: 2007 | POTENTIAL: Reserve LF/RF | **7C**

Bats R Age 26	Year	Lev	Team	AB	R	H	HR	RBI	Avg	OB	Slg	OPS	bb%	ct%	Eye	SB	CS	X/H%	Iso	RC/G
2004 (25) Texas A&M	2005	A+	Vero Beach	242	47	75	9	37	310	381	517	898	10	73	0.43	16	5	37	207	6.96
Pwr +++	2005	AA	Jacksonville	161	23	55	6	29	342	404	528	932	10	65	0.30	8	3	31	186	7.91
BAvg ++	2006	AA	Jack/Mont	405	102	112	13	73	277	377	484	861	14	74	0.62	14	9	46	207	6.64
4.30 Spd +++	2007	AAA	Durham	482	78	149	20	73	309	378	502	880	10	69	0.35	26	11	34	193	6.84
Def +++	2007	MLB	Tampa Bay	14	2	3	0	3	214	267	214	481	7	64	0.20	0	0	0	0	0.95

Strong/athletic outfielder with good secondary skills. Bat speed generates power to all fields and hit for BA despite a high strikeout rate. Steals bases via speed and instincts. Range and arm strength are average in corner outfield, but bat will have to play up if he wants to start.

Salome,Angel — 2 — Milwaukee

EXP MLB DEBUT: 2009 | POTENTIAL: Starting CA | **8C**

Bats R Age 22	Year	Lev	Team	AB	R	H	HR	RBI	Avg	OB	Slg	OPS	bb%	ct%	Eye	SB	CS	X/H%	Iso	RC/G
2004 (5) Geo Washingto	2004	Rk	AZL Brewers	81	7	19	0	8	235	271	321	592	5	83	0.29	2	0	37	86	2.82
Pwr +++	2005	Rk	Helena	159	34	66	8	50	415	466	673	1138	9	90	0.94	6	2	38	258	9.17
BAvg +++	2005	A-	W. Virginia	118	15	30	4	21	254	302	432	734	6	86	0.47	1	0	40	178	4.49
Spd +	2006	A-	W. Virginia	418	63	122	10	85	292	352	447	800	9	85	0.62	7	3	35	156	5.43
Def +++	2007	A+	Brevard Co	258	33	82	6	53	318	348	465	813	4	88	0.38	1	0	32	147	5.31

Short/stocky receiver with BA ability and line-drive power. Walks and strikes-out infrequently. Arm strength and release (1.9) are fine, but footwork is lacking accounting for a 13% CS%. Missed two months following ankle surgery and was suspended 50 games for using PED's.

Sanchez,Gaby — 352 — Florida

EXP MLB DEBUT: 2009 | POTENTIAL: Platoon 1B/3B | **7C**

Bats R Age 24	Year	Lev	Team	AB	R	H	HR	RBI	Avg	OB	Slg	OPS	bb%	ct%	Eye	SB	CS	X/H%	Iso	RC/G
2005 (4) Miami-FL	2005	A-	Jamestown	234	34	83	5	42	355	396	487	883	6	90	0.67	11	5	25	132	6.23
Pwr +++	2006	Rk	GCL Marlins	6	1	2	0	3	333	636	500	1136	45	100	0.00	0	0	50	167	12.30
BAvg +++	2006	A-	Greensboro	189	43	60	14	39	317	434	603	1037	17	89	1.95	6	2	43	286	8.52
Spd ++	2006	AAA	Albuquerque	55	13	10	1	7	182	328	327	656	18	78	1.00	1	0	50	145	4.08
Def +	2007	A+	Jupiter	473	89	132	9	70	279	365	433	798	12	84	0.86	6	6	39	154	5.67

Bat speed and plate discipline have always accounted for solid BA and power, but hits didn't fall and power regressed. Drilled 40 doubles, but for a corner player, more power will be mandated. Played less catcher and more 1B as his arm strength and stiff hands were a liability.

Sanders,Marcus — 4 — San Francisco

EXP MLB DEBUT: 2007 | POTENTIAL: Starting 2B | **7C**

Bats R Age 22	Year	Lev	Team	AB	R	H	HR	RBI	Avg	OB	Slg	OPS	bb%	ct%	Eye	SB	CS	X/H%	Iso	RC/G
2003 (17) So Florida CC	2004	Rk	AZL Giants	209	54	61	3	21	292	393	431	824	14	78	0.78	28	4	31	139	6.16
Pwr +	2005	A-	Augusta	420	86	126	5	40	300	399	400	799	14	79	0.77	57	9	22	100	5.79
BAvg +++	2006	Rk	AZL Giants	33	7	4	0	3	121	275	152	427	18	67	0.64	4	0	25	30	0.44
4.00 Spd +++++	2006	A+	San Jose	211	39	45	0	17	213	297	265	562	11	80	0.58	23	5	22	52	2.62
Def +++	2007	A-	Augusta	292	53	77	0	26	264	364	342	706	14	81	0.82	29	6	26	79	4.67

Athletic infielder with plus speed that is basis of game. Draws walks and sprays ball to the whole field, but mediocre bat speed results in negligible power. Shoulder surgery left him with a below average arm, so was moved to 2B where his range and quick DP turn stand-out.

BATTERS

Sandoval,Pablo — 235 — San Francisco — EXP MLB DEBUT: 2009 — POTENTIAL: Platoon 3B/1B — 7D

Bats B Age 21
2003 FA (Venezuela)

			Year	Lev	Team	AB	R	H	HR	RBI	Avg	OB	Slg	OPS	bb%	ct%	Eye	SB	CS	X/H%	Iso	RC/G
	Pwr	+++	2004	Rk	AZL Giants	177	21	47	0	26	266	286	373	659	3	90	0.29	4	1	30	107	3.68
	BAvg	++	2005	A-	Salem-Keizer	294	46	97	3	50	330	375	425	800	7	89	0.64	2	3	21	95	5.35
	Spd	++	2006	A-	Augusta	441	43	117	1	49	265	300	322	622	5	83	0.29	3	4	19	57	3.09
	Def	+++	2007	A+	San Jose	401	56	115	11	52	287	314	476	790	4	87	0.31	3	1	43	190	5.06

Strong/stocky player with strong bat and defensive versatility. Drives ball hard to gaps with moderate bat speed and hits for BA despite lackluster plate discipline, though his hits lack loft. Defense at catcher and 3B is below average with low agility, but throws well and has soft hands.

Santana,Carlos — 257 — Los Angeles (N) — EXP MLB DEBUT: 2010 — POTENTIAL: Platoon CA/3B — 8E

Bats B Age 22
2004 FA (DR)

			Year	Lev	Team	AB	R	H	HR	RBI	Avg	OB	Slg	OPS	bb%	ct%	Eye	SB	CS	X/H%	Iso	RC/G
	Pwr	+++	2005	Rk	GCL Dodgers	78	14	23	1	14	295	415	410	825	17	90	2.00	0	2	26	115	6.39
	BAvg	++++	2006	Rk	Ogden	132	31	40	7	27	303	432	515	947	19	86	1.58	4	0	33	212	7.66
	Spd	++	2006	A+	Vero Beach	198	16	53	3	18	268	344	384	728	10	78	0.53	0	3	28	116	4.66
	Def	+	2007	A-	Great Lakes	292	32	65	7	36	223	316	370	686	12	85	0.89	5	3	43	147	4.29

Strong/athletic player who was moved to catcher from 3B to take advantage of his agility and plus arm strength. Threw-out 38% of attempted runners, but struggle to receive ball. Extreme contact hitter, he will draw walks, use the whole field, and turn on mistake pitches with moderate power.

Santana,Cristian — 2 — Texas — EXP MLB DEBUT: 2012 — POTENTIAL: Starting CA — 8E

Bats R Age 18
2005 FA (DR)

			Year	Lev	Team	AB	R	H	HR	RBI	Avg	OB	Slg	OPS	bb%	ct%	Eye	SB	CS	X/H%	Iso	RC/G
	Pwr	++++																				
	BAvg	++																				
4.30	Spd	+++	2007	Rk	AZL Rangers	96	20	29	3	15	302	380	531	911	11	72	0.44	3	3	45	229	7.34
	Def	+++	2007	A-	Spokane	25	1	8	1	4	320	320	520	840	0	76	0.00	0	0	38	200	5.44

Compact/athletic catcher possesses ability to impact game defensively and offensively. Solid bat speed produces moderate power and hit for BA at both stops. Features solid arm strength and receiving skills, but only threw-out 18% of attempted runners and needs to block pitches better.

Santos,Sergio — 6 — Toronto — EXP MLB DEBUT: 2008 — POTENTIAL: Starting SS/3B — 6A

Bats R Age 24
2002 (1) HS (CA)

			Year	Lev	Team	AB	R	H	HR	RBI	Avg	OB	Slg	OPS	bb%	ct%	Eye	SB	CS	X/H%	Iso	RC/G
			2004	AA	El Paso	347	53	98	11	52	282	329	461	790	6	74	0.27	3	2	36	179	5.26
	Pwr	+++	2005	AAA	Tucson	490	55	117	12	68	239	288	367	656	6	78	0.31	2	2	31	129	3.47
	BAvg	+	2006	AAA	Syracuse	481	48	103	5	38	214	251	299	551	5	80	0.25	1	3	29	85	2.16
4.35	Spd	+++	2007	AA	New Hamp	432	63	108	20	62	250	318	477	795	9	78	0.44	2	0	52	227	5.35
	Def	++	2007	AAA	Syracuse	47	4	9	0	4	191	208	234	442	2	79	0.10	2	0	22	43	0.67

Wiry strong athlete gained some semblance of offense, showing moderate power. Struggles to hit for BA due to mediocre plate discipline and a long swing which gets exploited by good pitching. Plus arm strength compensates for average range and stiff hands.

Sapp,Max — 2 — Houston — EXP MLB DEBUT: 2010 — POTENTIAL: Starting CA — 8D

Bats L Age 20
2006 (1) HS (FL)

			Year	Lev	Team	AB	R	H	HR	RBI	Avg	OB	Slg	OPS	bb%	ct%	Eye	SB	CS	X/H%	Iso	RC/G
	Pwr	++++																				
	BAvg	+++																				
	Spd	+	2006	A-	Tri City	166	20	38	1	20	229	319	301	620	12	78	0.59	0	0	26	72	3.35
	Def	++	2007	A-	Lexington	315	25	76	2	32	241	330	333	663	11	78	0.54	0	0	32	92	3.55

Strong/stocky catcher with plus bat speed and uppercut swing that gives him above average power. Plate discipline is strong for experience level and should hit for better BA. Defense is questionable as his receiving skills and agility hardly measure-up to his strong throwing arm.

Saunders,Michael — 9 — Seattle — EXP MLB DEBUT: 2009 — POTENTIAL: Platoon RF/LF — 7C

Bats L Age 21
2004 (11) Tallahassee C

			Year	Lev	Team	AB	R	H	HR	RBI	Avg	OB	Slg	OPS	bb%	ct%	Eye	SB	CS	X/H%	Iso	RC/G
	Pwr	+++	2005	A-	Everett	196	24	53	7	39	270	359	474	833	12	62	0.36	2	7	43	204	6.76
	BAvg	++	2006	A-	Wisconsin	360	47	86	4	39	239	328	344	673	12	71	0.47	22	6	26	106	4.03
4.15	Spd	+++	2007	A+	High Desert	431	91	129	14	77	299	385	473	858	12	73	0.52	27	10	33	174	6.50
	Def	+++	2007	AA	West Tenn	52	8	15	1	7	288	373	442	815	12	62	0.35	2	1	27	154	6.61

Tall/athletic outfielder with excellent secondary skills, but a poor contact rate could suppress BA. Moderate bat speed produces doubles power and runs the bases efficiently and aggressively. Possesses range in the outfield, but a fringe-average arm may limit time in CF.

Schafer,Jordan — 9 — Atlanta — EXP MLB DEBUT: 2009 — POTENTIAL: Starting CF — 9C

Bats L Age 21
2005 (3) HS (FL)

			Year	Lev	Team	AB	R	H	HR	RBI	Avg	OB	Slg	OPS	bb%	ct%	Eye	SB	CS	X/H%	Iso	RC/G
	Pwr	+++	2005	Rk	GCL Braves	182	18	37	3	19	203	256	352	608	7	73	0.27	13	6	49	148	2.95
	BAvg	++++	2006	A-	Rome	388	49	93	8	60	240	291	376	667	7	76	0.30	15	9	32	137	3.67
4.05	Spd	++++	2007	A-	Rome	129	16	48	5	20	372	441	636	1077	11	76	0.52	4	4	46	264	9.34
	Def	++++	2007	A+	Myrtle Beach	436	70	128	10	43	294	353	477	830	8	78	0.42	19	11	41	183	5.90

Strong/athletic hitter with five above average tools and led minors in hits. Drives ball to all fields and improved power through a shortened swing and added strength. Plus speed is useful for steals and on defense, where paired with his plus arm, makes him above average in CF.

Schierholtz,Nate — 9 — San Francisco — EXP MLB DEBUT: 2007 — POTENTIAL: Starting RF — 8C

Bats L Age 24
2003 (2) Chabot JC

			Year	Lev	Team	AB	R	H	HR	RBI	Avg	OB	Slg	OPS	bb%	ct%	Eye	SB	CS	X/H%	Iso	RC/G
			2004	A+	San Jose	258	39	76	3	31	295	333	469	802	5	84	0.37	3	1	39	174	5.41
	Pwr	++++	2005	A+	San Jose	502	83	160	15	86	319	360	514	873	6	74	0.24	5	7	38	195	6.41
	BAvg	++	2006	AA	Connecticut	470	55	126	14	54	268	308	438	746	5	83	0.33	8	3	37	170	4.57
4.30	Spd	++	2007	AAA	Fresno	411	67	137	16	68	333	360	560	919	4	86	0.29	10	4	39	226	6.49
	Def	++	2007	MLB	San Francisco	112	9	34	0	10	304	316	402	718	2	83	0.11	3	1	24	98	4.12

Strong/muscular hitter with bat speed and power to all fields. Plate discipline and long swing cause fluctuations in BA, but does hit ball hard when he makes contact. Takes better routes in RF after moving from infield and possesses a strong/accurate throwing arm.

Schnurstein,Micah — 35 — Chicago (A) — EXP MLB DEBUT: 2009 — POTENTIAL: Reserve 3B/1B — 7C

Bats R Age 24
2002 (7) HS (NV)

			Year	Lev	Team	AB	R	H	HR	RBI	Avg	OB	Slg	OPS	bb%	ct%	Eye	SB	CS	X/H%	Iso	RC/G
			2003	Rk	Great Falls	193	35	51	1	16	264	304	337	641	5	80	0.28	0	1	22	73	3.31
	Pwr	+++	2004	A-	Kannapolis	491	52	135	6	58	275	311	379	690	5	79	0.25	14	4	29	104	3.89
	BAvg	++	2005	A+	Win-Sal	488	78	131	15	68	268	324	416	740	8	80	0.41	12	8	30	148	4.56
	Spd	++	2006	AA	Birmingham	480	48	105	9	46	219	256	335	591	5	79	0.24	8	6	34	117	2.63
	Def	+++	2007	A+	Win-Sal	508	83	139	25	84	274	343	508	851	10	80	0.52	7	8	47	234	6.05

Tall/strong hitter found offensive groove and led CAR in HR and SLG. Solid bat speed propels bat through zone and improve loft on hits. Low contact rate will keep BA low, but BABIP remains high. Defense is much better at 1B where his lack of agility is less of an issue.

Schoop,Sharlon — 64 — San Francisco — EXP MLB DEBUT: 2010 — POTENTIAL: Starting SS/2B — 8E

Bats R Age 21
2004 FA (Curacao)

			Year	Lev	Team	AB	R	H	HR	RBI	Avg	OB	Slg	OPS	bb%	ct%	Eye	SB	CS	X/H%	Iso	RC/G
			2005	Rk	AZL Giants	169	29	43	1	19	254	311	296	607	8	89	0.78	10	4	12	41	3.25
	Pwr	+	2006	Rk	AZL Giants	126	29	39	1	21	310	428	405	832	17	88	1.73	8	3	23	95	6.47
	BAvg	+++	2006	A-	Salem-Keizer	7	1	2	0	1	286	444	286	730	22	100		0	0	0	0	6.05
	Spd	++++	2007	A-	Salem-Keizer	190	30	54	4	29	284	337	463	800	7	82	0.43	2	4	39	179	5.43
	Def	+++++	2007	A-	Augusta	136	18	32	1	19	235	278	301	579	6	76	0.25	4	3	22	66	2.47

Athletic middle infielder with strong defensive skills, featuring plus range, soft hands, and arm strength. Makes excellent contact and draws walks which enhances BA and allows him to utilize speed. Lacks physical strength so doesn't hit for power and struggled in full-season league.

Sellers,Justin — 46 — Oakland — EXP MLB DEBUT: 2009 — POTENTIAL: Reserve SS/2B — 7D

Bats R Age 22
2005 (6) HS (CA)

			Year	Lev	Team	AB	R	H	HR	RBI	Avg	OB	Slg	OPS	bb%	ct%	Eye	SB	CS	X/H%	Iso	RC/G
	Pwr	++	2005	A-	Vancouver	175	31	48	0	13	274	345	331	677	10	86	0.79	8	3	19	57	4.15
	BAvg	+++	2006	A-	Kane Co	411	75	99	5	46	241	335	338	673	12	84	0.89	17	5	28	97	4.17
4.20	Spd	+++	2007	A+	Stockton	434	72	119	4	37	274	344	378	722	10	84	0.67	11	4	28	104	4.62
	Def	+++++	2007	AA	Midland	45	2	7	0	3	156	208	178	386	6	78	0.30	2	0	14	22	0.08

Small/athletic infielder with outstanding defense, featuring arm strength, range, and soft/quick hands. Slap-type approach attenuates BA and will draw walks, which gives opportunities to steal bases. Lacks power in his swing and is under consideration to switch-hit.

Shelby, John — 4 — Chicago (A)

Bats R **Age** 22 — 2006 (5) Kentucky — **EXP MLB DEBUT:** 2009 — **POTENTIAL:** Starting 2B — **7D**

Pwr +++ / BAvg +++ / 4.00 Spd ++++ / Def ++

Year	Lev	Team	AB	R	H	HR	RBI	Avg	OB	Slg	OPS	bb%	ct%	Eye	SB	CS	X/H%	Iso	RC/G
2006	Rk	Great Falls	250	37	68	8	36	272	321	432	753	7	78	0.33	7	4	32	160	4.69
2007	A-	Kannapolis	488	83	147	16	79	301	348	508	856	7	84	0.45	19	8	41	207	5.98

Solid full-season debut, showing good secondary skills. Provides moderate power and makes contact, but power may lessen with promotion due to a long swing and mediocre plate discipline. Exhibits range, but average arm, stiff hands, and poor infield actions could send him to CF.

Sinisi, Vince — 37 — San Diego

Bats L **Age** 26 — 2003 (2) Rice — **EXP MLB DEBUT:** 2008 — **POTENTIAL:** Reserve LF/1B — **6B**

Pwr +++ / BAvg +++ / 4.35 Spd ++ / Def ++

Year	Lev	Team	AB	R	H	HR	RBI	Avg	OB	Slg	OPS	bb%	ct%	Eye	SB	CS	X/H%	Iso	RC/G
2005	A+	Bakersfield	135	25	49	6	22	363	434	600	1034	11	86	0.89	5	0	37	237	8.30
2005	AA	Frisco	248	27	64	4	29	258	300	343	643	6	84	0.38	4	4	20	85	3.36
2006	AA	Fris/Mob	448	61	122	7	55	272	353	404	757	11	82	0.68	9	4	35	132	5.10
2006	AAA	Oklahoma	50	6	11	0	7	220	304	300	604	11	82	0.67	0	0	36	80	3.26
2007	AAA	Portland	303	44	94	9	36	310	353	475	828	6	86	0.49	5	3	33	165	5.57

Strong/muscular hitter with bat speed that provides only gap power. Improved BA with controlled-aggressive approach and better contact rate. Speed is below average and lacks arm strength, so is a below average fielder at 1B and both corner outfield positions.

Sizemore, Scott — 46 — Detroit

Bats R **Age** 23 — 2006 (5) Virginia Comm — **EXP MLB DEBUT:** 2009 — **POTENTIAL:** Platoon 2B/SS — **7C**

Pwr ++ / BAvg +++ / 4.30 Spd +++ / Def ++++

Year	Lev	Team	AB	R	H	HR	RBI	Avg	OB	Slg	OPS	bb%	ct%	Eye	SB	CS	X/H%	Iso	RC/G
2006	A-	Oneonta	294	49	96	3	37	327	393	435	828	10	84	0.68	7	5	23	109	5.89
2007	A-	W. Michigan	438	78	116	4	48	265	370	390	760	14	86	1.22	16	10	36	126	5.43

Hard-nosed athlete with excellent instincts and average tools. Possesses strong plate discipline and contact ability, which keeps his OBP high. Lacks bat speed and power, but can drive doubles. Steals bases despite average speed and can be solid-average defensively at 2B.

Skelton, James — 2 — Detroit

Bats L **Age** 22 — 2004 (14) HS (CA) — **EXP MLB DEBUT:** 2010 — **POTENTIAL:** Reserve CA — **7E**

Pwr ++ / BAvg ++++ / 4.25 Spd +++ / Def ++

Year	Lev	Team	AB	R	H	HR	RBI	Avg	OB	Slg	OPS	bb%	ct%	Eye	SB	CS	X/H%	Iso	RC/G
2004	Rk	GCL Tigers	43	3	6	0	2	140	260	163	423	14	74	0.64	0	0	17	23	0.67
2005	Rk	GCL Tigers	33	6	6	0	1	182	413	212	625	28	73	1.44	0	0	17	30	3.91
2005	A+	Lakeland	1	0	0	0	0	0	0	0	0	0	0	0.00	0	0	0	0	0.00
2006	A-	Oneonta	130	20	39	1	22	300	397	400	797	14	78	0.72	1	1	26	100	5.80
2007	A-	W. Michigan	353	60	109	7	52	309	402	448	850	13	85	1.04	18	5	30	139	6.36

Athletic catcher with solid contact/BA ability and plate discipline. Lacks bat speed and ability to pull baseball which cuts-down power, but adds dimension of the stolen base with his speed. Footwork and release needs improvement in order to off-set average arm strength.

Smith, David — 9 — Toronto

Bats R **Age** 27 — 2005 (12) West Virginia St — **EXP MLB DEBUT:** 2008 — **POTENTIAL:** Platoon RF/LF — **7C**

Pwr ++++ / BAvg ++ / 4.30 Spd +++ / Def +++

Year	Lev	Team	AB	R	H	HR	RBI	Avg	OB	Slg	OPS	bb%	ct%	Eye	SB	CS	X/H%	Iso	RC/G
2003	A-	Charleston	342	44	83	8	29	243	307	523	670	9	80	0.48	7	1	28	120	3.78
2004	A-	Charleston	436	74	121	12	68	278	356	431	787	11	73	0.45	5	0	34	154	5.48
2005	A+	Dunedin	391	65	115	14	73	294	352	473	825	8	81	0.48	4	2	35	179	5.66
2006	AA	New Hamp	483	67	122	19	74	253	310	443	753	8	76	0.34	7	4	43	190	4.76
2007	AA	New Hamp	463	85	128	24	70	276	351	512	863	10	77	0.50	4	5	47	235	6.32

Tall/athletic outfielder with power to all fields, bat speed, and ability to draw walks. Mediocre plate discipline and contact rate will keep BA down and struggles against RH pitching. Average defender in corner outfield possessing a strong arm and average range.

Smith, Seth — 8 — Colorado

Bats R **Age** 25 — 2004 (2) Mississippi — **EXP MLB DEBUT:** 2007 — **POTENTIAL:** Platoon LF/CF — **7B**

Pwr +++ / BAvg +++ / 4.40 Spd ++ / Def +++

Year	Lev	Team	AB	R	H	HR	RBI	Avg	OB	Slg	OPS	bb%	ct%	Eye	SB	CS	X/H%	Iso	RC/G
2004	Rk	Casper	233	46	86	9	61	369	430	601	1031	10	80	0.53	9	1	38	232	8.40
2005	A+	Modesto	533	87	160	9	72	300	354	458	811	8	78	0.38	5	3	38	158	5.62
2006	AA	Tulsa	524	79	154	15	71	294	357	483	839	9	86	0.69	4	4	42	189	5.94
2007	AAA	Colo Springs	451	68	143	17	82	317	371	528	899	8	84	0.53	7	3	38	211	6.54
2007	MLB	Colorado	8	4	5	0	0	625	625	875	1500	0	88	0.00	0	0	20	250	12.85

Impressed coaches with his all-around style of play. Bat speed, contact ability, and plate discipline account for both BA and moderate power. Runs bases well despite below average speed. Plays all three outfield positions, possessing good range and average arm strength.

Smith, Tim — 7 — Texas

Bats L **Age** 21 — 2007 (7) Arizona St — **EXP MLB DEBUT:** 2009 — **POTENTIAL:** Platoon LF — **7D**

Pwr ++ / BAvg ++++ / 4.25 Spd ++ / Def +++

Year	Lev	Team	AB	R	H	HR	RBI	Avg	OB	Slg	OPS	bb%	ct%	Eye	SB	CS	X/H%	Iso	RC/G
2007	A-	Spokane	81	18	23	1	9	284	370	383	752	12	80	0.69	1	2	26	99	5.06

Lean/athletic outfielder with solid barrel awareness and plate discipline which allows him to hit for BA and get on-base. Lacks loft in swing which depresses power, but has gap power. Runs bases well despite slightly below average speed and has average arm strength in LF.

Smolinski, Jake — 73 — Washington

Bats R **Age** 19 — 2007 (2) HS (IL) — **EXP MLB DEBUT:** 2011 — **POTENTIAL:** Starting RF/LF — **8E**

Pwr ++++ / BAvg +++ / Spd ++ / Def +++

Year	Lev	Team	AB	R	H	HR	RBI	Avg	OB	Slg	OPS	bb%	ct%	Eye	SB	CS	X/H%	Iso	RC/G
2007	Rk	GCL Nationals	105	18	32	1	16	305	381	410	791	11	77	0.54	7	2	28	105	5.55

Strong and athletic, he had an impressive debut hitting for BA and driving ball to gaps. HR power projects to come late, but will have to tighten-up strike zone. Possesses below average speed, but picks spots to steal. Made defensive transition from SS to LF where he shows plus arm strength.

Snider, Travis — 9 — Toronto

Bats L **Age** 20 — 2006 (1) HS (WA) — **EXP MLB DEBUT:** 2009 — **POTENTIAL:** Starting RF — **9B**

Pwr ++++ / BAvg ++++ / 4.45 Spd + / Def ++

Year	Lev	Team	AB	R	H	HR	RBI	Avg	OB	Slg	OPS	bb%	ct%	Eye	SB	CS	X/H%	Iso	RC/G
2006	Rk	Pulaski	194	36	63	11	41	325	415	567	982	13	76	0.64	6	3	38	242	8.02
2007	A-	Lansing	457	72	143	16	93	313	379	525	905	10	72	0.38	3	10	41	212	7.12

Bat speed, strong hands, and contact ability produce above average power, which allowed him to lead MWL in SLG, doubles, and RBI. Plate discipline slipped, which could make it hard to maintain +.300 BA, but will use whole field. Lacks range in RF, but possesses arm strength.

Snyder, Brad — 9 — Cleveland

Bats L **Age** 26 — 2003 (1) Ball St — **EXP MLB DEBUT:** 2008 — **POTENTIAL:** Reserve RF/LF — **7D**

Pwr +++ / BAvg ++ / 4.40 Spd +++ / Def +++

Year	Lev	Team	AB	R	H	HR	RBI	Avg	OB	Slg	OPS	bb%	ct%	Eye	SB	CS	X/H%	Iso	RC/G
2004	A+	Kinston	110	20	39	6	21	355	423	600	1023	11	75	0.46	4	2	36	245	8.48
2005	A+	Kinston	209	36	58	6	28	278	352	431	783	10	69	0.38	12	1	31	153	5.48
2005	AA	Akron	304	56	85	16	54	280	334	539	874	8	69	0.27	5	3	49	260	6.64
2006	AA	Akron	523	86	141	18	72	270	347	446	793	11	70	0.39	20	3	36	176	5.60
2007	AAA	Buffalo	259	41	68	10	35	263	353	448	800	12	65	0.40	12	0	37	185	5.98

Broken left thumb caused him to miss half of season, but really hasn't improved game in three years. Moderate bat speed allows him to drill mistakes, but trigger is slow and struggles with pitch recognition. Intelligent baserunner and is solid defensively in both outfield corners.

Snyder, Brandon — 3 — Baltimore

Bats R **Age** 21 — 2005 (1) HS (VA) — **EXP MLB DEBUT:** 2009 — **POTENTIAL:** Starting 1B — **8D**

Pwr ++++ / BAvg ++ / Spd ++ / Def +++

Year	Lev	Team	AB	R	H	HR	RBI	Avg	OB	Slg	OPS	bb%	ct%	Eye	SB	CS	X/H%	Iso	RC/G
2005	Rk	Bluefield	144	26	39	8	35	271	390	493	883	16	75	0.78	7	2	41	222	6.82
2005	A-	Aberdeen	28	4	11	0	6	393	433	464	898	7	75	0.29	0	0	18	71	6.76
2006	A-	Aberdeen	123	14	28	1	20	228	258	333	591	4	65	0.12	1	1	36	106	2.69
2006	A-	Delmarva	144	12	28	3	20	194	242	340	582	6	62	0.16	0	0	54	146	2.65
2007	A-	Delmarva	448	63	127	11	58	283	348	422	769	9	76	0.41	0	2	29	138	5.08

Strong/muscular hitter with good bat speed and power potential. Plate discipline will cause BA to suffer, but made adjustments in second half. Rotator cuff surgery decreased arm strength and lacked mobility behind plate, so was moved to 1B where offense will be more of a factor.

Sogard,Eric — 4 — San Diego

EXP MLB DEBUT: 2009 | POTENTIAL: Starting 2B | 7C

Bats L Age 22
2007 (2-C) Arizona St

Pwr +
BAvg ++++
4.10 Spd ++++
Def +++

Year	Lev	Team	AB	R	H	HR	RBI	Avg	OB	Slg	OPS	bb%	ct%	Eye	SB	CS	X/H%	Iso	RC/G
2007	A-	Eugene	125	20	32	2	18	256	354	376	730	13	87	1.19	4	2	34	120	4.97
2007	A-	Ft. Wayne	83	7	21	2	15	253	303	349	653	7	84	0.46	2	2	19	96	3.49
2007	AAA	Portland	3	0	0	0	0	0	0	0	0	0	0	0.00	0	0	0	0	0.00

Short/athletic infielder with excellent BA ability due to plate discipline, contact rate, and speed. Short stroke and lack of bat speed precludes him hitting for power, but should hit share of doubles. Defense is well-suited for 2B with range, soft hands, and average arm strength.

Soto,Geovany — 23 — Chicago (N)

EXP MLB DEBUT: 2005 | POTENTIAL: Starting CA | 7A

Bats R Age 25
2001 (11) HS (PR)

Pwr ++++
BAvg +++
4.70 Spd +
Def ++++

Year	Lev	Team	AB	R	H	HR	RBI	Avg	OB	Slg	OPS	bb%	ct%	Eye	SB	CS	X/H%	Iso	RC/G
2005	AAA	Iowa	292	30	74	4	39	253	359	342	701	14	74	0.62	0	1	24	89	4.46
2006	AAA	Iowa	342	34	92	6	38	269	347	383	730	11	78	0.55	0	1	29	114	4.68
2006	MLB	Chicago (N)	25	1	5	0	2	200	200	240	440	0	80	0.00	0	0	20	40	0.58
2007	AAA	Iowa	385	75	136	26	109	353	432	652	1083	12	76	0.56	0	0	44	299	9.29
2007	MLB	Chicago (N)	54	12	21	3	8	389	441	667	1107	8	74	0.36	0	0	43	278	9.57

PCL MVP leading league in RBI and the minors in SLG. Drove ball consistently, making hard contact with his compact swing, generating more uppercut, and turning on inside pitches. Solid catch-and-throw receiver, preventing running game (31% CS%) and showing newfound agility.

Soto,Neftali — 65 — Cincinnati

EXP MLB DEBUT: 2010 | POTENTIAL: Starting 3B | 8E

Bats R Age 19
2007 (3) HS (PR)

Pwr +++
BAvg +++
4.30 Spd +++
Def +++

Year	Lev	Team	AB	R	H	HR	RBI	Avg	OB	Slg	OPS	bb%	ct%	Eye	SB	CS	X/H%	Iso	RC/G
2007	Rk	GCL Reds	152	18	46	2	28	303	350	454	804	7	80	0.35	2	0	30	151	5.48

Strong athlete with moderate bat speed and ability to center baseball providing moderate power. Hits for BA, but doesn't recognize pitches well. Average speed is likely to decline and already shows limited range at SS. Arm speed and soft/quick hands will play just as well at 3B.

Span,Denard — 8 — Minnesota

EXP MLB DEBUT: 2008 | POTENTIAL: Reserve CF/LF | 7E

Bats L Age 24
2002 (1) HS (FL)

Pwr +
BAvg +++
4.00 Spd ++++
Def +++

Year	Lev	Team	AB	R	H	HR	RBI	Avg	OB	Slg	OPS	bb%	ct%	Eye	SB	CS	X/H%	Iso	RC/G
2004	A-	Quad Cities	240	29	64	0	14	267	358	308	666	12	80	0.69	15	8	11	42	4.01
2005	A+	Fort Myers	186	38	63	1	19	339	409	403	812	11	87	0.88	13	4	11	65	5.74
2005	AA	New Britain	267	47	76	0	26	285	339	345	684	8	85	0.54	10	8	14	60	4.06
2006	AA	New Britain	536	80	153	2	45	285	335	349	684	7	85	0.51	23	11	16	63	4.01
2007	AAA	Rochester	487	59	130	3	55	267	323	355	678	8	82	0.44	25	14	23	88	3.94

Speed in only positive to game as he is a threat on the bases and chases down flyballs in CF. Slap-type approach generate some infield hits, but doesn't hit for BA consistently and has no power. Arm strength is well below average and limits value defensively.

Spencer,Matt — 7 — Philadelphia

EXP MLB DEBUT: 2009 | POTENTIAL: Platoon LF/RF | 7D

Bats L Age 22
2007 (3) Arizona St

Pwr +++
BAvg +++
4.40 Spd ++
Def ++

Year	Lev	Team	AB	R	H	HR	RBI	Avg	OB	Slg	OPS	bb%	ct%	Eye	SB	CS	X/H%	Iso	RC/G
2007	A-	Williamsport	179	21	47	9	26	263	305	469	775	6	74	0.24	3	3	40	207	4.89

Lean/athletic outfielder produced BA and moderate power as collegian, but can be pitched to and plate discipline is lacking, which makes offense hard to project. Instinctive player on the bases and defensively, but may be relegated to LF due to below average range and arm strength.

Stansberry,Craig — 4 — San Diego

EXP MLB DEBUT: 2007 | POTENTIAL: Reserve 2B | 5A

Bats R Age 26
2003 (5) Rice

Pwr ++
BAvg +++
4.25 Spd +++
Def +++

Year	Lev	Team	AB	R	H	HR	RBI	Avg	OB	Slg	OPS	bb%	ct%	Eye	SB	CS	X/H%	Iso	RC/G
2005	AA	Altoona	421	62	100	18	67	238	310	470	780	9	73	0.39	14	5	51	233	5.30
2006	AA	Altoona	260	46	67	10	30	258	337	465	802	11	76	0.50	8	3	46	208	5.59
2006	AAA	Indianapolis	197	30	44	3	25	223	341	340	681	15	82	1.00	10	3	34	117	4.36
2007	AAA	Portland	466	83	127	14	75	273	368	446	814	13	80	0.74	10	10	39	174	5.86
2007	MLB	San Diego	7	1	2	0	1	286	286	286	571	0	57	0.00	0	0	0	0	2.38

Plays above tools with aggressive style, showing above average speed and ability to walk. Makes fair contact, uses whole field, and can hit for BA, but most of power is to pull field. Soft/quick hands and arm strength allow him to make plays at 2B despite lack of range.

Stanton,Mike — 9 — Florida

EXP MLB DEBUT: 2011 | POTENTIAL: Starting RF | 8E

Bats R Age 18
2007 (2) HS (CA)

Pwr ++++
BAvg ++
Spd ++++
Def +++

Year	Lev	Team	AB	R	H	HR	RBI	Avg	OB	Slg	OPS	bb%	ct%	Eye	SB	CS	X/H%	Iso	RC/G
2007	Rk	GCL Marlins	26	6	7	0	1	269	296	346	642	4	77	0.17	0	0	29	77	3.27
2007	A-	Jamestown	30	2	2	1	2	67	152	200	352	9	50	0.20	0	0	100	133	-1.44

Tall/athletic outfielder with plus speed and excellent raw power. Lacks strike zone judgment and contact ability, but is still new to game, as he split his time with football. Runs with long strides and has solid closing range, which coupled with his arm strength, could make him a solid defender.

Statia,Hainley — 6 — Los Angeles (A)

EXP MLB DEBUT: 2009 | POTENTIAL: Reserve SS/2B | 7C

Bats B Age 22
2004 (9) HS (FL)

Pwr +
BAvg +++
4.20 Spd ++++
Def ++++

Year	Lev	Team	AB	R	H	HR	RBI	Avg	OB	Slg	OPS	bb%	ct%	Eye	SB	CS	X/H%	Iso	RC/G
2005	Rk	Orem	277	44	83	2	41	300	353	426	779	8	86	0.58	12	10	30	126	5.24
2005	A+	Rancho Cuc	106	12	26	1	8	245	279	292	572	5	88	0.38	6	3	12	47	2.57
2006	A-	Cedar Rapids	417	68	125	1	39	300	377	386	763	11	87	0.96	23	15	26	86	5.28
2006	A+	Rancho Cuc	60	8	18	0	8	300	382	367	749	12	88	1.14	1	1	17	67	5.18
2007	A+	Rancho Cuc	549	86	158	3	74	288	345	379	724	8	86	0.61	29	8	23	91	4.58

Small/athletic infielder possesses bat handling ability, plate discipline, and speed, making him a potential, #2 hitter. Hits well from both sides of the plate, but lacks power. Improved arm strength, which in-concert with his soft hands and range, makes him a solid defensive SS.

Stavinoha,Nick — 9 — St. Louis

EXP MLB DEBUT: 2008 | POTENTIAL: Platoon RF/LF | 7C

Bats R Age 26
2005 (7) Louisiana St

Pwr +++
BAvg ++
4.45 Spd ++
Def +++

Year	Lev	Team	AB	R	H	HR	RBI	Avg	OB	Slg	OPS	bb%	ct%	Eye	SB	CS	X/H%	Iso	RC/G
2005	A-	Quad Cities	250	54	86	14	53	344	399	564	963	8	90	0.92	4	0	29	220	7.12
2006	AA	Springfield	417	55	124	12	73	297	342	460	802	6	81	0.35	2	1	33	163	5.29
2007	AAA	Memphis	501	50	131	13	49	261	305	373	678	6	84	0.38	7	1	23	112	3.73

Offense has stagnated at upper levels where he doesn't provide enough HR power and plate discipline is declining. Uses whole field to drive ball and has periods where he'll hit for BA. Possesses strong arm in RF, but below average speed leaves him with mediocre range.

Stewart,Caleb — 9 — New York (N)

EXP MLB DEBUT: 2008 | POTENTIAL: Reserve LF/RF | 6C

Bats R Age 26
2004 (22) Kentucky

Pwr ++++
BAvg ++
Spd +
Def ++

Year	Lev	Team	AB	R	H	HR	RBI	Avg	OB	Slg	OPS	bb%	ct%	Eye	SB	CS	X/H%	Iso	RC/G
2004	A-	Capital City	86	20	27	5	15	314	404	558	962	13	87	1.18	0	1	41	244	7.47
2005	A-	Brooklyn	265	39	72	10	45	272	381	487	868	15	76	0.73	6	3	49	215	6.71
2005	A+	St. Lucie	56	12	16	3	7	286	365	554	919	11	77	0.54	3	1	56	268	7.08
2006	A+	St. Lucie	242	38	63	14	42	260	327	521	848	9	79	0.46	1	1	52	260	5.96
2007	AA	Binghamton	433	63	109	16	69	252	309	400	709	8	76	0.35	4	7	28	148	4.12

Strong/muscular hitter with excellent pull power and co-led the AFL in HR. Pitches with a wrinkle give him fits and too much back load makes his swing late on occasion. Lack of speed gives him very little range, but does possesses excellent arm strength in corner outfield.

Stewart,Ian — 5 — Colorado

EXP MLB DEBUT: 2007 | POTENTIAL: Starting 3B | 9C

Bats L Age 23
2003 (1) HS (CA)

Pwr ++++
BAvg +++
4.30 Spd ++
Def +++

Year	Lev	Team	AB	R	H	HR	RBI	Avg	OB	Slg	OPS	bb%	ct%	Eye	SB	CS	X/H%	Iso	RC/G
2004	A-	Asheville	505	92	161	30	101	319	398	594	992	12	78	0.59	19	9	43	275	7.97
2005	A+	Modesto	435	83	119	17	86	274	351	497	848	11	74	0.46	2	2	47	223	6.27
2006	AA	Tulsa	462	75	124	10	71	268	340	452	792	10	77	0.48	3	8	47	184	5.52
2007	AAA	Colo Springs	414	72	126	15	65	304	378	478	856	11	78	0.53	11	2	32	174	6.22
2007	MLB	Colorado	43	3	9	1	9	209	227	372	599	2	60	0.06	0	0	56	163	2.92

Offense starting to return to projected levels, though home ballpark played a big role. Bat speed with uppercut swing generates power to all fields and mature approach enhances BA. Defense at 3B is strong featuring good arm strength, and may get opportunity at 2B in spring.

Still, Jon — 32 — Boston
EXP MLB DEBUT: 2009 — POTENTIAL: Platoon 1B/CA — 7D
Bats R — Age 23 — 2006 (4) NC State
Pwr ++++ | BAvg +++ | Spd + | Def ++

Year	Lev	Team	AB	R	H	HR	RBI	Avg	OB	Slg	OPS	bb%	ct%	Eye	SB	CS	X/H%	Iso	RC/G
2006	A-	Lowell	232	23	51	2	27	220	298	293	592	10	82	0.63	0	0	24	73	3.00
2007	A+	Lancaster	80	19	23	4	19	288	418	488	906	18	78	1.00	0	1	35	200	7.21
2007	AA	Greenville	360	71	105	21	79	292	430	542	971	19	76	1.02	2	0	45	250	8.17

Strong wrists and bat speed produce power to pull field, and has the plate discipline and contact ability to hit for BA. Drafted as a catcher, but with little agility and mediocre receiving skills, he began playing 1B. Possesses arm strength and should be able to catch occasionally.

Stubbs, Drew — 8 — Cincinnati
EXP MLB DEBUT: 2009 — POTENTIAL: Starting CF — 8C
Bats R — Age 23 — 2006 (1) Texas
Pwr ++++ | BAvg ++ | Spd ++++ (4.10) | Def +++++

Year	Lev	Team	AB	R	H	HR	RBI	Avg	OB	Slg	OPS	bb%	ct%	Eye	SB	CS	X/H%	Iso	RC/G
2006	Rk	Billings	210	39	53	6	25	252	351	400	751	13	70	0.50	19	4	30	148	5.13
2007	A-	Dayton	497	93	134	12	43	270	359	421	779	12	71	0.49	23	15	34	151	5.49

Athletic outfielder possesses two plus tools in his speed and CF defense. Bat speed and wiry strength generate power, and shortened a lengthy swing, but questionable contact rate will always keep BA low. Instinctive baserunner who can steal bases and led MWL in runs scored.

Sublett, Damon — 4 — New York (A)
EXP MLB DEBUT: 2010 — POTENTIAL: Platoon 2B — 7C
Bats L — Age 22 — 2007 (7) Wichita St
Pwr ++ | BAvg ++++ | Spd ++++ (4.10) | Def +++

Year	Lev	Team	AB	R	H	HR	RBI	Avg	OB	Slg	OPS	bb%	ct%	Eye	SB	CS	X/H%	Iso	RC/G
2007	A-	Staten Island	239	43	78	8	53	326	429	531	960	15	80	0.91	10	4	38	205	7.86

Offensive-minded infielder with short/compact stroke, bat speed, and contact ability giving him moderate power and BA ability. Led NY-P in RBI being a good situational/clutch hitter. Average defender at 2B with soft hands and arm strength, but lacks range and DP turn.

Sulentic, Matt — 7 — Oakland
EXP MLB DEBUT: 2010 — POTENTIAL: Platoon LF/RF — 8E
Bats L — Age 20 — 2006 (3) HS (TX)
Pwr +++ | BAvg ++++ | Spd +++ (4.20) | Def ++

Year	Lev	Team	AB	R	H	HR	RBI	Avg	OB	Slg	OPS	bb%	ct%	Eye	SB	CS	X/H%	Iso	RC/G
2006	A-	Kane Co	98	12	23	1	13	235	318	327	645	11	81	0.63	1	2	26	92	3.67
2006	A-	Vancouver	144	24	51	2	22	354	411	479	891	9	79	0.47	3	4	25	125	6.65
2007	A-	Kane Co	206	14	36	1	16	175	234	218	452	6	82	0.35	2	0	19	44	-1.01
2007	A-	Vancouver	276	41	72	4	40	261	362	388	750	13	71	0.53	2	5	35	127	5.11

Pure hitter with fluid stroke and moderate bat speed, but offense tapered-off from debut season. Bat speed should allow him to approach moderate power and is patient enough to hit good pitches. Average arm strength and range likely limits him to LF.

Sutil, Wladimir — 46 — Houston
EXP MLB DEBUT: 2009 — POTENTIAL: Reserve 2B/SS — 6C
Bats R — Age 23 — 2004 FA (Venezuela)
Pwr + | BAvg +++ | Spd ++++ (4.10) | Def ++++

Year	Lev	Team	AB	R	H	HR	RBI	Avg	OB	Slg	OPS	bb%	ct%	Eye	SB	CS	X/H%	Iso	RC/G
2005	A-	Tri City	231	42	76	0	21	329	387	385	773	9	95	1.83	13	6	17	56	5.35
2005	A-	Lexington	23	2	6	0	3	261	261	304	565	0	78	0.00	2	0	17	43	2.04
2006	A-	Lexington	195	31	52	0	12	267	332	308	639	9	92	1.27	20	5	15	41	3.85
2006	A+	Salem	97	14	22	0	9	227	292	278	571	8	90	0.90	8	3	23	52	2.98
2007	A+	Salem	393	42	107	0	41	272	333	310	644	8	88	0.77	36	10	14	38	3.70

Light-framed infielder with game-changing speed and projects as a solid number two hitter with ability to handle bat and draw walks. Medium bat speed limits power and needs to add strength. Possesses solid range, but arm strength is better suited for 2B.

Suttle, Brad — 5 — New York (A)
EXP MLB DEBUT: 2009 — POTENTIAL: Starting 3B — 8D
Bats B — Age 22 — 2007 (4) Texas
Pwr ++++ | BAvg +++ | Spd ++ | Def ++

Year	Lev	Team	AB	R	H	HR	RBI	Avg	OB	Slg	OPS	bb%	ct%	Eye	SB	CS	X/H%	Iso	RC/G
2007	Rk	GCL Yankees	8	1	1	0	1	125	222	125	347	11	75	0.50	0	0	0	0	-0.45

Draft-eligible sophomore who signed above slot. Switch-hits with fluid hitting mechanics and power/BA from both sides. He showed plate discipline in college and should carry it over. Possesses arm strength and soft hands at 3B, but a heavy lower half limits mobility and speed.

Sweeney, Matt — 5 — Los Angeles (A)
EXP MLB DEBUT: 2010 — POTENTIAL: Platoon 3B/1B — 8C
Bats L — Age 20 — 2006 (8) HS (MD)
Pwr | BAvg +++ | Spd + | Def ++

Year	Lev	Team	AB	R	H	HR	RBI	Avg	OB	Slg	OPS	bb%	ct%	Eye	SB	CS	X/H%	Iso	RC/G
2006	Rk	AZL Angels	170	38	58	5	39	341	420	576	996	12	84	0.85	4	1	40	235	8.07
2006	Rk	Orem	6	0	1	0	0	167	167	167	333	0	67	0.00	0	0	0	0	-1.38
2007	A-	Cedar Rapids	439	64	114	18	72	260	324	458	782	8	80	0.43	7	7	43	198	4.88

Bat speed and aggressive nature make him a constant power threat, but will need to tighten strike zone and make better contact to improve overall offensive package. Converted to 3B from catcher, he displays good arm strength, but may lack the hands and agility to remain there.

Sweeney, Ryan — 9 — Chicago (A)
EXP MLB DEBUT: 2006 — POTENTIAL: Starting RF — 8C
Bats L — Age 23 — 2003 (2) HS (IA)
Pwr +++ | BAvg +++ | Spd ++ (4.20) | Def ++++

Year	Lev	Team	AB	R	H	HR	RBI	Avg	OB	Slg	OPS	bb%	ct%	Eye	SB	CS	X/H%	Iso	RC/G
2005	AA	Birmingham	429	64	128	1	47	298	351	371	722	8	88	0.66	6	6	20	72	4.55
2006	AAA	Charlotte	449	64	133	13	70	296	347	452	799	7	84	0.48	7	7	31	156	5.29
2006	MLB	Chicago (A)	35	1	8	0	5	229	229	229	457	0	80	0.00	0	0	0	0	0.69
2007	AAA	Charlotte	397	50	107	10	49	270	348	398	746	11	82	0.68	8	5	27	128	4.86
2007	MLB	Chicago (A)	45	5	9	1	5	200	265	333	599	8	89	0.80	0	1	44	133	3.18

Tall/athletic outfielder was hampered by a wrist injury at mid-season and wasn't the same afterwards. Possesses bat speed and can hit for BA, but power has eluded him with little loft and loop to swing. Arm strength plays anywhere in OF and should be able to play CF for the next few years.

Szymanski, BJ — 8 — Cincinnati
EXP MLB DEBUT: 2009 — POTENTIAL: Reserve CF/RF — 7E
Bats B — Age 25 — 2004 (2) Princeton
Pwr ++++ | BAvg ++ | Spd +++ (4.20) | Def +++

Year	Lev	Team	AB	R	H	HR	RBI	Avg	OB	Slg	OPS	bb%	ct%	Eye	SB	CS	X/H%	Iso	RC/G
2004	Rk	Billings	81	13	21	3	17	259	333	469	802	10	68	0.35	2	1	43	210	5.84
2005	A-	Dayton	191	32	50	10	26	262	335	471	806	10	70	0.37	7	1	38	209	5.62
2006	A-	Dayton	482	68	115	16	59	239	305	415	720	9	60	0.24	21	10	43	176	4.93
2007	A+	Sarasota	434	63	105	14	59	242	291	396	687	10	68	0.35	2	1	33	210	4.24

Tall/athletic outfielder has yet to get out of Class-A. Bat speed produces good power, but makes such little contact that it shows. Gave-up switch-hitting in hopes of improving BA. Possesses above average range and arm strength, and can play all three outfield positions.

Tabata, Jose — 9 — New York (A)
EXP MLB DEBUT: 2009 — POTENTIAL: Starting RF/CF — 9C
Bats R — Age 19 — 2005 FA (Venezuela)
Pwr ++++ | BAvg ++++ | Spd +++ (4.25) | Def ++++

Year	Lev	Team	AB	R	H	HR	RBI	Avg	OB	Slg	OPS	bb%	ct%	Eye	SB	CS	X/H%	Iso	RC/G
2005	Rk	GCL Yankees	156	30	49	3	25	314	374	417	791	9	91	1.07	22	6	18	103	5.38
2006	A-	Charleston	319	50	95	5	51	298	358	420	778	9	79	0.45	15	5	29	122	5.20
2007	A+	Tampa	411	56	126	5	54	307	358	392	750	7	83	0.47	15	7	18	85	4.74

Power/speed prospect was able to hit for BA, but power was absent due to a right hamate injury that later required surgery. Excellent bat speed and draws power from his muscular frame. Plate discipline improved, but needs to walk more. Arm strength and range play anywhere in OF.

Taylor, Jason — 46 — Kansas City
EXP MLB DEBUT: 2010 — POTENTIAL: Reserve 3B/2B — 7D
Bats R — Age 20 — 2006 (2) HS (VA)
Pwr ++ | BAvg ++++ | Spd +++ (4.30) | Def +++

Year	Lev	Team	AB	R	H	HR	RBI	Avg	OB	Slg	OPS	bb%	ct%	Eye	SB	CS	X/H%	Iso	RC/G
2006	Rk	AZL Royals	151	27	39	0	22	258	367	325	692	15	80	0.87	7	2	23	66	4.51
2007																			

Athletic player with average tools who missed 2007 with injury. Gets on-base via solid contact rate and plate discipline, but doesn't have the bat speed to hit for power. Runs bases well despite average speed and is adapting to 3B where he shows arm strength and first-step quickness.

Teagarden, Taylor — 2 — Texas

EXP MLB DEBUT: 2008 **POTENTIAL:** Starting CA **8B**

Bats R Age 24 — 2005 (3) Texas
Pwr +++ | BAvg +++ | Spd ++ | Def ++++

Year	Lev	Team	AB	R	H	HR	RBI	Avg	OB	Slg	OPS	bb%	ct%	Eye	SB	CS	X/H%	Iso	RC/G
2005	A-	Spokane	96	23	27	7	16	281	420	635	1056	19	67	0.72	1	1	59	354	9.97
2006	Rk	AZL Rangers	20	4	1	0	1	50	345	50	395	31	65	1.29	1	0	0	0	-0.24
2007	A+	Bakersfield	292	75	92	20	67	315	440	606	1046	18	70	0.73	2	1	49	291	9.49
2007	AA	Frisco	102	19	30	7	16	294	357	529	887	9	62	0.26	0	0	33	235	7.23

Noted for his outstanding defense, but had a breakout offensively. Receiving skills, agility, release time (1.9), and arm strength are above average, and nabbed 33% of attempted runners. BA and power are enhanced by home ballpark, but shows moderate power and draws walks.

Tejada, Ruben — 6 — New York (N)

EXP MLB DEBUT: 2012 **POTENTIAL:** Starting SS **9E**

Bats R Age 18 — 2006 FA (Panama)
Pwr + | BAvg ++++ | Spd ++++ | Def ++++

Year	Lev	Team	AB	R	H	HR	RBI	Avg	OB	Slg	OPS	bb%	ct%	Eye	SB	CS	X/H%	Iso	RC/G
2007	Rk	GCL Mets	120	13	34	0	16	283	401	367	768	14	87	1.19	2	1	21	83	4.92

Exciting athlete with plus speed and advanced hitting approach. Incredibly patient for experience level, he makes solid contact and uses entire field. Unlikely to develop more than average power due to size. Plays outstanding defense with all the tools, and just needs consistency.

Tejeda, Oscar — 6 — Boston

EXP MLB DEBUT: 2012 **POTENTIAL:** Starting SS **9E**

Bats R Age 18 — 2006 FA (DR)
Pwr +++ | BAvg ++++ | Spd +++ | Def ++++

Year	Lev	Team	AB	R	H	HR	RBI	Avg	OB	Slg	OPS	bb%	ct%	Eye	SB	CS	X/H%	Iso	RC/G
2007	Rk	GCL Red Sox	173	23	51	1	21	295	351	399	750	8	84	0.56	6	2	29	104	4.88
2007	A-	Lowell	94	14	28	0	12	298	340	394	734	6	72	0.23	4	1	25	96	4.68

Wiry strong athlete with excellent defensive skills, showing solid arm strength, soft/quick hands, and range. Projected to hit for power, but hasn't filled-out frame and struggles with plate discipline. Possesses good speed and can be an impact, top-of-the-order hitter if he can improve OBP.

Thomas, Clete — 9 — Detroit

EXP MLB DEBUT: 2008 **POTENTIAL:** Reserve RF/LF **7C**

Bats L Age 24 — 2005 (6) Auburn
Pwr +++ | BAvg +++ | Spd +++ | Def +++

Year	Lev	Team	AB	R	H	HR	RBI	Avg	OB	Slg	OPS	bb%	ct%	Eye	SB	CS	X/H%	Iso	RC/G
2005	A-	Oneonta	70	19	27	1	14	386	476	529	1004	15	84	1.09	9	0	26	143	8.36
2005	A-	W. Michigan	194	39	55	0	11	284	353	376	730	10	81	0.57	11	3	24	93	4.76
2006	A+	Lakeland	529	67	135	6	40	255	326	365	691	10	76	0.44	33	13	30	110	4.17
2007	AA	Erie	528	97	148	8	53	280	353	405	758	10	79	0.54	18	11	30	125	5.04

Muscular athlete whose game doesn't fit appearance. Possesses bat speed, but uses middle of the field, so doesn't have HR power, but can hit for BA. Led EL in runs scored and steals bases with slightly above average speed. Range and arm strength are solid in corner outfield.

Thomas, Tony — 4 — Chicago (N)

EXP MLB DEBUT: 2009 **POTENTIAL:** Starting 2B **7C**

Bats R Age 21 — 2007 (3) Florida St
Pwr + | BAvg +++ | Spd ++++ | Def ++

Year	Lev	Team	AB	R	H	HR	RBI	Avg	OB	Slg	OPS	bb%	ct%	Eye	SB	CS	X/H%	Iso	RC/G
2007	Rk	AZL Cubs	17	7	3	0	6	176	263	412	675	11	71	0.40	0	0	67	235	4.39
2007	A-	Boise	182	44	56	5	33	308	391	544	935	12	77	0.61	28	2	45	236	7.53

Athletic infielder with plus speed and bat handling capability, he hit for BA, got on-base, and used the entire field. Hit for surprising power, but his flat bat plane will limit power at upper levels. Below average defender with stiff hands and a weak throwing arm that doesn't figure to improve.

Timpner, Clay — 8 — San Francisco

EXP MLB DEBUT: 2008 **POTENTIAL:** Reserve CF/LF **6B**

Bats L Age 25 — 2004 (4) Central Florida
Pwr + | BAvg ++ | Spd ++++ | Def +++

Year	Lev	Team	AB	R	H	HR	RBI	Avg	OB	Slg	OPS	bb%	ct%	Eye	SB	CS	X/H%	Iso	RC/G
2004	A-	Salem-Keizer	294	37	86	5	28	293	338	381	719	6	88	0.57	16	5	16	88	4.35
2005	A+	San Jose	549	85	160	4	39	291	333	397	730	6	83	0.37	34	13	24	106	4.49
2006	AA	Connecticut	261	26	58	3	13	222	259	314	573	5	88	0.42	11	6	28	92	2.69
2006	AAA	Fresno	238	33	68	3	19	286	315	382	697	4	87	0.32	5	7	21	97	3.98
2007	AAA	Fresno	392	51	118	6	39	301	361	395	757	9	83	0.54	9	11	18	94	4.89

Plus athlete with excellent speed and baserunning instincts, making him a threat on the bases. Makes solid contact, but doesn't walk much or possess power which will keep him from starting in the Majors. Ranges well in CF with fringe-average arm strength.

Tolbert, Matt — 456 — Minnesota

EXP MLB DEBUT: 2007 **POTENTIAL:** Reserve 2B/3B **6B**

Bats B Age 26 — 2004 (16) Mississippi
Pwr + | BAvg +++ | Spd +++ | Def ++++

Year	Lev	Team	AB	R	H	HR	RBI	Avg	OB	Slg	OPS	bb%	ct%	Eye	SB	CS	X/H%	Iso	RC/G
2004	Rk	Elizabethton	104	23	32	3	18	308	379	500	879	10	88	0.92	3	2	38	192	6.50
2005	A+	Fort Myers	417	55	111	3	46	266	323	385	688	8	81	0.44	11	4	26	98	4.06
2006	A+	Fort Myers	155	20	47	4	24	303	361	458	819	8	89	0.82	7	2	28	155	5.65
2006	AA	New Britain	247	33	63	3	35	255	336	360	696	11	83	0.70	5	1	30	105	4.34
2007	AAA	Rochester	417	65	122	6	53	293	350	427	777	8	87	0.66	11	3	30	134	5.21

Fundamentally sound infielder capable of playing three infield positions and is a plus defender at 2B with soft hands, range, and average arm strength. Contact hitter with line-drive stroke that is capable of hitting for BA, but a flat bat plane lessens power. Runs bases well with average speed.

Tolisano, John — 4 — Toronto

EXP MLB DEBUT: 2011 **POTENTIAL:** Starting 2B **8D**

Bats B Age 19 — 2007 (2) HS (FL)
Pwr ++++ | BAvg ++++ | Spd +++ | Def ++

Year	Lev	Team	AB	R	H	HR	RBI	Avg	OB	Slg	OPS	bb%	ct%	Eye	SB	CS	X/H%	Iso	RC/G
2007	Rk	GCL Blue Jays	183	35	45	10	33	246	340	437	777	12	78	0.65	7	1	33	191	5.14

Offensive-minded infielder led GCL in HR and hits for BA with plate discipline and controlled aggression. Speed is slightly above average and shows good instincts on the bases. Arm strength is solid, but footwork and hands are questionable, which may force a position switch.

Towles, J.R. — 2 — Houston

EXP MLB DEBUT: 2007 **POTENTIAL:** Starting CA **7A**

Bats R Age 24 — 2004 (2) Collin Co CC
Pwr +++ | BAvg +++ | Spd +++ | Def +++

Year	Lev	Team	AB	R	H	HR	RBI	Avg	OB	Slg	OPS	bb%	ct%	Eye	SB	CS	X/H%	Iso	RC/G
2006	A-	Lexington	285	39	89	12	55	317	364	525	889	7	84	0.46	13	5	37	207	6.30
2007	A+	Salem	90	14	18	0	11	200	339	278	617	12	83	0.80	3	5	28	78	3.32
2007	AA	Corpus Christi	216	47	70	11	49	324	425	551	976	10	84	0.66	9	4	36	227	7.77
2007	AAA	Round Rock	43	5	12	0	2	279	364	279	643	9	84	0.57	2	4	0	0	3.89
2007	MLB	Houston	40	9	15	1	12	375	432	575	1007	9	84	3.00	1	0	40	200	8.41

Wiry athlete with solid offensive game, hitting for BA, lining extra-base hits, and stealing bases. Exercises plate discipline and rarely gets himself out. Possesses arm strength and a quick release (2.0), but receiving skills and ability to halt running game (26 % CS%) could improve.

Tracy, Chad — 723 — Texas

EXP MLB DEBUT: 2009 **POTENTIAL:** Platoon LF/1B **7C**

Bats R Age 22 — 2006 (3) Pepperdine
Pwr +++ | BAvg +++ | Spd +++ | Def +

Year	Lev	Team	AB	R	H	HR	RBI	Avg	OB	Slg	OPS	bb%	ct%	Eye	SB	CS	X/H%	Iso	RC/G
2006	A-	Spokane	252	41	67	11	35	266	327	460	788	8	82	0.50	4	1	39	194	5.16
2007	A-	Clinton	509	64	127	14	84	250	317	409	725	9	82	0.54	9	1	40	159	4.52

Strong/athletic player with some offensive upside with his bat speed, contact ability, and instincts. Showed massive platoon split which could suppress BA. Defense behind plate was dreadful, so played mostly LF where he showed fringe-average range and arm strength.

Tripp, Brandon — 9 — Baltimore

EXP MLB DEBUT: 2010 **POTENTIAL:** Platoon LF/RF **8D**

Bats L Age 23 — 2006 (12) Cal St Fullerton
Pwr ++++ | BAvg ++ | Spd ++ | Def ++

Year	Lev	Team	AB	R	H	HR	RBI	Avg	OB	Slg	OPS	bb%	ct%	Eye	SB	CS	X/H%	Iso	RC/G
2006	A-	Aberdeen	145	20	32	2	15	221	298	317	615	10	66	0.33	1	2	31	97	3.13
2007	A-	Delmarva	371	72	107	19	79	288	362	531	893	10	70	0.38	7	1	45	243	6.99

Strong athlete with moderate bat speed displayed power in a pitcher-friendly environment. Mediocre contact ability and plate discipline will catch up to him at upper levels, so will have to adjust to hit for BA. Defense in RF is solid, featuring arm strength and adequate range.

Triunfel,Carlos — 6 — Seattle

EXP MLB DEBUT: 2011 | POTENTIAL: Starting SS | 9C

Bats R Age 18 — 2006 FA (DR)

Pwr ++ | BAvg ++++ | Spd +++ (4.30) | Def +++

Year	Lev	Team	AB	R	H	HR	RBI	Avg	OB	Slg	OPS	bb%	ct%	Eye	SB	CS	X/H%	Iso	RC/G
2007	Rk	AZL Mariners	11	1	3	0	3	273	273	273	545	0	91	0.00	0	0	0	0	2.09
2007	A-	Wisconsin	152	18	47	0	14	309	331	388	719	3	85	0.22	4	8	21	79	4.22
2007	A+	High Desert	208	32	60	0	22	288	327	356	683	5	85	0.39	3	4	20	67	3.94

Solid athlete handled bat and glove well despite being youngest regular in both leagues. Aggressive hitter with excellent contact ability and average speed, but power was limited to doubles. Possesses arm strength and soft hands, but made 36 errors and low range may not work at SS.

Trumbo,Mark — 3 — Los Angeles (A)

EXP MLB DEBUT: 2009 | POTENTIAL: Platoon 1B | 8E

Bats R Age 22 — 2004 (18) HS (CA)

Pwr ++++ | BAvg + | Spd + (4.50) | Def +

Year	Lev	Team	AB	R	H	HR	RBI	Avg	OB	Slg	OPS	bb%	ct%	Eye	SB	CS	X/H%	Iso	RC/G
2005	Rk	Orem	299	45	82	10	45	274	322	458	780	7	78	0.31	2	2	41	184	5.07
2006	A-	Cedar Rapids	428	43	94	13	58	220	292	355	648	9	77	0.44	5	5	34	136	3.45
2007	A-	Cedar Rapids	471	57	128	14	76	272	321	427	748	7	79	0.35	10	8	34	155	4.63

Possesses plus power potential with plus bat speed, but lack of plate discipline and tendency to pull baseball limits offense. Instinctive baserunner who steals bases despite below average speed. Defense at 1B is poor with stiff hands and low range, but arm strength is a plus.

Tuiasosopo,Matt — 5 — Seattle

EXP MLB DEBUT: 2008 | POTENTIAL: Platoon 3B/LF | 7C

Bats R Age 22 — 2004 (3) HS (WA)

Pwr +++ | BAvg +++ | Spd +++ (4.30) | Def ++

Year	Lev	Team	AB	R	H	HR	RBI	Avg	OB	Slg	OPS	bb%	ct%	Eye	SB	CS	X/H%	Iso	RC/G
2004	A-	Everett	101	18	25	2	14	248	315	386	701	9	64	0.28	4	3	36	139	4.49
2005	A-	Wisconsin	409	72	113	6	45	276	347	386	733	10	77	0.46	8	5	27	110	4.69
2006	A+	Inland Emp	232	31	71	1	34	306	346	379	725	6	75	0.24	5	6	21	73	4.40
2006	AA	San Antonio	216	16	40	1	10	185	254	218	472	8	70	0.31	2	1	13	32	0.99
2007	AA	West Tenn	446	74	116	9	57	260	371	404	775	15	75	0.67	4	8	35	143	4.77

Strong athlete who took advantage of a hitter-friendly environment to improve offense. Possesses bat speed, but inside-out swing path limits power. Moved from SS to 3B where his lack of range and footwork problems were less of an issue, though he does have a strong infield arm.

Valaika,Chris — 6 — Cincinnati

EXP MLB DEBUT: 2009 | POTENTIAL: Starting 2B | 7C

Bats R Age 22 — 2006 (3) UCSB

Pwr +++ | BAvg +++ | Spd +++ (4.30) | Def ++

Year	Lev	Team	AB	R	H	HR	RBI	Avg	OB	Slg	OPS	bb%	ct%	Eye	SB	CS	X/H%	Iso	RC/G
2006	Rk	Billings	275	58	89	8	60	324	378	520	898	8	78	0.39	2	2	38	196	6.71
2007	A-	Dayton	300	38	92	10	56	307	344	493	837	5	76	0.24	1	4	36	187	5.77
2007	A+	Sarasota	217	26	55	2	23	253	296	332	627	6	81	0.31	0	3	22	78	3.15

Pure hitter and possessor of good bat speed, he is aggressive early in the count trying to drive ball, but will use whole field. Plate discipline is lacking, but power is a necessary trade-off. Stocky build doesn't give him much speed or range, and despite arm strength, will move to 2B.

Valbuena,Luis — 4 — Seattle

EXP MLB DEBUT: 2009 | POTENTIAL: Starting 2B | 7E

Bats L Age 22 — 2002 FA (Venezuela)

Pwr +++ | BAvg ++++ | Spd ++++ | Def ++

Year	Lev	Team	AB	R	H	HR	RBI	Avg	OB	Slg	OPS	bb%	ct%	Eye	SB	CS	X/H%	Iso	RC/G
2005	A-	Everett	287	47	75	12	51	261	333	443	776	10	87	0.84	14	6	33	181	5.14
2005	AAA	Tacoma	4	0	0	0	0	0	200	0	200	20	50	0.50	0	0		0	
2006	A-	Wisconsin	325	45	93	3	38	286	371	400	771	12	86	1.00	21	6	27	114	5.40
2006	A+	Inland Emp	163	18	41	2	10	252	311	362	673	8	84	0.54	1	3	32	110	3.92
2007	AA	West Tenn	444	55	106	11	44	239	313	378	691	10	81	0.58	10	6	35	140	4.14

Stocky athlete with good speed has shown ability to make solid contact and judge strike zone, which boosts BA/OBP. Power has dwindled with promotion, but adds value with stolen bases. Stiff hands and marginal range aren't conducive to good middle infield play.

Valencia,Danny — 53 — Minnesota

EXP MLB DEBUT: 2009 | POTENTIAL: Platoon 1B/3B | 8E

Bats R Age 23 — 2006 (19) Miami-FL

Pwr ++++ | BAvg +++ | Spd + | Def +

Year	Lev	Team	AB	R	H	HR	RBI	Avg	OB	Slg	OPS	bb%	ct%	Eye	SB	CS	X/H%	Iso	RC/G
2006	Rk	Elzbton	190	30	59	8	29	311	361	505	866	7	82	0.44	0	2	36	195	6.06
2007	A-	Beloit	242	44	73	11	35	302	374	500	874	10	78	0.52	3	3	36	198	6.39
2007	A+	Fort Myers	230	28	67	6	31	291	337	422	759	7	79	0.33	1	0	24	130	4.75

Pure hitter capable of hitting for BA and power with his bat speed and strong wrists. Aggressive approach drives-down walk rate and has no foot speed. Possesses average arm strength, but lacks first-step quickness and has stiff hands, making his defense below average.

Van Every,Jon — 8 — Boston

EXP MLB DEBUT: 2008 | POTENTIAL: Reserve CF/LF | 6B

Bats L Age 28 — 2000 (29) Itawamba CC

Pwr ++++ | BAvg + | Spd ++++ | Def +++

Year	Lev	Team	AB	R	H	HR	RBI	Avg	OB	Slg	OPS	bb%	ct%	Eye	SB	CS	X/H%	Iso	RC/G
2005	AA	Akron	389	71	95	27	64	244	354	499	853	15	60	0.43	16	6	45	254	7.00
2006	AA	Akron	233	33	59	9	39	253	326	481	806	10	66	0.32	4	1	51	227	6.00
2006	AAA	Buffalo	151	23	39	5	16	258	329	444	773	10	66	0.31	5	2	41	185	5.46
2007	AA	Akron	151	27	52	4	34	344	418	583	1000	11	68	0.40	4	5	44	238	8.96
2007	AAA	Buffalo	158	17	43	8	23	272	365	468	833	13	64	0.40	2	3	33	196	6.45

Wiry athlete with solid secondary skills, but a poor contact rate will always keep BA low. Bat speed gives him above average power, draws plenty of walks, and is an efficient basestealer with his speed. Ranges well in all three outfield positions and sports an average throwing arm.

Van Ostrand,Jimmy — 7 — Houston

EXP MLB DEBUT: 2009 | POTENTIAL: Reserve LF/RF | 6C

Bats R Age 23 — 2006 (8) Cal Poly

Pwr +++ | BAvg ++ | Spd ++ | Def +++

Year	Lev	Team	AB	R	H	HR	RBI	Avg	OB	Slg	OPS	bb%	ct%	Eye	SB	CS	X/H%	Iso	RC/G
2006	A-	Tri-City	149	14	32	2	13	215	272	295	567	5	84	0.25	2	3	25	80	2.80
2007	A-	Lexington	363	42	105	12	60	289	360	455	815	9	82	0.59	4	4	31	165	6.11

Wiry strong player with moderate bat speed and doubles power. Will struggle to hit for BA at higher levels with mediocre plate discipline and contact rate. Speed and range are slightly below average and has adequate arm strength in corner outfield.

Velez,Eugenio — 84 — San Francisco

EXP MLB DEBUT: 2008 | POTENTIAL: Reserve CF/2B | 7C

Bats B Age 26 — 2001 FA (DR)

Pwr ++ | BAvg +++ | Spd +++++ (3.90) | Def +++

Year	Lev	Team	AB	R	H	HR	RBI	Avg	OB	Slg	OPS	bb%	ct%	Eye	SB	CS	X/H%	Iso	RC/G
2005	A-	Lansing	239	25	68	4	34	285	310	406	716	4	83	0.23	7	5	26	121	4.13
2006	A-	Augusta	459	91	146	14	90	318	366	560	926	7	82	0.43	64	16	43	242	6.95
2007	AA	Connecticut	376	55	112	1	25	298	343	399	742	6	82	0.39	49	17	24	101	4.70
2007	AAA	Fresno	18	5	5	0	0	278	350	278	628	10	83	0.67	5	0	0	0	3.42
2007	MLB	San Francisco	11	5	3	0	2	273	385	636	1021	15	73	0.67	4	0	67	364	9.60

High-energy player with plus speed and secondary skills to impact game. Inside-out swing produces solid BA and drives ball from RH side. Took to CF well after moving from 2B, showing closing range and sufficient arm strength, but will likely be used in a utility role in the Majors.

Venable,Will — 8 — San Diego

EXP MLB DEBUT: 2009 | POTENTIAL: Starting CF/LF | 8D

Bats L Age 25 — 2005 (7) Princeton

Pwr +++ | BAvg +++ | Spd ++++ | Def +++

Year	Lev	Team	AB	R	H	HR	RBI	Avg	OB	Slg	OPS	bb%	ct%	Eye	SB	CS	X/H%	Iso	RC/G
2005	Rk	AZL Padres	59	13	19	1	12	322	344	508	853	3	85	0.22	4	0	37	186	5.81
2005	A-	Eugene	139	17	30	2	14	216	288	324	611	9	73	0.37	2	1	30	108	3.04
2006	A-	Ft. Wayne	473	86	148	11	92	313	384	476	860	10	83	0.68	18	5	34	163	6.29
2007	AA	San Antonio	515	66	143	8	68	278	327	373	700	7	84	0.45	21	2	21	95	4.12

Tall/lean athlete with BA ability, moderate power, and ability to draw walks, making him a top-of-the-order threat. SD had him skip a level and was overmatched early before adjusting. Above average speed nets steals and provides range in CF, but arm strength is below average.

Villalona,Angel — 5 — San Francisco

EXP MLB DEBUT: 2011 | POTENTIAL: Starting 3B | 9D

Bats R Age 17 — 2006 FA (DR)

Pwr ++++ | BAvg ++++ | Spd +++ (4.30) | Def ++++

Year	Lev	Team	AB	R	H	HR	RBI	Avg	OB	Slg	OPS	bb%	ct%	Eye	SB	CS	X/H%	Iso	RC/G
2007	Rk	AZL Giants	200	40	57	5	37	285	335	450	785	7	79	0.36	1	1	35	165	5.18
2007	A-	Salem-Keizer	12	1	2	0	1	167	167	167	333	0	83	0.00	1	0	0	0	-0.59

Strong/athletic hitter with plus bat speed and power potential. Centers ball with good contact, which should give him a solid BA despite lackluster plate discipline. Arm strength, first-step quickness, and hands are all above average, and can be a top-notch defender.

Vinyard, Chris — 3 — Baltimore

Bats R Age 22
2005 (38) Chandler-Gilbert

EXP MLB DEBUT: 2009 POTENTIAL: Starting 1B **7D**

	Pwr	++++
	BAvg	+++
	Spd	+
	Def	++

Year	Lev	Team	AB	R	H	HR	RBI	Avg	OB	Slg	OPS	bb%	ct%	Eye	SB	CS	X/H%	Iso	RC/G
2006	A-	Aberdeen	264	40	75	8	47	284	353	489	841	10	77	0.45	0	0	48	205	6.11
2007	A-	Delmarva	480	61	129	16	82	269	335	440	775	9	76	0.42	1	0	39	171	5.13

Skills point to a one-dimensional power hitter as foray into full-season baseball didn't turn out well. Power to all fields, but struggles to make contact and judge strike zone, culminating in a low BA. Below average defensively at 1B and lacks speed on the bases.

Vitters, Josh — 5 — Chicago (N)

Bats R Age 18
2007 (1) HS (CA)

EXP MLB DEBUT: 2011 POTENTIAL: Starting 3B **9D**

	Pwr	++++
	BAvg	++++
	Spd	++
	Def	+++

Year	Lev	Team	AB	R	H	HR	RBI	Avg	OB	Slg	OPS	bb%	ct%	Eye	SB	CS	X/H%	Iso	RC/G
2007	Rk	AZL Cubs	30	0	2	0	2	67	97	67	163	3	70	0.11	0	0	0	0	-3.49
2007	A-	Boise	21	2	4	0	1	190	261	190	451	9	76	0.40	1	1	0	0	0.90

Pure hitter with bat speed and a compact swing, giving him ability to hit for both power and BA. Stays behind ball and extends well, but may need to tighten strike zone. Arm strength and first-step quickness are sound, but needs to read groundball hops more consistently.

Votto, Joey — 37 — Cincinnati

Bats L Age 24
2002 (2) Richview

EXP MLB DEBUT: 2007 POTENTIAL: Starting 1B **8A**

	Pwr	++++
	BAvg	++++
4.50	Spd	++
	Def	++

Year	Lev	Team	AB	R	H	HR	RBI	Avg	OB	Slg	OPS	bb%	ct%	Eye	SB	CS	X/H%	Iso	RC/G
2004	A+	Potomac	84	11	25	5	20	298	379	560	938	12	75	0.52	1	1	48	262	7.37
2005	A+	Sarasota	464	64	119	17	83	256	331	425	756	10	74	0.43	4	5	35	168	4.93
2006	AA	Chattanooga	508	85	162	22	77	319	410	547	957	13	79	0.72	23	8	43	228	7.68
2007	AAA	Louisville	496	74	146	22	92	294	382	478	859	12	78	0.64	17	10	31	183	6.30
2007	MLB	Cincinnati	84	11	27	4	17	321	360	548	907	6	82	0.33	1	0	41	226	6.44

Bat speed and strong wrists unleashed BA and power to all fields. Made better contact after getting new contact lenses, but is still prone to striking-out. Runs well bases well despite below average speed. Defense at 1B was better than advertised and even logged innings in LF.

Wagner, Mark — 2 — Boston

Bats R Age 24
2005 (9) UC-Irvine

EXP MLB DEBUT: 2009 POTENTIAL: Platoon CA **8D**

	Pwr	+++
	BAvg	+++
	Spd	+
	Def	++++

Year	Lev	Team	AB	R	H	HR	RBI	Avg	OB	Slg	OPS	bb%	ct%	Eye	SB	CS	X/H%	Iso	RC/G
2005	A-	Lowell	69	10	14	0	6	203	295	261	556	12	90	1.29	1	1	21	58	3.02
2006	A+	Wilmington	65	8	11	1	5	169	250	277	527	10	86	0.78	0	0	45	108	2.36
2006	AA	Greenville	355	49	107	7	45	301	375	456	832	11	85	0.81	1	3	37	155	5.98
2007	A+	Lancaster	368	71	117	14	82	318	407	533	939	13	88	1.20	0	1	43	215	7.33

Strong-framed catcher noted for his solid defense, where he shows arm strength, receiving skills, and agility. Power output enhanced by hitter friendly environment, but makes good contact and judges strike zone which will keep BA respectable. True test of overall ability will come in Double-A.

Walker, Andrew — 2 — Pittsburgh

Bats R Age 22
2007 (5) TCU

EXP MLB DEBUT: 2010 POTENTIAL: Platoon CA **7D**

	Pwr	+++
	BAvg	++
	Spd	+
	Def	+++

Year	Lev	Team	AB	R	H	HR	RBI	Avg	OB	Slg	OPS	bb%	ct%	Eye	SB	CS	X/H%	Iso	RC/G
2007	A-	State College	161	17	51	2	24	317	385	441	826	10	78	0.50	1	1	29	124	5.95

Solid/all-around catcher that produces gap power with moderate bat speed, but could struggle to hit for BA with marginal contact rate and a long swing. Possesses agility and receiving skills behind the plate, and compensates for average arm strength with a quick release.

Walker, Neil — 5 — Pittsburgh

Bats B Age 22
2004 (1) HS (PA)

EXP MLB DEBUT: 2008 POTENTIAL: Starting 3B **8B**

	Pwr	++++
	BAvg	++++
4.35	Spd	++
	Def	++

Year	Lev	Team	AB	R	H	HR	RBI	Avg	OB	Slg	OPS	bb%	ct%	Eye	SB	CS	X/H%	Iso	RC/G
2005	A-	Hickory	485	78	146	12	68	301	329	452	780	4	85	0.28	7	4	32	151	4.89
2006	A+	Lynchburg	264	32	75	3	35	284	332	409	741	7	84	0.46	3	5	35	125	4.69
2006	AA	Altoona	31	5	5	2	3	161	188	355	542	3	87	0.25	0	0	40	194	1.95
2007	AA	Altoona	431	77	124	13	66	288	366	462	827	11	83	0.73	9	4	37	174	5.89
2007	AAA	Indianapolis	64	7	13	0	0	203	227	250	477	3	80	0.15	1	1	23	47	1.19

Smooth swinging hitter with bat speed and ability to size-up barrel. Plate discipline improved and stripped of the rigors of catching allowed him to relax. Runs well for size and will steal occasional base. Adapted well to 3B showing average arm strength and soft hands.

Waring, Brandon — 5 — Cincinnati

Bats R Age 21
2007 (7) Wofford

EXP MLB DEBUT: 2010 POTENTIAL: Platoon 1B/LF **8E**

	Pwr	++++
	BAvg	++
	Spd	++
	Def	+

Year	Lev	Team	AB	R	H	HR	RBI	Avg	OB	Slg	OPS	bb%	ct%	Eye	SB	CS	X/H%	Iso	RC/G
2007	Rk	Billings	267	63	83	20	61	311	361	614	975	7	69	0.25	1	0	47	303	7.94
2007	A-	Dayton	1	0	1	0	2	1000	1000	1000	2000	0	100		0	0	0	0	16.32

Strong/athletic player with bat speed and power, helping him lead PIO in HR. Making contact is a problem, as he struck-out almost a third of the time, making BA projection difficult. Possesses strong arm, but mediocre range and stiff hands make him a defensive liability.

Webster, Anthony — 8 — Texas

Bats L Age 25
2001 (15) HS (TN)

EXP MLB DEBUT: 2007 POTENTIAL: Reserve CF/LF **6B**

	Pwr	++
	BAvg	++
4.10	Spd	++++
	Def	+++

Year	Lev	Team	AB	R	H	HR	RBI	Avg	OB	Slg	OPS	bb%	ct%	Eye	SB	CS	X/H%	Iso	RC/G
2004	A+	Stockton	380	66	109	8	44	287	353	439	793	9	82	0.57	20	4	32	153	5.41
2005	A+	Bakersfield	498	93	150	11	73	301	342	484	826	6	89	0.56	25	5	39	183	5.64
2006	A+	Frisco	216	37	67	5	19	310	363	463	826	8	88	0.72	3	5	28	153	5.70
2006	AAA	Oklahoma	242	30	65	3	19	269	306	384	690	5	85	0.36	16	4	31	116	3.98
2007	AA	Frisco	411	66	114	8	39	277	313	411	724	5	87	0.38	30	11	32	134	4.34

Wiry athlete with excellent speed underway allowing him to steal bases and track flyballs in CF. Opened-up swing and became more aggressive which gave him more power and BA, but his OBP is low and that will be the key to his playing time. Could fare well as reserve outfielder.

Weglarz, Nick — 73 — Cleveland

Bats L Age 20
2005 (3) HS (Canada)

EXP MLB DEBUT: 2010 POTENTIAL: Starting LF/1B **8D**

	Pwr	++++
	BAvg	++
	Spd	++
	Def	++

Year	Lev	Team	AB	R	H	HR	RBI	Avg	OB	Slg	OPS	bb%	ct%	Eye	SB	CS	X/H%	Iso	RC/G
2005	Rk	Burlington	147	22	34	2	13	231	311	347	658	10	71	0.40	2	1	38	116	3.75
2006	Rk	GCL Indians	2	0	0	0	0	0	0	0	0	0	0	0.00	0	0		0	
2007	A-	Lake County	439	75	121	23	82	276	390	497	886	16	71	0.64	1	1	42	221	7.03
2007	A+	Kinston	7	1	1	1	1	143	250	571	821	13	71	0.50	0	0	100	429	5.34

Possesses best power in organization, combining excellent bat speed and plate discipline. Drives ball hard to all fields, but will struggle to hit for BA with his long swing and high strikeout rate. Average arm strength and mediocre range will keep him at either 1B or LF.

West, Matt — 456 — Texas

Bats R Age 19
2007 (2) HS (TX)

EXP MLB DEBUT: 2012 POTENTIAL: Starting 3B **9E**

	Pwr	++++
	BAvg	+++
4.35	Spd	++
	Def	+++

Year	Lev	Team	AB	R	H	HR	RBI	Avg	OB	Slg	OPS	bb%	ct%	Eye	SB	CS	X/H%	Iso	RC/G
2007	Rk	AZL Rangers	103	21	31	0	17	301	357	388	745	8	80	0.43	1	3	16	87	4.84

Athletic infielder with excellent bat speed that produces power to pull field. Is at mercy of plate discipline and does struggle on pitches with a wrinkle. Possesses arm strength and soft hands while playing three infield positions, but range is better-suited for 3B.

Whitesell, Josh — 3 — Washington

Bats L Age 26
2004 (6) Loyola Marymount

EXP MLB DEBUT: 2008 POTENTIAL: Platoon 1B **7D**

	Pwr	++++
	BAvg	++
	Spd	+
	Def	++++

Year	Lev	Team	AB	R	H	HR	RBI	Avg	OB	Slg	OPS	bb%	ct%	Eye	SB	CS	X/H%	Iso	RC/G
2003	A-	Vermont	167	13	41	5	19	246	354	407	761	14	68	0.53	0	0	39	162	5.36
2004	A-	Savannah	380	56	95	16	54	250	349	453	802	13	76	0.64	0	1	47	203	5.67
2005	A+	Potomac	389	59	114	18	66	293	406	524	930	16	68	0.59	1	1	46	231	7.93
2006	AA	Harrisburg	403	47	106	19	56	263	349	432	780	12	69	0.42	2	6	28	169	5.35
2007	AA	Harrisburg	387	78	110	21	74	284	416	512	927	18	72	0.81	6	2	41	227	7.65

Bat speed, a shortened swing, and plate discipline produced above average power and gave him a strong OBP. Mediocre pitch recognition and a slow trigger will negatively affect BA. Possesses below average speed and defense, so will need to maintain offensive level.

Whitney,Matt — 3 — Washington — EXP MLB DEBUT: 2009 — POTENTIAL: Platoon 1B/3B — 7D

Bats R Age 24	Year	Lev	Team	AB	R	H	HR	RBI	Avg	OB	Slg	OPS	bb%	ct%	Eye	SB	CS	X/H%	Iso	RC/G
2002 (1-S) HS (FL)	2004	A-	Lake County	195	21	50	5	31	256	335	390	725	11	58	0.28	0	0	32	133	5.18
Pwr ++++	2005	A-	Lake County	277	38	67	6	27	242	325	332	657	11	77	0.53	0	3	19	90	3.65
BAvg ++	2006	A+	Kinston	344	40	71	10	38	206	293	363	656	11	62	0.32	0	2	45	157	3.84
Spd ++	2007	A-	Lake County	286	52	88	16	64	308	375	542	917	10	78	0.50	0	1	40	234	6.86
Def ++	2007	A+	Kinston	226	43	65	16	49	288	351	549	899	9	74	0.37	1	0	42	261	6.63

Wiry strong hitter with bat speed and moderate power to all fields, but struggles to make contact against breaking pitches, driving BA down. Possesses arm strength, but a fractured tibia/fibula suffered in 2003 has left him with no first-step quickness and is relegated to 1B defensively.

Whittleman,Johnny — 5 — Texas — EXP MLB DEBUT: 2009 — POTENTIAL: Starting 3B — 8C

Bats L Age 21	Year	Lev	Team	AB	R	H	HR	RBI	Avg	OB	Slg	OPS	bb%	ct%	Eye	SB	CS	X/H%	Iso	RC/G
2005 (2) HS (TX)																				
Pwr ++++	2005	Rk	AZL Rangers	190	31	53	0	35	279	391	426	817	16	78	0.83	11	4	38	147	6.30
BAvg +++	2006	A-	Clinton	466	56	106	9	43	227	316	343	659	11	79	0.62	6	6	31	116	3.80
4.40 Spd ++	2007	A-	Clinton	336	56	91	14	57	271	386	476	862	16	73	0.69	5	3	44	205	6.69
Def ++	2007	A+	Bakersfield	104	18	25	3	15	240	378	413	791	18	68	0.70	0	3	48	173	5.98

Power hitter with bat speed and plate discipline received off-season Lasik surgery, which improved vision. High strikeout rate will keep BA low, but draws walks, elevating OBP. Possesses strong arm, but hands are stiff and lacks proper throwing mechanics, leading to 29 errors.

Wieters,Matt — 2 — Baltimore — EXP MLB DEBUT: 2009 — POTENTIAL: Starting CA — 9B

Bats B Age 22	Year	Lev	Team	AB	R	H	HR	RBI	Avg	OB	Slg	OPS	bb%	ct%	Eye	SB	CS	X/H%	Iso	RC/G
2007 (1) Georgia Tech																				
Pwr ++++																				
BAvg ++++																				
Spd ++																				
Def +++	2007																			

Tall/strong catcher with potential for a high impact bat, combining BA, power, and plate discipline. Derives bat speed and power from the LH side, with an inside-out swing tailored for BA from the RH side. Possesses arm strength and receives the ball well, but size could jeopardize agility.

Williams,Jackson — 2 — San Francisco — EXP MLB DEBUT: 2010 — POTENTIAL: Starting CA — 7D

Bats R Age 22	Year	Lev	Team	AB	R	H	HR	RBI	Avg	OB	Slg	OPS	bb%	ct%	Eye	SB	CS	X/H%	Iso	RC/G
2007 (1-S) Oklahoma																				
Pwr ++																				
BAvg +++																				
Spd +																				
Def ++++	2007	A-	Salem-Keizer	130	20	30	5	20	231	315	369	684	11	79	0.59	0	0	27	138	3.96

Strong/well-proportioned catcher with excellent defensive skills, including arm strength, quick release (1.9), and receiving skills. Moderate bat speed and level bat plane produces doubles power and can hit for BA with good contact rate, use of whole field, and strike zone judgment.

Wilson,Bobby — 2 — Los Angeles (A) — EXP MLB DEBUT: 2008 — POTENTIAL: Reserve CA — 6B

Bats R Age 25	Year	Lev	Team	AB	R	H	HR	RBI	Avg	OB	Slg	OPS	bb%	ct%	Eye	SB	CS	X/H%	Iso	RC/G
2002 (48) St. Pete JC	2004	A-	Cedar Rapids	396	45	106	8	64	268	319	386	706	7	86	0.55	5	2	29	119	4.23
Pwr +++	2005	A+	Rancho Cuc	466	66	135	14	77	290	333	453	785	6	87	0.49	2	1	35	163	5.08
BAvg ++	2006	AA	Arkansas	374	45	107	9	53	286	344	428	772	8	87	0.70	1	6	33	142	5.08
Spd +	2007	AA	Arkansas	181	24	49	6	27	271	350	420	770	11	86	0.85	5	3	31	149	5.14
Def +++	2007	AAA	Salt Lake	132	15	39	3	22	295	336	477	813	6	86	0.44	1	0	44	182	5.46

Low upside receiver, but has enough offense and defense to be a reserve catcher. Possesses average arm strength and receiving skills, nailing 37% of attempted runners. Produces moderate power and BA ability with his quick stroke and contact ability.

Wimberly,Corey — 4 — Colorado — EXP MLB DEBUT: 2009 — POTENTIAL: Starting 2B — 7D

Bats B Age 24	Year	Lev	Team	AB	R	H	HR	RBI	Avg	OB	Slg	OPS	bb%	ct%	Eye	SB	CS	X/H%	Iso	RC/G
2005 (6) Alcorn St																				
Pwr +																				
BAvg ++++	2005	Rk	Casper	281	58	107	1	22	381	418	427	845	6	90	0.67	36	13	10	46	5.78
3.90 Spd ++++	2006	A+	Modesto	342	72	111	2	24	325	379	383	762	8	88	0.71	50	16	11	58	4.99
Def ++	2007	AA	Tulsa	365	63	98	4	33	268	305	348	653	5	86	0.37	36	9	20	79	3.49

Short/stocky infielder with plus speed that allowed him to lead TL in SB. Possesses contact skills and can bunt, but lacks power and will need to improve walk rate to maintain OBP. Defense is average at best as he lacks arm strength and footwork around 2B bag.

Winfree,David — 5 — Minnesota — EXP MLB DEBUT: 2008 — POTENTIAL: Reserve 3B/1B — 7D

Bats R Age 22	Year	Lev	Team	AB	R	H	HR	RBI	Avg	OB	Slg	OPS	bb%	ct%	Eye	SB	CS	X/H%	Iso	RC/G
2003 (13) HS (VA)	2004	Rk	Elzbton	217	31	62	8	37	286	340	433	774	8	76	0.35	1	1	26	147	4.95
Pwr ++++	2005	A-	Beloit	562	80	165	16	101	294	320	452	772	4	83	0.24	3	2	32	158	4.76
BAvg ++	2006	Rk	GCL Twins	15	2	3	0	1	200	250	267	517	6	73	0.25	0	0	33	67	1.71
Spd ++	2006	A+	Fort Myers	261	43	72	13	48	276	325	490	815	7	77	0.32	2	0	39	215	5.43
Def +++	2007	AA	New Britain	460	57	123	12	51	267	307	426	733	5	77	0.25	0	0	36	159	4.43

Strong/athletic player with good bat speed that generates moderate power to pull field. Struggles to make contact and aggressive approach tempers BA. Features plus arm strength, but stiff hands, lack of agility, and a strained shoulder put him at 1B for part of the season.

Wood,Brandon — 56 — Los Angeles (A) — EXP MLB DEBUT: 2007 — POTENTIAL: Starting 3B — 9C

Bats R Age 23	Year	Lev	Team	AB	R	H	HR	RBI	Avg	OB	Slg	OPS	bb%	ct%	Eye	SB	CS	X/H%	Iso	RC/G
2003 (1) HS (AZ)	2005	A+	Rancho Cuc	536	109	172	43	115	321	377	672	1048	8	76	0.36	7	3	57	351	8.53
Pwr +++++	2005	AAA	Salt Lake	19	1	6	0	1	316	316	526	842	0	68	0.00	0	0	50	211	6.33
BAvg +++	2006	AA	Arkansas	453	74	125	25	83	276	353	552	905	11	67	0.36	18	3	57	276	7.37
4.40 Spd ++	2007	AAA	Salt Lake	437	73	119	23	77	272	340	497	837	9	73	0.38	10	1	43	224	5.97
Def +++	2007	MLB	Los Angeles (A)	33	2	5	1	3	152	152	273	424	0	64	0.00	0	0	40	121	-0.11

Plus power with excellent loft, fueled by bat speed and fluid swing mechanics. Strikeout rate will always be excessive and aggressive approach will suppress walk rate/OBP. Runs bases well despite below average speed. Arm strength and soft/quick hands play at both 3B and SS.

Worth,Daniel — 6 — Detroit — EXP MLB DEBUT: 2009 — POTENTIAL: Starting SS — 7C

Bats R Age 22	Year	Lev	Team	AB	R	H	HR	RBI	Avg	OB	Slg	OPS	bb%	ct%	Eye	SB	CS	X/H%	Iso	RC/G
2007 (2) Pepperdine																				
Pwr +																				
BAvg +++																				
4.30 Spd +++	2007	A+	Lakeland	171	22	43	2	21	251	325	363	888	10	77	0.46	6	0	30	111	6.96
Def ++++	2007	AA	Erie	14	4	6	0	4	429	438	714	1152	7	93	1.00	1	0	50	286	12.54

Athletic infielder who rates as a plus defender with arm strength, soft hands, and range. Offense reliant on BA, as bat speed and the use of the middle of the field limits power and only has average speed. Defense should get him to Majors, but bat will determine his role and playing time.

Young,Delwyn — 7 — Los Angeles (N) — EXP MLB DEBUT: 2006 — POTENTIAL: Reserve LF/RF — 7C

Bats B Age 25	Year	Lev	Team	AB	R	H	HR	RBI	Avg	OB	Slg	OPS	bb%	ct%	Eye	SB	CS	X/H%	Iso	RC/G
2002 (4) Santa Barbara (	2005	AAA	Las Vegas	160	23	52	4	14	325	357	475	832	5	78	0.23	0	0	31	150	5.61
Pwr +++	2006	AAA	Las Vegas	532	76	145	18	98	273	326	457	783	7	80	0.40	3	4	42	184	5.11
BAvg ++++	2006	MLB	Los Angeles (N)	5	0	0	0	0	0	0	0	0	0	80	0.00	0	0	0	0	0.00
4.40 Spd ++	2007	AAA	Las Vegas	490	107	165	17	97	337	384	571	956	7	79	0.36	4	3	46	235	7.38
Def +	2007	MLB	Los Angeles (N)	34	4	13	2	3	382	417	647	1064	6	85	0.40	1	0	31	265	8.16

Pure hitter with exceptional contact ability, bat speed, and barrel awareness, he led PCL in runs scored. HR power enhanced by home environement, but can lace gaps consistently. Doesn't walk or strike-out very much. Possesses fringe-average arm strength, but needs to take better routes.

Young,Eric — 4 — Colorado — EXP MLB DEBUT: 2009 — POTENTIAL: Starting 2B — 7C

Bats B Age 23	Year	Lev	Team	AB	R	H	HR	RBI	Avg	OB	Slg	OPS	bb%	ct%	Eye	SB	CS	X/H%	Iso	RC/G
2003 (30) HS (NJ)																				
Pwr +	2004	Rk	Casper	87	20	23	0	7	264	402	345	747	19	85	1.54	14	1	26	80	5.53
BAvg +++	2005	Rk	Casper	219	48	66	3	25	301	398	438	836	14	76	0.67	25	10	26	137	6.33
3.95 Spd +++++	2006	A-	Asheville	482	92	142	5	49	295	381	409	789	12	84	0.89	87	31	27	114	5.60
Def +++	2007	A+	Modesto	540	113	157	8	63	291	346	430	776	8	81	0.44	73	18	31	139	5.16

Compact athlete with plus speed which allowed him to lead CAL in SB. Draws walks and makes contact to all fields, but lacks power and struggles versus LH pitching. Makes plays defensively with excellent range, but arm strength is poor and needs work on turning double-play.

PITCHERS

ROLE: Pitchers are classified as Starters (SP) or Relievers (RP).

THROWS: Handedness — right (RH) or left (LH).

AGE: Pitcher's age, as of April 1, 2008.

DRAFTED: The year, round, and school that the pitcher performed at as an amateur if drafted, or the year and country where the player was signed from, if a free agent.

EXP MLB DEBUT: The year a player is expected to debut in the Major Leagues.

PROJ ROLE: The role that the pitcher is expected to have at the peak of his Major League career.

PITCHES: Each pitch that a pitcher throws is graded and designated with a "+", indicating how well that pitch will fare in the Majors at his peak. Pitches are graded for their velocity, movement, and command. An average pitch will receive three "+" marks. When possible, a pitcher's velocity for each pitch is indicated.

FB	fastball
CB	curveball
SP	split-fingered fastball
SL	slider
CU	change-up
CT	cut-fastball
KC	knuckle-curve
KB	knuckle-ball
SC	screwball
SU	slurve

PLAYER STAT LINES: Pitchers receive statistics for the last five teams that they played for (if applicable), including the Major Leagues.

TEAM DESIGNATIONS: Each team that the pitcher performed for during a given year is included. "JPN" means Japan, "MEX" means Mexico, "KOR" means Korea, "TWN" means Taiwan, "CUB" means Cuba and "IND" means independent league.

LEVEL DESIGNATIONS: The level for each team a player performed is included. "AAA" means Triple-A, "AA" means Double-A, "A" means Class-A, and "Rk" means rookie level.

SABERMETRIC CATEGORIES: Descriptions of all the sabermetric categories appear in the glossary. The decimal point has been suppressed on several categories to conserve space.

CAPSULE COMMENTARIES: For each pitcher, a brief analysis of their skills/statistics, and their future potential is provided.

ELIGIBILITY: Eligibility for inclusion is the standard for which Major League Baseball adheres to; 50 innings pitched or 45 days on the 25-man roster, not including the month of September.

POTENTIAL RATINGS

The Potential Ratings are a two-part system in which a player is assigned a number rating based on his upside potential (1-10) and a letter rating based on the probability of reaching that potential (A-E).

Potential

10: Hall of Famer	5: MLB reserve
9: Elite player	4: Top minor leaguer
8: Solid regular	3: Averge minor leaguer
7: Average regular	2: Minor league reserve
6: Platoon player	1: Minor league roster filler

Probability Rating

A: 90% probability of reaching potential
B: 70% probability of reaching potential
C: 50% probability of reaching potential
D: 30% probability of reaching potential
E: 10% probability of reaching potential

FASTBALL

Scouts grade a fastball in terms of both velocity and movement. Movement of a pitch is purely subjective, but one can always watch the hitter, to see how he reacts to a pitch or if he swings and misses. Pitchers throw three types of fastballs with varying movement. A two-seam fastball is often referred to as a sinker, a four-seam fastball appears to maintain its plane at high velocities, and a cutter can move in different directions and is caused by the pitcher both cutting-off his extension out front and by varying the grip. Velocity is often graded on the 20-80 scale and is indicated by the chart below.

Scout Grade	Velocity (MPH)
80	96+
70	94-95
60	92-93
50 (average)	89-91
40	87-88
30	85-86
20	82-84

PITCHER RELEASE TIMES

The speed (in seconds) that a pitcher releases a pitch is extremely important in terms of halting the running game and establishing good pitching mechanics. Pitchers are timed from the movement of the front leg until the baseball reaches the catcher's mitt. The phrases "slow to the plate" or "quick to the plate" may often appear in the capsule commentary box.

1.0-1.2	+
1.3-1.4	MLB average
1.5+	-

Abreu, Winston — RP — Washington — EXP MLB DEBUT: 2006 — POTENTIAL: Setup reliever — 6C

Thrws R   Age 31
1994 FA (DR)
89-94 FB ++++
CB +++

Year	Lev	Team	W	L	Sv	IP	K	ERA	WHIP	BF/G	OBA	H%	S%	xERA	Ctl	Dom	Cmd	hr/9	BPV
2005	AAA	Tucson	2	3	2	33	42	6.53	1.57	5.4	284	38	61	5.58	4.1	11.4	2.8	1.6	77
2006	AAA	Ottawa	9	4	1	65	78	2.49	1.14	5.6	227	32	80	2.71	2.8	10.8	3.9	0.6	140
2006	MLB	Baltimore	0	0	0	8	6	10.13	2.00	5.5	307	35	47	6.58	6.8	6.8	1.0	1.1	21
2007	AAA	Columbus	3	0	5	52	82	1.21	0.84	5.2	140	25	88	0.76	3.5	14.2	4.1	0.3	188
2007	MLB	Washington	0	1	0	30	26	5.98	1.53	5.0	304	34	67	6.23	2.7	7.8	2.9	2.1	39

Hard-throwing reliever had career interrupted twice by elbow and shoulder surgeries. Produces strikeouts with electric FB and CB, but game came together by improving command. Needs to trust stuff when behind in count and get ahead of hitters more consistently.

Acosta, Manny — RP — Atlanta — EXP MLB DEBUT: 2007 — POTENTIAL: Setup reliever — 7C

Thrws R   Age 27
1998 FA (Panama)
90-95 FB ++++
80-82 CB +++

Year	Lev	Team	W	L	Sv	IP	K	ERA	WHIP	BF/G	OBA	H%	S%	xERA	Ctl	Dom	Cmd	hr/9	BPV
2005	A+	Myrtle Beach	2	2	7	22	18	4.43	1.40	5.2	261	32	75	4.69	3.7	7.3	2.0	0.4	51
2006	AA	Mississippi	0	0	4	15	13	2.35	1.46	5.0	141	30	73	2.40	8.9	7.7	0.9	0.6	91
2006	AAA	Richmond	1	6	17	43	43	3.63	1.60	5.2	233	31	72	3.50	6.7	9.0	1.3	0.8	70
2007	AAA	Richmond	9	3	12	59	56	2.26	1.37	6.2	216	33	78	2.12	5.3	8.5	1.6	0.0	89
2007	MLB	Atlanta	1	1	0	23	22	2.28	1.16	4.4	166	30	80	2.00	5.4	8.5	1.6	0.7	66

Tall/projectable reliever with explosive four seamer and hard CB that generates swings and misses. Arm action provides movement and resiliency, and is aggressive in approach. Throws too many pitches to get job done, which can is easily correctable.

Adenhart, Nick — SP — Los Angeles (A) — EXP MLB DEBUT: 2008 — POTENTIAL: #2 starter — 9C

Thrws R   Age 21
2004 (14) HS (MD)
88-94 FB ++++
74-76 CB ++++
80-83 CU +++

Year	Lev	Team	W	L	Sv	IP	K	ERA	WHIP	BF/G	OBA	H%	S%	xERA	Ctl	Dom	Cmd	hr/9	BPV
2005	Rk	AZL Angels	2	3	0	44	52	3.68	1.43	14.4	239	35	71	3.09	4.9	10.6	2.2	0.0	116
2005	Rk	Orem	1	0	0	6	7	0.00	0.50	19.9	151	23	100	0.00	0.0	10.5	0.0	0.0	88
2006	A-	Cedar Rapids	10	2	0	106	99	2.04	1.04	25.6	219	29	80	2.02	2.2	8.4	3.8	0.2	136
2006	A+	Rancho Cuc.	5	2	0	52	46	3.80	1.29	23.8	258	33	68	3.15	2.8	7.9	2.9	0.2	106
2007	AA	Arkansas	10	8	0	153	116	3.65	1.46	25.2	268	32	75	3.96	3.8	6.8	1.8	0.4	67

Projectable arm possessing fluid arm action, velocity, and a plus pitch (CB). Command and dominance regressed, but was focusing on mechanics and dealt with minor shoulder soreness. Pitched over 150 innings once again, putting to rest concerns over prior TJS.

Adkins, James — SP — Los Angeles (N) — EXP MLB DEBUT: 2009 — POTENTIAL: #3 starter — 8D

Thrws L   Age 22
2007 (1-S) Tennessee
85-91 FB +++
78-80 SL +++
73-79 CB +++
77-81 CU ++

Year	Lev	Team	W	L	Sv	IP	K	ERA	WHIP	BF/G	OBA	H%	S%	xERA	Ctl	Dom	Cmd	hr/9	BPV
2007	A-	Great Lakes	0	1	0	26	30	2.42	1.04	9.1	188	27	77	1.80	3.5	10.4	3.0	0.3	132

Finesse pitcher with excellent command and ability to mix four pitches. Likes to pitch backwards, compensating for mediocre velocity. Low ¾ slot provides deception and extends well to plate with long arms. History of shoulder soreness, so innings need to be monitored.

Alaniz, Adrian — SP — Washington — EXP MLB DEBUT: 2010 — POTENTIAL: #5 starter — 6C

Thrws R   Age 24
2007 (8) Texas
86-91 FB +++
77-80 SL +++
70-72 CB +++
79-80 CU ++

Year	Lev	Team	W	L	Sv	IP	K	ERA	WHIP	BF/G	OBA	H%	S%	xERA	Ctl	Dom	Cmd	hr/9	BPV
2007	A-	Vermont	8	2	0	60	62	2.40	0.83	16.9	199	27	71	1.37	1.2	9.3	7.8	0.3	225

Finesse-type that features solid command and ability to mix two breaking pitches with his two-seam FB. Provides deception with ¾ delivery, but despite an athletic frame, he doesn't repeat the arm speed on CU consistently, which he will need at upper levels to survive.

Albaladejo, Jonathan — RP — New York (A) — EXP MLB DEBUT: 2007 — POTENTIAL: Setup reliever — 6B

Thrws R   Age 25
2001 (19) Miami-Dade CC
87-91 FB +++
SL ++
CB +++

Year	Lev	Team	W	L	Sv	IP	K	ERA	WHIP	BF/G	OBA	H%	S%	xERA	Ctl	Dom	Cmd	hr/9	BPV
2006	Rk	GCL Pirates	1	0	0	12	16	2.92	1.24	16.4	260	31	72	2.95	2.2	11.9	5.3	0.8	97
2006	AA	Altoona	1	2	1	37	29	4.00	1.27	8.4	287	30	80	5.15	1.2	7.1	5.8	1.0	45
2007	AA	Harrisburg	4	3	2	36	35	4.17	1.24	7.0	227	32	78	5.00	3.7	8.7	2.3	0.7	66
2007	AAA	Columbus	3	0	0	24	21	1.13	0.88	5.9	171	30	82	2.44	2.6	7.9	3.0	0.7	65
2007	MLB	Washington	1	1	0	14	12	1.88	0.64	3.5	150	29	80	2.67	1.3	7.7	6.0	0.6	69

Tall/strong-framed pitcher with two years of relieving under his belt. Not a hard thrower, but sports excellent command and gets downward plane to pitches, which enhances look of FB and CB. Doesn't have much to offer LH batters and will need to keep body in-check.

Alderson, Tim — SP — San Francisco — EXP MLB DEBUT: 2011 — POTENTIAL: #3 starter — 8C

Thrws R   Age 19
2007 (1-C) HS (AZ)
88-93 FB ++++
78-81 CB +++
80-82 CU ++

Year	Lev	Team	W	L	Sv	IP	K	ERA	WHIP	BF/G	OBA	H%	S%	xERA	Ctl	Dom	Cmd	hr/9	BPV
2007	Rk	AZL Giants	0	0	0	5	12	0.00	0.80	6.0	221	66	100	1.15	0.0	21.6		0.0	140

Tall/projectable pitcher with tons of polish for age/level. Pitches on downward plane with FB and CB getting swings and misses. Command is outstanding and gets pitch movement through quick arm action. Will need to improve circle-CU and smooth-out his ¾ delivery.

Alexander, Mark — RP — Los Angeles (N) — EXP MLB DEBUT: 2008 — POTENTIAL: Setup reliever — 6B

Thrws R   Age 27
2004 (20) Missouri
87-91 FB +++
74-78 SL +++
77-80 CU ++

Year	Lev	Team	W	L	Sv	IP	K	ERA	WHIP	BF/G	OBA	H%	S%	xERA	Ctl	Dom	Cmd	hr/9	BPV
2005	A+	Vero Beach	5	4	23	65	91	3.04	1.34	5.2	259	39	80	3.86	3.2	12.6	4.0	0.8	137
2006	AA	Jacksonville	3	2	26	47	72	0.96	0.86	4.3	164	38	92	1.01	2.5	13.8	5.5	0.4	210
2006	AAA	Las Vegas	2	1	1	14	13	3.19	1.49	5.1	217	29	76	2.97	6.4	8.3	1.3	0.0	89
2007	AA	Jacksonville	5	1	5	67	81	4.43	1.33	7.7	222	28	72	3.99	4.7	10.9	2.3	1.5	80
2007	AAA	Las Vegas	0	0	0	12	14	14.25	3.00	5.8	334	45	49	9.15	14.3	10.5	0.7	0.8	44

Strong/stocky reliever who compensates for below average velocity with a tight SL, ability to keep ball down, and outstanding command. CU to LH batters regressed slightly and can be hittable if pitches are left in zone. Closing days are over, but can thrive in a matchup role.

Ambriz, Hector — SP — Arizona — EXP MLB DEBUT: 2009 — POTENTIAL: #5 starter — 6B

Thrws R   Age 24
2006 (2) UCLA
87-92 FB +++
82-84 SL +++
73-75 CB ++
85-87 SP +++

Year	Lev	Team	W	L	Sv	IP	K	ERA	WHIP	BF/G	OBA	H%	S%	xERA	Ctl	Dom	Cmd	hr/9	BPV
2006	Rk	Missoula	1	3	3	42	52	1.92	0.95	10.6	196	30	79	1.54	2.4	11.1	4.7	0.2	175
2007	A+	Visalia	10	8	0	150	133	4.08	1.25	21.8	245	30	68	3.39	3.0	8.0	2.7	0.7	88

Finesse pitcher with outstanding command and movement, using FB to set-up SPL and SL. Strong/athletic frame provided stamina for first time and has had previous shoulder surgery. Pitched well in a hitter-friendly environment, but will need to change speeds at next level.

Anderson, Brett — SP — Oakland — EXP MLB DEBUT: 2010 — POTENTIAL: #3 starter — 8C

Thrws L   Age 20
2006 (2) HS (OK)
86-90 FB +++
80-81 SL ++
73-78 CB +++
77-80 CU +++

Year	Lev	Team	W	L	Sv	IP	K	ERA	WHIP	BF/G	OBA	H%	S%	xERA	Ctl	Dom	Cmd	hr/9	BPV
2007	A-	South Bend	8	4	0	81	85	2.22	1.06	22.5	249	34	80	2.61	1.1	9.4	8.5	0.3	230
2007	A+	Visalia	3	3	0	39	40	4.85	1.56	19.0	313	39	73	5.78	2.5	9.2	3.6	1.4	83

Polished and durable pitcher with three average to above pitches and a repetitive delivery that keeps them disguised and under command. Strikeout rate accented by solid CB, but can be guilty of overusing it. Non-athletic frame and soft body could affect stamina if left unchecked.

Anderson, Brian — RP — San Francisco — EXP MLB DEBUT: 2008 — POTENTIAL: Setup reliever — 6C

Thrws R   Age 25
2005 (14) Long Beach St
86-89 FB ++
77-80 SL +++

Year	Lev	Team	W	L	Sv	IP	K	ERA	WHIP	BF/G	OBA	H%	S%	xERA	Ctl	Dom	Cmd	hr/9	BPV
2005	Rk	Salem-Keizer	3	1	19	28	42	1.93	0.68	3.6	168	27	76	0.93	1.0	13.5	14.0	0.6	377
2006	A+	San Jose	1	1	37	67	85	1.88	0.89	4.6	185	27	84	1.69	2.3	11.4	5.0	0.7	171
2007	AA	Connecticut	1	5	29	50	46	3.95	1.50	4.6	280	35	75	4.51	3.6	8.3	2.3	0.7	75

Soft-tosser led EL in saves a year removed from leading entire minors in saves. Exhibits plus command and can notch strikeouts, but lack of velocity makes him more hittable. Keeps ball down, is adept at discovering hitters' weaknesses, and makes pitches.

Andrade,Steve — RP — Tampa Bay

EXP MLB DEBUT: 2006 | POTENTIAL: Setup reliever | 6C

Thrws R Age 30
2001 (32) Cal St Stanislaus
88-92 FB +++
SL +
CB ++++

Year	Lev	Team	W	L	Sv	IP	K	ERA	WHIP	BF/G	OBA	H%	S%	xERA	Ctl	Dom	Cmd	hr/9	BPV
2004	AAA	Salt Lake	0	1	3	13	17	4.77	1.74	5.0	287	41	73	5.16	5.5	11.6	2.1	0.7	91
2005	AA	New Hamp.	3	2	3	50	71	1.98	0.78	5.2	140	22	78	0.79	2.9	12.8	4.4	0.5	181
2006	AAA	Omaha/Port	3	2	0	67	67	3.21	1.26	7.2	225	29	75	3.00	4.0	9.0	2.2	0.5	95
2006	MLB	Kansas City	0	0	0	4	5	10.71	2.14	5.2	297	42	44	5.68	8.6	10.7	1.3	0.0	86
2007	AAA	Durham	3	2	0	59	50	4.57	1.42	6.6	241	30	68	3.69	4.7	7.6	1.6	0.6	68

Minor league veteran has yet to have extended opportunity despite performance and stuff that say different. Utilizes multiple arm angles to deceive hitters, commands plate, and possesses a plus CB and life to FB. Arm action is long, which makes him susceptible to SB.

Arredondo,Jose — RP — Los Angeles (A)

EXP MLB DEBUT: 2008 | POTENTIAL: Setup reliever | 8C

Thrws R Age 24
2002 FA (DR)
90-97 FB ++++
82-86 SL ++
81-84 SP +++
CU ++

Year	Lev	Team	W	L	Sv	IP	K	ERA	WHIP	BF/G	OBA	H%	S%	xERA	Ctl	Dom	Cmd	hr/9	BPV
2006	A+	Rancho Cuc.	5	6	0	90	115	2.30	1.08	23.4	196	29	80	2.04	3.5	11.5	3.3	0.4	142
2006	AA	Arkansas	2	3	0	60	48	6.58	1.69	24.7	320	37	62	6.08	3.3	7.2	2.2	1.2	44
2007	A+	Rancho Cuc.	2	4	4	35	34	6.43	1.63	5.6	318	39	62	5.94	2.8	8.7	3.1	1.3	70
2007	AA	Arkansas	0	1	10	25	28	2.52	1.12	4.3	185	25	81	2.33	4.3	10.1	2.3	0.7	106
2007	AAA	Salt Lake	0	0	0	3	1	3.00	1.33	6.2	191	21	75	2.33	6.0	3.0	0.5	0.0	45

Energetic reliever with plus velocity, movement to SPL, and command, allowing him to get strikeouts. Arm action is quick, but does present some effort, which prompted move to relief. Maturity issues cost him a mid-season demotion, but problems seem to be corrected.

Arrieta,Jacob — SP — Baltimore

EXP MLB DEBUT: 2009 | POTENTIAL: #3 starter | 8C

Thrws R Age 22
2007 (5) TCU
87-94 FB ++++
78-82 SL +++
74-77 SP +++
79-81 CU +++

Year	Lev	Team	W	L	Sv	IP	K	ERA	WHIP	BF/G	OBA	H%	S%	xERA	Ctl	Dom	Cmd	hr/9	BPV
2007																			

Power pitcher with four offerings, but lacks strikeout ability. Keeps hitters off-balance by mixing pitches and maintains velocity which allows him to stay in games longer. Command suffers from not repeating ¾ drop-and-drive delivery, but has the arm action to improve.

Ascanio,Jose — RP — Chicago (N)

EXP MLB DEBUT: 2007 | POTENTIAL: Setup reliever/closer | 8C

Thrws R Age 23
2001 FA (Venezuela)
90-96 FB ++++
83-87 SL +++
77-78 CB ++

Year	Lev	Team	W	L	Sv	IP	K	ERA	WHIP	BF/G	OBA	H%	S%	xERA	Ctl	Dom	Cmd	hr/9	BPV
2005	A+	Myrtle Beach	3	1	0	20	12	6.24	1.73	18.4	313	32	70	7.05	4.0	5.3	1.3	2.2	-14
2006	A+	Myrtle Beach	1	1	0	31	23	4.94	1.87	18.2	303	37	71	5.13	5.8	6.7	1.2	0.0	59
2006	AA	Mississippi	4	2	0	38	37	4.26	1.42	6.7	257	33	69	3.75	4.0	8.8	2.2	0.5	88
2007	AA	Mississippi	2	2	10	78	71	2.54	1.08	6.9	231	30	75	2.22	2.1	8.2	3.9	0.1	137
2007	MLB	Atlanta	1	1	0	16	13	5.06	1.44	5.2	274	30	70	5.19	3.4	7.3	2.2	1.7	39

Wiry reliever made a successful comeback from a fractured lower back in 2005. Gets plus movement to FB and SL with his whip-like arm action and command is outstanding. Likes to challenge hitters and get strikeouts, but success will come with greater G/F ratio.

Atkins,Mitch — SP — Chicago (N)

EXP MLB DEBUT: 2009 | POTENTIAL: #5 starter | 7D

Thrws R Age 22
2004 (7) HS (NC)
88-91 FB +++
CB +++
CU +++

Year	Lev	Team	W	L	Sv	IP	K	ERA	WHIP	BF/G	OBA	H%	S%	xERA	Ctl	Dom	Cmd	hr/9	BPV
2004	Rk	AZL Cubs	2	2	0	29	20	8.01	1.92	13.8	338	40	54	5.82	4.3	6.2	1.4	0.0	54
2005	A-	Boise	3	6	0	73	59	5.05	1.57	21.4	292	34	69	5.13	3.7	7.3	2.0	1.0	52
2006	A-	Peoria	13	4	0	138	127	2.41	1.19	22.2	223	28	83	2.92	3.5	8.3	2.4	0.7	91
2007	A+	Daytona	8	7	0	115	88	3.13	1.13	22.7	234	26	78	3.33	2.4	6.9	2.8	1.1	76
2007	AA	Tennessee	1	1	0	26	18	5.54	1.58	16.3	290	31	69	5.83	3.8	6.2	1.6	1.7	17

Projectable pitcher with three average pitches and the ability to attack hitters. Command was better at lower level, but efficiency has been problem each step of the way. Repeats ¾ delivery consistently, giving him deception, but may always struggle to get strikeout.

Aumont,Phillippe — SP — Seattle

EXP MLB DEBUT: 2011 | POTENTIAL: #2 starter | 9E

Thrws R Age 19
2007 (1) HS (Canada)
88-94 FB ++++
78-82 SL +++
79-81 CU +

Year	Lev	Team	W	L	Sv	IP	K	ERA	WHIP	BF/G	OBA	H%	S%	xERA	Ctl	Dom	Cmd	hr/9	BPV
2007																			

Canadian prepster with heavy FB and darting SL that produces both groundball outs and strikeouts. Gains deception with low ¾ slot, but throws with effort and arm action is less than ideal. Perfecting CU and command should improve with a more consistent delivery.

Bachanov,Jonathon — SP — Los Angeles (A)

EXP MLB DEBUT: 2012 | POTENTIAL: #3 starter | 8D

Thrws R Age 19
2007 (1-S) HS (FL)
88-92 FB +++
87-88 CT +++
73-76 SU +++
76-78 CU ++

Year	Lev	Team	W	L	Sv	IP	K	ERA	WHIP	BF/G	OBA	H%	S%	xERA	Ctl	Dom	Cmd	hr/9	BPV
2007																			

Tall/strong-framed pitcher works effectively by mixing FB, CT, and SU. Gets hitters to chase pitches out of the zone, but costs him efficiency. Coaches love his aggressiveness and has good command. Effort to delivery gave rise to minor elbow pain and stamina a concern.

Bailey,Andrew — SP — Oakland

EXP MLB DEBUT: 2009 | POTENTIAL: #3 starter | 8C

Thrws R Age 24
2006 (6) Wagner
87-93 FB ++++
75-78 CB +++
83-86 CU +

Year	Lev	Team	W	L	Sv	IP	K	ERA	WHIP	BF/G	OBA	H%	S%	xERA	Ctl	Dom	Cmd	hr/9	BPV
2006	A-	Vancouver	2	5	0	58	53	2.02	1.02	17.1	193	25	81	1.79	3.1	8.2	2.7	0.3	112
2007	A-	Kane County	1	4	0	51	74	3.35	1.25	18.9	226	34	78	3.44	3.9	13.1	3.4	1.1	127
2007	A+	Stockton	3	4	0	66	72	3.82	1.32	24.8	231	30	75	3.73	4.2	9.8	2.3	1.1	84
2007	AAA	Sacramento	1	0	0	8	4	1.13	0.50	26.6	117	14	75	0.00	1.1	4.5	4.0	0.0	143

Power pitcher with quick arm action and ability to sustain velocity. Missed bats with excellent movement to FB and CB, command, and a deceptive delivery. TJS in 2005 stalled progress and is slowly regaining feel for comps, in which his circle-CU needs the most attention.

Bailey,Homer — SP — Cincinnati

EXP MLB DEBUT: 2007 | POTENTIAL: #1 starter | 9B

Thrws R Age 22
2004 (1) HS (TX)
89-96 FB ++++
84-86 CT +++
75-80 CB ++++
81-84 CU ++

Year	Lev	Team	W	L	Sv	IP	K	ERA	WHIP	BF/G	OBA	H%	S%	xERA	Ctl	Dom	Cmd	hr/9	BPV
2006	A+	Sarasota	3	5	0	70	79	3.33	1.01	20.7	198	27	69	2.25	2.8	10.1	3.6	0.8	128
2006	AA	Chattanooga	7	1	0	68	77	1.59	1.15	20.8	207	30	86	2.10	3.7	10.2	2.8	0.1	129
2007	A+	Sarasota	0	1	0	8	7	10.13	2.50	21.3	399	46	61	10.54	5.6	7.9	1.4	2.3	-16
2007	AAA	Louisville	6	3	0	67	59	3.08	1.21	22.5	206	26	75	2.64	4.3	7.9	1.8	0.5	84
2007	MLB	Cincinnati	4	2	0	45	28	5.79	1.57	22.0	253	29	62	4.24	5.6	5.6	1.0	0.6	41

Pitched better by focusing on movement and incorporating entire arsenal, though the cost was velocity and strikeout ability. CB and FB move extremely well and gains deception from drop-and-drive delivery. Missed innings with a strained groin and still struggles with efficiency.

Balester,Collin — SP — Washington

EXP MLB DEBUT: 2008 | POTENTIAL: #3 starter | 8C

Thrws R Age 22
2004 (4) HS (CA)
88-93 FB ++++
76-80 CB +++
82-85 CU ++

Year	Lev	Team	W	L	Sv	IP	K	ERA	WHIP	BF/G	OBA	H%	S%	xERA	Ctl	Dom	Cmd	hr/9	BPV
2005	A-	Savannah	8	6	0	125	95	3.67	1.18	20.8	230	27	71	3.10	3.0	6.8	2.3	0.8	74
2006	A+	Potomac	4	5	0	117	87	5.22	1.52	22.1	274	32	66	4.69	4.1	6.7	1.6	0.9	47
2006	AA	Harrisburg	1	0	0	19	10	1.88	1.09	25.0	217	25	81	2.01	2.8	4.7	1.7	0.0	75
2007	AA	Harrisburg	2	7	0	98	77	3.76	1.30	23.8	271	32	73	4.00	2.3	7.1	3.1	0.8	83
2007	AAA	Columbus	2	3	0	51	40	4.22	1.41	21.6	253	31	70	3.74	4.0	7.0	1.7	0.5	67

Well-proportioned pitcher with fluid arm action and easy velocity. Stuff doesn't match performance as he doesn't miss bats and pitches uphill from his drop-and-drive delivery. Command improved slightly, but will need to get greater separation between FB and CU.

Banks,Josh — SP — Toronto

EXP MLB DEBUT: 2007 | POTENTIAL: #5 starter | 6B

Thrws R Age 25
2003 (2) Florida Int
86-92 FB +++
81-84 SL +++
83-84 SP ++++
73-77 CB ++

Year	Lev	Team	W	L	Sv	IP	K	ERA	WHIP	BF/G	OBA	H%	S%	xERA	Ctl	Dom	Cmd	hr/9	BPV
2004	AA	New Hamp.	6	6	0	91	76	5.04	1.28	20.8	257	29	65	4.38	2.8	7.5	2.7	1.5	61
2005	AA	New Hamp.	8	12	0	162	145	3.83	1.05	23.2	258	31	66	3.34	0.6	8.1	13.2	1.0	299
2006	AAA	Syracuse	10	11	0	170	126	5.24	1.25	23.9	277	30	64	4.91	1.5	6.7	4.5	1.9	79
2007	AAA	Syracuse	12	10	0	169	101	4.63	1.28	25.7	287	31	66	4.51	1.3	5.4	4.2	1.2	83
2007	MLB	Toronto	0	0	0	7	2	7.61	1.83	11.0	355	36	58	7.12	2.5	2.5	1.0	1.3	-18

Strike thrower with six pitches, but is highly hittable and struggles to get strikeout. SPL is best pitch and tends to overuse it, but can keep hitters honest by sinking and cutting FB. Changes arm slots for effect and rarely gives-in to hitters, which doesn't always work.

Banwart,Travis — SP — Oakland

EXP MLB DEBUT: 2010 | POTENTIAL: #5 starter | 7C

Thrws R Age 22
2007 (4) Wichita St

Velo	Pitch	Grade
87-92	FB	+++
	SL	++
	CB	++
80-82	CU	+++

Year	Lev	Team	W	L	Sv	IP	K	ERA	WHIP	BF/G	OBA	H%	S%	xERA	Ctl	Dom	Cmd	hr/9	BPV
2007	A-	Kane County	2	1	1	45	41	2.60	1.02	14.4	221	28	75	2.22	2.0	8.2	4.1	0.4	134

Tall/well-proportioned pitcher with good arm action and advanced ability to change speeds. FB command will be the key to success unless he can learn to spin baseball better. Presents effort to his delivery and doesn't always repeat his arm slot, but has proved durable thus far.

Bard,Daniel — SP — Boston

EXP MLB DEBUT: 2009 | POTENTIAL: #3 starter/closer | 9D

Thrws R Age 22
2006 (1-C) No Carolina

Velo	Pitch	Grade
90-98	FB	++++
77-79	CB	+++
84-87	CU	++

Year	Lev	Team	W	L	Sv	IP	K	ERA	WHIP	BF/G	OBA	H%	S%	xERA	Ctl	Dom	Cmd	hr/9	BPV
2007	A+	Lancaster	0	2	0	13	9	10.31	3.28	16.0	362	40	68	10.99	15.1	6.2	0.4	1.4	-13
2007	AA	Greenville	3	5	0	61	38	6.47	1.81	16.7	242	28	62	4.55	8.2	5.6	0.7	0.4	41

Tall/projectable pitcher with plus movement and velocity generated by quick arm action. FB and CB are strong enough to elicit strikeouts, but doesn't always trust off-speed stuff and struggles to repeat delivery which leaves him with below average command.

Barnese,Nick — SP — Tampa Bay

EXP MLB DEBUT: 2012 | POTENTIAL: #4 starter | 8E

Thrws R Age 19
2007 (3) HS (CA)

Velo	Pitch	Grade
87-92	FB	++++
77-79	SU	+++
78-81	CU	++

Year	Lev	Team	W	L	Sv	IP	K	ERA	WHIP	BF/G	OBA	H%	S%	xERA	Ctl	Dom	Cmd	hr/9	BPV
2007	Rk	Princeton	2	2	0	36	37	0.25	0.94	15.1	228	21	157	4.76	1.0	9.2	9.3	3.2	162

Quick arm action provides solid FB movement and gains deception from his low ¾ slot. Shows poise and excellent command for experience level, and has the athletic frame to project more velocity. Will need to tighten rotation of breaking pitch and throw CU more often.

Barone,Daniel — SP — Florida

EXP MLB DEBUT: 2007 | POTENTIAL: #5 starter | 6B

Thrws R Age 25
2004 (11) Mont Peninsula

Velo	Pitch	Grade
87-93	FB	+++
78-82	SL	++
81-84	CU	+++

Year	Lev	Team	W	L	Sv	IP	K	ERA	WHIP	BF/G	OBA	H%	S%	xERA	Ctl	Dom	Cmd	hr/9	BPV
2006	A+	Jupiter	3	5	0	73	57	4.31	1.40	18.1	290	33	72	4.77	2.2	7.0	3.2	1.1	72
2006	AA	Carolina	1	0	0	20	13	1.80	0.95	25.1	187	22	83	1.71	2.7	5.9	2.2	0.5	85
2007	AA	Carolina	1	3	0	74	60	3.88	1.16	22.7	245	29	68	3.31	2.2	7.3	3.3	0.8	94
2007	AAA	Albuquerque	7	0	0	61	31	4.12	1.21	24.7	258	28	68	3.66	2.1	4.6	2.2	0.9	51
2007	MLB	Florida	1	3	0	41	18	5.71	1.68	11.5	302	29	74	6.94	4.2	4.0	0.9	2.4	-34

Unheralded arm was able to impress FLA brass with his command and ability to change speeds. FB is hard, but lacks movement and has trouble spinning baseball. Strikeout rate will always be low, so has to hit corners and keep ball down or upside will be very little.

Barthmaier,Jimmy — SP — Pittsburgh

EXP MLB DEBUT: 2009 | POTENTIAL: #4 starter/setup reliever | 7C

Thrws R Age 24
2003 (13) HS (TX)

Velo	Pitch	Grade
89-94	FB	++++
80-82	CB	+++
79-81	CU	+++

Year	Lev	Team	W	L	Sv	IP	K	ERA	WHIP	BF/G	OBA	H%	S%	xERA	Ctl	Dom	Cmd	hr/9	BPV
2004	Rk	Greeneville	4	3	0	69	65	3.78	1.33	22.0	265	34	71	3.57	2.9	8.5	3.0	0.4	103
2005	A-	Lexington	11	6	0	134	142	2.28	1.21	21.7	222	31	81	2.52	3.7	9.5	2.6	0.2	116
2005	A+	Salem	1	0	0	6	6	1.50	0.83	21.9	191	22	100	2.42	1.5	9.0	6.0	1.5	152
2006	A+	Salem	11	8	0	146	134	3.63	1.40	22.8	249	32	73	3.50	4.1	8.2	2.0	0.4	86
2007	AA	Corpus Christi	2	9	0	90	73	6.20	1.78	17.2	314	37	66	6.09	4.4	7.3	1.7	1.1	38

Large framed pitcher battled through an elbow nerve injury in April and wasn't the same pitcher upon return. Possesses overpowering FB and feels comfortable with both comps. Command declined and throws with effort and across body, which may signal a move to relief.

Bastardo,Antonio — SP — Philadelphia

EXP MLB DEBUT: 2010 | POTENTIAL: #5 starter | 7D

Thrws L Age 22
2006 FA (DR)

Velo	Pitch	Grade
86-91	FB	+++
	SL	+++
	CU	+++

Year	Lev	Team	W	L	Sv	IP	K	ERA	WHIP	BF/G	OBA	H%	S%	xERA	Ctl	Dom	Cmd	hr/9	BPV
2007	A-	Lakewood	9	0	0	91	98	1.88	1.15	24.1	197	27	84	2.15	4.1	9.7	2.3	0.3	114
2007	A+	Clearwater	1	0	0	5	12	7.20	1.60	22.1	262	70	50	3.70	5.4	21.6	4.0	0.0	216

Small/athletic pitcher allowed very few hits and struck-out plenty by mixing three pitches with solid command. Repeats delivery and hides baseball providing deception. Short stature could affect stamina and will have to have best stuff without above average FB velocity.

Baumgarner,Madison — SP — San Francisco

EXP MLB DEBUT: 2011 | POTENTIAL: #2 starter | 9D

Thrws L Age 18
2007 (1) HS (NC)

Velo	Pitch	Grade
87-95	FB	++++
76-80	SU	++
71-73	CB	+++
79-82	CU	++

Year	Lev	Team	W	L	Sv	IP	K	ERA	WHIP	BF/G	OBA	H%	S%	xERA	Ctl	Dom	Cmd	hr/9	BPV
2007																			

Promising pitcher with smooth arm action which begets pitch movement and easy velocity. Keeps ball low with sinker, uses two variations of his CB, and is tough on LH batters with his low ¾ slot. Needs to incorporate CU and build-up arm strength to improve stamina.

Bazardo,Yorman — SP — Detroit

EXP MLB DEBUT: 2007 | POTENTIAL: #5 starter | 6B

Thrws R Age 23
2000 FA (Venezuela)

Velo	Pitch	Grade
87-94	FB	+++
81-83	SL	++
80-84	CU	++++

Year	Lev	Team	W	L	Sv	IP	K	ERA	WHIP	BF/G	OBA	H%	S%	xERA	Ctl	Dom	Cmd	hr/9	BPV
2005	AA	San Ant/Car	11	8	0	142	99	4.06	1.36	23.7	267	30	73	4.28	3.0	6.3	2.1	1.0	53
2005	MLB	Florida	0	0	0	1	2	30.00	5.83	10.4	596	78	43	22.84	15.0	15.0	1.0	0.0	47
2006	AA	San Antonio	6	5	0	138	80	3.65	1.37	23.1	270	30	74	4.01	2.9	5.2	1.8	0.7	50
2007	AAA	Toledo	10	6	0	136	69	3.77	1.30	24.4	259	29	71	3.57	2.8	4.6	1.6	0.5	48
2007	MLB	Detroit	2	1	0	23	15	2.33	1.03	8.1	225	25	82	2.68	1.9	5.8	3.0	0.8	85

Extreme groundball pitcher with plus CU and good velocity, but doesn't miss many bats and struggles with command. Stiff arm action contributes to poor rotation of SL and overall pitch movement. Pitched a fair amount of innings and has a tendency to tire late in season.

Beam,TJ — RP — Pittsburgh

EXP MLB DEBUT: 2006 | POTENTIAL: Setup reliever | 6B

Thrws R Age 27
2002 (11) Mississippi

Velo	Pitch	Grade
89-95	FB	++++
79-82	SL	++
70-75	CB	++
80-83	CU	+++

Year	Lev	Team	W	L	Sv	IP	K	ERA	WHIP	BF/G	OBA	H%	S%	xERA	Ctl	Dom	Cmd	hr/9	BPV
2006	AA	Trenton	4	0	3	42	34	0.86	0.90	8.7	180	23	92	1.28	2.6	7.3	2.8	0.2	116
2006	AAA	Columbus	2	0	1	31	37	1.73	0.93	6.2	154	23	82	1.10	3.8	10.7	2.8	0.3	139
2006	MLB	New York (A)	2	0	0	18	12	8.50	1.78	4.1	339	36	56	7.84	3.0	6.0	2.0	2.5	-10
2007	Rk	GCL Yanks	0	0	0	7	7	2.57	1.00	6.7	233	28	80	2.01	1.3	9.0	7.0	0.0	132
2007	AAA	Scranton/WB	4	3	3	47	45	3.59	1.29	6.7	277	27	82	3.22	1.9	8.6	4.5	1.1	51

Tall/lanky reliever with advanced ability to change speeds and has explosive FB to ride alongside. Repeats ¾ delivery giving him above average command, but despite strikeout ability, he remains hittable. May have to morph SL and CB into one pitch as neither are solid by itself.

Beato,Pedro — SP — Baltimore

EXP MLB DEBUT: 2009 | POTENTIAL: #3 starter | 8C

Thrws R Age 21
2006 (1-S) St. Pete JC

Velo	Pitch	Grade
87-93	FB	++++
82-84	SL	++++
73-75	CB	+++
80-82	CU	++

Year	Lev	Team	W	L	Sv	IP	K	ERA	WHIP	BF/G	OBA	H%	S%	xERA	Ctl	Dom	Cmd	hr/9	BPV
2006	A-	Aberdeen	3	2	0	57	52	3.47	1.23	16.5	226	27	75	3.32	3.6	8.2	2.3	0.9	78
2007	A-	Delmarva	7	8	0	142	106	4.05	1.39	22.2	258	30	71	3.87	3.7	6.7	1.8	0.6	63

Velocity decreased, which affected dominance, but learned how to use comps and pitch to contact. Pitches aggressively with FB and SL, but throws with effort and a stiff landing leg elevates pitches. Will need to find a balance with pitching style and improve CU.

Beaven,Blake — SP — Texas

EXP MLB DEBUT: 2012 | POTENTIAL: #2 starter | 9D

Thrws R Age 19
2007 (1-C) HS (TX)

Velo	Pitch	Grade
88-95	FB	++++
79-83	SL	++++
80-83	CU	++

Year	Lev	Team	W	L	Sv	IP	K	ERA	WHIP	BF/G	OBA	H%	S%	xERA	Ctl	Dom	Cmd	hr/9	BPV
2007																			

Tall/projectable pitcher possessing arm strength and quick arm action. Pitches aggressively with FB and SL, showing command and the ability to get strikeouts and groundball outs. Doesn't repeat arm speed or ¾ slot consistently which affects CU and presents some recoil at finish.

Begg,Chris — SP — San Francisco

EXP MLB DEBUT: 2008 | POTENTIAL: #5 starter | 6C

Thrws R Age 28
2001 NDFA Niagara
86-89 FB ++
76-79 SL +++
80-81 CU +++

Year	Lev	Team	W	L	Sv	IP	K	ERA	WHIP	BF/G	OBA	H%	S%	xERA	Ctl	Dom	Cmd	hr/9	BPV
2004	AAA	Fresno	2	5	0	41	17	7.01	1.78	21.0	322	31	65	7.28	3.9	3.7	0.9	2.2	-33
2005	AA	Norwich	8	7	0	138	86	3.07	1.20	24.1	267	30	76	3.47	1.5	5.6	3.7	0.6	96
2006	AA	Connecticut	13	10	0	174	97	3.41	1.08	26.2	243	28	68	2.71	1.6	5.0	3.1	0.4	90
2007	AA	Connecticut	2	0	0	25	16	2.14	1.07	24.5	268	31	81	2.95	0.4	5.7	16.0	0.4	361
2007	AAA	Fresno	12	5	0	140	67	4.37	1.41	25.8	305	32	72	5.11	1.6	4.3	2.7	1.2	42

Tall/athletic pitcher with horrible base skills, but is able to win by mixing pitches and being deceptive with low ¾ delivery. Shows pinpoint command, but can be hittable when ball leaks-out over plate. Eats innings and keeps team in the game, which could prove useful.

Bell,Trevor — SP — Los Angeles (A)

EXP MLB DEBUT: 2010 | POTENTIAL: #3 starter | 7D

Thrws R Age 21
2005 (1-S) HS (CA)
88-94 FB ++++
73-75 CB +++
CU +

Year	Lev	Team	W	L	Sv	IP	K	ERA	WHIP	BF/G	OBA	H%	S%	xERA	Ctl	Dom	Cmd	hr/9	BPV
2005	Rk	AZL Angels	0	0	0	8	7	4.50	1.63	8.9	307	39	69	4.57	3.4	7.9	2.3	0.0	90
2006	Rk	Orem	4	2	0	82	53	3.51	1.18	20.5	262	29	73	3.63	1.6	5.8	3.5	0.9	85
2007	A-	Cedar Rapids	8	4	0	115	90	4.14	1.38	23.0	295	35	70	4.37	1.8	7.0	3.9	0.6	102

Projectable pitcher with outstanding movement to FB and CB due to his quick arm action. Demonstrates plus command and improved CU by repeating delivery more frequently. Learned to pitch more to contact, but needs to increase strikeout rate at upper levels.

Below,Duane — SP — Detroit

EXP MLB DEBUT: 2010 | POTENTIAL: #5 starter | 7

Thrws L Age 22
2006 (19) Lk Mich CC
85-88 FB ++
71-74 CB +++
76-79 CU +++

Year	Lev	Team	W	L	Sv	IP	K	ERA	WHIP	BF/G	OBA	H%	S%	xERA	Ctl	Dom	Cmd	hr/9	BPV
2006	A-	Oneonta	0	0	0	9	8	3.96	1.76	20.8	300	38	75	4.79	4.9	7.9	1.6	0.0	76
2006	Rk	GCL Tigers	2	0	0	34	31	2.11	1.14	9.0	219	28	82	2.37	3.2	8.2	2.6	0.3	107
2007	A-	W. Michigan	13	5	0	145	160	2.98	1.28	22.9	238	33	77	3.05	3.6	9.9	2.8	0.4	114

Led MWL in strikeouts featuring a highly deceptive, high ¾ delivery and an advanced ability to change speeds. Height creates downward plane which enhances look and sinking action of FB. Command is outstanding and will need tighter CB to survive upper levels.

Bergesen,Brad — SP — Baltimore

EXP MLB DEBUT: 2010 | POTENTIAL: #4 starter | 8D

Thrws R Age 22
2004 (4) HS (CA)
88-94 FB ++++
80-83 SL +++
CU +

Year	Lev	Team	W	L	Sv	IP	K	ERA	WHIP	BF/G	OBA	H%	S%	xERA	Ctl	Dom	Cmd	hr/9	BPV
2004	Rk	Bluefield	0	0	0	5	6	8.65	1.92	4.9	323	41	56	7.17	5.2	10.4	2.0	1.7	43
2005	A-	Aberdeen	1	3	0	71	54	4.82	1.45	20.2	308	36	66	4.74	1.8	6.8	3.9	0.6	97
2006	A-	Delmarva	5	4	0	86	49	4.29	1.24	19.4	285	32	65	3.89	1.0	5.1	4.9	0.6	113
2007	A-	Delmarva	7	3	0	94	73	2.20	0.98	23.8	220	27	78	2.01	1.6	7.0	4.3	0.3	134
2007	A+	Frederick	3	6	0	56	35	5.78	1.55	24.5	330	38	61	5.38	1.4	5.6	3.9	0.6	85

Strong framed pitcher with plus command and solid groundball tendencies. Good velocity doesn't generate strikeout and can be hittable, but rarely gives-up extra base hits. Repeats delivery well, though his CU is underdeveloped. Some upside here, but needs to put game together.

Berken,Jason — SP — Baltimore

EXP MLB DEBUT: 2009 | POTENTIAL: #4 starter | 7C

Thrws R Age 24
2006 (6) Clemson
87-92 FB +++
75-77 CB +++
79-81 CU ++

Year	Lev	Team	W	L	Sv	IP	K	ERA	WHIP	BF/G	OBA	H%	S%	xERA	Ctl	Dom	Cmd	hr/9	BPV
2006	A-	Aberdeen	1	4	0	45	46	2.80	0.98	19.0	235	30	75	2.66	1.0	9.2	9.2	0.8	232
2007	A+	Frederick	9	9	0	151	124	4.53	1.38	23.5	273	33	68	4.13	2.9	7.4	2.5	0.7	76

Strong-armed pitcher coming off TJS in 2005 has learned to pitch to contact and to get groundball outs. Command remains essential to his survival, but doesn't have the same pitch movement, which has decreased strikeout rate. CB is the comp of choice.

Betances,Dellin — SP — New York (A)

EXP MLB DEBUT: 2011 | POTENTIAL: #2 starter | 9D

Thrws R Age 20
2006 (8) HS (NJ)
88-95 FB ++++
77-82 KC +++
78-81 CU +

Year	Lev	Team	W	L	Sv	IP	K	ERA	WHIP	BF/G	OBA	H%	S%	xERA	Ctl	Dom	Cmd	hr/9	BPV
2006	Rk	GCL Yankees	0	1	0	23	27	1.17	0.91	12.3	177	25	90	1.39	2.7	10.5	3.9	0.4	152
2007	A-	Staten Island	1	2	0	25	29	3.60	1.64	18.6	254	37	76	3.81	6.1	10.4	1.7	0.0	103

Tall/projectable pitcher with smooth arm action and excellent velocity. Gets solid movement to FB and KC and his hard to hit, but command suffers from not repeating overhand slot, which he tends to drop. Possesses tons of upside if he can harness stuff and mechanics.

Bibens-Dirkx,Austin — RP — Seattle

EXP MLB DEBUT: 2009 | POTENTIAL: Setup reliever | 7D

Thrws R Age 23
2006 (16) Portland
87-93 FB ++++
79-81 SL +++
80-83 CU +

Year	Lev	Team	W	L	Sv	IP	K	ERA	WHIP	BF/G	OBA	H%	S%	xERA	Ctl	Dom	Cmd	hr/9	BPV
2006	A-	Wisconsin	2	2	4	32	38	1.96	0.97	4.9	210	31	77	1.54	2.0	10.7	5.4	0.0	191
2006	A-	Everett	0	0	1	4	6	0.00	0.50	4.4	81	16	100	0.00	2.3	13.5	6.0	0.0	246
2006	AAA	Tacoma	0	0	0	2	5	0.00	1.50	8.6	262	76	100	3.44	4.5	22.5	5.0	0.0	243
2007	A+	High Desert	3	1	8	38	26	4.48	1.57	5.4	271	32	71	4.35	4.7	6.1	1.3	0.5	51

Athletic reliever with deceptive low ¾ slot and ability to mix pitches. Generates groundball outs with two-seamer and goes to SL for strikeouts. Doesn't possess much confidence in his CU and command was very inconsistent from outing-to-outing.

Bierd,Randor — SP — Baltimore

EXP MLB DEBUT: 2008 | POTENTIAL: #5 starter | 7C

Thrws R Age 24
2003 FA (DR)
86-92 FB +++
82-83 SL +++
76-78 CU +++

Year	Lev	Team	W	L	Sv	IP	K	ERA	WHIP	BF/G	OBA	H%	S%	xERA	Ctl	Dom	Cmd	hr/9	BPV
2005	A+	Lakeland	1	3	0	20	18	5.79	1.29	20.7	279	32	59	4.96	1.8	8.0	4.5	1.8	88
2005	AA	Erie	1	3	0	21	10	5.52	1.70	23.9	319	34	68	5.77	3.4	4.2	1.3	0.8	17
2006	A-	Oneonta	5	0	0	38	41	6.61	1.65	8.5	309	41	57	5.09	3.5	9.7	2.7	0.5	95
2007	A-	W Michigan	1	1	0	22	29	2.05	1.05	5.7	215	33	82	2.18	2.5	11.9	4.8	0.4	172
2007	AA	Erie	3	2	1	45	52	3.38	0.91	6.2	196	28	60	1.42	2.0	10.4	5.2	0.2	181

Tall/athletic pitcher with solid G/F and plus command. FB has excellent sinking action and will throw both of his comps at any point in the count. Repeats high ¾ delivery well, giving him deception, and is adept at missing bats. DET was cautious with his workload, following TJS in 2005.

Billings,Bruce — SP — Colorado

EXP MLB DEBUT: 2010 | POTENTIAL: #5 starter | 7D

Thrws R Age 22
2007 (30) San Diego St
87-93 FB +++
79-82 SL +++
73-77 CB ++
79-80 CU ++

Year	Lev	Team	W	L	Sv	IP	K	ERA	WHIP	BF/G	OBA	H%	S%	xERA	Ctl	Dom	Cmd	hr/9	BPV
2007	A-	Tri-City	4	2	0	78	89	2.99	0.96	19.7	211	28	73	2.41	1.8	10.2	5.6	0.9	163

Stocky pitcher with excellent FB movement due to his fluid arm action and extension, which helped him lead NWL in strikeouts. Provides three comps that he commands and mixes well. Will need to adjust to hitters as he progresses and repeat delivery more frequently.

Bisenius,Joe — RP — Philadelphia

EXP MLB DEBUT: 2007 | POTENTIAL: Setup reliever | 7D

Thrws R Age 25
2004 (12) Oklahoma City
87-94 FB ++++
82-85 SL +++
84-87 CU ++

Year	Lev	Team	W	L	Sv	IP	K	ERA	WHIP	BF/G	OBA	H%	S%	xERA	Ctl	Dom	Cmd	hr/9	BPV
2005	A-	Lakewood	6	4	4	64	56	5.90	1.61	7.1	267	33	62	4.59	5.2	7.9	1.5	0.7	59
2006	A+	Clearwater	4	1	2	60	62	1.94	1.16	6.9	220	29	86	2.75	3.3	9.3	2.8	0.6	108
2006	AA	Reading	4	2	5	23	33	3.12	0.95	5.4	177	27	70	1.84	3.1	12.9	4.1	0.8	160
2007	AAA	Ottawa	3	4	0	46	41	5.48	1.80	6.1	286	35	71	5.62	6.1	8.0	1.3	1.0	44
2007	MLB	Philadelphia	0	0	0	2	3	0.00	2.00	4.8	262	43	100	4.79	9.0	13.5	1.5	0.0	115

Tall/strong-framed reliever induces groundball outs with power sinker and notches strikeouts with SL. Holds velocity well due to above average arm strength, but throws with effort and isn't very resilient. Will need to establish FB command and lessen velocity on CU.

Blackburn,Nick — SP — Minnesota

EXP MLB DEBUT: 2007 | POTENTIAL: #5 starter | 6B

Thrws R Age 26
2001 (29) Seminole St CC
88-94 FB +++
83-87 SL +++
75-80 CB ++
85-88 CU +++

Year	Lev	Team	W	L	Sv	IP	K	ERA	WHIP	BF/G	OBA	H%	S%	xERA	Ctl	Dom	Cmd	hr/9	BPV
2005	AAA	Rochester	0	0	0	14	7	5.14	1.64	20.8	336	36	71	6.33	1.9	4.5	2.3	1.3	25
2006	AA	New Britain	7	8	0	132	81	4.43	1.36	18.4	276	31	68	4.15	2.5	5.5	2.2	0.7	56
2007	AA	New Britain	3	1	0	38	18	3.08	1.13	18.8	251	28	71	2.78	1.7	4.3	2.6	0.2	77
2007	AAA	Rochester	7	3	0	110	57	2.12	0.98	24.6	236	26	81	2.50	1.0	4.7	4.8	0.6	118
2007	MLB	Minnesota	0	2	0	11	8	8.04	1.88	8.8	376	42	58	7.91	1.6	6.4	4.0	1.6	54

Solid season highlighted by 41.1 consecutive scoreless innings. Showed plus command and rarely left ball up, but will live on the edge with below average strikeout rate. Works effectively with four-pitch mix and mechanical adjustments accounted for success.

Blackley,Travis — SP — Philadelphia

EXP MLB DEBUT: 2004 | POTENTIAL: #5 starter | 6B

Thrws L Age 25 | 2000 FA (Australia)

85-88 FB ++ | 82-83 CT +++ | 74-76 CB ++ | 78-81 CU ++++

Year	Lev	Team	W	L	Sv	IP	K	ERA	WHIP	BF/G	OBA	H%	S%	xERA	Ctl	Dom	Cmd	hr/9	BPV
2004	AAA	Tacoma	8	6	0	110	80	3.84	1.34	24.1	244	27	75	4.02	3.8	6.5	1.7	1.1	47
2006	AA	San Antonio	8	11	0	144	100	4.06	1.27	23.6	254	28	72	3.97	2.8	6.3	2.2	1.1	55
2006	AAA	Tacoma	1	1	0	11	5	4.09	1.36	23.0	244	24	77	4.58	4.1	4.1	1.0	1.6	3
2007	AAA	Fresno	10	8	0	162	121	4.66	1.38	24.3	254	29	69	4.30	3.8	6.7	1.8	1.2	47
2007	MLB	San Fran	0	0	0	8	5	7.68	1.83	19.1	302	31	62	7.09	5.5	5.5	1.0	2.2	-17

Finesse-type pitcher with plus CU and ability to mix pitches. Missed more bats than in previous seasons, but because he nibbles, his walk rate and command aren't that great. Subtracts from FB well, but will need a tighter CB and can't be overexposed.

Blevins,Jerry — RP — Oakland

EXP MLB DEBUT: 2007 | POTENTIAL: Situational reliever | 6B

Thrws L Age 24 | 2004 (17) Dayton

87-94 FB +++ | 72-76 CB +++ | CU ++

Year	Lev	Team	W	L	Sv	IP	K	ERA	WHIP	BF/G	OBA	H%	S%	xERA	Ctl	Dom	Cmd	hr/9	BPV
2006	AA	W. Tennessee	0	0	1	6	8	1.48	0.98	4.6	225	35	83	1.77	1.5	11.8	8.0	0.0	249
2007	A+	Daytona	1	0	6	23	32	0.39	0.78	5.6	166	28	94	0.55	1.9	12.4	6.4	0.0	231
2007	AA	Mid/Ten	3	5	4	51	66	2.29	1.06	4.9	222	33	80	2.41	2.3	11.6	5.1	0.5	171
2007	AAA	Sacramento	1	0	0	2	4	0.00	0.45	7.2	139	31	100	0.00	0.0	16.4		0.0	125
2007	MLB	Oakland	0	1	0	4	3	10.71	2.38	3.6	403	44	56	10.24	4.3	6.4	1.5	2.1	-20

Tall/thin reliever that is deadly versus LH batters with his CB and deceptive FB. Commands all quadrants of the plate, keeps ball down, and misses bats. Lacks ability to change speeds which gives him nothing to offer RH batters and keeps him in a situational role.

Boggs,Mitchell — SP — St. Louis

EXP MLB DEBUT: 2008 | POTENTIAL: #5 starter | 7C

Thrws R Age 24 | 2005 (5) Georgia

88-95 FB ++++ | 83-85 CT +++ | 79-83 CB +++ | CU +

Year	Lev	Team	W	L	Sv	IP	K	ERA	WHIP	BF/G	OBA	H%	S%	xERA	Ctl	Dom	Cmd	hr/9	BPV
2005	A-	New Jersey	4	4	0	71	61	3.92	1.42	20.1	277	34	73	4.19	3.0	7.7	2.5	0.6	80
2006	A+	Palm Beach	10	6	0	145	126	3.41	1.41	22.7	272	34	76	3.91	3.2	7.8	2.5	0.4	86
2007	AA	Springfield	11	7	0	152	117	3.85	1.51	25.3	280	33	77	4.70	3.7	6.9	1.9	0.9	53

Projectable pitcher with strong frame and arm action that allows him to sustain velocity and generate pitch movement. FB is primary pitch featuring sinking and cutting action. Not a lot of finesse to his game, as his CU is below average and command is inconsistent.

Bogusevic,Brian — SP — Houston

EXP MLB DEBUT: 2009 | POTENTIAL: #4 starter | 7C

Thrws L Age 24 | 2005 (1) Tulane

87-92 FB +++ | 82-84 SL +++ | 75-79 SU +++ | 79-83 CU +++

Year	Lev	Team	W	L	Sv	IP	K	ERA	WHIP	BF/G	OBA	H%	S%	xERA	Ctl	Dom	Cmd	hr/9	BPV
2005	A-	Tri City	0	2	3	21	17	7.68	1.85	7.6	335	40	57	6.39	3.8	7.3	1.9	0.9	46
2006	A-	Lexington	2	5	0	70	60	4.75	1.43	17.5	278	34	67	4.35	3.1	7.7	2.5	0.8	75
2006	A-	Tri City	0	0	0	11	6	4.09	1.36	15.3	244	26	71	3.80	4.1	4.9	1.2	0.8	36
2007	A+	Salem	9	7	0	114	91	4.02	1.51	23.5	292	35	73	4.57	3.1	7.2	2.3	0.6	72
2007	AA	Corpus Christi	1	1	0	24	17	7.47	1.78	18.5	299	35	55	5.21	5.2	6.3	1.2	0.4	48

Athletic pitcher finally got over the hump. FB has always possessed good sink, but tightened CB and disguised CU better, giving him another two options. Threw more quality strikes and was stingy with HR, but will need to lower oppBA and set-up pitches better.

Bostick,Adam — SP — New York (N)

EXP MLB DEBUT: 2008 | POTENTIAL: #5 starter | 6C

Thrws R Age 25 | 2001 (6) HS (PA)

88-92 FB +++ | 75-77 CB ++++ | 81-84 CU +

Year	Lev	Team	W	L	Sv	IP	K	ERA	WHIP	BF/G	OBA	H%	S%	xERA	Ctl	Dom	Cmd	hr/9	BPV
2005	A+	Jupiter	4	5	0	91	94	3.85	1.44	22.8	270	35	74	4.18	3.6	9.3	2.6	0.7	91
2005	AA	Carolina	4	3	0	44	39	4.69	1.52	21.3	252	31	69	4.08	5.1	8.0	1.6	0.6	67
2006	AA	Carolina	8	7	0	115	108	3.52	1.45	22.3	236	30	76	3.63	5.2	8.5	1.6	0.5	76
2006	AAA	Albuquerque	1	2	0	27	30	4.67	1.93	25.6	339	43	79	7.07	4.3	10.0	2.3	1.3	56
2007	AAA	New Orleans	6	7	0	97	91	5.66	1.56	20.2	279	32	69	5.71	4.2	8.4	2.0	1.9	37

Strong-framed pitcher with plus CB and deceptive delivery. Strikeout rate and command suffice, but FB lacks movement and doesn't change speeds well, making him highly hittable. Will need to repeat delivery and prevent from opening-up front side prior to pitch release.

Bowden,Michael — SP — Boston

EXP MLB DEBUT: 2009 | POTENTIAL: #3 starter | 9D

Thrws R Age 21 | 2005 (1-S) HS (IL)

89-94 FB ++++ | 81-83 SL ++ | 76-80 CB ++++ | 79-82 CU +++

Year	Lev	Team	W	L	Sv	IP	K	ERA	WHIP	BF/G	OBA	H%	S%	xERA	Ctl	Dom	Cmd	hr/9	BPV
2005	Rk	GCL Red Sox	1	0	0	6	10	0.00	1.33	6.2	191	37	100	2.21	6.0	15.0	2.5	0.0	159
2006	A+	Wilmington	0	0	0	5	3	9.00	2.00	24.1	390	45	50	7.00	1.8	5.4	3.0	0.0	72
2006	AA	Greenville	9	6	0	107	118	3.53	1.14	17.7	231	31	71	2.96	2.6	9.9	3.8	0.8	125
2007	A+	Lancaster	2	0	0	46	46	1.37	0.93	21.6	212	29	86	1.70	1.6	9.0	5.8	0.2	181
2007	AA	Portland	8	6	0	96	82	4.30	1.43	21.5	279	34	71	4.46	3.1	7.7	2.5	0.8	72

Athletic pitcher works primarily off of CB and FB, but improved CU, giving him three pitches to go to. Repeats overhand delivery well, with command being main beneficiary. Recoil of arm at finish of delivery is concerning, but holds velocity and pitches deep into games.

Brackman,Andrew — SP — New York (A)

EXP MLB DEBUT: 2010 | POTENTIAL: #2 starter | 9D

Thrws R Age 22 | 2007 (1) North Carolina

89-96 FB ++++ | 76-81 KC ++++ | 81-84 CU ++

Year	Lev	Team	W	L	Sv	IP	K	ERA	WHIP	BF/G	OBA	H%	S%	xERA	Ctl	Dom	Cmd	hr/9	BPV
2007																			

Tall/projectable pitcher with huge upside if he can harness mechanics and pitches. Repeats high ¾ delivery well and has two plus pitches with his FB and KC, but his command is spotty. Will miss 2008 after TJS in September and will need to refrain from throwing across body.

Braddock,Zach — SP — Milwaukee

EXP MLB DEBUT: 2010 | POTENTIAL: #4 starter | 8D

Thrws L Age 20 | 2005 (18) HS (NJ)

87-91 FB +++ | 74-78 SL +++ | 78-80 CU ++

Year	Lev	Team	W	L	Sv	IP	K	ERA	WHIP	BF/G	OBA	H%	S%	xERA	Ctl	Dom	Cmd	hr/9	BPV
2006	Rk	Helena	2	2	0	39	30	5.52	1.61	12.4	225	27	65	4.04	7.1	6.9	1.0	0.7	51
2007	A-	W. Virginia	3	1	0	47	68	1.15	0.91	17.6	174	29	88	1.17	2.9	13.0	4.5	0.2	188

Tall/projectable pitcher who had shown recovery from TJS, but missed last two months with minor elbow injury. Misses bats with regularity and keeps ball low utilizing his above average sinker and SL. Command was outstanding, but needs a better CU and to prove his arm is sound.

Bresnahan,Pat — RP — Pittsburgh

EXP MLB DEBUT: 2009 | POTENTIAL: Setup reliever | 7D

Thrws R Age 23 | 2006 (5) Arizona St

89-93 FB +++ | SL +++ | CB +++ | CU ++

Year	Lev	Team	W	L	Sv	IP	K	ERA	WHIP	BF/G	OBA	H%	S%	xERA	Ctl	Dom	Cmd	hr/9	BPV
2006	A-	Williamsport	4	5	0	68	59	2.25	0.99	17.3	207	31	75	3.70	2.3	7.8	3.5	0.4	76
2007	A+	Lynchburg	4	3	6	60	63	4.18	1.43	7.5	242	30	76	4.78	4.8	9.4	2.0	0.5	54
2007	AA	Altoona	1	0	0	6	3	4.50	1.17	8.0	228	33	80	5.77	3.0	4.5	1.5	0.0	48

Power reliever who improved mechanics, gaining him better rotation of breaking pitches. Arm strength/action provides solid velocity and most of his pitches possess late life. Command can be a struggle at times and doesn't have much to offer LH batters.

Britton,Zach — SP — Baltimore

EXP MLB DEBUT: 2010 | POTENTIAL: #3 starter | 7C

Thrws L Age 20 | 2006 (3) HS (TX)

85-92 FB +++ | 74-76 SL +++ | 77-79 CU ++

Year	Lev	Team	W	L	Sv	IP	K	ERA	WHIP	BF/G	OBA	H%	S%	xERA	Ctl	Dom	Cmd	hr/9	BPV
2006	Rk	Bluefield	0	4	0	34	21	5.29	1.62	13.7	267	29	69	4.98	5.3	5.6	1.1	1.1	25
2007	A-	Aberdeen	6	4	0	63	45	3.68	1.36	17.6	264	31	72	3.99	3.1	6.4	2.0	0.1	88

Athletic pitcher with arm speed and plus FB movement, showing sinking/cutting action. Base skills on the mediocre side, but was young for level and hasn't grown into body. CBI was thrown with more consistency, but needs to repeat delivery on CU and improve stamina.

Broadway,Lance — SP — Chicago (A)

EXP MLB DEBUT: 2007 | POTENTIAL: #4 starter | 7B

Thrws R Age 21 | 2005 (1) Texas Christian

88-92 FB +++ | 84-86 CT +++ | 75-81 CB ++++ | 75-79 CU ++

Year	Lev	Team	W	L	Sv	IP	K	ERA	WHIP	BF/G	OBA	H%	S%	xERA	Ctl	Dom	Cmd	hr/9	BPV
2005	A+	Win-Salem	1	3	0	55	58	4.58	1.60	22.1	305	40	71	5.06	3.3	9.5	2.9	0.7	92
2006	AA	Birmingham	8	8	0	154	111	2.74	1.30	25.4	269	32	81	3.74	2.3	6.5	2.8	0.6	81
2006	AAA	Charlotte	0	0	0	6	6	3.00	1.00	22.9	228	31	67	1.87	1.5	9.0	6.0	0.0	189
2007	AAA	Charlotte	8	9	0	155	108	4.65	1.50	24.8	262	30	71	4.54	4.5	6.3	1.4	1.0	40
2007	MLB	Chicago (A)	1	1	0	10	14	0.89	0.99	9.6	149	26	90	0.91	4.5	12.5	2.8	0.0	159

Athletic pitcher who has survived mediocre base skills and velocity by mixing three average pitches and keeping the ball down. CB can be a plus pitch at times, CU improved, and does a nice job of repeating high ¾ delivery. Strikeouts will be elusive and needs better efficiency.

Bromberg, David — SP — Minnesota

| | | | EXP MLB DEBUT: 2011 | POTENTIAL: #4 starter | 8D |

Thrws R Age 20
2005 (32) HS (CA)

88-92 FB	++++
77-80 CB	+++
CU	+

Year	Lev	Team	W	L	Sv	IP	K	ERA	WHIP	BF/G	OBA	H%	S%	xERA	Ctl	Dom	Cmd	hr/9	BPV
2006	Rk	GCL Twins	3	3	0	50	31	2.69	1.20	20.2	229	27	78	2.74	3.2	5.6	1.7	0.4	68
2007	Rk	Elizabethton	9	0	0	58	81	2.79	1.33	18.5	215	33	81	3.08	5.0	12.5	2.5	0.6	122

Won Pitcher of the Year in APPY, leading league in wins and strikeouts. Projectable arm who pitches tall, giving downward plane to sinker and CB and creating an obscene strikeout rate. Doesn't repeat high ¾ delivery which affects CU, but demonstrated command.

Browning, Barret — RP — Los Angeles (A)

| | | | EXP MLB DEBUT: 2009 | POTENTIAL: Setup reliever | 6C |

Thrws L Age 23
2006 (18) Florida St

86-92 FB	+++
SL	+++
CU	+++

Year	Lev	Team	W	L	Sv	IP	K	ERA	WHIP	BF/G	OBA	H%	S%	xERA	Ctl	Dom	Cmd	hr/9	BPV
2006	Rk	Orem	3	2	1	41	40	3.07	1.09	7.0	216	28	74	2.59	2.8	8.8	3.1	0.7	109
2007	A-	Cedar Rapids	9	4	8	74	74	2.80	1.08	6.0	206	28	73	2.03	3.2	9.0	2.8	0.2	120

Athletic pitcher with outstanding command and ability to mix three pitches. SL allows him to get strikeouts and has enough velocity to sneak past hitters. He has issues mechanically, as his arm action is stiff and struggles to repeat arm slot, fluctuating between ¾ and low ¾.

Brown, Brooks — SP — Arizona

| | | | EXP MLB DEBUT: 2008 | POTENTIAL: #4 starter/setup reliever | 8C |

Thrws R Age 23
2006 (1-S) Georgia

87-91 FB	+++
80-83 SL	+++
77-78 CB	+++
CU	+++

Year	Lev	Team	W	L	Sv	IP	K	ERA	WHIP	BF/G	OBA	H%	S%	xERA	Ctl	Dom	Cmd	hr/9	BPV
2006	A-	Yakima	0	2	0	23	30	3.49	1.51	7.7	260	37	79	4.28	4.7	11.6	2.5	0.8	102
2007	A+	Visalia	6	3	0	80	74	2.81	1.11	22.5	226	30	74	2.35	2.6	8.3	3.2	0.2	120
2007	AA	Mobile	4	4	0	66	54	3.68	1.51	23.9	256	32	74	3.80	4.9	7.4	1.5	0.3	71

College closer converted to a starter, where he has altered style of pitching to cope with decreased velocity and having to pace himself. Pitches aggressively with four pitches that he can command, and despite missing fewer bats, he limited the HR and had a strong G/F ratio.

Bryson, Rob — SP — Milwaukee

| | | | EXP MLB DEBUT: 2011 | POTENTIAL: #3 starter | 8E |

Thrws R Age 20
2006 (31) HS (DE)

88-94 FB	++++
78-82 SL	+++
CU	++

Year	Lev	Team	W	L	Sv	IP	K	ERA	WHIP	BF/G	OBA	H%	S%	xERA	Ctl	Dom	Cmd	hr/9	BPV
2007	Rk	Helena	3	0	8	54	70	2.67	1.13	11.8	243	29	72	2.77	2.0	11.7	5.8	0.3	119

Draft-and-follow put-up obscene strikeout numbers and topped it off by showing excellent command. Arm action and physical strength provides solid velocity and hammers hitters with a nasty slider. Needs to change speeds better and adjust to greater workloads.

Bucardo, Wilber — SP — San Francisco

| | | | EXP MLB DEBUT: 2011 | POTENTIAL: #3 starter | 9E |

Thrws R Age 19
2005 FA (DR)

89-94 FB	++++
SL	+++
CU	+

Year	Lev	Team	W	L	Sv	IP	K	ERA	WHIP	BF/G	OBA	H%	S%	xERA	Ctl	Dom	Cmd	hr/9	BPV
2007	A-	Salem-Keizer	1	0	0	5	3	3.60	1.60	22.1	332	39	75	4.93	1.8	5.4	3.0	0.0	84
2007	Rk	AZL Giants	6	2	0	60	34	1.95	0.93	20.5	213	25	78	1.70	1.5	5.1	3.4	0.1	110

Promising hurler with plus power sinker that generates groundball outs and broken bats. Arm action is behind pitch movement and presents easy velocity. Command is outstanding for experience level and may be able to survive with a below average strikeout rate.

Buchholz, Clay — SP — Boston

| | | | EXP MLB DEBUT: 2007 | POTENTIAL: #1 starter | 9A |

Thrws R Age 23
2005 (1-S) Angelina CC

88-95 FB	++++
81-84 SL	++
71-77 CB	+++
76-81 CU	++++

Year	Lev	Team	W	L	Sv	IP	K	ERA	WHIP	BF/G	OBA	H%	S%	xERA	Ctl	Dom	Cmd	hr/9	BPV
2006	A+	Wilmington	2	0	0	16	23	1.13	0.88	19.7	181	31	86	0.97	2.3	12.9	5.8	0.0	217
2006	AA	Greenville	9	4	0	103	117	2.62	1.04	18.9	212	28	79	2.58	2.5	10.2	4.0	0.9	133
2007	AA	Portland	7	2	0	86	116	1.77	0.89	20.0	185	29	82	1.45	2.3	12.1	5.3	0.4	189
2007	AAA	Pawtucket	1	3	0	38	55	4.01	1.18	19.1	229	34	70	3.40	3.1	13.0	4.2	1.2	140
2007	MLB	Boston	3	1	0	22	22	1.62	1.08	21.7	183	26	83	1.54	4.1	8.9	2.2	0.0	118

Incredible base skills backed-up by impressive stuff and threw no-hitter in second MLB appearance. Possesses three above average pitches; all with excellent movement. High ¾ slot doesn't allow much deception and isn't always efficient, but has ingredients to dominate.

Buckner, Billy — SP — Arizona

| | | | EXP MLB DEBUT: 2007 | POTENTIAL: #4 starter | 7C |

Thrws R Age 24
2004 (2) So Carolina

87-92 FB	+++
77-81 KC	+++
78-82 CU	+++

Year	Lev	Team	W	L	Sv	IP	K	ERA	WHIP	BF/G	OBA	H%	S%	xERA	Ctl	Dom	Cmd	hr/9	BPV
2006	A+	High Desert	7	1	0	90	85	3.90	1.53	24.5	264	33	75	4.26	4.7	8.5	1.8	0.6	73
2006	AA	Wichita	5	3	0	75	63	4.67	1.56	25.3	269	32	71	4.62	4.7	7.5	1.6	0.8	55
2007	AA	Wichita	1	3	0	19	13	4.71	1.36	20.0	271	32	73	5.15	2.8	6.1	2.2	1.9	27
2007	AAA	Omaha	9	7	0	104	83	3.80	1.29	15.8	269	32	73	4.04	2.2	7.2	3.2	1.0	83
2007	MLB	Kansas City	1	2	0	34	17	5.29	1.56	21.3	278	29	69	5.25	4.2	4.5	1.1	1.3	9

Polished pitcher with good arm action, command, and a deceptive ¾ delivery, which compensates for his lack of a strikeout pitch. Lands stiffly on front leg, which elevates pitches and makes him susceptible to home runs. Will need to trust stuff and repeat delivery consistently.

Buck, Dallas — SP — Arizona

| | | | EXP MLB DEBUT: 2009 | POTENTIAL: #5 starter | 7D |

Thrws R Age 23
2006 (3) Oregon St

85-90 FB	+++
77-81 SL	+++
79-82 SP	++

Year	Lev	Team	W	L	Sv	IP	K	ERA	WHIP	BF/G	OBA	H%	S%	xERA	Ctl	Dom	Cmd	hr/9	BPV
2007	A+	Visalia	4	4	0	97	88	3.43	1.18	24.3	235	28	74	3.29	2.9	8.1	2.8	0.9	89

Tall/athletic hurler missed second half with TJS, which would explain drop in velocity. Pitches well without best stuff because he keeps ball down and base skills were solid in high-offensive league. Will need to change speeds better and smooth-out a max-effort delivery.

Bulger, Jason — RP — Los Angeles (A)

| | | | EXP MLB DEBUT: 2005 | POTENTIAL: Setup reliever/closer | 7C |

Thrws R Age 29
2001 (1) Valdosta St

90-96 FB	++++
80-84 CB	+++

Year	Lev	Team	W	L	Sv	IP	K	ERA	WHIP	BF/G	OBA	H%	S%	xERA	Ctl	Dom	Cmd	hr/9	BPV
2005	AAA	Tucson	3	6	4	56	55	3.54	1.38	4.2	240	31	74	3.43	4.3	8.8	2.0	0.5	88
2006	AAA	Salt Lake	2	2	4	34	44	4.75	1.32	5.2	238	37	60	2.78	4.0	11.6	2.9	0.0	139
2006	MLB	Los Angeles (A)	0	0	0	1	1	22.50	3.33	3.7	228	30	25	7.77	22.5	7.5	0.3	0.0	61
2007	AAA	Salt Lake	5	2	10	53	81	3.72	1.43	4.6	254	41	75	3.87	4.2	13.7	3.2	0.7	134
2007	MLB	Los Angeles (A)	0	0	0	6	8	2.95	1.31	4.2	225	35	75	2.59	4.4	11.8	2.7	0.0	137

Hard-throwing reliever overpowers hitters with FB movement and a hard CB. Command has improved incrementally and does have closer experience. Is slow to plate (1.6) and a max-effort ¾ delivery will always make stamina a concern.

Bullington, Brian — SP — Pittsburgh

| | | | EXP MLB DEBUT: 2005 | POTENTIAL: #4 starter | 7D |

Thrws R Age 27
2002 (1) Ball St

86-92 FB	+++
80-84 SL	+++
71-74 CB	+++
78-81 CU	++

Year	Lev	Team	W	L	Sv	IP	K	ERA	WHIP	BF/G	OBA	H%	S%	xERA	Ctl	Dom	Cmd	hr/9	BPV
2005	AAA	Indianapolis	9	5	0	109	82	0.91	1.19	24.3	253	22	134	5.88	2.1	6.8	3.2	3.4	10
2005	MLB	Pittsburgh	0	0	0	1	1	0.00	1.82	5.1	244				8.2	8.2	1.0	16.4	-415
2006																		
2007	AAA	Indianapolis	11	9	0	150	89	0.60	1.36	24.2	256	19	141	6.97	3.5	5.3	1.5	4.0	-53
2007	MLB	Pittsburgh	0	3	0	17	7	1.59	1.71	15.4	334	25	137	10.22	2.6	3.7	1.4	5.3	-119

Recovered from shoulder surgery to make it to the Majors. Athletic pitcher with good arm action and a complete arsenal, but because of his soft base skills, he has to mix pitches and pitch backwards. Improved CU to average level, but without better command, he'll get killed.

Burnett, Alex — SP — Minnesota

| | | | EXP MLB DEBUT: 2010 | POTENTIAL: #4 starter | 7D |

Thrws R Age 20
2005 (12) HS (CA)

88-92 FB	+++
72-76 CB	+++
78-81 CU	++

Year	Lev	Team	W	L	Sv	IP	K	ERA	WHIP	BF/G	OBA	H%	S%	xERA	Ctl	Dom	Cmd	hr/9	BPV
2005	Rk	GCL Twins	4	2	0	48	33	4.12	1.33	15.4	269	30	72	4.34	2.6	6.2	2.4	1.1	54
2006	Rk	Elizabethton	4	3	0	71	71	4.05	1.11	21.5	248	32	64	3.12	1.6	9.0	5.5	0.8	151
2007	A-	Beloit	9	8	0	155	117	3.02	1.15	22.8	243	29	75	2.95	2.2	6.8	3.1	0.5	96

Short/athletic pitcher with poise and ability to exploit hitters' weaknesses. Commands plate and pitches to contact, getting groundball outs with sinker. CB is used to get strikeouts and should be able to increase velocity with physical maturity, giving him increased dominance.

Butler, Josh — SP — Tampa Bay

EXP MLB DEBUT: 2009 | POTENTIAL: #4 starter | 7C

Thrws R — Age 23
2006 (2) San Diego
88-94 FB ++++
80-82 SL +++
CU +

Year	Lev	Team	W	L	Sv	IP	K	ERA	WHIP	BF/G	OBA	H%	S%	xERA	Ctl	Dom	Cmd	hr/9	BPV
2006	A-	Hudson Valley	0	3	0	13	12	5.50	1.53	11.4	260	34	60	3.63	4.8	8.2	1.7	0.0	88
2007	A-	Columbus	5	1	0	77	54	2.33	1.08	23.1	225	27	79	2.38	2.3	6.3	2.7	0.4	94
2007	A+	Vero Beach	4	3	0	49	34	4.95	1.47	21.0	269	29	71	5.17	3.8	6.2	1.6	1.6	23

Projectable pitcher with good velocity and ability to diagnose hitters' weaknesses. Possesses excellent command and strong G/F, but isn't one to get a lot of strikeouts. Tinkers too much with delivery and has stiff arm action which could be behind arm injuries that effect stamina.

Butler, Tony — SP — Seattle

EXP MLB DEBUT: 2010 | POTENTIAL: #3 starter | 8C

Thrws L — Age 20
2006 (3) HS (WI)
88-92 FB ++++
76-80 CB +++
79-81 CU ++

Year	Lev	Team	W	L	Sv	IP	K	ERA	WHIP	BF/G	OBA	H%	S%	xERA	Ctl	Dom	Cmd	hr/9	BPV
2006	Rk	AZL Mariners	2	0	0	14	25	2.57	1.00	10.7	112	26	71	0.54	5.8	16.1	2.8	0.0	187
2006	A-	Everett	1	2	0	42	52	2.78	1.14	18.5	162	24	76	4.05	5.3	11.1	2.1	0.4	120
2007	A-	Wisconsin	4	7	0	85	73	4.75	1.46	18.2	245	28	75	5.15	4.9	7.7	1.6	1.1	44

Tall/projectable pitcher experienced a tired arm and sore back which limited effectiveness. Arm action gives rise to excellent pitch movement and repeats ¾ delivery. Command is inconsistent and needs to change speeds better, but should improve both if healthy.

Cahill, Trevor — SP — Oakland

EXP MLB DEBUT: 2010 | POTENTIAL: #3 starter | 8C

Thrws R — Age 20
2006 (2) HS (CA)
86-92 FB +++
SL ++
79-82 KC +++
CU ++

Year	Lev	Team	W	L	Sv	IP	K	ERA	WHIP	BF/G	OBA	H%	S%	xERA	Ctl	Dom	Cmd	hr/9	BPV
2006	Rk	AZL Athletics	0	0	0	9	11	3.00	1.00	8.6	73	12	67	0.23	7.0	11.0	1.6	0.0	139
2007	A-	Kane County	11	4	0	105	117	2.74	1.19	21.1	223	31	76	2.52	3.4	10.0	2.9	0.3	124

Athletic pitcher adapted well to full-season baseball, showing plus movement to FB and KC, and maintaining velocity. Repeats delivery, giving him command, and pitches on a downward plane, which helped him miss bats. Got off to a slow start, battling a viral infection.

Campillo, Jorge — SP — Seattle

EXP MLB DEBUT: 2005 | POTENTIAL: #5 starter | 6B

Thrws R — Age 29
2005 FA (Mexico)
87-92 FB +++
84-86 CT +++
71-75 CT ++
79-82 CU ++++

Year	Lev	Team	W	L	Sv	IP	K	ERA	WHIP	BF/G	OBA	H%	S%	xERA	Ctl	Dom	Cmd	hr/9	BPV
2006	AA	San Antonio	2	0	0	10	3	2.65	1.37	21.4	294	32	79	3.79	1.8	2.6	1.5	0.0	44
2006	MLB	Seattle	0	0	0	2	1	17.14	1.90	9.9	403	45	0	7.04	0.0	4.3		0.0	0
2006	Rk	AZL Mariners	0	0	0	13	15	4.15	1.00	8.3	262	38	54	2.30	0.0	10.4		0.0	65
2007	AAA	Tacoma	9	6	0	149	99	3.08	1.21	25.4	264	30	78	3.69	2.4	6.0	2.5	0.7	71
2007	MLB	Seattle	0	0	0	13	9	6.87	1.83	12.2	328	36	64	6.72	4.1	6.2	1.5	1.4	17

Returned from TJS and led PCL in ERA. Possesses good arm strength, but doesn't rely on velocity, keeping hitters off-balance by subtracting from FB with CT and CU. Command and keeping ball down will remain essential, but may always lack stamina.

Capellan, Jose — SP — San Francisco

EXP MLB DEBUT: 2008 | POTENTIAL: #4 starter | 7D

Thrws L — Age 21
2003 FA (DR)
88-91 FB +++
73-76 CB ++++
77-79 CU ++

Year	Lev	Team	W	L	Sv	IP	K	ERA	WHIP	BF/G	OBA	H%	S%	xERA	Ctl	Dom	Cmd	hr/9	BPV
2006	Rk	GCL Red Sox	4	1	0	48	48	2.81	1.06	16.9	237	31	75	2.67	1.7	9.0	5.3	0.6	157
2007	A-	Lowell	4	3	0	75	71	3.71	1.05	20.8	243	32	62	2.31	1.3	8.5	6.5	0.1	189

Strong-framed/bad-bodied reliever with plus CB that nets strikeouts and impressive command for his age. Keeps ball down effectively with FB that bores into LH batters. Has yet to be challenged past short-season ball, so questions about performance remain.

Carignan, Andrew — RP — Oakland

EXP MLB DEBUT: 2009 | POTENTIAL: Setup reliever | 7C

Thrws R — Age 21
2007 (5) North Carolina
88-95 FB ++++
86-87 CT +++
79-84 SL ++

Year	Lev	Team	W	L	Sv	IP	K	ERA	WHIP	BF/G	OBA	H%	S%	xERA	Ctl	Dom	Cmd	hr/9	BPV
2007	A-	Kane County	1	1	4	13	19	2.03	1.30	4.5	140	32	72	2.50	7.6	13.1	1.7	0.0	157

Short/stocky reliever who pitches aggressively with his high-octane FB and CT, enabling him to get strikeouts. The ball gets on-top of hitters quickly from a ¾ slot. Needs to repeat delivery which would help command and tighten rotation of SL.

Carpenter, Drew — SP — Philadelphia

EXP MLB DEBUT: 2009 | POTENTIAL: #5 starter | 6B

Thrws R — Age 23
2006 (2) Long Beach St
86-91 FB +++
SL +++
SP ++
CU +++

Year	Lev	Team	W	L	Sv	IP	K	ERA	WHIP	BF/G	OBA	H%	S%	xERA	Ctl	Dom	Cmd	hr/9	BPV
2006	Rk	GCL Phillies	0	0	0	3	4	0.00	0.67	5.2	191	31	100	0.56	0.0	12.0		0.0	89
2006	A-	Batavia	0	0	0	11	12	0.80	1.34	15.5	240	34	93	3.63	4.0	9.6	2.4	0.0	115
2007	A+	Clearwater	17	6	1	163	116	3.20	1.25	24.5	246	32	76	4.02	2.9	6.4	2.2	0.9	72

Extreme groundball pitcher led FSL in wins, succeeding via excellent command, keeping ball low, and mixing pitches. Repeats arm speed, giving him deception and command, but doesn't miss a lot of bats and lacks a consistent breaking pitch, so could struggle at upper levels.

Carrasco, Carlos — SP — Philadelphia

EXP MLB DEBUT: 2008 | POTENTIAL: #2 starter | 9C

Thrws R — Age 21
2004 FA (Venezuela)
88-94 FB ++++
72-78 CB ++
79-82 CU ++++

Year	Lev	Team	W	L	Sv	IP	K	ERA	WHIP	BF/G	OBA	H%	S%	xERA	Ctl	Dom	Cmd	hr/9	BPV
2005	A-	Lakewood	1	7	0	62	46	7.09	1.70	21.6	308	34	60	6.28	4.1	6.7	1.6	1.6	20
2005	A-	Batavia	0	3	0	15	12	13.71	2.25	19.1	405	41	42	12.41	3.0	7.2	2.4	4.8	-76
2006	A-	Lakewood	12	6	0	159	159	2.26	1.06	23.7	187	25	79	1.84	3.7	9.0	2.4	0.3	113
2007	A+	Clearwater	6	2	0	69	53	2.86	1.03	22.2	201	22	78	2.60	2.9	6.9	2.4	1.0	76
2007	AA	Reading	6	4	0	70	49	4.88	1.58	22.0	247	27	72	4.71	5.9	6.3	1.1	1.2	31

Projectable pitcher with outstanding velocity and ability to sequence pitches properly. Struggled with command and HR rate on promotion, and strikeout rate was low all season. Quick arm action attenuates pitch movement, but pitches with effort which compromises stamina.

Carrillo, Cesar — SP — San Diego

EXP MLB DEBUT: 2009 | POTENTIAL: #4 starter | 8D

Thrws R — Age 24
2005 (1) Miami-FL
86-94 FB ++++
68-72 CB +++
79-82 CU +++

Year	Lev	Team	W	L	Sv	IP	K	ERA	WHIP	BF/G	OBA	H%	S%	xERA	Ctl	Dom	Cmd	hr/9	BPV
2005	A+	Lk Elsinore	1	2	0	25	29	7.14	1.55	15.7	297	39	53	5.19	3.2	10.4	3.2	1.1	93
2005	AA	Mobile	4	0	0	30	35	3.28	0.99	23.0	213	30	68	2.21	2.1	10.4	5.0	0.6	162
2006	AA	Mobile	1	3	0	50	43	3.05	1.20	22.4	241	29	78	3.39	2.7	7.7	2.9	0.9	86
2006	AAA	Portland	0	0	0	2	1	8.18	2.27	11.2	244	28	60	5.33	12.3	4.1	0.3	0.0	38
2007	AAA	Portland	0	2	0	15	8	8.88	2.37	15.8	339	36	62	8.11	8.3	4.7	0.6	1.2	-8

Missed most of 2007 season due to TJS which presented itself the previous season. Athletic pitcher with good arm action and a repetitive ¾ delivery, he shows good command and pitch movement. Lacks a strikeout pitch and needs to learn to pitch without best stuff.

Carroll, Scott — SP — Cincinnati

EXP MLB DEBUT: 2010 | POTENTIAL: #3 starter | 7D

Thrws R — Age 23
2007 (3) Missouri St
88-94 FB ++++
80-83 SL +++
79-81 SP +++
CU +

Year	Lev	Team	W	L	Sv	IP	K	ERA	WHIP	BF/G	OBA	H%	S%	xERA	Ctl	Dom	Cmd	hr/9	BPV
2007	Rk	Billings	0	1	0	15	15	2.98	1.26	10.3	247	34	74	2.77	3.0	8.9	3.0	0.0	122

Strong-armed pitcher with solid velocity and two breaking pitches that can be difficult to hit when his command is present. Throws strikes, but could used better command within strike zone. Needs to mask CU better and set-up his pitches more effectively.

Carr, Adam — RP — Washington

EXP MLB DEBUT: 2009 | POTENTIAL: Setup reliever | 7C

Thrws R — Age 24
2006 (18) Oklahoma St
88-94 FB ++++
79-83 SL +++
80-81 CU ++

Year	Lev	Team	W	L	Sv	IP	K	ERA	WHIP	BF/G	OBA	H%	S%	xERA	Ctl	Dom	Cmd	hr/9	BPV
2006	A-	Savannah	0	0	0	8	8	2.25	1.50	5.8	262	35	83	3.58	4.5	9.0	2.0	0.0	99
2006	Rk	GCL Nationals	1	0	1	18	19	2.98	1.22	7.3	203	27	76	2.57	4.5	9.4	2.1	0.5	101
2007	A+	Potomac	3	1	10	49	65	1.83	1.38	5.0	178	26	91	2.90	7.0	11.9	1.7	0.7	105
2007	AA	Harrisburg	1	0	2	11	13	1.64	1.45	6.7	184	25	93	3.25	7.4	10.6	1.4	0.8	88

Aggressive reliever who likes to register strikeouts and pitch inside. Quick arm action provides late movement to FB and SL, but may need CU to combat LH batters effectively. Command is below average, but is difficult to hit and operates by being effectively wild.

Carr,Nick — SP — New York (N)

EXP MLB DEBUT: 2011 | POTENTIAL: #3 starter/setup reliever | 8E

Thrws R Age 20 | 2005 (41) HS (ID)

88-95 FB ++++ | 83-86 SL +++ | 81-84 CU +

Year	Lev	Team	W	L	Sv	IP	K	ERA	WHIP	BF/G	OBA	H%	S%	xERA	Ctl	Dom	Cmd	hr/9	BPV
2006	Rk	Kingsport	3	3	0	48	44	4.88	1.50	17.3	266	33	69	4.52	4.3	8.3	1.9	0.9	63
2007	A-	Brooklyn	5	2	0	66	74	3.81	1.24	19.2	228	31	69	2.98	3.7	10.1	2.7	0.5	111

Athletic build and quick arm action provide excellent velocity and pitch movement. Pitches aggressively with power sinker and SL, but tends to rush delivery which negatively affects command. Lack of serviceable CU and high-effort delivery may prompt move to relief.

Cassel,Jack — SP — Houston

EXP MLB DEBUT: 2007 | POTENTIAL: #5 starter | 6B

Thrws R Age 27 | 2000 (25) Pierce JC

84-90 FB ++ | 72-77 SL +++ | 77-80 CU +++

Year	Lev	Team	W	L	Sv	IP	K	ERA	WHIP	BF/G	OBA	H%	S%	xERA	Ctl	Dom	Cmd	hr/9	BPV
2005	AAA	Portland	3	2	0	39	21	4.62	1.82	7.9	329	37	74	5.88	3.9	4.8	1.2	0.5	30
2006	AA	Mobile	6	3	0	78	75	2.30	1.07	25.4	230	30	79	2.42	2.1	8.6	4.2	0.3	138
2006	AAA	Portland	3	5	0	76	44	6.50	1.63	18.8	309	33	62	5.97	3.3	5.2	1.6	1.4	15
2007	AAA	Portland	7	14	0	156	117	3.92	1.57	25.4	315	37	76	5.27	2.4	6.7	2.8	0.7	68
2007	MLB	San Diego	1	1	0	22	11	4.05	1.58	16.3	324	36	74	5.13	2.0	4.5	2.2	0.4	51

Contact/command pitcher who compensates for low velocity and lack of movement with a deceptive delivery. Strong frame and arm strength allow him to hold velocity, and has proved durable. SL can get loose rotation at such low velocities and will always be hittable.

Castillo,Fabio — SP — Texas

EXP MLB DEBUT: 2012 | POTENTIAL: #2 starter | 9E

Thrws R Age 19 | 2006 FA (DR)

89-96 FB ++++ | 82-85 CB +++ | 80-82 CU ++

Year	Lev	Team	W	L	Sv	IP	K	ERA	WHIP	BF/G	OBA	H%	S%	xERA	Ctl	Dom	Cmd	hr/9	BPV
2006	Rk	AZL Rangers	0	0	0	3	4	0.00	1.00	11.5	106	18	100	0.52	6.0	12.0	2.0	0.0	148
2007	A-	Spokane	3	5	0	62	46	5.94	1.61	19.7	294	35	61	4.89	3.9	6.7	1.7	0.6	55

Tall/physical pitcher with impressive FB movement and SL that is tough on RH batters. Raw in ability, he needs to repeat his delivery more often, which would improve command and quality of CU. Base skills were not indicative of ability, but is purely projection at this stage.

Castro,Simon — SP — San Diego

EXP MLB DEBUT: 2012 | POTENTIAL: #3 starter | 9E

Thrws R Age 19 | 2006 FA (DR)

90-96 FB ++++ | SL ++ | CU +

Year	Lev	Team	W	L	Sv	IP	K	ERA	WHIP	BF/G	OBA	H%	S%	xERA	Ctl	Dom	Cmd	hr/9	BPV
2007	Rk	AZL Padres	2	6	0	50	55	6.27	1.81	16.6	301	40	64	5.60	5.4	9.9	1.8	0.7	71

Projectable pitcher who relies solely on FB which leaves him hittable when behind in count. Gets strikeouts with late life on FB but doesn't command SL and fails to repeat high ¾ delivery which makes his CU below average. Needs more experience on the mound.

Cecil,Brett — RP — Toronto

EXP MLB DEBUT: 2009 | POTENTIAL: #3 starter | 8C

Thrws R Age 21 | 2007 (1-S) Maryland

88-92 FB ++++ | 83-86 SL ++++ | 77-78 CB ++ | 78-80 SP ++

Year	Lev	Team	W	L	Sv	IP	K	ERA	WHIP	BF/G	OBA	H%	S%	xERA	Ctl	Dom	Cmd	hr/9	BPV
2007	A-	Auburn	1	0	0	49	56	1.28	0.96	13.3	206	30	87	1.65	2.0	10.2	5.1	0.2	177

Aggressive pitcher with a nasty SL and FB movement, which allowed him to miss bats. CB and SPL aren't used often and may switch to a true CU later on. His ¾ delivery can get long and doesn't project more velocity, but TOR believes he can make the adjustments to the rotation.

Ceda,Jose — SP — Chicago (N)

EXP MLB DEBUT: 2009 | POTENTIAL: #3 starter | 8C

Thrws R Age 21 | 2005 FA (DR)

90-97 FB ++++ | 82-84 SL +++ | 79-83 CU ++

Year	Lev	Team	W	L	Sv	IP	K	ERA	WHIP	BF/G	OBA	H%	S%	xERA	Ctl	Dom	Cmd	hr/9	BPV
2006	A-	Boise	1	0	0	11	11	3.27	0.64	12.7	139	17	50	0.72	1.6	9.0	5.5	0.8	172
2006	Rk	AZL Cubs	2	0	0	35	52	3.60	1.29	11.1	202	34	70	2.47	5.1	13.4	2.6	0.3	142
2007	A-	Peoria	2	2	0	46	66	3.12	0.98	8.3	97	17	66	0.55	6.1	12.9	2.1	0.2	152
2007	Rk	AZL Cubs	0	0	0	3	3	2.81	1.56	7.0	181	25	80	2.74	8.4	8.4	1.0	0.0	90

Tall/strong framed pitcher with plus FB, he was moved to relief after stint with a sore shoulder and flourished, tossing 23 hitless innings at one point. SL is deadly to RH batters, but must smooth-out arm action and repeat delivery which would greatly improve command.

Chamberlain,Joba — SP — New York (A)

EXP MLB DEBUT: 2007 | POTENTIAL: #1 starter | 9B

Thrws R Age 22 | 2006 (1-S) Nebraska

88-97 FB ++++ | 80-85 SL ++++ | 72-75 CB +++ | 80-82 CU ++

Year	Lev	Team	W	L	Sv	IP	K	ERA	WHIP	BF/G	OBA	H%	S%	xERA	Ctl	Dom	Cmd	hr/9	BPV
2007	A+	Tampa	4	0	0	40	51	2.03	0.90	21.3	181	29	75	1.04	2.5	11.5	4.6	0.0	185
2007	AA	Trenton	4	2	0	40	66	3.37	1.17	20.0	221	37	74	3.00	3.4	14.8	4.4	0.9	165
2007	AAA	Scranton/WB	1	0	0	8	18	0.00	0.75	9.5	181	52	100	0.58	1.1	20.3	18.0	0.0	518
2007	MLB	New York (A)	2	0	1	24	34	0.38	0.75	4.5	151	25	100	0.67	2.3	12.8	5.7	0.4	209

Tall/strong pitcher with overpowering stuff and command who matured into one of the better pitchers in the game. His FB and SL were a lethal combination as NYY used him in relief, but is still envisioned as a starter. Will need to keep his body in shape, but incurred no injuries in 2007.

Chavez,Jesse — RP — Pittsburgh

EXP MLB DEBUT: 2008 | POTENTIAL: Setup reliever | 6B

Thrws R Age 24 | 2002 (42) Riverside CC

89-94 FB ++++ | 80-84 SL +++ | 69-72 CB ++ | 81-84 CU ++

Year	Lev	Team	W	L	Sv	IP	K	ERA	WHIP	BF/G	OBA	H%	S%	xERA	Ctl	Dom	Cmd	hr/9	BPV
2005	A+	Bakersfield	0	0	2	24	31	2.24	1.04	8.5	191	27	83	2.19	3.4	11.6	3.4	0.7	136
2005	AA	Frisco	4	3	1	57	27	5.68	1.68	8.3	306	31	70	6.22	3.9	4.3	1.1	1.6	-5
2006	AA	Frisco	2	5	4	59	70	4.42	1.39	6.5	245	34	69	3.77	4.3	10.7	2.5	0.8	100
2006	AAA	Ind/Okl	2	1	0	19	18	4.26	1.58	6.4	282	37	70	4.06	4.3	8.5	2.0	0.0	92
2007	AAA	Indianapolis	3	3	2	80	65	3.93	1.39	7.3	294	36	71	4.19	1.9	7.3	3.8	0.4	107

Athletic/light-framed reliever focused more on contact/command which lowered strikeout rate. Possesses late life to FB with his quick arm action and SL is tough on RH batters. Was able to be used in back-to-back outings, but did tire towards end of season.

Cheng,Chi-Hung — SP — Toronto

EXP MLB DEBUT: 2009 | POTENTIAL: #5 starter | 7E

Thrws L Age 28 | 2003 FA (Taiwan)

85-89 FB ++ | 65-69 CB ++++ | 73-76 CB ++++ | CU ++

Year	Lev	Team	W	L	Sv	IP	K	ERA	WHIP	BF/G	OBA	H%	S%	xERA	Ctl	Dom	Cmd	hr/9	BPV
2004	Rk	Pulaski	3	1	0	60	74	2.84	1.36	18.0	217	31	81	3.19	5.2	11.1	2.1	0.6	104
2005	A-	Lansing	7	6	0	137	142	3.15	1.32	21.8	220	29	77	3.07	4.7	9.3	2.0	0.5	93
2006	A-	Lansing	11	5	0	143	154	2.70	1.38	21.4	242	33	80	3.29	4.3	9.7	2.3	0.3	103
2007	A-	Auburn	1	1	0	13	13	2.77	1.15	17.2	179	25	73	1.68	4.8	9.0	1.9	0.0	112
2007	Rk	GCL Blue Jays	0	2	0	9	11	6.85	1.74	10.5	258	29	69	6.86	6.8	10.8	1.6	2.9	13

Athletic pitcher recovering from labrum surgery in 2006 and needs to regain feel for pitching. Lacks good velocity, but keeps ball low and offers hitters two variations of his CB. Getting his command back should be easy, but will need to develop CU and miss more bats.

Cherry,Rocky — RP — Baltimore

EXP MLB DEBUT: 2007 | POTENTIAL: Setup reliever | 6B

Thrws R Age 28 | 2002 (14) Oklahoma

88-93 FB +++ | 81-84 SL ++++ | CU ++

Year	Lev	Team	W	L	Sv	IP	K	ERA	WHIP	BF/G	OBA	H%	S%	xERA	Ctl	Dom	Cmd	hr/9	BPV
2006	AA	W. Tennessee	4	1	2	48	50	2.24	1.18	6.2	240	32	83	3.01	2.6	9.3	3.6	0.6	121
2007	AAA	Iowa	2	0	7	51	56	4.59	1.33	4.9	258	34	67	3.92	3.2	9.9	3.1	0.9	102
2007	MLB	Chicago (N)	1	1	0	15	13	3.00	1.27	5.1	235	29	78	3.21	3.6	7.8	2.2	0.6	82
2007	MLB	Baltimore	0	0	0	16	10	7.83	1.86	7.5	272	28	59	6.25	7.3	5.6	0.8	1.7	0
2007	Rk	AZL Cubs	0	0	0	2	2	0.00	0.50	3.3	0	0	100	0.00	4.5	9.0	2.0	0.0	151

Aggressive reliever with power sinker and a hard SL that he throws often to RH batters. Tall/strong frame and arm strength allows him to hold velocity. Commands plate and can get strikeout when needed. Prior TJS (2005) and mild effort to ¾ delivery limits usage pattern.

Clarke,Darren — RP — Colorado

EXP MLB DEBUT: 2007 | POTENTIAL: Setup reliever | 7C

Thrws R Age 27 | 2000 (35) So Florida CC

91-98 FB +++++ | 84-87 SL +++

Year	Lev	Team	W	L	Sv	IP	K	ERA	WHIP	BF/G	OBA	H%	S%	xERA	Ctl	Dom	Cmd	hr/9	BPV
2005	A-	Tri-City	0	0	3	14	18	0.64	0.79	4.2	186	30	91	0.80	1.3	11.6	9.0	0.0	276
2005	A+	Modesto	0	0	0	6	4	9.00	2.67	6.6	434	46	71	12.46	4.5	6.0	1.3	3.0	-58
2006	A+	Modesto	1	1	5	26	37	1.37	0.76	3.8	150	25	84	0.67	2.4	12.7	5.3	0.3	202
2007	AA	Tulsa	1	1	0	11	16	1.64	0.55	3.7	139	17	100	1.22	0.8	13.1	16.0	1.6	393
2007	MLB	Colorado	0	0	0	1	1	0.00	2.73	3.1	392	49	100	8.85	8.2	8.2	1.0	0.0	47

Tall/strong-framed pitcher creates menacing downhill plane to high-octane FB and amasses strikeouts with hard SL. Commands plate and likes to pitch inside, and is stingy with long ball. Pitches with effort and had TJS in 2006, so workload has to be monitored closely.

Clippard,Tyler

SP | Washington | EXP MLB DEBUT: 2007 | POTENTIAL: #5 starter | 7B

Thrws R Age 23
2003 (9) HS (FL)
- 85-91 FB +++
- 73-77 SL +++
- 79-81 CU +++

Year	Lev	Team	W	L	Sv	IP	K	ERA	WHIP	BF/G	OBA	H%	S%	xERA	Ctl	Dom	Cmd	hr/9	BPV
2005	A+	Tampa	10	9	0	147	169	3.18	1.03	21.8	221	30	71	2.55	2.1	10.3	5.0	0.7	155
2006	AA	Trenton	12	10	0	166	175	3.36	1.04	22.9	201	26	70	2.36	3.0	9.5	3.2	0.8	116
2007	AA	Trenton	2	1	0	26	28	5.50	1.30	18.0	229	27	62	4.25	4.1	9.6	2.3	1.7	64
2007	AAA	Scranton/WB	4	4	0	69	55	4.17	1.69	22.3	296	35	77	5.43	4.6	7.2	1.6	0.9	44
2007	MLB	New York (A)	3	1	0	27	18	6.33	1.70	20.4	276	28	68	6.20	5.7	6.0	1.1	2.0	-2

Attacks hitters with multiple arm slots and a solid mix of pitches. None of his pitches stand out, but keeps ball down and out of hitting zone. Repeats delivery and is deceptive with a slight hesitation, but did struggle more with command and dominance than in previous seasons.

Clyne,Stephen

RP | New York (N) | EXP MLB DEBUT: 2009 | POTENTIAL: #4 starter | 8E

Thrws R Age 23
2007 (3) Clemson
- 88-94 FB ++++
- 78-81 SL +++
- 77-79 CU +

Year	Lev	Team	W	L	Sv	IP	K	ERA	WHIP	BF/G	OBA	H%	S%	xERA	Ctl	Dom	Cmd	hr/9	BPV
2007	A-	Brooklyn	1	1	8	26	30	2.07	1.53	5.7	222	33	85	3.12	6.6	10.3	1.6	0.0	106

Well-proportioned pitcher with solid velocity and two above average pitches that net him strikeouts and groundball outs. Knows how to set-up hitters and sports excellent command. Doesn't repeat arm speed or ¾ slot for CU and has had prior TJS (2004).

Corcoran,Roy

RP | Seattle | EXP MLB DEBUT: 2006 | POTENTIAL: Setup reliever | 6C

Thrws R Age 28
2001 NDFA LSU
- 88-93 FB +++
- 78-80 SL +++
- CU ++

Year	Lev	Team	W	L	Sv	IP	K	ERA	WHIP	BF/G	OBA	H%	S%	xERA	Ctl	Dom	Cmd	hr/9	BPV
2005	AAA	New Orleans	4	4	3	68	55	4.88	1.51	5.7	258	30	69	4.44	4.8	7.3	1.5	0.9	51
2006	AA	Harrisburg	0	2	16	26	40	0.69	0.85	4.5	141	25	95	0.77	3.5	13.8	4.0	0.3	184
2006	AAA	New Orleans	2	4	11	33	37	2.44	1.48	5.1	204	30	82	2.77	6.8	10.0	1.5	0.0	105
2006	MLB	Washington	0	1	0	5	6	12.12	3.08	5.1	450	56	60	12.63	6.9	10.4	1.5	1.7	7
2007	AAA	Albuquerque	4	4	15	61	52	3.54	1.57	5.1	268	34	76	4.00	4.9	7.7	1.6	0.1	76

Short/stocky reliever with quick arm action that makes FB deceptively fast and provides movement. SL is devastating to RH batters and keeps the ball on the ground effectively. Walk rate has been a problem and can be too aggressive, which can get him into trouble.

Cordier,Erik

SP | Atlanta | EXP MLB DEBUT: 2009 | POTENTIAL: #3 starter | 8D

Thrws R Age 22
2004 (2) HS (WI)
- 88-95 FB ++++
- CB ++
- CU +++

Year	Lev	Team	W	L	Sv	IP	K	ERA	WHIP	BF/G	OBA	H%	S%	xERA	Ctl	Dom	Cmd	hr/9	BPV
2004	Rk	AZL Royals	2	4	0	34	22	5.26	1.73	14.1	283	33	67	4.72	5.5	5.8	1.0	0.3	47
2006	A-	Burlington	3	1	0	36	23	2.98	1.13	20.4	209	23	76	2.71	3.5	5.7	1.6	0.7	60
2007	Rk	Idaho Falls	1	0	0	16	19	3.38	0.88	19.7	196	30	57	1.15	1.7	10.7	6.3	0.0	213

Missed 2007 season due to TJS, but will be ready by spring training. Possesses plus velocity and repeats arm speed, giving him ability to change speeds and command. Strikeout rate is excellent and could actually improve with a more consistent CB.

Correa,Hector

SP | Florida | EXP MLB DEBUT: 2012 | POTENTIAL: #3 starter | 8E

Thrws R Age 19
2006 (4) HS (PR)
- 88-93 FB ++++
- SL +++
- CU +

Year	Lev	Team	W	L	Sv	IP	K	ERA	WHIP	BF/G	OBA	H%	S%	xERA	Ctl	Dom	Cmd	hr/9	BPV
2006	Rk	GCL Marlins	1	2	0	41	38	1.76	1.29	16.9	247	32	87	3.07	3.3	8.3	2.5	0.2	102
2007	A-	Greensboro	1	5	0	31	20	9.29	2.29	19.8	386	42	61	9.56	4.6	5.8	1.3	2.0	-22
2007	A-	Jamestown	6	2	0	58	83	3.25	1.27	21.6	271	41	77	3.82	2.0	12.8	6.4	0.8	189

Tall/projectable pitcher was overmatched in full-season ball, where he pitched tentatively, but was dominant in NY-P. Tends to overuse SL which is a definite strikeout pitch and uses it to set-up FB. Will need to repeat arm speed on CU as he tends to tip the pitch.

Correa,Heitor

SP | Philadelphia | EXP MLB DEBUT: 2012 | POTENTIAL: #3 starter | 8E

Thrws R Age 18
2006 FA (Brazil)
- 89-93 FB ++++
- 73-76 CB +++
- CU +

Year	Lev	Team	W	L	Sv	IP	K	ERA	WHIP	BF/G	OBA	H%	S%	xERA	Ctl	Dom	Cmd	hr/9	BPV
2006	Rk	GCL Phillies	0	3	0	23	14	7.83	1.83	13.4	350	40	54	6.19	2.7	5.5	2.0	0.4	48
2007	Rk	GCL Phillies	3	3	0	65	49	3.74	1.20	20.1	240	29	69	3.08	2.8	6.8	2.5	0.6	82

Lively arm, but raw in ability, he gets excellent movement and velocity to FB and CB. Not a lot of finesse to game, as he tends to overthrow and doesn't have any kind of feel for CU. Needs to establish FB command and repeat mechanics on a more consistent basis.

Cortes,Daniel

SP | Kansas City | EXP MLB DEBUT: 2009 | POTENTIAL: #3 starter | 7C

Thrws R Age 21
2005 (7) HS (CA)
- 88-92 FB ++++
- 78-81 CB +++
- CU +

Year	Lev	Team	W	L	Sv	IP	K	ERA	WHIP	BF/G	OBA	H%	S%	xERA	Ctl	Dom	Cmd	hr/9	BPV
2005	Rk	Bristol	1	4	0	38	38	5.20	1.50	11.0	291	38	64	4.42	3.1	9.0	2.9	0.5	98
2006	A-	Burl/Kann	4	11	0	142	126	4.75	1.43	22.4	271	33	68	4.32	3.5	8.0	2.3	0.8	72
2007	A+	Wilmington	8	8	0	123	120	3.07	1.20	20.6	227	30	75	2.84	3.3	8.8	2.7	0.5	103

Tall/lanky pitcher who has developed nicely with an excellent CB and average velocity. Arm action can be stiff and doesn't repeat arm speed on CU, but was sound enough to establish command. Strikeout rate improved and was one of younger starting pitchers in high Class-A.

Cowart,Adam

SP | San Francisco | EXP MLB DEBUT: 2008 | POTENTIAL: Setup reliever | 6C

Thrws R Age 24
2006 (35) Kansas St
- 81-86 FB ++
- 76-79 SL +++
- 72-76 CU ++

Year	Lev	Team	W	L	Sv	IP	K	ERA	WHIP	BF/G	OBA	H%	S%	xERA	Ctl	Dom	Cmd	hr/9	BPV
2006	A-	Salem-Keizer	10	1	0	83	55	1.08	0.71	19.6	179	21	86	0.79	0.9	6.0	6.9	0.2	193
2007	A-	Augusta	14	7	0	169	95	2.39	1.06	23.5	242	28	77	2.45	1.5	5.1	3.4	0.2	102

Plus command and deceptive sidearm delivery allows him to post solid ERA despite below average velocity and strikeout rate. Keeps ball down effectively and can punch-out RH batters with SL. Will need to make constant adjustments and have his best stuff at all times.

Cox,Bryce

RP | Boston | EXP MLB DEBUT: 2009 | POTENTIAL: Setup reliever/closer | 8C

Thrws R Age 23
2006 (3) Rice
- 89-96 FB ++++
- 82-86 SL +++

Year	Lev	Team	W	L	Sv	IP	K	ERA	WHIP	BF/G	OBA	H%	S%	xERA	Ctl	Dom	Cmd	hr/9	BPV
2006	A-	Lowell	0	1	0	5	3	1.73	1.54	7.6	290	34	88	4.12	3.5	5.2	1.5	0.0	60
2006	A+	Wilmington	2	0	0	27	26	0.66	1.00	7.4	182	25	93	1.32	3.3	8.6	2.6	0.0	125
2007	AA	Greenville	1	1	0	33	24	5.44	1.24	6.4	249	28	57	3.80	2.7	6.5	2.4	1.1	62
2007	AA	Portland	1	1	0	14	3	5.07	1.83	7.3	273	27	72	5.23	7.0	1.9	0.3	0.6	-1

Tall/athletic pitcher who generates movement to FB and SL with quick arm action. Struggled to repeat delivery and poor mechanics were compounded by a nagging hamstring injury. Command has been very inconsistent and needs another pitch to offer something to LH batters.

Cox,J Brent

RP | New York (A) | EXP MLB DEBUT: 2009 | POTENTIAL: Setup reliever | 8C

Thrws R Age 24
2005 (2) Texas
- 87-92 FB +++
- 79-83 SL +++
- 71-72 CB ++
- 77-80 CU +++

Year	Lev	Team	W	L	Sv	IP	K	ERA	WHIP	BF/G	OBA	H%	S%	xERA	Ctl	Dom	Cmd	hr/9	BPV
2005	A+	Tampa	1	2	0	27	27	2.65	0.92	6.4	207	28	71	1.72	1.7	8.9	5.4	0.3	171
2006	AA	Trenton	6	2	3	77	60	1.75	1.01	7.2	199	25	83	3.22	2.8	7.0	2.5	0.2	103
2007																			

TJS in March cost him the 2007 season. As predicted, he ditched his CB, and will rely on SL to get strikeouts and sinker to get grounders. Will have to regain feel for pitches and command. With average FB velocity and dominance over RH batters, he likely becomes a setup reliever.

Crosby,Casey

SP | Detroit | EXP MLB DEBUT: 2011 | POTENTIAL: #3 starter | 8E

Thrws L Age 19
2007 (5) HS (IL)
- 86-92 FB +++
- 77-80 SL +++
- 68-71 CB +++
- 74-76 CU ++

Year	Lev	Team	W	L	Sv	IP	K	ERA	WHIP	BF/G	OBA	H%	S%	xERA	Ctl	Dom	Cmd	hr/9	BPV
2007																			

Tall/athletic pitcher with downward plane and deceptive high ¾ delivery that puts pitches on-top of hitters quickly. Offers two solid-average breaking pitches and good velocity, but FB tends to be straight. Slow arm action could be detriment in throwing CU and underwent TJS in Nov.

Cruceta,Francisco — RP — Detroit

EXP MLB DEBUT: 2004 | POTENTIAL: Setup reliever | 7C

Thrws R Age 26			Year	Lev	Team	W	L	Sv	IP	K	ERA	WHIP	BF/G	OBA	H%	S%	xERA	Ctl	Dom	Cmd	hr/9	BPV
1999 FA (DR)			2004	AAA	Buffalo	6	5	0	83	62	3.25	1.37	24.9	250	30	78	3.73	3.9	6.7	1.7	0.7	62
88-93	FB	+++	2005	AAA	Buff/Tac	7	5	0	111	102	5.18	1.52	15.1	300	35	70	5.63	2.8	8.3	2.9	1.5	60
78-82	SL	++++	2006	AAA	Tacoma	13	9	0	160	185	4.38	1.41	24.2	248	32	74	4.46	4.3	10.4	2.4	1.4	77
	SP	+++	2006	MLB	Seattle	0	0	0	6	2	11.61	2.58	8.4	364	34	57	10.72	8.7	2.9	0.3	2.9	-80
80-83	CU	++	2007	AAA	Oak. City	3	0	1	65	70	3.04	1.20	10.5	171	24	74	1.96	5.5	9.7	1.8	0.3	107

Strong-framed pitcher missed action after testing positive for performance-enhancing drugs. Moved to bullpen with excellent results, pumping-up strikeout rate and improving velocity. Delivery is deceptive with multiple arm slots and proved effective with his FB/SPL/SL trio.

Cueto,Johnny — SP — Cincinnati

EXP MLB DEBUT: 2008 | POTENTIAL: #3 starter | 9C

Thrws R Age 22			Year	Lev	Team	W	L	Sv	IP	K	ERA	WHIP	BF/G	OBA	H%	S%	xERA	Ctl	Dom	Cmd	hr/9	BPV
2004 FA (DR)			2006	A-	Dayton	8	1	0	76	83	2.60	0.88	20.1	195	26	73	1.72	1.8	9.8	5.5	0.6	173
88-94	FB	++++	2006	A+	Sarasota	7	2	0	61	61	3.53	1.16	20.3	218	27	72	2.98	3.4	9.0	2.7	0.9	95
82-85	SL	+++	2007	A+	Sarasota	4	5	0	78	72	3.34	1.19	22.4	246	32	71	2.92	2.4	8.3	3.4	0.3	117
78-80	CU	+++	2007	AA	Chattanooga	6	3	0	61	77	3.10	1.03	23.5	232	33	74	2.81	1.6	11.4	7.0	0.9	197
			2007	AAA	Louisville	2	1	0	22	21	2.05	1.09	21.5	262	33	86	3.32	0.8	8.6	10.5	0.8	250

Short/athletic pitcher armed with good velocity and two solid comps. Exhibits plus command and gets strikeouts via impressive pitch movement from his quick arm action. Short stature/light frame has not posed stamina concerns and could thrive in a variety of roles.

Cuevas,Jairo — SP — Atlanta

EXP MLB DEBUT: 2008 | POTENTIAL: #4 starter | 7D

Thrws R Age 24			Year	Lev	Team	W	L	Sv	IP	K	ERA	WHIP	BF/G	OBA	H%	S%	xERA	Ctl	Dom	Cmd	hr/9	BPV
2003 FA (DR)			2004	Rk	Danville	0	0	0	4	3	0.00	1.25	16.3	81	11	100	0.98	9.0	6.8	0.8	0.0	95
89-93	FB	++++	2004	Rk	GCL Braves	2	3	1	35	39	3.09	1.03	15.0	227	32	69	2.16	1.8	10.0	5.6	0.3	179
	CB	++	2005	Rk	Danville	6	1	0	55	69	1.96	1.03	17.7	184	27	83	1.87	3.6	11.3	3.1	0.5	137
	CU	++	2006	A-	Rome	7	12	0	129	117	5.57	1.46	20.5	252	31	61	4.00	4.5	8.2	1.8	0.7	70
			2007	A+	Myrtle Beach	6	12	0	132	116	3.55	1.39	22.2	233	29	75	3.51	4.8	7.9	1.6	0.6	72

Projectable in terms of velocity and was able to notch strikeout with FB and CU, but wasn't efficient and pitched behind in the count, resulting in too many walks and hits. Will need to establish command with FB to improve comps and efficiency, and will need tighter spin to his CB.

Culp,Nate — SP — San Diego

EXP MLB DEBUT: 2009 | POTENTIAL: #5 starter | 7D

Thrws L Age 23			Year	Lev	Team	W	L	Sv	IP	K	ERA	WHIP	BF/G	OBA	H%	S%	xERA	Ctl	Dom	Cmd	hr/9	BPV
2006 (4) Missouri																						
86-90	FB	+++	2006	A-	Eugene	0	1	0	18	8	4.09	1.28	12.3	272	31	72	4.62	2.0	4.0	2.0	0.5	35
80-84	CT	+++	2006	A-	Fort Wayne	4	2	0	33	16	1.50	1.48	20.3	279	31	87	3.21	3.5	4.4	1.2	0.0	67
71-73	CB	++	2007	A-	Fort Wayne	8	3	0	79	54	3.16	1.11	22.2	251	29	74	4.49	1.5	6.1	4.2	0.5	70
76-79	CU	+++	2007	A+	Lk Elsinore	5	4	0	63	39	4.81	1.60	23.3	336	30	75	5.02	1.6	5.6	3.5	0.7	41

Athletic pitcher who pitches to contact, commands plate, and subtracts from FB. Strikeout rate is low and can be hittable, which is mostly due to a below average CB. Stamina no longer seems an issue, but he can't afford to have any deficiencies with the way he pitches.

Davidson,David — RP — Pittsburgh

EXP MLB DEBUT: 2007 | POTENTIAL: Situational reliever | 6A

Thrws L Age 24			Year	Lev	Team	W	L	Sv	IP	K	ERA	WHIP	BF/G	OBA	H%	S%	xERA	Ctl	Dom	Cmd	hr/9	BPV
2002 (10) HS (Canada)			2006	A-	Hickory	2	1	0	56	72	1.93	1.05	8.0	194	30	82	1.87	3.4	11.6	3.4	0.3	148
86-90	FB	+++	2006	AA	Altoona	1	1	0	11	13	2.41	1.61	5.0	202	30	83	3.07	8.0	10.4	1.3	0.0	105
74-77	CB	+++	2007	AA	Altoona	3	1	2	59	55	4.26	1.25	6.2	209	27	65	2.70	4.6	8.4	1.8	0.5	88
			2007	AAA	Indianapolis	1	0	0	7	9	1.25	1.25	4.9	228	35	89	2.48	3.8	11.3	3.0	0.0	140
			2007	MLB	Pittsburgh	0	0	0	2	0	22.50	4.00	6.8	515	47	43	19.51	9.0	0.0	0.0	4.5	-183

Projectable pitcher with deceptive arm action. Velocity is below average, but depth/command of CB enhances FB appearance and generates good pitch movement. Tough on LH batters and can carve out matchup role, but must pitch aggressively and sharpen command.

Davis,Wade — SP — Tampa Bay

EXP MLB DEBUT: 2008 | POTENTIAL: #2 starter | 9C

Thrws R Age 22			Year	Lev	Team	W	L	Sv	IP	K	ERA	WHIP	BF/G	OBA	H%	S%	xERA	Ctl	Dom	Cmd	hr/9	BPV
2004 (3) HS (FL)			2004	Rk	Princeton	3	5	0	57	38	6.14	1.57	19.3	306	34	62	5.61	3.0	6.0	2.0	1.3	34
87-94	FB	++++	2005	A-	Hudson Valley	7	4	0	86	97	2.72	1.14	22.7	236	32	77	2.81	2.4	10.2	4.2	0.5	142
85-86	CT	+++	2006	A-	SW Michigan	7	12	0	146	165	3.02	1.29	22.2	231	33	76	2.92	3.9	10.2	2.6	0.3	115
75-78	CB	+++	2007	A+	Vero Beach	3	0	0	78	88	1.84	0.96	22.7	197	27	84	1.93	2.4	10.1	4.2	0.6	147
78-82	CU	++	2007	AA	Montgomery	7	3	0	80	81	3.15	1.30	23.5	247	33	75	3.19	3.4	9.1	2.7	0.3	107

Pitched consistently well at two levels, possessing three average to above pitches, along with exceptional command. FB tends to be straight at higher velocities, but can go to comps when needed. Misses bats with regularity and has stamina to pitch deep into games.

Day,Dewon — RP — Chicago (A)

EXP MLB DEBUT: 2007 | POTENTIAL: Setup reliever | 7C

Thrws R Age 27			Year	Lev	Team	W	L	Sv	IP	K	ERA	WHIP	BF/G	OBA	H%	S%	xERA	Ctl	Dom	Cmd	hr/9	BPV
2002 (26) Southern			2005	A-	Lansing	0	0	0	13	14	4.12	1.83	6.8	289	36	82	6.08	6.2	9.6	1.6	1.4	46
89-95	FB	++++	2006	A+	Win-Salem	1	4	8	45	62	3.38	1.31	4.9	234	35	75	3.25	4.0	12.3	3.1	0.6	129
83-86	SL	++++	2007	AA	Birmingham	2	3	3	25	48	3.60	1.52	5.4	269	53	76	3.99	4.3	17.3	4.0	0.4	178
82-84	CU	+	2007	AAA	Charlotte	0	2	0	14	15	6.38	2.13	5.0	201	29	67	4.38	12.8	9.6	0.8	0.0	88
			2007	MLB	Chicago (A)	0	1	0	12	7	11.25	2.33	4.8	360	40	48	7.97	6.8	5.3	0.8	0.8	8

Tall/athletic reliever decimated Double-A hitters, striking-out almost two batters per inning. FB and SL have late life, which is traced to his smooth arm action, and will utilize different arm angles to derive deception. Will need CU for LH batters and show more consistent command.

De la Cruz,Eulogio — RP — Florida

EXP MLB DEBUT: 2007 | POTENTIAL: Setup reliever | 8C

Thrws R Age 24			Year	Lev	Team	W	L	Sv	IP	K	ERA	WHIP	BF/G	OBA	H%	S%	xERA	Ctl	Dom	Cmd	hr/9	BPV
2001 FA (DR)			2006	AA	Erie	5	6	2	106	88	3.40	1.42	11.8	258	32	75	3.57	3.9	7.5	1.9	0.3	81
92-98	FB	++++	2006	AAA	Toledo	0	0	0	2	3	12.86	2.86	11.9	403	51	60	13.39	8.6	12.9	1.5	4.3	-46
77-79	SL	+++	2007	AA	Erie	4	5	0	66	57	3.41	1.11	23.6	225	28	71	2.75	2.6	7.8	3.0	0.7	99
			2007	AAA	Toledo	3	0	0	38	25	3.54	1.55	7.6	276	33	75	3.93	4.3	5.9	1.4	0.0	64
			2007	MLB	Detroit	0	0	0	6	5	7.26	2.26	5.2	364	42	69	8.49	5.8	7.3	1.3	1.5	8

Small/compact pitcher gets movement and velocity through arm strength and quick arm action. Base skills and velocity declined, but was asked to start during first half and was working on repeating ¾ delivery. FB and SL are strong pitchers and can survive by being effectively wild.

De los Santos,Fautino — SP — Chicago (A)

EXP MLB DEBUT: 2009 | POTENTIAL: #2 starter | 9C

Thrws R Age 22			Year	Lev	Team	W	L	Sv	IP	K	ERA	WHIP	BF/G	OBA	H%	S%	xERA	Ctl	Dom	Cmd	hr/9	BPV
2005 FA (DR)																						
89-96	FB	++++																				
82-84	SL	++++																				
75-79	CB	++																				
80-83	CU	++	2007	A-	Kannapolis	9	4	0	97	121	0.46	0.87	17.1	152	13	136	2.92	3.3	11.2	3.4	2.4	90

Wiry athlete with plus pitch movement and velocity from whip-like delivery. FB and SL were too much for Class-A hitters, but key to success was improved command. CB and CU remain below average pitches and has a tendency to pitch up in the strike zone which could get exploited.

Deduno,Samuel — SP — Colorado

EXP MLB DEBUT: 2008 | POTENTIAL: #5 starter/setup reliever | 7C

Thrws R Age 24			Year	Lev	Team	W	L	Sv	IP	K	ERA	WHIP	BF/G	OBA	H%	S%	xERA	Ctl	Dom	Cmd	hr/9	BPV
2003 FA (DR)			2004	Rk	Casper	6	4	0	76	118	3.19	1.24	20.6	224	38	74	2.70	3.8	14.0	3.7	0.4	161
88-93	FB	++++	2005	A-	Asheville	8	8	0	89	110	5.65	1.65	19.9	246	34	66	4.57	6.6	11.1	1.7	0.9	81
75-80	CB	+++	2006	A+	Modesto	5	8	0	146	167	4.80	1.46	23.1	227	33	64	3.17	5.7	10.3	1.8	0.2	104
78-82	CU	++	2007	A+	Modesto	1	1	0	11	8	6.55	1.45	23.5	225	26	53	3.77	5.7	6.5	1.1	0.8	49
			2007	AA	Tulsa	5	8	0	124	121	5.44	1.50	25.5	255	32	64	4.38	4.8	8.8	1.8	0.9	67

Athletic pitcher with plus movement to CB and FB which helped him lead TL in strikeouts. Poor command has been nemesis during career and was victimized by the long ball for first time. Rarely pitches more than five innings and lacks a CU, so could be moved to relief.

Degerman,Eddie — SP — St. Louis

EXP MLB DEBUT: 2009 | POTENTIAL: #5 starter | 7D

Thrws R Age 24			Year	Lev	Team	W	L	Sv	IP	K	ERA	WHIP	BF/G	OBA	H%	S%	xERA	Ctl	Dom	Cmd	hr/9	BPV
2006 (4) Rice																						
87-92	FB	+++																				
75-78	CB	++++	2006	A-	State College	2	1	0	42	53	2.78	1.35	19.5	238	35	79	3.06	4.3	11.3	2.7	0.2	125
68-70	CB	+++	2007	A-	Quad Cities	1	1	1	47	71	2.48	0.95	14.8	163	26	78	1.68	3.6	13.5	3.7	0.8	159
75-78	CU	++	2007	A+	Palm Beach	4	4	0	54	57	5.98	1.59	21.7	246	33	60	4.05	6.0	9.5	1.6	0.5	81

Athletic-type pitcher with an incredibly deceptive overhand delivery and two CB's that he uses plenty. Strikeout rate remains high despite average velocity. Tends to leave the ball up and command is inconsistent. Needs to be challenged to gauge true level of ability.

Delaney,Robert | RP | Minnesota | EXP MLB DEBUT: 2009 | POTENTIAL: Setup reliever | 7C

Thrws R Age 23	Year	Lev	Team	W	L	Sv	IP	K	ERA	WHIP	BF/G	OBA	H%	S%	xERA	Ctl	Dom	Cmd	hr/9	BPV
2006 NDFA St. John's																				
87-92 FB +++	2006	Rk	GCL Twins	1	3	2	33	27	4.64	1.24	7.9	284	33	65	4.29	1.1	7.4	6.8	1.1	151
CB ++++	2006	A+	Ft. Myers	0	0	0	5	3	5.40	1.40	7.0	332	35	67	6.11	0.0	5.4		1.8	-33
CU ++	2007	A-	Beloit	1	0	28	46	56	0.78	0.67	4.5	161	24	90	0.43	1.2	10.9	9.3	0.2	278
	2007	A+	Ft. Myers	2	0	7	23	27	1.56	1.26	5.5	226	32	89	2.84	3.9	10.5	2.7	0.4	118

Strong-framed reliever dominated as a closer, utilizing a deceptive ¾ delivery, establishing FB command, and dropping CB for strikeouts. Likes to pitch aggressively and missed bat despite solid-average velocity. Will need to develop CU to combat LH batters.

Demel,Sam | RP | Oakland | EXP MLB DEBUT: 2009 | POTENTIAL: Setup reliever/closer | 8D

Thrws R Age 22	Year	Lev	Team	W	L	Sv	IP	K	ERA	WHIP	BF/G	OBA	H%	S%	xERA	Ctl	Dom	Cmd	hr/9	BPV
2007 (3) TCU																				
89-93 FB +++																				
78-80 SL ++++																				
SP +++	2007	A-	Kane County	0	1	4	9	10	0.99	0.77	3.6	105	16	86	0.00	4.0	9.9	2.5	0.0	146
	2007	A+	Stockton	0	0	0	14	13	7.07	2.21	6.4	288	35	69	6.97	9.6	8.4	0.9	1.3	27

College reliever with explosive FB movement and plus SL from a quick arm action and low ¾ slot. Pitches aggressive, but overuses SL when backed into corner and throws with effort. Command has always been solid and has no problem notching strikeouts.

DeSalvo,Matt | SP | New York (A) | EXP MLB DEBUT: 2007 | POTENTIAL: #5 starter | 6A

Thrws R Age 27	Year	Lev	Team	W	L	Sv	IP	K	ERA	WHIP	BF/G	OBA	H%	S%	xERA	Ctl	Dom	Cmd	hr/9	BPV
2003 NDFA Marietta	2005	AA	Trenton	9	5	0	149	151	3.02	1.16	23.7	201	27	75	2.41	4.0	9.1	2.3	0.5	102
86-91 FB +++	2006	AA	Trenton	5	4	0	78	53	5.88	1.78	22.5	266	30	67	5.13	6.8	6.1	0.9	0.8	33
79-81 SL ++	2006	AAA	Columbus	1	6	0	38	30	7.77	2.12	17.2	304	36	62	6.66	8.0	7.1	0.9	0.9	27
73-77 KC +++	2007	AAA	Scranton/WB	9	5	0	113	102	2.71	1.31	23.3	224	29	79	2.91	4.5	8.1	1.8	0.3	88
76-79 CU +++	2007	MLB	New York (A)	1	3	0	27	10	6.29	1.91	18.4	307	32	66	5.96	6.0	3.3	0.6	0.7	5

Unorthodox delivery and ability to throw seven pitches compensates for his short stature which puts pitches on a flat plane. Adds and subtracts from FB featuring good movement, and keeps ball down. Command wasn't as consistent and failed to trust stuff in Major League stint.

Detwiler,Ross | SP | Washington | EXP MLB DEBUT: 2007 | POTENTIAL: #2 starter | 9C

Thrws L Age 22	Year	Lev	Team	W	L	Sv	IP	K	ERA	WHIP	BF/G	OBA	H%	S%	xERA	Ctl	Dom	Cmd	hr/9	BPV
2007 (1) Missouri St																				
88-94 FB ++++																				
77-81 CB ++++	2007	A+	Potomac	2	2	0	21	13	4.27	1.71	19.1	312	36	74	5.27	3.8	5.5	1.4	0.4	43
78-80 CU ++	2007	MLB	Washington	0	0	0	1	1	0.00	0.00	2.8	0	0		0.00	0.0	9.0		0.0	109
	2007	Rk	GCL Nationals	0	0	0	12	15	2.25	1.17	12.0	245	35	85	3.20	2.3	11.3	5.0	0.8	156

Projectable, hard-throwing pitcher with excellent base skills and the intelligence/poise to get hitters out in numerous ways. Mixes FB and CB to get strikeouts, but needs better deception to CU. Arm action from a ¾ slot isn't fluid, but proved durable during college.

Devine,Joey | RP | Atlanta | EXP MLB DEBUT: 2005 | POTENTIAL: Setup reliever/closer | 8C

Thrws R Age 24	Year	Lev	Team	W	L	Sv	IP	K	ERA	WHIP	BF/G	OBA	H%	S%	xERA	Ctl	Dom	Cmd	hr/9	BPV
2005 (1) No Carolina St	2006	AA	Mississippi	2	0	0	11	20	0.82	0.55	6.2	61	8	100	0.00	3.3	16.4	5.0	0.8	222
88-95 FB ++++	2006	MLB	Atlanta	0	0	0	6	10	10.33	2.79	3.4	317	49	63	8.97	13.3	14.8	1.1	1.5	59
80-84 SL ++++	2007	AA	Mississippi	2	4	16	35	51	2.06	1.11	4.2	209	34	82	2.12	3.3	13.1	3.9	0.3	167
79-82 CU +	2007	AAA	Richmond	3	0	4	22	27	1.64	0.95	4.9	195	29	85	1.72	2.5	11.0	4.5	0.4	165
	2007	MLB	Atlanta	1	0	0	8	7	1.11	1.85	3.8	235	31	93	4.11	8.9	7.8	0.9	0.0	73

Bounced around from minors to ATL, but in-between, was incredibly effective. Uses FB/SL combination to attack hitters, getting both strikeouts and groundball outs. Command improved immensely by being more around plate, but pitched tentatively in his Major League stints.

Deza,Fredy | RP | Baltimore | EXP MLB DEBUT: 2007 | POTENTIAL: Setup reliever | 7C

Thrws R Age 25	Year	Lev	Team	W	L	Sv	IP	K	ERA	WHIP	BF/G	OBA	H%	S%	xERA	Ctl	Dom	Cmd	hr/9	BPV
1999 FA (DR)	2004	A-	Delmarva	8	11	0	119	93	3.32	1.03	20.9	233	28	68	2.53	1.6	7.0	4.4	0.5	128
88-95 FB ++++	2004	A+	Frederick	1	3	0	25	20	5.71	1.39	21.2	317	36	61	5.48	0.7	7.1	10.0	1.4	202
SL +++	2005	A+	Frederick	5	8	0	104	64	6.14	1.63	16.6	313	35	63	5.76	3.1	5.5	1.8	1.1	29
CU +	2006	A+	Frederick	3	4	0	83	68	4.76	1.49	8.3	282	34	68	4.56	3.5	7.4	2.1	0.8	65
	2007	AA	Bowie	7	8	0	124	101	4.43	1.40	14.5	273	30	74	5.00	3.1	7.3	2.3	1.6	46

Swingman with deadly FB/SL combination that is tough on RH batters. Arm action provides pitch movement and is compact with delivery. Doesn't strike-out as many as stuff would indicate and needs to keep ball down as he was victimized by the long ball.

Diamond,Thomas | SP | Texas | EXP MLB DEBUT: 2007 | POTENTIAL: #4 starter/setup reliever | 8D

Thrws R Age 25	Year	Lev	Team	W	L	Sv	IP	K	ERA	WHIP	BF/G	OBA	H%	S%	xERA	Ctl	Dom	Cmd	hr/9	BPV
2004 (1) New Orleans	2004	A-	Clinton	1	0	0	30	42	2.09	0.86	15.9	174	28	76	1.14	2.4	12.5	5.3	0.3	197
88-95 FB ++++	2005	A+	Bakersfield	8	0	0	81	101	2.00	1.04	22.3	188	28	81	1.78	3.4	11.2	3.3	0.3	143
83-86 SL ++	2005	AA	Frisco	5	4	0	69	68	5.35	1.51	21.3	253	31	66	4.46	5.0	8.9	1.8	1.0	64
72-76 CB +++	2006	AA	Frisco	12	5	0	129	145	4.25	1.41	20.2	222	29	72	3.74	5.4	10.1	1.9	1.0	81
77-81 CU +++	2007	AA	Frisco																	

Missed 2007 season with TJS and may resurface in relief. Overpowers hitters with FB and CB, and though he repeats his delivery and disguises his CU, his command wavers and wastes pitches. Will need to continue to smooth-out mechanics and build-up arm strength.

Dominguez,Jose | SP | Los Angeles (N) | EXP MLB DEBUT: 2012 | POTENTIAL: #4 starter | 8E

Thrws R Age 18	Year	Lev	Team	W	L	Sv	IP	K	ERA	WHIP	BF/G	OBA	H%	S%	xERA	Ctl	Dom	Cmd	hr/9	BPV
2007 FA (DR)																				
86-90 FB +++																				
CB +++																				
CU ++																				
	2007																			

Tall/projectable pitcher who belies age with ability to pitch. Quick arm action provides movement to average velocity FB and CB which helps in getting strikeouts. Command is exceptional and sets-up pitches well. Will need to repeat delivery more frequently to improve CU.

Doyne,Cory | RP | Baltimore | EXP MLB DEBUT: 2007 | POTENTIAL: Setup reliever | 6B

Thrws R Age 26	Year	Lev	Team	W	L	Sv	IP	K	ERA	WHIP	BF/G	OBA	H%	S%	xERA	Ctl	Dom	Cmd	hr/9	BPV
2000 (8) HS (FL)	2005	AA	Springfield	2	1	19	55	53	1.96	1.32	4.8	192	24	90	3.03	5.9	8.7	1.5	0.8	75
87-93 FB +++	2006	AA	Springfield	1	7	6	66	78	3.40	1.36	5.1	205	30	73	2.61	5.7	10.6	1.9	0.1	113
77-78 CB ++	2006	AAA	Memphis	0	0	0	5	3	0.00	1.20	10.1	175	21	100	1.79	5.4	5.4	1.0	0.0	73
80-82 CU +++	2007	AAA	Norfolk	0	1	29	44	49	2.24	0.88	3.9	156	23	72	0.74	3.3	10.0	3.1	0.0	148
	2007	MLB	Baltimore	0	0	0	3	2	16.88	3.13	3.8	437	46	44	13.50	8.4	5.6	0.7	2.8	-69

Closer who changes eye levels with four-seam FB and CB, is deceptive with overhand delivery, and changes speeds effectively. Commands all three pitches and can get strikeout when needed. Workload needs to be monitored as he struggles if overused.

Drabek,Kyle | SP | Philadelphia | EXP MLB DEBUT: 2011 | POTENTIAL: #2 starter/setup reliever | 9E

Thrws R Age 20	Year	Lev	Team	W	L	Sv	IP	K	ERA	WHIP	BF/G	OBA	H%	S%	xERA	Ctl	Dom	Cmd	hr/9	BPV
2006 (1-C) HS (TX)																				
89-94 FB ++++																				
83-86 SL +++																				
76-81 KC +++	2006	Rk	GCL Phillies	1	3	0	23	14	7.79	1.90	18.2	336	38	57	6.50	4.3	5.5	1.3	0.8	24
CU +	2007	A-	Lakewood	5	1	0	54	46	4.33	1.35	20.5	247	28	73	4.43	3.8	7.7	2.0	1.5	49

Low velocity that he experienced in June culminated in TJS in July. Athleticism and smooth delivery give him easy velocity and movement to pitches, and improved his command, ability to pitch, and overall performance. May not pitch until end of 2008, but should return strong.

Duensing,Brian | SP | Minnesota | EXP MLB DEBUT: 2008 | POTENTIAL: #5 starter | 7C

Thrws L Age 25	Year	Lev	Team	W	L	Sv	IP	K	ERA	WHIP	BF/G	OBA	H%	S%	xERA	Ctl	Dom	Cmd	hr/9	BPV
2005 (3-C) Nebraska	2006	A-	Beloit	2	3	0	70	55	2.95	1.17	25.4	256	31	75	3.04	1.8	7.1	3.9	0.4	117
86-92 FB +++	2006	A+	Fort Myers	2	5	0	40	33	4.49	1.37	24.0	294	35	69	4.57	1.8	7.4	4.1	0.9	100
78-82 SL +++	2006	AA	New Britain	1	2	0	49	30	3.67	1.41	20.7	269	29	78	4.51	3.3	5.5	1.7	1.1	36
72-74 CB ++	2007	AA	New Britain	4	1	0	50	38	2.69	1.08	21.7	249	30	75	2.70	1.3	6.8	5.4	0.4	149
76-80 CU +++	2007	AAA	Rochester	11	5	0	116	86	3.25	1.25	24.9	260	30	78	3.88	2.3	6.7	2.9	1.0	73

Short/athletic pitcher was consistent all season, baffling hitters with command and deception. Repeats ¾ delivery on all pitches and exploits hitters' weaknesses, but will struggle to get strikeouts. Pitches with some effort and has had prior TJS, so workload should be monitored.

Duffy, Dan — SP — Kansas City

EXP MLB DEBUT: 2011 **POTENTIAL:** #3 starter **8D**

Thrws L **Age** 19
2007 (3) HS (CA)

87-94	FB	++++
79-80	SL	+++
70-73	CB	+++
80-82	CU	++

Year	Lev	Team	W	L	Sv	IP	K	ERA	WHIP	BF/G	OBA	H%	S%	xERA	Ctl	Dom	Cmd	hr/9	BPV
2007	Rk	GCL Royals	2	3	0	37	63	1.45	1.11	12.1	178	25	81	1.72	4.1	15.2	3.7	0.0	184

Maturely built pitcher with arm strength, velocity, and FB movement. Possesses two breaking pitches that can be thrown for strikes and commands all quadrants of plate. Mixes pitches well and didn't allow a HR in minors. Will need to repeat delivery and change speeds better.

Dumatrait, Phil — SP — Pittsburgh

EXP MLB DEBUT: 2007 **POTENTIAL:** #5 starter **5A**

Thrws L **Age** 26
2000 (1) Bakersfield CC

87-93	FB	+++
80-83	SL	+++
75-77	CB	+++
79-81	CU	+++

Year	Lev	Team	W	L	Sv	IP	K	ERA	WHIP	BF/G	OBA	H%	S%	xERA	Ctl	Dom	Cmd	hr/9	BPV
2005	AA	Chattanooga	4	12	0	127	101	3.18	1.45	22.7	243	30	77	3.49	5.0	7.1	1.4	3.2	71
2006	AA	Chattanooga	3	4	0	49	45	3.66	1.24	20.0	219	27	72	3.06	4.0	8.2	2.0	3.7	82
2006	AAA	Louisville	5	7	0	87	58	4.75	1.61	24.1	297	33	72	5.35	3.7	6.0	1.6	4.7	34
2007	AAA	Louisville	10	6	0	125	76	3.53	1.30	24.1	297	31	71	3.66	3.5	5.5	1.6	3.5	47
2007	MLB	Cincinnati	0	4	0	18	9	15.00	2.83	14.9	448	41	69	19.50	6.0	4.5	0.8	3.0	-98

Athletic pitcher survives by mixing pitches and repeating delivery. Throws hard and improved rotation of SL, but lacks FB movement and lost consistency to CB. Tends to nibble which elevates walk rate and causes him to pitch from behind, hurting oppBA.

Dunn, Michael — SP — New York (A)

EXP MLB DEBUT: 2010 **POTENTIAL:** #5 starter **7C**

Thrws L **Age** 23
2004 (33) S Nevada

86-91	FB	+++
	SL	+++
	CU	++

Year	Lev	Team	W	L	Sv	IP	K	ERA	WHIP	BF/G	OBA	H%	S%	xERA	Ctl	Dom	Cmd	hr/9	BPV
2006	A-	Staten Island	0	0	0	6	7	5.90	1.64	9.1	149	23	60	2.56	10.3	10.3	1.0	0.0	108
2006	Rk	GCL Yankees	3	0	4	24	26	0.74	0.91	8.2	160	24	91	0.85	3.3	9.7	2.9	0.0	142
2007	A-	Charleston	12	5	0	144	138	3.43	1.26	21.8	251	31	75	3.63	2.8	8.6	3.1	0.9	95

Drafted as a position player, but was quickly converted to the mound due to his arm strength. Doesn't have overpowering velocity, but gets strikeouts through a deceptive delivery and being able to pinpoint FB and SL. Strides too much to the plate, which elevates pitches.

Durkin, Matt — SP — New York (N)

EXP MLB DEBUT: 2009 **POTENTIAL:** #4 starter **7E**

Thrws R **Age** 25
2004 (2) San Jose St

88-92	FB	++++
77-80	SL	+++
71-73	CB	+++
75-77	CU	++

Year	Lev	Team	W	L	Sv	IP	K	ERA	WHIP	BF/G	OBA	H%	S%	xERA	Ctl	Dom	Cmd	hr/9	BPV
2005	A-	Hagerstown	4	5	0	76	79	3.78	1.42	17.0	201	25	77	3.60	6.4	9.3	1.5	1.1	70
2006	A-	Hagerstown	0	0	0	3	4	0.00	1.67	13.5	191	31	100	3.08	9.0	12.0	1.3	0.0	117
2006	Rk	GCL Mets	0	1	0	14	13	8.87	2.25	12.0	333	40	60	7.76	7.6	8.2	1.1	1.3	23
2006	Rk	Kingsport	0	0	0	4	4	0.00	0.95	5.3	78	11	100	0.18	6.4	8.6	1.3	0.0	119
2007	A-	Savannah	4	8	2	114	71	4.02	1.43	19.4	249	28	73	3.93	4.4	5.6	1.3	0.7	44

Strong-framed pitcher with history of shoulder problems. Possesses arsenal of a starter and has excellent velocity, but struggles with command, stamina, and changing speeds. Making him a reliever could improve his lot and get him advanced past Class-A.

Edwards, Justin — SP — Chicago (A)

EXP MLB DEBUT: 2010 **POTENTIAL:** #5 starter **7E**

Thrws L **Age** 20
2006 (3) HS (FL)

85-89	FB	++
69-72	CB	+++
77-79	CU	+++

Year	Lev	Team	W	L	Sv	IP	K	ERA	WHIP	BF/G	OBA	H%	S%	xERA	Ctl	Dom	Cmd	hr/9	BPV
2006	Rk	Bristol	3	7	0	52	42	5.34	1.72	19.8	319	37	70	5.98	3.6	7.2	2.0	1.0	46
2007	A-	Kannapolis	6	9	0	115	87	5.79	1.50	18.4	283	33	60	4.62	3.4	6.8	2.0	0.8	57

Short/athletic pitcher with three average pitches and plus command. Strikeout rate will always be low without good velocity, so he has to keep ball down and continue to mix pitches. Stamina is a concern as he doesn't hold velocity and struggles through lineup the second time.

Egbert, Jack — SP — Chicago (A)

EXP MLB DEBUT: 2009 **POTENTIAL:** #3 starter **7B**

Thrws R **Age** 25
2004 (13) Rutgers

85-91	FB	+++
81-83	CT	++
72-73	CB	++
75-77	CU	++++

Year	Lev	Team	W	L	Sv	IP	K	ERA	WHIP	BF/G	OBA	H%	S%	xERA	Ctl	Dom	Cmd	hr/9	BPV
2004	Rk	Great Falls	4	1	0	58	52	3.40	1.44	14.6	237	30	76	3.40	5.1	8.0	1.6	0.3	80
2005	A-	Kannapolis	10	5	0	147	107	3.12	1.19	19.7	235	28	73	2.75	2.9	6.6	2.2	0.3	85
2006	A+	Win-Salem	9	8	0	140	120	2.70	1.24	22.8	245	31	77	2.83	3.0	7.7	2.6	0.1	103
2006	AA	Birmingham	0	2	0	21	24	0.86	1.19	21.1	223	33	92	2.28	3.4	10.3	3.0	0.0	135
2007	AA	Birmingham	12	8	0	161	165	3.07	1.13	22.7	233	32	71	2.41	2.5	9.2	3.8	0.2	137

Doubles as one of the better groundball and command pitchers in the minors. Repeats delivery so well that he gets swings and misses despite average velocity. CB is a below average offering and will have to improve, but does provide deception and hesitation to delivery.

Elbert, Scott — SP — Los Angeles (N)

EXP MLB DEBUT: 2009 **POTENTIAL:** #2 starter **9C**

Thrws L **Age** 23
2004 (1) HS (MO)

89-93	FB	+++
71-74	CB	+++
79-81	CU	+++

Year	Lev	Team	W	L	Sv	IP	K	ERA	WHIP	BF/G	OBA	H%	S%	xERA	Ctl	Dom	Cmd	hr/9	BPV
2004	Rk	Ogden	2	3	0	49	45	5.30	1.57	18.0	253	31	67	4.49	5.5	8.2	1.5	0.9	58
2005	A-	Columbus	8	5	0	115	128	2.66	1.22	18.6	204	28	80	2.70	4.5	10.0	2.2	0.6	103
2006	A+	Vero Beach	5	5	0	83	97	2.38	1.18	19.6	195	28	81	2.32	4.4	10.5	2.4	0.4	116
2006	AA	Jacksonville	6	4	0	62	76	3.62	1.35	23.6	186	23	81	3.74	6.4	11.0	1.7	1.6	72
2007	AA	Jacksonville	0	1	0	14	24	3.86	1.14	18.5	132	28	63	1.09	6.4	15.4	2.4	0.0	172

Projectable pitcher missed most of 2007 with minor shoulder surgery in June, but should be 100% by spring training. Arm action gives rise to easy velocity and is able to get strikeouts with any of his three pitches. Keeps ball low and shows command, but isn't always efficient.

Ely, John — SP — Chicago (A)

EXP MLB DEBUT: 2009 **POTENTIAL:** #4 starter **7D**

Thrws R **Age** 22
2007 (3) Miami-OH

88-93	FB	+++
74-78	CB	++
76-78	CU	++++

Year	Lev	Team	W	L	Sv	IP	K	ERA	WHIP	BF/G	OBA	H%	S%	xERA	Ctl	Dom	Cmd	hr/9	BPV
2007	Rk	Great Falls	6	1	0	56	56	3.86	1.23	17.5	258	32	71	3.76	2.3	9.0	4.0	1.0	112

Dominant in debut with plus CU, though was pitching against younger hitters. Pitches above stuff, as he gets little FB movement from his stiff arm action and effort to delivery. Commands plate, is deceptive, and competes on the mound, but will have to prove self at upper levels.

Enright, Barry — SP — Arizona

EXP MLB DEBUT: 2010 **POTENTIAL:** #4 starter **7C**

Thrws R **Age** 22
2007 (2) Pepperdine

86-90	FB	+++
76-80	SL	+++
77-79	CU	+++

Year	Lev	Team	W	L	Sv	IP	K	ERA	WHIP	BF/G	OBA	H%	S%	xERA	Ctl	Dom	Cmd	hr/9	BPV
2007	A-	South Bend	0	0	1	2	1	0.00	0.50	6.6	151	18	100	0.00	0.0	4.5		0.0	52
2007	A-	Yakima	0	0	0	8	12	0.00	0.88	5.9	151	27	100	0.63	3.4	13.5	4.0	0.0	190
2007	A+	Visalia	0	0	1	5	4	0.00	1.00	4.8	175	23	100	1.27	3.6	7.2	2.0	0.0	105

Durable/inning-eating type pitcher with average repertoire, but demonstrates plus command and provides deception by repeating ¾ delivery and showing quick arm action. Missing bats could be a problem, so will have to mix pitches effectively and out-think hitters.

Erbe, Brandon — SP — Baltimore

EXP MLB DEBUT: 2009 **POTENTIAL:** #2 starter **9D**

Thrws R **Age** 20
2005 (3) HS (MD)

89-95	FB	++++
85-86	CT	++++
77-78	SL	++
77-78	CU	+++

Year	Lev	Team	W	L	Sv	IP	K	ERA	WHIP	BF/G	OBA	H%	S%	xERA	Ctl	Dom	Cmd	hr/9	BPV
2005	A-	Aberdeen	1	1	0	7	9	7.71	1.43	9.9	233	36	40	2.99	5.1	11.6	2.3	0.0	125
2005	Rk	Bluefield	1	1	1	23	48	3.12	0.78	7.6	109	29	59	0.29	3.9	18.7	4.8	0.4	234
2006	A-	Delmarva	5	9	0	114	133	3.23	1.18	16.3	215	31	71	2.30	3.7	10.5	2.8	0.2	130
2007	A+	Frederick	6	8	0	119	111	6.27	1.59	21.0	274	33	61	4.97	4.7	8.4	1.8	1.1	56

Athletic pitcher with organization's best FB, but struggled with command and consistency of comps. High ¾ slot doesn't give him much deception and his flyball tendencies will be problematic at higher levels. Ability for rebound, but lack of CU could mean a move to relief.

Estrada, Marco — RP — Washington

EXP MLB DEBUT: 2009 **POTENTIAL:** #5 starter **7D**

Thrws R **Age** 25
2005 (6) Long Beach St

88-92	FB	+++
79-81	CB	+++
76-79	CU	+++

Year	Lev	Team	W	L	Sv	IP	K	ERA	WHIP	BF/G	OBA	H%	S%	xERA	Ctl	Dom	Cmd	hr/9	BPV
2006	A-	Savannah	1	4	0	37	29	5.59	1.57	20.3	297	34	67	5.64	3.4	7.1	2.1	1.5	38
2006	Rk	GCL Nationals	2	0	0	23	27	1.55	0.86	17.1	176	25	84	1.26	2.3	10.5	4.5	0.4	165
2007	A-	Hagerstown	1	5	0	36	35	5.25	1.56	19.7	278	34	67	4.88	4.3	8.8	2.1	1.0	65
2007	A+	Potomac	5	3	0	58	54	4.96	1.45	22.5	290	35	68	4.87	2.6	8.4	3.2	1.1	81
2007	Rk	GCL Nationals	0	0	0	11	13	3.24	1.98	13.3	378	50	86	7.43	2.4	10.5	4.3	0.8	109

Strong-framed pitcher with average stuff, but sets-up pitches well and improved command, which worked for him at the lower levels. Likes to get strikeouts with SU and keeps ball low, but can be hittable due to his flat plane to the plate and average FB velocity.

Estrada, Paul — RP — Houston
Thrws R **Age** 25 — 1999 FA (DR) — EXP MLB DEBUT: 2008 — POTENTIAL: Setup reliever — **7C**

FB 88-94 ++++ · CB 75-78 ++++ · SP 82-85 ++

Year	Lev	Team	W	L	Sv	IP	K	ERA	WHIP	BF/G	OBA	H%	S%	xERA	Ctl	Dom	Cmd	hr/9	BPV
2003	Rk	Martinsville	1	0	1	21	25	5.55	1.90	8.3	232	32	71	4.97	9.4	10.7	1.1	0.9	71
2004	A-	Tri City	5	1	8	41	56	2.84	1.04	6.9	183	27	77	2.23	3.7	12.2	3.3	0.9	135
2005	A-	Lexington	6	7	3	90	94	2.70	1.10	7.7	204	27	77	2.38	3.4	9.4	2.8	0.6	111
2006	AA	Corpus Christi	8	5	15	87	131	3.10	1.11	6.2	196	30	77	2.70	3.8	13.5	3.5	1.0	140
2007	AAA	Round Rock	1	8	8	70	69	5.14	1.63	5.9	267	34	69	4.69	5.4	8.9	1.6	0.8	66

Base skills declined across board and was in no position to help HOU bullpen. Features a plus CB and solid velocity, but command reverted back to days of old and was more hittable. Will need to sequence pitches better and find some way to establish better command.

Evans, Dustin — SP — Atlanta
Thrws R **Age** 23 — 2006 (2-C) Georgia So — EXP MLB DEBUT: 2009 — POTENTIAL: #4 starter/setup reliever — **7D**

FB 88-95 ++++ · SL 81-84 +++ · CU +

Year	Lev	Team	W	L	Sv	IP	K	ERA	WHIP	BF/G	OBA	H%	S%	xERA	Ctl	Dom	Cmd	hr/9	BPV
2006	A-	Rome	2	2	0	40	25	2.91	1.19	20.2	246	29	74	2.84	2.5	5.6	2.3	0.2	80
2006	Rk	Danville	1	1	0	10	10	1.76	0.88	18.9	148	21	78	0.67	3.5	8.8	2.5	0.0	131
2007	A+	Myrtle Beach	2	10	0	99	72	4.72	1.47	20.3	284	32	70	4.78	3.2	6.5	2.1	1.0	51

Tall/athletic pitcher had a dismal season in a pitcher's park, being very hittable. Arm action is stiff, which hurts his attempt to change speeds and hold velocity. SL is a potential plus pitch and throws hard, but may be better off in relief due to stamina issues and inability to throw CU.

Evarts, Steven — SP — Atlanta
Thrws L **Age** 20 — 2006 (1-S) HS (FL) — EXP MLB DEBUT: 2010 — POTENTIAL: #3 starter — **8D**

FB 87-91 +++ · CT 84-86 +++ · SU ++ · CU 78-81 ++++

Year	Lev	Team	W	L	Sv	IP	K	ERA	WHIP	BF/G	OBA	H%	S%	xERA	Ctl	Dom	Cmd	hr/9	BPV
2006	Rk	GCL Braves	2	2	0	43	33	2.93	1.26	15.9	257	32	74	2.92	2.5	6.9	2.8	0.0	103
2007	Rk	Danville	4	0	0	37	34	1.95	0.89	17.2	217	29	76	1.48	1.0	8.3	8.5	0.0	240

Tall/projectable pitcher with advanced ability to add and subtract from FB, using CT and CU from a repeatable delivery. Demonstrates excellent command and keeps ball low, but strikeout rate is likely to decline with promotion. Will need to improve rotation of SU.

Farina, Alan — RP — Toronto
Thrws R **Age** 21 — 2007 (3) Clemson — EXP MLB DEBUT: 2009 — POTENTIAL: #4 starter — **7D**

FB 87-93 ++++ · SL 81-84 +++ · CB 72-75 +++ · CU 78-81 ++

Year	Lev	Team	W	L	Sv	IP	K	ERA	WHIP	BF/G	OBA	H%	S%	xERA	Ctl	Dom	Cmd	hr/9	BPV
2007	A-	Auburn	0	2	0	11	14	4.91	1.82	8.5	244	35	74	4.88	8.2	11.5	1.4	0.8	80

Vast repertoire and ability to mix pitches allowed him to notch strikeouts without a plus pitch. Strong/athletic frame keeps his velocity stable and high ¾ slot makes short stature less of an issue. Repeating delivery could help him achieve better command and make CU more effective.

Feliz, Neftali — SP — Texas
Thrws R **Age** 20 — 2005 FA (DR) — EXP MLB DEBUT: 2011 — POTENTIAL: #2 starter — **9E**

FB 90-96 ++++ · SL 82-84 +++ · CU 80-83 +

Year	Lev	Team	W	L	Sv	IP	K	ERA	WHIP	BF/G	OBA	H%	S%	xERA	Ctl	Dom	Cmd	hr/9	BPV
2006	Rk	GCL Braves	0	2	2	29	42	4.03	1.17	10.5	197	33	62	1.89	4.3	13.0	3.0	0.0	157
2007	A-	Spokane	0	2	0	15	27	3.60	1.67	8.4	235	42	83	4.70	7.2	16.2	2.3	1.2	116
2007	Rk	Danville	2	0	0	27	28	1.99	1.11	13.3	191	27	80	1.69	4.0	9.3	2.3	0.0	122

Flamethrower with easy velocity and plus pitch movement, allowing him to miss bats with ease. Likes to overuse FB as he lacks confidence in comps, but his SL can be plus pitch at times. Despite ability to throw strikes, he will need to be finer within strike zone as he moves up.

Fisher, Brent — SP — Kansas City
Thrws L **Age** 20 — 2005 (7) HS (AZ) — EXP MLB DEBUT: 2010 — POTENTIAL: #4 starter — **7C**

FB 87-91 +++ · CB +++ · CU ++

Year	Lev	Team	W	L	Sv	IP	K	ERA	WHIP	BF/G	OBA	H%	S%	xERA	Ctl	Dom	Cmd	hr/9	BPV
2005	Rk	AZL Royals	5	2	1	50	69	3.05	1.22	15.6	254	39	75	3.06	2.3	12.4	5.3	0.4	179
2006	Rk	AZL Royals	3	1	0	68	98	2.11	0.88	18.0	176	29	76	1.17	2.5	13.0	5.2	0.3	198
2006	Rk	Idaho Falls	0	0	1	4	9	2.25	0.50	13.3	151	30	100	1.73	0.0	20.3		2.3	79
2007	A-	Burlington	1	4	1	35	28	5.13	1.71	17.7	317	38	70	5.67	3.6	7.2	2.0	0.8	54

Overpowering pitcher with excellent pitch movement, command, and a deceptive overhand delivery. Keeps ball low with power sinker and drops CB for strikeouts. CU is still a work in progress and missed most of the season with an elbow injury that required rest instead of surgery.

Fister, Doug — SP — Seattle
Thrws R **Age** 24 — 2006 (7) Fresno St — EXP MLB DEBUT: 2009 — POTENTIAL: #5 starter — **6B**

FB 86-90 +++ · SL ++ · CB +++ · CU ++

Year	Lev	Team	W	L	Sv	IP	K	ERA	WHIP	BF/G	OBA	H%	S%	xERA	Ctl	Dom	Cmd	hr/9	BPV
2006	A-	Everett	3	5	4	40	35	2.25	1.15	7.9	237	30	82	2.80	2.5	7.9	3.2	0.5	108
2007	AA	W. Tennessee	7	8	0	131	85	4.60	1.44	23.2	297	33	70	4.85	2.2	5.8	2.7	1.0	58

Tall/athletic pitcher with outstanding G/F ratio and command which off-sets low velocity. Fluid arm action helps with movement, but doesn't repeat arm speed on CU or get around on his SL. Doesn't pitch deep into games, but that's more a function of performance than stamina.

Font, Wilmer — SP — Texas
Thrws R **Age** 18 — 2006 FA (DR) — EXP MLB DEBUT: 2012 — POTENTIAL: #2 starter — **8E**

FB 89-97 +++++ · CB + · CU ++

Year	Lev	Team	W	L	Sv	IP	K	ERA	WHIP	BF/G	OBA	H%	S%	xERA	Ctl	Dom	Cmd	hr/9	BPV
2007	Rk	AZL Rangers	2	3	0	45	61	4.58	1.44	13.7	243	37	67	3.52	4.8	12.1	2.5	0.4	121

Strong-framed pitcher with fluid arm action which produces easy velocity and ability to change speeds. FB may be best in organization and has the command to along with hit. CB could stand to be tighter in its rotation and is still figuring-out how to use his entire repertoire.

Frieri, Ernesto — SP — San Diego
Thrws R **Age** 22 — 2004 FA (Columbia) — EXP MLB DEBUT: 2009 — POTENTIAL: Setup reliever — **7D**

FB 87-92 ++++ · SL 84-87 +++ · CB 78-79 +++ · CU 77-81 ++

Year	Lev	Team	W	L	Sv	IP	K	ERA	WHIP	BF/G	OBA	H%	S%	xERA	Ctl	Dom	Cmd	hr/9	BPV
2006	A-	Fort Wayne	0	0	0	1	1	9.00	6.00	8.8	262	35	83	14.92	45.0	9.0	0.2	0.0	61
2006	A-	Eugene	3	3	2	37	38	3.87	1.24	5.6	228	30	70	3.15	3.6	9.2	2.5	0.7	96
2006	A+	Lake Elsinore	0	0	0	6	4	6.00	1.83	14.0	321	38	64	5.33	4.5	6.0	1.3	0.0	55
2007	A-	Fort Wayne	1	2	0	64	65	2.66	1.11	6.3	210	27	78	2.44	3.2	9.1	2.8	0.6	110
2007	A+	Lake Elsinore	1	0	1	21	27	1.27	0.80	5.9	155	23	88	0.91	2.5	11.5	4.5	0.4	174

Pitched well in setup role where he could focus on lively FB and getting hitters to chase breaking pitches. Command was more consistent and achieves balance between strikeouts and groundball outs. Repeating delivery and developing CU could give him a more responsible role.

Fruto, Emiliano — RP — Arizona
Thrws R **Age** 24 — 2000 FA (Columbia) — EXP MLB DEBUT: 2006 — POTENTIAL: Setup reliever — **7C**

FB 86-91 ++++ · SL 80-82 +++ · CB 77-79 ++ · CU 76-79 +++

Year	Lev	Team	W	L	Sv	IP	K	ERA	WHIP	BF/G	OBA	H%	S%	xERA	Ctl	Dom	Cmd	hr/9	BPV
2005	AA	San Antonio	2	3	12	66	62	2.58	1.18	6.6	231	29	82	3.13	3.0	8.6	2.9	0.8	96
2005	AAA	Tacoma	1	2	0	11	12	13.09	2.00	5.9	262	34	29	5.60	9.0	9.8	1.1	0.8	60
2006	AAA	Tacoma	1	3	10	45	55	3.19	1.20	6.5	206	31	72	2.27	4.2	11.0	2.6	0.2	129
2006	MLB	Seattle	2	2	1	36	34	5.50	1.61	6.9	251	31	67	4.65	6.0	8.5	1.4	1.0	56
2007	AAA	Col/Tuc	3	10	0	98	82	4.95	1.58	18.0	237	29	68	3.98	6.3	7.5	1.2	0.6	61

Pitched in a variety of roles and dealt with decreased velocity and the lesser base skills that followed it. FB does possess late life and goes to his SL as his primary secondary pitch. Uses multiple arm angles on purpose, providing deception, but at the cost of command.

Furbush, Charlie — SP — Detroit
Thrws L **Age** 22 — 2007 (4) LSU — EXP MLB DEBUT: 2009 — POTENTIAL: #4 starter — **7C**

FB 86-92 +++ · CB 71-74 +++ · CU 79-82 ++

Year	Lev	Team	W	L	Sv	IP	K	ERA	WHIP	BF/G	OBA	H%	S%	xERA	Ctl	Dom	Cmd	hr/9	BPV
2007	Rk	GCL Tigers	2	0	0	16	23	1.13	0.88	14.8	196	21	133	3.77	1.7	12.9	7.7	2.8	170

Successful collegiate starter who adapted well to professional baseball. Showed excellent base skills and sets up pitches well, adding to his effectiveness. Arm action gives movement to FB and SU. Presents a deceptive delivery, but doesn't repeat arm speed on CU.

PITCHERS

Galarraga,Armando — SP — Texas

EXP MLB DEBUT: 2007 | POTENTIAL: #4 starter | 7B

Thrws R Age 26
1999 FA (Venezuela)
88-94 FB ++++
82-86 SL +++
79-82 CU +

Year	Lev	Team	W	L	Sv	IP	K	ERA	WHIP	BF/G	OBA	H%	S%	xERA	Ctl	Dom	Cmd	hr/9	BPV
2006	AA	Frisco	1	6	0	41	38	5.71	1.71	20.6	330	40	68	6.17	2.9	8.3	2.9	1.1	67
2006	Rk	AZL Rangers	0	2	0	16	16	3.35	1.49	11.6	284	38	75	3.87	3.4	8.9	2.7	0.0	108
2007	AA	Frisco	9	6	0	127	114	4.03	1.33	22.9	254	31	72	3.98	3.3	8.1	2.4	1.0	74
2007	AAA	Okl City	2	2	0	24	21	4.83	1.40	25.6	252	32	64	3.57	4.1	7.8	1.9	0.4	80
2007	MLB	Texas	0	0	0	8	6	6.59	1.83	12.7	257	26	69	6.43	7.7	6.6	0.9	2.2	-5

Athletic pitcher with fluid arm action which provides above average movement to FB and SL. Struggles to repeat delivery giving him a below average CU and overuses SL, but command remains solid. Showed no ill-effects from TJS in 2006 and has sleeper potential.

Gallagher,Nolan — SP — Seattle

EXP MLB DEBUT: 2009 | POTENTIAL: #4 starter | 7D

Thrws R Age 22
2007 (4) Stanford
86-90 FB +++
73-77 CB +++
77-79 CU +++

Year	Lev	Team	W	L	Sv	IP	K	ERA	WHIP	BF/G	OBA	H%	S%	xERA	Ctl	Dom	Cmd	hr/9	BPV
2007	A-	Wisconsin	0	2	0	19	15	4.69	1.93	22.8	298	34	79	6.52	6.6	7.0	1.1	1.4	18
2007	A-	Everett	1	1	0	32	24	0.84	0.78	19.2	174	20	96	1.24	1.7	6.8	4.0	0.6	128

Strong/athletic pitcher with three average to above pitches and a repeatable ¾ delivery that provides deception. Velocity fluctuated throughout season, barely hitting 88 MPH by season's end, but can pitch without best stuff. Strikeouts will be tough to get and needs to establish FB.

Gallagher,Sean — SP — Chicago (N)

EXP MLB DEBUT: 2007 | POTENTIAL: #4 starter | 7B

Thrws R Age 22
2004 (12) HS (FL)
87-93 FB +++
70-72 CB +++
78-83 CU +++

Year	Lev	Team	W	L	Sv	IP	K	ERA	WHIP	BF/G	OBA	H%	S%	xERA	Ctl	Dom	Cmd	hr/9	BPV
2006	A+	Daytona	4	0	0	78	80	2.30	1.23	24.3	254	33	84	3.33	2.4	9.2	3.8	0.6	122
2006	AA	W. Tennessee	7	5	0	86	91	2.72	1.50	24.8	234	32	82	3.59	5.7	9.5	1.7	0.4	88
2007	AA	Tennessee	7	2	0	61	54	3.39	1.28	22.7	239	30	73	3.14	3.5	8.0	2.3	0.4	89
2007	AAA	Iowa	3	1	0	40	37	2.69	1.14	19.9	225	30	76	2.42	2.9	8.3	2.8	0.2	113
2007	MLB	Chicago (N)	0	0	1	14	5	8.87	2.18	8.9	322	31	61	8.04	7.6	3.2	0.4	1.9	-39

Strong/durable pitcher with three average to above pitches and ability to get hitters out without best stuff. Keeps ball down, prevents the long ball, and has good FB command, keeping hitters off-balance by throwing all three pitches at any time. Improved velocity, but CB regressed.

Garceau,Shaun — SP — St. Louis

EXP MLB DEBUT: 2010 | POTENTIAL: #5 starter | 7D

Thrws R Age 20
2005 (20) HS (FL)
88-93 FB +++
70-73 CB +++
77-79 CU ++

Year	Lev	Team	W	L	Sv	IP	K	ERA	WHIP	BF/G	OBA	H%	S%	xERA	Ctl	Dom	Cmd	hr/9	BPV
2005	Rk	Johnson City	2	7	0	44	42	7.74	1.76	16.9	306	37	56	6.24	4.7	8.6	1.8	1.4	41
2007	A-	Quad Cities	8	11	0	111	110	4.86	1.63	16.5	293	36	73	5.50	4.1	8.9	2.2	1.2	59

Athletic/projectable pitcher recovered well from a staph infection in 2006. Possesses good velocity and power CB which elicits strikeouts, and throws strikes. Struggles to repeat delivery which hinders CU and needs to be finer within strike zone to prevent high oppBA.

Garcia,Christian — SP — New York (A)

EXP MLB DEBUT: 2010 | POTENTIAL: #4 starter | 8D

Thrws R Age 21
2004 (3) HS (FL)
87-94 FB ++++
76-80 CB +++
79-82 CU ++

Year	Lev	Team	W	L	Sv	IP	K	ERA	WHIP	BF/G	OBA	H%	S%	xERA	Ctl	Dom	Cmd	hr/9	BPV
2004	Rk	GCL Yankees	3	4	0	38	47	2.84	1.13	11.6	195	29	74	2.01	4.0	11.1	2.8	0.2	134
2005	A-	Charleston	5	6	0	106	103	3.91	1.46	21.6	254	34	72	3.62	4.5	8.7	1.9	0.3	90
2005	Rk	GCL Yankees	0	0	0	6	7	4.50	1.50	13.0	191	29	67	2.68	7.5	10.5	1.4	0.0	109
2006	A-	Charleston	2	3	0	41	45	3.50	1.19	23.6	242	33	70	2.92	2.6	9.8	3.8	0.4	131
2006	Rk	GCL Yankees	0	1	0	11	15	9.73	1.71	10.1	324	46	39	5.77	3.2	12.2	3.8	0.8	118

Projectable ar, but has difficulty staying healthy, missing 2007 season recovering from elbow surgery. Has outstanding CB along with easy velocity from a smooth arm action. Repeating delivery and changing speeds are his biggest hurdles following the health of his arm.

Garcia,Edgar — SP — Philadelphia

EXP MLB DEBUT: 2009 | POTENTIAL: #4 starter | 7C

Thrws R Age 20
2004 FA (DR)
89-94 FB ++++
78-80 CB +++
CU ++

Year	Lev	Team	W	L	Sv	IP	K	ERA	WHIP	BF/G	OBA	H%	S%	xERA	Ctl	Dom	Cmd	hr/9	BPV
2005	Rk	GCL Phillies	4	4	0	55	42	3.59	1.38	23.2	288	34	75	4.27	2.1	6.8	3.2	0.7	87
2006	A-	Batavia	3	5	0	66	46	3.00	1.09	21.5	250	29	75	3.04	1.4	6.3	4.6	0.7	119
2007	A-	Lakewood	4	9	0	113	83	4.13	1.33	23.5	272	32	70	4.06	2.5	6.6	2.6	0.8	71
2007	A-	Williamsport	1	0	0	8	11	2.22	0.99	15.4	208	34	75	1.56	2.2	12.2	5.5	0.0	202

Strong armed pitcher who is learning to pitch. Possesses electric FB and ability to get strikeout, but tends to overthrow, reducing movement. CB graduated to an average pitch, showing good depth, but lacks ability to change speeds due to not repeating delivery consistently.

Garcia,Harvey — RP — Florida

EXP MLB DEBUT: 2007 | POTENTIAL: Setup reliever | 7C

Thrws R Age 24
2000 FA (Venezuela)
89-96 FB ++++
80-83 CB +++
81-83 CU +

Year	Lev	Team	W	L	Sv	IP	K	ERA	WHIP	BF/G	OBA	H%	S%	xERA	Ctl	Dom	Cmd	hr/9	BPV
2005	AA	Greenville	3	5	6	44	54	2.04	1.52	6.0	282	39	89	4.46	3.7	11.0	3.0	0.6	109
2006	A+	Jupiter	0	7	20	63	81	2.99	1.36	4.9	233	34	80	3.48	4.6	11.5	2.5	0.7	109
2007	AA	Carolina	2	2	0	24	25	4.11	1.58	5.9	236	30	77	4.48	6.3	9.3	1.5	1.1	61
2007	AAA	Albuquerque	4	1	1	48	45	6.19	1.69	5.2	304	36	67	6.25	4.1	8.4	2.0	1.7	37
2007	MLB	Florida	0	1	0	12	15	4.46	1.74	6.9	291	37	83	6.66	5.2	11.2	2.1	2.2	42

Thin/athletic reliever possesses easy velocity and plus FB movement from a quick arm action. Command is inconsistent, but misses bats by getting hitters to chase SL, which he added in lieu of his CB. Throws with effort which makes move to bullpen more palatable.

Garcia,Jaime — SP — St. Louis

EXP MLB DEBUT: 2009 | POTENTIAL: #3 starter | 8B

Thrws L Age 21
2005 (22) HS (TX)
87-92 FB +++
74-78 CB ++++
79-81 CU ++

Year	Lev	Team	W	L	Sv	IP	K	ERA	WHIP	BF/G	OBA	H%	S%	xERA	Ctl	Dom	Cmd	hr/9	BPV
2006	A-	Quad City	5	4	0	77	80	2.91	1.10	23.3	235	32	71	2.33	2.1	9.3	4.4	0.1	154
2006	A+	Palm Beach	4	3	0	60	40	3.90	1.15	26.5	252	30	64	2.87	1.8	6.0	3.3	0.3	102
2007	AA	Springfield	5	9	0	103	97	3.75	1.34	23.8	242	29	77	4.06	3.9	8.5	2.2	1.2	66

Athletic pitcher with easy velocity, plus CB, and outstanding command. Pitches efficiently and is adept at getting strikeout and keeping ball low. Light-frame attenuates stamina issues as he was shut-down in July after experiencing a strained elbow ligament.

Garcia,Jose — SP — Oakland

EXP MLB DEBUT: 2006 | POTENTIAL: #4 starter | 8D

Thrws R Age 23
2001 FA (DR)
87-93 FB ++++
73-76 SL +++
70-71 CB ++
76-77 CU +++

Year	Lev	Team	W	L	Sv	IP	K	ERA	WHIP	BF/G	OBA	H%	S%	xERA	Ctl	Dom	Cmd	hr/9	BPV
2005	A-	Greensboro	3	0	0	28	39	1.29	0.54	18.8	122	20	79	0.00	1.3	12.5	9.8	0.3	301
2006	A+	Jupiter	6	2	1	78	71	1.96	0.99	22.8	217	28	81	2.04	1.8	8.2	4.4	0.3	144
2006	AA	Carolina	6	7	0	84	87	3.42	1.22	24.3	247	31	76	3.68	2.7	9.3	3.5	1.1	102
2006	AAA	Albuquerque	0	1	0	4	5	11.25	2.25	20.3	307	44	44	6.11	9.0	11.3	1.3	0.0	87
2007																			

Missed 2007 season with TJS in March. Wiry athlete who derives plus pitch movement and easy velocity from smooth arm action and whip-like delivery. Misses bats easily and commands plate. Will need to tighten CB and build up arm strength to improve stamina.

Garrison,Steve — SP — San Diego

EXP MLB DEBUT: 2010 | POTENTIAL: #5 starter | 7C

Thrws L Age 21
2006 (10) HS (NJ)
86-90 FB +++
72-76 CB ++
77-80 CU +++

Year	Lev	Team	W	L	Sv	IP	K	ERA	WHIP	BF/G	OBA	H%	S%	xERA	Ctl	Dom	Cmd	hr/9	BPV
2005	Rk	AZL Brewers	2	2	2	34	28	2.89	1.29	12.8	288	36	75	3.43	1.3	7.4	5.6	0.0	159
2006	A-	West Virginia	7	6	0	88	77	3.47	1.22	21.0	257	31	76	3.79	2.2	7.9	3.5	1.0	94
2007	A+	LE/BC	10	7	0	146	102	3.26	1.17	21.6	249	29	72	3.07	2.1	6.3	3.0	0.5	91

Athletic pitcher with ability to out-smart hitters and plus command. Changes speeds and repeats delivery, but lacks velocity and CB movement, which paints him in a corner when behind. Keeps ball low and yields few homers, which could give him a chance as a backend starter.

Gearrin,Cory — SP — Atlanta

EXP MLB DEBUT: 2009 | POTENTIAL: Setup reliever | 7D

Thrws R Age 22
2007 (4) Mercer
86-90 FB +++
76-79 SL +++

Year	Lev	Team	W	L	Sv	IP	K	ERA	WHIP	BF/G	OBA	H%	S%	xERA	Ctl	Dom	Cmd	hr/9	BPV
2007	Rk	Danville	1	1	0	26	37	0.34	1.42	6.1	222	18	150	7.02	5.5	12.8	2.3	4.5	1

Sidearm, college reliever who is adept at missing bats and is tough on RH batters. Velocity is average, but gets late sinking movement to FB, and SL sweeps across zone. Pitches with effort and has recoil at finish, but his durability has yet to be affected.

Geer,Josh — SP — San Diego

EXP MLB DEBUT: 2008 | POTENTIAL: #5 starter | 6A

Thrws R Age 25
2005 (3) Rice
86-90 FB +++
74-76 CB +++
77-80 CU +++

Year	Lev	Team	W	L	Sv	IP	K	ERA	WHIP	BF/G	OBA	H%	S%	xERA	Ctl	Dom	Cmd	hr/9	BPV
2005	A-	Eugene	3	1	0	31	13	3.75	1.25	18.1	285	29	73	6.85	1.2	3.8	3.3	1.4	46
2006	A-	Fort Wayne	6	2	0	72	46	3.12	1.18	24.1	261	30	73	5.72	1.6	5.7	3.5	0.4	100
2006	A+	Lake Elsinore	7	4	0	89	56	4.69	1.48	25.5	316	36	66	9.03	1.6	5.7	3.5	0.7	78
2007	AA	San Antonio	16	6	0	171	102	3.20	1.11	25.9	253	33	72	3.21	1.4	5.4	3.8	0.3	109
2007	AAA	Portland	1	0	0	6	6	3.00	1.17	23.9	262	32	72	3.00	1.5	9.0	6.0	0.0	93

TL Pitcher of the Year, leading league in ERA and wins. Features plus command and ability to change speeds, but lost ability to miss bats. Dropped SL from arsenal and picked-up CB. Upside is limited, but can survive if he keeps ball down and mixes pitches.

Gervacio,Samuel — RP — Houston

EXP MLB DEBUT: 2008 | POTENTIAL: Setup reliever | 7C

Thrws R Age 23
2002 FA (DR)
85-89 FB ++
CB ++
77-79 SP ++++

Year	Lev	Team	W	L	Sv	IP	K	ERA	WHIP	BF/G	OBA	H%	S%	xERA	Ctl	Dom	Cmd	hr/9	BPV
2005	Rk	Greenville	3	2	8	33	53	2.71	0.90	5.9	204	36	69	1.54	1.6	14.4	8.8	0.3	278
2005	A-	Lexington	1	0	0	9	11	0.99	0.55	6.1	135	21	80	0.00	1.0	10.9	11.0	0.0	324
2006	A-	Lexington	7	5	10	83	89	2.49	1.03	6.8	198	26	81	2.40	3.0	9.6	3.2	0.9	114
2007	A+	Salem	1	3	18	55	80	2.45	1.03	5.4	213	35	75	1.88	2.5	13.1	5.3	0.2	198
2007	AA	Corpus Christi	3	2	0	22	24	2.03	1.17	6.8	193	27	84	2.26	4.5	9.7	2.2	0.4	108

Short/light-framed reliever with a plus SPL that moves violently downward, giving him ability to notch strikeouts and prevent hits. Needs to establish FB and use it more in pressure situations. Will need to keep ball down as he lacks velocity to pitch in middle of strike zone.

Gibson,Glenn — SP — Tampa Bay

EXP MLB DEBUT: 2011 | POTENTIAL: #4 starter | 8C

Thrws L Age 20
2006 (4) HS (NY)
85-90 FB +++
75-77 CB ++
76-79 CU ++++

Year	Lev	Team	W	L	Sv	IP	K	ERA	WHIP	BF/G	OBA	H%	S%	xERA	Ctl	Dom	Cmd	hr/9	BPV
2006	A-	Vermont	0	0	0	6	7	0.00	0.33	6.3	106	17	100	0.00	0.0	10.5		0.0	97
2007	A-	Vermont	4	3	0	58	58	3.10	1.07	18.8	223	29	71	2.42	2.3	9.0	3.9	0.5	132

Tall/thin pitcher who brings three plus skills (groundball ability, command, and changing speeds) to the table. FB isn't overpowering, but his smooth arm action gives him late life and CB bite. Performance has been solid and just needs to develop more stamina.

Ginley,Kyle — SP — Toronto

EXP MLB DEBUT: 2010 | POTENTIAL: #3 starter | 8D

Thrws R Age 21
2006 (17) St. Petersburg JC
88-94 FB ++++
81-84 SL ++
78-81 CU ++

Year	Lev	Team	W	L	Sv	IP	K	ERA	WHIP	BF/G	OBA	H%	S%	xERA	Ctl	Dom	Cmd	hr/9	BPV
2006	A-	Auburn	1	0	0	10	6	0.00	1.00	19.1	151	18	100	1.02	4.5	5.4	1.2	0.0	82
2006	Rk	Pulaski	1	1	0	26	42	4.81	1.26	13.4	229	37	63	3.46	3.8	14.4	3.8	1.0	145
2007	A-	Lansing	7	6	0	121	129	4.75	1.51	20.2	294	38	69	4.82	3.0	9.6	3.1	0.8	95

Projectable pitcher with power sinker that generates groundball outs and strikeouts. Throws strikes, but could have better command within strike zone. Comps lag severely and really only trusts FB when behind which made him hittable throughout the season.

Gonzalez,Giovanny — SP — Chicago (A)

EXP MLB DEBUT: 2008 | POTENTIAL: #2 starter | 8B

Thrws L Age 22
2004 (1-S) HS (FL)
85-92 FB ++++
75-80 CB ++++
75-81 CU +++

Year	Lev	Team	W	L	Sv	IP	K	ERA	WHIP	BF/G	OBA	H%	S%	xERA	Ctl	Dom	Cmd	hr/9	BPV
2004	A-	Kannapolis	1	1	0	32	27	3.03	1.34	22.3	248	32	72	3.11	3.6	7.5	2.1	0.3	51
2005	A-	Kannapolis	5	3	0	57	84	1.89	1.01	19.9	182	30	84	1.77	3.5	13.2	3.8	0.5	164
2005	A+	Win-Salem	8	3	0	73	79	3.57	1.18	22.5	228	31	70	2.89	3.1	9.7	3.2	0.6	116
2006	AA	Reading	7	12	0	154	166	4.67	1.43	24.3	244	30	72	4.47	4.7	9.7	2.0	1.4	65
2007	AA	Birmingham	9	7	0	150	185	3.18	1.15	22.1	215	33	69	3.94	3.4	11.1	3.2	0.6	94

Small/athletic pitcher improved in every aspect of pitching and led minors with 185 strikeouts. CB is a plus pitch and gains deception from his high leg kick, making his FB and CU play-up. Pitched over 150 innings for second straight year, alleviating stamina concern.

Graham,Connor — SP — Colorado

EXP MLB DEBUT: 2009 | POTENTIAL: #4 starter | 7D

Thrws R Age 22
2007 (5) Miami-OH
88-94 FB ++++
74-77 SL ++
77-80 SP +++

Year	Lev	Team	W	L	Sv	IP	K	ERA	WHIP	BF/G	OBA	H%	S%	xERA	Ctl	Dom	Cmd	hr/9	BPV
2007	A-	Tri-City	1	0	0	19	18	2.37	1.53	13.8	300	37	89	5.10	2.8	8.5	3.0	0.9	81

Tall/projectable pitcher with arm strength and easy velocity. Strikeout rate is strong and gets tremendous movement to SPL which drops out of the zone. Placement of landing foot is inconsistent which affects command and will need to tighten rotation and increase velocity of SL.

Green,Matt — SP — Arizona

EXP MLB DEBUT: 2008 | POTENTIAL: #5 starter/setup reliever | 6C

Thrws R Age 26
2005 (2) Lou-Monroe
89-93 FB ++++
81-83 SL +++
CU ++

Year	Lev	Team	W	L	Sv	IP	K	ERA	WHIP	BF/G	OBA	H%	S%	xERA	Ctl	Dom	Cmd	hr/9	BPV
2005	Rk	Missoula	4	3	0	60	59	5.55	1.72	18.1	313	39	68	5.72	3.9	8.9	2.3	0.9	66
2006	A+	Lancaster	5	12	0	136	96	5.55	1.72	22.9	323	36	69	6.18	3.4	6.3	1.9	1.2	32
2007	AA	Mobile	12	6	0	148	128	3.95	1.39	22.3	266	32	74	4.23	3.3	7.8	2.3	0.9	70

Tall/athletic pitcher with smooth arm action that leads to movement to FB and SL. Throws strikes, but needs better command within strike zone, and improved strikeout rate. Doesn't use CU that much and will need that pitch to survive upper levels as a starter.

Green,Nick — SP — Los Angeles (A)

EXP MLB DEBUT: 2008 | POTENTIAL: #5 starter | 6B

Thrws R Age 23
2004 (35) Darton JC
87-91 FB +++
75-78 CB ++
76-80 CU ++++

Year	Lev	Team	W	L	Sv	IP	K	ERA	WHIP	BF/G	OBA	H%	S%	xERA	Ctl	Dom	Cmd	hr/9	BPV
2004	Rk	Provo	4	3	0	51	44	4.05	1.49	12.9	280	34	74	4.47	3.5	7.7	2.2	0.7	71
2005	A-	Cedar Rapids	3	3	2	100	74	3.59	1.09	15.1	252	29	70	3.35	1.3	6.6	5.3	1.0	126
2006	A+	Rancho Cuc.	5	3	0	65	57	4.15	1.48	25.4	296	35	76	5.19	2.6	7.9	3.0	1.2	69
2006	AA	Arkansas	8	5	0	112	78	4.42	1.20	26.5	265	28	71	4.64	1.7	6.3	3.7	1.8	62
2007	AA	Arkansas	10	8	0	178	107	3.69	1.10	24.9	246	27	69	3.20	1.6	5.4	3.3	0.9	83

Advanced ability to change speeds, induce groundball outs, and command plate. Repeats delivery effectively, providing deception, and was less hittable than his stuff would indicate. Strikeout rate remains low and needs to get on-top of CB to improve effectiveness.

Griffin,Dan — SP — San Francisco

EXP MLB DEBUT: 2009 | POTENTIAL: #4 starter | 7C

Thrws R Age 23
2005 (5) Niagara
87-93 FB ++++
73-76 CB +++
79-82 CU ++

Year	Lev	Team	W	L	Sv	IP	K	ERA	WHIP	BF/G	OBA	H%	S%	xERA	Ctl	Dom	Cmd	hr/9	BPV
2005	A-	Salem-Keizer	3	2	0	37	49	2.42	1.21	18.7	239	36	80	2.74	2.9	11.9	4.1	0.2	157
2005	Rk	AZL Giants	0	0	0	12	20	0.75	1.25	12.2	210	39	93	2.22	4.5	15.0	3.3	0.0	173
2006	A-	Augusta	5	5	0	72	78	4.49	1.54	19.7	277	36	72	4.70	4.1	9.7	2.4	0.9	81
2007	A-	Augusta	6	6	1	79	67	4.33	1.44	13.0	285	34	71	4.53	2.8	7.6	2.7	0.8	76

Tall/projectable pitcher with excellent pitch movement, owing to a whip-like arm action. FB bores into RH batters and CB is strong enough to get strikeouts. Repeats delivery, giving him solid command, but doesn't change speeds well which may mean a move to relief.

Griffith,Nevin — SP — Chicago (A)

EXP MLB DEBUT: 2011 | POTENTIAL: #3 starter | 8E

Thrws R Age 19
2007 (2) HS (FL)
88-94 FB ++++
79-83 SL +++
75-80 CB +++
80-82 CU +

Year	Lev	Team	W	L	Sv	IP	K	ERA	WHIP	BF/G	OBA	H%	S%	xERA	Ctl	Dom	Cmd	hr/9	BPV
2007	Rk	Bristol	0	0	0	8	7	5.49	2.44	5.4	377	46	75	7.83	6.6	7.7	1.2	0.0	50

Projectable arm with loose arm action that gives him movement to FB and both breaking pitches. Mixes pitches well and throws with a purpose. Gets strikeouts and groundball outs, but needs better command. Lacks deception with delivery and tends to show baseball at release.

Gronkiewicz,Lee — RP — Boston

EXP MLB DEBUT: 2007 | POTENTIAL: Setup reliever | 6B

Thrws R Age 29
2001 NDFA So Carolina
87-90 FB +++
75-76 SL +++
68-70 CB +++
78-80 CU ++

Year	Lev	Team	W	L	Sv	IP	K	ERA	WHIP	BF/G	OBA	H%	S%	xERA	Ctl	Dom	Cmd	hr/9	BPV
2005	AAA	Syracuse	0	1	6	28	26	2.24	1.21	4.0	209	25	87	3.08	4.2	8.3	2.0	1.0	76
2006	AAA	Syracuse	2	3	17	44	33	3.27	1.25	4.4	275	32	76	3.92	1.6	6.8	4.1	0.8	103
2007	AA	New Hamp.	3	2	11	30	37	1.80	1.17	5.0	268	37	91	3.65	1.2	11.1	9.3	0.9	235
2007	AAA	Syracuse	3	1	2	44	46	2.85	1.00	7.3	234	30	75	2.69	1.2	9.4	7.7	0.8	201
2007	MLB	Toronto	0	0	0	4	2	2.25	1.00	15.3	151	10	100	3.15	4.5	4.5	1.0	2.3	5

Light-framed reliever works effectively to RH batters with a solid FB/CT/CB trio. Keeps ball low and command is impeccable. Resiliency of arm is one of his strengths and needs to be given an opportunity based on his stuff and consistent performance.

Guerra, Deolis — SP — New York (N)

EXP MLB DEBUT: 2010 | POTENTIAL: #3 starter | 9D

Thrws R Age 19
2005 FA (Venezuela)
87-92 FB +++
74-75 CB ++
78-80 CU +++

Year	Lev	Team	W	L	Sv	IP	K	ERA	WHIP	BF/G	OBA	H%	S%	xERA	Ctl	Dom	Cmd	hr/9	BPV
2006	A-	Hagerstown	6	7	0	81	64	2.22	1.18	19.1	205	25	82	2.38	4.1	7.1	1.7	0.3	83
2006	A+	St. Lucie	1	1	0	7	5	6.34	2.11	17.5	310	35	71	7.05	7.6	6.3	0.8	1.3	10
2007	A+	St. Lucie	2	6	0	89	66	4.04	1.18	17.0	241	28	68	3.36	2.5	6.7	2.6	0.9	75

Tall pitcher with downward plane and sinking action to pitches. Improved his command and already is accomplished at changing speeds. Reports of him hitting 94 MPH were exaggerated, but is projectable. Will need to slow-down delivery, tighten CB, and improve stamina.

Guevara, Carlos — RP — San Diego

EXP MLB DEBUT: 2008 | POTENTIAL: Situational reliever | 6B

Thrws R Age 26
2003 (7) St. Mary's
86-89 FB ++
77-79 SC ++++
CB +++

Year	Lev	Team	W	L	Sv	IP	K	ERA	WHIP	BF/G	OBA	H%	S%	xERA	Ctl	Dom	Cmd	hr/9	BPV
2003	A-	Dayton	0	1	0	39	39	3.45	1.30	13.4	251	32	77	3.81	3.2	9.0	2.8	0.9	89
2004	A-	Dayton	3	4	9	56	90	2.88	1.26	5.2	229	37	82	3.39	3.8	14.4	3.8	1.0	146
2005	A+	Sarasota	4	3	14	51	65	2.47	1.04	4.5	213	32	76	2.09	2.5	11.4	4.6	0.4	168
2006	AA	Chattanooga	2	3	1	77	89	3.74	1.31	6.5	254	35	73	3.63	3.2	10.4	3.3	0.7	115
2007	AA	Chattanooga	1	2	16	62	87	2.32	1.19	4.9	226	35	83	2.84	3.3	12.6	3.8	0.6	148

Small/light-framed reliever is difficult to hit, nailing hitters with a plus screwball and demonstrating pinpoint command. CB is a solid pitch and though he doesn't throw hard, he keeps the ball down and consistently posts outstanding strikeout rate.

Gunderson, Kevin — RP — Atlanta

EXP MLB DEBUT: 2008 | POTENTIAL: Situational reliever | 7C

Thrws L Age 23
2006 (5) Oregon St
85-90 FB +++
75-77 SL +++

Year	Lev	Team	W	L	Sv	IP	K	ERA	WHIP	BF/G	OBA	H%	S%	xERA	Ctl	Dom	Cmd	hr/9	BPV
2006	A-	Rome	4	0	3	24	21	1.13	0.83	6.3	191	24	89	1.37	1.5	7.9	5.3	0.4	163
2006	Rk	Danville	0	0	0	1	0	0.00	0.00	2.8	0	0		0.00	0.0	0.0	0.0	0.0	55
2007	A+	Myrtle Beach	4	5	7	52	47	3.10	1.57	5.2	257	32	81	4.19	5.3	8.1	1.5	0.5	68
2007	AA	Mississippi	0	0	0	4	0	2.25	2.50	10.6	415	41	90	8.84	4.5	0.0	0.0	0.0	-28

Short/athletic pitcher with a deceptive low ¾ delivery that makes him tough on LH batters. Lacks velocity, but pitches have late downward movement and can bury hitters with his SL. Likes to command inside part of plate and arm has proved resilient in back-to-back outings.

Gutierrez, Juan — SP — Arizona

EXP MLB DEBUT: 2007 | POTENTIAL: #4 starter | 8C

Thrws R Age 24
2000 FA (Venezuela)
88-94 FB ++++
72-77 CB +++
78-82 CU ++

Year	Lev	Team	W	L	Sv	IP	K	ERA	WHIP	BF/G	OBA	H%	S%	xERA	Ctl	Dom	Cmd	hr/9	BPV
2005	A-	Lexington	9	5	0	120	100	3.22	1.24	22.2	238	29	76	3.32	3.2	7.5	2.3	0.7	79
2005	A+	Salem	1	1	0	12	9	3.00	1.50	17.3	228	27	82	3.86	6.0	6.8	1.1	0.8	51
2006	AA	Corpus Christi	8	4	0	103	106	3.05	1.24	21.0	244	31	79	3.50	3.0	9.2	3.1	0.9	101
2007	AAA	Round Rock	5	10	0	156	108	4.15	1.39	25.3	259	29	73	4.22	3.6	6.2	1.7	1.0	47
2007	MLB	Houston	1	1	0	21	16	5.97	1.47	12.9	296	34	61	5.21	2.6	6.8	2.7	1.3	54

Strong-framed pitcher with a durable arm who uses all three pitches, striking a balance between pitching to contact and getting strikeouts. Establishes FB and will to use CB off the plate. Needs to repeat ¾ slot and arm speed on his CU, which will be the final piece of the puzzle.

Haeger, Charles — SP — Chicago (A)

EXP MLB DEBUT: 2006 | POTENTIAL: #5 starter | 7D

Thrws R Age 24
2001 (25) HS (MI)
81-86 CT ++
69-74 KN +++
79-81 SL +

Year	Lev	Team	W	L	Sv	IP	K	ERA	WHIP	BF/G	OBA	H%	S%	xERA	Ctl	Dom	Cmd	hr/9	BPV
2005	AA	Birmingham	6	3	0	85	48	3.80	1.51	28.4	259	30	73	3.71	4.8	5.1	1.1	0.1	53
2006	AAA	Charlotte	14	6	0	170	130	3.07	1.30	26.9	230	28	77	3.12	4.1	6.9	1.7	0.5	71
2006	MLB	Chicago (A)	1	1	1	18	19	3.48	1.38	10.9	190	27	72	2.38	6.5	9.4	1.5	0.0	104
2007	AAA	Charlotte	5	16	0	147	126	4.10	1.39	25.8	250	30	73	4.07	4.1	7.7	1.9	1.0	61
2007	MLB	Chicago (A)	0	1	0	11	1	7.30	2.25	7.0	352	32	73	9.25	6.5	0.8	0.1	2.4	-81

Most advanced knuckle-ball pitcher in last decade, but performances fluctuate from outing to outings. Throws 90% knuckle-balls, but will mix-in an occasional CT and SL. Missed more bats in 2007, but command slipped slightly. CHW will have to catch him at the right moment.

Hagadone, Nick — SP — Boston

EXP MLB DEBUT: 2009 | POTENTIAL: #3 starter | 8C

Thrws L Age 22
2007 (1-S) Washington
88-95 FB ++++
82-85 SL +++
79-82 CU ++

Year	Lev	Team	W	L	Sv	IP	K	ERA	WHIP	BF/G	OBA	H%	S%	xERA	Ctl	Dom	Cmd	hr/9	BPV
2007	A-	Lowell	0	1	0	24	33	1.87	0.91	9.0	171	27	81	1.30	3.0	12.3	4.1	0.4	170

Polished collegiate who uses command, a deceptive delivery, and an aggressive approach to get hitters out. He throws hard and can get strikeouts with SL, but his CU lags behind. Strong frame and arm strength give him durability, but lacks fluidity in his delivery.

Haigwood, Daniel — SP — Boston

EXP MLB DEBUT: 2008 | POTENTIAL: #5 starter | 6C

Thrws L Age 24
2002 (16) HS (AR)
84-90 FB +++
76-77 SU ++
72-74 CB ++++
78-79 CU +++

Year	Lev	Team	W	L	Sv	IP	K	ERA	WHIP	BF/G	OBA	H%	S%	xERA	Ctl	Dom	Cmd	hr/9	BPV
2005	A+	Win-Salem	8	2	0	76	84	3.78	1.47	21.8	269	35	77	4.48	3.9	9.9	2.5	0.9	86
2005	AA	Birmingham	6	1	0	67	76	1.74	1.04	23.6	171	26	81	1.30	4.2	10.2	2.5	0.0	133
2006	AA	Frisco/Read	3	7	0	146	142	3.58	1.53	23.5	251	32	73	4.16	5.3	8.8	1.7	0.7	72
2007	AA	Portland	3	5	0	69	72	5.74	1.70	18.3	259	31	70	5.50	6.4	9.4	1.5	1.6	43
2007	Rk	GCL Red Sox	1	0	0	7	10	1.27	1.27	14.5	231	37	89	2.54	3.8	12.7	3.3	0.0	155

Missed half of season with a nagging groin injury and never got comfortable on the mound. Offers a plus CB and ability to change speeds which masks average velocity and lack of movement. Command is essential to survival and helps himself by keeping ball down.

Hamilton, Brandon — SP — Detroit

EXP MLB DEBUT: 2012 | POTENTIAL: #3 starter | 9E

Thrws R Age 19
2007 (1-S) HS (AL)
87-94 FB ++++
80-84 KC +++
CU +

Year	Lev	Team	W	L	Sv	IP	K	ERA	WHIP	BF/G	OBA	H%	S%	xERA	Ctl	Dom	Cmd	hr/9	BPV
2007	Rk	GC Tigers	1	1	0	20	23	3.13	1.19	11.5	175	23	77	2.56	5.4	10.3	1.9	0.9	95

Tall/muscular pitcher with excellent velocity and plus movement to FB and KC. Can miss bats with anyone, but struggles with command and efficiency. Pitches with effort and doesn't have much of a CU, so could be moved to relief at some point in the future.

Hammes, Zach — SP — Los Angeles (N)

EXP MLB DEBUT: 2009 | POTENTIAL: #5 starter | 7E

Thrws R Age 24
2002 (2-C) HS (IA)
89-95 FB ++++
77-82 SL +++
79-82 CU +

Year	Lev	Team	W	L	Sv	IP	K	ERA	WHIP	BF/G	OBA	H%	S%	xERA	Ctl	Dom	Cmd	hr/9	BPV
2004	A-	Columbus	5	8	0	112	73	4.57	1.78	21.5	316	35	77	6.25	4.3	5.9	1.4	1.2	19
2005	A-	Columbus	3	4	1	63	46	4.84	1.91	13.6	279	32	76	5.82	7.4	6.6	0.9	1.0	27
2006	A+	Vero Beach	6	3	1	91	90	4.24	1.55	9.7	270	34	74	4.64	4.5	8.9	2.0	0.9	69
2006	AAA	Las Vegas	0	0	0	8	8	5.63	1.50	17.3	237	29	64	4.30	5.6	9.0	1.6	1.1	61
2007	AA	Jacksonville	5	8	0	94	76	5.25	1.49	15.6	293	34	66	4.99	2.9	7.3	2.5	1.1	62

Tall/projectable pitcher with plus FB, but stuff hasn't translated to performance. Strikeout rate lags as he lacks confidence in his SL and doesn't change speeds well, which forces him to go to FB. Doesn't repeat ¾ delivery, leaving him with below average command.

Hammond, Steve — SP — Milwaukee

EXP MLB DEBUT: 2008 | POTENTIAL: #5 starter | 6B

Thrws L Age 26
2005 (6) Long Beach St
86-91 FB +++
79-81 SL +++
77-80 CU ++

Year	Lev	Team	W	L	Sv	IP	K	ERA	WHIP	BF/G	OBA	H%	S%	xERA	Ctl	Dom	Cmd	hr/9	BPV
2005	A+	Brevard Co	1	3	0	35	30	2.81	1.19	17.7	250	31	78	3.13	2.3	7.7	3.3	0.5	106
2005	Rk	Helena	1	0	0	17	23	1.06	0.76	15.2	213	32	92	1.56	0.0	12.2		0.5	70
2006	A+	Brevard Co	6	5	0	85	70	2.54	1.07	23.6	221	26	80	2.67	2.4	7.4	3.0	0.7	97
2006	AA	Huntsville	5	6	0	73	58	2.95	1.20	22.6	234	27	79	3.28	3.1	7.1	2.3	0.9	74
2007	AA	Huntsville	7	9	1	142	109	4.69	1.45	20.9	289	33	71	5.00	2.7	6.9	2.5	1.2	56

Strong-framed pitcher releases ball late, providing deception and enhancing look of FB. Attacks hitters aggressively and keeps ball down, but lacks strikeout ability and was subject to the long ball. Mechanics get out-of-whack easily, which decreases command and velocity.

Hansack, Devern — SP — Boston

EXP MLB DEBUT: 2006 | POTENTIAL: Setup/middle reliever | 6B

Thrws R Age 25
1999 (Nicaragua)
87-92 FB +++
80-83 SL +++
79-82 CU +++
+

Year	Lev	Team	W	L	Sv	IP	K	ERA	WHIP	BF/G	OBA	H%	S%	xERA	Ctl	Dom	Cmd	hr/9	BPV
2005																			
2006	AA	Portland	8	7	1	132	124	3.27	1.20	17.1	247	30	76	3.51	2.5	8.4	3.4	1.0	100
2006	MLB	Boston	1	1	0	10	8	2.70	0.70	17.6	175	17	80	2.21	0.9	7.2	8.0	1.8	177
2007	AAA	Pawtucket	10	7	0	139	131	3.62	1.19	22.3	243	30	73	3.53	2.6	8.5	3.3	1.0	95
2007	MLB	Boston	0	1	0	7	5	5.00	1.94	11.4	307	31	83	7.74	6.3	6.3	1.0	2.5	-23

Thin/athletic pitcher that attacks hitters with four pitches and uses multiple arm angles for effect. Command and strikeout rate remained stable and has learned to pitch with movement as opposed to velocity. Versatile and resilient arm allows him to handle a multitude of roles.

Hanson,Tommy — SP — Atlanta
EXP MLB DEBUT: 2009 | POTENTIAL: #2 starter | 9D

Thrws R Age 21 — 2005 (22) Riverside CC
- 88-95 FB ++++
- 73-76 CB +++
- 78-81 CU ++

Year	Lev	Team	W	L	Sv	IP	K	ERA	WHIP	BF/G	OBA	H%	S%	xERA	Ctl	Dom	Cmd	hr/9	BPV
2007	A-	Rome	2	6	0	73	90	2.59	1.05	18.9	199	31	72	3.01	3.2	11.1	3.5	0.7	111
2007	A+	Myrtle Beach	3	3	0	60	64	4.20	1.42	23.1	239	33	73	4.15	4.8	9.6	2.0	1.5	65

Draft-and-follow improved velocity and CB rotation which accented his plus command and ability to keep the ball down. Extension and downward plane allows to the ball to get on top of hitters quickly. Will need to improve CU and hold velocity deeper into games.

Happ,JA — SP — Philadelphia
EXP MLB DEBUT: 2007 | POTENTIAL: #4 starter | 7C

Thrws L Age 25 — 2004 (3) Northwestern
- 84-91 FB +++
- 75-78 CB +++
- 78-81 CU +++

Year	Lev	Team	W	L	Sv	IP	K	ERA	WHIP	BF/G	OBA	H%	S%	xERA	Ctl	Dom	Cmd	hr/9	BPV
2006	A+	Clearwater	3	7	0	80	77	2.81	1.03	23.7	218	27	78	2.77	2.1	8.7	4.1	1.0	118
2006	AA	Reading	6	2	0	74	81	2.67	1.17	24.7	217	30	76	2.39	3.5	9.8	2.8	0.2	122
2006	AAA	Scranton/WB	1	0	0	6	4	1.50	0.67	20.9	151	13	100	1.59	1.5	6.0	4.0	1.5	100
2007	AAA	Ottawa	4	6	0	118	117	5.02	1.52	21.4	262	29	75	5.88	4.7	8.9	1.9	0.9	20
2007	MLB	Philadelphia	0	1	0	4	5	11.25	2.25	20.3	383	24	78	14.50	4.5	11.3	2.5	6.8	-109

Tall/projectable pitcher was able to improve strikeout rate, but was more hittable. Possesses deceptive ¾ delivery and induces tons of groundballs, but lacked CB rotation. Walk rate was slightly elevated and will need to improve efficiency, but still exhibits fair control.

Harben,Adam — SP — Chicago (N)
EXP MLB DEBUT: 2009 | POTENTIAL: #5 starter | 7D

Thrws R Age 24 — 2002 (15) Ark-Ft. Smith
- 88-93 FB ++++
- 75-79 CB +++
- 80-83 CU +

Year	Lev	Team	W	L	Sv	IP	K	ERA	WHIP	BF/G	OBA	H%	S%	xERA	Ctl	Dom	Cmd	hr/9	BPV
2003	A-	Quad City	5	6	0	87	77	4.34	1.45	23.2	270	34	69	4.06	3.6	8.0	2.2	0.5	79
2004	A-	Quad City	9	7	0	142	171	3.10	1.28	22.4	221	32	75	2.77	4.3	10.8	2.5	0.3	119
2005	A+	Fort Myers	10	5	0	135	119	2.66	1.21	21.8	211	27	78	2.59	4.1	7.9	1.9	0.4	89
2006	AA	New Britain	4	9	1	122	74	3.98	1.51	18.3	255	29	73	3.90	4.9	5.5	1.1	0.4	49
2007	Rk	AZL Cubs	0	1	0	5	6	1.80	1.20	6.7	124	20	83	1.21	7.2	10.8	1.5	0.0	126

Athletic hurler with complete arsenal missed most of 2007 recovering from TJS. Generates easy velocity and pitch movement with his smooth arm action. Not repeating delivery leaves him with below average command and CU, and will need to regain feel for pitching.

Hardy,Rowdy — SP — Kansas City
EXP MLB DEBUT: 2009 | POTENTIAL: reliever | 5B

Thrws L Age 25 — 2005 UDFA Austin Peay
- 78-84 FB ++
- 63-65 CB ++
- 68-71 CU ++++

Year	Lev	Team	W	L	Sv	IP	K	ERA	WHIP	BF/G	OBA	H%	S%	xERA	Ctl	Dom	Cmd	hr/9	BPV
2006	Rk	Idaho Falls	5	3	0	80	52	2.70	1.04	20.6	257	30	75	2.79	0.6	5.8	10.4	0.4	244
2007	A+	Wilmington	15	5	1	167	91	2.48	0.96	24.3	234	27	74	2.19	0.9	4.9	5.7	0.3	147

Athletic pitcher led CAR in wins by demonstrating plus command with a deceptive delivery. Changes speeds well, but velocity is below average and struggles to get strikeouts. Upside is limited, but if he can bring CB to average, he could have a career in middle relief.

Harrell,Lucas — SP — Chicago (A)
EXP MLB DEBUT: 2009 | POTENTIAL: #4 starter | 7D

Thrws R Age 23 — 2004 (4) HS (MO)
- 87-92 FB +++
- 76-80 CB +++
- 78-81 CU +++

Year	Lev	Team	W	L	Sv	IP	K	ERA	WHIP	BF/G	OBA	H%	S%	xERA	Ctl	Dom	Cmd	hr/9	BPV
2004	Rk	Bristol	3	5	0	48	33	5.61	1.77	17.0	281	32	69	5.43	6.0	6.2	1.0	0.9	29
2005	A-	Kannapolis	7	11	0	133	85	3.65	1.50	22.1	254	29	76	4.00	4.8	5.7	1.2	0.5	48
2006	A+	Win-Salem	7	2	0	91	70	2.57	1.12	21.1	184	23	77	1.95	4.3	6.9	1.6	0.3	84
2006	AA	Birmingham	0	2	0	9	4	10.76	2.83	17.3	316	33	60	8.70	13.7	3.9	0.3	1.0	-8

Missed 2007 season after arthroscopic elbow surgery. Changes speeds effectively and gets late movement to FB which helps him avoid bats. Struggles to repeat ¾ delivery which causes shaky command. Will need to smooth-out arm action and speed-up delivery.

Harrison,Matt — SP — Texas
EXP MLB DEBUT: 2008 | POTENTIAL: #3 starter | 8C

Thrws L Age 22 — 2003 (3) HS (NC)
- 87-92 FB +++
- 75-80 CB ++
- 78-81 CU ++++

Year	Lev	Team	W	L	Sv	IP	K	ERA	WHIP	BF/G	OBA	H%	S%	xERA	Ctl	Dom	Cmd	hr/9	BPV
2004	Rk	Danville	4	4	0	66	49	4.09	1.24	20.6	279	33	66	3.58	1.4	6.7	4.9	0.4	130
2005	A-	Rome	12	7	0	167	118	3.23	1.08	24.1	243	28	74	3.16	1.6	6.4	3.9	0.9	100
2006	A+	Myrtle Beach	8	4	0	81	60	3.11	1.15	24.7	252	30	75	3.20	1.8	6.7	3.8	0.7	103
2006	AA	Mississippi	3	4	0	77	54	3.74	1.31	24.5	279	32	73	4.02	2.0	6.3	3.2	0.7	83
2007	AA	Mississippi	5	7	0	116	78	3.41	1.31	24.0	265	31	74	3.60	2.6	6.0	2.3	0.5	73

Large-framed pitcher missed last month with shoulder soreness. Changes speeds effectively, keeps ball on the ground, and commands FB, which allows him to win with average velocity and strikeout ability. CB needs tightened and will have to alleviate stamina concern.

Hart,Kevin — SP — Chicago (N)
EXP MLB DEBUT: 2007 | POTENTIAL: #5 starter | 6A

Thrws R Age 25 — 2004 (11) Maryland
- 87-91 FB +++
- 84-85 CT +++
- 72-74 CB ++
- 78-80 CU +++

Year	Lev	Team	W	L	Sv	IP	K	ERA	WHIP	BF/G	OBA	H%	S%	xERA	Ctl	Dom	Cmd	hr/9	BPV
2005	A-	Delmarva	9	8	0	152	164	4.56	1.47	23.3	284	38	68	4.31	3.2	9.7	3.0	0.5	104
2006	A+	Frederick	6	11	0	148	122	4.68	1.44	22.6	263	31	70	4.50	4.0	7.4	1.9	1.1	53
2007	AA	Tennessee	8	5	0	102	92	4.24	1.25	23.0	258	31	69	3.97	2.4	8.1	3.4	1.1	89
2007	AAA	Iowa	4	1	0	56	39	3.54	1.41	26.3	262	30	78	4.28	3.7	6.3	1.7	1.0	47
2007	MLB	Chicago (N)	0	0	0	11	13	0.82	1.00	5.3	184	28	91	1.33	3.3	10.6	3.3	0.0	150

Tall/well-proportioned pitcher with average velocity, but plenty of sink to FB. Subtracts from FB with CT and CU, keeping hitters off-balance and does a fair job of pitching to contact. Commands plate well, but lacks tight rotation to CB and doesn't miss many bats.

Hawksworth,Blake — SP — St. Louis
EXP MLB DEBUT: 2008 | POTENTIAL: #4 starter | 7C

Thrws R Age 25 — 2001 (28) HS (WA)
- 88-93 FB ++++
- 72-74 CB ++
- 79-82 CU ++++

Year	Lev	Team	W	L	Sv	IP	K	ERA	WHIP	BF/G	OBA	H%	S%	xERA	Ctl	Dom	Cmd	hr/9	BPV
2004	A+	Palm Beach	1	0	0	10	11	6.18	1.27	20.9	258	31	55	4.61	2.6	9.7	3.7	1.8	86
2005	A-	New Jersey	0	3	0	14	12	8.24	1.97	9.7	310	39	54	5.49	6.3	7.6	1.2	0.0	64
2006	A+	Palm Beach	7	2	0	83	55	2.49	1.13	23.5	242	29	76	2.41	2.1	5.9	2.9	0.0	103
2006	AA	Springfield	4	2	0	79	66	3.41	1.30	25.1	244	29	77	3.70	3.5	7.5	2.1	0.9	69
2007	AAA	Memphis	4	13	0	129	88	5.29	1.48	22.2	292	31	69	5.55	2.9	6.1	2.1	1.7	28

Athletic pitcher finally achieved full health, but base skills declined across board. Repeats ¾ delivery with gives him above average command and ability to change speeds. FB has velocity, but stayed straight and CB was inconsistent. Will have to learn to pitch to contact.

Haynes,Jeremy — SP — Los Angeles (A)
EXP MLB DEBUT: 2010 | POTENTIAL: Setup reliever | 8E

Thrws R Age 22 — 2005 (37) Tallahassee CC
- 88-94 FB ++++
- 79-82 CB +++
- CU +

Year	Lev	Team	W	L	Sv	IP	K	ERA	WHIP	BF/G	OBA	H%	S%	xERA	Ctl	Dom	Cmd	hr/9	BPV
2006	Rk	Orem	3	1	1	58	68	2.78	1.49	15.7	219	30	84	3.72	6.3	10.5	1.7	0.8	86
2007	A-	Cedar Rapids	5	6	0	94	75	3.06	1.48	21.3	270	33	79	3.92	3.9	7.2	1.8	0.3	74

Athletic frame, arm strength, and velocity project him as solid starter. Strikeout rate regressed with promotion and needs stamina, but still has overpowering FB and solid CB. Lacks finesse and a repeatable delivery which negatively affects CU and command.

Hedrick,Justin — RP — San Francisco
EXP MLB DEBUT: 2008 | POTENTIAL: Setup reliever | 6B

Thrws R Age 26 — 2004 (6) Northwestern
- 87-91 FB +++
- 79-82 SL ++
- 76-79 CB +++
- SP ++

Year	Lev	Team	W	L	Sv	IP	K	ERA	WHIP	BF/G	OBA	H%	S%	xERA	Ctl	Dom	Cmd	hr/9	BPV
2004	A-	Salem-Keizer	1	2	0	33	44	3.27	1.18	12.0	191	28	75	2.63	4.6	12.0	2.6	0.8	119
2004	Rk	AZL Giants	0	0	0	2	4	12.27	3.18	6.6	492	73	57	12.33	4.1	16.4	4.0	0.0	139
2005	A+	San Jose	3	4	12	58	75	3.56	1.12	4.5	204	28	72	2.87	3.6	11.6	3.3	1.1	120
2006	A+	San Jose	6	4	6	85	110	2.01	0.97	5.8	181	28	80	1.52	3.2	11.6	3.7	0.3	156
2007	AA	Connecticut	4	6	1	71	72	2.15	1.29	7.1	215	28	85	2.93	4.7	9.1	1.9	0.5	92

Tall/strong-framed reliever who doesn't rely on one pitch for strikeouts, but has three breaking pitches in addition to FB. Commands plate, keeping hitters off stride and is equally tough on all batters. Sometimes tips pitches by not repeating ¾ release point and pitches with effort.

Hellickson,Jeremy — SP — Tampa Bay
EXP MLB DEBUT: 2010 | POTENTIAL: #3 starter | 8C

Thrws R Age 21 — 2005 (4) HS (IA)
- 87-92 FB +++
- 76-79 CB +++
- 77-80 CU +++

Year	Lev	Team	W	L	Sv	IP	K	ERA	WHIP	BF/G	OBA	H%	S%	xERA	Ctl	Dom	Cmd	hr/9	BPV
2005	Rk	Princeton	0	0	0	6	11	6.00	1.17	6.0	262	46	50	4.07	1.5	16.5	11.0	1.5	288
2006	A-	Hudson Valley	4	3	0	77	96	2.45	0.92	19.2	202	30	74	1.66	1.9	11.2	6.0	0.3	197
2007	A-	Columbus	13	3	0	111	106	2.67	1.09	20.7	217	28	77	2.50	2.8	8.6	3.1	0.6	112

Short/athletic pitcher with quick arm action, providing explosive FB movement. Repeats ¾ delivery well which allows him to command arsenal and disguise CU. TAM still has him on a pitch count as they are concerned about piling a heavy workload to his slight frame.

Heredia, Jairo — SP — New York (A)

EXP MLB DEBUT: 2012 POTENTIAL: #3 starter **9E**

Thrws R Age 18
2006 FA (DR)

88-93	FB	+ + + +
	SU	+ + +
	CU	+

Year	Lev	Team	W	L	Sv	IP	K	ERA	WHIP	BF/G	OBA	H%	S%	xERA	Ctl	Dom	Cmd	hr/9	BPV
2007	Rk	GCL Yankees	2	2	0	46	52	2.73	1.08	16.4	231	31	78	2.84	2.1	10.2	4.7	0.8	146

Wiry/athletic pitcher with a fluid, whip-like arm action that generates plus movement to pitches, which nets strikeouts. SU is tough to hit, though it could be tighter, and will need to repeat delivery more frequently for CU. Commands plate well and may just need to develop physically.

Hernandez, David — SP — Baltimore

EXP MLB DEBUT: 2010 POTENTIAL: #4 starter **8D**

Thrws R Age 23
2005 (16) Cons River JC

87-94	FB	+ + + +
80-82	SL	+ + +
79-82	CU	+

Year	Lev	Team	W	L	Sv	IP	K	ERA	WHIP	BF/G	OBA	H%	S%	xERA	Ctl	Dom	Cmd	hr/9	BPV
2005	A-	Aberdeen	1	2	0	41	47	3.93	1.41	14.5	261	36	71	3.73	3.7	10.3	2.8	0.4	109
2006	A-	Delmarva	7	8	0	140	149	4.24	1.41	22.0	246	32	71	3.87	4.4	9.6	2.2	0.8	85
2007	A+	Frederick	7	11	0	145	168	4.96	1.28	21.3	254	34	62	3.83	2.9	10.4	3.6	1.0	112

Projectable pitcher with quick arm action that gives him exceptional movement to FB and SL, which in turn, nets him strikeouts. Command within strike zone could improve and to remain in rotation, will need to repeat arm speed on CU on a more consistent basis.

Hernandez, Fernando — RP — Oakland

EXP MLB DEBUT: 2008 POTENTIAL: Setup reliever **6B**

Thrws R Age 23
2002 (49) HS (FL)

86-89	FB	+ + +
79-80	SL	+ + +

Year	Lev	Team	W	L	Sv	IP	K	ERA	WHIP	BF/G	OBA	H%	S%	xERA	Ctl	Dom	Cmd	hr/9	BPV
2004	A-	Kannapolis	3	3	4	45	59	2.99	1.31	6.6	253	38	77	3.32	3.2	11.8	3.7	0.4	141
2004	A+	Win-Salem	0	0	0	2	1	0.00	1.00	3.8	151	18	100	1.03	4.5	4.5	1.0	0.0	73
2005	A+	Win-Salem	4	1	1	70	59	5.14	1.61	6.9	296	36	68	5.10	3.9	7.6	2.0	0.8	59
2006	A+	Win-Salem	7	5	13	67	83	2.01	1.27	4.8	216	31	86	2.87	4.4	11.1	2.5	0.5	115
2007	AA	Birmingham	1	3	9	85	84	3.07	1.13	5.6	233	31	73	2.66	2.4	8.9	3.7	0.4	126

Rule 5 selection. Short/athletic reliever with smooth arm action and precise command. Tough on RH batters with sinker/SL combination and balances strikeouts with groundball outs. Repeats ¾ delivery which helps his pitches play-up.

Hernandez, Gaby — SP — Florida

EXP MLB DEBUT: 2008 POTENTIAL: #3 starter **8C**

Thrws R Age 22
2004 (3) HS (FL)

88-93	FB	+ + + +
75-79	CB	+ + +
80-83	CU	+ +

Year	Lev	Team	W	L	Sv	IP	K	ERA	WHIP	BF/G	OBA	H%	S%	xERA	Ctl	Dom	Cmd	hr/9	BPV
2004	Rk	GCL Mets	3	3	0	49	58	1.10	0.75	17.6	153	23	86	0.54	2.2	10.6	4.8	0.2	184
2005	A-	Hagerstown	6	1	0	92	99	2.44	0.97	19.4	185	25	75	1.63	2.9	9.7	3.3	0.4	134
2005	A+	St. Lucie	2	5	0	42	32	5.77	1.38	17.7	288	35	54	3.86	2.1	6.8	3.2	0.2	99
2006	A+	Jupiter	9	6	0	113	112	3.90	1.29	23.2	260	34	70	3.55	2.7	8.9	3.3	0.6	109
2007	AA	Carolina	9	11	0	153	113	4.23	1.31	22.6	250	29	69	3.72	3.3	6.6	2.0	0.8	63

Consistent winner and adapted well to newer mechanics, but base skills declined across the board. Strong frame and arm action gives him durability and ability to hold velocity. Works primarily off of FB and CB, but will interchange with his CU to keep hitters' honest.

Herrera, Daniel — RP — Cincinnati

EXP MLB DEBUT: 2008 POTENTIAL: Situational reliever **6C**

Thrws L Age 23
2006 (45) New Mexico

81-84	FB	+
74-75	SL	+ + +
57-60	CU	+ + + + +

Year	Lev	Team	W	L	Sv	IP	K	ERA	WHIP	BF/G	OBA	H%	S%	xERA	Ctl	Dom	Cmd	hr/9	BPV
2006	Rk	AZL Rangers	0	1	1	5	6	2.20	0.96	9.8	254	29	60	0.26	0.0	10.4		0.0	211
2006	A+	Bakersfield	4	2	1	53	61	1.36	0.96	14.3	207	31	84	1.50	2.0	10.3	5.1	0.0	182
2007	A+	Bakersfield	2	0	1	11	11	3.27	1.73	7.1	311	32	76	3.66	4.1	9.0	2.2	0.8	98
2007	AA	Frisco	5	2	0	52	64	3.78	1.21	6.2	226	31	75	3.92	3.5	11.1	3.2	0.5	89

Diminutive reliever with extreme groundball tendencies and ability to register strikeouts with below average velocity. Repeats delivery, giving him deception and possesses an outstanding CU. SL works well against LH batters and could do well in a situational role.

Herron, Tyler — SP — St. Louis

EXP MLB DEBUT: 2009 POTENTIAL: #5 starter **7C**

Thrws R Age 21
2005 (1-S) HS (FL)

86-91	FB	+ + +
71-74	CB	+ + + +
78-81	CU	+ +

Year	Lev	Team	W	L	Sv	IP	K	ERA	WHIP	BF/G	OBA	H%	S%	xERA	Ctl	Dom	Cmd	hr/9	BPV
2005	Rk	Johnson City	0	3	0	49	49	5.67	1.50	16.4	253	29	68	5.36	4.9	9.0	1.8	2.0	36
2006	A-	State College	0	1	0	6	3	3.00	1.33	24.9	293	30	86	5.05	1.5	4.5	3.0	1.5	41
2006	Rk	Johnson City	5	6	0	69	54	4.03	1.32	22.0	261	31	71	3.85	2.9	7.0	2.5	0.8	73
2007	A-	Quad Cities	10	7	1	137	130	3.74	1.09	17.9	241	31	65	2.70	1.7	8.5	5.0	0.5	149

Athletic pitcher with plus CB and pinpoint command of entire arsenal. Arm action provides good pitch movement and was able to get strikeouts by out-thinking hitters and mixing pitches. CU lacks deception and tends to leave the ball up when he is tired.

Hochevar, Luke — SP — Kansas City

EXP MLB DEBUT: 2007 POTENTIAL: #2 starter **9C**

Thrws R Age 24
2006 (1) Tennessee

88-95	FB	+ + + +
82-85	SL	+ + + +
76-80	CB	+ +
82-84	CU	+ + +

Year	Lev	Team	W	L	Sv	IP	K	ERA	WHIP	BF/G	OBA	H%	S%	xERA	Ctl	Dom	Cmd	hr/9	BPV
2006	A-	Burlington	0	1	0	15	16	1.19	0.60	12.9	141	16	100	0.99	1.2	9.5	8.0	1.2	216
2007	AA	Wichita	3	6	0	94	94	4.69	1.45	23.6	293	36	71	5.06	2.5	9.0	3.6	1.2	89
2007	AAA	Omaha	1	3	0	58	44	5.12	1.28	23.8	245	26	65	4.41	3.3	6.8	2.1	1.7	40
2007	MLB	Kansas City	0	1	0	12	5	2.21	1.23	12.4	242	25	86	3.38	3.0	3.7	1.3	0.7	33

Tall/projectable pitcher features velocity/movement, repeatable ¾ delivery, and two complementary pitches (SL and CU) that he'll throw at any time. Worked on adding CB to arsenal. HR rate was elevated, but was subject to two hitter friendly leagues and ballparks.

Hoey, James — RP — Baltimore

EXP MLB DEBUT: 2006 POTENTIAL: Setup reliever/closer **8C**

Thrws R Age 25
2003 (13) Rider

90-97	FB	+ + + +
84-87	SL	+ + +

Year	Lev	Team	W	L	Sv	IP	K	ERA	WHIP	BF/G	OBA	H%	S%	xERA	Ctl	Dom	Cmd	hr/9	BPV
2006	AA	Bowie	0	0	4	9	11	4.00	1.33	4.7	262	36	73	4.08	3.0	11.0	3.7	1.0	116
2006	MLB	Baltimore	0	1	0	9	6	10.76	2.07	3.7	350	39	44	7.34	4.9	5.9	1.2	1.0	16
2007	AA	Bowie	1	0	14	18	28	0.00	0.93	3.4	202	36	100	1.34	2.0	13.8	7.0	0.0	245
2007	AAA	Norfolk	2	0	2	27	41	1.33	0.93	5.1	165	28	88	1.22	3.3	13.7	4.1	0.3	180
2007	MLB	Baltimore	3	4	0	24	18	7.44	1.78	4.8	268	31	56	5.08	6.7	6.7	1.0	0.7	40

Obliterated minor league hitters once again with high-octane FB and deadly SL from a quick arm action. Base skills at top of chart, but can't be overused. Tendency to overthrow, which decreases movement, and intestinal fortitude are the things that are holding him back.

Holdzkom, John — RP — New York (N)

EXP MLB DEBUT: 2010 POTENTIAL: Setup reliever/closer **7D**

Thrws R Age 20
2006 (4) Salt Lake CC

91-96	FB	+ + + +
83-86	SL	+ + +
	CU	+

Year	Lev	Team	W	L	Sv	IP	K	ERA	WHIP	BF/G	OBA	H%	S%	xERA	Ctl	Dom	Cmd	hr/9	BPV
2006	Rk	GCL Mets	2	5	3	24	25	7.47	1.99	6.8	299	40	58	5.35	7.1	9.3	1.3	0.0	79
2007	Rk	GCL Mets	0	1	0	6	4	6.00	1.50	6.5	262	28	63	5.02	4.5	6.0	1.3	1.5	22
2007	Rk	Kingsport	1	0	0	5	6	3.60	1.60	7.4	221	33	75	3.28	7.2	10.8	1.5	0.0	107

Possesses top fastball in organization with boring action and high-octane velocity, which he owes to plus arm strength, and has a deadly SL. Has tendency to overthrow, which complicates delivery and prevents consistent command and ability to change speeds.

Holliman, Mark — SP — Chicago (N)

EXP MLB DEBUT: 2008 POTENTIAL: #5 starter **6C**

Thrws R Age 24
2005 (3) Mississippi

86-90	FB	+ +
78-80	SL	+ + +
74-77	CB	+ + +
77-79	CU	+ + +

Year	Lev	Team	W	L	Sv	IP	K	ERA	WHIP	BF/G	OBA	H%	S%	xERA	Ctl	Dom	Cmd	hr/9	BPV
2006	A+	Daytona	8	11	0	144	121	4.38	1.30	22.8	241	29	67	3.51	3.6	7.6	2.1	0.8	73
2007	AA	Tennessee	10	11	0	161	108	3.58	1.33	24.8	257	29	75	3.89	3.2	6.0	1.9	0.8	54

Short/stocky pitcher maximizes average stuff by mixing pitches, hitting spots, and keeping ball low. Lacks strikeout ability and deception to ¾ delivery which makes him hittable, but will throw two breaking pitches and CU in FB counts, which disrupts hitters' timing.

Horne, Alan — SP — New York (A)

EXP MLB DEBUT: 2008 POTENTIAL: #3 starter **8C**

Thrws R Age 25
2005 (11) Florida

87-95	FB	+ + + +
82-86	CT	+ + +
73-74	CB	+ + +
78-82	CU	+ +

Year	Lev	Team	W	L	Sv	IP	K	ERA	WHIP	BF/G	OBA	H%	S%	xERA	Ctl	Dom	Cmd	hr/9	BPV
2006	A+	Tampa	6	9	1	122	122	4.79	1.35	18.2	232	30	65	3.49	4.5	9.0	2.0	0.7	82
2007	AA	Trenton	12	4	0	153	165	3.12	1.35	23.6	257	34	78	3.66	3.4	9.7	2.9	0.6	105

Scouts have always liked his pitch movement and arm action, but improved command and CU allowed him to reach potential and lead EL in strikeouts and ERA. Whip-like delivery causes elbow stress and had prior TJS. Will need to firm-up delivery and get body in-sync.

Houser, James — SP — Tampa Bay

Thrws L | Age 23 | 2003 (2) HS (FL)
EXP MLB DEBUT: 2008 | POTENTIAL: #5 starter | 6B

86-90 FB ++ | 84-85 CT +++ | 75-78 CB ++ | 77-80 CU

Year	Lev	Team	W	L	Sv	IP	K	ERA	WHIP	BF/G	OBA	H%	S%	xERA	Ctl	Dom	Cmd	hr/9	BPV
2003	Rk	Princeton	0	4	0	41	44	3.73	1.37	17.2	271	37	71	3.57	2.9	9.7	3.4	0.2	123
2004	A-	Charleston	3	1	0	32	27	2.24	1.24	18.7	229	29	82	2.77	3.6	7.5	2.1	0.3	90
2005	A-	SW Michigan	8	8	0	115	109	3.76	1.14	20.7	236	29	70	3.21	2.4	8.5	3.5	0.9	105
2006	A+	Visalia	12	4	0	151	137	4.35	1.22	21.8	245	29	68	3.77	2.7	8.2	3.0	1.2	82
2007	AA	Montgomery	5	4	0	103	90	3.66	1.23	20.9	232	28	73	3.34	3.4	7.8	2.3	0.9	78

Light-framed pitcher with no body projection, which may have been reason behind his use of PED's earning him a 50-game suspension. Arm action provides him with movement to CT and CB, but lacks adequate velocity and ability to change speeds, limiting upside.

Hudgins, John — SP — San Diego

Thrws R | Age 26 | 2003 (3) Stanford
EXP MLB DEBUT: 2008 | POTENTIAL: #5 starter/setup reliever | 6C

87-91 FB +++ | 74-77 CB ++++ | SP + | 77-79 CU +++

Year	Lev	Team	W	L	Sv	IP	K	ERA	WHIP	BF/G	OBA	H%	S%	xERA	Ctl	Dom	Cmd	hr/9	BPV
2004	AAA	Oklahoma	0	1	0	12	8	7.50	2.00	19.3	360	41	61	7.12	3.8	6.0	1.6	0.8	30
2004	AA	Frisco	1	2	0	17	11	4.74	1.35	23.7	237	27	64	3.39	4.2	5.8	1.4	0.5	55
2005	AAA	Oklahoma	3	7	0	102	77	5.90	1.60	23.8	306	35	64	5.50	3.3	6.8	2.1	1.1	47
2006	AA	Mobile	4	3	0	51	55	2.81	1.11	22.4	221	30	75	2.40	2.8	9.7	3.4	0.4	130
2006	AAA	Okl/Port	2	2	0	25	23	5.40	1.48	11.9	291	34	67	5.31	2.9	8.3	2.9	1.4	64

Missed 2007 season due to TJS, but progress was favorable for a mid-2008 return. Sports a strong CB and knows how to change speeds, but will have to have best stuff to compensate for marginal velocity. Will need to regain feel for pitches and may return as a reliever.

Huff, David — SP — Cleveland

Thrws L | Age 23 | 2006 (1-S) UCLA
EXP MLB DEBUT: 2008 | POTENTIAL: #4 starter | 7C

86-90 FB +++ | 71-74 CB ++ | 74-78 CU ++++

Year	Lev	Team	W	L	Sv	IP	K	ERA	WHIP	BF/G	OBA	H%	S%	xERA	Ctl	Dom	Cmd	hr/9	BPV
2006	A-	Mahoning Val	0	1	0	7	8	6.25	2.22	9.1	307	42	69	6.05	8.8	10.0	1.1	0.0	78
2007	A+	Kinston	4	2	0	59	46	2.74	1.22	21.7	255	30	79	3.35	2.3	7.0	3.1	0.6	92

Finesse-type pitcher who relies on command, deception, and keeping ball down. Repeating high ¾ delivery is key to success, as he lacks velocity and ability to spin baseball. Doesn't give-in to hitters and makes adjustments. Missed second half with a sprained elbow ligament.

Hughes, Jared — SP — Pittsburgh

Thrws R | Age 22 | 2006 (4) Long Beach St
EXP MLB DEBUT: 2009 | POTENTIAL: #4 starter | 6C

87-92 FB +++ | 80-82 SL +++ | 77-80 CU +++

Year	Lev	Team	W	L	Sv	IP	K	ERA	WHIP	BF/G	OBA	H%	S%	xERA	Ctl	Dom	Cmd	hr/9	BPV
2006	A-	Hickory	5	4	0	48	25	5.80	1.60	21.3	253	27	65	4.81	5.8	4.7	0.8	1.1	16
2006	A-	Williamsport	1	2	0	23	11	2.74	0.91	17.2	178	18	74	1.84	2.7	4.3	1.6	0.8	55
2007	A-	Hickory	8	9	0	145	109	4.65	1.49	23.2	284	33	69	4.52	3.3	6.8	2.0	0.7	61

Tall/strong-framed pitcher likes to pitch to contact and sets-up hitters well, compensating for average stuff. Lacks strikeout ability and tends to walk too many, but keeps ball down and turns it up a notch with runners on base. Upside is limited, but can be a durable-type starter.

Humber, Phil — SP — New York (N)

Thrws R | Age 25 | 2004 (1) Rice
EXP MLB DEBUT: 2007 | POTENTIAL: #3 starter | 8C

88-93 FB ++++ | 76-80 CB +++ | 82-84 SP +++ | 81-84 CU +++

Year	Lev	Team	W	L	Sv	IP	K	ERA	WHIP	BF/G	OBA	H%	S%	xERA	Ctl	Dom	Cmd	hr/9	BPV
2006	A+	St. Lucie	3	1	0	38	36	2.37	0.87	20.0	183	22	79	1.90	2.1	8.5	4.0	0.9	125
2006	AA	Binghamton	2	2	0	34	36	2.90	1.03	21.9	206	26	77	2.66	2.6	9.5	3.6	1.1	115
2006	MLB	NY Mets	0	0	0	2	2	0.00	0.50	3.3	0	0	100	0.00	4.5	9.0	2.0	0.0	151
2007	AAA	NewOrleans	11	9	0	139	120	4.27	1.24	22.6	248	28	77	4.01	2.8	7.8	2.7	1.4	62
2007	MLB	NY Mets	0	0	0	7	2	7.71	1.57	10.2	313	30	73	8.11	2.6	2.6	1.0	1.3	-144

Strong/athletic pitcher hasn't dominated since TJS in 2005 and now projects to an inning-eater. Gains deception from drop-and-drive delivery and throws four pitches with precision. High HR/9 was uncharacteristic and will need keep ball low as he pitches more to contact.

Hunter, Tommy — RP — Texas

Thrws R | Age 21 | 2007 (1-S) Alabama
EXP MLB DEBUT: 2010 | POTENTIAL: #4 starter | 8E

88-94 FB ++++ | 81-84 SU +++ | 78-80 CU +

Year	Lev	Team	W	L	Sv	IP	K	ERA	WHIP	BF/G	OBA	H%	S%	xERA	Ctl	Dom	Cmd	hr/9	BPV
2007	A-	Spokane	2	3	1	17	13	2.62	0.93	6.5	236	30	69	1.82	0.5	6.8	13.0	0.0	322

Power pitcher build and plus arm strength gives him velocity and boring action on his FB. Lacks consistent comps and though he throws strikes, he needs to be finer within strike zone. TEX used him in relief, but may re-explore the starting rotation if he can develop his CU.

Hunt, Leroy — RP — Chicago (A)

Thrws R | Age 20 | 2007 (4) Sacramento CC
EXP MLB DEBUT: 2010 | POTENTIAL: Setup reliever | 7D

85-92 FB ++++ | 75-76 SL ++ | 77-79 CU ++

Year	Lev	Team	W	L	Sv	IP	K	ERA	WHIP	BF/G	OBA	H%	S%	xERA	Ctl	Dom	Cmd	hr/9	BPV
2007	Rk	Great Falls	2	0	0	30	30	3.87	1.62	9.6	267	34	77	4.51	5.4	8.9	1.7	0.6	72

Power reliever with electric FB and the arm strength to provide versatility. Pitches aggressively with FB, which he has relied on, but needs to tighten SL and show more consistent command. Not much finesse to his game and will need to tone-down maximum-effort delivery.

Hurley, Eric — SP — Texas

Thrws R | Age 22 | 2004 (1) HS (FL)
EXP MLB DEBUT: 2008 | POTENTIAL: #2 starter | 9C

88-94 FB ++++ | 80-83 SL +++ | 80-84 CU +++

Year	Lev	Team	W	L	Sv	IP	K	ERA	WHIP	BF/G	OBA	H%	S%	xERA	Ctl	Dom	Cmd	hr/9	BPV
2005	A-	Clinton	12	6	0	155	152	3.77	1.25	22.5	236	30	70	3.20	3.4	8.8	2.6	0.6	96
2006	A+	Bakersfield	5	6	0	100	106	4.13	1.24	22.6	246	31	70	3.70	2.9	9.5	3.3	1.1	100
2006	AA	Frisco	3	1	0	37	31	1.95	0.86	22.7	168	19	86	1.76	2.7	7.5	2.8	1.0	97
2007	AA	Frisco	7	2	0	88	76	3.27	1.11	23.1	222	25	78	3.34	2.8	7.8	2.8	1.3	76
2007	AAA	Oak. City	4	7	0	73	59	4.92	1.27	23.0	240	26	66	4.23	3.4	7.3	2.1	1.6	47

Tall/well-proportioned pitcher with fluid arm action and a repeatable delivery, providing velocity and pitch movement. Pitched more to contact, which lowered strikeout rate, but was hard to hit and commanded plate. Experience and maturity should improve performance.

Huseby, Chris — SP — Chicago (N)

Thrws R | Age 20 | 2006 (11) HS (FL)
EXP MLB DEBUT: 2011 | POTENTIAL: #4 starter | 8D

86-92 FB +++ | 76-79 CB +++ | CU ++

Year	Lev	Team	W	L	Sv	IP	K	ERA	WHIP	BF/G	OBA	H%	S%	xERA	Ctl	Dom	Cmd	hr/9	BPV
2006	Rk	AZL Cubs	0	2	0	17	14	5.26	1.58	12.5	303	37	65	4.89	3.2	7.4	2.3	0.5	72
2007	A-	Boise	2	5	0	66	53	3.39	1.39	18.6	247	33	69	3.13	4.2	7.2	1.7	0.9	54

Projectable pitcher with arm strength and fluid delivery. Suffered a decrease in velocity, trying to be more mechanically sound, but did a better job of incorporating comps into game plan. Command was inconsistent and needs a better CB to improve dominance.

Hynick, Brandon — SP — Colorado

Thrws R | Age 23 | 2006 (8) Birm-Southern
EXP MLB DEBUT: 2009 | POTENTIAL: #4 starter | 7C

87-92 FB ++++ | 75-79 CB ++ | 83-84 SP +++ | 78-82 CU +++

Year	Lev	Team	W	L	Sv	IP	K	ERA	WHIP	BF/G	OBA	H%	S%	xERA	Ctl	Dom	Cmd	hr/9	BPV
2006	A-	Tri-City	0	0	0	7	9	2.57	0.86	12.9	202	32	67	1.17	1.3	11.6	9.0	0.0	273
2006	Rk	Casper	4	3	0	64	70	2.11	0.97	20.2	230	32	80	2.21	1.1	9.8	8.8	0.4	239
2007	A+	Modesto	16	5	0	182	136	2.52	1.10	25.5	249	29	80	3.03	1.5	6.7	4.4	0.6	118

Led CAL in wins and ERA, torturing hitters with a deceptive delivery, plus command, and ability to mix four pitches. Strikeout rate and oppBA declined slightly, but pitched in a high-offensive league. Stamina wasn't a problem, so his unorthodox mechanics will not be altered.

Ingram, Jesse — RP — Texas

Thrws R | Age 26 | 2004 (36) California
EXP MLB DEBUT: 2008 | POTENTIAL: Setup reliever | 6B

87-92 FB +++ | 79-83 SL +++ | 74-77 CB +++ | 80-82 CU +

Year	Lev	Team	W	L	Sv	IP	K	ERA	WHIP	BF/G	OBA	H%	S%	xERA	Ctl	Dom	Cmd	hr/9	BPV
2004	A-	Spokane	4	1	4	31	45	1.44	1.12	5.6	178	30	88	1.82	4.6	13.0	2.8	0.3	148
2005	A+	Bakersfield	0	2	2	6	8	21.00	4.33	5.4	470	61	48	16.08	16.5	12.0	0.7	1.5	3
2006	A+	Bakersfield	6	0	9	59	95	2.44	0.95	8.2	169	30	75	1.43	3.4	14.5	4.3	0.5	185
2006	AA	Frisco	3	2	4	19	22	5.21	1.26	5.2	262	35	59	3.85	2.4	10.4	4.4	0.9	129
2007	AA	Frisco	3	1	26	62	70	4.21	1.15	4.4	197	24	69	3.22	4.1	10.2	2.5	1.5	85

Dominating closer who misses bats, despite an overpowering pitch. Mixes FB and two breaking balls, allowing him to nail hitters from both sides. Command was impressive and heavy workload didn't affect stamina, but tends to elevate FB, leaving him susceptible to homers.

Inman,Will — SP — San Diego

EXP MLB DEBUT: 2009 | POTENTIAL: #3 starter | 8C

Thrws R Age 21			Year	Lev	Team	W	L	Sv	IP	K	ERA	WHIP	BF/G	OBA	H%	S%	xERA	Ctl	Dom	Cmd	hr/9	BPV
2005 (3) HS (VA)			2005	Rk	AZL Brewers	0	0	0	2	1	0.00	0.50	6.6	0	0	100	0.00	4.5	4.5	1.0	0.0	103
87-92	FB	++++	2005	Rk	Helena	6	0	1	45	58	2.00	0.89	12.8	186	26	86	2.01	2.2	11.6	5.3	1.0	168
76-80	CB	+++	2006	A-	West Virginia	10	2	0	110	134	1.72	0.90	17.8	194	29	81	1.42	2.0	10.9	5.6	0.2	192
	SP	++	2007	A+	Brevard Co	4	3	0	78	98	1.73	1.01	23.0	203	30	85	2.00	2.6	11.3	4.3	0.5	158
	CU	+++	2007	AA	Hunt/SA	4	8	0	80	82	4.83	1.32	22.1	239	29	68	4.19	3.9	9.2	2.3	1.5	68

Flyball pitcher who could thrive at Petco Park as he misses bats and presents excellent FB command. Likes to pitch aggressively and has improved ability to change speeds. Strong build allows him to hold velocity, but effort to his delivery has resulted in a fatigued arm.

Italiano,Craig — SP — Oakland

EXP MLB DEBUT: 2010 | POTENTIAL: Setup reliever/closer | 8E

Thrws R Age 21			Year	Lev	Team	W	L	Sv	IP	K	ERA	WHIP	BF/G	OBA	H%	S%	xERA	Ctl	Dom	Cmd	hr/9	BPV
2005 (2) HS (TX)																						
90-97	FB	++++																				
80-83	SL	++	2005	Rk	AZL Athletics	1	2	0	18	27	6.92	1.54	9.9	280	45	50	3.89	4.0	13.4	3.4	0.0	150
	CU	+	2006	A-	Kane County	0	1	0	18	23	3.50	1.50	19.4	262	38	77	4.02	4.5	11.5	2.6	0.5	110
			2007	A-	Kane County	0	3	0	17	24	12.71	2.82	16.0	400	55	53	10.71	8.5	12.7	1.5	1.6	35

Tall/projectable frame and plus velocity give him tremendous upside. Missed 2006 with shoulder surgery and most of 2007 with skull fracture. Likes to pitch aggressively, but tendency to overthrow decreases pitch movement and lacks command. May be better-off in relief.

Jackson,Zach — SP — Milwaukee

EXP MLB DEBUT: 2006 | POTENTIAL: #5 starter | 6C

Thrws L Age 22			Year	Lev	Team	W	L	Sv	IP	K	ERA	WHIP	BF/G	OBA	H%	S%	xERA	Ctl	Dom	Cmd	hr/9	BPV
2004 (1-S) Texas A&M			2005	AA	New Hamp.	4	3	0	54	43	4.00	1.28	24.6	272	33	68	3.65	2.0	7.2	3.6	0.5	104
86-91	FB	+++	2005	AAA	Syracuse	4	4	0	47	33	5.16	1.74	26.9	315	37	70	5.53	4.0	6.3	1.6	0.6	46
83-85	CT	+++	2006	AAA	Nashville	4	6	0	107	58	4.21	1.40	25.1	260	28	72	4.21	3.7	4.9	1.3	0.9	32
76-81	SL	++	2006	MLB	Milwaukee	2	2	0	38	22	5.43	1.63	21.2	309	33	70	5.96	3.3	5.2	1.6	1.4	15
72-75	CU	+++	2007	AAA	Nashville	11	10	0	169	123	4.47	1.47	25.0	278	33	70	4.40	3.4	6.5	1.9	0.7	58

Finesse pitcher with soft base skills and no strikeout pitch, keeping his upside low. Subtracts from FB with CT and circle-CU and gains some deception from his low ¾ slot. Command has been inconsistent for two years and lacks the arm action to pull it off.

James,Brad — SP — Houston

EXP MLB DEBUT: 2009 | POTENTIAL: #4 starter | 7C

Thrws R Age 24			Year	Lev	Team	W	L	Sv	IP	K	ERA	WHIP	BF/G	OBA	H%	S%	xERA	Ctl	Dom	Cmd	hr/9	BPV
2004 (29) NC Texas CC			2004	Rk	Greeneville	2	6	0	52	38	4.48	1.44	17.1	250	31	66	3.44	4.5	6.6	1.5	0.2	70
88-93	FB	+++	2005	Rk	Greeneville	3	3	0	63	48	4.99	1.41	20.5	268	33	62	3.72	3.4	6.8	2.0	0.3	76
	SU	+++	2006	A-	Lexington	6	2	0	92	51	1.47	1.12	21.3	224	26	88	2.44	2.7	5.0	1.8	0.3	70
	CU	++	2007	A+	Salem	9	2	0	95	55	1.99	1.10	23.3	211	24	84	2.41	3.1	5.2	1.7	0.5	65
			2007	AA	Corpus Christi	1	5	0	47	22	5.17	1.55	22.8	286	32	65	4.46	3.8	4.2	1.1	0.4	35

Enigmatic pitcher with solid FB, but base skills do not support low ERA. Fails to repeat delivery, causing poor command and inability to change speeds. Lacks strikeout ability, but when SU is working, he can be tough to hit. How he does in Double-A will determine fate.

Jeffress,Jeremy — SP — Milwaukee

EXP MLB DEBUT: 2011 | POTENTIAL: #2 starter | 9D

Thrws R Age 20			Year	Lev	Team	W	L	Sv	IP	K	ERA	WHIP	BF/G	OBA	H%	S%	xERA	Ctl	Dom	Cmd	hr/9	BPV
2006 (1) HS (VA)																						
88-97	FB	+++++																				
78-82	SL	+++																				
	CU	++	2006	Rk	AZL Brewers	2	5	0	33	37	5.96	1.66	11.4	243	35	60	3.70	6.8	10.0	1.5	0.0	98
			2007	A-	West Virginia	9	5	0	86	95	3.14	1.23	19.4	203	27	78	2.93	4.6	9.9	2.2	0.8	94

Combination of arm strength/action and a tall/projectable frame give him a high upside. FB and SL are lethal pitches, and is virtually unhittable when everything is working. Will need to change speeds better and make-up for lost innings due to 50-game illegal substance suspension.

Jepsen,Kevin — RP — Los Angeles (A)

EXP MLB DEBUT: 2009 | POTENTIAL: Setup reliever | 8D

Thrws R Age 23			Year	Lev	Team	W	L	Sv	IP	K	ERA	WHIP	BF/G	OBA	H%	S%	xERA	Ctl	Dom	Cmd	hr/9	BPV
2002 (2) HS (VA)			2004	A-	Cedar Rapids	8	10	0	144	136	3.44	1.38	22.4	231	30	75	3.23	4.8	8.5	1.8	0.4	86
91-97	FB	++++	2005	A+	Rancho Cuc.	0	1	0	12	11	11.07	2.38	15.9	356	42	52	8.66	7.4	8.1	1.1	1.5	11
86-88	SL	+++	2005	Rk	AZL Angels	0	1	0	14	17	5.70	1.34	8.4	167	23	56	2.59	7.0	10.8	1.5	0.6	100
	CU	++	2006	A+	Rancho Cuc.	4	4	16	50	46	3.77	1.70	4.8	265	34	77	4.46	6.1	8.3	1.4	0.4	69
			2007	A+	Rancho Cuc.	1	5	3	53	50	4.23	1.86	5.7	289	37	76	5.20	6.4	8.5	1.3	0.3	65

Projectable athlete with best FB in the organization, but a max-effort delivery keeps him from holding his velocity. SL works well versus RH batters and notches strikeouts easily. Move to bullpen lessens need for CU, but could still show better command.

Joaquin,Waldis — SP — San Francisco

EXP MLB DEBUT: 2010 | POTENTIAL: #3 starter/setup reliever | 9E

Thrws L Age 21			Year	Lev	Team	W	L	Sv	IP	K	ERA	WHIP	BF/G	OBA	H%	S%	xERA	Ctl	Dom	Cmd	hr/9	BPV
2004 FA (DR)																						
89-96	FB	++++																				
84-87	SL	++++																				
80-83	CU	++	2005	Rk	AZL Giants	1	1	1	29	37	3.70	1.30	12.0	254	37	70	3.23	3.1	11.4	3.7	0.3	141
			2007	A-	Salem-Keizer	3	0	0	38	30	2.84	1.05	9.8	183	22	74	1.93	3.8	7.1	1.9	0.5	86

Returned from TJS with velocity intact, but hadn't regained command or feel for comps. Overpowers hitters with lively FB and darting SL, which is the result of quick arm action. Pitches with effort, so will need to smooth delivery, and needs to gain experience in setting-up pitches.

Johnson,Blake — SP — Kansas City

EXP MLB DEBUT: 2009 | POTENTIAL: #5 starter | 7D

Thrws R Age 23			Year	Lev	Team	W	L	Sv	IP	K	ERA	WHIP	BF/G	OBA	H%	S%	xERA	Ctl	Dom	Cmd	hr/9	BPV
2004 (2) HS (LA)																						
88-93	FB	++++	2004	Rk	Ogden	3	3	0	73	57	6.47	1.61	20.8	183	40	59	5.35	2.3	7.0	3.0	0.8	86
84-85	CT	+++	2005	A-	Columbus	9	4	0	83	88	3.33	1.19	16.7	227	29	71	2.69	3.9	9.5	2.4	0.4	98
76-77	CB	+++	2006	A+	VB/HD	5	6	0	136	82	5.00	1.32	21.1	292	33	63	4.46	1.5	6.3	4.3	0.9	97
	CU	+	2007	A+	Wilmington	9	6	0	119	80	3.28	1.15	18.2	244	33	68	3.02	2.5	6.1	2.4	0.5	77

Projectable pitcher with easy velocity and smooth arm action. FB loses movement when he overthrows and works best when he subtracts from the pitch. CB has improved to average pitch, but needs to repeat arm speed on CU and pitch off the corners more frequently.

Johnson,James — SP — Baltimore

EXP MLB DEBUT: 2006 | POTENTIAL: #4 starter | 7B

Thrws R Age 24			Year	Lev	Team	W	L	Sv	IP	K	ERA	WHIP	BF/G	OBA	H%	S%	xERA	Ctl	Dom	Cmd	hr/9	BPV
2001 (5) HS (NY)			2005	A+	Frederick	12	9	1	159	168	3.51	1.28	23.3	236	31	73	3.25	3.6	9.5	2.6	0.6	101
87-91	FB	+++	2005	AA	Bowie	0	0	0	7	6	0.00	0.71	24.7	132	18	100	0.09	2.6	7.7	3.0	0.0	138
72-75	CB	++++	2006	AA	Bowie	13	6	0	156	124	4.44	1.42	24.5	273	32	69	4.26	3.3	7.2	2.2	0.8	67
81-83	CU	++	2007	AAA	Norfolk	6	12	0	148	109	4.07	1.43	24.2	282	33	74	4.57	2.9	6.6	2.3	0.9	59
			2007	MLB	Baltimore	0	0	0	2	1	9.00	2.50	10.6	347	39	60	7.47	9.0	4.5	0.5	0.0	23

Tall/projectable pitcher utilizes CB from high ¾ slot and tries to keep hitters honest with average FBand CU. Pitches to contact and keeps ball low, but needs to miss more bats and show better command within strike zone. CU would be more effective if thrown slower.

Johnson,Kris — SP — Boston

EXP MLB DEBUT: 2009 | POTENTIAL: #4 starter | 7D

Thrws L Age 23			Year	Lev	Team	W	L	Sv	IP	K	ERA	WHIP	BF/G	OBA	H%	S%	xERA	Ctl	Dom	Cmd	hr/9	BPV
2006 (1-S) Wichita St																						
88-92	FB	+++																				
76-78	CB	+++																				
78-81	CU	+++	2006	A-	Lowell	0	2	0	30	27	0.89	1.06	8.4	227	30	91	2.02	2.1	8.0	3.9	0.0	139
			2007	A+	Lancaster	9	7	0	136	100	5.56	1.51	21.8	278	31	65	5.10	3.8	6.6	1.8	1.3	36

Athletic pitcher with repetitive delivery and is deceptively fast, making FB appear harder. Quality of CB and walk rate regressed, which are two things he'll have to have. Strikeout rate will likely always be low and will have to overcome stiff arm action in developing stamina.

Johnson,Steven — SP — Los Angeles (N)

EXP MLB DEBUT: 2010 | POTENTIAL: #4 starter | 8E

Thrws R Age 20			Year	Lev	Team	W	L	Sv	IP	K	ERA	WHIP	BF/G	OBA	H%	S%	xERA	Ctl	Dom	Cmd	hr/9	BPV
2005 (13) HS (MD)																						
89-91	FB	+++	2005	Rk	GCL Ddgers	0	2	0	11	14	9.73	1.98	8.9	365	50	48	7.18	3.2	11.4	3.5	0.8	99
	SL	+++	2006	Rk	Ogden	5	5	0	78	86	3.91	1.33	23.2	264	36	70	3.60	2.9	9.9	3.4	0.5	120
	CB	+++	2006	AA	Jacksonville	0	0	0	4	3	0.00	0.95	7.9	144	18	100	0.83	4.3	6.4	1.5	0.0	96
	CU	++	2007	A-	Great Lakes	3	6	0	81	65	4.85	1.60	19.9	282	35	72	4.90	4.4	7.2	1.6	0.3	72

Fluid arm action provides excellent pitch movement and is adept at exploiting hitters' weaknesses. Strikeout rate and command plummeted in full-season league. Offers three breaking pitches which compensates for average velocity, but needs a better CU and stamina.

Jones, Beau — SP — Texas

| | EXP MLB DEBUT: 2009 | POTENTIAL: #3 starter/setup reliever | 8E |

Thrws L Age 21
2005 (1-S) HS (LA)

			Year	Lev	Team	W	L	Sv	IP	K	ERA	WHIP	BF/G	OBA	H%	S%	xERA	Ctl	Dom	Cmd	hr/9	BPV
87-93	FB	+++	2005	Rk	GCL Braves	3	2	0	35	41	3.86	1.17	17.5	202	30	63	1.97	4.1	10.5	2.6	0.0	132
76-78	CB	++++	2006	A-	Rome	5	5	1	110	101	5.55	1.89	20.8	287	36	70	5.53	6.8	8.2	1.2	0.7	53
	CU	+	2007	A-	Clin/Rome	9	1	3	75	75	2.87	1.13	10.6	223	29	75	2.59	2.9	9.0	3.1	0.5	115
			2007	A+	Myrtle Beach	0	0	0	7	3	16.25	3.33	8.9	330	37	46	9.28	17.5	3.8	0.2	0.0	16

Strong-framed pitcher features plus CB and improved base skills after trade to TEX. FB has above average velocity and appears quicker with his deceptive delivery. Needs to repeat delivery more frequently which will improve CU and help maintain command.

Jukich, Ben — SP — Cincinnati

| | EXP MLB DEBUT: 2008 | POTENTIAL: #5 starter/setup reliever | 7C |

Thrws L Age 25
2006 (13) Dak Wesleyan

			Year	Lev	Team	W	L	Sv	IP	K	ERA	WHIP	BF/G	OBA	H%	S%	xERA	Ctl	Dom	Cmd	hr/9	BPV
87-92	FB	+++																				
73-77	SL	++	2006	A-	Kane Cty	3	2	0	41	40	2.40	1.60	14.0	261	34	85	4.03	5.5	8.7	1.6	0.2	82
79-81	CB	++++	2006	A-	Vancouver	0	0	2	8	10	3.33	1.73	12.3	283	41	79	4.42	5.6	11.1	2.0	0.0	107
	CU	++	2007	A+	Sara/Stock	11	6	0	76	117	4.35	1.21	13.0	236	35	77	4.88	2.8	7.8	2.8	0.3	84

Tall/projectable pitcher with plus CB and FB movement, giving him excellent strikeout ability. Command improved over last season, but still doesn't repeat delivery or change speeds effectively, which could put him in relief. Will need to build arm strength to throw more innings.

Jung, Sung-Ki — RP — Atlanta

| | EXP MLB DEBUT: 2009 | POTENTIAL: Setup reliever | 7C |

Thrws R Age 28
2002 FA (Korea)

			Year	Lev	Team	W	L	Sv	IP	K	ERA	WHIP	BF/G	OBA	H%	S%	xERA	Ctl	Dom	Cmd	hr/9	BPV
87-89	FB	+++																				
78-81	SL	++																				
77-81	CU	++++	2007	A+	Myrtle Beach	0	1	22	39	49	1.15	0.87	4.4	167	34	81	2.33	2.8	11.3	4.1	0.5	112
			2007	AA	Mississipp	0	1	1	9	8	1.93	1.10	5.1	260	33	80	2.49	1.0	7.9	8.0	0.0	140

Short/thin reliever missed three years to serve in Korean army, but returned with a vengeance. Deceptive sidearm delivery and ability to change speeds makes him tough on RH batters. Misses bats despite below average velocity, but needs to tighten rotation of SL and get stronger.

Jung, Young-Il — SP — Los Angeles (A)

| | EXP MLB DEBUT: 2011 | POTENTIAL: #3 starter | 8E |

Thrws R Age 19
2006 FA (Korea)

			Year	Lev	Team	W	L	Sv	IP	K	ERA	WHIP	BF/G	OBA	H%	S%	xERA	Ctl	Dom	Cmd	hr/9	BPV
88-92	FB	+++																				
82-85	SL	++																				
81-82	CU	+++	2007	Rk	Orem	0	1	0	9	9	9.00	1.78	13.8	283	35	47	5.51	6.0	9.0	1.5	1.0	54

Short/strong-framed pitcher missed most of 2007 with a strained forearm. Drop-and-drive delivery is repeatable and coupled with his fluid arm action, helps derive movement to FB and CU. SL needs tighter rotation and will need to improve command within strike zone.

Jurrjens, Jair — SP — Atlanta

| | EXP MLB DEBUT: 2008 | POTENTIAL: #4 starter | 8C |

Thrws R Age 22
2003 FA (Curacao)

			Year	Lev	Team	W	L	Sv	IP	K	ERA	WHIP	BF/G	OBA	H%	S%	xERA	Ctl	Dom	Cmd	hr/9	BPV
			2005	A-	W. Michigan	12	6	0	142	108	3.42	1.18	21.9	248	30	70	2.90	2.3	6.8	3.0	0.3	100
88-94	FB	++++	2006	A+	Lakeland	5	0	0	73	59	2.09	0.86	22.5	204	25	78	1.71	1.2	7.3	5.9	0.5	167
76-79	CB	++	2006	AA	Erie	4	3	0	67	53	3.36	1.37	23.4	273	32	79	4.32	2.8	7.1	2.5	0.9	68
81-84	CU	+++	2007	AA	Erie	7	5	0	112	94	3.21	1.27	24.2	261	32	76	3.54	2.5	7.5	3.0	0.6	95
			2007	MLB	Detroit	3	1	0	30	13	4.77	1.16	17.2	220	22	61	3.34	3.3	3.9	1.2	1.2	23

Athletic pitcher with excellent combination of velocity, command, and pitchability. Changes speeds well and learned to pitch more to contact, which lowered strikeout rate. CBI is inconsistent, FB lacks movement at upper velocities, and presents some effort at finish of delivery.

Kennedy, Ian — SP — New York (A)

| | EXP MLB DEBUT: 2007 | POTENTIAL: #3 starter | 8B |

Thrws R Age 23
2006 (1-C) USC

			Year	Lev	Team	W	L	Sv	IP	K	ERA	WHIP	BF/G	OBA	H%	S%	xERA	Ctl	Dom	Cmd	hr/9	BPV
			2006	A-	Staten Island	0	0	0	2	2	0.00	1.82	10.2	244	32	100	4.14	8.2	8.2	1.0	0.0	76
85-91	FB	+++	2007	A+	Tampa	6	1	0	63	72	1.29	0.97	21.7	180	26	88	1.48	3.1	10.3	3.3	0.3	141
81-83	SL	++	2007	AA	Trenton	1	0	0	48	57	2.61	0.91	20.0	166	24	71	1.26	3.2	10.6	3.4	0.4	145
72-76	CB	+++	2007	AAA	Scranton/WB	1	1	0	34	34	2.11	1.05	22.1	206	27	82	2.23	2.9	8.9	3.1	0.5	117
78-81	CU	++++	2007	MLB	New York (A)	1	0	0	19	15	1.89	1.16	25.2	195	24	86	2.34	4.3	7.1	1.7	0.5	79

Flew through minors giving NYY rotation a boost in Sept. Master at changing speeds and shows excellent command. Keeps ball down with sinker and has solid CB, helping him lead minors in oppBA. Short stature brings pitches flat to the plate and lacks projection.

Kershaw, Clayton — SP — Los Angeles (N)

| | EXP MLB DEBUT: 2009 | POTENTIAL: #1 starter | 10D |

Thrws L Age 20
2006 (1) HS (TX)

			Year	Lev	Team	W	L	Sv	IP	K	ERA	WHIP	BF/G	OBA	H%	S%	xERA	Ctl	Dom	Cmd	hr/9	BPV
87-94	FB	++++																				
74-77	CB	++++	2006	Rk	GCL Dodgers	2	0	1	37	54	1.95	0.89	13.7	212	36	76	1.36	1.2	13.1	10.8	0.0	318
79-82	CU	++++	2007	A-	Great Lakes	7	5	0	97	134	2.78	1.26	19.8	208	32	79	2.68	4.6	12.4	2.7	0.5	130
			2007	AA	Jacksonville	1	2	0	24	29	3.72	1.40	20.4	199	25	80	3.93	6.3	10.8	1.7	1.5	71

Tall/projectable pitcher with overpowering FB and good depth to CB, being able to strike-out anyone. Repeats ¾ delivery well giving him a solid CU and command. Delivery lacks fluidity and tends to push baseball when tired. Dominated as one of league's youngest players.

Kiker, Kasey — SP — Texas

| | EXP MLB DEBUT: 2010 | POTENTIAL: #2 starter | 9C |

Thrws L Age 20
2006 (1) HS (TX)

			Year	Lev	Team	W	L	Sv	IP	K	ERA	WHIP	BF/G	OBA	H%	S%	xERA	Ctl	Dom	Cmd	hr/9	BPV
88-93	FB	++++																				
74-78	CB	++++																				
78-83	CU	+++	2006	A-	Spokane	0	7	0	53	52	4.41	1.60	14.7	243	31	74	4.37	6.3	8.8	1.4	0.8	63
			2007	A-	Clinton	7	4	0	96	112	2.90	1.30	19.8	237	32	82	3.60	3.8	10.5	2.7	0.9	100

Short/athletic pitcher with smooth arm action and incredible movement to three pitches, making him adept at missing bats. Repeats high ¾ delivery, which improved command and helped disguise pitches. TEX hasn't given him much rope, so needs to build stamina.

King, Blake — SP — St. Louis

| | EXP MLB DEBUT: 2010 | POTENTIAL: #4 starter | 7C |

Thrws R Age 21
2005 (44) HS (OK)

			Year	Lev	Team	W	L	Sv	IP	K	ERA	WHIP	BF/G	OBA	H%	S%	xERA	Ctl	Dom	Cmd	hr/9	BPV
87-92	FB	+++																				
81-84	SL	++++	2006	Rk	Johnson City	4	3	0	62	74	3.04	1.06	18.6	174	25	71	1.78	4.2	10.7	2.6	0.4	125
	CU	+	2007	A-	Quad Cities	2	3	0	57	62	5.21	1.54	13.1	215	29	65	3.52	6.9	9.8	1.4	0.5	86
			2007	A-	Batavia	1	4	0	53	65	4.74	1.54	14.5	242	35	68	3.88	5.8	11.0	1.9	0.5	97

Strong-framed pitcher misses bats with a plus SL and late life to FB. Delivery and extension provide deception, but pitches with effort and doesn't repeat arm speed which leaves CU flat and command inconsistent. Stamina is an issue and profiles better as a power reliever.

Kinney, Josh — RP — St. Louis

| | EXP MLB DEBUT: 2006 | POTENTIAL: Setup reliever | 7B |

Thrws R Age 29
2001 NDFA Quincy

			Year	Lev	Team	W	L	Sv	IP	K	ERA	WHIP	BF/G	OBA	H%	S%	xERA	Ctl	Dom	Cmd	hr/9	BPV
88-94	FB	++++	2004	A+	Palm Beach	0	1	0	8	12	4.44	1.73	5.3	259	39	77	5.12	6.7	13.3	2.0	1.1	92
81-84	SL	+++	2004	AA	Tennessee	3	8	4	55	48	5.54	1.83	5.1	301	36	71	5.90	5.5	7.8	1.4	0.0	42
77-80	CB	+++	2005	AA	Springfield	5	2	11	42	42	1.29	0.95	5.0	191	25	89	1.71	2.6	9.0	3.5	0.4	131
			2005	AAA	Memphis	1	2	0	25	25	7.50	2.34	5.0	360	44	69	8.60	6.8	8.9	1.3	1.4	21
			2006	AAA	Memphis	2	2	3	71	76	1.52	1.06	5.4	187	26	86	1.75	3.7	9.6	2.6	0.3	123

Torn elbow ligament, suffered during spring training caused TJS for the second time in three years. Lives at the bottom of strike zone with sinker and SL, is deceptively quick, and misses bats. Should return by mid-season, but career will always be hanging by a thread.

Kline, William — SP — Tampa Bay

| | EXP MLB DEBUT: 2009 | POTENTIAL: #5 starter | 7D |

Thrws R Age 23
2007 (2) Mississippi

			Year	Lev	Team	W	L	Sv	IP	K	ERA	WHIP	BF/G	OBA	H%	S%	xERA	Ctl	Dom	Cmd	hr/9	BPV
87-92	FB	+++																				
80-82	SL	++																				
78-81	CU	+++	2007	A-	Columbus	0	4	0	29	27	4.97	1.69	14.5	317	29	68	4.48	3.4	8.4	2.5	1.2	44

TJS survivor (2004), he has turned into an inning-eating type pitcher that pitches above his average repertoire. Doesn't present much pitch movement, which makes him hittable, but mixes pitches and hits spots. Strikeout rate was fine in debut, but may drop with promotions.

Kluber,Corey — SP — San Diego

EXP MLB DEBUT: 2010 | POTENTIAL: #4 starter | 7D

Thrws R Age 22
2007 (4-C) Stetson

Velo	Pitch	Grade
88-92	FB	+ + +
	SL	+ + +
	CB	+ +
	CU	+ + +

Year	Lev	Team	W	L	Sv	IP	K	ERA	WHIP	BF/G	OBA	H%	S%	xERA	Ctl	Dom	Cmd	hr/9	BPV
2007	A-	Eugene	1	1	0	33	33	3.53	1.30	13.6	231	31	71	2.92	4.1	9.0	2.2	0.3	101

Polished college pitcher with four-pitch arsenal and repeatable delivery that masks pitches and gives solid command. Smooth arm action provides movement and allows him to hold velocity, and though his strikeout rate was fine in debut, he could struggle at higher levels.

Kobayashi,Masahide — RP — Cleveland

EXP MLB DEBUT: 2008 | POTENTIAL: Setup reliever | 7B

Thrws R Age 34
2007 FA (Japan)

Velo	Pitch	Grade
87-92	FB	+ + +
	SL	+ + +
	SP	+ + + +

Year	Lev	Team	W	L	Sv	IP	K	ERA	WHIP	BF/G	OBA	H%	S%	xERA	Ctl	Dom	Cmd	hr/9	BPV
2003	Intl	Ciba Lotta	0	2	33	47	30	2.87	1.19	4.3	253	30	76	3.08	2.1	5.7	2.7	0.4	85
2004	Intl	Ciba Lotta	8	5	20	57	50	3.90	1.22	4.5	240	29	68	3.11	3.0	7.9	2.6	0.6	91
2005	Intl	Ciba Lotta	2	2	29	45	33	2.58	1.29	4.0	278	31	87	4.43	1.8	6.6	3.7	1.2	80
2006	Intl	Ciba Lotta	6	2	34	53	48	2.68	1.07	3.9	246	30	77	2.85	1.4	8.1	6.0	0.7	160
2007	Intl	Ciba Lotta	2	7	27	47	35	3.61	1.38	4.0	285	33	75	4.36	2.3	6.7	2.9	0.8	76

Signed in Nov to serve as the primary setup reliever. Successful Japanese closer with plus movement to FB, SL, and SPL. Athleticism allows him to repeat a deceptive delivery and maintain consistent command. Strikeout rate is likely to drop, but will be very tough to hit.

Komine,Shane — SP — Oakland

EXP MLB DEBUT: 2006 | POTENTIAL: #5 starter | 6B

Thrws R Age 27
2002 (9) Nebraska

Velo	Pitch	Grade
86-92	FB	+ + +
82-84	CT	+ + +
72-76	CB	+ + + +
78-81	CU	+ +

Year	Lev	Team	W	L	Sv	IP	K	ERA	WHIP	BF/G	OBA	H%	S%	xERA	Ctl	Dom	Cmd	hr/9	BPV
2005	AA	Midland	2	1	0	31	33	3.18	1.09	24.3	235	29	79	3.55	2.0	9.5	4.7	1.4	121
2006	AAA	Sacramento	11	8	0	140	116	4.05	1.31	24.1	269	32	71	3.98	2.4	7.5	3.1	0.8	85
2006	MLB	Oakland	0	0	0	9	1	5.00	2.00	21.7	283	22	87	8.03	8.0	1.0	0.1	3.0	-83
2007	AAA	Sacramento	5	12	0	133	99	4.87	1.42	24.5	276	31	70	4.93	3.1	6.7	2.2	1.4	43
2007	MLB	Oakland	0	0	0	7	1	5.00	0.97	13.7	228	17	60	4.23	1.3	1.3	1.0	2.5	-37

Plus athlete with plethora of pitches, but base skills regressed significantly and struggled. Short stature brings pitches on a flat plane, but changes high level with his plus CB. Subtracts from FB with CT and CU, destroying hitters' timing. Will always have to battle for opportunities.

Kontos,George — SP — New York (A)

EXP MLB DEBUT: 2009 | POTENTIAL: #4 starter | 8D

Thrws R Age 23
2006 (5) Northwestern

Velo	Pitch	Grade
89-94	FB	+ + + +
82-85	SL	+ + +
78-82	CB	+
78-80	CU	+ +

Year	Lev	Team	W	L	Sv	IP	K	ERA	WHIP	BF/G	OBA	H%	S%	xERA	Ctl	Dom	Cmd	hr/9	BPV
2006	A-	Staten Island	7	3	0	78	82	2.54	1.06	21.7	225	31	76	2.31	2.2	9.4	4.3	0.3	147
2007	A+	Tampa	4	6	0	94	101	4.02	1.33	20.5	264	33	75	4.52	2.9	9.7	3.4	1.4	88

Projectable pitcher thrived in jump to high Class-A where he showed excellent command and strikeout ability. Keeps ball low with sinker/SL combination and improved CU to give him a third option. Unlikely to develop anymore velocity, but adding muscle could allow him to hold it.

Kopp,David — SP — St. Louis

EXP MLB DEBUT: 2010 | POTENTIAL: #4 starter/setup reliever | 8E

Thrws R Age 22
2007 (2-C) Clemson

Velo	Pitch	Grade
90-95	FB	+ + + +
80-83	SL	+ + +
80-84	CU	+

Year	Lev	Team	W	L	Sv	IP	K	ERA	WHIP	BF/G	OBA	H%	S%	xERA	Ctl	Dom	Cmd	hr/9	BPV
2007	A-	Batavia	0	1	0	4	3	0.00	1.50	8.6	210	27	100	2.93	6.8	6.8	1.0	0.0	74

Athletic/projectable pitcher with above average velocity and biting SL, but didn't miss bats like stuff would indicate. Struggles to repeat ¾ delivery which poses problems with command and changing speeds, and pitches with effort, affecting stamina.

Kunz,Edward — RP — New York (N)

EXP MLB DEBUT: 2009 | POTENTIAL: Setup reliever/closer | 7C

Thrws R Age 22
2007 (1-S) Oregon St

Velo	Pitch	Grade
89-94	FB	+ + + +
80-83	SL	+ + + +
75-79	CU	+ +

Year	Lev	Team	W	L	Sv	IP	K	ERA	WHIP	BF/G	OBA	H%	S%	xERA	Ctl	Dom	Cmd	hr/9	BPV
2007	A-	Brooklyn	0	1	5	12	9	0.00	1.33	4.2	191	0	0	8.64	6.0	6.8	1.1	6.8	-122

Tall/strong framed reliever produces a heavy sinker that gets groundball outs and a SL which he uses for strikeouts. Repeats ¾ delivery which helps his command. Scouts question his aggressiveness and his arm action is stiff which hinders his durability in the bullpen.

Kuroda,Hiroki — SP — Los Angeles (N)

EXP MLB DEBUT: 2008 | POTENTIAL: #3 starter | 8B

Thrws R Age 33
2007 FA (Japan)

Velo	Pitch	Grade
88-94	FB	+ + + +
84-87	CT	+ + +
82-85	SL	+ + + +
81-85	SP	+ + +

Year	Lev	Team	W	L	Sv	IP	K	ERA	WHIP	BF/G	OBA	H%	S%	xERA	Ctl	Dom	Cmd	hr/9	BPV
2003	Intl	Hiroshima	13	9	0	205	137	3.11	1.18	29.3	254	29	76	3.41	2.0	6.0	3.0	0.8	81
2004	Intl	Hiroshima	7	9	0	147	138	4.65	1.47	30.0	311	38	70	5.20	1.8	8.4	4.8	1.0	112
2005	Intl	Hiroshima	15	12	0	212	165	3.17	1.06	28.4	234	28	72	2.78	1.8	7.0	3.9	0.7	111
2006	Intl	Hiroshima	13	6	1	189	144	1.85	0.96	27.5	241	29	85	2.61	1.0	6.9	6.9	0.6	175
2007	Intl	Hiroshima	12	8	0	179	123	3.56	1.21	27.7	257	29	74	3.76	2.1	6.2	2.9	1.0	72

Athletic import with excellent velocity and tendency to throw everything hard. Possesses good arm action, but his deliberate delivery makes him susceptible to running game. Commands plate, but is hittable due to overuse of FB and lacks strikeout ability.

Laffey,Aaron — SP — Cleveland

EXP MLB DEBUT: 2007 | POTENTIAL: #5 starter á | 7B

Thrws L Age 23
2003 (16) HS (MD)

Velo	Pitch	Grade
85-90	FB	+ + +
76-80	SL	+ + +
79-82	CU	+ +

Year	Lev	Team	W	L	Sv	IP	K	ERA	WHIP	BF/G	OBA	H%	S%	xERA	Ctl	Dom	Cmd	hr/9	BPV
2006	A+	Kinston	4	1	1	41	24	2.19	1.07	16.0	247	29	77	2.33	1.3	5.3	4.0	0.0	121
2006	AA	Akron	8	3	0	112	61	3.53	1.37	24.7	277	31	76	4.19	2.6	4.9	1.8	0.7	46
2007	AA	Akron	4	1	0	35	24	2.31	1.03	22.5	227	27	79	2.44	1.8	6.2	3.4	0.5	103
2007	AAA	Buffalo	9	3	0	96	75	3.09	1.17	23.9	247	30	74	3.00	2.2	7.0	3.3	0.5	102
2007	MLB	Cleveland	4	2	0	49	25	4.58	1.34	22.7	281	31	64	3.84	2.2	4.6	2.1	0.4	59

Extreme groundball pitcher who gave CLE a shot in the arm in Aug. Improved fortune by improving CU and faring better against RH batters. Quick arm action provides deception and movement, especially to his slurve-type SL, which he needs with below average velocity.

Lahey,Tim — RP — Chicago (N)

EXP MLB DEBUT: 2008 | POTENTIAL: Setup reliever | 6C

Thrws R Age 26
2004 (20) Princeton

Velo	Pitch	Grade
89-94	FB	+ + + +
82-85	SL	+ + +
79-82	SP	+ + + +
78-82	CU	+

Year	Lev	Team	W	L	Sv	IP	K	ERA	WHIP	BF/G	OBA	H%	S%	xERA	Ctl	Dom	Cmd	hr/9	BPV
2005	Rk	Elizabethton	0	1	15	25	30	3.59	1.16	3.8	229	34	66	2.26	2.9	10.8	3.8	0.0	153
2006	A+	Fort Myers	7	1	8	71	56	4.42	1.38	6.8	261	33	65	3.39	3.4	7.1	2.1	0.1	85
2007	AA	New Britain	8	4	13	78	56	3.46	1.42	6.6	262	30	79	4.27	3.8	6.5	1.7	0.9	49
2007	AAA	Rochester	0	0	1	3	3	9.00	2.00	7.2	321	42	50	5.72	6.0	9.0	1.5	0.0	76

Top pick in 2007 Rule 5 Draft, the former catcher possesses excellent arm strength and durability. Works primarily off of FB and SPL, being very effective to RH batters, but lacks confidence in his CU and struggles with his command within the strike zone.

Lambert,Chris — RP — Detroit

EXP MLB DEBUT: 2008 | POTENTIAL: Setup reliever | 7D

Thrws R Age 28
2004 (1) Boston College

Velo	Pitch	Grade
86-94	FB	+ + + +
76-80	SL	+ + +
71-73	CB	+
75-79	CU	+ + +

Year	Lev	Team	W	L	Sv	IP	K	ERA	WHIP	BF/G	OBA	H%	S%	xERA	Ctl	Dom	Cmd	hr/9	BPV
2006	AA	Springfield	10	9	0	120	113	5.32	1.57	23.0	271	32	70	5.30	4.7	8.5	1.8	1.5	44
2007	AA	Springfield	0	2	0	26	17	3.45	1.23	21.1	246	25	81	4.32	2.8	5.9	2.1	1.7	34
2007	AAA	Memphis	1	4	0	57	50	7.55	1.80	9.4	314	37	59	6.60	4.6	7.9	1.7	1.6	28
2007	AAA	Toledo	0	0	0	6	10	0.00	0.50	19.9	56	13	100	0.00	3.0	15.0	5.0	0.0	239
2007	AAA	Mem/Tol	1	4	0	63	60	6.84	1.68	9.8	296	35	60	5.86	4.4	8.5	1.9	1.4	45

Moved to bullpen and pitched better, reducing arsenal. Strikeout rate improved, held velcoity longer, and SL proved tough to RH batters. Doesn't repeat compact delivery and arm action is slow (1.6), making him susceptible to the running game.

Lannan,John — SP — Washington

EXP MLB DEBUT: 2007 | POTENTIAL: #4 starter | 7C

Thrws L Age 23
2005 (11) Siena

Velo	Pitch	Grade
87-91	FB	+ + +
74-77	CB	+ + +
79-82	CU	+ + + +

Year	Lev	Team	W	L	Sv	IP	K	ERA	WHIP	BF/G	OBA	H%	S%	xERA	Ctl	Dom	Cmd	hr/9	BPV
2006	A-	Savannah	6	8	0	138	114	4.70	1.47	21.9	277	33	68	4.40	3.5	7.4	2.1	0.7	67
2007	A+	Potomac	6	0	0	50	35	2.15	0.92	23.4	180	21	79	1.62	2.7	6.3	2.3	0.5	90
2007	AA	Harrisburg	3	2	0	36	20	3.25	1.28	24.6	234	26	75	3.16	3.8	5.0	1.3	0.5	51
2007	AAA	Columbus	3	1	0	38	19	1.66	1.11	21.3	219	25	85	2.29	2.8	4.5	1.6	0.2	64
2007	MLB	Washington	2	2	0	34	10	4.21	1.55	24.9	272	28	74	4.65	4.5	2.6	0.6	0.8	5

Finesse pitcher with plus CU and ability to mix pitches. Keeps ball off plate, but needs better command. Strikeouts will be tough to come by, though helps himself with a good pickoff move. Deliberate ¾ delivery aids in deception, but also makes him slow to plate (1.7).

Lansford,Jared — SP — Oakland

EXP MLB DEBUT: 2010 | POTENTIAL: #4 starter | 8E

Thrws R Age 21 | 2005 (2-C) HS (CA)

Velo	Pitch	Grade	Year	Lev	Team	W	L	Sv	IP	K	ERA	WHIP	BF/G	OBA	H%	S%	xERA	Ctl	Dom	Cmd	hr/9	BPV
87-94	FB	++++	2005	Rk	AZL Athletics	0	1	0	21	20	1.28	1.00	11.5	212	29	86	1.67	2.1	8.5	4.0	0.0	148
72-74	CB	++	2006	A-	Kane County	11	6	0	104	50	2.86	1.24	23.5	229	26	75	2.61	3.6	4.3	1.2	0.1	58
78-80	CU	++	2006	A+	Stockton	0	1	0	11	9	14.59	2.61	20.1	434	47	44	12.53	4.1	7.3	1.8	3.2	-48
			2007	A+	Stockton	0	1	0	4	2	9.00	2.00	19.3	307	35	50	5.54	6.8	4.5	0.7	0.0	35

Pitched very little in 2007 while nursing a shoulder strain. Quick arm action gives him good movement on all pitches and does keep ball down, but lacks strikeout ability. Command can be inconsistent and lacks quality CU, which comes down to not repeating delivery.

Latos,Matt — SP — San Diego

EXP MLB DEBUT: 2010 | POTENTIAL: #2 starter | 9D

Thrws R Age 20 | 2006 (11) HS (FL)

Velo	Pitch	Grade	Year	Lev	Team	W	L	Sv	IP	K	ERA	WHIP	BF/G	OBA	H%	S%	xERA	Ctl	Dom	Cmd	hr/9	BPV
89-96	FB	++++																				
79-82	SL	++																				
	CB	+++																				
80-83	CU	+++	2007	A-	Eugene	1	4	0	56	74	3.83	1.43	14.9	268	29	73	3.99	3.5	11.9	3.4	0.2	145

Draft-and-follow pitched well for Broward County CC (2.03 ERA), possessing a good combination projectable size, arm action, and a plus FB. Commands plate and misses bats. SL lacks consistent bite and delivery gets lengthy, creating problems with running game.

LeBlanc,Wade — SP — San Diego

EXP MLB DEBUT: 2008 | POTENTIAL: #5 starter | 7C

Thrws R Age 23 | 2006 (2) Alabama

Velo	Pitch	Grade	Year	Lev	Team	W	L	Sv	IP	K	ERA	WHIP	BF/G	OBA	H%	S%	xERA	Ctl	Dom	Cmd	hr/9	BPV
84-89	FB	++	2006	A-	Fort Wayne	4	1	0	32	27	2.24	1.27	18.8	255	32	83	3.18	2.8	7.5	2.7	0.3	98
82-83	CT	+++	2006	A-	Eugene	1	0	0	21	20	4.29	1.19	12.0	243	33	60	2.55	2.6	8.6	3.3	0.0	128
64-69	CB	++	2007	A+	Lake Elsinore	6	5	0	92	90	2.64	0.97	21.8	217	28	74	2.12	1.7	8.8	5.3	0.5	161
73-76	CU	++++	2007	AA	San Antonio	7	3	0	57	55	3.47	1.17	19.0	230	27	76	3.52	3.0	8.7	2.9	1.3	84

Polished pitcher who pitches above stuff by keeping ball low, mixing pitches, and displaying pinpoint command. Possesses below average velocity, but nets strikeouts by subtracting from FB and getting good movement. Tends to hang CB and will need pitch to succeed.

Lebron,Luis — RP — Baltimore

EXP MLB DEBUT: 2009 | POTENTIAL: Setup reliever | 8E

Thrws R Age 23 | 2004 FA (DR)

Velo	Pitch	Grade	Year	Lev	Team	W	L	Sv	IP	K	ERA	WHIP	BF/G	OBA	H%	S%	xERA	Ctl	Dom	Cmd	hr/9	BPV
91-98	FB	+++++	2006	A-	Delmarva	1	0	0	1	1	32.73	3.64	3.6	492	49	0	21.24	8.2	8.2	1.0	8.2	-219
83-85	SL	+++	2006	A-	Aberdeen	0	2	20	30	46	1.19	1.06	3.7	166	28	93	1.82	4.5	13.7	3.1	0.6	150
	CU	+	2007	A-	Delmarva	1	2	5	55	86	5.06	1.87	5.6	236	40	71	4.27	9.0	14.0	1.6	0.2	120
			2007	AA	Bowie	0	0	0	2	4	4.29	0.95	4.0	144	34	50	0.72	4.3	17.1	4.0	0.0	213

Thin/athletic who regressed statistically, essentially becoming a two-outcome reliever (strikeout or walk). Quick arm action may produce too much movement, but can overpower hitters with system's best velocity. Not a lot of finesse to game and will need CU to combat LH batters.

LeCure,Sam — SP — Cincinnati

EXP MLB DEBUT: 2009 | POTENTIAL: #4 starter | 7C

Thrws R Age 24 | 2005 (4) Texas

Velo	Pitch	Grade	Year	Lev	Team	W	L	Sv	IP	K	ERA	WHIP	BF/G	OBA	H%	S%	xERA	Ctl	Dom	Cmd	hr/9	BPV
88-93	FB	++++	2005	Rk	Billings	5	1	0	41	44	3.28	1.41	13.4	271	36	77	3.88	3.3	9.6	2.9	0.4	107
81-84	SL	+++	2006	A+	Sarasota	7	12	0	141	115	3.44	1.25	21.3	246	29	74	3.46	2.9	7.3	2.5	0.8	79
78-81	CU	++	2007	A+	Sarasota	1	0	0	5	8	1.80	0.40	16.1	124	25	50	0.00	0.0	14.4		0.0	117
			2007	AA	Chattanooga	7	5	0	110	104	4.17	1.50	22.6	277	34	75	4.72	3.8	8.5	2.3	1.0	69

Athletic pitcher possesses two above average pitches in his SL and FB that he sets-up and commands well. Held velocity and pitched later in games, alleviating any stamina concerns. Spent most of the year focusing on repeating his delivery and improving deception of CU.

Lerew,Anthony — SP — Atlanta

EXP MLB DEBUT: 2005 | POTENTIAL: #4 starter | 7D

Thrws R Age 25 | 2001 (11) HS (PA)

Velo	Pitch	Grade	Year	Lev	Team	W	L	Sv	IP	K	ERA	WHIP	BF/G	OBA	H%	S%	xERA	Ctl	Dom	Cmd	hr/9	BPV
			2006	AA	Mississippi	4	2	0	48	37	2.80	1.16	21.3	240	30	75	2.63	2.4	6.9	2.8	0.2	103
88-94	FB	+++	2006	AAA	Richmond	3	5	0	71	69	7.48	1.80	20.5	315	38	59	6.56	4.6	8.7	1.9	1.5	39
76-80	SL	++	2006	MLB	Atlanta	0	0	0	2	1	22.50	4.00	13.6	470	52	38	13.90	13.5	4.5	0.3	0.0	-5
79-84	CU	++++	2007	AAA	Richmond	1	0	0	26	15	1.38	1.07	20.3	214	25	86	1.92	2.8	5.2	1.9	0.0	83
			2007	MLB	Atlanta	0	2	0	11	9	8.04	1.88	17.5	307	31	65	8.22	5.6	7.2	1.3	3.2	-32

Athletic pitcher was off to a hot start until derailed by TJS in July. Repeats his ¾ delivery enabling him to show command and mask his plus SPL, while enhancing look of FB. Will need to regain feel for pitching, strengthen arm, and learn to trust stuff.

Lewis,Scott — SP — Cleveland

EXP MLB DEBUT: 2008 | POTENTIAL: #5 starter | 7C

Thrws L Age 24 | 2004 (3) Ohio St

Velo	Pitch	Grade	Year	Lev	Team	W	L	Sv	IP	K	ERA	WHIP	BF/G	OBA	H%	S%	xERA	Ctl	Dom	Cmd	hr/9	BPV
84-88	FB	++	2004	A-	Mahoning Val	0	2	0	5	13	5.29	1.18	6.8	258	78	50	2.57	1.8	22.9	13.0	0.0	414
72-75	CB	+++	2005	A-	Mahoning Val	0	1	0	15	24	4.74	1.25	8.8	233	37	65	3.62	3.6	14.2	4.0	1.2	142
78-81	CU	+++	2006	A+	Kinston	3	3	0	115	123	1.48	0.97	16.2	205	29	85	1.74	2.2	9.6	4.4	0.2	157
			2007	AA	Akron	7	9	0	134	121	3.69	1.26	20.3	263	32	73	3.81	2.3	8.1	3.6	0.9	100

CLE gave him more rope, pitching a career-high in IP, as his prior elbow and shoulder surgeries had held him back. Command is outstanding, is deceptive with ¾ delivery, and has three pitches he can interchange. Below average velocity will keep him at backend of rotation.

Lincoln,Brad — SP — Pittsburgh

EXP MLB DEBUT: 2009 | POTENTIAL: #2 starter/setup reliever | 9D

Thrws R Age 23 | 2006 (1) Houston

Velo	Pitch	Grade	Year	Lev	Team	W	L	Sv	IP	K	ERA	WHIP	BF/G	OBA	H%	S%	xERA	Ctl	Dom	Cmd	hr/9	BPV
88-96	FB	++++																				
82-84	CB	++++																				
	CU	++	2006	A-	Hickory	1	2	0	16	10	6.75	2.00	19.3	366	41	67	7.59	3.4	5.6	1.7	1.1	17
			2006	Rk	GCL Pirates	0	0	0	7	9	0.00	0.97	13.7	228	35	100	1.78	1.3	11.3	9.0	0.0	266

Elbow ligament irritation led to TJS in Apr. Short/strong-framed pitcher features plus velocity and hard CB that registers strikeouts. Arm action is smooth and exhibits excellent command, but doesn't repeat ¾ delivery or change speeds adequately, so may struggle intially.

Liz,Radhames — SP — Baltimore

EXP MLB DEBUT: 2007 | POTENTIAL: #2 starter | 9C

Thrws R Age 25 | 2003 FA (DR)

Velo	Pitch	Grade	Year	Lev	Team	W	L	Sv	IP	K	ERA	WHIP	BF/G	OBA	H%	S%	xERA	Ctl	Dom	Cmd	hr/9	BPV
			2005	A-	Delmarva	2	3	0	38	55	4.49	1.47	16.3	235	37	69	3.55	5.4	13.0	2.4	0.5	122
89-98	FB	++++	2006	A+	Frederick	6	5	0	83	95	2.82	1.22	20.9	196	26	81	2.83	4.8	10.3	2.2	0.9	97
82-84	SL	+++	2006	AA	Bowie	3	1	0	50	54	5.39	1.72	22.7	280	35	73	5.89	5.6	9.7	1.7	1.6	45
73-78	CB	++++	2007	AA	Bowie	11	4	0	137	161	3.22	1.25	22.3	207	28	77	3.03	4.6	10.6	2.3	0.9	100
80-83	CU	+++	2007	MLB	Baltimore	0	2	0	24	24	7.07	1.98	12.9	268	33	64	5.93	8.6	8.9	1.0	1.1	43

Athletic/live-armed pitcher with two plus pitches (FB and CB) and quick arm action, making him tough to hit. Improved command, repetitiveness of delivery, and stamina may allow him to remain a starter. Needs to trust stuff and be more precise in the strike zone.

Locke,Jeff — SP — Atlanta

EXP MLB DEBUT: 2010 | POTENTIAL: #3 starter | 8C

Thrws L Age 20 | 2006 (2-C) HS (NH)

Velo	Pitch	Grade	Year	Lev	Team	W	L	Sv	IP	K	ERA	WHIP	BF/G	OBA	H%	S%	xERA	Ctl	Dom	Cmd	hr/9	BPV
87-93	FB	++++																				
72-78	CB	+++																				
	CU	++	2006	Rk	GCL Braves	4	3	0	32	38	4.22	1.34	13.3	296	39	72	4.72	1.4	10.7	7.6	1.1	186
			2007	Rk	Danville	7	1	1	61	74	2.66	0.92	17.5	218	34	73	3.12	1.2	10.9	9.3	0.3	166

Athletic pitcher showed impressive command and dominance, proving very hard to hit. Works primarily off of FB, but can drop CB in for strikeouts. Arm action is present to repeat delivery and improve quality of CU, and projects to more velocity with maturity.

Lofgren,Chuck — SP — Cleveland

EXP MLB DEBUT: 2008 | POTENTIAL: #3 starter | 8B

Thrws L Age 22 | 2004 (4) HS (CA)

Velo	Pitch	Grade	Year	Lev	Team	W	L	Sv	IP	K	ERA	WHIP	BF/G	OBA	H%	S%	xERA	Ctl	Dom	Cmd	hr/9	BPV
			2004	Rk	Burlington	0	0	0	22	23	6.11	1.72	11.1	286	35	68	6.00	5.3	9.4	1.8	1.6	42
86-92	FB	++++	2005	A-	Lake County	5	5	0	93	89	2.81	1.25	21.0	218	28	79	2.92	4.2	8.6	2.1	0.6	89
81-84	SL	+++	2006	A+	Kinston	17	5	0	139	125	2.33	1.16	22.1	214	28	80	2.41	3.5	8.1	2.3	0.3	100
70-74	CB	++	2007	AA	Akron	12	7	0	146	123	4.37	1.51	24.3	271	32	72	4.56	4.2	7.6	1.8	0.9	58
77-80	CU	+++	2007	AAA	Buffalo	0	1	0	5	7	10.80	2.00	24.1	332	46	44	7.55	5.4	12.6	2.3	1.8	59

Relied more on movement and incorporating all pitches, which cost him efficiency and command. Repeats a deceptive high ¾ delivery, although he sometimes gets out of sync with runners on base. FB exhibits natural cutting action and throws strikes with SL and CU.

 PITCHERS

Long,Matt — RP — Chicago (A)

EXP MLB DEBUT: 2009 | POTENTIAL: Setup reliever/closer | 7D

Thrws R Age 24
2006 (2) Miami-OH

Velo	Pitch	Grade
88-93	FB	++++
76-79	CB	+++
78-81	CU	+

Year	Lev	Team	W	L	Sv	IP	K	ERA	WHIP	BF/G	OBA	H%	S%	xERA	Ctl	Dom	Cmd	hr/9	BPV
2006	A-	Kannapolis	3	5	1	33	20	8.13	1.93	7.2	353	38	58	7.39	3.5	5.4	1.5	1.4	9
2007	A-	Kannapolis	9	3	0	104	73	5.54	1.55	17.5	307	35	65	5.36	2.7	6.3	2.4	1.0	50

Successful college closer hasn't adjusted well to starting, showing decrease in velocity, strikeout rate, and hit rate. Derives movement to FB and CB with his smooth arm action and creates downward plane with his height. Will have to develop CU to continue in role.

Lotzkar,Kyle — SP — Cincinnati

EXP MLB DEBUT: 2011 | POTENTIAL: #3 starter | 8E

Thrws R Age 18
2007 (1-S) HS (Canada)

Velo	Pitch	Grade
88-93	FB	++++
79-82	SU	+++
	CU	+

Year	Lev	Team	W	L	Sv	IP	K	ERA	WHIP	BF/G	OBA	H%	S%	xERA	Ctl	Dom	Cmd	hr/9	BPV
2007	Rk	Billings	0	0	0	8	12	1.13	0.50	13.3	42	0	100	0.00	3.4	13.5	4.0	1.1	178
2007	Rk	GCL Reds	0	2	0	21	24	3.86	1.33	12.5	262	35	73	3.95	3.0	10.3	3.4	0.9	111

Top-flight Canadian arm with smooth arm action that generates excellent movement. Velocity projects higher and gets strikeouts with SU. Likes to pitch aggressively, but pitches move so well that he has difficulty commanding them and lacks finesse to game.

Lowe,Mark — RP — Seattle

EXP MLB DEBUT: 2006 | POTENTIAL: Setup reliever/closer | 7B

Thrws R Age 25
2004 (5) Tex-Arlington

Velo	Pitch	Grade
88-94	FB	++++
82-86	SL	+++
78-81	CU	++

Year	Lev	Team	W	L	Sv	IP	K	ERA	WHIP	BF/G	OBA	H%	S%	xERA	Ctl	Dom	Cmd	hr/9	BPV
2006	MLB	Seattle	1	0	0	18	20	1.98	1.15	4.8	190	26	85	2.25	4.5	9.9	2.2	0.5	108
2007	A-	Everett	0	0	0	1	0	0.00	0.00	2.8	0	0		0.00	0.0	0.0		0.0	55
2007	AA	W. Tennessee	0	0	0	2	1	4.09	1.82	3.4	244	28	75	4.18	8.2	4.1	0.5	0.0	41
2007	AAA	Tacoma	0	0	0	6	5	5.90	2.46	4.6	411	47	79	9.96	4.4	7.4	1.7	1.5	8
2007	MLB	Seattle	0	0	0	2	3	8.18	2.27	2.8	244	24	75	9.09	12.3	12.3	1.0	4.1	-22

Missed most of 2007 with clean-out elbow surgery, but remains part of SEA bullpen plans. Dominates hitters with FB and SL that are both plus pitches, but unlike most flame-throwers, he has a sense of command. CU is a distant third and could take next step if it improves.

Luebke,Cory — SP — San Diego

EXP MLB DEBUT: 2009 | POTENTIAL: #4 starter | 8D

Thrws L Age 23
2007 (1-S) Ohio St

Velo	Pitch	Grade
87-91	FB	+++
78-81	SL	+++
77-81	CU	+++

Year	Lev	Team	W	L	Sv	IP	K	ERA	WHIP	BF/G	OBA	H%	S%	xERA	Ctl	Dom	Cmd	hr/9	BPV
2007	A-	Eugene	3	0	0	24	26	1.49	0.83	11.0	209	27	89	1.89	0.7	9.7	13.0	0.7	322
2007	A-	Fort Wayne	1	2	0	27	30	3.33	1.26	22.0	276	37	75	3.78	1.7	10.0	6.0	0.7	166
2007	A+	Lake Elsinore	1	1	0	7	5	7.71	1.57	15.4	336	38	50	6.13	1.3	6.4	5.0	1.3	93

Athletic/projectable pitcher with intelligence and three average to above pitches that feed off each other. Keeps hitters off-balance by mixing pitchees and repeating delivery, and commands plate. Strikeout rate isn't high, but induces enough groundballs to compensate.

Lumsden,Tyler — SP — Kansas City

EXP MLB DEBUT: 2008 | POTENTIAL: #5 starter | 7C

Thrws L Age 25
2004 (1-S) Clemson

Velo	Pitch	Grade
87-92	FB	++++
81-84	SL	+++
70-75	CB	+++
79-83	CU	++

Year	Lev	Team	W	L	Sv	IP	K	ERA	WHIP	BF/G	OBA	H%	S%	xERA	Ctl	Dom	Cmd	hr/9	BPV
2004	A+	Win-Salem	3	1	0	39	31	4.14	1.66	11.7	290	35	75	4.84	4.6	7.1	1.6	0.5	59
2006	AA	Birm/Wich	11	5	0	159	96	2.77	1.31	24.3	249	28	81	3.61	3.4	5.4	1.6	0.7	51
2007	AAA	Omaha	9	6	0	119	74	5.89	1.68	21.4	296	33	65	5.33	4.5	5.6	1.3	0.8	31

Projectable pitcher with good velocity and two average breaking pitches. Deceptive ¾ delivery makes pitches appear better and can be tough on LH batters. Poor base skills can't totally be blamed on hitter-friendly environment, as he has always struggled with command.

Lyman,Jeff — SP — Atlanta

EXP MLB DEBUT: 2010 | POTENTIAL: #4 starter | 7D

Thrws R Age 21
2005 (2-C) HS (CA)

Velo	Pitch	Grade
88-91	FB	+++
76-79	SU	+++
78-81	CU	+++

Year	Lev	Team	W	L	Sv	IP	K	ERA	WHIP	BF/G	OBA	H%	S%	xERA	Ctl	Dom	Cmd	hr/9	BPV
2005	Rk	GCL Braves	0	3	0	34	28	4.24	1.41	18.0	300	36	70	4.41	1.9	7.4	4.0	0.5	108
2006	A-	Rome	6	6	0	100	80	4.50	1.65	20.3	295	36	71	4.70	4.2	7.2	1.7	0.3	67
2006	Rk	GCL Braves	0	0	0	6	9	1.50	0.50	10.0	106	20	67	0.00	1.5	13.5	9.0	0.0	304
2007	A-	Rome	5	8	0	104	77	4.59	1.55	22.7	294	34	72	4.99	3.4	6.7	2.0	0.9	52
2007	A+	Myrtle Beach	0	5	0	31	17	8.97	1.90	18.3	308	33	51	6.38	5.8	4.9	0.9	1.2	6

Possesses arm strength and is deceptive with low ¾ slot, making him tough on RH batters. Lacks strikeout ability and velocity, but commands three average pitches. Aggressive style can be too much at times and needs to smooth-out delivery.

Machi,Jean — RP — Toronto

EXP MLB DEBUT: 2008 | POTENTIAL: Setup reliever | 7D

Thrws R Age 25
2002 FA (Venezuela)

Velo	Pitch	Grade
90-96	FB	++++
82-85	SL	+
80-82	CU	+++

Year	Lev	Team	W	L	Sv	IP	K	ERA	WHIP	BF/G	OBA	H%	S%	xERA	Ctl	Dom	Cmd	hr/9	BPV
2003	A-	Batavia	2	4	0	32	19	4.78	1.34	16.7	250	29	62	3.32	3.7	5.3	1.5	0.3	59
2005	A+	Visalia	3	11	3	97	106	6.03	1.76	14.3	292	39	65	5.36	5.4	9.8	1.8	0.7	72
2005	AA	Montgomery	0	0	0	0	0			5.6							0.0		
2006	AA	Montgomery	6	1	16	70	67	2.56	1.44	6.2	247	32	82	3.47	4.6	8.6	1.9	0.3	88
2007	AA	New Hamp.	2	4	2	81	56	3.55	1.13	6.7	229	26	71	3.08	2.7	6.2	2.3	0.9	69

Strong/stocky reliever with best velocity in system, but is more of a groundball pitcher than one that gets strikeouts. Repeats delivery which gives him above average command and ability to change speeds. Doesn't spin ball well which plays into low strikeout rate.

Madrigal,Warner — RP — Texas

EXP MLB DEBUT: 2009 | POTENTIAL: Setup reliever | 8E

Thrws R Age 24
2003 FA (DR)

Velo	Pitch	Grade
91-97	FB	++++
82-86	SL	+++

Year	Lev	Team	W	L	Sv	IP	K	ERA	WHIP	BF/G	OBA	H%	S%	xERA	Ctl	Dom	Cmd	hr/9	BPV
2006	Rk	AZL Angels	2	1	4	11	12	4.09	1.18	4.0	244	34	62	2.52	2.5	9.8	4.0	0.0	149
2007	A-	Cedar Rapids	5	4	20	61	75	2.07	1.10	4.4	204	30	83	2.22	3.4	11.1	3.3	0.4	136

Strong/athletic pitcher made successful transition to pitching after spending time as an outfielder. FB and SL form a deadly combination in getting strikeouts and command is solid for experience level. Pitches with effort, so will have to have usage patterns monitored.

Madsen,Mike — SP — Oakland

EXP MLB DEBUT: 2008 | POTENTIAL: #5 starter | 7C

Thrws R Age 25
2005 (21) Ohio St

Velo	Pitch	Grade
86-92	FB	+++
69-71	CB	+++
80-82	CU	+++

Year	Lev	Team	W	L	Sv	IP	K	ERA	WHIP	BF/G	OBA	H%	S%	xERA	Ctl	Dom	Cmd	hr/9	BPV
2006	A+	Stockton	6	11	0	121	102	6.69	1.59	22.2	302	36	57	5.23	3.3	7.6	2.3	0.9	62
2006	AA	Midland	0	0	0	7	5	19.01	3.10	21.0	487	56	32	12.08	3.8	6.3	1.7	0.0	31
2007	A+	Stockton	1	2	0	24	20	3.75	1.25	24.4	237	30	69	2.98	3.4	7.5	2.2	0.4	88
2007	AA	Midland	5	2	0	65	69	2.76	1.18	23.7	217	30	76	2.46	3.6	9.5	2.7	0.3	116
2007	AAA	Sacramento	5	1	0	58	40	5.11	1.45	24.8	248	27	67	4.44	4.6	6.2	1.3	1.2	33

Workhorse pitcher found early success, using his three-pitch mix to keep hitters off-balance and showing good command. None of his pitches rate better than average, but repeats high ¾ delivery and has a nice downward plane to the plate. Upside is limited, but can eat innings.

Maestri,Alessandro — RP — Chicago (N)

EXP MLB DEBUT: 2009 | POTENTIAL: Setup reliever/closer | 8E

Thrws R Age 23
2006 FA (Italy)

Velo	Pitch	Grade
88-92	FB	+++
80-82	SL	++++
	CU	+

Year	Lev	Team	W	L	Sv	IP	K	ERA	WHIP	BF/G	OBA	H%	S%	xERA	Ctl	Dom	Cmd	hr/9	BPV
2006	A-	Boise	4	3	1	42	35	3.80	1.16	7.6	232	32	75	3.99	2.8	7.5	2.7	0.8	84
2007	A-	Peoria	6	3	12	83	83	2.26	0.87	6.4	195	30	75	3.28	1.6	9.0	5.5	0.8	111

Short/athletic pitcher switched to relief after four starts and dominated as the closer. SL is a nasty pitch to RH batters and has improved his velocity over the past two seasons. Commands plate well and can miss bats, but needs to develop CU to combat LH batters.

Magee,Brandon — SP — Toronto

EXP MLB DEBUT: 2009 | POTENTIAL: #4 starter | 7D

Thrws R Age 24
2006 (4) Bradley

Velo	Pitch	Grade
88-94	FB	++++
81-84	SL	+++
78-81	CU	+

Year	Lev	Team	W	L	Sv	IP	K	ERA	WHIP	BF/G	OBA	H%	S%	xERA	Ctl	Dom	Cmd	hr/9	BPV
2006	A-	Auburn	3	1	0	52	40	3.11	1.32	19.6	254	31	75	3.21	3.3	6.9	2.1	0.2	85
2007	A+	Dunedin	9	8	0	156	76	3.92	1.38	23.4	268	29	73	4.15	3.1	4.4	1.4	0.8	33

Tall/projectable pitcher who had to rely on above average FB, as command and confidence in comps deserted him. Exhibits quick arm action, giving him movement to pitches, and will keep the ball down, but poor efficiency made him very hittable. Will need to improve comps.

Magnuson,Trystan — RP — Toronto

EXP MLB DEBUT: 2009 | POTENTIAL: Setup reliever/closer | 7B

Thrws R Age 23
2007 (1-S) Louisville
87-94 FB ++++
80-84 SL +++

Year	Lev	Team	W	L	Sv	IP	K	ERA	WHIP	BF/G	OBA	H%	S%	xERA	Ctl	Dom	Cmd	hr/9	BPV
2007																			

Tall/lanky reliever is tough on RH batters with low ¾ slot and whip-like motion. Power sinker and SL move extremely well and induces tons of groundballs, but isn't one to get many strikeouts. Upside isn't high, but could thrive and arrive quickly as a matchup reliever.

Maine,Scott — SP — Arizona

EXP MLB DEBUT: 2009 | POTENTIAL: #4 starter | 7D

Thrws L Age 23
2007 (6) Miami-FL
86-91 FB +++
73-76 CB +++
75-80 CU +++

Year	Lev	Team	W	L	Sv	IP	K	ERA	WHIP	BF/G	OBA	H%	S%	xERA	Ctl	Dom	Cmd	hr/9	BPV
2007	A-	Yakima	1	0	1	10	20	6.24	1.78	5.8	174	41	61	3.12	10.7	17.8	1.7	0.0	162

Pitchability hurler with three average pitches that play-up based on repeatable delivery, command, whip-like arm action, and aggressiveness. FB fades away from LH batters and gets sinking action to CU. May struggle to get strikeouts, but keeps ball down effectively.

Main,Michael — SP — Texas

EXP MLB DEBUT: 2011 | POTENTIAL: #2 starter | 9D

Thrws R Age 19
2007 (1-C) HS (FL)
90-97 FB +++++
77-82 SL +++
73-76 CB ++++
76-80 CU +++

Year	Lev	Team	W	L	Sv	IP	K	ERA	WHIP	BF/G	OBA	H%	S%	xERA	Ctl	Dom	Cmd	hr/9	BPV
2007	A-	Spokane	2	0	0	15	18	4.77	1.39	12.7	247	35	65	3.65	4.2	10.7	2.6	0.6	106
2007	Rk	AZL Rangers	0	1	0	12	16	1.48	1.23	9.9	207	30	93	2.86	4.4	11.8	2.7	0.7	118

Projectable/athletic pitcher with overpowering velocity and the ability to both miss bats and keep ball low. Has two breaking pitches at his disposal and showed better command than he did in high school. There is mild effort to his ¾ delivery and has a tendency to overthrow.

Maiques,Kenny — RP — St. Louis

EXP MLB DEBUT: 2009 | POTENTIAL: Setup reliever | 7D

Thrws R Age 23
2005 (37) Rio Hondo JC
89-94 FB ++++
80-83 SL ++++

Year	Lev	Team	W	L	Sv	IP	K	ERA	WHIP	BF/G	OBA	H%	S%	xERA	Ctl	Dom	Cmd	hr/9	BPV
2006	A-	State College	0	0	0	4	3	6.75	0.75	14.3	210	32	80	7.39	0.0	6.8	9.0	1.3	50
2007	A-	Quad Cties	1	5	31	53	20	1.53	0.70	3.6	185	33	84	3.21	0.5	3.4	6.7	0.8	97

Light-framed reliever with easy velocity and ability to nail RH batters with SL. Possesses solid command and limits long-ball with sinker, but doesn't have anything to offer LH batters. Throws with effort and has had prior TJS, so usage patterns need to be watched closely.

Maloney,Matt — SP — Cincinnati

EXP MLB DEBUT: 2008 | POTENTIAL: #5 starter | 7C

Thrws L Age 24
2005 (3) Mississippi
85-89 FB +++
77-80 SL +++
69-73 CB +++
78-79 CU +++

Year	Lev	Team	W	L	Sv	IP	K	ERA	WHIP	BF/G	OBA	H%	S%	xERA	Ctl	Dom	Cmd	hr/9	BPV
2005	A-	Batavia	2	1	0	37	36	3.89	1.43	19.7	267	35	73	3.94	3.6	8.8	2.4	0.5	90
2006	A-	Lakewood	16	9	0	168	180	2.09	1.15	24.7	202	28	82	2.17	3.9	9.6	2.5	0.3	116
2007	AA	Chat/Read	11	9	9	153	154	3.70	1.19	24.6	237	30	72	3.39	2.8	9.0	3.2	1.0	99
2007	AAA	Louisville	2	1	0	17	23	3.18	0.94	21.3	173	24	71	2.04	3.2	12.2	3.8	1.1	142

Finesse pitcher who wins and produces better base skills than stuff would indicate. Commands and mixes four pitches, and proved that he can get upper level hitters out. Needs to maintain command and prevent elevation of pitches, but look like a backend starter.

Manship,Jeff — SP — Minnesota

EXP MLB DEBUT: 2009 | POTENTIAL: #4 starter | 8C

Thrws R Age 23
2006 (14) Notre Dame
87-92 FB +++
SL +
CB ++++
CU ++

Year	Lev	Team	W	L	Sv	IP	K	ERA	WHIP	BF/G	OBA	H%	S%	xERA	Ctl	Dom	Cmd	hr/9	BPV
2006	A+	Fort Myers	0	0	0	8	12	2.20	1.10	8.0	232	39	78	2.13	2.2	13.2	6.0	0.0	214
2006	Rk	GCL Twins	0	0	0	5	10	0.00	0.77	9.3	170	39	100	0.53	1.7	17.3	10.0	0.0	335
2007	A-	Beloit	7	1	0	77	77	1.52	0.78	21.4	190	25	84	1.29	1.0	9.0	8.6	0.5	237
2007	A+	Fort Myers	8	5	0	71	59	3.16	1.43	23.3	277	34	79	4.24	3.2	7.5	2.4	0.6	75

Nearly untouchable in MWL with his plus CB and properly spotted FB, but numbers posted in FSL are more in-tune with his age/level. Intelligent pitcher who uses all four pitches. Light frame and average arm action could cause stamina issues, but pitched healthy all season.

Marek,Stephen — RP — Los Angeles (A)

EXP MLB DEBUT: 2008 | POTENTIAL: Setup reliever/closer | 8D

Thrws R Age 24
2004 (40) San Jacinto JC
88-96 FB ++++
78-82 CB +++
CU +

Year	Lev	Team	W	L	Sv	IP	K	ERA	WHIP	BF/G	OBA	H%	S%	xERA	Ctl	Dom	Cmd	hr/9	BPV
2005	Rk	Orem	1	3	0	66	55	4.50	1.50	19.0	284	34	72	4.81	3.4	7.5	2.2	1.0	61
2006	A-	Cedar Rapids	10	2	0	119	100	1.96	1.00	23.9	220	27	84	2.36	1.8	7.6	4.2	0.6	126
2006	A+	Rancho Cuc.	2	3	0	32	33	3.94	1.22	21.5	224	28	71	3.42	3.7	9.3	2.5	1.1	86
2007	A+	Rancho Cuc.	8	10	0	134	106	4.30	1.36	22.4	260	30	72	4.29	3.3	7.1	2.2	1.1	57

Slowly transforming from a thrower to a pitcher, his strong frame and arm strength allow him to maintain velocity. Works off FB and CB with success, but because his command was inconsistent, his dominance decreased. Will need to improve CU or get moved to relief.

Marquez,Jeff — SP — New York (A)

EXP MLB DEBUT: 2009 | POTENTIAL: #4 starter | 8C

Thrws R Age 23
2004 (1-S) Sacramento CC
89-94 FB ++++
76-79 CB ++
76-80 CU +++

Year	Lev	Team	W	L	Sv	IP	K	ERA	WHIP	BF/G	OBA	H%	S%	xERA	Ctl	Dom	Cmd	hr/9	BPV
2004	A-	Staten Island	2	4	0	50	36	3.05	1.41	19.3	265	32	78	3.76	3.6	6.5	1.8	0.4	68
2005	A-	Charleston	9	13	0	139	107	3.43	1.43	21.9	260	32	75	3.64	3.9	6.9	1.8	0.3	74
2006	A+	Tampa	7	5	0	92	82	3.62	1.42	21.7	282	36	74	4.04	2.8	8.0	2.8	0.4	94
2006	Rk	GCL Yankees	0	1	0	5	8	3.46	1.54	11.3	323	47	86	6.17	1.7	13.8	8.0	1.7	190
2007	AA	Trenton	15	9	0	155	94	3.66	1.35	24.0	275	31	74	4.03	2.6	5.5	2.1	0.6	58

Smooth delivery and quick arm action provide sinking movement to FB and ability to change speeds. Improved CB and learned to use all pitches, helping him lead EL in wins, but had to sacrifice strikeout rate. Stamina issues were alleviated after pitching 150+ innings.

Martinez,Carlos — RP — Florida

EXP MLB DEBUT: 2006 | POTENTIAL: Setup reliever/closer | 7C

Thrws R Age 26
2004 FA (Venezuela)
88-94 FB ++++
82-85 SL +++

Year	Lev	Team	W	L	Sv	IP	K	ERA	WHIP	BF/G	OBA	H%	S%	xERA	Ctl	Dom	Cmd	hr/9	BPV
2006	MLB	Florida	0	1	0	10	11	1.78	1.49	3.6	240	34	87	3.24	5.3	9.8	1.8	0.0	104
2007	A+	Jupiter	0	0	0	2	1	4.50	1.50	4.3	347	30	100	9.18	0.0	4.5		4.5	-122
2007	AA	Carolina	1	1	0	21	18	3.41	1.23	4.5	261	31	75	3.70	2.1	7.7	3.6	0.9	99
2007	AAA	Albuquerque	0	0	0	1	2	8.18	3.64	2.4	492	73	75	13.47	8.2	16.4	2.0	0.0	97
2007	MLB	Florida	0	0	0	2	2	16.36	2.27	5.6	392	19	50	19.24	4.1	8.2	2.0	12.3	-300

Returned from TJS in 2006 to contribute to the big club in September. Possesses extreme movement to FB and SL, and quickly gained feel for pitches and command. Stamina may always be a concern due to his slight frame and effort to ¾ delivery, but can effective in relief.

Martinez,Joey — SP — San Francisco

EXP MLB DEBUT: 2009 | POTENTIAL: #5 starter | 7D

Thrws R Age 25
2005 (12) Boston College
84-89 FB ++
70-72 CB +++
75-79 CU ++++

Year	Lev	Team	W	L	Sv	IP	K	ERA	WHIP	BF/G	OBA	H%	S%	xERA	Ctl	Dom	Cmd	hr/9	BPV
2005	A-	Salem-Keizer	4	3	0	69	59	4.30	1.22	18.6	262	33	74	4.44	2.0	7.7	3.9	1.2	54
2006	A-	Augusta	15	5	0	165	134	3.01	1.08	24.8	247	30	75	3.78	1.4	7.3	5.2	0.5	80
2007	A+	San Jose	10	10	0	162	151	4.26	1.28	23.8	273	33	72	4.30	2.0	8.4	4.2	0.6	89

Soft-tossing hurler with an excellent CU. Pitches backwards in an aggressive fashion, adding and subtracting from FB. Lacks velocity and strikeout capability, but keeps ball low and command is solid. Real test will come at upper levels, where his style will be scrutinized.

Martis,Shairon — SP — Washington

EXP MLB DEBUT: 2009 | POTENTIAL: #4 starter | 7D

Thrws R Age 21
2004 FA (Curacao)
87-91 FB +++
SL ++
CB ++
CU +++

Year	Lev	Team	W	L	Sv	IP	K	ERA	WHIP	BF/G	OBA	H%	S%	xERA	Ctl	Dom	Cmd	hr/9	BPV
2005	Rk	AZL Giants	2	1	1	34	50	1.85	1.09	12.1	226	37	83	2.28	2.4	13.2	5.6	0.3	198
2006	A-	Aug/Sav	7	5	0	98	80	3.49	1.26	21.0	262	32	72	3.41	2.3	7.3	3.2	0.5	100
2006	A+	Potomac	0	2	0	12	7	3.00	1.00	22.9	210	25	67	1.69	2.3	5.3	2.3	0.0	93
2006	AA	Harrisburg	0	1	0	5	1	12.60	2.20	25.1	362	23	57	13.77	5.4	1.8	0.3	7.2	-216
2007	A+	Potomac	14	8	0	151	108	4.23	1.34	23.3	260	31	68	3.68	3.1	6.4	2.1	0.5	69

Wiry athlete with body type and arm action to project more velocity. K/9 and oppBA were soft, but knows how to attack hitters' weaknesses, changes speeds well, and commands plate. Doesn't spin ball well and may need to eliminate a breaking pitch.

Mason,Chris — SP — Tampa Bay

EXP MLB DEBUT: 2008 | POTENTIAL: #5 starter | 7C

Thrws R Age 23
2005 (2) UNC Greensboro

Velo	Pitch	Grade
88-92	FB	+ + +
78-81	SL	+ + +
	CU	+ +

Year	Lev	Team	W	L	Sv	IP	K	ERA	WHIP	BF/G	OBA	H%	S%	xERA	Ctl	Dom	Cmd	hr/9	BPV
2005	A-	SW Michigan	1	0	0	18	16	1.48	1.21	7.3	249	32	86	2.68	2.5	7.9	3.2	0.0	120
2005	A-	Hudson Valley	1	1	2	15	14	2.40	1.27	6.8	206	28	79	2.29	4.8	8.4	1.8	0.0	101
2006	A+	Visalia	12	10	0	152	111	5.03	1.45	23.2	292	33	67	4.86	2.6	6.6	2.5	1.0	59
2007	AA	Montgomery	15	4	0	161	136	2.57	1.19	23.0	244	31	79	2.93	2.5	7.6	3.1	0.4	105

Aggressive pitcher with deceptive delivery and command, allowing him to lead SL in ERA and wins. Pitches to hitters' weaknesses and induces plenty of groundballs, combating his marginal strikeout ability and velocity. CU is much improved and projects as an inning-eater.

Masterson,Justin — RP — Boston

EXP MLB DEBUT: 2008 | POTENTIAL: #4 starter/setup reliever | 8B

Thrws R Age 23
2006 (2) San Diego St

Velo	Pitch	Grade
88-93	FB	+ + + +
81-84	SL	+ + +
80-83	CU	+ +

Year	Lev	Team	W	L	Sv	IP	K	ERA	WHIP	BF/G	OBA	H%	S%	xERA	Ctl	Dom	Cmd	hr/9	BPV
2006	A-	Lowell	3	1	0	31	33	0.87	0.71	7.9	185	27	86	0.61	0.6	9.5	16.5	0.0	422
2007	A+	Lancaster	8	5	0	95	56	4.35	1.31	23.1	277	32	65	3.71	2.1	5.3	2.5	0.4	73
2007	AA	Portland	4	3	0	58	59	4.34	1.16	23.1	231	30	62	2.88	2.8	9.2	3.3	0.6	114

Tall/well-proportioned pitcher with plus sinking movement to FB, as evidenced by a 3.5 G/F in Double-A. Pitches with low ¾ slot that adds to his deception and compliments his groundball prowess with strikeouts. CU could be used more frequently.

Mateo,Juan — SP — Chicago (N)

EXP MLB DEBUT: 2006 | POTENTIAL: #5 starter/setup reliever | 7C

Thrws R Age 25
2002 FA (DR)

Velo	Pitch	Grade
87-94	FB	+ + + +
78-80	SL	+ + +
82-84	CU	+ +

Year	Lev	Team	W	L	Sv	IP	K	ERA	WHIP	BF/G	OBA	H%	S%	xERA	Ctl	Dom	Cmd	hr/9	BPV
2005	A+	Daytona	10	5	2	109	123	3.22	1.15	13.6	243	33	74	3.15	2.2	10.1	4.6	0.7	141
2006	AA	W. Tennessee	7	4	0	92	70	2.83	1.13	20.2	231	27	77	2.80	2.5	6.8	2.7	0.6	89
2006	MLB	Chicago (N)	1	3	0	45	35	5.38	1.64	18.3	286	33	69	5.40	4.6	7.0	1.5	1.2	36
2007	A-	Peoria	2	1	0	22	14	5.29	1.58	16.2	302	35	65	4.79	3.3	5.7	1.8	0.4	53
2007	AAA	Iowa	2	3	0	40	29	4.05	1.53	21.7	307	33	81	6.02	2.5	6.5	2.6	1.8	34

CHC was counting on some contribution from him, but struggled with minor injuries and ineffectiveness. Possesses live FB and SL, being extremely tough on RH batters. Struggles to repeat ¾ slot and arm speed for CU which could make him more suitable for relief.

Mathieson,Scott — SP — Philadelphia

EXP MLB DEBUT: 2006 | POTENTIAL: #3 starter | 8D

Thrws R Age 24
2002 (17) HS (Canada)

Velo	Pitch	Grade
89-95	FB	+ + + +
83-86	SL	+ + +
79-82	CB	+
80-82	CU	+ + +

Year	Lev	Team	W	L	Sv	IP	K	ERA	WHIP	BF/G	OBA	H%	S%	xERA	Ctl	Dom	Cmd	hr/9	BPV
2006	AAA	Scranton/WB	3	1	0	34	36	3.96	1.06	26.4	213	29	62	2.32	2.6	9.5	3.6	0.5	129
2006	MLB	Philadelphia	1	4	0	37	28	7.52	1.73	18.7	315	34	59	6.77	3.9	6.8	1.8	1.9	11
2007	A+	Clearwater	0	0	0	4	5	4.50	1.50	5.8	210	32	67	2.89	6.8	11.3	1.7	0.0	115
2007	AA	Reading	0	0	0	2	1	9.00	2.50	5.3	347	30	75	11.70	9.0	4.5	0.5	4.5	-112
2007	Rk	GCL Phillies	0	0	0	2	3	0.00	0.50	3.3	0	0	100	0.00	4.5	13.5	3.0	0.0	199

Longer recovery from TJS than expected, undergoing a minor procedure in Sept. Arm action provides easy velocity and pitch movement, and repeats ¾ delivery giving him ability to change speeds and command. Needs to find a workable breaking pitch and build-up arm strength.

Matos,Osiris — SP — San Francisco

EXP MLB DEBUT: 2008 | POTENTIAL: Short reliever/closer | 7C

Thrws R Age 23
2002 FA (DR)

Velo	Pitch	Grade
89-94	FB	+ + + +
81-83	SL	+ + +
79-82	CU	+ +

Year	Lev	Team	W	L	Sv	IP	K	ERA	WHIP	BF/G	OBA	H%	S%	xERA	Ctl	Dom	Cmd	hr/9	BPV
2005	A-	Augusta	8	8	0	135	79	5.00	1.43	19.8	298	33	65	4.71	2.1	5.3	2.5	0.8	56
2006	A-	Augusta	7	3	13	61	81	1.77	0.89	5.1	196	30	82	1.59	1.8	12.0	6.8	0.4	216
2006	AA	Connecticut	0	0	2	9	5	3.91	1.41	6.5	298	34	69	3.92	2.0	4.9	2.5	0.0	77
2007	A-	Augusta	0	0	4	9	9	0.00	0.22	3.9	38	6	100	0.00	1.0	9.0	9.0	0.0	290
2007	AA	Connecticut	5	0	4	56	43	2.89	1.27	6.5	240	29	78	3.18	3.4	6.9	2.0	0.5	77

Strong framed reliever with aggressive approach. FB has power and movement, and has two comps to combat hitters from both sides, giving him an option to close. Command wavers from outing to outing and pitches with some effort, but hasn't affected resiliency of arm.

McAllister,Zach — SP — New York (A)

EXP MLB DEBUT: 2010 | POTENTIAL: #5 starter | 7C

Thrws R Age 20
2006 (3) Illinois Valley

Velo	Pitch	Grade
87-92	FB	+ + +
78-81	SL	+ + +
77-80	CU	+ +

Year	Lev	Team	W	L	Sv	IP	K	ERA	WHIP	BF/G	OBA	H%	S%	xERA	Ctl	Dom	Cmd	hr/9	BPV
2006	Rk	GCL Yankees	5	2	0	35	28	0.26	1.34	13.2	262	25	128	5.86	3.1	7.2	2.3	2.8	10
2007	A-	Staten Island	4	6	0	71	75	0.38	1.52	19.3	285	24	157	8.83	3.5	9.5	2.7	5.2	-45

Tall/projectable hurler was able to adjust to a higher arm slot which culminated in better command and pitch movement. Works primarily off of FB and can nail RH batters with SL. Needs to incorporate CU and will need to show he can handle a heavy workload.

McBeth,Marcus — RP — Cincinnati

EXP MLB DEBUT: 2007 | POTENTIAL: Setup reliever | 7C

Thrws R Age 27
2001 (4) So Carolina

Velo	Pitch	Grade
87-92	FB	+ + + +
80-84	SL	+ +
79-83	CU	+ + +

Year	Lev	Team	W	L	Sv	IP	K	ERA	WHIP	BF/G	OBA	H%	S%	xERA	Ctl	Dom	Cmd	hr/9	BPV
2006	A+	Stockton	0	0	7	8	14	0.00	0.37	3.3	41	10	100	0.00	2.2	15.4	7.0	0.0	286
2006	AA	Midland	3	2	24	53	63	2.54	1.17	4.8	219	30	81	2.80	3.4	10.7	3.2	0.7	121
2006	AAA	Sacramento	0	1	0	7	7	11.41	1.83	5.5	259	23	40	7.95	7.6	8.9	1.2	3.8	-33
2007	AAA	Lou/Sac	2	1	17	41	35	2.40	1.21	4.4	256	31	85	3.61	2.2	7.6	3.5	0.9	97
2007	MLB	Cincinnati	3	2	0	19	17	6.09	1.51	3.6	289	35	59	4.88	3.3	8.0	2.4	0.9	68

Athletic reliever with arm strength and good pitch movement, his FB/CU creates a solid one-two punch that feed off each other. Command improved and pitched effectively to hitters from both sides. SL could be tighter and needs to pitch with less effort to improve resiliency.

McCardell,Michael — SP — Minnesota

EXP MLB DEBUT: 2009 | POTENTIAL: #4 starter | 8D

Thrws R Age 23
2007 (6) Kutztown

Velo	Pitch	Grade
88-92	FB	+ + + +
	SL	+ +
	CU	+ +

Year	Lev	Team	W	L	Sv	IP	K	ERA	WHIP	BF/G	OBA	H%	S%	xERA	Ctl	Dom	Cmd	hr/9	BPV
2005	Rk	Elizabethton	5	1	0	45	70	0.60	0.76	20.1	186	25	129	2.59	1.0	14.0	14.0	2.0	336
2007	Rk	GCL Twins	2	0	1	18	25	1.00	0.78	16.2	178	19	133	3.04	1.5	12.5	8.3	2.5	194

Tall/athletic pitcher blitzed through two short-season leagues. Pitches off lively FB and commands it so well that he generates swings and misses. Though he repeats high ¾ delivery consistently, his CU isn't that effective and needs to tighten rotation of SL.

McCormick,Mark — SP — St. Louis

EXP MLB DEBUT: 2009 | POTENTIAL: #4 starter/closer | 8E

Thrws R Age 24
2005 (1-S) Baylor

Velo	Pitch	Grade
90-97	FB	+ + + +
81-84	SL	+ +
77-81	CB	+ + +
80-81	CU	+ +

Year	Lev	Team	W	L	Sv	IP	K	ERA	WHIP	BF/G	OBA	H%	S%	xERA	Ctl	Dom	Cmd	hr/9	BPV
2005	A-	Quad City	1	2	0	42	45	5.55	1.64	20.9	256	33	66	4.64	6.0	9.6	1.6	0.9	69
2006	A-	Quad City	2	4	0	52	63	3.97	1.46	20.3	205	29	73	3.22	6.6	10.9	1.7	0.5	98
2006	A+	Palm Beach	0	0	0	4	5	11.25	2.00	9.6	307	44	38	5.48	6.8	11.3	1.7	0.0	96
2007	A+	Palm Beach	0	0	0	3	2	0.00	0.67	10.5	191	24	100	0.62	0.0	6.0		0.0	53
2007	Rk	AZL Cardinals	0	0	0	4	4	2.14	0.71	4.9	78	11	67	0.00	4.3	8.6	2.0	0.0	133

Missed most of 2007 with minor shoulder surgery. Possesses lively arm with plus movement and velocity to FB and a CB that is impossible to hit. Mechanics are not consistent, affecting command and efficiency. Without quality CU and stamina issues, he may move to relief.

McCrory,Bob — RP — Baltimore

EXP MLB DEBUT: 2008 | POTENTIAL: Setup reliever | 7C

Thrws R Age 26
2003 (4) So Miss

Velo	Pitch	Grade
91-98	FB	+ + + +
83-86	SL	+
77-78	SU	+ +

Year	Lev	Team	W	L	Sv	IP	K	ERA	WHIP	BF/G	OBA	H%	S%	xERA	Ctl	Dom	Cmd	hr/9	BPV
2004	Rk	Bluefield	4	3	0	51	51	1.93	1.45	19.9	225	29	89	3.46	5.6	9.0	1.6	0.5	81
2005	A-	Aberdeen	2	1	0	24	21	3.35	1.20	19.4	235	29	74	3.17	3.0	7.8	2.6	0.7	88
2006	A-	Aberdeen	2	2	2	38	57	2.36	1.26	7.8	229	37	83	2.93	3.8	13.4	3.6	0.5	150
2007	A+	Frederick	0	0	14	22	22	1.23	1.27	4.1	205	27	93	2.66	4.9	9.0	1.8	0.4	94
2007	AA	Bowie	1	2	13	23	22	3.91	1.70	4.7	262	35	74	4.07	6.3	8.6	1.4	0.0	83

Strong-framed reliever who pitches aggressive with plus velocity and fair CU. Operates by being effectively wild, but will need to throw SL for strikes instead of off the plate. Tends to rush delivery and throws with effort which could have been culprit behind TJS in 2005.

McCulloch,Kyle — SP — Chicago (A)

EXP MLB DEBUT: 2008 | POTENTIAL: #4 starter | 7C

Thrws R Age 23
2006 (1) Texas

Velo	Pitch	Grade
85-92	FB	+ + +
75-78	CB	+ + +
78-79	SP	+ + + +
77-80	CU	

Year	Lev	Team	W	L	Sv	IP	K	ERA	WHIP	BF/G	OBA	H%	S%	xERA	Ctl	Dom	Cmd	hr/9	BPV
2006	A+	Win-Salem	2	5	0	35	21	4.10	1.54	21.9	272	30	76	4.82	4.4	5.4	1.2	1.0	28
2006	Rk	Great Falls	1	1	0	22	27	1.63	1.18	14.7	234	34	88	2.75	2.9	11.0	3.9	0.4	143
2007	A+	Win-Salem	7	7	0	121	88	3.64	1.31	22.7	254	30	72	3.49	3.1	6.5	2.1	0.5	72
2007	AA	Birmingham	1	2	0	26	16	6.53	1.87	20.5	340	37	67	7.03	3.8	5.5	1.5	1.4	9

Pitches to contact and works backwards, preferring to use CU and CB to set-up FB. Repeats ¾ slot and stays tall through delivery giving sink to pitches and consistency to command. Won't miss many bats, so it's imperative that he be efficient and have all pitches working.

McCutchen,Daniel

SP | **New York (A)** | EXP MLB DEBUT: 2009 | POTENTIAL: #4 starter | **7D**

Thrws R Age 25
2006 (13) Oklahoma
89-94 FB ++++
79-81 KC +++
77-80 SP +++

Year	Lev	Team	W	L	Sv	IP	K	ERA	WHIP	BF/G	OBA	H%	S%	xERA	Ctl	Dom	Cmd	hr/9	BPV
2006	A-	Charleston	1	0	1	21	18	2.14	0.86	11.0	180	21	81	1.76	2.1	7.7	3.6	0.9	115
2006	A-	Staten Island	1	0	0	9	12	2.00	0.67	15.7	165	18	100	2.15	1.0	12.0	12.0	2.0	286
2007	A+	Tampa	11	2	0	101	67	2.50	1.06	23.0	232	27	79	2.69	1.9	6.0	3.2	0.6	93
2007	AA	Trenton	3	2	0	41	36	2.41	1.02	22.5	206	26	78	2.09	2.6	7.9	3.0	0.4	111

Athletic pitcher who wins utilizing pitch movement, command, and ability to induce groundballs. Despite good velocity and three average to above pitches, he lacks strikeout ability. Only negative is the effort to his ¾ delivery, but is making adjustments to smooth it out.

McDonald,James

SP | **Los Angeles (N)** | EXP MLB DEBUT: 2009 | POTENTIAL: #3 starter | **8C**

Thrws R Age 23
2002 (11) HS (CA)
88-93 FB +++
79-81 CB +
71-75 CU ++++
77-80 +++

Year	Lev	Team	W	L	Sv	IP	K	ERA	WHIP	BF/G	OBA	H%	S%	xERA	Ctl	Dom	Cmd	hr/9	BPV
2003	Rk	GCL Dodgers	2	4	0	48	47	3.36	1.12	15.8	223	29	71	2.64	2.8	8.8	3.1	0.6	112
2005	Rk	Ogden	0	0	0	6	9	1.50	1.00	5.7	191	34	83	1.39	3.0	13.5	4.5	0.0	192
2006	A-	Columbus	5	10	1	143	147	3.97	1.28	19.5	228	29	71	3.46	4.0	9.3	2.3	0.9	85
2007	A+	Inland Emp	6	7	0	82	104	3.95	1.22	20.7	255	36	70	3.57	2.3	11.4	5.0	0.9	150
2007	AA	Jacksonville	7	2	0	52	64	1.72	1.11	20.5	222	31	91	2.87	2.8	11.0	4.0	0.9	135

Tall/slender pitcher uses a deceptive high ¾ delivery, pinpoint command, and four-pitch mix to get hitters out. Lacks FB movement, but will throw any pitch at any time. Tends to rush delivery in pressure situations and pitches up in the zone, but those should vanquish with experience.

McGeary,Jack

SP | **Washington** | EXP MLB DEBUT: 2012 | POTENTIAL: #4 starter | **8E**

Thrws L Age 19
2007 (6) HS (MA)
84-89 FB +++
74-77 CB ++++
77-80 CU ++

Year	Lev	Team	W	L	Sv	IP	K	ERA	WHIP	BF/G	OBA	H%	S%	xERA	Ctl	Dom	Cmd	hr/9	BPV
2007	A-	Vermont	0	1	0	2	4	16.36	3.64	7.1	326	58	50	9.85	20.5	16.4	0.8	0.0	105

Athletic pitcher with plus CB and advanced pitching style. Despite low velocity, he succeeds by keeping ball low, hitting spots, and mixing pitches. CU needs work and is unlikely to get many strikeouts. Upside is limited, but should improve with physical maturity.

McGee,Jacob

SP | **Tampa Bay** | EXP MLB DEBUT: 2008 | POTENTIAL: #2 starter | **9C**

Thrws L Age 21
2004 (5) HS (NV)
88-95 FB ++++
69-76 CB +++
78-80 CU +++

Year	Lev	Team	W	L	Sv	IP	K	ERA	WHIP	BF/G	OBA	H%	S%	xERA	Ctl	Dom	Cmd	hr/9	BPV
2004	Rk	Princeton	4	1	0	56	53	4.00	1.32	19.4	236	29	71	3.53	4.0	8.5	2.1	0.8	79
2005	A-	Hudson Valley	5	4	0	76	89	3.66	1.14	20.1	229	32	67	2.68	2.7	10.5	3.9	0.5	139
2006	A-	SW Michigan	7	9	0	134	171	3.02	1.25	21.0	214	32	76	2.76	4.4	11.5	2.6	0.5	122
2007	A+	Vero Beach	5	4	0	116	145	2.94	1.08	21.6	208	30	74	2.38	3.0	11.2	3.7	0.6	140
2007	AA	Montgomery	3	2	0	23	30	4.29	1.39	19.4	226	33	70	3.52	5.1	11.7	2.3	0.8	105

Projectable pitcher who has led league in strikeouts the past two years. Throws hard and repeats high ¾ delivery, giving him a solid CU and command. CB has good movement and is improving command of pitch. Maintained base skills in promotion to Double-A.

Medlen,Kris

RP | **Atlanta** | EXP MLB DEBUT: 2009 | POTENTIAL: Setup reliever | **7D**

Thrws R Age 22
2006 (10) Santa Ana JC
88-93 FB ++++
CB ++++
CU +

Year	Lev	Team	W	L	Sv	IP	K	ERA	WHIP	BF/G	OBA	H%	S%	xERA	Ctl	Dom	Cmd	hr/9	BPV
2006	Rk	Danville	1	0	10	22	36	0.41	0.73	3.9	184	32	79	1.37	0.8	14.7	18.0	0.8	460
2007	A-	Rome	0	1	8	20	33	0.87	0.79	4.3	186	31	81	1.63	1.3	14.7	11.0	0.9	310
2007	A+	Myrtle Beach	2	0	2	24	28	1.13	1.21	5.4	245	32	83	3.66	2.6	10.5	4.0	1.1	119
2007	AA	Mississippi	0	0	1	2	2	11.57	2.86	4.0	403	20	80	21.49	8.6	8.6	1.0	12.9	-339

Athletic reliever overpowers hitters with electric FB and CB that breaks out of strike zone. Arm action is fluid and repeats delivery well, giving him consistent command, but doesn't have much of a CU and thus isn't that effective to LH batters.

Medlock,Calvin

RP | **Tampa Bay** | EXP MLB DEBUT: 2008 | POTENTIAL: Setup reliever | **6C**

Thrws R Age 25
2002 (39) N. Texas CC
86-91 FB +++
79-81 CB +++
78-81 CU ++

Year	Lev	Team	W	L	Sv	IP	K	ERA	WHIP	BF/G	OBA	H%	S%	xERA	Ctl	Dom	Cmd	hr/9	BPV
2004	A+	Potomac	3	4	1	47	46	6.36	1.52	14.7	265	35	77	7.01	4.2	9.5	2.1	1.5	57
2005	A+	Sarasota	6	3	0	109	98	3.06	1.08	16.4	234	32	81	3.30	1.8	7.9	4.5	0.5	80
2006	AA	Chattanooga	7	2	2	64	70	2.97	1.29	7.2	226	34	80	3.22	4.0	7.6	2.5	0.5	78
2007	AA	Chattanooga	2	2	2	48	59	2.64	0.84	5.4	202	32	75	2.79	0.9	11.1	11.8	0.6	111
2007	AAA	Dur/Lou	4	1	0	32	25	4.55	1.53	4.0	226	33	77	4.66	6.5	7.1	1.1	0.6	40

Short/compact reliever who relies on mixing pitches and command to get hitters' out. Lacks good arm action which decreases movement, and tends to lose velocity from the stretch. Does get good extension to high 3/4 delivery which makes FB appear harder.

Melancon,Mark

RP | **New York (A)** | EXP MLB DEBUT: 2009 | POTENTIAL: Setup reliever | **8D**

Thrws R Age 23
2006 (9) Arizona
90-95 FB ++++
81-84 CB +++
CU +

Year	Lev	Team	W	L	Sv	IP	K	ERA	WHIP	BF/G	OBA	H%	S%	xERA	Ctl	Dom	Cmd	hr/9	BPV
2006	A-	Staten Island	0	1	2	6	7	1.45	1.13	4.1	222	32	86	2.11	2.9	10.2	3.5	0.0	145
2007																			

Power reliever missed 2007 season recovering from TJS. Keeps ball low with power sinker and registers strikeouts with hard CB. Commands plate and loves to pitch inside. Possesse effor to his delivery, so may take time to adjust to new mechanics upon his return.

Meloan,Jonathon

SP | **Los Angeles (N)** | EXP MLB DEBUT: 2007 | POTENTIAL: Setup reliever/closer | **9C**

Thrws R Age 23
2005 (5) Arizona
88-94 FB ++++
83-85 SL +++
77-81 KC ++++
79-82 CU ++

Year	Lev	Team	W	L	Sv	IP	K	ERA	WHIP	BF/G	OBA	H%	S%	xERA	Ctl	Dom	Cmd	hr/9	BPV
2006	A+	Vero Beach	1	0	0	18	27	2.50	1.06	17.4	228	35	82	2.91	2.0	13.5	6.8	1.0	202
2006	AA	Jacksonville	1	0	0	10	23	1.76	0.78	7.4	94	26	86	0.58	4.4	20.3	4.6	0.8	228
2007	AA	Jacksonville	5	2	19	45	70	2.18	0.93	4.8	155	33	80	2.44	3.6	14.0	3.9	0.6	199
2007	AAA	Las Vegas	2	0	1	21	21	1.69	1.00	5.8	168	30	81	2.02	3.8	9.0	2.3	0.9	179
2007	MLB	Los Angeles (N)	0	0	0	7	7	11.05	2.25	7.2	285	37	67	16.54	10.1	8.9	0.9	1.3	-145

Tall/strong-framed reliever with ability to subtract from plus FB and two above average breaking pitches at his disposal. Repeats ¾ delivery giving him stellar command, but likes to pitch up in the zone which could be problematic. Has mentality and power arsenal to close.

Mendoza,Thomas

SP | **Los Angeles (A)** | EXP MLB DEBUT: 2010 | POTENTIAL: #3 starter | **8D**

Thrws R Age 20
2005 (5) HS (FL)
88-94 FB ++++
80-82 SL +++
72-76 CB +++
78-81 CU ++

Year	Lev	Team	W	L	Sv	IP	K	ERA	WHIP	BF/G	OBA	H%	S%	xERA	Ctl	Dom	Cmd	hr/9	BPV
2005	Rk	AZL Angels	3	3	0	52	56	1.55	1.06	15.5	222	31	85	3.40	2.2	9.7	4.3	0.2	154
2005	A+	Rancho Cuc	1	0	1	10	12	0.00	0.40	16.1	124	20	100	0.00	0.0	10.8		0.0	95
2006	A-	Cedar Rapids	11	6	0	170	134	4.18	1.18	25.2	260	31	66	3.52	1.7	7.1	4.2	0.0	110
2007	Rk	AZL Angels	1	0	0	5	4	0.00	1.40	21.1	262	32	100	0.00	3.6	7.2	2.0	0.0	296
2007	A-	Cedar Rapids	2	4	0	53	38	4.86	1.56	19.4	309	32	70	4.77	2.7	6.4	2.4	0.0	92

Sore arm kept him out of action for two months and never got comfortable. Projectable with good arm action, he gets velocity and movement to his FB and two breaking pitches. Command wasn't a problem, but needs to repeat delivery more often and refrain from overthrowing.

Meyers,Brad

SP | **Washington** | EXP MLB DEBUT: 2010 | POTENTIAL: #4 starter | **7E**

Thrws R Age 22
2007 (5) Loyola-Mary
88-92 FB +++
SL +++
CU ++

Year	Lev	Team	W	L	Sv	IP	K	ERA	WHIP	BF/G	OBA	H%	S%	xERA	Ctl	Dom	Cmd	hr/9	BPV
2007	A-	Hagerstown	1	1	0	20	9	0.45	1.04	19.5	186	20	100	1.94	3.6	4.0	1.1	0.4	52
2007	A+	Potomac	0	0	0	10	7	5.29	2.35	17.6	343	39	78	7.83	7.9	6.2	0.8	0.9	13
2007	Rk	GCL Nationals	0	0	0	9	9	0.00	0.22	9.1	73	11	100	0.00	0.0	9.0		0.0	94

Tall/projectable pitcher with quick arm action that produces downward movement to FB and bite to SL. Mechanics have lots of moving parts and tends to drop ¾ slot which tips pitches. Commands plate and gets groundball outs, but strikeout rate will always be low.

Meyer,Dan

SP | **Oakland** | EXP MLB DEBUT: 2004 | POTENTIAL: #4 starter | **7C**

Thrws L Age 26
2002 (1-S) James Madison
85-91 FB +++
79-82 SL +++
72-74 CB ++
77-80 CU ++++

Year	Lev	Team	W	L	Sv	IP	K	ERA	WHIP	BF/G	OBA	H%	S%	xERA	Ctl	Dom	Cmd	hr/9	BPV
2005	AAA	Sacramento	2	8	0	89	63	5.36	1.62	20.8	287	31	71	5.68	4.3	6.4	1.5	1.5	21
2006	AAA	Sacramento	3	3	0	49	29	5.67	1.71	22.3	316	33	72	6.65	3.7	5.3	1.5	1.8	-1
2007	AA	Midland	0	0	0	4	2	6.75	2.25	20.3	307	24	86	10.40	9.0	4.5	0.5	4.5	-104
2007	AAA	Sacramento	8	2	0	115	105	3.28	1.34	22.8	241	29	79	3.78	4.0	8.2	2.1	0.9	71
2007	MLB	Oakland	0	2	0	16	11	8.94	1.80	12.4	306	34	48	6.06	5.0	6.1	1.2	1.1	23

Recovered well from shoulder surgery, but didn't show the same velocity. Achieved better feel for pitches as season progressed and was able to incorporate all pitches. Key to success still hinges on deceptive delivery, command, and keeping ball out of hitting zone.

PITCHERS

Mickolio,Kam — RP — Seattle

EXP MLB DEBUT: 2008 | POTENTIAL: Setup reliever/closer | 8B

Thrws R Age 24
2006 (18) Utah Valley St
88-95 FB ++++
85-87 CT +++
82-83 SL +++
CU +

Year	Lev	Team	W	L	Sv	IP	K	ERA	WHIP	BF/G	OBA	H%	S%	xERA	Ctl	Dom	Cmd	hr/9	BPV
2006	A-	Everett	1	0	4	32	26	2.80	1.28	6.3	273	34	78	3.45	2.0	7.3	3.7	0.3	114
2007	AA	W. Tennessee	3	1	2	29	27	1.85	1.23	6.6	226	30	83	2.44	3.7	8.3	2.3	0.0	107
2007	AAA	Tacoma	3	3	1	24	28	3.75	1.21	6.9	219	29	73	3.33	3.8	10.5	2.8	1.1	99

Tall/projectable pitcher who intimidates on mound with a downward plane and above average velocity. Pounds strike zone with FB, CT, and SL, and threw more quality strikes in 2007. Keeps ball low and notches strikeouts, but needs to improve CU to combat LH batters.

Mijares,Jose — SP — Minnesota

EXP MLB DEBUT: 2008 | POTENTIAL: Setup reliever | 7D

Thrws L Age 23
2002 FA (Venezuela)
88-94 FB ++++
77-81 SL ++++
72-75 CB +++
77-82 CU ++

Year	Lev	Team	W	L	Sv	IP	K	ERA	WHIP	BF/G	OBA	H%	S%	xERA	Ctl	Dom	Cmd	hr/9	BPV
2005	A-	Beloit	6	3	2	54	78	4.33	1.53	11.8	220	33	74	4.01	6.7	13.0	2.0	1.0	100
2005	A+	Fort Myers	0	0	0	12	17	1.50	0.83	8.8	129	19	89	1.01	3.8	12.8	3.4	0.8	155
2006	A+	Fort Myers	3	5	0	63	77	3.57	1.27	9.6	229	30	79	3.89	3.9	11.0	2.9	1.4	92
2007	AA	New Britain	5	3	9	61	75	3.54	1.44	5.7	189	25	79	3.47	7.1	11.1	1.6	1.0	85
2007	AAA	Rochester	0	1	0	8	6	6.59	1.71	7.4	280	26	73	7.48	5.5	6.6	1.2	3.3	-35

Short/stocky reliever achieves easy velocity and plus pitch movement with excellent arm action. Likes to challenge hitters and get strikeout, but mediocre command keeps him from having that breakthrough season. Move to relief was prompted by lack of third pitch.

Miller,Adam — SP — Cleveland

EXP MLB DEBUT: 2008 | POTENTIAL: #1 starter | 9C

Thrws R Age 23
2003 (1-S) HS (TX)
89-98 FB +++++
84-88 SL ++++
82-86 CU ++

Year	Lev	Team	W	L	Sv	IP	K	ERA	WHIP	BF/G	OBA	H%	S%	xERA	Ctl	Dom	Cmd	hr/9	BPV
2005	A-	Mahoning Val	0	0	0	10	6	5.29	2.06	16.6	371	43	71	6.79	3.5	5.3	1.5	0.0	44
2005	A+	Kinston	2	4	0	59	45	4.86	1.57	21.7	313	37	69	5.24	2.6	6.8	2.6	0.8	66
2006	AA	Akron	15	6	0	153	157	2.76	1.12	23.2	229	30	77	2.67	2.5	9.2	3.7	0.5	125
2006	AAA	Buffalo	0	0	0	4	4	6.43	1.67	18.8	252	34	57	3.87	6.4	8.6	1.3	0.0	84
2007	AAA	Buffalo	5	4	0	65	68	4.84	1.37	14.3	270	36	64	3.87	2.9	9.4	3.2	0.6	109

Elbow inflammation kept his innings down and prevented him from pitching in the Majors. Generates plus movement to FB and SL with quick ¾ arm action and was able to improve command. CU still lags and could benefit by being eased into starting rotation by pitching in relief.

Miller,Drew — SP — San Diego

EXP MLB DEBUT: 2010 | POTENTIAL: #3 starter | 8D

Thrws R Age 22
2005 (37) Seminole St JC
89-96 FB ++++
CB +++
CU +

Year	Lev	Team	W	L	Sv	IP	K	ERA	WHIP	BF/G	OBA	H%	S%	xERA	Ctl	Dom	Cmd	hr/9	BPV
2006	Rk	AZL Padres	3	0	0	23	14	3.51	1.26	13.4	226	26	71	2.89	3.9	5.4	1.4	0.4	60
2006	A-	Eugene	2	1	0	37	23	3.64	1.59	18.2	272	32	75	3.97	4.9	5.6	1.2	0.0	58
2007	A-	Fort Wayne	4	6	0	80	87	4.69	1.22	20.3	247	31	75	4.84	2.7	9.8	3.6	1.3	108

Tall/projectable pitcher with explosive fastball and big-bending CB that he can get strikeouts with. Improved CU and consistency of command by repeating delivery more frequently. Velocity tends to fall-off after 50 pitches and was placed on DL for a sore shoulder.

Miller,Greg — SP — Los Angeles (N)

EXP MLB DEBUT: 2007 | POTENTIAL: Situational reliever | 7C

Thrws L Age 23
2002 (1-S) HS (CA)
87-93 FB ++++
81-85 CT +++
77-80 CB +++
78-81 CU +++

Year	Lev	Team	W	L	Sv	IP	K	ERA	WHIP	BF/G	OBA	H%	S%	xERA	Ctl	Dom	Cmd	hr/9	BPV
2005	Rk	GCL Dodgers	0	0	0	12	14	2.25	0.92	11.2	171	26	73	0.98	3.0	10.5	3.5	0.0	157
2006	AA	Jacksonville	1	0	1	22	24	0.81	1.13	8.0	161	24	92	1.41	5.3	9.7	1.8	0.0	120
2006	AAA	Las Vegas	3	0	0	37	32	4.38	1.78	5.2	240	31	74	4.24	8.0	7.8	1.0	0.2	67
2007	AA	Jacksonville	1	2	1	48	65	4.69	1.85	11.2	254	38	74	4.68	8.1	12.2	1.5	0.4	98
2007	AAA	Las Vegas	1	1	0	28	32	7.98	2.30	10.3	193	27	63	5.03	14.7	10.2	0.7	0.3	83

Enigmatic pitcher who can dominate with solid CB and ability to subtract from lively FB, but can blow-up the next outing. Gains deception from lower slot, but is slow to plate (1.45) and command is never consistent. Shows effort to delivery and throws across body.

Miller,Jim — RP — Baltimore

EXP MLB DEBUT: 2007 | POTENTIAL: Setup reliever | 7C

Thrws R Age 26
2004 (8) Louisiana-Monroe
90-95 FB ++++
72-74 SU +++
80-84 CU ++

Year	Lev	Team	W	L	Sv	IP	K	ERA	WHIP	BF/G	OBA	H%	S%	xERA	Ctl	Dom	Cmd	hr/9	BPV
2005	A+	Modesto	1	3	25	47	68	3.81	1.19	3.9	227	36	68	2.82	3.2	13.0	4.0	0.6	154
2005	AA	Tulsa	1	1	9	15	19	0.60	0.93	3.5	124	15	108	1.66	4.8	11.4	2.4	1.2	112
2006	AA	Tulsa	0	3	12	44	41	3.88	1.45	4.2	287	32	83	5.73	2.9	8.4	2.9	2.0	48
2007	AA	Bowie	2	3	4	38	49	2.83	1.34	5.3	194	31	76	2.29	5.9	11.5	2.0	0.0	127
2007	AAA	Norfolk	1	2	3	27	30	4.30	1.51	5.4	246	32	74	4.30	5.3	9.9	1.9	1.0	75

FB and SU worked in preventing hits and getting strikeouts. Tends to overthrow FB, but achieves better movement and success when he lets pitches work for him. Works quickly and aggressively, being highly successful versus RH batters. Needs to throw quality strikes.

Mills,Brad — SP — Toronto

EXP MLB DEBUT: 2009 | POTENTIAL: #4 starter | 7D

Thrws L Age 23
2007 (4) Arizona
85-91 FB +++
72-74 CB ++++
77-80 CU +++

Year	Lev	Team	W	L	Sv	IP	K	ERA	WHIP	BF/G	OBA	H%	S%	xERA	Ctl	Dom	Cmd	hr/9	BPV
2007	A-	Auburn	2	0	0	18	21	2.00	0.83	11.0	151	23	73	0.55	3.0	10.5	3.5	0.0	161

Athletic pitcher had his way with short-season hitters, demonstrating excellent command and ability to miss bats. Plus CB and solid CU make average FB better. Tends to leave the ball up, which coupled with his mediocre velocity, could make life tough at upper levels.

Misch,Pat — SP — San Francisco

EXP MLB DEBUT: 2007 | POTENTIAL: reliever | 6B

Thrws L Age 26
2003 (7) Western Michigan
84-89 FB ++
80-84 SL +++
74-76 CB +++
79-82 CU +++

Year	Lev	Team	W	L	Sv	IP	K	ERA	WHIP	BF/G	OBA	H%	S%	xERA	Ctl	Dom	Cmd	hr/9	BPV
2006	AA	Connecticut	5	4	0	103	79	2.27	1.14	22.7	244	29	83	3.03	2.1	6.9	3.3	0.6	98
2006	AAA	Fresno	4	2	0	65	57	4.02	1.31	26.8	288	35	72	4.38	1.5	7.9	5.2	1.0	125
2006	MLB	San Fran	0	0	0	1	1	0.00	2.00	4.8	415	52	100	7.49	0.0	9.0		0.0	26
2007	AAA	Fresno	2	5	1	66	74	2.31	1.10	7.6	224	31	81	2.59	2.6	10.1	3.9	0.5	136
2007	MLB	San Fran	0	4	0	40	26	4.26	1.47	9.6	294	34	71	4.62	2.7	5.8	2.2	0.7	57

Finesse pitcher with below average velocity and strikeout rate, but gets hitters to hit his pitches and is deceptive with ¾ delivery. Possesses command, mixes four pitches, and isn't afraid to pitch to contact. Likes to work backwards with his vast arsenal, but has no margin for error.

Mock,Garrett — SP — Washington

EXP MLB DEBUT: 2007 | POTENTIAL: Setup reliever/closer | 6C

Thrws R Age 25
2004 (3) Houston
89-94 FB +++
84-87 CT +++
77-78 CB +++
78-81 CU ++

Year	Lev	Team	W	L	Sv	IP	K	ERA	WHIP	BF/G	OBA	H%	S%	xERA	Ctl	Dom	Cmd	hr/9	BPV
2005	A+	Lancaster	14	7	0	174	160	4.19	1.35	25.9	292	36	71	4.55	1.7	8.3	4.8	1.0	119
2006	AA	Harr/Tenn	4	12	0	147	126	5.56	1.55	23.8	294	35	65	5.10	3.4	7.7	2.3	1.0	61
2007	A+	Potomac	1	0	0	6	5	0.00	0.67	20.9	151	20	100	0.16	1.5	7.5	5.0	0.0	175
2007	AA	Harrisburg	1	5	0	51	41	5.81	1.84	21.6	314	37	69	6.05	4.9	7.2	1.5	0.9	40
2007	Rk	GCL Nationals	0	2	0	7	8	5.00	1.67	10.8	351	39	89	8.91	1.3	10.0	8.0	3.8	100

Missed first month following knee surgery. Movement and velocity doesn't always translate to missed bats, especially when FB command is lacking. Repeats high ¾ delivery, but doesn't change speeds well or show much deception, so must stay on corners.

Morales,Alexis — RP — Washington

EXP MLB DEBUT: 2009 | POTENTIAL: Setup reliever | 7D

Thrws R Age 25
2003 (46) Oakton CC
89-95 FB ++++
75-78 SU +++
80-84 CU +

Year	Lev	Team	W	L	Sv	IP	K	ERA	WHIP	BF/G	OBA	H%	S%	xERA	Ctl	Dom	Cmd	hr/9	BPV
2006	AA	Harrisburg	0	0	0	15	15	5.74	2.43	8.9	272	30	69	5.66	12.4	8.9	0.7	1.7	-109
2007	Rk	GCL Nationals	0	0	0	1	2	9.00	2.00	4.7	75	41	72	9.00	4.8	13.1	2.7	0.0	12
2007	A+	Potomac	1	0	3	13	19	0.00	0.76	4.7	75	29	100	0.00	4.8	13.1	2.7	0.0	175
2007	AA	Harrisburg	3	2	2	23	34	3.04	1.64	6.5	152	30	75	3.55	10.1	13.2	1.3	0.0	97
2007	AAA	Columbus	1	1	0	14	17	6.91	2.29	7.0	273	28	73	7.02	3.0	10.5	3.5	1.3	-66

Short/athletic reliever with quick arm action and strength, which sparks plus velocity. Pitches aggressively to inside part of plate and drops SU into zone for strikeouts. Command improved slightly, but needs to be more precise and improve deception of CU.

Morales,Franklin — SP — Colorado

EXP MLB DEBUT: 2007 | POTENTIAL: #1 starter | 9C

Thrws L Age 22
2002 FA (DR)
89-96 FB +++++
71-76 CB ++++
78-81 CU +++

Year	Lev	Team	W	L	Sv	IP	K	ERA	WHIP	BF/G	OBA	H%	S%	xERA	Ctl	Dom	Cmd	hr/9	BPV
2005	A-	Asheville	8	4	1	96	108	3.09	1.26	18.7	212	29	77	2.85	4.5	10.1	2.3	0.6	104
2006	A+	Modesto	10	9	0	154	179	3.68	1.40	24.0	225	31	74	3.31	5.2	10.5	2.0	0.5	99
2007	AA	Tulsa	3	4	0	95	77	3.50	1.28	23.0	223	26	75	3.24	4.3	7.3	1.7	0.8	67
2007	AAA	Colo Springs	2	0	0	17	16	3.71	1.94	27.0	294	37	81	5.66	6.9	8.5	1.2	0.5	57
2007	MLB	Colorado	3	2	0	39	26	3.45	1.23	19.8	236	28	72	3.01	3.2	6.0	1.9	0.5	69

Strong frame and quick arm action provide easy velocity, and misses bats. Creates deception with deliberate delivery that features a slight hesitation, but doesn't repeat mechanics. High walk rate hurts efficiency and pitches with effort, though it hasn't affected stamina.

Moreno,Juan

SP | **Chicago (A)** | EXP MLB DEBUT: 2011 | POTENTIAL: #3 starter | **8E**

Thrws R Age 21
2004 FA (DR)

Velocity	Pitch	Rating
87-92	FB	++++
	SL	+++
	CU	++

Year	Lev	Team	W	L	Sv	IP	K	ERA	WHIP	BF/G	OBA	H%	S%	xERA	Ctl	Dom	Cmd	hr/9	BPV
2006	Rk	Bristol	7	5	0	72	65	4.62	1.35	23.1	285	35	67	4.46	2.0	8.1	4.1	1.0	102
2007	Rk	Great Falls	6	4	0	90	77	2.40	1.04	21.8	246	31	78	2.60	1.1	7.7	7.0	0.4	187

PIO Pitcher of the Year, leading league in ERA and was untouchable over last month. Works quickly with a FB and SL combination, getting good movement due to his fluid arm action. Command is exceptional for age/level and just needs to repeat arm speed for CU.

Morillo,Juan

RP | **Colorado** | EXP MLB DEBUT: 2006 | POTENTIAL: Setup reliever/closer | **8C**

Thrws R Age 24
2001 FA (DR)

Velocity	Pitch	Rating
90-99	FB	+++++
83-88	SL	+++

Year	Lev	Team	W	L	Sv	IP	K	ERA	WHIP	BF/G	OBA	H%	S%	xERA	Ctl	Dom	Cmd	hr/9	BPV
2006	AA	Tulsa	12	8	0	140	132	4.63	1.48	22.3	245	30	70	4.10	5.1	8.5	1.7	0.8	67
2006	MLB	Colorado	0	0	0	4	4	15.75	2.75	22.3	415	41	50	15.73	6.8	9.0	1.3	6.8	-148
2007	AA	Tulsa	6	4	0	57	59	2.36	1.24	5.0	215	29	81	2.61	4.3	9.3	2.2	0.3	104
2007	AAA	Colo Springs	0	1	0	9	12	3.91	1.20	5.3	212	33	64	2.15	3.9	11.7	3.0	0.0	146
2007	MLB	Colorado	0	0	0	3	3	11.25	1.25	3.3	250	25	0	5.43	2.8	8.4	3.0	2.8	34

Athletic pitcher was moved to relief after failing to change speeds and pace self. FB and SL are incredibly explosive with his whip-like delivery, making him tough to hit. Aggressive approach plays right into relief role and just needs not to overthrow and establish FB command.

Morlan,Eduardo

RP | **Tampa Bay** | EXP MLB DEBUT: 2009 | POTENTIAL: Setup reliever/closer | **8C**

Thrws R Age 22
2004 (3) HS (FL)

Velocity	Pitch	Rating
90-96	FB	++++
80-84	SL	+++
77-78	CB	+++

Year	Lev	Team	W	L	Sv	IP	K	ERA	WHIP	BF/G	OBA	H%	S%	xERA	Ctl	Dom	Cmd	hr/9	BPV
2005	A-	Beloit	4	4	0	51	55	4.40	1.37	21.4	213	28	69	3.44	5.5	9.7	1.8	0.9	81
2005	Rk	Elizabethton	2	0	0	22	30	0.82	0.55	18.5	88	16	83	0.00	2.5	12.3	5.0	0.0	216
2006	A-	Beloit	5	5	2	106	125	2.29	1.09	14.8	207	29	81	2.31	3.2	10.6	3.3	0.5	131
2007	A+	Fort Myers	4	3	18	65	92	3.17	1.10	6.2	230	34	75	3.03	2.3	12.7	5.4	1.0	170
2007	AA	New Britain	1	0	0	4	7	2.25	1.50	8.6	210	41	83	2.84	6.8	15.8	2.3	0.0	156

Strong-framed reliever with an obscene strikeout rate and above average command. Pitches aggressively with explosive FB, and uses SL as his primary comp. Move to relief was prompted by low stamina, as he possesses a max-effort delivery and short stature.

Morris,Bryan

SP | **Los Angeles (N)** | EXP MLB DEBUT: 2010 | POTENTIAL: #4 starter/setup reliever | **8D**

Thrws R Age 21
2006 (1-C) Motlow St CC

Velocity	Pitch	Rating
88-94	FB	++++
80-83	SL	+++
74-78	CB	++++
		++

Year	Lev	Team	W	L	Sv	IP	K	ERA	WHIP	BF/G	OBA	H%	S%	xERA	Ctl	Dom	Cmd	hr/9	BPV
2006	Rk	Ogden	4	5	0	59	79	5.17	1.76	19.4	277	41	69	4.84	6.1	12.0	2.0	0.5	99
2007																			

Missed 2007 season with TJS which was workload related. Possesses explosive FB and hard break to CB from a smooth arm action, giving him ability to miss bats. Needs to repeat delivery more frequently which would improve quality of CU and provide consistent command.

Morris,Ryan

SP | **Cleveland** | EXP MLB DEBUT: 2011 | POTENTIAL: #5 starter | **7D**

Thrws L Age 20
2006 (4) HS (NC)

Velocity	Pitch	Rating
85-90	FB	+++
75-78	SL	+++
77-79	CU	++

Year	Lev	Team	W	L	Sv	IP	K	ERA	WHIP	BF/G	OBA	H%	S%	xERA	Ctl	Dom	Cmd	hr/9	BPV
2006	Rk	Burlington	0	0	0	1	1	15.00	2.50	6.4	371	30	50	14.93	7.5	7.5	1.0	7.5	-178
2006	Rk	GCL Indians	1	5	0	27	21	4.65	1.44	14.4	261	31	68	4.06	4.0	7.0	1.8	0.7	61
2007	A-	Lake County	0	2	0	39	31	5.28	1.38	18.3	219	27	60	3.16	5.3	7.1	1.3	0.5	68
2007	Rk	GCL Indians	3	0	0	25	22	1.80	0.84	18.3	156	21	76	0.65	2.9	7.9	2.8	0.0	129

Tall/athletic pitcher with projectable velocity and outstanding command. Mixes three pitches equally, getting groundball outs with sinker and strikeouts with SL. Needs to add muscle to frame which would increase velocity and needs to repeat ¾ delivery more consistently.

Mortensen,Clayton

SP | **St. Louis** | EXP MLB DEBUT: 2009 | POTENTIAL: #3 starter | **8C**

Thrws R Age 23
2007 (1-S) Gonzaga

Velocity	Pitch	Rating
88-92	FB	++++
80-83	SL	+++
80-83	CU	+++

Year	Lev	Team	W	L	Sv	IP	K	ERA	WHIP	BF/G	OBA	H%	S%	xERA	Ctl	Dom	Cmd	hr/9	BPV
2007	A-	Quad Cities	0	2	0	40	45	3.14	1.30	16.5	280	38	76	3.73	1.8	10.1	5.6	0.4	164
2007	A-	Batavia	1	1	0	20	23	1.79	1.19	13.4	187	28	83	1.85	4.9	10.3	2.1	0.0	123

Tall/projectable pitcher with a host of skills that are conducive to winning. Commands three pitches with a heavy FB that supports a solid G/F and delivers strikeouts. Quick high ¾ delivery gets the ball on-top of hitters right now and his repetitiveness provides him deception.

Morton,Charlie

RP | **Atlanta** | EXP MLB DEBUT: 2008 | POTENTIAL: Setup reliever | **6B**

Thrws R Age 24
2002 (3) HS (CT)

Velocity	Pitch	Rating
88-94	FB	++++
	SL	++
	CB	++++
	CU	++

Year	Lev	Team	W	L	Sv	IP	K	ERA	WHIP	BF/G	OBA	H%	S%	xERA	Ctl	Dom	Cmd	hr/9	BPV
2003	Rk	Danville	2	5	0	54	46	4.67	1.67	17.3	299	30	74	4.89	4.2	7.7	1.8	0.5	51
2004	A-	Rome	7	9	2	117	102	4.82	1.77	19.9	298	33	76	5.11	5.2	7.8	1.5	0.5	37
2005	A-	Rome	5	9	1	124	86	5.20	1.50	20.6	261	32	72	5.30	4.5	6.2	1.4	0.5	38
2006	A+	Myrtle Bch	6	7	2	100	75	5.49	1.70	15.1	291	31	70	5.33	4.9	6.8	1.4	1.3	40
2007	AA	Mississippi	4	6	0	79	67	4.29	1.48	8.3	264	29	74	4.58	4.2	7.6	1.8	0.3	79

Tall/strong-framed pitcher with a plus CB, solid velocity, and ability to mix pitches effectively. Lacks ability to change speeds, FB is straight, and command is inconsistent, but gets downward plane to his overhand delivery. Can pitch in variety of roles.

Moskos,Daniel

SP | **Pittsburgh** | EXP MLB DEBUT: 2008 | POTENTIAL: #3 starter/closer | **8C**

Thrws L Age 22
2007 (1) Clemson

Velocity	Pitch	Rating
89-94	FB	++++
81-85	SU	+++
74-79	CB	+++

Year	Lev	Team	W	L	Sv	IP	K	ERA	WHIP	BF/G	OBA	H%	S%	xERA	Ctl	Dom	Cmd	hr/9	BPV
2007	A-	State College	0	0	1	12	13	4.43	2.05	5.4	356	46	79	7.13	4.4	9.6	2.2	0.7	65
2007	Rk	GCL Pirates	0	0	0	3	3	0.00	1.33	6.2	321	42	100	4.04	0.0	9.0		0.0	45

Successful college reliever who will be used as a starter initially. Athletic frame and possesses velocity and two versions of a CB that hitters struggle to touch. Pittsburgh has him working on smoothing-out effort to high ¾ delivery, which should provide more stamina.

Moviel,Scott

SP | **New York (N)** | EXP MLB DEBUT: 2012 | POTENTIAL: #2 starter | **9E**

Thrws R Age 20
2007 (2-C) HS (OH)

Velocity	Pitch	Rating
87-93	FB	++++
80-83	CB	+++
79-82	CU	+

Year	Lev	Team	W	L	Sv	IP	K	ERA	WHIP	BF/G	OBA	H%	S%	xERA	Ctl	Dom	Cmd	hr/9	BPV
2007	Rk	GCL Mets	0	2	0	40	37	3.38	1.40	14.1	285	36	76	4.08	2.5	8.3	3.4	0.5	105

Tall/athletic pitcher with long arm action, his 6'11" height creates a frightening downward plane and extends well to the plate. Solid command in debut, though he doesn't always repeat high ¾ delivery consistently. FB amd CB have potential to be plus pitches.

Mujica,Edwad

RP | **Cleveland** | EXP MLB DEBUT: 2006 | POTENTIAL: Setup reliever | **7C**

Thrws R Age 24
2001 FA (Venezuela)

Velocity	Pitch	Rating
89-93	FB	++++
83-87	SL	+++
79-80	SP	+++

Year	Lev	Team	W	L	Sv	IP	K	ERA	WHIP	BF/G	OBA	H%	S%	xERA	Ctl	Dom	Cmd	hr/9	BPV
2006	AA	Akron	1	0	8	19	17	0.00	1.05	6.1	170	23	100	1.34	4.3	8.1	1.9	0.0	109
2006	AAA	Buffalo	3	1	5	32	29	2.52	1.12	5.8	255	33	77	3.47	1.4	8.1	5.8	0.3	166
2006	MLB	Cleveland	0	1	0	18	12	2.98	1.38	7.6	329	36	79	4.79	0.0	6.0		0.5	142
2007	AAA	Buffalo	2	1	14	37	44	5.02	1.18	4.4	250	34	77	5.66	2.2	10.6	4.9	0.9	104
2007	MLB	Cleveland	0	0	0	13	7	8.31	1.62	5.8	341	33	76	10.84	1.4	4.8	3.5	1.9	-72

Command and dominance stayed at prior levels, but was more hittable in 2007. Deceptive delivery and ability to throw three pitches for strikes makes him a tough customer, but needs to repeat ¾ slot on all pitches and trust stuff. Season ended with knee surgery in Sept.

Mullins,Ryan

SP | **Minnesota** | EXP MLB DEBUT: 2009 | POTENTIAL: #5 starter | **6C**

Thrws L Age 24
2005 (3) Vanderbilt

Velocity	Pitch	Rating
86-90	FB	++
77-81	SL	++
70-75	CB	+++
77-82	CU	+++

Year	Lev	Team	W	L	Sv	IP	K	ERA	WHIP	BF/G	OBA	H%	S%	xERA	Ctl	Dom	Cmd	hr/9	BPV
2005	Rk	Elizabethton	3	0	0	53	60	2.20	0.88	17.9	185	25	79	1.69	2.2	10.2	4.6	0.7	156
2006	A-	Beloit	5	8	0	156	139	3.86	1.34	24.0	262	32	73	3.94	3.1	8.0	2.6	0.8	82
2007	A+	Fort Myers	3	3	0	54	56	1.99	1.14	21.5	246	32	86	3.09	2.0	9.3	4.7	0.7	140
2007	AA	New Britain	4	3	0	85	68	4.01	1.29	25.0	266	32	69	3.62	2.4	7.2	3.0	0.5	91
2007	AAA	Rochester	0	3	0	15	11	10.73	2.19	18.9	397	45	48	8.72	3.0	6.6	2.2	1.2	25

Tall/slender pitcher with outstanding command, and ability to mix pitches. Repeats ¾ delivery and features hesitation with motion, providing deception, which allows his average repertoire to play up. Misses bats better than you would think.

Mulvey,Kevin — SP — New York (N) — EXP MLB DEBUT: 2008 — POTENTIAL: #4 starter — 7B

Thrws R Age 23
2006 (2) Villanova
87-91 FB +++
83-85 SL +++
71-72 CB ++
75-79 CU +++

Year	Lev	Team	W	L	Sv	IP	K	ERA	WHIP	BF/G	OBA	H%	S%	xERA	Ctl	Dom	Cmd	hr/9	BPV
2006	Rk	GCL Mets	0	0	0	2	1	0.00	0.50	6.6	151	18	100	0.00	0.0	4.5		0.0	52
2006	AA	Binghamton	0	1	0	13	10	1.37	1.15	17.3	213	25	93	2.72	3.4	6.9	2.0	0.7	75
2007	AA	Binghamton	11	10	0	151	110	3.33	1.24	23.6	254	31	72	3.07	2.6	6.5	2.6	0.2	90
2007	AAA	New Orleans	1	0	0	6	3	0.00	0.33	18.9	106	13	100	0.00	0.0	4.5		0.0	61

Contact pitcher who subtracts from FB with outstanding command, keeping hitters off-balance. Possesses good arm action and repeats delivery well. Low strikeout rate is a cause of concern and may need to improve CB rotation to give hitters something on a different plane.

Munoz,Arnaldo — RP — Washington — EXP MLB DEBUT: 2004 — POTENTIAL: Situational reliever — 6B

Thrws L Age 26
1998 FA (DR)
87-91 FB +++
80-82 CB ++++
74-78 CB +++

Year	Lev	Team	W	L	Sv	IP	K	ERA	WHIP	BF/G	OBA	H%	S%	xERA	Ctl	Dom	Cmd	hr/9	BPV
2005	AAA	Charlotte	8	14	1	132	109	4.29	1.59	14.6	287	34	76	5.20	4.1	7.4	1.8	1.1	48
2006	AA	Birmingham	2	4	2	46	48	3.72	1.13	7.0	227	29	69	2.91	2.7	9.4	3.4	0.8	115
2006	AAA	Charlotte	0	1	0	6	5	14.75	2.79	4.9	368	42	44	9.92	10.3	7.4	0.7	1.5	-4
2007	AAA	Columbus	3	1	0	52	46	2.59	1.23	3.9	238	29	83	3.39	3.1	7.9	2.6	0.9	83
2007	MLB	Washington	0	0	0	5	3	7.06	2.55	2.1	294	26	82	10.04	12.4	5.3	0.4	3.5	-69

Short/compact reliever is very effective to LH batters with two different types of CB and a deceptive high ¾ delivery. Velocity is average, but keeps ball down and limits long ball. Command showed marked improvement and has little left to prove in minors.

Nestor,Scott — RP — Florida — EXP MLB DEBUT: 2008 — POTENTIAL: Setup reliever — 7D

Thrws R Age 23
2003 (14) Chaffey JC áá
89-94 FB ++++
85-87 CT +++
83-85 SL +++
80-82 CU +

Year	Lev	Team	W	L	Sv	IP	K	ERA	WHIP	BF/G	OBA	H%	S%	xERA	Ctl	Dom	Cmd	hr/9	BPV
2004	A-	Greensboro	2	0	0	39	34	6.43	1.81	7.9	294	36	63	5.48	5.7	7.8	1.4	0.7	51
2005	A-	Greensboro	4	6	2	72	80	3.99	1.45	5.3	225	30	74	3.78	5.7	10.0	1.7	0.9	80
2006	A+	Jupiter	2	2	10	39	48	2.53	1.15	4.7	147	23	76	1.31	6.0	11.0	1.8	0.0	131
2006	AA	Carolina	2	2	0	13	13	7.56	2.37	5.7	328	42	67	7.40	8.9	8.9	1.0	0.7	43
2007	AA	Carolina	2	4	1	75	86	4.44	1.41	5.5	235	32	68	3.55	4.9	10.3	2.1	0.6	96

Tall/strong-framed reliever with overpowering FB and ability to generate strikeouts with tight SL. Struggles to repeat ¾ delivery, giving him below average command and CU, and needs to setup pitches better. Tough on RH batters and could thrive in a setup role.

Newmann,David — SP — Tampa Bay — EXP MLB DEBUT: 2009 — POTENTIAL: #5 starter — 7D

Thrws L Age 23
2007 (4) Texas A&M
88-92 FB +++
75-77 CB +++
79-82 CU +++

Year	Lev	Team	W	L	Sv	IP	K	ERA	WHIP	BF/G	OBA	H%	S%	xERA	Ctl	Dom	Cmd	hr/9	BPV
2007																			

Polished college pitcher with ability to exploit hitters' weaknesses and has three average pitches that he'll interchange. Command is inconsistent and isn't a strikeout pitcher, but induces groundball outs with ease. Mechanics aren't very smooth and did undergo TJS in 2005.

Newman,Josh — RP — Colorado — EXP MLB DEBUT: 2008 — POTENTIAL: Middle reliever — 6C

Thrws L Age 26
2004 (9) Ohio St
87-91 FB ++
72-75 CB ++
76-79 CU ++++

Year	Lev	Team	W	L	Sv	IP	K	ERA	WHIP	BF/G	OBA	H%	S%	xERA	Ctl	Dom	Cmd	hr/9	BPV
2004	Rk	Casper	1	2	1	33	46	3.52	1.14	4.9	243	37	69	2.90	2.2	12.5	5.8	0.5	186
2005	A+	Modesto	5	2	0	63	99	3.14	1.35	6.4	202	34	79	3.05	5.7	14.1	2.5	0.7	130
2006	AA	Tulsa	9	5	2	77	77	3.16	1.04	4.8	205	26	74	2.57	2.8	9.0	3.2	0.9	107
2007	AAA	Colo Springs	3	2	0	62	49	4.06	1.66	5.1	295	36	75	4.88	4.4	7.1	1.6	0.4	60
2007	MLB	Colorado	0	0	0	2	3	4.50	1.00	3.8	262	43	50	2.27	0.0	13.5		0.0	84

Contact pitcher that thrives on deception, repeating a delivery that masks CU and hiding baseball with his overhand delivery. Doesn't miss bats with average velocity and marginal CB, but rarely do hitters get good swings. Stiff arm action leaves him with poor stamina.

Nickerson,Jonah — RP — Detroit — EXP MLB DEBUT: 2009 — POTENTIAL: #5 starter — 7C

Thrws R Age 23
2006 (7) Oregon St
85-90 FB +++
83-86 CT +++
70-78 CB ++++
78-82 CU +++

Year	Lev	Team	W	L	Sv	IP	K	ERA	WHIP	BF/G	OBA	H%	S%	xERA	Ctl	Dom	Cmd	hr/9	BPV
2007	A-	W. Michigan	11	7	0	150	116	4.25	1.29	24.7	269	32	66	3.62	2.3	7.0	3.1	0.5	93

Workhorse pitcher possesses plus CB and outstanding command of four pitches due to good arm action and a repeatable ¾ delivery. Lacks strikeout ability and is prone to the extra-base hit, but extends well to plate, creating deception. Will need to prove himself at upper levels.

Niemann,Jeff — SP — Tampa Bay — EXP MLB DEBUT: 2008 — POTENTIAL: #2 starter — 9C

Thrws R Age 25
2004 (1) Rice
88-96 FB ++++
81-85 SL +++
74-75 KC +++
79-80 CU ++

Year	Lev	Team	W	L	Sv	IP	K	ERA	WHIP	BF/G	OBA	H%	S%	xERA	Ctl	Dom	Cmd	hr/9	BPV
2005	A+	Visalia	0	1	0	20	28	4.03	1.09	15.7	175	24	68	2.71	4.5	12.5	2.8	1.3	114
2005	AA	Montgomery	0	1	0	10	14	4.46	1.19	6.7	197	33	58	1.94	4.5	12.5	2.8	0.0	149
2006	AA	Montgomery	5	5	0	77	84	2.68	1.10	21.6	205	27	78	2.50	3.4	9.8	2.9	0.7	113
2007	AAA	Durham	12	6	0	131	123	3.98	1.45	22.4	280	35	75	4.56	3.2	8.5	2.7	0.9	79

Tall/strong pitcher with downward plane and three pitches he can notch strikeouts with. Repeats delivery and knows how to attack hitters weaknesses. Can be slow to plate (1.8) and despite apparently smooth arm action, has battled shoulder soreness for the past three years.

Niesen,Eric — SP — New York (N) — EXP MLB DEBUT: 2009 — POTENTIAL: Setup reliever/closer — 7D

Thrws L Age 22
2007 (3-C) Wake Forest
89-95 FB ++++
79-83 SL ++
79-81 CU +

Year	Lev	Team	W	L	Sv	IP	K	ERA	WHIP	BF/G	OBA	H%	S%	xERA	Ctl	Dom	Cmd	hr/9	BPV
2007	A-	Brooklyn	0	3	0	30	27	3.30	1.83	15.5	262	33	81	4.71	7.5	8.1	1.1	0.3	65

Short/athletic reliever who relies solely on his electric FBI. Low ¾ delivery and semblance of a SL makes him tough on LH batters, but struggles with command and ability to change speeds. Will need to improve game or risk getting pigeon-holed as a situational reliever.

Niese,Jonathon — SP — New York (N) — EXP MLB DEBUT: 2009 — POTENTIAL: #3 starter — 8C

Thrws L Age 21
2005 (7) HS (OH)
85-91 FB +++
69-72 CB +++
77-80 CU ++

Year	Lev	Team	W	L	Sv	IP	K	ERA	WHIP	BF/G	OBA	H%	S%	xERA	Ctl	Dom	Cmd	hr/9	BPV
2005	Rk	GCL Mets	1	0	0	24	24	3.65	1.36	14.5	252	33	72	3.33	3.7	8.9	2.4	0.4	97
2006	A-	Hagerstown	11	9	0	123	132	3.94	1.49	21.2	258	35	73	3.97	4.5	9.6	2.1	0.5	91
2006	A+	St. Lucie	0	2	0	10	10	4.50	1.30	20.6	221	31	62	2.54	4.5	9.0	2.0	0.0	107
2007	A+	St. Lucie	11	7	0	137	113	4.29	1.36	20.5	285	32	69	4.14	2.1	7.4	3.5	0.6	81

Projectable hurler made solid progress, learning to mix pitches and showing better FB command. Strikeout rate declined slightly, which may be a continuing trend. Pitched more to contact and improved CU deception. Pitches above stuff and knows how to win.

Norris,Bud — SP — Houston — EXP MLB DEBUT: 2009 — POTENTIAL: #3 starter — 8D

Thrws R Age 23
2006 (6) Cal Poly
90-95 FB ++++
79-82 CB ++
84-87 CU ++

Year	Lev	Team	W	L	Sv	IP	K	ERA	WHIP	BF/G	OBA	H%	S%	xERA	Ctl	Dom	Cmd	hr/9	BPV
2006	A-	Tri City	2	0	2	38	46	3.79	1.08	9.9	207	31	63	2.02	3.1	10.9	3.5	0.2	146
2007	A-	Lexington	2	8	0	96	117	4.77	1.31	18.1	239	33	64	3.47	3.8	10.9	2.9	0.7	110
2007	A+	Salem	1	0	0	6	2	1.50	0.83	21.9	191	21	80	1.07	1.5	3.0	2.0	0.0	77

Strong-armed pitcher with overpowering FB that grades well for velocity and movement. Demonstrates good command and is efficient with pitches. CB lacks consistent rotation and doesn't have enough velocity separation between FB and CU, making the bullpen an option.

Nova,Ivan — SP — New York (A) — EXP MLB DEBUT: 2010 — POTENTIAL: #4 starter — 8D

Thrws R Age 21
2005 FA (DR)
89-94 FB ++++
74-76 CB ++
83-84 CU +++

Year	Lev	Team	W	L	Sv	IP	K	ERA	WHIP	BF/G	OBA	H%	S%	xERA	Ctl	Dom	Cmd	hr/9	BPV
2006	Rk	GCL Yankees	3	0	1	43	36	2.72	1.00	16.4	229	27	79	2.88	1.5	7.5	5.1	1.0	131
2007	A-	Charleston	6	8	0	99	54	4.99	1.53	20.5	302	33	67	4.97	2.8	4.9	1.7	0.7	39

Tall/projectable pitcher possesses good velocity, but it is his ability to change speeds and spot pitches that drives success. Throws too many strikes which makes him hittable and lowers strikeout rate. Improved rotation of CB, but needs to repeat delivery and get stronger.

Nunez,Jhonny — SP — Washington

EXP MLB DEBUT: 2010 | POTENTIAL: #4 starter | 7D

Thrws R Age 21
2003 FA (DR)

Velo	Pitch	Grade
88-93	FB	+ + +
	SL	+ + +
	CU	+ +

Year	Lev	Team	W	L	Sv	IP	K	ERA	WHIP	BF/G	OBA	H%	S%	xERA	Ctl	Dom	Cmd	hr/9	BPV
2006	Rk	GCL Dodgers	6	0	0	57	56	1.58	0.95	21.5	179	25	81	1.16	3.0	8.8	2.9	0.0	134
2007	A-	Hagerstown	4	6	0	106	86	4.07	1.37	19.3	245	29	72	3.82	4.1	7.3	1.8	0.8	62

Projectable arm with good arm action and velocity. SL has chance to be a plus pitch and is the pitch he uses to get strikeouts and groundball outs. Repeating his delivery would help command and quality of CU. WAS has been cautious with workload, so needs to build stamina.

O'Sullivan,Sean — SP — Los Angeles (A)

EXP MLB DEBUT: 2009 | POTENTIAL: #3 starter | 8C

Thrws R Age 20
2005 (3) Grossmont JC

Velo	Pitch	Grade
87-93	FB	+ + + +
78-80	SL	+ + +
74-76	CB	+ + +
77-79	CU	+ +

Year	Lev	Team	W	L	Sv	IP	K	ERA	WHIP	BF/G	OBA	H%	S%	xERA	Ctl	Dom	Cmd	hr/9	BPV
2006	Rk	Orem	4	0	0	71	55	2.15	1.01	19.5	245	30	79	2.38	0.9	7.0	7.9	0.3	205
2007	A-	Cedar Rapids	10	7	0	158	125	2.22	1.11	24.9	234	31	77	2.44	2.3	7.1	3.1	0.3	84

Athletic/projectable pitcher who has led league in ERA the past two seasons. Arm action and a repeatable delivery allows him to mask pitches and show plus command. Keeps ball down and limits hits due to extraordinary movement. Fared well with innings increase.

Ohlendorf,Ross — RP — New York (A)

EXP MLB DEBUT: 2007 | POTENTIAL: Setup reliever | 7B

Thrws R Age 25
2004 (4) Princeton

Velo	Pitch	Grade
88-96	FB	+ + + +
82-85	SL	+ +
80-82	SP	+ +
79-82	CU	+ + + +

Year	Lev	Team	W	L	Sv	IP	K	ERA	WHIP	BF/G	OBA	H%	S%	xERA	Ctl	Dom	Cmd	hr/9	BPV
2006	AA	Tennessee	10	8	0	177	124	3.30	1.18	26.2	265	31	73	3.46	1.5	6.3	4.3	0.7	110
2006	AAA	Tucson	0	0	0	5	4	1.80	1.20	20.1	299	37	83	3.37	0.0	7.2		0.0	38
2007	AAA	Scranton/WB	3	3	0	66	48	5.04	1.66	14.1	316	36	71	5.71	3.3	6.5	2.0	1.0	44
2007	MLB	New York (A)	0	0	0	6	9	2.95	1.15	4.0	225	33	83	3.55	3.0	13.3	4.5	1.5	140
2007	Rk	GCL Yankees	1	1	0	16	17	3.94	0.88	14.8	224	28	58	2.55	0.6	9.6	17.0	1.1	391

Strong-framed pitcher converted to relief late in season allowing him to max-out FB and pitch more aggressively. Threw more quality strikes and picked-up a SPL, though his strikeout rate plummeted in Triple-A. Pitches with effort and doesn't repeat ¾ slot, but can pitch through them.

Olson,Garrett — SP — Baltimore

EXP MLB DEBUT: 2007 | POTENTIAL: #4 starter | 7B

Thrws L Age 24
2005 (1-S) Cal Poly

Velo	Pitch	Grade
87-92	FB	+ + +
74-78	SU	+ + + +
78-81	CU	+ +

Year	Lev	Team	W	L	Sv	IP	K	ERA	WHIP	BF/G	OBA	H%	S%	xERA	Ctl	Dom	Cmd	hr/9	BPV
2005	A+	Frederick	0	0	0	14	19	3.19	1.21	18.9	201	33	71	2.03	4.5	12.1	2.7	0.0	145
2006	A+	Frederick	4	4	0	81	77	2.77	1.22	23.4	259	32	80	3.57	2.1	8.5	4.1	0.8	116
2006	AA	Bowie	6	5	0	84	85	3.42	1.30	24.7	247	32	74	3.37	3.3	9.1	2.7	0.5	102
2007	AAA	Norfolk	9	7	0	128	120	3.16	1.05	22.5	208	25	74	2.61	2.7	8.4	3.1	0.9	101
2007	MLB	Baltimore	1	3	0	32	28	7.85	2.18	22.9	317	38	64	7.17	7.9	7.9	1.0	1.1	26

Base skills were solid across board despite marginal FB, but mixes pitches, shows command, keeps ball low, and is deceptive with high ¾ slot. Tends to fly open, causing arm to lag, which then suppresses velocity. Fared better with balls in play, which lowered oppBA.

Omogrosso,Brian — RP — Chicago (A)

EXP MLB DEBUT: 2009 | POTENTIAL: Setup reliever | 6C

Thrws R Age 24
2006 (6) Indiana St

Velo	Pitch	Grade
88-92	FB	+ + +
78-81	SL	+ + +

Year	Lev	Team	W	L	Sv	IP	K	ERA	WHIP	BF/G	OBA	H%	S%	xERA	Ctl	Dom	Cmd	hr/9	BPV
2006	A-	Kannapolis	1	2	1	36	23	3.23	1.10	6.5	209	24	71	2.41	3.2	5.7	1.8	0.5	70
2007	A+	Win-Salem	8	8	5	120	108	3.75	1.26	12.2	217	27	70	2.89	4.3	8.1	1.9	0.5	84

Survivor of TJS in 2005, he pitches aggressively from a sidearm delivery that is tough on RH batters. Sports velocity and sinking movement to FB, but tends to float SL. Generates groundball outs and strikeouts, though he lives dangerously by throwing too many pitches.

Orenduff,Justin — SP — Los Angeles (N)

EXP MLB DEBUT: 2008 | POTENTIAL: #4 starter | 7C

Thrws R Age 25
2004 (1) Virginia Comm.

Velo	Pitch	Grade
87-91	FB	+ + +
79-82	SL	+ + + +
78-82	CU	+ + +

Year	Lev	Team	W	L	Sv	IP	K	ERA	WHIP	BF/G	OBA	H%	S%	xERA	Ctl	Dom	Cmd	hr/9	BPV
2004	Rk	Ogden	2	3	0	43	57	4.79	1.64	14.8	274	39	72	4.86	5.2	11.9	2.3	0.8	94
2005	A+	Vero Beach	5	3	0	60	81	2.25	1.01	19.2	171	27	79	1.63	3.9	12.1	3.1	0.4	145
2005	AA	Jacksonville	5	2	0	66	65	4.08	1.26	19.2	240	30	69	3.44	3.3	8.9	2.7	0.8	92
2006	AA	Jacksonville	4	2	0	50	54	3.41	1.18	20.0	221	29	73	2.90	3.4	9.7	2.8	0.7	107
2007	AA	Jacksonville	8	5	0	109	113	4.21	1.44	17.2	267	33	75	4.74	3.7	9.3	2.5	1.3	71

Armed with a plus SL and FB movement, he registers strikeouts easily. Commands plate, changes speeds, and gains deception from a deliberate motion, but can also be slow to the plate and doesn't repeat ¾ release point. Suffered through shoulder impingement.

Ortegano,Jose — SP — Atlanta

EXP MLB DEBUT: 2010 | POTENTIAL: #3 starter | 8E

Thrws L Age 20
2003 FA (Venezuela)

Velo	Pitch	Grade
86-89	FB	+ +
	CB	+ +
	CU	+ + + +

Year	Lev	Team	W	L	Sv	IP	K	ERA	WHIP	BF/G	OBA	H%	S%	xERA	Ctl	Dom	Cmd	hr/9	BPV
2006	Rk	GCL Braves	3	3	0	46	31	3.32	1.15	15.3	249	29	72	3.09	2.0	6.1	3.1	0.6	89
2007	Rk	Danville	6	1	0	60	55	1.50	0.91	17.3	206	26	87	1.81	1.6	8.2	5.0	0.4	155

Athletic pitcher with advanced approach, showing rare ability to change speeds and command plate for age/level. Lacks velocity, but keeps ball low and possesses late movement. CB is loose in its rotation and hasn't been extended, so will need to build arm strength.

Ottavino,Adam — SP — St. Louis

EXP MLB DEBUT: 2009 | POTENTIAL: #3 starter | 8C

Thrws R Age 22
2006 (1) Northeastern

Velo	Pitch	Grade
88-93	FB	+ + + +
77-79	SL	+ + +
72-75	CB	+ +
78-81	CU	+ +

Year	Lev	Team	W	L	Sv	IP	K	ERA	WHIP	BF/G	OBA	H%	S%	xERA	Ctl	Dom	Cmd	hr/9	BPV
2006	A-	Quad City	2	3	0	36	38	3.48	1.30	18.6	215	28	75	3.16	4.7	9.4	2.0	0.7	88
2006	A-	State College	2	2	0	28	26	3.19	1.28	19.3	224	29	74	2.83	4.1	8.3	2.0	0.3	92
2007	A+	Palm Beach	12	8	0	143	128	3.08	1.35	22.1	244	30	79	3.55	4.0	8.1	2.0	0.6	78

Strong-framed pitcher supports velocity and durability. Gains deception from drop-and-drive delivery and pitches on a downward plane, which assists in getting groundball outs. Tends to show baseball and needs to throw breaking pitches for strikes instead of out of the zone.

Outman,Josh — SP — Philadelphia

EXP MLB DEBUT: 2008 | POTENTIAL: #4 starter | 7C

Thrws L Age 23
2005 (10) Cent Missouri St

Velo	Pitch	Grade
88-94	FB	+ + + +
80-84	SL	+ + +
73-74	CB	+
78-80	CU	+ +

Year	Lev	Team	W	L	Sv	IP	K	ERA	WHIP	BF/G	OBA	H%	S%	xERA	Ctl	Dom	Cmd	hr/9	BPV
2005	A-	Batavia	2	1	0	29	31	2.78	1.27	10.8	219	30	78	2.73	4.3	9.6	2.2	0.3	106
2006	A-	Lakewood	14	6	0	155	161	2.95	1.25	23.4	214	29	76	2.60	4.4	9.3	2.1	0.3	105
2007	A+	Clearwater	10	4	0	117	117	2.45	1.35	24.4	240	31	77	2.32	4.2	9.0	2.2	0.5	108
2007	AA	Reading	2	3	0	42	34	4.50	1.45	25.6	243	32	76	4.40	4.9	7.3	1.5	1.1	61

Led FSL in ERA by interchanging all three pitches and achieving a balance between strikeouts and groundball outs. None of his pitches are strikeout pitches on their own, but will go to SL when pressure is on. Command took a hit with promotion and will need to improve CU.

Oxspring,Chris — SP — Milwaukee

EXP MLB DEBUT: 2005 | POTENTIAL: #5 starter/setup reliever | 7C

Thrws R Age 31
2000 FA (Australia)

Velo	Pitch	Grade
88-92	FB	+ + +
81-82	SL	+ + +
75-76	CB	+ +
79-80	CU	+

Year	Lev	Team	W	L	Sv	IP	K	ERA	WHIP	BF/G	OBA	H%	S%	xERA	Ctl	Dom	Cmd	hr/9	BPV
2003	AA	Mobile	10	6	0	135	129	2.93	1.24	13.7	218	28	77	2.73	4.1	8.6	2.1	0.4	95
2004	AAA	Portland	6	4	0	85	81	4.01	1.48	21.5	254	32	74	4.12	4.6	8.6	1.8	0.7	72
2005	AAA	Portland	12	6	0	160	125	4.04	1.19	24.7	247	29	67	3.39	2.4	7.0	3.0	0.8	85
2005	MLB	San Diego	0	0	0	12	11	3.75	1.25	9.8	210	23	77	3.70	4.5	8.3	1.8	1.5	56
2007	AAA	Nashville	7	5	0	96	106	3.56	1.39	22.4	250	33	77	3.90	4.0	9.9	2.5	0.8	91

Strong-framed pitcher returned after one season in Japan. Learned to trust stuff, repeat ¾ delivery, and not overthrow, which improved movement, command, and strikeout rate. Primarily a sinker/SL pitcher, but began to incorporate CU into game plan.

Parisi,Michael — SP — St. Louis

EXP MLB DEBUT: 2008 | POTENTIAL: #5 starter | 6C

Thrws R Age 25
2004 (9) Manhattan

Velo	Pitch	Grade
86-92	FB	+ + +
75-80	CB	+ + +
80-81	CU	+ +

Year	Lev	Team	W	L	Sv	IP	K	ERA	WHIP	BF/G	OBA	H%	S%	xERA	Ctl	Dom	Cmd	hr/9	BPV
2004	A-	Peoria	1	1	0	35	36	3.32	1.28	24.0	232	31	73	2.86	3.8	9.2	2.4	0.3	107
2005	A-	Quad City	5	5	0	86	66	4.08	1.43	26.1	288	35	71	4.28	2.6	6.9	2.6	0.5	79
2005	A+	Palm Beach	5	6	0	78	63	3.23	1.29	24.7	264	32	77	3.76	2.5	7.3	2.9	0.7	85
2006	AA	Springfield	9	8	0	150	107	4.61	1.54	24.2	284	33	71	4.74	3.8	6.4	1.7	0.8	49
2007	AAA	Memphis	8	13	0	165	111	4.91	1.56	25.8	292	33	71	5.26	3.5	6.1	1.7	1.1	34

Short/athletic pitcher gets most out of average repertoire by setting-up pitches and throwing strikes. Lacks velocity, but gets late movement to pitches by quick arm action and keeps ball down. Needs to repeat delivery, but unlikely to survive more than twice through lineup.

Parker,Jarrod — SP — Arizona — EXP MLB DEBUT: 2011 — POTENTIAL: #2 starter — 9D

Thrws R Age 19	Year	Lev	Team	W	L	Sv	IP	K	ERA	WHIP	BF/G	OBA	H%	S%	xERA	Ctl	Dom	Cmd	hr/9	BPV
2007 (1) HS (IN)																				
89-97 FB ++++																				
79-82 SL ++++																				
73-76 CB ++																				
77-81 CU +++	2007																			

Athletic pitcher with quick arm action and clean mechanics giving him easy velocity. Repeats ¾ delivery on SL and CU, but tends to shorten stride when throwing them. Achieves balance of strikeouts and groundball outs, and loves to work quickly on the mound.

Parnell,Robert — SP — New York (N) — EXP MLB DEBUT: 2009 — POTENTIAL: #4 starter — 7C

Thrws R Age 23	Year	Lev	Team	W	L	Sv	IP	K	ERA	WHIP	BF/G	OBA	H%	S%	xERA	Ctl	Dom	Cmd	hr/9	BPV
2005 (9) Charleston So	2005	A-	Brooklyn	2	3	0	73	67	1.73	1.05	18.9	189	25	83	1.67	3.6	8.3	2.3	0.1	112
88-95 FB +++	2006	A-	Hagerstown	5	10	0	93	84	4.06	1.33	21.5	242	30	70	3.53	3.9	8.1	2.1	0.7	79
82-85 SL +++	2006	A+	St. Lucie	0	1	0	11	13	9.64	2.23	18.9	336	41	59	8.81	7.2	10.4	1.4	2.4	8
78-80 SP +++	2007	A+	St. Lucie	3	3	0	55	62	3.27	1.42	19.4	265	37	74	3.39	3.6	10.1	2.8	0.0	122
	2007	AA	Binghamton	5	5	0	88	74	4.80	1.54	22.6	283	34	70	4.85	3.9	7.6	1.9	0.9	57

Projectable pitcher added a few ticks to FB and got hitters to chase SL which improved strikeout rate. Keeps ball low and possesses good movement with his quick arm action. Command remains inconsistent and doesn't always bring a quality SPLCU to the mound.

Parra,Manny — SP — Milwaukee — EXP MLB DEBUT: 2007 — POTENTIAL: #2 starter — 9C

Thrws L Age 25	Year	Lev	Team	W	L	Sv	IP	K	ERA	WHIP	BF/G	OBA	H%	S%	xERA	Ctl	Dom	Cmd	hr/9	BPV
2001 (26) American River JC	2006	A+	Brevard Co	1	2	0	54	61	2.99	1.46	15.5	235	32	81	3.73	5.3	10.1	1.9	0.7	89
87-93 FB ++++	2006	AA	Huntsville	3	0	0	31	29	2.89	1.09	20.3	229	31	71	2.12	2.3	8.4	3.6	0.0	136
81-85 SP ++	2007	AA	Huntsville	7	3	0	80	81	2.69	1.20	24.8	236	32	77	2.68	2.9	9.1	3.1	0.2	121
73-78 CB ++++	2007	AAA	Nashville	3	1	0	26	25	1.73	0.85	23.8	170	22	81	1.13	2.4	8.7	3.6	0.3	138
80-84 CU +++	2007	MLB	Milwaukee	0	1	0	26	26	3.79	1.42	12.3	254	34	72	3.58	4.1	9.0	2.2	0.3	93

All he needed was heatlh to live-up to his potential. Flashes plus CB and is able to add/subtract from FB with his smooth arm action. Repeats high ¾ delivery, giving him consistent command and ability to disguise pitches. Has chance to dominate with ability to miss bats.

Pascual,Rolando — SP — Milwaukee — EXP MLB DEBUT: 2011 — POTENTIAL: #3 starter — 8E

Thrws R Age 19	Year	Lev	Team	W	L	Sv	IP	K	ERA	WHIP	BF/G	OBA	H%	S%	xERA	Ctl	Dom	Cmd	hr/9	BPV
2005 FA (DR)																				
87-93 FB ++++																				
CB ++																				
CU ++	2006	Rk	AZL Brewers	2	7	0	41	22	10.05	1.97	14.1	275	31	44	5.18	8.1	4.8	0.6	0.2	35
	2007	Rk	AZL Brewers	0	1	0	5	6	9.00	2.60	9.0	299	43	62	6.86	12.6	10.8	0.9	0.0	78

Tall/projectable pitcher with explosive FB and quick arm action, but missed season recovering from TJS. Lacks consistency of comps (CB/CU) which falls back to not repeating his mechanics. Experience and physical maturity will solve a multitude of problems.

Patterson,Scott — RP — New York (A) — EXP MLB DEBUT: 2008 — POTENTIAL: Setup reliever — 7C

Thrws R Age 29	Year	Lev	Team	W	L	Sv	IP	K	ERA	WHIP	BF/G	OBA	H%	S%	xERA	Ctl	Dom	Cmd	hr/9	BPV
2006 UDFA WV St																				
88-92 FB +++																				
CB +++	2006	AA	Trenton	0	1	1	38	44	2.36	0.89	5.5	194	24	86	2.51	1.9	10.4	5.5	1.4	151
	2007	AA	Trenton	4	2	2	74	91	1.09	0.81	6.3	177	27	86	0.89	1.8	11.1	6.1	0.1	210
	2007	AAA	Scranton/WB	0	0	0	3	1	0.00	0.00	8.5	0	0	100	0.00	0.0	3.0		0.0	73

Tall/lanky reliever with incredible base skills. Scary to RH batters with his overhand delivery and extension which puts the baseball on-top of them in a hurry. Generates swings and misses with CB and FB that possesses late life. Could be effective as a match-up reliever.

Patton,Troy — SP — Baltimore — EXP MLB DEBUT: 2007 — POTENTIAL: #3 starter — 8B

Thrws R Age 22	Year	Lev	Team	W	L	Sv	IP	K	ERA	WHIP	BF/G	OBA	H%	S%	xERA	Ctl	Dom	Cmd	hr/9	BPV
2004 (9) HS (TX)	2006	A+	Salem	7	7	0	101	102	2.85	1.27	21.7	242	32	77	3.05	3.3	9.1	2.8	0.4	108
86-93 FB ++++	2006	AA	Corpus Christi	2	5	0	45	37	4.39	1.35	23.5	274	32	71	4.52	2.6	7.4	2.8	1.2	68
83-86 CT +++	2007	AA	Corpus Christi	6	6	0	102	68	3.00	1.26	26.1	250	28	80	3.68	2.9	6.0	2.1	0.9	58
78-81 SL ++	2007	AAA	Round Rock	4	2	0	49	25	4.59	1.12	24.1	242	26	60	3.26	2.0	4.6	2.3	0.9	54
79-81 CU +++	2007	MLB	Houston	0	2	0	12	8	3.69	1.15	16.1	225	21	82	4.32	3.0	5.9	2.0	2.2	21

Athletic pitcher with pitch movement and a deceptively quick arm, none of his pitches stand-out, but work in-concert with each other to derive results. Command is solid and repeated arm slot more effectively. His flyball tendencies could be a detriment at Camden Yards.

Pauley,David — SP — Boston — EXP MLB DEBUT: 2006 — POTENTIAL: #5 starter — 6B

Thrws R Age 25	Year	Lev	Team	W	L	Sv	IP	K	ERA	WHIP	BF/G	OBA	H%	S%	xERA	Ctl	Dom	Cmd	hr/9	BPV
2001 (8) HS (CO)	2005	AA	Portland	9	7	0	156	104	3.81	1.30	23.8	278	31	74	4.30	2.0	6.0	3.1	1.0	69
86-92 FB +++	2006	AA	Portland	2	3	0	60	47	2.40	1.18	24.0	242	28	85	3.37	2.5	7.0	2.8	0.9	80
73-77 CB ++++	2006	AAA	Pawtucket	1	3	0	50	25	5.39	1.54	24.3	295	30	70	5.87	3.2	4.5	1.4	1.8	-2
79-82 CU +++	2006	MLB	Boston	0	2	0	16	10	7.88	2.31	27.4	407	46	64	8.67	3.4	5.6	1.7	0.6	25
	2007	AAA	Pawtucket	6	6	0	153	110	4.35	1.39	23.9	275	31	71	4.51	2.9	6.5	2.2	1.1	54

Low upside hurler who pitches to contact and relies on keeping ball low and command arsenal. Goes to CB when in trouble as he possesses very little movement to FB. Tends to tip pitches by not repeating high ¾ slot and showing baseball at top of release.

Paulino,Felipe — SP — Houston — EXP MLB DEBUT: 2007 — POTENTIAL: #3 starter/setup reliever — 9D

Thrws R Age 24	Year	Lev	Team	W	L	Sv	IP	K	ERA	WHIP	BF/G	OBA	H%	S%	xERA	Ctl	Dom	Cmd	hr/9	BPV
2002 FA (Venezuela)	2005	A-	Lexington	1	1	0	24	30	1.87	1.12	13.6	236	33	88	2.96	2.2	11.2	5.0	0.7	158
92-98 FB +++++	2005	A-	Tri City	2	2	1	30	34	3.87	1.06	9.0	198	27	63	2.21	3.3	10.1	3.1	0.6	123
85-87 SL +++	2006	A+	Salem	9	7	0	126	91	4.35	1.41	19.8	251	29	71	4.10	4.2	6.5	1.5	0.9	48
80-83 CB +++	2007	AA	Corpus Christi	6	9	0	112	110	3.62	1.36	21.3	246	32	73	3.46	3.9	8.8	2.2	0.5	92
75-80 CU ++	2007	MLB	Houston	2	1	0	19	11	7.11	1.53	16.5	291	29	58	6.32	3.3	5.2	1.6	2.4	-10

Live-armed pitcher with soaring velocity and solid movement to both breaking pitches. Gets by on FB, but improved command and pitchability. Doesn't change speeds effectively and pitches with effort, so needs a smoother delivery and develop repertoire to remain a starter.

Pawelek,Mark — SP — Chicago (N) — EXP MLB DEBUT: 2010 — POTENTIAL: #3 starter — 8E

Thrws R Age 21	Year	Lev	Team	W	L	Sv	IP	K	ERA	WHIP	BF/G	OBA	H%	S%	xERA	Ctl	Dom	Cmd	hr/9	BPV
2005 (1) HS (UT)	2005	Rk	AZL Cubs	0	3	0	43	56	2.72	1.07	11.9	171	28	72	1.35	4.4	11.7	2.7	0.0	147
88-93 FB ++++	2006	A-	Boise	3	5	0	61	52	2.66	1.26	16.6	239	31	78	2.82	3.4	7.7	2.3	0.1	96
73-75 CB +++	2007	A-	Peoria	0	0	0	4	3	6.75	1.50	8.6	151	19	50	2.27	9.0	6.8	0.8	0.0	81
78-81 CU ++	2007	A-	Boise	1	2	0	12	10	9.59	1.89	7.2	274	33	45	5.43	7.4	7.4	1.0	0.7	43
	2007	Rk	AZL Cubs	0	0	0	1	1	0.00	3.00	5.8	415	52	100	10.01	9.0	9.0	1.0	0.0	47

Athletic/projectable pitcher took most of the year to build-up arm strength and work on mechanics on the side. Possesses strikeout ability and excellent movement to CB and FB, featuring smooth arm action. Command and CU suffers by not repeating delivery.

Pelland,Tyler — SP — Cincinnati — EXP MLB DEBUT: 2008 — POTENTIAL: #5 starter — 6C

Thrws L Age 24	Year	Lev	Team	W	L	Sv	IP	K	ERA	WHIP	BF/G	OBA	H%	S%	xERA	Ctl	Dom	Cmd	hr/9	BPV
2002 (9) HS (VT)	2004	Rk	Billings	9	3	0	73	82	3.44	1.45	17.4	245	34	76	3.56	4.8	10.1	2.1	0.4	100
87-92 FB +++	2005	A+	Sarasota	5	8	0	102	103	4.05	1.63	15.1	263	35	75	4.33	5.6	9.1	1.6	0.4	78
74-78 CB +++	2006	AA	Chattanooga	9	5	0	142	107	3.99	1.64	22.6	264	31	77	4.64	5.6	6.8	1.2	0.7	47
81-84 CU ++	2007	AA	Chattanooga	5	4	2	66	71	3.95	1.44	8.0	253	33	74	4.06	4.4	9.7	2.2	0.8	85
	2007	AAA	Louisville	1	1	0	23	27	3.10	1.03	4.7	206	29	70	2.04	2.7	10.5	3.9	0.4	146

Athletic pitcher was moved to long relief after failing to develop CU and stamina. Tough on LH batters with solid CB and velocity, but needs command within strike zone. Pitches with effort and long ¾ delivery makes him susceptible to running game.

Pena,Luis — SP — Milwaukee — EXP MLB DEBUT: 2008 — POTENTIAL: #4 starter/setup reliever — 7D

Thrws L Age 25	Year	Lev	Team	W	L	Sv	IP	K	ERA	WHIP	BF/G	OBA	H%	S%	xERA	Ctl	Dom	Cmd	hr/9	BPV
1999 FA (Venezuela)	2004	A-	Kannapolis	0	4	0	24	25	6.35	1.37	10.1	284	35	55	4.97	2.2	9.3	4.2	1.5	97
89-95 FB ++++	2004	Rk	Bristol	2	0	4	18	22	1.48	0.77	6.5	135	19	85	0.69	3.0	10.9	3.7	0.5	155
CB +++	2005	Rk	Great Falls	0	1	0	33	25	6.80	1.99	8.9	320	36	67	6.99	6.0	6.8	1.1	1.4	15
SP ++	2007	A+	Brevard Co	5	0	6	21	27	2.12	0.99	5.0	190	28	80	1.76	3.0	11.5	3.9	0.4	154
CU +++	2007	AA	Huntsville	0	4	12	46	42	2.92	1.08	5.2	216	28	71	2.13	2.7	8.2	3.0	0.2	118

Tall/projectable pitcher found success in bullpen where he was able to air-out FB and show command, which improved strikeout rate. CU is preferred comp as he has difficulty spinning baseball. Repeats delivery and has quick arm action, providing movement/deception.

Pereira,Nick | SP | San Francisco | EXP MLB DEBUT: 2007 | POTENTIAL: #4 starter | 7C

Thrws R Age 25 — 2005 (10) San Francisco
- 86-91 FB +++
- 75-80 SL +++
- 79-80 CU ++

Year	Lev	Team	W	L	Sv	IP	K	ERA	WHIP	BF/G	OBA	H%	S%	xERA	Ctl	Dom	Cmd	hr/9	BPV
2005	A-	Salem-Keizer	5	3	0	50	41	3.05	1.36	14.9	277	35	75	3.44	2.5	7.4	2.9	0.0	105
2006	A+	San Jose	7	1	0	78	76	1.96	1.02	23.1	225	30	80	2.00	1.8	8.7	4.8	0.1	159
2006	AAA	Fresno	4	3	0	79	60	5.92	1.71	23.9	281	32	66	5.46	5.5	6.8	1.3	1.1	32
2007	AA	Connecticut	9	9	0	143	123	3.40	1.32	22.8	235	28	78	3.67	4.1	7.7	1.9	0.9	66

Short/athletic pitcher amassed groundball outs with sinker and gets enough strikeouts to be effective. Command suffered for first time in career, but was trying to be too fine. Stiff arm action makes it difficult to repeat ¾ delivery and leaves him with a below average CU.

Perez,Chris | RP | St. Louis | EXP MLB DEBUT: 2008 | POTENTIAL: Setup reliever/closer | 8C

Thrws R Age 22 — 2006 (1-S) Miami-FL
- 90-95 FB ++++
- 82-86 SL +++
- 75-78 CB +++

Year	Lev	Team	W	L	Sv	IP	K	ERA	WHIP	BF/G	OBA	H%	S%	xERA	Ctl	Dom	Cmd	hr/9	BPV
2006	A-	Quad City	2	0	12	29	32	2.16	1.34	4.8	196	29	82	2.33	5.9	9.9	1.7	0.0	111
2007	A-	Eugene	4	2	0	51	52	6.00	1.67	8.8	258	34	61	4.27	6.2	9.2	1.5	0.4	79
2007	AA	Springfield	2	0	27	40	62	2.46	1.12	4.1	130	21	81	1.67	6.3	13.9	2.2	0.7	139
2007	AAA	Memphis	0	1	9	14	15	4.50	1.36	3.9	132	14	71	2.90	8.4	9.6	1.2	1.3	72

Dominating closer with high-octane velocity and two breaking pitches at his disposal, of which his SL is his strikeout pitch. Command improved slightly, but operates by being effectively wild. Keeps ball down, misses bats, has a durable arm, and loves to pitch under pressure.

Perez,Juan | RP | Pittsburgh | EXP MLB DEBUT: 2007 | POTENTIAL: Situational reliever | 6C

Thrws L Age 27 — 1998 FA (DR)
- 86-92 FB +++
- 78-80 SU +++

Year	Lev	Team	W	L	Sv	IP	K	ERA	WHIP	BF/G	OBA	H%	S%	xERA	Ctl	Dom	Cmd	hr/9	BPV
2005	AAA	Pawtucket	4	5	1	62	74	4.50	1.45	6.6	259	35	71	4.35	4.2	10.7	2.6	1.0	91
2006	AAA	Ind/Nor	0	1	0	70	61	2.57	1.50	6.4	256	32	84	3.99	4.8	7.8	1.6	0.5	70
2006	MLB	Pittsburgh	0	1	0	3	3	8.71	1.94	2.1	364	41	60	9.03	2.9	8.7	3.0	2.9	10
2007	AAA	Indianapolis	3	2	2	55	63	4.73	1.39	5.8	250	34	67	3.91	4.1	10.3	2.5	0.8	95
2007	MLB	Pittsburgh	0	0	0	12	10	4.46	1.82	3.3	291	33	80	6.21	6.0	7.4	1.3	1.5	23

Situational reliever misses bats with power sinker and began to throw SU for strikes instead of off the plate. ¾ delivery provides deception, but tends to slow-down arm speed when throwing SU. Command improved slightly, but needs to be more efficient in attacking hitters.

Perez,Oneli | RP | Chicago (A) | EXP MLB DEBUT: 2008 | POTENTIAL: Situational reliever | 6A

Thrws R Age 25 — 2003 FA (DR)
- 84-89 FB ++
- 75-79 SL +++
- 80-82 CU +++

Year	Lev	Team	W	L	Sv	IP	K	ERA	WHIP	BF/G	OBA	H%	S%	xERA	Ctl	Dom	Cmd	hr/9	BPV
2005	A-	Kannapolis	4	2	2	80	62	3.71	1.45	9.5	271	32	76	4.34	3.6	7.0	1.9	0.8	60
2006	A-	Kannapolis	3	1	8	35	40	1.03	0.80	4.5	175	25	89	0.97	1.8	10.3	5.7	0.3	194
2006	A+	Win-Salem	1	0	0	25	29	0.72	0.88	5.4	194	28	95	1.49	1.8	10.4	5.8	0.4	190
2006	AA	Birmingham	0	1	1	16	20	0.56	0.75	8.2	117	16	100	0.51	3.4	11.2	3.3	0.6	152
2007	AA	Birmingham	6	2	16	77	89	2.10	1.06	5.1	222	31	83	2.50	2.3	10.4	4.5	0.6	149

Successful closer featuring deceptive low ¾ slot and frisbee SL that ties-up RH batters. Commands plate, keeps ball low, and will use any pitch, which could allow him to be more than a situational reliever. Athleticism allows him to repeat delivery, adding to his effectiveness.

Perez,Sergio | SP | Houston | EXP MLB DEBUT: 2009 | POTENTIAL: #4 starter/setup reliever | 8E

Thrws R Age 23 — 2006 (2) Tampa
- 88-95 FB ++++
- 80-83 SL +++
- CU +

Year	Lev	Team	W	L	Sv	IP	K	ERA	WHIP	BF/G	OBA	H%	S%	xERA	Ctl	Dom	Cmd	hr/9	BPV
2006	A-	Lexington	3	0	0	16	21	2.24	1.06	5.7	165	27	76	1.26	4.5	11.7	2.6	0.0	147
2007	A+	Salem	7	10	0	128	84	4.00	1.34	21.3	263	30	71	3.82	3.0	5.9	2.0	0.6	60

Strong/projectable pitcher with smooth arm action and easy velocity. Strikeout rate was absurdly low in 2007, but was focusing more on pitching to contact and keeping ball low. Will need to repeat ¾ delivery on CU and learn how to set-up pitches better.

Petrick,Billy | RP | Chicago (N) | EXP MLB DEBUT: 2007 | POTENTIAL: Setup reliever | 6C

Thrws R Age 24 — 2002 (3) HS (IL)
- 88-93 FB +++
- 80-83 SL +++
- CU +

Year	Lev	Team	W	L	Sv	IP	K	ERA	WHIP	BF/G	OBA	H%	S%	xERA	Ctl	Dom	Cmd	hr/9	BPV
2006	A+	Daytona	1	2	0	16	9	6.15	1.61	23.8	346	37	65	6.78	1.1	5.0	4.5	1.7	60
2007	A+	Daytona	0	1	0	11	10	3.21	1.25	7.6	275	36	71	3.14	1.6	8.0	5.0	0.0	153
2007	AA	Tennessee	1	1	2	30	33	2.39	1.00	6.4	206	27	81	2.43	2.4	9.9	4.1	0.9	133
2007	AAA	Iowa	1	1	0	12	7	5.21	1.57	5.9	333	34	75	6.96	1.5	5.2	3.5	2.2	26
2007	MLB	Chicago (N)	0	0	0	9	6	7.83	1.63	5.1	236	20	58	6.35	6.8	5.9	0.9	2.9	-27

Tall/strong-framed pitcher resurrected career with move to bullpen. Primarily a sinker/SL pitcher, getting downward movement due to quick arm action. Fails to repeat release point on "show-me" CU, and lacks stamina to be used on back-to-back days.

Phillips,Paul | RP | Toronto | EXP MLB DEBUT: 2009 | POTENTIAL: Setup reliever | 7E

Thrws R Age 24 — 2005 (9) Oakland
- 89-95 FB ++++
- 83-85 SL +++
- CU +

Year	Lev	Team	W	L	Sv	IP	K	ERA	WHIP	BF/G	OBA	H%	S%	xERA	Ctl	Dom	Cmd	hr/9	BPV
2006	A-	Lansing	5	3	14	39	35	2.07	1.20	5.2	241	30	84	2.99	2.8	8.1	2.9	0.5	103
2006	A+	Dunedin	1	3	0	20	21	7.13	1.68	6.1	322	42	55	5.35	3.1	9.4	3.0	0.4	96
2006	AA	New Hamp.	0	0	0	2	5	8.57	2.38	3.6	252	68	60	5.54	12.9	21.4	1.7	0.0	168
2007	A-	Lansing	1	1	11	29	34	2.47	1.10	4.6	234	33	77	2.47	2.2	10.5	4.9	0.3	164
2007	A+	Dunedin	4	1	1	27	25	6.31	1.48	4.5	282	31	64	5.99	3.3	8.3	2.5	2.3	31

Strong-armed reliever with plus velocity and ability to overpower hitters with hard SL. Not a lot of finesse to game as he tends to overthrow which decreases pitch movement, but still gets share of strikeouts. Command holds up well despite struggles to repeat delivery.

Phillips,Zach | SP | Texas | EXP MLB DEBUT: 2010 | POTENTIAL: #5 starter | 7D

Thrws L Age 21 — 2004 (23) Sacramento CC
- 86-90 FB +++
- CB +++
- CU ++

Year	Lev	Team	W	L	Sv	IP	K	ERA	WHIP	BF/G	OBA	H%	S%	xERA	Ctl	Dom	Cmd	hr/9	BPV
2005	Rk	AZL Rangers	1	3	0	50	73	3.95	1.30	14.7	269	42	69	3.63	2.3	13.1	5.6	0.5	182
2005	A-	Clinton	0	0	0	4	4	6.75	1.75	9.1	383	49	57	6.20	0.0	9.0		0.0	32
2006	A-	Clinton	5	12	0	142	126	5.96	1.72	23.0	308	39	63	5.11	4.2	8.0	1.9	0.3	72
2007	A-	Clinton	11	7	0	151	157	2.92	1.20	22.5	246	33	76	2.95	2.6	9.3	3.7	0.4	128

Athletic pitcher who succeeds with mediocre velocity by showing extreme groundball tendencies and outstanding command. Notches strikeouts with CB and doesn't waste pitches. Despite athleticism, he needs to repeat delivery more consistently to improve look of CU.

Pichardo,Kelvin | SP | San Francisco | EXP MLB DEBUT: 2009 | POTENTIAL: #5 starter/setup reliever | 7D

Thrws R Age 22 — 2003 FA (DR)
- 88-94 FB ++++
- CB +++
- CU ++

Year	Lev	Team	W	L	Sv	IP	K	ERA	WHIP	BF/G	OBA	H%	S%	xERA	Ctl	Dom	Cmd	hr/9	BPV
2005	Rk	GCL Phillies	3	2	0	54	37	4.17	1.15	21.4	279	32	64	3.59	0.5	6.2	12.3	0.7	275
2006	A-	Augusta	2	4	0	36	35	3.23	1.33	12.5	233	31	74	2.99	4.2	8.7	2.1	0.2	96
2006	A-	Salem-Keizer	2	0	1	15	24	4.74	1.38	10.6	284	44	68	4.65	2.4	14.2	6.0	1.2	174
2007	A+	San Jose	2	3	3	46	71	3.12	1.17	6.4	221	37	73	2.53	3.3	13.8	4.2	0.4	170
2007	AA	Connecticut	2	2	2	21	16	3.86	1.43	5.2	191	22	75	3.34	6.9	6.9	1.0	0.9	53

Short/athletic with obscene strikeout and command numbers in high Class-A. Overpowers hitters with above average velocity and CB, but lacks ability to change speeds. Has a tendency to overthrow which reduces movement and pitched tentatively in exposure to Double-A.

Pignatiello,Carmen | RP | Chicago (N) | EXP MLB DEBUT: 2007 | POTENTIAL: Situational reliever | 6B

Thrws L Age 25 — 2000 (20) HS (IL)
- 84-87 FB ++
- 77-80 CB ++++

Year	Lev	Team	W	L	Sv	IP	K	ERA	WHIP	BF/G	OBA	H%	S%	xERA	Ctl	Dom	Cmd	hr/9	BPV
2006	AA	W. Tennessee	3	1	0	59	73	2.74	1.17	6.4	231	33	77	2.74	2.9	11.1	3.8	0.5	143
2006	AAA	Iowa	0	0	0	6	4	2.90	1.45	3.3	286	34	78	3.83	2.9	5.8	2.0	0.0	75
2007	AA	Tennessee	1	0	2	6	6	0.00	0.65	4.3	103	15	100	0.00	2.9	8.7	3.0	0.0	150
2007	AAA	Iowa	1	0	2	49	44	2.76	1.14	4.3	224	27	80	3.06	2.9	8.1	2.8	0.9	89
2007	MLB	Chicago (N)	0	0	0	2	3	4.50	1.50	2.2	347	43	100	9.09	0.0	13.5		4.5	-68

Plus CB nets strikeouts and off-sets low velocity in making him extremely tough on LH batters. Provides little deception by showing baseball at top of release and will purposely alter arm slot, which hasn't tipped pitches to the batter or affected command.

Pimentel,Carlos | SP | Texas | EXP MLB DEBUT: 2012 | POTENTIAL: #3 starter | 9E

Thrws R Age 18 — 2006 FA (DR)
- 88-94 FB ++++
- CB ++
- CU +

Year	Lev	Team	W	L	Sv	IP	K	ERA	WHIP	BF/G	OBA	H%	S%	xERA	Ctl	Dom	Cmd	hr/9	BPV
2007	Rk	AZL Rangers	0	5	1	42	59	5.56	1.45	13.8	270	41	60	4.13	3.6	12.6	3.5	0.6	130

Projectable pitcher with easy velocity and the ability to overpower hitters. Sports fair command despite not repeating high ¾ delivery, but doesn't change speeds well, CB rotation is inconsistent, and is hittable by LH batters. May spend another year in rookie ball to gain confidence.

Pimentel, Julio — SP — Kansas City

Thrws R **Age** 22
2003 FA (DR)

87-93	FB	++++	
77-81	CB	+++	
80-84	CU	+++	

EXP MLB DEBUT: 2008 | POTENTIAL: #4 starter | **7C**

Year	Lev	Team	W	L	Sv	IP	K	ERA	WHIP	BF/G	OBA	H%	S%	xERA	Ctl	Dom	Cmd	hr/9	BPV
2004	A-	Columbus	10	8	0	111	102	3.48	1.38	20.3	253	30	79	4.22	3.8	8.3	2.2	1.1	66
2005	A+	Vero Beach	8	10	0	124	105	5.08	1.55	20.8	299	36	67	4.86	3.1	7.6	2.4	0.7	73
2006	A+	Vbeach/Hdes	5	9	4	97	103	5.10	1.65	10.3	277	36	69	4.78	5.1	9.6	1.9	0.6	77
2007	A+	Wilmington	12	4	0	152	73	2.66	1.24	22.9	253	28	79	3.27	2.5	4.3	1.7	0.5	52

Low ERA and ability to win based on extreme groundball tendencies and ability to change speeds. Possesses velocity, but lacks movement and strikeout ability. Athletic frame helps in repeating delivery. Command within strike zone has to improve and will need to tighten CB.

Pino, Yohan — SP — Minnesota

Thrws R **Age** 24
2004 FA (Venezuela)

86-90	FB	+++	
83-85	CT	+++	
79-80	SL	++	
70-73	CB	+++	

EXP MLB DEBUT: 2009 | POTENTIAL: #4 starter | **7D**

Year	Lev	Team	W	L	Sv	IP	K	ERA	WHIP	BF/G	OBA	H%	S%	xERA	Ctl	Dom	Cmd	hr/9	BPV
2005	Rk	Elizabethton	9	2	0	67	64	3.75	1.21	22.5	264	34	68	3.25	1.7	8.6	4.9	0.4	145
2006	A-	Beloit	14	2	3	94	99	1.91	0.95	8.4	207	28	81	1.83	1.9	9.5	5.0	0.4	163
2007	A+	Fort Myers	4	3	0	67	64	1.74	0.95	13.3	199	26	82	1.65	2.3	8.6	3.8	0.3	138
2007	AA	New Britain	2	4	0	47	40	5.16	1.40	22.1	300	35	65	4.98	1.7	7.6	4.4	1.1	100

Combats hitters with sinker/CT/SL trio that he keeps low in strike zone and can command with precision. Makes up for low velocity with movement and as promotion to Double-A showed, will need to be more sharper at upper levels. Could have upside as match-up reliever.

Pinto, Julio — RP — Toronto

Thrws R **Age** 23
2001 FA (Venezuela)

88-92	FB	+++	
85-86	CT	+++	
	CB	+++	
78-82	CU	++	

EXP MLB DEBUT: 2010 | POTENTIAL: #5 starter | **7E**

Year	Lev	Team	W	L	Sv	IP	K	ERA	WHIP	BF/G	OBA	H%	S%	xERA	Ctl	Dom	Cmd	hr/9	BPV
2007	A-	Lansing	3	4	1	83	85	4.21	1.19	5.2	238	26	76	4.10	2.4	9.2	3.9	0.5	88

Athletic/light-framed reliever with quick arm action that gives him excellent movement to FB. Likes to subtract with CT and CU, and will use CB to change eye level. Command and dominance are outstanding and may get an opportunity to move to starting rotation in 2008.

Plummer, Jarod — RP — Kansas City

Thrws R **Age** 24
2002 (26) HS (TX)

88-92	FB	+++	
74-77	CB	++	
80-82	SP	++++	

EXP MLB DEBUT: 2008 | POTENTIAL: Setup reliever | **7C**

Year	Lev	Team	W	L	Sv	IP	K	ERA	WHIP	BF/G	OBA	H%	S%	xERA	Ctl	Dom	Cmd	hr/9	BPV
2005	A+	Vero Beach	1	1	0	25	23	3.23	1.16	11.1	237	31	71	2.72	2.5	8.2	3.3	0.4	115
2006	A+	High Desert	11	5	10	95	114	3.97	1.18	9.8	255	34	69	3.63	1.9	10.8	5.7	1.0	157
2006	AA	Wichita	1	0	0	2	3	0.00	1.50	8.6	151	27	100	2.20	9.0	13.5	1.5	0.0	137
2007	AA	Wichita	5	6	11	79	90	3.08	1.03	6.9	226	28	79	3.29	1.8	10.3	5.6	1.5	145
2007	AAA	Omaha	0	0	0	3	1	15.00	2.33	7.7	371	29	40	13.15	6.0	3.0	0.5	6.0	-171

Tall/lanky reliever pitches aggressively with a whip-like delivery and SPL that allows him to miss bats. FB command is exceptional and has enough velocity to keep hitters honest, but is too much of a flyball pitcher. Could survive in setup role with two pitches, but is working on CB.

Pomeranz, Stuart — SP — St. Louis

Thrws R **Age** 23
2003 (2) HS (TN)

87-92	FB	+++	
75-77	KC	+++	
79-81	CU	++	

EXP MLB DEBUT: 2009 | POTENTIAL: #5 starter | **7E**

Year	Lev	Team	W	L	Sv	IP	K	ERA	WHIP	BF/G	OBA	H%	S%	xERA	Ctl	Dom	Cmd	hr/9	BPV
2005	A+	Palm Beach	2	5	0	48	29	3.37	1.37	25.2	292	34	74	3.90	1.9	5.4	2.9	0.2	84
2005	AA	Springfield	5	6	0	98	66	5.32	1.53	23.7	284	32	67	5.03	3.7	6.0	1.7	1.1	36
2006	AA	Springfield	7	4	0	98	64	4.40	1.40	23.0	279	31	72	4.71	2.8	5.9	2.1	1.2	43
2007	Rk	AZL Cardinals	0	0	0	4	4	6.43	1.19	5.6	252	28	50	4.69	2.1	8.6	4.0	2.1	76
2007	A+	Palm Beach	1	2	0	9	5	6.85	1.52	13.3	316	28	70	8.16	2.0	4.9	2.5	3.9	-44

Tall/strong-framed pitcher missed much of season with arthroscopic shoulder surgery in June. Keeps ball low with sinker, but can get strikeouts with KC, but doesn't have dominating stuff. Possesses stiff arm action and low arm slot doesn't allow him to stay tall.

Pope, Ryan — SP — New York (A)

Thrws R **Age** 22
2007 (3) Savannah A&D

88-93	FB	++++	
73-77	CB	+++	
80-81	CU	++	

EXP MLB DEBUT: 2010 | POTENTIAL: #5 starter | **7C**

Year	Lev	Team	W	L	Sv	IP	K	ERA	WHIP	BF/G	OBA	H%	S%	xERA	Ctl	Dom	Cmd	hr/9	BPV
2007	A-	Staten Island	3	0	0	43	46	2.51	1.18	17.3	252	34	80	3.03	2.1	9.6	4.6	0.4	146

Strong framed pitcher with good arm action, giving him movement to FB and CB, and the ability to maintain his velocity. Demonstrated plus command and was able to register strikeout. Will need to repeat arm speed on CU to take him to the next level.

Porcello, Rick — SP — Detroit

Thrws R **Age** 19
2007 (1) HS (NJ)

89-97	FB	++++	
78-81	SL	+++	
72-76	CB	++++	
83-85	CU	++	

EXP MLB DEBUT: 2010 | POTENTIAL: #1 starter | **9C**

Year	Lev	Team	W	L	Sv	IP	K	ERA	WHIP	BF/G	OBA	H%	S%	xERA	Ctl	Dom	Cmd	hr/9	BPV
2007																			

Top rated high school pitcher in 2007 Draft with projectable frame and explosive velocity. Sports smooth arm action and repeats ¾ delivery, but tends to throw across body. Commands plate and has three above average pitches, which will propel him through minors quickly.

Poreda, Aaron — SP — Chicago (A)

Thrws L **Age** 21
2007 (1) San Francisco

88-97	FB	++++	
75-76	SL	++	
	CU	++	

EXP MLB DEBUT: 2010 | POTENTIAL: #3 starter | **9D**

Year	Lev	Team	W	L	Sv	IP	K	ERA	WHIP	BF/G	OBA	H%	S%	xERA	Ctl	Dom	Cmd	hr/9	BPV
2007	Rk	Great Falls	4	0	0	46	48	1.17	0.85	14.1	182	25	87	1.12	2.0	9.4	4.8	0.2	170

Hard-throwing pitcher with arm action allowing him to get both strikeouts and groundball outs. Predominantly a FB pitcher, but low ¾ delivery makes his SL tough on RH batters. Command was strong in debut, but his comps lag and needs experience in setting-up pitches.

Poveda, Omar — SP — Texas

Thrws R **Age** 20
2004 FA (Venezuela)

87-92	FB	+++	
70-75	CB	+++	
75-80	CU	+++	

EXP MLB DEBUT: 2009 | POTENTIAL: #3 starter | **8D**

Year	Lev	Team	W	L	Sv	IP	K	ERA	WHIP	BF/G	OBA	H%	S%	xERA	Ctl	Dom	Cmd	hr/9	BPV
2005	Rk	AZL Rangers	2	6	0	52	56	5.71	1.46	15.9	304	41	57	4.25	2.1	9.7	4.7	0.2	145
2006	A-	Clinton	4	13	0	149	133	4.83	1.36	24.0	283	35	64	4.22	2.2	8.0	3.6	0.7	100
2006	AA	Frisco	0	1	0	5	1	1.80	1.80	23.1	221	23	89	3.87	9.0	1.8	0.2	0.0	26
2007	A-	Clinton	11	4	0	125	120	2.80	1.01	22.8	210	26	75	2.35	2.3	8.6	3.8	0.7	122
2007	A+	Bakersfield	1	2	0	28	33	5.14	1.43	23.8	255	33	67	4.49	4.2	10.6	2.5	1.3	82

Tall/strong-framed pitcher with solid repertoire. FB lacks movement, but thrived when he used all pitches and kept hitters off-balance. Fluid arm action allows him to repeat delivery. Needs to show better command within strike zone and incorporate legs into delivery.

Price, David — SP — Tampa Bay

Thrws L **Age** 22
2007 (1) Vanderbilt

89-95	FB	++++	
84-87	SL	++++	
77-79	SU	+++	
83-86	CU	+++	

EXP MLB DEBUT: 2008 | POTENTIAL: #1 starter | **9B**

Year	Lev	Team	W	L	Sv	IP	K	ERA	WHIP	BF/G	OBA	H%	S%	xERA	Ctl	Dom	Cmd	hr/9	BPV
2007																			

Tall/lanky pitcher with above average repertoire and the ability to use it. Sports excellent arm action and despite not repeating ¾ slot consistently, demonstrates command and ability to mask pitches. FB and two versions of SL are plus pitches and should dominate.

Pucetas, Kevin — SP — San Francisco

Thrws R **Age** 23
2006 (17) Limestone

85-89	FB	++	
	SL	+++	
	CB	++	
76-79	CU	+++	

EXP MLB DEBUT: 2010 | POTENTIAL: #5 starter | **7D**

Year	Lev	Team	W	L	Sv	IP	K	ERA	WHIP	BF/G	OBA	H%	S%	xERA	Ctl	Dom	Cmd	hr/9	BPV
2006	A-	Salem-Keizer	7	1	0	72	61	2.75	1.14	19.0	231	29	77	2.74	2.6	7.6	2.9	0.5	101
2007	A-	Augusta	15	4	1	145	104	1.86	1.00	20.5	233	28	83	2.36	1.3	6.5	5.0	0.4	138

Minor league leader in ERA showing plus command and being extremely difficult to hit. Lacks velocity and strikeout rate, but is confident in pitching to contact, works quickly, and rarely puts ball in the middle. Tall/projectable frame and smooth arm action could bump-up velocity.

Purcey,David — SP — Toronto

EXP MLB DEBUT: 2008 | POTENTIAL: #4 starter | 8D

Thrws L Age 26	Year	Lev	Team	W	L	Sv	IP	K	ERA	WHIP	BF/G	OBA	H%	S%	xERA	Ctl	Dom	Cmd	hr/9	BPV
2004 (1) Oklahoma	2005	A+	Dunedin	5	4	0	94	116	3.63	1.45	19.1	232	33	77	3.74	5.4	11.1	2.1	0.8	96
89-93 FB ++++	2005	AA	New Hamp.	4	3	0	43	45	2.93	1.33	22.3	209	28	78	2.85	5.2	9.4	1.8	0.4	95
76-79 CB +++	2006	AA	New Hamp.	4	5	0	88	81	5.62	1.65	24.6	289	35	66	5.20	4.5	8.3	1.8	0.9	58
79-83 CU ++	2006	AAA	Syracuse	2	7	0	51	45	5.45	1.70	17.8	253	30	70	5.13	6.7	7.9	1.2	1.2	40
	2007	AA	New Hamp.	3	5	0	62	55	5.37	1.34	23.4	277	34	58	3.94	2.3	8.0	3.4	0.6	102

Missed most of season to an elbow strain and upon return, his velocity wasn't there. Command is solid and will miss bats, but tends to pitch up and hung too many CB's. Hides the ball well with high ¾ delivery, but doesn't repeat arm speed on CU, which limits his options.

Putkonen,Luke — SP — Detroit

EXP MLB DEBUT: 2009 | POTENTIAL: #4 starter/setup reliever | 7E

Thrws R Age 22	Year	Lev	Team	W	L	Sv	IP	K	ERA	WHIP	BF/G	OBA	H%	S%	xERA	Ctl	Dom	Cmd	hr/9	BPV
2007 (3) North Carolina																				
86-93 FB ++++																				
73-78 CB ++																				
80-84 CU +++																				
	2007	Rk	GCL Tigers	0	1	0	8	9	4.39	0.98	10.4	257	36	50	2.18	0.0	9.9		0.0	63

Tall/projectable pitcher with quick arm action from a high ¾ slot. Displays good command and strikeout ability, though he doesn't have much FB movement and CB is inconsistent. Throws across body which hinders stamina (elbow surgery 2005) and needs to be more aggressive.

Rainville,Jay — SP — Minnesota

EXP MLB DEBUT: 2009 | POTENTIAL: #4 starter | 7D

Thrws R Age 22	Year	Lev	Team	W	L	Sv	IP	K	ERA	WHIP	BF/G	OBA	H%	S%	xERA	Ctl	Dom	Cmd	hr/9	BPV
2004 (1-S) HS (RI)																				
87-92 FB +++	2004	Rk	GCL Twins	3	2	0	34	38	1.85	1.23	17.3	289	40	85	3.52	0.8	10.0	12.7	0.3	316
78-80 CB +++	2005	A-	Beloit	8	2	0	88	77	3.78	1.25	22.4	250	29	76	4.14	2.8	7.9	2.9	1.4	69
79-81 CU ++	2005	A+	Fort Myers	4	3	0	54	35	2.67	1.11	23.6	262	29	83	3.72	1.0	5.8	5.8	1.2	125
	2007	A+	Fort Myers	9	11	0	142	110	3.29	1.24	21.4	266	32	74	3.53	2.0	7.0	3.5	0.6	101

Strong-framed pitcher rebounded nicely from shoulder surgery tossing a career-high in IP. Possesses average velocity, but lacks movement so relies on command and groundball outs, instead of strikeouts. Needs to repeat arm speed on CU and pitch with less effort.

Ramirez,Edwar — RP — New York (A)

EXP MLB DEBUT: 2007 | POTENTIAL: Setup reliever | 7B

Thrws R Age 27	Year	Lev	Team	W	L	Sv	IP	K	ERA	WHIP	BF/G	OBA	H%	S%	xERA	Ctl	Dom	Cmd	hr/9	BPV
2001 FA (DR)	2005	AAA	Salt Lake	0	0	0	2	2	0.00	0.00	5.6	0	0		0.00	0.0	9.0		0.0	109
86-92 FB +++	2006	A+	Tampa	4	1	3	30	47	1.19	0.66	5.5	141	27	80	0.00	1.8	14.0	7.8	0.0	275
79-83 SL +	2007	AA	Trenton	3	0	1	16	33	0.56	0.86	6.6	116	28	100	0.73	4.4	18.3	4.1	0.6	212
79-82 CU +++++	2007	AAA	Scranton/WB	1	0	6	40	69	0.90	0.85	5.9	151	31	88	0.54	3.2	15.5	4.9	0.0	222
	2007	MLB	New York (A)	1	1	1	21	31	8.14	1.81	4.6	288	39	59	7.11	6.0	13.3	2.2	2.6	46

Featuring one of the minors' deadliest CU's, he put up obscene strikeout numbers in the high minors, and coupled with outstanding command, was virtually untouchable. Repeats his ¾ delivery, which helps make-up for fringe-average velocity. Didn't trust stuff upon promotion.

Ramirez,Juan — SP — Seattle

EXP MLB DEBUT: 2010 | POTENTIAL: #3 starter | 9E

Thrws R Age 19	Year	Lev	Team	W	L	Sv	IP	K	ERA	WHIP	BF/G	OBA	H%	S%	xERA	Ctl	Dom	Cmd	hr/9	BPV
2005 FA (Nicaragua)																				
90-95 FB ++++																				
73-75 CB ++																				
79-82 CU +++																				
	2007	A-	Everett	3	7	0	75	73	4.31	1.38	21.1	224	29	67	3.13	5.2	8.7	1.7	0.4	88

Projectable pitcher with quick arm action giving him plus FB movement, ability to change speeds, and strikeout capability. Command is inconsistent, pitches up in zone, and doesn't spin ball well, but those should be corrected once he repeats his ¾ slot and slows-down arm speed.

Ramirez,Neil — SP — Texas

EXP MLB DEBUT: 2012 | POTENTIAL: #3 starter | 8E

Thrws R Age 19	Year	Lev	Team	W	L	Sv	IP	K	ERA	WHIP	BF/G	OBA	H%	S%	xERA	Ctl	Dom	Cmd	hr/9	BPV
2007 (1-S) HS (VA)																				
88-94 FB ++++																				
74-78 CB +++																				
79-81 CU ++																				
	2007																			

Tall/projectable pitcher with excellent arm strength and fluid arm action. Establishes lively FB and will go to CB to get strikeouts. Throws strikes, but doesn't repeat high ¾ delivery which alters command within strike zone and gives him a below average CU.

Ramos,Cesar — SP — San Diego

EXP MLB DEBUT: 2008 | POTENTIAL: #5 starter | 7C

Thrws L Age 24	Year	Lev	Team	W	L	Sv	IP	K	ERA	WHIP	BF/G	OBA	H%	S%	xERA	Ctl	Dom	Cmd	hr/9	BPV
2005 (1-S) Long Beach St																				
85-89 FB ++	2005	A-	Fort Wayne	3	2	0	38	32	4.24	1.28	22.4	281	36	63	3.31	1.6	7.5	4.6	0.0	140
83-84 CT +++	2005	A-	Eugene	0	1	0	20	13	6.68	1.68	15.2	322	35	61	6.22	3.1	5.8	1.9	1.3	24
68-70 CB +++	2006	A+	Lake Elsinore	7	8	0	141	70	3.64	1.45	23.1	287	32	75	4.38	2.8	4.5	1.6	0.6	41
80-82 CU ++++	2007	AA	San Antonio	13	9	0	163	90	3.42	1.20	24.3	250	27	74	3.47	2.4	5.0	2.1	0.8	54

Athletic pitcher prefers to work backward using CU and SL to make his low velocity FB appear quicker. Repeats arm speed and hides ball which masks pitches and provides good command. Doesn't miss many bats, so will have to out-think hitters and be efficient to succeed.

Ray,Jason — SP — Oakland

EXP MLB DEBUT: 2009 | POTENTIAL: #4 starter/setup reliever | 7D

Thrws R Age 23	Year	Lev	Team	W	L	Sv	IP	K	ERA	WHIP	BF/G	OBA	H%	S%	xERA	Ctl	Dom	Cmd	hr/9	BPV
2005 (8) Azusa Pacific																				
87-93 FB +++	2005	A-	Vancouver	0	1	0	29	56	2.16	1.37	6.1	171	38	85	2.34	7.1	17.3	2.4	0.3	166
70-72 CB +++	2006	A-	Kane County	6	1	0	65	68	3.04	1.27	20.5	207	29	74	2.43	4.8	9.4	1.9	0.1	107
75-79 CU +	2006	A+	Stockton	5	6	0	62	49	4.78	1.51	14.2	258	29	72	4.81	4.8	7.1	1.5	1.3	38
	2007	A+	Stockton	1	1	0	10	14	2.65	1.37	5.3	148	25	79	1.87	7.9	12.4	1.6	0.0	132

Missed most of 2007 with elbow soreness. Possesses overpowering FB that allows him to miss bats, but lacks consistent break to CB and command is spotty. Move to relief decreases need for CU, but stamina could be a factor with his short stature and recoil to delivery.

Reckling,Trevor — SP — Los Angeles (A)

EXP MLB DEBUT: 2012 | POTENTIAL: #3 starter | 8E

Thrws L Age 19	Year	Lev	Team	W	L	Sv	IP	K	ERA	WHIP	BF/G	OBA	H%	S%	xERA	Ctl	Dom	Cmd	hr/9	BPV
2007 (8) HS (NJ)																				
84-87 FB +++																				
70-73 CB ++++																				
77-80 CU ++																				
	2007	Rk	AZL Angels	3	1	2	36	55	2.75	1.11	15.7	245	40	76	2.80	1.8	13.8	7.9	0.5	238

Highly projectable pitcher with a plus 12-6 CB and deceptive high ¾ delivery. Base skills were incredible and though he doesn't have great velocity, he gets good movement based on his quick arm action. Will need to improve CU and hold velocity deeper in games.

Redmond,Todd — SP — Pittsburgh

EXP MLB DEBUT: 2008 | POTENTIAL: #3 starter | 7C

Thrws R Age 23	Year	Lev	Team	W	L	Sv	IP	K	ERA	WHIP	BF/G	OBA	H%	S%	xERA	Ctl	Dom	Cmd	hr/9	BPV
2004 (39) St Pete JC																				
88-93 FB ++++	2005	A-	Williamsport	1	2	0	72	63	1.99	1.15	19.1	233	30	83	2.56	2.6	7.9	3.0	0.2	111
CB +++	2006	A-	Hickory	13	6	0	160	148	2.81	1.06	23.0	233	29	76	2.78	1.9	8.3	4.5	0.7	131
CU +++	2007	A+	Lynchburg	7	12	0	142	95	4.56	1.29	23.4	274	31	65	4.01	2.0	6.0	3.0	0.8	74
	2007	AA	Altoona	1	1	0	17	12	3.16	1.05	22.1	237	26	75	3.14	1.6	6.3	4.0	1.1	98

Draft-and-follow offers hitters a three-pitch mix with plus command. Makes in-game adjustments to hitters, but needs better command within strike zone and prevent elevation of pitches. Despite velocity, he pitches to contact and lacks strikeout ability due to a below average CB.

Reed,Evan — SP — Texas

EXP MLB DEBUT: 2009 | POTENTIAL: #3 starter/setup reliever | 8E

Thrws R Age 22	Year	Lev	Team	W	L	Sv	IP	K	ERA	WHIP	BF/G	OBA	H%	S%	xERA	Ctl	Dom	Cmd	hr/9	BPV
2007 (3) Cal Poly																				
89-95 FB ++++																				
82-85 SL +++																				
80-83 CU +	2007	A-	Spokane	0	0	1	17	23	2.09	1.05	9.5	157	26	78	1.14	4.7	12.0	2.6	0.0	150
	2007	A-	Clinton	1	1	0	20	11	1.80	0.80	18.1	138	17	75	0.39	3.2	5.0	1.6	0.0	90

Tall/strong-framed pitcher who pitches aggressively with electric FB and hard SL. Lacks deception and doesn't repeat arm speed which affects both command and quality of CU. Keeps ball low and has the velocity in his back pocket to overpower hitters when he needs to.

Register,Steven — RP — New York (N)

EXP MLB DEBUT: 2008 | POTENTIAL: Setup reliever | 6C

Thrws R Age 25
2004 (3) Auburn
87-92 FB + + +
79-83 SL + + +
SP + + +
78-82 CU + +

Year	Lev	Team	W	L	Sv	IP	K	ERA	WHIP	BF/G	OBA	H%	S%	xERA	Ctl	Dom	Cmd	hr/9	BPV
2004	Rk	Tri-City	6	7	0	79	63	3.64	1.11	20.7	234	28	67	2.78	2.3	7.2	3.2	0.6	100
2005	A+	Modesto	9	11	0	156	108	4.44	1.40	24.4	295	34	70	4.70	2.0	6.2	3.1	0.9	71
2006	AA	Tulsa	4	10	0	155	77	5.57	1.56	25.2	302	31	67	5.72	3.1	4.5	1.5	1.5	8
2007	AA	Tulsa	1	3	37	58	48	4.03	1.36	4.0	278	34	70	3.91	2.5	7.4	3.0	0.5	93

Wiry/athletic pitcher was unsuccessful as starter, due to inconsistent mechanics and a straight FB, so was moved to relief. Provides deception with high ¾ delivery and keeps ball down effectively with solid command. SL and SPL are solid comps, giving him something for all hitters.

Reineke,Chad — RP — Houston

EXP MLB DEBUT: 2008 | POTENTIAL: Setup reliever á | 7C

Thrws R Age 26
2004 (13) Miami-OH
87-93 FB + + + +
82-85 SL + + +
75-80 CU + +

Year	Lev	Team	W	L	Sv	IP	K	ERA	WHIP	BF/G	OBA	H%	S%	xERA	Ctl	Dom	Cmd	hr/9	BPV
2004	A-	Tri City	1	2	3	36	52	2.49	1.38	6.6	209	35	80	2.56	5.7	12.9	2.3	0.0	138
2005	A-	Lexington	10	8	4	102	108	3.53	1.30	10.0	226	31	73	3.02	4.3	9.5	2.2	0.4	100
2006	A+	Salem	6	5	0	99	87	2.99	1.12	23.0	227	29	74	2.59	2.6	7.9	3.0	0.5	106
2006	AA	Corpus Christi	1	3	0	44	45	3.06	1.34	12.2	210	27	79	3.07	5.3	9.2	1.7	0.6	86
2007	AAA	Round Rock	5	5	0	100	95	4.68	1.51	13.5	260	33	69	4.17	4.7	8.6	1.8	0.6	74

Tall/projectable pitcher who pitches aggressively with FB and SL and gives hitters an excellent downward plane. Delivery lacks fluidness and struggles to repeat ¾ slot which negatively affects command and CU. Can be very tough on RH batters and may fare better in relief.

Reyes,Angel — SP — New York (A)

EXP MLB DEBUT: 2011 | POTENTIAL: #4 starter | 8E

Thrws L Age 20
2005 FA (DR)
87-93 FB + + + +
75-77 CB + + + +
79-81 CU +

Year	Lev	Team	W	L	Sv	IP	K	ERA	WHIP	BF/G	OBA	H%	S%	xERA	Ctl	Dom	Cmd	hr/9	BPV
2006	A-	Staten Island	1	1	0	17	16	1.57	1.05	22.2	198	27	83	1.64	3.1	8.4	2.7	0.0	122
2006	Rk	GCL Yankees	3	2	3	46	45	1.36	0.84	15.4	161	22	84	0.89	2.7	8.8	3.2	0.2	137
2007	A-	Charleston	0	2	0	31	33	4.65	1.48	19.1	222	29	70	3.83	6.1	9.6	1.6	0.9	75
2007	A-	Staten Island	0	0	0	4	3	15.37	5.37	11.2	464	54	68	17.16	26.3	6.6	0.3	0.0	7
2007	Rk	GCL Yankees	0	0	0	10	13	3.53	1.96	8.1	238	36	80	4.40	9.7	11.5	1.2	0.0	101

Small/athletic pitcher with quick arm action that provides easy velocity and pitch movement. Strikeouts are easy to come by, using primarily his FB and CB, and keeps ball down. Command was inconsistent, but was battling nagging arm injuries and was rarely comfortable.

Reynolds,Greg — SP — Colorado

EXP MLB DEBUT: 2009 | POTENTIAL: #3 starter | 8C

Thrws R Age 22
2006 (1) Stanford
88-94 FB + + + +
74-77 CB + + +
79-83 CU + +

Year	Lev	Team	W	L	Sv	IP	K	ERA	WHIP	BF/G	OBA	H%	S%	xERA	Ctl	Dom	Cmd	hr/9	BPV
2006	A+	Modesto	2	1	0	48	29	3.36	1.35	18.3	273	32	73	3.56	2.6	5.4	2.1	0.2	71
2007	AA	Tulsa	4	1	0	50	35	1.43	0.82	22.8	184	22	85	1.25	1.6	6.3	3.9	0.4	127

Tall/athletic pitcher with excellent stuff including a power sinker and two variations of CB. Repeats delivery with exceptional command and it tough to hit, but struggles to get strikeouts. Surgery corrected labrum fraying and should be ready for spring training.

Richardson,Dustin — SP — Boston

EXP MLB DEBUT: 2010 | POTENTIAL: #5 starter | 7C

Thrws L Age 24
2006 (5) Texas Tech
88-92 FB + + +
CB + + +
CU + +

Year	Lev	Team	W	L	Sv	IP	K	ERA	WHIP	BF/G	OBA	H%	S%	xERA	Ctl	Dom	Cmd	hr/9	BPV
2006	A-	Lowell	4	1	2	39	44	3.21	1.05	9.5	202	28	69	2.09	3.0	10.1	3.4	0.5	132
2007	A+	Lancaster	4	0	0	23	25	2.74	0.83	21.0	178	25	67	1.20	2.0	9.8	5.0	0.4	171
2007	AA	Greenville	5	7	0	99	98	3.36	1.34	19.7	235	31	74	3.16	4.3	8.9	2.1	0.4	94

Tall/athletic pitcher with aggressive approach and downward plane to pitches. Very tough to hit as he gets excellent movement to FB and CB, and command improved immensely upon promotion. Lack of a CU could force him to relief, but will continue as a starter for now.

Richmond,Jamie — SP — Atlanta

EXP MLB DEBUT: 2010 | POTENTIAL: #4 starter | 7D

Thrws R Age 22
2004 (31) Cawthraw SS
88-91 FB + + +
CB + + +
CU + +

Year	Lev	Team	W	L	Sv	IP	K	ERA	WHIP	BF/G	OBA	H%	S%	xERA	Ctl	Dom	Cmd	hr/9	BPV
2005	Rk	GCL Braves	2	0	0	11	12	3.21	0.80	5.1	181	26	56	0.82	1.6	9.6	6.0	0.0	203
2006	Rk	Danville	7	1	0	67	52	1.21	0.82	17.4	213	27	84	1.25	0.5	7.0	13.0	0.0	327
2007	A-	Rome	7	6	0	138	98	3.06	1.20	22.2	266	31	76	3.45	1.6	6.4	3.9	0.6	105

Draft-and-follow with exquisite command and ability to induce groundball outs. What he lacks in velocity and strikeout rate, he makes-up with movement, emanating from his fluid arm action. Will need to repeat arm speed on CU, which will prevent him from tipping it.

Robertson,Connor — RP — Arizona

EXP MLB DEBUT: 2007 | POTENTIAL: Setup reliever | 6C

Thrws R Age 26
2004 (31) Birmingham So
85-90 FB + + +
78-83 SL + + +
80-82 CU + +

Year	Lev	Team	W	L	Sv	IP	K	ERA	WHIP	BF/G	OBA	H%	S%	xERA	Ctl	Dom	Cmd	hr/9	BPV
2005	A+	Stockton	5	2	1	42	68	2.78	1.43	5.6	238	42	80	3.21	4.9	14.5	3.0	0.2	150
2006	AA	Midland	6	2	7	84	98	2.78	1.13	6.0	235	34	73	2.37	2.4	10.5	4.5	0.1	161
2007	AAA	Sacramento	4	1	2	39	40	4.37	1.64	5.6	281	36	74	4.83	4.8	9.2	1.9	0.7	73
2007	MLB	Oakland	0	0	0	2	2	18.00	4.00	4.5	515	62	50	15.19	9.0	9.0	1.0	0.0	27
2007	Rk	AZL Athletics	1	0	0	1	2	0.00	0.00	2.8	0	0	100	0.00	0.0	18.0		0.0	163

Quick arm action generates downward movement to sinker/SL combination, making him effective to RH batters. Strikeout rate remained strong, but tends to tip pitches by altering high ¾ slot which makes him hittable and makes command inconsistent.

Robertson,Tyler — RP — Minnesota

EXP MLB DEBUT: 2010 | POTENTIAL: #3 starter | 8C

Thrws L Age 20
2006 (3) HS (CA)
86-92 FB + + +
CB + + +
CU + +

Year	Lev	Team	W	L	Sv	IP	K	ERA	WHIP	BF/G	OBA	H%	S%	xERA	Ctl	Dom	Cmd	hr/9	BPV
2006	Rk	GCL Twins	4	2	0	48	54	4.29	1.43	18.6	284	39	69	4.06	2.8	10.1	3.6	0.4	123
2007	A-	Beloit	9	5	1	102	123	2.29	1.18	22.7	232	34	80	2.59	2.9	10.8	3.7	0.3	144

Tall/projectable pitcher who has a solid combination of velocity, command, and deception, faring well as a teenager in full-season baseball. FB and CB possess good movement, but stiff arm action makes throwing his CU difficult and could be cause for injury concern.

Rodgers,Chad — SP — Atlanta

EXP MLB DEBUT: 2011 | POTENTIAL: #5 starter | 7D

Thrws L Age 20
2006 (3) HS (OH)
86-91 FB + + +
CB + + +
CU + + +

Year	Lev	Team	W	L	Sv	IP	K	ERA	WHIP	BF/G	OBA	H%	S%	xERA	Ctl	Dom	Cmd	hr/9	BPV
2006	Rk	GCL Braves	3	2	1	39	30	2.54	1.13	14.0	220	27	77	2.33	3.0	6.9	2.3	0.2	94
2007	Rk	Danville	3	1	1	48	46	3.92	1.06	17.0	227	30	61	2.36	2.1	8.6	4.2	0.4	138

Tall/projectable pitcher shows an advanced feel for pitching by throwing three pitches for strikes and being able to setup hitters. Command is essential as none of his pitches project as true strikeout pitches. ATL has been cautious with workload and needs to be extended.

Rodriguez,Aneury — SP — Colorado

EXP MLB DEBUT: 2010 | POTENTIAL: #3 starter | 8D

Thrws R Age 20
2005 FA (DR)
87-92 FB + + +
76-79 CB + + +
80-83 CU + + +

Year	Lev	Team	W	L	Sv	IP	K	ERA	WHIP	BF/G	OBA	H%	S%	xERA	Ctl	Dom	Cmd	hr/9	BPV
2005	Rk	Casper	3	4	0	62	47	7.55	1.66	18.5	306	35	53	5.60	3.8	6.8	1.8	1.0	42
2006	A-	Tri-City	4	4	0	76	69	4.14	1.42	21.5	267	34	69	3.68	3.6	8.2	2.3	0.2	92
2007	A-	Asheville	9	9	0	152	160	5.15	1.51	23.5	298	38	68	5.18	2.8	9.5	3.3	1.1	88

Athletic/projectable pitcher led SAL in strikeouts, mixing his three-pitch arsenal with impressive command. Delivery lacks fluidity and lands stiffly on front leg, which elevates pitches and makes him hittable. ERA not as bad when taking home ballpark into context.

Rodriguez,Henry — SP — Oakland

EXP MLB DEBUT: 2010 | POTENTIAL: #2 starter | 9E

Thrws R Age 21
2005 FA (Venezuela)
89-95 FB + + + +
CB + +
CU +

Year	Lev	Team	W	L	Sv	IP	K	ERA	WHIP	BF/G	OBA	H%	S%	xERA	Ctl	Dom	Cmd	hr/9	BPV
2006	Rk	AZL Athletics	5	2	1	43	59	7.42	2.22	14.5	274	33	63	6.78	10.4	12.3	1.2	0.2	99
2007	A-	Kane County	6	8	0	99	106	3.07	1.34	20.6	211	32	74	2.99	5.3	9.6	1.8	0.2	188

Armed with organization's liveliest FB, he once hit 100 MPH, but has toned-down his delivery to derive more movement. Command waivers from outing to outing and doesn't have much trust in comps. Ability to miss bats is impressive and may just need experience and stamina.

Roemer,Wes — SP — Arizona

EXP MLB DEBUT: 2009 | POTENTIAL: #4 starter | 7B

Thrws R Age 21
2007 (1-S) Cal St Fullerton

Velocity	Pitch	Grade
85-92	FB	+++
79-84	SL	+++
79-82	CU	+++

Year	Lev	Team	W	L	Sv	IP	K	ERA	WHIP	BF/G	OBA	H%	S%	xERA	Ctl	Dom	Cmd	hr/9	BPV
2007	A-	Yakima	1	0	0	12	18	4.50	1.08	5.9	245	39	58	2.96	1.5	13.5	9.0	0.8	253

Advanced pitcher with plus command and penchant for pitching inside, he loves to get the strikeout, but relies on movement as opposed to velocity. Repeats delivery for all three pitches and is deceptive with low ¾ slot. Arm action is very quick, but does pitch with effort.

Roenicke,Josh — RP — Cincinnati

EXP MLB DEBUT: 2008 | POTENTIAL: Setup reliever | 7C

Thrws R Age 25
2006 (10) UCLA

Velocity	Pitch	Grade
88-94	FB	++++
82-86	SL	+++

Year	Lev	Team	W	L	Sv	IP	K	ERA	WHIP	BF/G	OBA	H%	S%	xERA	Ctl	Dom	Cmd	hr/9	BPV
2006	Rk	Billings	1	0	6	15	24	6.51	1.45	4.6	189	32	52	3.04	7.1	14.2	2.0	0.6	127
2006	Rk	GCL Reds	1	0	0	7	9	1.25	1.53	4.5	283	41	91	3.92	3.8	11.3	3.0	0.0	129
2007	A+	Sarasota	2	1	16	27	41	3.31	1.40	4.2	231	38	76	3.17	5.0	13.6	2.7	0.3	138
2007	AA	Chattanooga	1	1	8	19	15	0.95	0.95	3.8	183	24	89	1.22	2.8	7.1	2.5	0.0	114

Strong frame and arm strength allow him to generate and hold velocity, and hard SL is killer to RH batters. Pitches aggressively to both sides of plate and can hit spots with both pitches. Throws with effort from ¾ slot which limits usage patterns.

Roe,Chaz — SP — Colorado

EXP MLB DEBUT: 2010 | POTENTIAL: #3 starter | 8D

Thrws R Age 21
2005 (1-S) HS (KY)

Velocity	Pitch	Grade
86-93	FB	+++
75-80	CB	++++
	CU	++

Year	Lev	Team	W	L	Sv	IP	K	ERA	WHIP	BF/G	OBA	H%	S%	xERA	Ctl	Dom	Cmd	hr/9	BPV
2005	Rk	Casper	5	2	0	49	55	4.21	1.36	17.1	183	26	68	2.58	6.6	10.1	1.5	0.4	100
2006	A-	Asheville	7	4	0	99	80	4.35	1.53	22.7	273	34	70	4.17	4.3	7.3	1.7	0.4	69
2007	A+	Modesto	7	11	0	170	131	4.34	1.30	24.2	236	27	68	3.59	3.9	6.9	1.8	0.9	60

Tall/athletic pitcher with projectable velocity and downward plane to pitches. Possesses plus CB and enough velocity to keep hitters honest. Command and strikeout rate fell in the high-offense CAL. Arm action is quick, but stiff, making it difficult to change speeds.

Rogers,Mark — SP — Milwaukee

EXP MLB DEBUT: 2010 | POTENTIAL: #3 starter | 9E

Thrws R Age 22
2004 (1) HS (ME)

Velocity	Pitch	Grade
91-99	FB	+++++
83-89	SL	+++
73-76	CB	++
80-83	CU	++

Year	Lev	Team	W	L	Sv	IP	K	ERA	WHIP	BF/G	OBA	H%	S%	xERA	Ctl	Dom	Cmd	hr/9	BPV
2004	Rk	AZL Brewers	0	3	0	26	35	4.81	1.68	13.1	289	44	68	4.38	4.8	12.0	2.5	0.0	122
2005	A-	West Virginia	2	9	1	98	109	5.13	1.60	17.4	239	31	69	4.46	6.4	10.0	1.6	1.0	70
2006	Rk	AZL Brewers	0	0	0	4	5	2.25	1.75	6.1	307	44	86	4.85	4.5	11.3	2.5	0.0	114
2006	A+	Brevard Co	1	2	0	71	96	5.07	1.70	20.1	254	37	70	4.66	6.7	12.2	1.8	0.8	93
2007																			

Missed 2007 season with shoulder surgery in Dec, which explained velocity decrease. Possesses plus FB and easy velocity while gaining deception from drop-and-drive delivery. Will need to regain feel for all three comps and smooth-out mechanics upon return.

Rohrbaugh,Robert — SP — Seattle

EXP MLB DEBUT: 2009 | POTENTIAL: #5 starter | 6C

Thrws L Age 24
2005 (7) Clemson

Velocity	Pitch	Grade
85-90	FB	++
	SU	++
78-81	CU	++++

Year	Lev	Team	W	L	Sv	IP	K	ERA	WHIP	BF/G	OBA	H%	S%	xERA	Ctl	Dom	Cmd	hr/9	BPV
2005	Rk	Everett	5	2	0	68	71	3.84	1.26	19.8	262	34	72	3.85	2.4	9.4	3.9	0.9	114
2006	A+	Inland Emp	7	1	0	55	47	1.47	0.93	20.6	217	27	86	1.86	1.3	7.7	5.9	0.3	171
2006	AA	San Antonio	5	5	0	85	64	3.80	1.34	25.3	266	31	74	4.14	2.9	6.8	2.4	1.0	64
2007	AA	W Tennessee	7	5	0	85	62	3.28	1.24	23.0	259	31	74	3.40	2.2	6.6	3.0	0.5	89
2007	AAA	Tacoma	6	3	0	85	49	2.96	1.29	26.9	259	28	82	4.05	2.7	5.2	1.9	1.1	42

Tall/athletic pitcher with good downward plane that assists in keeping sinker down in the zone. Changes speeds well, features a deceptive high ¾ delivery, and is adept at pitching to contact, which he needs being that his strikeout rate and velocity are low.

Rohrbough,Cole — SP — Atlanta

EXP MLB DEBUT: 2011 | POTENTIAL: #2 starter | 9D

Thrws L Age 21
2006 (22) W Nevada CC

Velocity	Pitch	Grade
88-93	FB	+++
	KC	++++
	CU	+

Year	Lev	Team	W	L	Sv	IP	K	ERA	WHIP	BF/G	OBA	H%	S%	xERA	Ctl	Dom	Cmd	hr/9	BPV
2007	A-	Rome	2	0	0	28	38	1.29	0.89	17.3	141	23	88	0.89	3.9	12.2	3.2	0.3	157
2007	Rk	Danville	3	2	0	33	58	1.09	0.85	15.2	176	35	89	1.06	2.2	15.8	7.3	0.3	258

Draft-and-follow was lights-out at two stops, mesmerizing hitters with his FB and KC from a low ¾ slot. Commands plate extremely well and could pick-up more velocity as he matures. CU is still a work in progress and could get more CB tilt with a raised arm slot.

Rollins,Heath — SP — Tampa Bay

EXP MLB DEBUT: 2010 | POTENTIAL: #5 starter | 7D

Thrws R Age 23
2006 (13) Winthrop

Velocity	Pitch	Grade
87-91	FB	+++
85-86	CT	+++
76-79	SL	+++
	CU	++

Year	Lev	Team	W	L	Sv	IP	K	ERA	WHIP	BF/G	OBA	H%	S%	xERA	Ctl	Dom	Cmd	hr/9	BPV
2007	A-	Columbus	17	4	0	159	149	2.55	1.07	22.9	227	29	79	2.63	2.1	8.4	3.9	0.6	124

Athletic/low upside pitcher who led SAL in wins, utilizing plus command and mixing his four-pitch arsenal. Despite average velocity, he misses bats by repeating ¾ delivery and keeping ball down. This style of pitching works in the low minors, so needs to be challenged to find true ability.

Romero,Ricky — SP — Toronto

EXP MLB DEBUT: 2008 | POTENTIAL: #4 starter | 7B

Thrws L Age 23
2005 (1) Cal St Fullerton

Velocity	Pitch	Grade
87-92	FB	+++
79-84	CT	+++
72-76	CB	+++
78-82	CU	++

Year	Lev	Team	W	L	Sv	IP	K	ERA	WHIP	BF/G	OBA	H%	S%	xERA	Ctl	Dom	Cmd	hr/9	BPV
2005	A+	Dunedin	1	0	0	30	22	3.87	1.42	16.0	297	35	73	4.48	2.1	6.6	3.1	0.6	83
2006	A+	Dunedin	2	1	0	58	61	2.48	1.07	22.6	227	29	81	2.75	2.2	9.4	4.4	0.8	135
2006	AA	New Hamp.	2	6	0	67	41	5.10	1.36	23.4	256	28	63	4.05	3.5	5.5	1.6	0.9	42
2007	A+	Dunedin	0	0	0	4	2	4.29	1.19	16.8	252	29	60	2.72	2.1	4.3	2.0	0.0	72
2007	AA	New Hamp.	3	6	0	88	80	4.90	1.69	22.1	283	35	72	5.23	5.2	8.2	1.6	0.9	53

Athletic pitcher who relies on command and pitching to contact, but struggled to find strike zone and pitched behind too often. Pitches move well due to his whip-like arm action and changed speeds better, but lacks velocity and confidence in comps, which hinders strikeout rate.

Romo,Sergio — RP — San Francisco

EXP MLB DEBUT: 2009 | POTENTIAL: Setup reliever | 8D

Thrws R Age 25
2005 (28) Mesa St

Velocity	Pitch	Grade
86-90	FB	+++
	SL	+++
	CB	+++
	CU	++

Year	Lev	Team	W	L	Sv	IP	K	ERA	WHIP	BF/G	OBA	H%	S%	xERA	Ctl	Dom	Cmd	hr/9	BPV
2005	A-	Salem-Keizer	7	1	0	68	65	2.77	1.16	18.1	267	33	81	3.66	1.2	8.6	7.2	0.9	177
2006	A-	Augusta	10	2	4	103	95	2.53	0.94	12.5	212	26	77	2.27	1.7	8.3	5.0	0.8	144
2007	A+	San Jose	6	2	9	66	106	1.36	0.76	5.8	158	28	87	0.91	2.0	14.4	7.1	0.5	242

Short/strong-framed pitcher led minor league relievers in K/9. Arm action provides exceptional pitch movement and will alter ¾ slot purposely to add deception. CB is his big pitch and keeps ball down with sinker. Velocity projects upwards, but will need better CU to close.

Rondon,Hector — SP — Cleveland

EXP MLB DEBUT: 2011 | POTENTIAL: #4 starter | 8E

Thrws R Age 20
2006 FA (Venezuela)

Velocity	Pitch	Grade
87-93	FB	++++
71-73	CB	++
78-82	CU	+++

Year	Lev	Team	W	L	Sv	IP	K	ERA	WHIP	BF/G	OBA	H%	S%	xERA	Ctl	Dom	Cmd	hr/9	BPV
2006	Rk	GCL Indians	3	4	0	52	32	5.17	1.25	19.3	296	33	59	4.44	0.5	5.5	10.7	1.0	222
2007	A-	Lake County	7	10	0	136	113	4.37	1.25	20.5	272	32	66	3.91	1.8	7.5	4.2	0.9	108

Tall/projectable pitcher with lively FB and a deceptive high ¾ delivery. Not afraid to go to CU to get strikeouts and because he repeats his delivery, his command is fairly consistent. Rotation of CB is loopy and needs to be more fine within strike zone to lower oppBA.

Roquet,Rocky — RP — Chicago (N)

EXP MLB DEBUT: 2008 | POTENTIAL: Setup reliever/closer | 7C

Thrws R Age 25
2006 NDFA Cal Poly

Velocity	Pitch	Grade
91-97	FB	+++++
83-85	SL	+++
81-84	CU	+

Year	Lev	Team	W	L	Sv	IP	K	ERA	WHIP	BF/G	OBA	H%	S%	xERA	Ctl	Dom	Cmd	hr/9	BPV
2006	A-	Boise	0	0	3	19	31	5.63	1.35	4.2	279	46	56	3.84	2.3	14.5	6.2	0.5	202
2007	A-	Peoria	0	0	11	25	29	0.36	1.12	5.2	194	29	96	1.75	4.0	10.4	2.6	0.0	134
2007	A+	Daytona	1	0	0	6	9	1.50	1.00	7.6	228	39	83	1.83	1.5	13.5	9.0	0.0	279
2007	AA	Tennessee	4	0	7	39	42	3.67	1.28	5.7	224	29	74	3.38	4.1	9.6	2.3	0.9	89

Strong-armed reliever with plus velocity and a deadly SL that allows him to miss bats with ease. Throws strikes, but could used better command within strike zone and needs to perfect CU to give him something to offer LH batters. Stamina is always a concern with his delivery style.

Rosales,Leo — SP — Arizona

EXP MLB DEBUT: 2008 | POTENTIAL: Setup reliever | 7C

Thrws R Age 27	Year	Lev	Team	W	L	Sv	IP	K	ERA	WHIP	BF/G	OBA	H%	S%	xERA	Ctl	Dom	Cmd	hr/9	BPV
2003 (2) Cal St Northridge	2004	A-	Fort Wayne	6	1	26	57	66	1.42	0.93	4.0	191	26	90	1.82	2.4	10.4	4.4	0.6	153
89-92 FB +++	2005	A+	Lake Elsinore	8	7	27	65	77	3.18	1.18	4.3	224	31	75	2.92	3.3	10.7	3.2	0.7	121
77-82 SL ++	2006	A+	Lake Elsinore	1	0	0	6	7	0.00	0.49	4.0	55	9	100	0.00	3.0	10.3	3.5	0.0	179
73-77 CB ++	2006	AA	Mobile	5	6	0	61	54	3.09	1.13	4.6	228	28	76	3.03	2.6	7.9	3.0	0.9	94
76-80 CU ++++	2007	AAA	Portland	1	1	14	24	27	3.35	1.36	4.2	252	33	80	4.14	3.7	10.0	2.7	1.1	88

Strong-physical reliever missed half season with a broken hand. Impressive ability to change speeds with a repeatable overhand delivery that also provides deception. FB has late life, but struggles to spin baseball and command can be inconsistent.

Rosa,Carlos — SP — Kansas City

EXP MLB DEBUT: 2008 | POTENTIAL: #4 starter/setup reliever | 7C

Thrws R Age 23	Year	Lev	Team	W	L	Sv	IP	K	ERA	WHIP	BF/G	OBA	H%	S%	xERA	Ctl	Dom	Cmd	hr/9	BPV
2003 FA (DR)	2004	A-	Burlington	0	5	0	34	23	4.74	1.70	19.3	298	35	70	4.87	4.5	6.1	1.4	0.3	52
89-94 FB ++++	2006	A-	Burlington	8	6	0	138	102	2.54	1.27	23.5	237	29	80	3.05	3.5	6.6	1.9	0.4	75
80-83 SL ++	2006	A+	High Desert	0	1	0	11	13	7.30	2.16	18.4	390	51	65	8.12	3.2	10.5	3.3	0.8	84
82-84 CU +++	2007	A+	Wilmington	2	1	0	23	15	0.39	0.91	21.5	217	27	95	1.55	1.2	5.9	5.0	0.0	152
	2007	AA	Wichita	6	6	1	97	70	4.36	1.48	19.9	270	31	71	4.37	4.0	6.5	1.6	0.7	52

Thin/athletic pitcher possesses quick arm action which basis for solid pitch movement and easy velocity. Command and quality of CU improved, but the jump to Double-A decreased ability to get strikeouts. Will need to learn to pitch without best stuff and tighten break on SL.

Rowland-Smith,Ryan — SP — Seattle

EXP MLB DEBUT: 2007 | POTENTIAL: #5 starter | 7C

Thrws L Age 25	Year	Lev	Team	W	L	Sv	IP	K	ERA	WHIP	BF/G	OBA	H%	S%	xERA	Ctl	Dom	Cmd	hr/9	BPV
2001 FA (Australia)	2005	AA	San Antonio	6	7	0	122	102	4.35	1.51	16.0	279	32	77	4.94	3.8	7.5	2.0	0.5	85
86-92 FB ++	2006	A+	Inland Emp	0	1	0	6	9	5.68	1.64	3.9	317	33	74	5.91	3.0	13.3	4.5	1.4	92
78-82 SL ++++	2006	AA	San Antonio	1	3	4	41	48	2.83	1.36	7.5	247	31	73	3.05	3.9	10.5	2.7	0.4	128
70-74 CB ++	2007	AAA	Tacoma	3	4	1	41	50	3.67	1.38	6.9	232	34	78	4.12	4.8	10.9	2.3	0.4	120
78-82 CU ++	2007	MLB	Seattle	1	0	0	38	42	3.96	1.41	6.2	266	32	74	4.24	3.5	9.9	2.8	0.9	98

Projectable arm who may get consideration as a starter after two years of relieving. Not overpowering, but sports excellent command and movement, which allows him to miss bats. Will need to repeat arm speed on CU and build-up arm strength over off-season.

Runion,Samuel — SP — Kansas City

EXP MLB DEBUT: 2011 | POTENTIAL: #4 starter | 8E

Thrws R Age 19	Year	Lev	Team	W	L	Sv	IP	K	ERA	WHIP	BF/G	OBA	H%	S%	xERA	Ctl	Dom	Cmd	hr/9	BPV
2007 (2) HS (NC)																				
87-92 FB +++																				
79-82 SL ++																				
80-83 CU +++																				
	2007	Rk	AZL Royals	3	4	0	51	51	5.82	1.53	18.5	298	29	74	6.02	3.0	9.0	3.0	0.7	121

Strong-framed pitcher with fluid arm action, giving him FB movement and ability to repeat ¾ delivery. Can notch strikeouts and throws strikes, but could use better command within strike zone. SL is loose in its rotation and will need to adjust to a professional workload.

Russell,Adam — RP — Chicago (A)

EXP MLB DEBUT: 2008 | POTENTIAL: Setup reliever | 6B

Thrws R Age 25	Year	Lev	Team	W	L	Sv	IP	K	ERA	WHIP	BF/G	OBA	H%	S%	xERA	Ctl	Dom	Cmd	hr/9	BPV
2004 (6) Ohio	2004	A-	Kannapolis	0	2	0	10	3	9.00	2.50	26.6	390	37	68	10.82	6.3	2.7	0.4	2.7	-79
88-94 FB ++++	2005	A-	Kannapolis	9	7	0	126	82	3.78	1.36	21.9	246	28	73	3.70	3.9	5.9	1.5	0.7	51
76-78 SL ++	2006	A+	Win-Salem	7	3	0	97	62	2.69	1.27	23.3	233	27	80	3.08	3.7	5.8	1.6	0.5	62
70-75 CB +++	2006	AA	Birmingham	3	3	0	55	47	4.75	1.42	23.3	276	33	67	4.34	3.1	7.7	2.5	0.8	73
77-79 CU +	2007	AA	Birmingham	9	11	1	138	95	4.82	1.57	16.0	290	34	68	4.67	3.8	6.2	1.6	0.5	53

Moved back to bullpen after failed stint as starter, and should fare better. Lacks strikeout ability despite above average velocity as he doesn't get much pitch movement. Uses all five pitches, but struggles to disguise them due to his stiff arm action and unrepeatable delivery.

Rustich,Brant — RP — New York (N)

EXP MLB DEBUT: 2009 | POTENTIAL: Setup reliever | 8C

Thrws R Age 24	Year	Lev	Team	W	L	Sv	IP	K	ERA	WHIP	BF/G	OBA	H%	S%	xERA	Ctl	Dom	Cmd	hr/9	BPV
2007 (2-C) UCLA																				
88-94 FB ++++																				
84-87 SL ++++																				
SP ++	2007	A-	Brooklyn	2	0	2	12	11	2.21	0.41	3.9	104	8	67	0.44	0.7	8.1	11.0	1.5	270
CU ++	2007	Rk	Kingsport	1	0	0	10	10	0.89	0.69	7.1	174	25	86	0.46	0.9	8.9	10.0	0.0	284

Power reliever with above average FB and SL, but relies more on command and keeping ball out of the middle of the plate. Strong frame and natural arm strength provide him with durability. Has tendency to show baseball and grip on SPL may have caused recent finger injury.

Rzepczynski,Marc — SP — Toronto

EXP MLB DEBUT: 2010 | POTENTIAL: #4 starter | 7D

Thrws L Age 22	Year	Lev	Team	W	L	Sv	IP	K	ERA	WHIP	BF/G	OBA	H%	S%	xERA	Ctl	Dom	Cmd	hr/9	BPV
2007 (5) UC Riverside																				
87-92 FB +++																				
80-84 SL +++																				
78-81 CB +++																				
78-80 CU ++	2007	A-	Auburn	5	0	0	45	49	2.79	1.11	16.1	206	28	75	2.23	3.4	9.8	2.9	0.4	121

Finesse pitcher with four workable pitches, and was able to keep hitters at-bay by commanding strike zone and keeping hitters off-balance. Did not allow any long balls and achieved a solid balance of strikeouts and groundball outs. This style works at lower levels.

Sadler,Billy — RP — San Francisco

EXP MLB DEBUT: 2006 | POTENTIAL: Setup reliever/closer | 7C

Thrws R Age 26	Year	Lev	Team	W	L	Sv	IP	K	ERA	WHIP	BF/G	OBA	H%	S%	xERA	Ctl	Dom	Cmd	hr/9	BPV
2003 (6) LSU	2006	AA	Connecticut	4	3	20	44	66	2.65	1.13	4.1	150	26	76	1.46	5.7	13.4	2.4	0.2	149
87-93 FB ++++	2006	AAA	Fresno	2	0	1	10	12	1.80	0.70	5.0	151	20	83	1.06	1.8	10.8	6.0	0.9	189
78-81 SL ++	2006	MLB	San Fran	0	0	0	4	6	6.75	1.75	3.7	307	36	80	9.05	4.5	13.5	3.0	4.5	3
75-78 CB +++	2007	AA	Connecticut	0	0	1	12	18	0.74	0.74	4.8	81	11	100	0.33	4.5	13.4	3.0	0.7	160
	2007	AAA	Fresno	3	2	6	42	59	5.99	1.69	4.7	233	34	65	4.63	7.5	12.6	1.7	1.1	87

Small/athletic reliever with quick arm action and deceptive delivery. Pitches aggressively with FB and CB, posting one of the better strikeout rates in the minors. Struggles to repeat low ¾ arm slot and arm speed, making his command inconsistent and CU ineffective.

Salas,Marino — RP — Pittsburgh

EXP MLB DEBUT: 2007 | POTENTIAL: Setup reliever | 7C

Thrws R Age 27	Year	Lev	Team	W	L	Sv	IP	K	ERA	WHIP	BF/G	OBA	H%	S%	xERA	Ctl	Dom	Cmd	hr/9	BPV
1998 FA (DR)	2004	A-	Delmarva	2	4	13	50	46	2.16	1.36	5.2	265	33	89	4.11	3.1	8.3	2.7	0.9	81
90-95 FB ++++	2005	A+	Frederick	4	2	16	62	63	3.63	1.32	5.1	236	30	76	3.74	4.1	9.1	2.3	1.0	79
82-85 SL ++	2006	AA	Bowie	2	6	19	49	46	2.93	1.12	4.4	215	27	75	2.54	3.1	8.4	2.7	0.5	103
	2007	AA	Huntsville	0	0	17	38	29	1.42	1.03	4.0	189	23	89	1.94	3.3	6.9	2.1	0.5	88
	2007	AAA	Nashville	0	1	0	23	25	5.04	1.51	7.2	292	33	79	6.58	3.1	9.7	3.1	2.7	39

Resilient arm featuring arm strength and high-octane FB with late life. Overpowers hitters with FB and gets them to chase SL out of zone. Command is inconsistent, but can survive by being effectively wild. Tough on RH batters and being a match-up reliever may be his ceiling.

Samardzija,Jeff — SP — Chicago (N)

EXP MLB DEBUT: 2009 | POTENTIAL: #2 starter | 9D

Thrws R Age 23	Year	Lev	Team	W	L	Sv	IP	K	ERA	WHIP	BF/G	OBA	H%	S%	xERA	Ctl	Dom	Cmd	hr/9	BPV
2006 (5) Notre Dame																				
88-95 FB +++++	2006	A-	Peoria	0	1	0	11	4	3.27	1.09	21.5	162	16	73	2.16	4.9	3.3	0.7	0.8	32
78-82 SL ++	2006	A-	Boise	1	1	0	19	13	2.37	1.26	15.5	251	30	83	3.31	2.8	6.2	2.2	0.5	73
77-81 CU +	2007	A+	Daytona	3	8	0	107	45	4.96	1.65	20.0	320	34	70	5.51	2.9	3.8	1.3	0.7	21
	2007	AA	Tennessee	3	3	0	34	20	3.43	1.23	23.0	255	25	85	4.84	2.4	5.3	2.2	2.1	19

Tall/athletic pitcher with incredible velocity and sink to FB but doesn't miss many bats or have a good feel for pitching. Pitched better with promotion to Double-A, including better command. Repeating ¾ slot has been a problem and prevents comps from being consistent.

Sanchez,Humberto — SP — New York (A)

EXP MLB DEBUT: 2009 | POTENTIAL: #4 starter/setup reliever | 8C

Thrws R Age 25	Year	Lev	Team	W	L	Sv	IP	K	ERA	WHIP	BF/G	OBA	H%	S%	xERA	Ctl	Dom	Cmd	hr/9	BPV
2001 (31) Connors St JC	2004	A+	Lakeland	7	11	0	105	115	5.22	1.47	23.7	258	34	64	4.15	4.4	9.8	2.3	0.8	87
88-93 FB ++++	2005	AA	Erie	3	5	0	64	65	5.61	1.54	18.7	285	35	66	5.32	3.8	9.1	2.4	1.4	61
80-83 SL +++	2006	AA	Erie	5	3	0	71	86	1.77	1.04	25.0	190	28	83	1.73	3.4	10.9	3.2	0.3	142
78-82 CB +++	2006	AAA	Toledo	5	3	0	51	43	3.87	1.37	23.8	258	32	71	3.54	3.5	7.6	2.2	0.4	84
82-84 CU ++	2007																			

Underwent TJS prior to season and is expected to be ready by June. Features good velocity and two solid breaking pitches and his high ¾ slot provides downward plane. Strong frame hasn't translated into stamina as he recoils at finish of delivery. May shift to relief.

Sarfate,Dennis — SP — Baltimore

EXP MLB DEBUT: 2006 | POTENTIAL: Setup reliever/closer | 7C

Thrws R Age 27
2001 (9) Chandler-Gilbert JC
- 90-96 FB ++++
- 82-85 SL +++

Year	Lev	Team	W	L	Sv	IP	K	ERA	WHIP	BF/G	OBA	H%	S%	xERA	Ctl	Dom	Cmd	hr/9	BPV
2005	AA	Huntsville	9	9	0	130	110	3.88	1.38	22.7	247	29	74	3.92	4.1	7.6	1.9	0.9	64
2006	AAA	Nashville	10	7	0	125	117	3.67	1.62	16.3	262	33	78	4.37	5.6	8.4	1.5	0.5	70
2006	MLB	Milwaukee	0	0	0	8	11	4.44	1.60	4.5	283	43	69	4.10	4.4	12.2	2.8	0.0	130
2007	AAA	Nashville	2	7	4	61	68	4.56	1.76	6.2	261	34	75	5.05	6.9	10.0	1.4	0.9	67
2007	MLB	Houston	1	0	0	8	14	1.11	0.74	4.1	180	36	83	0.58	1.1	15.6	14.0	0.0	406

Strong-framed reliever with explosive FB and biting SL that allows him to miss bats. Arm action is relatively smooth, but tends to overthrow, which lessens movement. Achieving consistent command and efficiency has always been his biggest hurdle during career.

Savery,Joe — SP — Philadelphia

EXP MLB DEBUT: 2009 | POTENTIAL: #3 starter | 8C

Thrws L Age 22
2007 (1) Rice
- 86-92 FB +++
- 78-82 CB +++
- 74-77 CU +++

Year	Lev	Team	W	L	Sv	IP	K	ERA	WHIP	BF/G	OBA	H%	S%	xERA	Ctl	Dom	Cmd	hr/9	BPV
2007	A-	Williamsport	2	3	0	26	22	2.76	1.34	15.5	230	30	77	2.77	4.5	7.6	1.7	0.0	90

Athletic pitcher who relies on command, utilizing all pitches, and out-thinking hitters. Possesses average velocity, but pitches feed off each other and disguises them by repeating high ¾ delivery. Strikeout rate may never be high, but induces groundballs and is tough to hit.

Scherzer,Max — RP — Arizona

EXP MLB DEBUT: 2008 | POTENTIAL: #3 starter/setup reliever | 9C

Thrws R Age 23
2006 (1) Missouri
- 88-95 FB ++++
- 79-84 SL ++++
- 81-84 CU ++

Year	Lev	Team	W	L	Sv	IP	K	ERA	WHIP	BF/G	OBA	H%	S%	xERA	Ctl	Dom	Cmd	hr/9	BPV
2007	A+	Visalia	2	0	0	17	30	0.53	0.41	18.3	94	22	86	0.00	1.1	15.9	15.0	0.0	446
2007	AA	Mobile	4	4	0	73	76	3.93	1.42	22.2	237	32	71	3.38	4.9	9.3	1.9	0.4	93

Blessed with arm strength and quick arm action, he generates plus velocity to FB and movement to SL. Deceptive with low ¾ slot and loves to challenge hitters inside. Struggles to change speeds and hasn't shown much stamina which may prompt move to relief.

Schmidt,Josh — RP — New York (A)

EXP MLB DEBUT: 2008 | POTENTIAL: Setup reliever | 7C

Thrws R Age 25
2005 (15) Pacific
- 87-92 FB +++
- 81-84 SL +++
- CU +++

Year	Lev	Team	W	L	Sv	IP	K	ERA	WHIP	BF/G	OBA	H%	S%	xERA	Ctl	Dom	Cmd	hr/9	BPV
2005	A-	Staten Island	5	1	13	33	47	0.27	0.67	4.4	131	23	95	0.00	2.2	12.8	5.9	0.0	229
2006	A+	Tampa	4	4	1	68	66	4.37	1.28	7.1	226	29	65	3.05	4.1	8.7	2.1	0.5	91
2007	A+	Tampa	6	1	3	67	92	2.81	1.22	7.0	222	34	77	2.69	3.8	12.3	3.3	0.4	142

Athletic reliever with a power sinker that generates groundball outs and a SL that he puts-away RH batters with. Strikeout rate is exceptional and improved walk rate. Tends to throw across body which causes stamina issues and doesn't really have a way to combat LH batters.

Schmidt,Nick — SP — San Diego

EXP MLB DEBUT: 2010 | POTENTIAL: #3 starter | 8D

Thrws L Age 22
2007 (1) Arkansas
- 87-91 FB +++
- 77-80 CB +++
- 79-81 CU ++++

Year	Lev	Team	W	L	Sv	IP	K	ERA	WHIP	BF/G	OBA	H%	S%	xERA	Ctl	Dom	Cmd	hr/9	BPV
2007	A-	Fort Wayne	0	1	0	7	6	6.43	2.00	11.2	288	37	64	5.23	7.7	7.7	1.0	0.0	65

Projectable pitcher who relies on command, movement, and ability to change speeds. Repeats delivery well giving him a plus CU and keeps ball low with sinking FB. Will need to be more efficient with pitches. Elbow discomfort encountered in Aug, resulted in TJS.

Schultz,Mike — RP — Arizona

EXP MLB DEBUT: 2006 | POTENTIAL: Setup reliever | 5B

Thrws R Age 28
2000 (2) Loyola Marymount
- 87-92 FB +++
- 78-81 CB +++
- 78-80 CU +++

Year	Lev	Team	W	L	Sv	IP	K	ERA	WHIP	BF/G	OBA	H%	S%	xERA	Ctl	Dom	Cmd	hr/9	BPV
2005	AA	Tennessee	4	6	6	65	68	3.59	1.71	4.7	276	37	79	4.68	5.7	9.4	1.7	0.4	79
2006	AA	Tennessee	1	0	3	11	7	1.61	0.71	4.4	112	14	75	0.00	3.2	5.6	1.8	0.0	103
2006	AAA	Tucson	2	4	4	52	40	3.55	1.44	4.6	279	34	74	3.86	3.1	6.9	2.2	0.2	81
2007	AAA	Tucson	4	5	4	78	50	3.92	1.55	6.2	279	35	77	4.54	4.2	5.8	1.4	0.5	72
2007	MLB	Arizona	0	0	0	1	1	0.00	1.00	3.8	333	35	100	2.32	0.0	9.0		0.0	122

Tall/lanky pitcher moved to bullpen due to stamina issues caused by throwing across body. Pitches to contact with solid command and downward plane, forgoing strikeouts, but limiting home runs. Arsenal is average across board, but needs to repeat high ¾ delivery.

Severino,Sergio — SP — Houston

EXP MLB DEBUT: 2009 | POTENTIAL: #4 starter/setup reliever | 8E

Thrws L Age 23
2005 FA (DR)
- 89-93 FB ++++
- 81-84 SL +++
- 78-81 CU +

Year	Lev	Team	W	L	Sv	IP	K	ERA	WHIP	BF/G	OBA	H%	S%	xERA	Ctl	Dom	Cmd	hr/9	BPV
2005	Rk	Greeneville	3	5	0	61	69	4.71	1.36	19.7	214	30	64	3.00	5.3	10.1	1.9	0.4	100
2006	Rk	Greeneville	6	3	0	68	90	3.17	1.15	20.8	210	32	73	2.48	3.6	11.9	3.3	0.5	139
2007	A-	Lexington	5	8	3	84	84	4.17	1.33	11.3	225	27	72	3.77	4.6	9.0	2.0	1.2	70

Small/athletic pitcher with strikeout ability, getting solid movement to FB and SL with quick arm action. Likes to pitch aggressively and shows command, but tends to elevate pitches, loses focus, and pitches with too much effort. Ingredients to close are present, but is inconsistent.

Shafer,David — RP — Oakland

EXP MLB DEBUT: 2008 | POTENTIAL: Setup reliever | 6C

Thrws R Age 26
2001 (32) Cent Ariz JC
- 88-92 FB +++
- 79-82 SL ++++
- CU ++

Year	Lev	Team	W	L	Sv	IP	K	ERA	WHIP	BF/G	OBA	H%	S%	xERA	Ctl	Dom	Cmd	hr/9	BPV
2005	A+	Sarasota	1	0	5	13	18	0.00	0.83	4.8	195	32	100	1.02	1.4	12.3	9.0	0.0	279
2005	AA	Chattanooga	1	6	6	39	41	4.13	1.40	4.9	219	29	71	3.42	5.5	9.4	1.7	0.7	83
2006	AA	Chattanooga	1	2	26	49	52	2.38	1.08	4.4	211	29	78	2.19	2.9	9.5	3.3	0.4	127
2007	AA	Midland	0	0	8	23	21	2.33	1.16	3.7	225	29	81	2.62	3.1	8.1	2.6	0.4	102
2007	AAA	Sacramento	1	1	0	34	23	7.89	1.78	6.1	277	28	58	6.52	6.3	6.1	1.0	2.1	-7

Setup reliever who pitches aggressively with sinker/SL combination that quiets RH bats. Notches strikeouts and groundball outs and has provided steady command the past two years. CU to LH batters is ineffective and hasn't shown much stamina, so usage is limited.

Sharpless,Josh — RP — Pittsburgh

EXP MLB DEBUT: 2006 | POTENTIAL: Setup reliever | 6B

Thrws R Age 27
2003 (24) Allegheny College
- 87-92 FB +++
- 79-80 SL +++
- 80-83 CU ++

Year	Lev	Team	W	L	Sv	IP	K	ERA	WHIP	BF/G	OBA	H%	S%	xERA	Ctl	Dom	Cmd	hr/9	BPV
2006	AA	Altoona	2	0	8	21	30	0.86	0.81	5.4	119	21	88	0.15	3.9	12.9	3.3	0.0	178
2006	AAA	Indianapolis	1	1	1	33	30	2.45	1.42	6.1	256	33	83	3.57	4.1	8.2	2.0	0.3	87
2006	MLB	Pittsburgh	0	0	0	12	7	1.50	1.50	3.7	171	21	89	2.51	8.3	5.3	0.6	0.0	66
2007	AAA	Indianapolis	1	5	3	64	69	4.35	1.56	6.5	252	31	77	4.91	5.5	9.7	1.8	1.4	58
2007	MLB	Pittsburgh	0	1	0	4	1	13.17	1.95	3.3	377	27	40	12.85	2.2	2.2	1.0	6.6	-184

Pitches aggressively with sinker and SL achieving a solid balance of strikeouts and groundball outs. Command can be spotty and lacks quality CU due to not repeating high ¾ delivery. Pitches with effort and can be inefficient which affects stamina.

Shearn,Tom — SP — Cincinnati

EXP MLB DEBUT: 2007 | POTENTIAL: #5 starter/mid reliever | 6B

Thrws R Age 30
1996 (29) HS (OH)
- 86-91 FB +++
- 79-82 CB +++
- 66-69 CU ++
- 80-83 +++

Year	Lev	Team	W	L	Sv	IP	K	ERA	WHIP	BF/G	OBA	H%	S%	xERA	Ctl	Dom	Cmd	hr/9	BPV
2005	AAA	Louisville	4	5	1	93	93	4.26	1.37	8.8	240	30	72	3.95	4.3	9.0	2.1	1.1	73
2006	AA	Chattanooga	0	0	0	2	4	8.57	2.38	10.9	403	68	60	8.12	4.3	17.1	4.0	0.0	161
2006	AAA	Louisville	9	4	0	96	79	2.53	1.30	12.4	234	28	85	3.61	3.9	7.4	1.9	0.9	64
2007	AAA	Louisville	7	10	0	143	109	4.21	1.42	23.4	275	33	70	4.12	3.2	6.9	2.1	0.6	69
2007	MLB	Cincinnati	3	0	0	32	16	5.03	1.40	19.4	261	24	73	5.45	3.6	4.5	1.2	2.2	-12

Tall/strong-framed veteran pitched extremely well as starter in Sept. Throws any pitch at any time, will challenge hitters, and is deceptive with overhand delivery. Must have FB command and prevent choking of CB if he is to get MLB hitters out consistently.

Simmons,James — SP — Oakland

EXP MLB DEBUT: 2009 | POTENTIAL: #3 starter | 8C

Thrws R Age 21
2007 (1) UC Riverside
- 86-92 FB +++
- 83-84 SL +++
- 72-75 CB ++
- 77-80 CU +++

Year	Lev	Team	W	L	Sv	IP	K	ERA	WHIP	BF/G	OBA	H%	S%	xERA	Ctl	Dom	Cmd	hr/9	BPV
2007	AA	Midland	0	0	0	29	23	4.01	1.51	9.7	304	36	74	4.81	2.5	7.1	2.9	0.6	79

Polished college pitcher who relies on plus command and mixing pitches. Tall/athletic frame allows him to repeat delivery and likes to subtract from his FB with CU and SL/CT hybrid. May not strike-out many, but it tough to get good wood on and doesn't beat himself.

Sinkbeil,Brett
RP | **Florida** | EXP MLB DEBUT: 2009 | POTENTIAL: Setup reliever/closer | **8C**

Thrws R Age 23
2006 (1) Missouri St

Velo	Pitch	Grade
89-94	FB	++++
79-81	SL	+++
	CU	++

Year	Lev	Team	W	L	Sv	IP	K	ERA	WHIP	BF/G	OBA	H%	S%	xERA	Ctl	Dom	Cmd	hr/9	BPV
2006	A-	Greensboro	1	1	0	39	32	5.05	1.51	21.2	289	34	69	5.08	3.2	7.3	2.3	1.1	55
2006	A-	Jamestown	2	0	0	22	22	1.23	1.00	16.8	184	25	90	1.73	3.3	9.0	2.8	0.4	118
2007	A+	Jupiter	6	4	0	79	49	3.42	1.22	22.8	269	30	75	3.85	1.6	5.6	3.5	0.9	81

Power pitcher missed half of season with separate forearm and back problems, which likely led to his lower strikeout rate. Pounds strike zone with natural cutting FB and SL. Repeats ¾ delivery which enhances command, but hasn't done much to improve quality of CU.

Sipp,Tony
RP | **Cleveland** | EXP MLB DEBUT: 2009 | POTENTIAL: Setup reliever | **7C**

Thrws L Age 24
2004 (5) Clemson

Velo	Pitch	Grade
86-93	FB	++++
77-80	SL	+++
79-80	CU	++

Year	Lev	Team	W	L	Sv	IP	K	ERA	WHIP	BF/G	OBA	H%	S%	xERA	Ctl	Dom	Cmd	hr/9	BPV
2004	A-	Mahoning Val	3	1	0	42	74	3.20	1.09	16.5	217	38	76	2.90	2.8	15.8	5.7	1.1	194
2005	A-	Lake County	4	1	0	69	71	2.22	0.96	20.0	195	25	80	1.97	2.5	9.3	3.7	0.7	131
2005	A+	Kinston	2	2	2	47	59	2.68	1.21	8.6	204	29	81	2.80	4.4	11.3	2.6	0.8	113
2006	AA	Akron	4	2	3	60	80	3.14	1.10	8.1	210	32	70	2.15	3.1	12.0	3.8	0.3	156
2007																			

Missed 2007 with elbow injury that resulted in TJS in July. Athleticism allows him to repeat high ¾ delivery giving him solid command and ability to disguise pitches. FB and SL are lethal pitches he can get strikeouts with. Will need to tone-down the effort to his delivery.

Slocum,Brian
SP | **Cleveland** | EXP MLB DEBUT: 2006 | POTENTIAL: #5 starter | **6B**

Thrws R Age 27
2002 (2) Villanova

Velo	Pitch	Grade
89-93	FB	+++
81-84	SL	+++
79-82	CU	++

Year	Lev	Team	W	L	Sv	IP	K	ERA	WHIP	BF/G	OBA	H%	S%	xERA	Ctl	Dom	Cmd	hr/9	BPV
2004	A+	Kinston	15	6	0	135	102	4.33	1.31	22.3	263	31	68	3.96	2.7	6.8	2.5	0.9	69
2005	AA	Akron	7	5	0	102	95	4.41	1.31	20.1	254	32	67	3.75	3.2	8.4	2.6	0.8	86
2006	AAA	Buffalo	6	3	1	94	91	3.35	1.21	14.0	225	29	72	2.82	3.5	8.7	2.5	0.5	100
2006	MLB	Cleveland	0	0	0	17	11	5.76	2.09	10.6	358	39	76	8.09	4.7	5.8	1.2	1.6	-3
2007	AAA	Buffalo	2	2	0	26	28	4.15	1.42	22.1	223	28	74	3.84	5.5	9.7	1.8	1.0	74

Tall/well-proportioned pitcher was off to solid start before suffering elbow soreness. Generates easy velocity from his fluid ¾ delivery and can get both groundball outs and strikeouts with FB and SL. Lacks stamina and consistent CU which may force him to bullpen.

Smith,Brett
SP | **New York (A)** | EXP MLB DEBUT: 2009 | POTENTIAL: #5 starter | **7D**

Thrws R Age 24
2004 (2) UC-Irvine

Velo	Pitch	Grade
88-92	FB	+++
77-80	CB	+++
78-81	CU	+++

Year	Lev	Team	W	L	Sv	IP	K	ERA	WHIP	BF/G	OBA	H%	S%	xERA	Ctl	Dom	Cmd	hr/9	BPV
2005	A-	Charleston	3	2	0	66	61	4.08	1.23	22.3	264	33	67	3.57	1.9	8.3	4.4	0.7	123
2005	A+	Tampa	4	7	0	74	34	5.22	1.19	21.2	254	26	57	3.75	2.1	4.1	2.0	1.1	38
2006	A+	Tampa	8	9	0	158	119	3.76	1.40	23.9	271	32	75	4.24	3.2	6.8	2.1	0.8	62
2007	A+	Tampa	0	6	0	34	15	7.68	2.00	20.5	324	32	65	7.81	5.8	4.0	0.7	2.1	-35
2007	AA	Trenton	7	4	0	91	80	2.97	1.19	21.4	192	23	77	2.57	4.6	7.9	1.7	0.7	79

Durable-type starter struggled initially, but actually pitched better with promotion to Double-A. Lacks strikeout ability with three average pitches, but is an extreme groundball pitcher and is helped by a downward plane created by his high ¾ slot and deceptive arm action.

Smith,Dan
RP | **Atlanta** | EXP MLB DEBUT: 2008 | POTENTIAL: Situational reliever | **6C**

Thrws L Age 24
2003 NDFA HS (FL)

Velo	Pitch	Grade
87-91	FB	+++
77-79	CB	++
76-77	CU	+++

Year	Lev	Team	W	L	Sv	IP	K	ERA	WHIP	BF/G	OBA	H%	S%	xERA	Ctl	Dom	Cmd	hr/9	BPV
2006	A+	Myrtle Beach	1	0	5	8	13	1.13	1.13	3.9	181	29	100	2.64	4.5	14.6	3.3	1.1	141
2006	AA	Mississippi	3	6	0	60	86	3.14	1.21	8.7	195	31	74	2.40	4.8	12.9	2.7	0.4	136
2007	AA	Mississippi	4	2	0	51	41	1.94	1.12	22.3	205	26	82	2.07	3.5	7.2	2.1	0.2	95
2007	AAA	Richmond	3	5	0	58	39	5.43	1.67	18.6	262	29	68	4.91	6.1	6.1	1.0	0.9	32
2007	Rk	GCL Braves	0	1	0	5	5	1.80	0.60	8.6	175	25	67	0.25	0.0	9.0		0.0	74

Tall/strong reliever who gets downward plane to pitches, helping to keep ball low, and is deceptive with delivery. Improved CU, and command remains a strength, but regressed the consistent rotation of his CB and was less dominant overall.

Smith,Greg
SP | **Oakland** | EXP MLB DEBUT: 2008 | POTENTIAL: #5 starter | **6B**

Thrws L Age 24
2005 (6) Louisiana St

Velo	Pitch	Grade
86-91	FB	++
81-85	CT	+++
72-75	CB	++
76-80	CU	+++

Year	Lev	Team	W	L	Sv	IP	K	ERA	WHIP	BF/G	OBA	H%	S%	xERA	Ctl	Dom	Cmd	hr/9	BPV
2005	Rk	Missoula	8	5	0	82	100	4.17	1.06	19.9	230	32	62	2.85	2.0	11.0	5.6	0.9	165
2006	A+	Lancaster	9	0	0	88	71	1.63	1.00	25.9	187	23	85	1.68	3.2	7.3	2.3	0.3	100
2006	AA	Tennessee	5	4	0	60	38	3.90	1.47	23.4	278	32	74	4.31	3.5	5.7	1.7	0.6	50
2007	AA	Mobile	5	3	0	69	62	3.38	1.13	22.8	247	30	73	3.30	1.8	8.1	4.4	0.9	120
2007	AAA	Tucson	4	2	0	52	34	3.80	1.52	22.6	293	34	76	4.75	3.1	5.9	1.9	0.7	51

Finesse-type pitcher who subtracts from average FB, keeping hitters off-balance with a repeatable ¾ delivery. Commands plate well, keeps ball low, and was able to maintain average strikeout rate. CB has loose rotation and needs to be extended past six innings.

Smith,Sean
SP | **Cleveland** | EXP MLB DEBUT: 2008 | POTENTIAL: #4 starter | **7C**

Thrws R Age 24
2001 (16) Sacramento CC

Velo	Pitch	Grade
86-92	FB	++++
	SL	+++
76-78	CB	+++
	CU	+++

Year	Lev	Team	W	L	Sv	IP	K	ERA	WHIP	BF/G	OBA	H%	S%	xERA	Ctl	Dom	Cmd	hr/9	BPV
2004	A-	Lake County	7	2	0	61	48	3.39	1.28	19.2	225	27	74	3.11	4.1	7.1	1.7	0.6	71
2005	A+	Kinston	5	8	2	142	120	3.61	1.37	20.5	235	28	77	3.79	4.5	7.6	1.7	1.0	61
2006	A+	Kinston	1	2	0	25	23	3.60	1.04	24.1	221	27	67	2.57	2.2	8.3	3.8	0.7	119
2006	AA	Akron	10	5	0	144	94	3.81	1.28	23.6	255	29	71	3.54	2.8	5.9	2.1	0.6	64
2007	AAA	Buffalo	9	7	0	133	90	4.26	1.41	23.5	257	29	73	4.34	3.9	6.1	1.6	1.1	40

Projectable pitcher continued his focus on pitching to contact which ate into his strikeout rate. Fluid arm action generates movement to FB and breaking pitches. Despite being able to repeat ¾ delivery, he hasn't been efficient with his pitches and sports a high walk rate.

Smit,Alexander
SP | **Cincinnati** | EXP MLB DEBUT: 2010 | POTENTIAL: #5 starter | **7D**

Thrws L Age 22
2002 FA (Netherlands)

Velo	Pitch	Grade
86-92	FB	+++
74-77	KC	++
78-80	CU	+++

Year	Lev	Team	W	L	Sv	IP	K	ERA	WHIP	BF/G	OBA	H%	S%	xERA	Ctl	Dom	Cmd	hr/9	BPV
2005	Rk	Elizabethton	6	1	3	45	86	1.99	0.82	7.8	164	36	79	1.15	2.4	17.1	7.2	0.6	258
2005	A-	Beloit	1	9	0	49	54	6.04	1.75	16.1	295	37	69	6.21	5.1	9.9	1.9	1.6	46
2006	A-	Beloit	7	2	0	108	141	1.18	1.03	12.8	202	30	76	2.50	4.4	11.7	2.7	0.5	126
2007	A-	Dayton	2	2	0	22	19	1.19	1.19	17.9	233	34	77	2.48	3.2	7.7	2.4	0.4	74
2007	A+	Sar/FM	1	6	1	67	57	5.32	1.61	13.5	281	35	75	5.61	4.6	7.6	1.7	0.5	69

Tall/projectable pitcher with ability to elicit strikeouts with deceptive FB and KC. Lacks feel for comps and struggles with mechanics as he tends to short-arm baseball and flops wrist in the back of his delivery. Experience could cure a host of ills, but has a solid upside.

Smoker,Josh
SP | **Washington** | EXP MLB DEBUT: 2012 | POTENTIAL: #2 starter | **9E**

Thrws L Age 19
2007 (1-S) HS (GA)

Velo	Pitch	Grade
86-92	FB	++++
78-81	SL	++
72-76	CB	+++
81-83	SP	+++

Year	Lev	Team	W	L	Sv	IP	K	ERA	WHIP	BF/G	OBA	H%	S%	xERA	Ctl	Dom	Cmd	hr/9	BPV
2007	A-	Vermont	0	0	0	4	5	4.50	1.25	8.1	151	24	60	1.60	6.8	11.3	1.7	0.0	127

Athletic pitcher with long arm action and extension, giving appearance of the baseball coming down on hitters quickly. FB and CB used more to get strikeouts. Despite quick arm action, he doesn't repeat ¾ deliver consistently resulting in marginal command and poor SL rotation.

Snyder,Ben
SP | **San Francisco** | EXP MLB DEBUT: 2010 | POTENTIAL: #5 starter | **7D**

Thrws L Age 22
2006 (4) Ball St

Velo	Pitch	Grade
86-90	FB	+++
	SL	++
	CB	+++
	CU	+++

Year	Lev	Team	W	L	Sv	IP	K	ERA	WHIP	BF/G	OBA	H%	S%	xERA	Ctl	Dom	Cmd	hr/9	BPV
2006	A-	Salem-Keizer	4	1	0	66	57	3.00	1.08	18.4	231	29	73	2.63	2.0	7.8	3.8	0.5	119
2007	A-	Augusta	16	5	1	151	145	2.09	1.06	20.9	231	29	84	2.74	1.9	8.6	4.5	0.7	134

Polished college pitcher who frustrated low level hitters with plus command. Despite low velocity and focus on pitching to contact, he did strike-out batters by mixing pitches and hitting spots. May have trouble duplicating strikeout rate and will need a tighter SL.

Sosa,Henry
SP | **San Francisco** | EXP MLB DEBUT: 2009 | POTENTIAL: #2 starter | **9D**

Thrws R Age 22
2006 FA (DR)

Velo	Pitch	Grade
90-96	FB	++++
80-84	CB	+++
82-86	CU	++

Year	Lev	Team	W	L	Sv	IP	K	ERA	WHIP	BF/G	OBA	H%	S%	xERA	Ctl	Dom	Cmd	hr/9	BPV
2006	Rk	AZL Giants	2	1	0	32	41	3.93	1.00	13.6	181	26	62	2.07	3.4	11.5	3.4	0.8	134
2007	A-	Augusta	6	0	1	62	61	0.73	0.89	17.7	146	20	94	0.93	3.6	8.9	2.4	0.3	121
2007	A+	San Jose	5	5	0	63	78	4.41	1.61	20.0	270	37	76	5.03	5.1	11.1	2.2	1.1	79

Athletic pitcher with terrifying FB and hard CB that registers strikeouts and makes him tough on RH batters. Command within strike zone improved during season, but needs to reduce walk rate. High ¾ delivery is associated with effort and does tend to overthrow.

Sosa,Oswaldo — SP — Minnesota

EXP MLB DEBUT: 2008 | POTENTIAL: #4 starter/setup reliever | 7C

Thrws R Age 22	Year	Lev	Team	W	L	Sv	IP	K	ERA	WHIP	BF/G	OBA	H%	S%	xERA	Ctl	Dom	Cmd	hr/9	BPV
2002 FA (Venezuela)	2005	Rk	Elizabethton	6	5	0	56	40	4.97	1.43	19.9	272	32	64	4.15	3.4	6.4	1.9	0.6	60
88-93 FB ++++	2006	A-	Beloit	9	7	0	117	95	2.76	1.18	23.4	236	30	74	2.51	2.8	7.3	2.6	0.1	105
80-82 SL +++	2006	A+	Fort Myers	4	1	0	34	27	1.84	1.20	22.9	193	24	85	2.21	4.7	7.1	1.5	0.3	83
CB ++	2007	A+	Fort Myers	5	5	0	105	82	2.23	1.24	22.4	241	30	81	2.82	3.1	7.0	2.3	0.2	92
79-82 CU +++	2007	AA	New Britain	1	4	0	48	35	4.50	1.40	22.5	250	29	68	3.88	4.1	6.6	1.6	0.8	55

Extreme groundball pitcher, working primarily off of FB and SL. Pitches tall, attenuating sinking action, but struggled with command and saw a regression in his strikeout rate. Will need to find a third pitch from his CB or CU if he wants to remain a starting pitcher.

Speier,Ryan — RP — Colorado

EXP MLB DEBUT: 2005 | POTENTIAL: Setup reliever | 6B

Thrws R Age 28	Year	Lev	Team	W	L	Sv	IP	K	ERA	WHIP	BF/G	OBA	H%	S%	xERA	Ctl	Dom	Cmd	hr/9	BPV
2001 NDFA Radford	2004	AA	Tulsa	3	1	37	62	71	2.03	0.95	3.8	159	22	80	1.34	3.8	10.3	2.7	0.4	129
87-90 SL +++	2005	AAA	Colo Springs	2	2	6	52	45	5.01	1.69	5.2	323	40	69	5.30	3.1	7.8	2.5	0.3	79
79-83 CU +++	2005	MLB	Colorado	2	1	0	24	10	3.72	1.61	4.9	276	31	74	4.11	4.8	3.7	0.8	0.0	38
75-76 ++	2007	AAA	Colo Springs	1	4	33	49	40	4.40	1.43	4.2	253	31	69	3.81	4.2	7.3	1.7	0.5	68
	2007	MLB	Colorado	3	1	0	18	13	4.00	1.56	3.9	283	33	74	4.51	4.0	6.5	1.6	0.5	57

PCL leader in saves gets great deception with his sidearm-low ¾ slot which provides boring and sinking movement to both FB and SL. Throws strikes, but due to marginal velocity, he has to live on corners for success. Ability to neutralize RH batters could give him matchup role.

Spoone,Chorye — SP — Baltimore

EXP MLB DEBUT: 2009 | POTENTIAL: #3 starter | 8C

Thrws R Age 22	Year	Lev	Team	W	L	Sv	IP	K	ERA	WHIP	BF/G	OBA	H%	S%	xERA	Ctl	Dom	Cmd	hr/9	BPV
2005 (8) Catonsville CC																				
88-93 FB +++																				
SL ++	2005	Rk	Bluefield	2	5	0	24	27	8.18	1.65	7.2	283	37	49	5.31	4.8	10.0	2.1	1.1	69
CB ++++	2006	A-	Delmarva	7	9	0	129	90	3.56	1.53	21.6	245	29	76	3.79	5.6	6.3	1.1	0.3	57
CU ++	2007	A+	Frederick	10	9	0	152	133	3.26	1.15	23.2	201	25	72	2.38	4.0	7.9	2.0	0.5	89

Strong/stocky pitcher with plus CB and solid-average FB who has proved difficult to get good wood on. Struggles to repeat delivery which affects quality of CU and command. Becoming more efficient and throwing quality strikes could elevate his game to the next level.

Stange,Daniel — RP — Arizona

EXP MLB DEBUT: 2009 | POTENTIAL: Setup reliever | 7D

Thrws R Age 22	Year	Lev	Team	W	L	Sv	IP	K	ERA	WHIP	BF/G	OBA	H%	S%	xERA	Ctl	Dom	Cmd	hr/9	BPV
2006 (7) UC Riverside																				
89-96 FB ++++																				
82-84 SL +++	2006	Rk	Missoula	5	2	13	36	48	4.25	1.56	5.8	278	41	72	4.38	4.3	12.0	2.8	0.5	116
CU +	2007	A+	Visalia	4	5	16	42	53	3.21	1.31	4.6	238	34	77	3.35	3.8	11.3	2.9	0.6	118
	2007	AA	Mobile	1	0	1	6	5	5.81	1.77	5.7	340	39	70	6.85	2.9	7.3	2.5	1.5	40

Strong-framed reliever with overpowering FB and nasty SL that freezes RH batters. Pitches aggressively to inside part of plate and has closer experience. FB command isn't always present and pitches with some effort, which led to TJS in the fall. He will miss all of 2008.

Strop,Pedro — RP — Colorado

EXP MLB DEBUT: 2009 | POTENTIAL: Setup reliever | 8D

Thrws R Age 23	Year	Lev	Team	W	L	Sv	IP	K	ERA	WHIP	BF/G	OBA	H%	S%	xERA	Ctl	Dom	Cmd	hr/9	BPV
2002 FA (DR)																				
89-94 FB ++++																				
80-83 SL ++	2006	Rk	Casper	1	0	0	13	22	2.08	0.85	4.3	197	35	80	1.70	1.4	15.2	11.0	0.7	317
	2006	A-	Asheville	2	1	0	13	13	4.81	1.15	4.7	213	23	67	3.99	3.4	8.9	2.6	2.1	59
	2007	A+	Modesto	5	2	7	54	75	4.32	1.33	4.7	220	33	68	3.18	4.8	12.5	2.6	0.7	120

Overpowering reliever with excellent base skills, but ERA was killed by relievers that followed. FB explodes in strike zone and will get hitters to chase SL off the plate. Command and ability to prevent long ball improved immensely, giving him ability to close in the future.

Sullivan,Josh — SP — Colorado

EXP MLB DEBUT: 2009 | POTENTIAL: #4 starter | 8E

Thrws R Age 23	Year	Lev	Team	W	L	Sv	IP	K	ERA	WHIP	BF/G	OBA	H%	S%	xERA	Ctl	Dom	Cmd	hr/9	BPV
2005 (5) Auburn																				
88-92 FB ++++																				
82-84 SI +++	2005	A-	Tri-City	0	1	0	1	1	27.00	4.00	6.8	515	62	25	15.19	9.0	9.0	1.0	0.0	27
CU ++	2006	A-	Tri-City	3	4	0	69	74	2.73	1.01	20.4	201	28	72	1.81	2.7	9.6	3.5	0.3	139
	2007	A-	Asheville	3	2	0	49	45	3.29	1.36	15.8	232	29	77	3.36	4.6	8.2	1.8	0.5	79

Missed half of 2007 with shoulder tendinitis. Polished pitcher who pitched well in a hitter-friendly environment, showing strikeout ability and groundball tendencies with his power sinker and tight SL. CU will need to be masked better and can sometimes be predictable.

Swarzak,Anthony — SP — Minnesota

EXP MLB DEBUT: 2008 | POTENTIAL: #3 starter | 8B

Thrws R Age 22	Year	Lev	Team	W	L	Sv	IP	K	ERA	WHIP	BF/G	OBA	H%	S%	xERA	Ctl	Dom	Cmd	hr/9	BPV
2004 (2) HS (FL)	2005	A-	Beloit	9	5	0	91	101	4.05	1.24	20.6	240	32	68	3.27	3.2	10.0	3.2	0.7	112
87-93 FB ++++	2005	A+	Fort Myers	3	4	0	59	55	3.66	1.41	24.9	302	38	74	4.36	1.7	8.4	5.0	0.5	136
78-80 SL ++	2006	A+	Fort Myers	11	7	0	145	131	3.10	1.32	22.2	242	31	77	3.33	3.7	8.1	2.2	0.5	86
72-75 CB +++	2007	A+	Fort Myers	0	0	0	15	18	2.37	1.25	20.6	246	36	79	2.72	3.0	10.7	3.6	0.0	145
78-79 CU +++	2007	AA	New Britain	5	4	0	86	76	3.24	1.17	22.9	243	30	74	3.10	2.4	7.9	3.3	0.6	105

Strong/athletic pitcher with good arm action, that provides plus movement and ability to repeat high ¾ delivery. Showed improved command and found balance of dominance and pitching to contact. Missed first two months following a suspension for a banned substance.

Talbot,Mitch — SP — Tampa Bay

EXP MLB DEBUT: 2008 | POTENTIAL: #4 starter | 8C

Thrws R Age 24	Year	Lev	Team	W	L	Sv	IP	K	ERA	WHIP	BF/G	OBA	H%	S%	xERA	Ctl	Dom	Cmd	hr/9	BPV
2002 (2) HS (UT)	2003	Rk	Martinsville	4	4	0	54	46	2.83	1.04	17.4	228	29	71	2.14	1.8	7.7	4.2	0.2	138
88-92 FB ++++	2004	A-	Lexington	10	10	0	152	115	3.84	1.27	23.1	253	29	72	3.79	2.9	6.8	2.3	0.9	66
80-83 SL +++	2005	A+	Salem	8	11	0	151	100	4.35	1.42	23.7	284	32	71	4.57	2.7	6.0	2.2	0.9	53
CB ++	2006	AA	CC/Mont	10	7	1	156	155	2.77	1.23	22.6	248	33	77	3.03	2.7	8.9	3.3	0.3	118
79-82 CU +++	2007	AAA	Durham	13	9	0	161	124	4.53	1.42	23.5	271	32	68	4.20	3.3	6.9	2.1	0.7	65

Contact pitcher with impressive G/F ratio, minimizing extra-base hits and leading IL in wins. Loose arm action is basis of movement and added a CT to repertoire. Pitch command will be key to existence and needs to repeat his ¾ delivery to be effective the second time through order.

Tanner,Clayton — SP — San Francisco

EXP MLB DEBUT: 2010 | POTENTIAL: #4 starter | 7C

Thrws L Age 21	Year	Lev	Team	W	L	Sv	IP	K	ERA	WHIP	BF/G	OBA	H%	S%	xERA	Ctl	Dom	Cmd	hr/9	BPV
2006 (3) HS (CA)																				
85-90 FB ++																				
77-81 SL ++++																				
CU ++	2006	A-	Salem-Keizer	2	2	1	26	25	3.46	0.96	7.6	188	25	63	1.63	2.8	8.7	3.1	0.3	125
	2007	A-	Augusta	12	8	0	135	104	3.60	1.41	21.2	278	34	74	3.93	2.9	6.9	2.4	0.3	81

Athletic pitcher with plus SL and FB location, which compensates for below average velocity. Decline in strikeout rate and oppBA expected with jump to full-season ball and a hitter-friendly ballpark. Arm action is conducive to repeating delivery and disguising CU.

Tata,Jordan — SP — Detroit

EXP MLB DEBUT: 2006 | POTENTIAL: #4 starter | 7C

Thrws R Age 26	Year	Lev	Team	W	L	Sv	IP	K	ERA	WHIP	BF/G	OBA	H%	S%	xERA	Ctl	Dom	Cmd	hr/9	BPV
2003 (16) Sam Houston St	2005	A+	Lakeland	13	2	0	155	134	2.79	1.15	24.6	240	29	78	3.08	2.4	7.8	3.3	0.7	101
88-94 FB ++++	2006	AAA	Toledo	10	6	0	122	86	3.84	1.36	24.3	254	29	74	3.90	3.6	6.3	1.8	0.8	55
84-86 CT +++	2006	MLB	Detroit	0	0	0	14	6	6.34	1.48	7.6	259	28	55	4.13	4.4	3.8	0.9	0.6	25
75-77 KC ++	2007	AAA	Toledo	4	5	0	82	50	3.07	1.16	23.3	224	25	77	3.08	3.1	5.5	1.8	0.9	54
80-82 CU +++	2007	MLB	Detroit	1	1	0	14	8	7.71	1.71	21.2	288	32	52	5.14	5.1	5.1	1.0	0.6	30

DET would have loved more contribution from him, but struggled with shoulder inflammation and never got into groove. Subtracts from FB with CT and straight-CU, and pitches down in strike zone with a repetitive delivery. KC still lacks consistent rotation.

Taylor,Graham — SP — Florida

EXP MLB DEBUT: 2009 | POTENTIAL: #5 starter | 7C

Thrws L Age 24	Year	Lev	Team	W	L	Sv	IP	K	ERA	WHIP	BF/G	OBA	H%	S%	xERA	Ctl	Dom	Cmd	hr/9	BPV
2006 (10) Miami-OH																				
85-88 FB ++																				
78-80 SL ++++	2006	A-	Jamestown	3	5	0	65	48	2.48	0.97	19.0	243	30	74	2.26	0.6	6.6	12.0	0.3	290
76-79 CU ++	2007	A-	Greensboro	11	3	0	164	135	2.69	0.93	24.6	226	27	76	2.51	1.0	7.4	7.5	0.9	185
	2007	A+	Jupiter	1	1	0	10	3	8.10	2.10	24.6	362	39	57	6.74	4.5	2.7	0.6	0.0	11

Combines plus command and extreme groundball tendencies to get hitters out. SL is only pitch that rates above average, but has to lower arm slot to throw it. Stiff arm action and inability to repeat delivery for CU could force him to relief despite his low ERA and solid win total.

Teheran,Julio — SP — Atlanta
EXP MLB DEBUT: 2012 | POTENTIAL: #2 starter | 9E

Thrws R Age 17
2007 FA (DR)

Velo	Pitch	Grade
86-93	FB	++++
75-79	CB	+++
79-82	CU	++++

Year	Lev	Team	W	L	Sv	IP	K	ERA	WHIP	BF/G	OBA	H%	S%	xERA	Ctl	Dom	Cmd	hr/9	BPV
2007																			

Top rated international pitcher sports an advanced feel for pitching and a plus CU. FB and CB are solid pitches with good movement, and command is supposed to be a plus. Scouts weren't enamored with his arm action and does have some effort to his delivery.

Thatcher,Joe — RP — San Diego
EXP MLB DEBUT: 2007 | POTENTIAL: Situational reliever | 6B

Thrws L Age 27
2005 NDFA Indiana St

Velo	Pitch	Grade
87-91	FB	+++
78-81	SL	+++

Year	Lev	Team	W	L	Sv	IP	K	ERA	WHIP	BF/G	OBA	H%	S%	xERA	Ctl	Dom	Cmd	hr/9	BPV
2006	A+	Brevard Co	3	1	2	30	32	0.30	0.70	6.6	124	17	100	0.22	2.7	9.5	3.6	0.3	153
2006	AA	Huntsville	1	0	0	5	6	1.76	0.78	4.6	122	19	75	0.14	3.5	10.6	3.0	0.0	157
2007	AA	Huntsville	1	0	0	16	20	0.56	0.81	4.2	195	30	92	0.97	1.1	11.2	10.0	0.0	293
2007	AAA	Port/Nash	3	1	1	30	44	1.79	1.23	3.8	254	41	84	2.74	2.4	13.1	5.5	0.0	198
2007	MLB	San Diego	2	2	0	21	16	1.29	0.90	3.6	180	22	89	1.49	2.6	6.9	2.7	0.4	103

Medium-framed pitcher who is adept at getting LH batters out with a deceptive, low ¾ slot and ability to keep ball down. FB lacks velocity and movement, but keeps it away from strike zone and gets strikeouts with SL. Commands plate and can succeed if role is limited.

Thomas,Justin — SP — Seattle
EXP MLB DEBUT: 2008 | POTENTIAL: #5 starter | 7C

Thrws L Age 24
2005 (4) Youngstown St

Velo	Pitch	Grade
85-92	FB	+++
78-80	SL	+++
77-80	CU	++

Year	Lev	Team	W	L	Sv	IP	K	ERA	WHIP	BF/G	OBA	H%	S%	xERA	Ctl	Dom	Cmd	hr/9	BPV
2005	A-	Everett	3	3	0	59	48	3.81	1.41	13.9	275	34	72	3.82	3.1	7.3	2.4	0.3	85
2006	A-	Wisconsin	5	5	0	61	51	3.10	1.41	23.5	286	35	79	4.27	2.5	7.5	3.0	0.6	88
2006	A+	Inland Emp	9	4	0	105	111	4.20	1.45	26.4	265	34	73	4.29	3.9	9.5	2.5	0.9	85
2007	AA	W. Tennessee	4	9	0	119	100	5.52	1.75	22.7	304	37	69	5.61	4.6	7.6	1.6	0.8	49

Strong/athletic hurler who pitches to contact and has to keep ball down. Throws strikes, but command within strike zone was marginal, making him hittable. Goes to SL when he needs a strikeout, but is going to struggle to miss bats unless he improves quality of CU.

Thompson,Aaron — SP — Florida
EXP MLB DEBUT: 2009 | POTENTIAL: #4 starter á | 7C

Thrws L Age 21
2005 (1-C) HS (TX)

Velo	Pitch	Grade
86-90	FB	+++
77-80	SL	++++
69-72	CB	++
80-82	CU	++

Year	Lev	Team	W	L	Sv	IP	K	ERA	WHIP	BF/G	OBA	H%	S%	xERA	Ctl	Dom	Cmd	hr/9	BPV
2005	Rk	GCL Marlins	2	4	0	32	41	4.50	1.63	17.8	318	45	71	4.96	2.8	11.5	4.1	0.3	138
2005	A-	Jamestown	1	2	0	20	17	3.13	1.74	18.3	306	38	82	5.27	4.5	7.6	1.7	0.4	62
2006	A-	Greensboro	8	8	0	134	114	3.63	1.30	23.0	269	32	74	3.94	2.4	7.7	3.3	0.8	91
2007	A+	Jupiter	4	6	0	115	84	3.37	1.36	24.0	272	33	73	3.52	2.7	6.6	2.4	0.2	86

Intelligent/poised pitcher achieves results with a deceptive delivery and being able to throw four pitches for strikes. Command within strike zone improved, and prefers to get groundball outs, as he lacks a strikeout pitch and can be hittable. Shoulder tendinitis halted season early.

Thompson,Daryl — SP — Cincinnati
EXP MLB DEBUT: 2009 | POTENTIAL: #4 starter | 8D

Thrws R Age 22
2003 (8) HS (MD)

Velo	Pitch	Grade
88-94	FB	++++
74-76	CB	+++
	CU	++

Year	Lev	Team	W	L	Sv	IP	K	ERA	WHIP	BF/G	OBA	H%	S%	xERA	Ctl	Dom	Cmd	hr/9	BPV
2005	A-	Savannah	2	3	0	53	48	3.38	1.32	20.0	235	30	75	3.24	4.1	8.1	2.0	0.5	84
2006	A-	Vermont	0	1	0	6	8	7.26	1.61	6.9	222	35	50	3.32	7.3	11.6	1.6	0.0	114
2006	Rk	GCL Reds	0	0	0	14	16	2.57	1.00	10.7	202	28	77	2.15	2.6	10.3	4.0	0.6	141
2007	A-	Dayton	5	0	0	28	24	0.96	0.64	19.4	168	21	88	0.59	0.6	7.7	12.0	0.3	310
2007	A+	Sarasota	9	5	0	105	97	3.77	1.30	19.7	264	30	79	4.65	2.7	8.3	3.1	1.6	69

Unheralded bounty from Lopez/Kearns deal, he was finally 100% after shoulder surgery in 2005. Possesses lively FB and 12-6 CB which has always netted him strikeouts. Command was much improved, but still needs to repeat drop-and-drive delivery and quality of CU.

Thompson,Rich — RP — Los Angeles (A)
EXP MLB DEBUT: 2008 | POTENTIAL: Setup reliever | 7C

Thrws R Age 23
2002 FA (Australia)

Velo	Pitch	Grade
87-95	FB	++++
77-80	CB	++++

Year	Lev	Team	W	L	Sv	IP	K	ERA	WHIP	BF/G	OBA	H%	S%	xERA	Ctl	Dom	Cmd	hr/9	BPV
2006	AA	Arkansas	3	4	10	66	60	12.46	1.19	6.3	218	30	78	15.11	3.7	8.2	2.2	2.1	-78
2007	A+	Rancho Cuc	0	0	0	2	3	0.00	0.50	6.6	151	27	100	0.00	0.0	13.5		0.0	106
2007	AA	Arkansas	2	3	0	49	50	2.01	0.98	8.9	197	29	77	2.79	2.6	9.2	3.6	0.9	85
2007	AAA	Salt Lake	3	0	1	23	32	2.28	0.95	5.8	206	30	79	3.63	1.9	12.4	6.4	0.8	153
2007	MLB	Los Angeles (A)	0	0	0	6	9	10.80	2.10	4.4	364	25	82	17.58	4.4	13.1	3.0	5.4	-225

Athletic pitcher improved lot with move to relief, where he generated more pitch movement and gained 4 MPH by lowering slot. Primarily works off hard CB and high-octane FB, getting tons of strikeouts. Command is exceptional, but stamina is still a concern with his max-effort delivery.

Thompson,Sean — SP — Colorado
EXP MLB DEBUT: 2008 | POTENTIAL: #5 starter | 7E

Thrws L Age 25
2002 (5) HS (CO)

Velo	Pitch	Grade
85-89	FB	++
70-74	CB	++++
76-78	CU	+++

Year	Lev	Team	W	L	Sv	IP	K	ERA	WHIP	BF/G	OBA	H%	S%	xERA	Ctl	Dom	Cmd	hr/9	BPV
2004	A-	Fort Wayne	9	6	0	148	157	3.10	1.22	22.2	229	30	78	3.30	3.5	9.5	2.8	0.9	97
2005	A+	Lake Elsinore	4	1	0	33	45	2.18	1.18	22.1	218	31	89	3.18	3.5	12.2	3.5	1.1	125
2005	AA	Mobile	4	5	0	113	94	4.69	1.61	25.1	285	34	72	4.93	4.4	7.5	1.7	0.8	55
2007	AA	Tul/San Ant	9	8	0	132	81	3.74	1.36	23.0	250	28	74	3.80	3.8	5.5	1.4	0.7	46
2007	AAA	Omaha	0	0	0	1	0	0.00	4.00	2.3	415	41	100	12.62	18.0	0.0	0.0	0.0	-28

Short/light-framed pitcher possesses plus CB and outstanding command which compensates for low velocity. Strikeout rate declined in return to Double-A, but kept ball on the ground and mixed pitches well. Well-versed in holding runners and fielding position.

Tiffany,Chuck — SP — Tampa Bay
EXP MLB DEBUT: 2009 | POTENTIAL: #4 starter | 8E

Thrws L Age 23
2003 (2) HS (CA)

Velo	Pitch	Grade
87-92	FB	+++
74-78	CB	++++
78-81	CU	+++

Year	Lev	Team	W	L	Sv	IP	K	ERA	WHIP	BF/G	OBA	H%	S%	xERA	Ctl	Dom	Cmd	hr/9	BPV
2003	Rk	Ogden	0	0	0	2	4	12.27	2.73	4.1	392	64	50	8.77	8.2	16.4	2.0	0.0	117
2004	A-	Columbus	5	2	0	99	141	3.72	1.17	18.0	214	32	71	3.02	3.6	12.8	3.5	1.0	133
2005	A+	Vero Beach	11	7	0	110	134	3.93	1.22	20.2	227	30	74	3.69	3.5	11.0	3.1	1.4	99
2006	AA	Montgomery	0	2	0	15	12	7.11	2.24	19.2	318	36	71	7.96	8.3	7.1	0.9	1.8	-1
2007																			

Missed 2007 season recovering from rotator cuff surgery. Projectable pitcher who had a plus CB and solid-average velocity before the injury, along with an ability to change speeds. Strong frame and fluid arm action should help him in building back his arm strength.

Tillman,Chris — SP — Seattle
EXP MLB DEBUT: 2010 | POTENTIAL: #3 starter | 8C

Thrws R Age 20
2006 (2) HS (CA)

Velo	Pitch	Grade
87-91	FB	+++
74-78	CB	+++
79-81	SP	+++

Year	Lev	Team	W	L	Sv	IP	K	ERA	WHIP	BF/G	OBA	H%	S%	xERA	Ctl	Dom	Cmd	hr/9	BPV
2006	Rk	AZL Mariners	2	0	1	11	16	0.82	1.27	9.0	225	37	93	2.48	4.1	13.1	3.2	0.0	156
2006	A-	Everett	1	3	0	19	29	7.97	2.08	18.8	316	46	64	7.56	7.0	13.6	1.9	1.9	58
2007	A-	Wisconsin	1	4	0	33	34	3.55	1.33	17.1	250	35	72	3.60	3.5	9.3	2.6	0.3	133
2007	A+	High Dsert	6	7	0	102	105	5.26	1.52	22.2	271	35	75	5.67	4.2	9.2	2.2	1.0	102

Projectable pitcher with athletic frame and clean arm action which should improve velocity with maturation. Mixes three pitches with outstanding command and repeats overhand delivery, giving him deception. Pitched better over last two months in a hitter-friendly environment.

Tobin,Mason — SP — Los Angeles (A)
EXP MLB DEBUT: 2010 | POTENTIAL: #4 starter | 8D

Thrws R Age 20
2007 (16) Everett CC

Velo	Pitch	Grade
87-92	FB	+++
80-83	SL	++++
77-81	CU	++

Year	Lev	Team	W	L	Sv	IP	K	ERA	WHIP	BF/G	OBA	H%	S%	xERA	Ctl	Dom	Cmd	hr/9	BPV
2007	Rk	AZL Angels	2	0	0	28	32	0.95	0.85	12.9	177	28	79	1.79	2.2	10.2	4.6	0.3	148
2007	Rk	Orem	2	1	0	28	23	3.21	1.07	18.2	230	30	66	4.06	2.3	7.4	3.3	0.0	98

Wiry/well-proportioned pitcher with outstanding life to his FB and a SL that generates swings and misses. Presents excellent arm action and should be able to repeat his delivery with experience. Likes to command inside part of the plate and go right after hitters.

Todd,Jesse — RP — St. Louis
EXP MLB DEBUT: 2009 | POTENTIAL: Setup reliever | 8E

Thrws R Age 22
2007 (2) Arkansas

Velo	Pitch	Grade
87-94	FB	++++
82-84	SL	++++
	CU	++

Year	Lev	Team	W	L	Sv	IP	K	ERA	WHIP	BF/G	OBA	H%	S%	xERA	Ctl	Dom	Cmd	hr/9	BPV
2007	A-	Batavia	4	1	0	58	69	2.78	1.06	14.1	227	32	80	4.63	2.2	10.7	4.9	0.3	114

Short/stocky reliever with a plus SL and a FB that moves in several directions. Pitches aggressively in establishing inside part of plate and has a circle-CU that he can offer to LH batters. Presents some effort to his delivery, but has proved durable for entire career.

Townsend,Wade — SP — Tampa Bay

EXP MLB DEBUT: 2009 | POTENTIAL: Setup reliever | 8E

Thrws R Age 25 | 2005 (1) Rice

Velo	Pitch	Grade
87-92	FB	++++
80-82	SL	++
77-80	KC	+++
	CU	++

Year	Lev	Team	W	L	Sv	IP	K	ERA	WHIP	BF/G	OBA	H%	S%	xERA	Ctl	Dom	Cmd	hr/9	BPV
2005	A-	Hudson Vall	0	4	0	39	33	5.52	1.74	14.9	285	34	69	5.39	5.5	7.6	1.4	0.9	45
2006																			
2007	A-	Columbus	6	10	0	102	92	5.11	1.41	20.6	240	28	67	4.39	4.7	8.1	1.7	1.4	50

Strong-framed pitcher who hasn't been healthy (elbow in 2006 and forearm in 2007). Elicits strikeouts with lively FB and KC, though he gets in trouble by elevating pitches. Began getting feel for pitches, but needs to repeat ¾ delivery to improve quality of CU.

Trahern,Dallas — SP — Florida

EXP MLB DEBUT: 2008 | POTENTIAL: #5 starter | 6B

Thrws R Age 22 | 2004 (34) HS (OK)

Velo	Pitch	Grade
88-92	FB	+++
80-83	CB	+++
78-81	CU	+++

Year	Lev	Team	W	L	Sv	IP	K	ERA	WHIP	BF/G	OBA	H%	S%	xERA	Ctl	Dom	Cmd	hr/9	BPV
2004	Rk	GCL Tigers	1	2	0	30	24	0.60	0.96	16.3	205	26	96	1.79	2.1	7.2	3.4	0.3	120
2005	A-	W. Michigan	7	11	0	156	66	3.58	1.33	24.9	264	28	73	3.73	2.9	3.8	1.3	0.5	37
2006	A+	Lakeland	6	11	0	144	86	3.25	1.18	23.1	241	27	73	3.05	2.6	5.4	2.1	0.6	66
2007	AA	Erie	12	6	0	162	92	3.88	1.41	26.4	279	31	73	4.24	2.8	5.1	1.8	0.7	48
2007	AAA	Toledo	1	0	0	6	2	2.95	1.31	25.2	225	25	75	2.68	4.4	3.0	0.7	0.0	42

Low ERA indicative of extreme groundball tendencies, as command and dominance were below average. Athletic build allows him to repeat delivery and mixes three pitches well. Throws strikes, but needs better command within strike zone and remain comfortable pitching to contact.

Troncoso,Ramon — RP — Los Angeles (N)

EXP MLB DEBUT: 2009 | POTENTIAL: Setup reliever/closer | 8E

Thrws R Age 25 | 2002 FA (DR)

Velo	Pitch	Grade
90-95	FB	++++
	SL	++
	SP	+++

Year	Lev	Team	W	L	Sv	IP	K	ERA	WHIP	BF/G	OBA	H%	S%	xERA	Ctl	Dom	Cmd	hr/9	BPV
2005	Rk	Ogden	6	2	13	36	30	3.73	1.44	5.3	282	36	71	3.71	3.0	7.5	2.5	0.0	96
2006	A-	Columbus	4	0	15	33	22	2.44	1.05	5.6	230	27	76	2.32	1.9	6.0	3.1	0.3	103
2006	A+	Vero Beach	1	3	0	29	31	6.80	1.92	7.7	344	45	62	6.20	4.0	9.6	2.4	0.3	85
2007	A+	Inland Emp	3	1	7	26	30	1.04	0.81	5.9	197	29	86	1.00	1.0	10.4	10.0	0.0	288
2007	AA	Jacksonville	7	3	7	52	39	3.12	1.35	6.2	262	31	78	3.70	3.1	6.8	2.2	0.5	73

Tall/thin reliever with outstanding velocity and downward tilt to pitches. Pitches aggressively with FB and hitters will chase SPLCU, but needs tighter rotation of SL and demonstrate better command within strike zone. Strikeout rate declined with promotion, so will need to adjust.

Tucker,Ryan — SP — Florida

EXP MLB DEBUT: 2009 | POTENTIAL: #3 starter/setup reliever | 8C

Thrws R Age 21 | 2005 (1-S) HS (CA)

Velo	Pitch	Grade
90-95	FB	++++
80-84	SL	++
70-74	CB	+++
77-81	CU	++

Year	Lev	Team	W	L	Sv	IP	K	ERA	WHIP	BF/G	OBA	H%	S%	xERA	Ctl	Dom	Cmd	hr/9	BPV
2005	Rk	GCL Marlins	3	3	0	31	23	3.75	1.63	17.4	285	35	75	4.26	4.6	6.6	1.4	0.0	68
2005	A-	Jamestown	1	1	0	14	18	8.36	2.07	17.1	347	46	62	8.13	5.1	11.6	2.3	1.9	44
2006	A-	Greensboro	7	13	0	131	133	5.01	1.45	22.4	250	32	66	4.19	4.6	9.1	2.0	1.0	73
2007	A+	Jupiter	5	7	0	138	104	3.52	1.35	24.0	265	32	73	3.62	3.0	6.8	2.3	0.4	79

Strong-framed pitcher with quick arm action featureing FB with late, explosive movement. CB is better of two breaking pitches and still needs to repeat delivery for CU. Command improved, but tends to elevates pitches and doesn't miss as many bats as stuff would indicate.

Valiquette,Philippe — SP — Cincinnati

EXP MLB DEBUT: 2010 | POTENTIAL: #4 starter | 8E

Thrws L Age 21 | 2004 (7) HS (Canada)

Velo	Pitch	Grade
88-94	FB	++++
	CB	++
	CU	+++

Year	Lev	Team	W	L	Sv	IP	K	ERA	WHIP	BF/G	OBA	H%	S%	xERA	Ctl	Dom	Cmd	hr/9	BPV
2005	Rk	Billings	2	1	0	21	18	6.43	1.57	13.2	280	35	56	4.42	4.3	7.7	1.8	0.4	70
2005	A-	Dayton	2	5	0	64	42	6.32	1.95	16.1	309	36	66	5.84	6.2	5.9	1.0	0.4	36
2006	A-	Dayton	2	4	0	37	24	7.54	1.97	14.8	333	37	62	7.02	5.1	5.8	1.1	1.2	11
2007	Rk	Billings	3	1	3	40	29	1.79	1.04	14.1	215	27	81	1.85	2.5	6.5	2.6	0.0	106
2007	A-	Dayton	1	2	0	10	8	7.06	1.86	6.8	371	44	61	7.11	1.8	7.1	4.0	0.9	81

Projectable frame and arm showed what he could do when healthy and in shape. Possesses fluid arm action and repeats ¾ delivery providing velocity, movement, and ability to change speeds. Command could be finer and needs to tighten CB if he's to have success past Class-A.

Van Buren,Jermaine — RP — Oakland

EXP MLB DEBUT: 2005 | POTENTIAL: Setup reliever | 6B

Thrws R Age 27 | 1998 (2) HS (MS)

Velo	Pitch	Grade
87-92	FB	+++
83-84	SL	+++
	CB	++
	CU	+

Year	Lev	Team	W	L	Sv	IP	K	ERA	WHIP	BF/G	OBA	H%	S%	xERA	Ctl	Dom	Cmd	hr/9	BPV
2005	AAA	Iowa	2	3	25	54	65	1.99	1.01	4.0	178	24	86	2.08	3.7	10.8	3.0	0.8	121
2005	MLB	Chicago (N)	0	2	0	6	3	3.00	1.83	4.7	106	13	82	2.69	13.5	4.5	0.3	0.0	68
2006	AAA	Pawtucket	4	0	16	45	46	2.99	1.22	5.5	225	30	75	2.76	3.6	9.2	2.6	0.4	107
2006	MLB	Boston	1	0	0	13	8	11.77	2.23	6.6	276	31	43	6.31	10.4	5.5	0.5	0.7	23
2007	AAA	Sac/Colu	1	3	3	64	58	3.66	1.38	5.7	237	28	78	4.13	4.5	8.2	1.8	1.3	57

Strong/athletic reliever with outstanding performance, but hasn't gotten extended opportunity. Induces groundballs with power sinker and gets strikeouts with SL that hitters tend to chase. Deceptive, drop-and-drive delivery adds to effectiveness, but does pitch with effort.

Varvaro,Anthony — SP — Seattle

EXP MLB DEBUT: 2009 | POTENTIAL: #4 starter | 7C

Thrws R Age 23 | 2005 (12) St. John's

Velo	Pitch	Grade
87-93	FB	+++
86-87	CT	+++
77-80	CB	+++
82-84	CU	++

Year	Lev	Team	W	L	Sv	IP	K	ERA	WHIP	BF/G	OBA	H%	S%	xERA	Ctl	Dom	Cmd	hr/9	BPV
2006	Rk	AZL Mariners	0	2	0	11	15	1.64	1.09	8.6	184	30	83	1.55	4.1	12.3	3.0	0.0	155
2007	A-	Wisconsin	4	11	1	103	112	4.71	1.41	19.8	244	33	66	3.67	4.4	9.8	2.2	0.6	93

Strong comeback from TJS, showing ability to miss bats and regaining command that was his staple in college. Not a hard thrower, but has excellent pitch movement and is deceptive with low ¾ slot. Hasn't regained feel for CU and will have to overcome stamina concerns.

Vasquez,Esmerling — SP — Arizona

EXP MLB DEBUT: 2008 | POTENTIAL: #4 starter | 8D

Thrws R Age 24 | 2003 FA (DR)

Velo	Pitch	Grade
88-95	FB	++++
80-83	SL	++
78-81	CU	+++

Year	Lev	Team	W	L	Sv	IP	K	ERA	WHIP	BF/G	OBA	H%	S%	xERA	Ctl	Dom	Cmd	hr/9	BPV
2004	Rk	Missoula	3	2	5	30	33	3.58	1.42	6.7	205	29	74	2.93	6.3	9.8	1.6	0.3	97
2004	A-	Yakima	0	0	1	5	7	6.92	1.92	4.9	405	54	67	8.69	0.0	12.1		1.7	-5
2005	A-	South Bend	6	4	3	71	79	3.67	1.54	5.9	239	33	75	3.61	5.9	10.0	1.7	0.3	95
2006	A+	Lancaster	4	9	0	117	115	5.91	1.54	15.0	281	36	60	4.58	3.9	8.8	2.3	0.7	78
2007	AA	Mobile	10	6	0	165	151	3.00	1.12	22.4	212	27	75	2.55	3.3	8.2	2.5	0.6	97

Thin/athletic pitcher with quick arm action and whip-like motion providing easy velocity and plus pitch movement. Changes speeds well and displays good command. SL rotation could be tighter and needs to get stronger to maintain velocity. Suffered torn labrum during AFL.

Vasquez,Sendy — SP — Detroit

EXP MLB DEBUT: 2009 | POTENTIAL: #5 starter | 6C

Thrws R Age 25 | 2003 FA (DR)

Velo	Pitch	Grade
89-94	FB	++++
	CB	++
80-83	CU	+++

Year	Lev	Team	W	L	Sv	IP	K	ERA	WHIP	BF/G	OBA	H%	S%	xERA	Ctl	Dom	Cmd	hr/9	BPV
2004	Rk	GCL Tigers	2	2	3	28	32	5.46	1.79	7.6	269	38	66	4.38	6.8	10.3	1.5	0.0	95
2005	A-	Oneonta	7	0	0	67	60	3.63	1.30	18.4	219	28	72	3.03	4.6	8.1	1.8	0.5	80
2006	A-	W. Michigan	13	6	0	142	112	2.98	1.25	22.3	244	30	77	3.14	3.1	7.1	2.3	0.4	84
2007	A-	Oneonta	6	5	0	76	61	4.25	1.52	23.6	240	30	71	3.70	5.7	7.2	1.3	0.4	66
2007	A+	Lakeland	0	3	0	18	12	8.41	1.98	21.8	328	39	53	5.80	5.4	5.9	1.1	0.0	48

Solid arm action provides late life to FB and repeats a deceptive delivery well which makes his CU more effective. Will need to improve rotation of CB and it is questionable as to if his command and dominance will survive the upper levels. Projects as an inning-eater at best.

Vasquez,Virgil — SP — Detroit

EXP MLB DEBUT: 2007 | POTENTIAL: #5 starter | 6A

Thrws R Age 26 | 2003 (7) UC Santa Barbara

Velo	Pitch	Grade
85-92	FB	+++
82-84	SL	+++
74-75	CB	+++
79-82	CU	+++

Year	Lev	Team	W	L	Sv	IP	K	ERA	WHIP	BF/G	OBA	H%	S%	xERA	Ctl	Dom	Cmd	hr/9	BPV
2003	A-	Oneonta	3	4	0	53	35	6.95	1.62	21.4	337	38	56	5.85	1.7	5.9	3.5	0.8	71
2004	A-	W. Michigan	14	6	0	168	120	3.64	1.13	24.6	248	29	69	3.18	1.8	6.4	3.5	0.7	96
2005	A+	Lakeland	4	1	0	47	31	4.21	1.26	23.9	282	31	70	4.35	1.3	5.9	4.4	1.1	93
2005	AA	Erie	2	8	0	83	53	5.30	1.29	22.8	284	31	60	4.40	1.5	5.7	3.8	1.1	80
2006	AA	Erie	7	12	0	174	129	3.72	1.30	26.6	264	30	75	4.13	2.6	6.7	2.6	1.1	64

Intelligent pitcher stays tall through deliberate delivery with fluid arm action that allows him to repeat his arm speed on all four pitches. Lacks FB movement, so doesn't register many strikeouts, but commands plate well and keeps ball inside the ballpark.

Veal,Donald — SP — Chicago (N)

EXP MLB DEBUT: 2009 | POTENTIAL: #3 starter | 8D

Thrws L Age 23 | 2005 (2) Pima CC

Velo	Pitch	Grade
87-93	FB	++++
75-79	CB	+++
79-81	CU	++

Year	Lev	Team	W	L	Sv	IP	K	ERA	WHIP	BF/G	OBA	H%	S%	xERA	Ctl	Dom	Cmd	hr/9	BPV
2005	Rk	AZL Cubs	0	1	0	10	14	5.29	1.27	10.4	218	29	64	4.06	4.4	12.4	2.8	1.8	91
2005	A-	Boise	1	2	0	29	34	2.48	1.14	16.4	180	25	81	2.22	4.7	10.6	2.3	0.6	111
2006	A-	Peoria	5	3	0	73	86	2.83	1.15	20.7	176	25	76	2.07	4.9	10.6	2.2	0.5	114
2006	A+	Daytona	6	2	0	80	88	1.68	1.10	22.4	169	24	86	1.74	4.7	9.9	2.1	0.3	114
2007	AA	Tennessee	8	10	0	130	131	4.98	1.53	20.2	256	33	68	4.28	5.0	9.1	1.8	0.8	73

Possessor of an electric FB and solid CB, but has yet to live-up to projections. Lanky frame and mechanics non in-sync, preventing him from repeating delivery, which is the root of his poor command and inconsistent CU. Will need a consolidating season in upper minors.

PITCHERS

Veras,Jose — RP — New York (A)

EXP MLB DEBUT: 2006 | POTENTIAL: Setup reliever | 7C

Thrws R Age 27 | 1998 FA (DR) | 91-96 FB ++++ | 77-80 SL +++ | 81-83 SP +

Year	Lev	Team	W	L	Sv	IP	K	ERA	WHIP	BF/G	OBA	H%	S%	xERA	Ctl	Dom	Cmd	hr/9	BPV
2006	AAA	Columbus	5	3	21	60	68	2.54	1.18	4.8	234	33	79	2.82	2.8	10.2	3.6	0.4	131
2007	A+	Tampa	0	0	0	3	5	0.00	0.67	5.2	0	0	100	0.00	6.0	15.0	2.5	0.0	198
2007	AAA	Scranton/WB	2	0	4	16	17	4.50	1.50	5.8	274	36	70	4.26	3.9	9.6	2.4	0.6	92
2007	MLB	New York (A)	0	0	2	9	7	5.93	1.43	4.3	190	24	54	2.51	6.9	6.9	1.0	0.0	80
2007	Rk	GCL Yankees	0	0	0	2	1	0.00	1.00	3.8	262	30	100	2.36	0.0	4.5		0.0	30

Strong-framed reliever with overpowering stuff, possessing both a FB and SL that are tough to hit. Command improved, but gets into trouble when he attempts to get strikeout. Lacks ability to repeat ¾ slot which doesn't disguise SPL. Season ended early due to elbow surgery.

Vineyard,Nate — SP — New York (N)

EXP MLB DEBUT: 2012 | POTENTIAL: #3 starter | 8D

Thrws L Age 19 | 2007 (1-S) HS (GA) | 86-91 FB +++ | 79-82 SL ++++ | CU ++

Year	Lev	Team	W	L	Sv	IP	K	ERA	WHIP	BF/G	OBA	H%	S%	xERA	Ctl	Dom	Cmd	hr/9	BPV
2007	Rk	GCL Mets	0	3	0	27	33	5.27	1.44	12.8	282	24	74	7.11	3.0	11.0	3.7	1.3	77

Projectable pitcher with easy velocity and a fluid delivery, he doesn't throw overly hard yet, but gets good pitch movement and his SL is a legitimate strikeout pitch. Showed better command than expected, but needs to repeat delivery more often, which should also improve CU.

Viola,Pedro — RP — Cincinnati

EXP MLB DEBUT: 2008 | POTENTIAL: Setup reliever | 7C

Thrws L Age 24 | 2006 FA (DR) | 87-92 FB ++++ | SL +++

Year	Lev	Team	W	L	Sv	IP	K	ERA	WHIP	BF/G	OBA	H%	S%	xERA	Ctl	Dom	Cmd	hr/9	BPV
2007	A-	Dayton	3	1	2	43	49	1.88	1.07	7.6	193	26	86	2.19	3.5	10.2	2.9	0.6	120
2007	A+	Sarasota	0	1	2	20	28	0.90	1.05	7.7	199	33	90	1.61	3.2	12.6	4.0	0.0	175
2007	AA	Chattanooga	0	0	2	19	17	0.95	0.95	5.1	183	21	100	2.10	2.8	8.1	2.8	0.9	98

Athletic reliever decimated hitters with a blend of pitch movement and command. Generates terrific movement to FB and SL through quick arm action, which allows him to miss bats. Likes to work inside and pitches well to hitters from both sides, which could expand bullpen role.

Volstad,Chris — SP — Florida

EXP MLB DEBUT: 2008 | POTENTIAL: #2 starter | 8C

Thrws R Age 21 | 2005 (1) HS (FL) | 87-93 FB ++++ | 75-80 CB ++++ | 76-80 CU ++

Year	Lev	Team	W	L	Sv	IP	K	ERA	WHIP	BF/G	OBA	H%	S%	xERA	Ctl	Dom	Cmd	hr/9	BPV
2005	Rk	GCL Marlins	1	1	0	27	26	2.33	1.07	17.5	247	32	79	2.62	1.3	8.7	6.5	0.3	184
2005	A-	Jamestown	3	2	0	38	29	2.13	1.42	23.0	286	35	83	3.75	2.6	6.9	2.6	0.0	94
2006	A-	Greensboro	11	8	0	152	99	3.08	1.30	24.1	273	31	78	3.92	2.1	5.9	2.8	0.7	72
2007	A+	Jupiter	8	9	0	126	93	4.50	1.50	25.9	300	35	70	4.68	2.6	6.6	2.5	0.6	71
2007	AA	Carolina	4	2	0	42	25	3.20	1.21	24.3	256	28	77	3.60	2.1	5.3	2.5	0.9	63

Projectable pitcher with good movement which is more conducive to groundball outs than strikeouts. Fails to repeat arm speed and high ¾ slot which leaves him with a below average CU. Stuff is too good to be pitching this much to contact and needs to be finer with command.

Walden,Jordan — SP — Los Angeles (A)

EXP MLB DEBUT: 2010 | POTENTIAL: #2 starter | 9D

Thrws R Age 20 | 2006 (12) HS (TX) | 89-96 FB ++++ | 81-83 SL +++ | CU ++

Year	Lev	Team	W	L	Sv	IP	K	ERA	WHIP	BF/G	OBA	H%	S%	xERA	Ctl	Dom	Cmd	hr/9	BPV
2007	Rk	Orem	1	1	0	64	63	3.09	1.03	16.5	213	28	70	2.16	2.4	8.8	3.7	0.4	131

Made correct decision to attend Grayson County CC, as he needed to mature physically and develop comps. Quick arm action gives him easy velocity and pitch movement. Struggles to repeat arm speed for CU and tends to get away from his high ¾ slot, but can be overpowering.

Waldrop,Kyle — SP — Minnesota

EXP MLB DEBUT: 2009 | POTENTIAL: #5 starter | 7D

Thrws R Age 22 | 2004 (1) HS (TN) | 87-90 FB +++ | SL + | CB +++ | CU +++

Year	Lev	Team	W	L	Sv	IP	K	ERA	WHIP	BF/G	OBA	H%	S%	xERA	Ctl	Dom	Cmd	hr/9	BPV
2005	A-	Beloit	6	11	0	151	108	5.00	1.36	23.4	299	34	64	4.73	1.4	6.4	4.7	1.0	102
2006	A-	Beloit	6	3	0	110	62	3.85	1.15	24.3	262	29	67	3.36	1.4	5.1	3.6	0.7	90
2006	A+	Fort Myers	3	2	0	45	25	3.59	1.44	24.0	274	30	77	4.39	3.4	5.0	1.5	0.8	37
2007	A+	Fort Myers	7	5	0	92	57	3.42	1.24	23.4	257	30	71	3.16	2.3	5.6	2.4	0.3	78
2007	AA	New Britain	3	6	0	59	33	5.34	1.58	23.6	308	33	67	5.49	2.9	5.0	1.7	1.1	28

Plus command and ability to mix three pitches has kept ERA low, but low dominance and high hit rate will snare him at upper levels. Repeats delivery, providing deception, which offsets lack of pitch movement. Velocity projection that was expected has not occurred.

Walker,Matt — SP — Tampa Bay

EXP MLB DEBUT: 2009 | POTENTIAL: #4 starter/setup reliever | 8D

Thrws R Age 21 | 2004 (10) HS (LA) | 89-94 FB ++++ | 77-80 CB +++ | 79-82 CU ++

Year	Lev	Team	W	L	Sv	IP	K	ERA	WHIP	BF/G	OBA	H%	S%	xERA	Ctl	Dom	Cmd	hr/9	BPV
2005	Rk	Princeton	2	3	1	57	71	5.35	1.49	18.9	281	40	61	4.08	3.5	11.2	3.2	0.3	124
2005	A-	Hudson Valley	0	0	0	3	5	11.61	2.90	17.7	364	57	56	8.68	11.6	14.5	1.3	0.0	96
2006	A-	SW Michigan	5	5	0	82	68	3.18	1.30	22.5	222	27	76	3.10	4.5	7.5	1.7	0.5	74
2007	A+	Vero Beach	4	9	0	95	76	5.58	1.87	14.4	263	31	70	5.26	7.8	7.2	0.9	0.8	42

Blessed with athleticism, arm strength, and arm action, he is extremely projectable with velocity and pitch movement, but lost command of the strike zone and pitches from behind. Stamina has never been good, and coupled with his mediocre CU, he may end up in relief.

Wall,Josh — SP — Los Angeles (N)

EXP MLB DEBUT: 2010 | POTENTIAL: #4 starter | 7D

Thrws R Age 21 | 2005 (2) HS (LA) | 86-90 FB +++ | 74-79 CB +++ | CU ++

Year	Lev	Team	W	L	Sv	IP	K	ERA	WHIP	BF/G	OBA	H%	S%	xERA	Ctl	Dom	Cmd	hr/9	BPV
2005	Rk	GCL Dodgers	1	3	0	14	5	3.86	1.50	12.1	248	24	79	4.65	5.1	3.2	0.6	1.3	-1
2006	Rk	Ogden	3	5	0	66	41	5.86	1.71	21.4	301	34	65	5.35	4.5	5.6	1.2	0.7	34
2007	A-	Great Lakes	6	10	1	129	103	4.18	1.43	21.1	272	33	70	4.07	3.3	7.2	2.1	0.6	72

Tall/projectable pitcher with smooth arm action that provides movement to generate strikeouts. Velocity and ability to change speeds are improving which accents strong CB and keeps pitches low. Needs to improve command which would keep him in ballgames longer.

Walters,PJ — SP — St. Louis

EXP MLB DEBUT: 2009 | POTENTIAL: #5 starter | 7C

Thrws R Age 23 | 2006 (11) So Alabama | 85-88 FB +++ | 76-77 SL ++ | 69-71 CB +++ | 75-78 CU ++++

Year	Lev	Team	W	L	Sv	IP	K	ERA	WHIP	BF/G	OBA	H%	S%	xERA	Ctl	Dom	Cmd	hr/9	BPV
2006	A-	State College	2	1	8	30	31	3.56	1.26	4.7	255	31	79	6.25	2.7	9.3	3.4	0.3	111
2007	A-	Quad Cties	6	1	1	68	73	2.62	1.04	15.5	235	32	77	4.13	1.6	9.6	6.1	0.3	139
2007	A+	Palm Beach	3	1	0	33	37	2.67	1.05	25.7	236	31	76	4.65	1.6	10.0	6.2	0.5	150
2007	AA	Springfield	3	4	0	49	37	2.37	1.16	24.4	233	29	77	4.30	2.7	6.8	2.5	0.7	89

Pitches to contact with excellent command and ability to change speeds. Lacks velocity, but keeps ball low and has late life to all pitches due to smooth arm action. Strikeout rate likely to decline at upper levels and can compensate by pitching to hitters' weaknesses.

Warden,Jim Ed — RP — Washington

EXP MLB DEBUT: 2008 | POTENTIAL: Setup reliever | 6B

Thrws R Age 29 | 2001 (6) Tennessee Tech | 86-92 FB +++ | 79-82 SL +++

Year	Lev	Team	W	L	Sv	IP	K	ERA	WHIP	BF/G	OBA	H%	S%	xERA	Ctl	Dom	Cmd	hr/9	BPV
2004	A-	Lake County	5	1	13	54	63	3.00	1.30	5.4	220	29	81	3.45	4.5	10.5	2.3	1.0	93
2005	A+	Kinston	3	5	4	67	72	3.75	1.49	6.3	264	34	78	4.58	4.3	9.6	2.3	1.1	75
2006	AA	Akron	5	2	11	59	47	3.05	1.08	4.2	174	21	72	1.90	4.4	7.2	1.6	0.5	84
2007	AA	Akron	4	4	6	51	48	2.82	1.29	5.3	258	32	81	3.66	2.8	8.5	3.0	0.7	96
2007	AAA	Buffalo	1	1	0	23	20	7.40	2.16	7.2	368	44	65	7.71	4.7	7.8	1.7	0.8	40

Tall/lanky reliever with sidearm delivery makes him death on RH batters and hard for hitters to lift baseball. SL is pitch he goes to when he needs strikeouts as his FB lacks movement. Command is outstanding as his delivery is very repetitive, and has quick arm action.

Ward,Zach — SP — Minnesota

EXP MLB DEBUT: 2008 | POTENTIAL: Setup/middle reliever | 6C

Thrws R Age 24 | 2005 (3) Gardner-Webb | 86-93 FB +++ | 82-87 SL +++ | 78-80 CB ++ | 79-82 ++

Year	Lev	Team	W	L	Sv	IP	K	ERA	WHIP	BF/G	OBA	H%	S%	xERA	Ctl	Dom	Cmd	hr/9	BPV
2006	A-	Bel/Day	8	4	0	144	0	3.06	0.69	19.5	197	19	53	1.00	0.0	0.0		0.2	10
2007	A+	Fort Myers	5	17	1	130	107	4.08	1.31	18.5	266	33	67	3.49	2.6	7.4	2.9	0.3	97

Heavy sinker and deceptive velocity generated lots of groundball outs, but didn't miss bats like he did at lower levels. Repeats ¾ delivery, but has tendency to short-arm baseball. Very efficient with pitches, which is essential since he loses velocity after four innings.

Watson, Sean — SP — Cincinnati

Thrws: R Age 22
2006 (2) Tennessee

EXP MLB DEBUT: 2009 POTENTIAL: #5 starter/setup reliever **7C**

88-91	FB	++++	Year	Lev	Team	W	L	Sv	IP	K	ERA	WHIP	BF/G	OBA	H%	S%	xERA	Ctl	Dom	Cmd	hr/9	BPV

Year	Lev	Team	W	L	Sv	IP	K	ERA	WHIP	BF/G	OBA	H%	S%	xERA	Ctl	Dom	Cmd	hr/9	BPV
88-91 FB ++++																			
80-83 SL ++	2006	Rk	Billings	0	0	1	23	19	1.55	0.91	12.3	197	26	81	1.27	1.9	7.4	3.8	0.0	140
81-85 KC +++	2006	A-	Dayton	1	2	0	14	16	8.87	1.90	6.7	355	45	52	7.23	3.2	10.1	3.2	1.3	74
78-80 CU +	2007	A-	Dayton	5	2	0	71	85	1.90	1.00	20.9	224	31	88	2.63	1.6	10.7	6.5	0.9	185
	2007	A+	Sarasota	4	4	0	54	50	5.48	1.38	16.3	261	31	63	4.53	3.5	8.3	2.4	1.3	63

Large-framed/stocky pitcher with heavy sinker and KC that generates groundball outs and strikeouts. A reliever in college, but CIN kept him in low minors to work as a starter, where he still lacks stamina. Lack of arm action and not repeating delivery limits SL and CU.

Watson, Tony — SP — Pittsburgh

Thrws: L Age 23
2007 (9) Nebraska

EXP MLB DEBUT: 2009 POTENTIAL: #5 starter **7D**

Year	Lev	Team	W	L	Sv	IP	K	ERA	WHIP	BF/G	OBA	H%	S%	xERA	Ctl	Dom	Cmd	hr/9	BPV
87-92 FB +++																			
81-83 SL ++																			
79-81 CU ++++	2007	A-	State College	6	1	0	53	40	2.54	1.02	20.4	239	28	78	2.70	1.2	6.8	5.7	0.7	148
	2007	A-	Hickory	1	1	0	14	18	3.86	1.07	18.2	262	30	71	3.68	0.6	11.6	18.0	1.3	412

Tall/projectable pitcher who disabled short-season hitter with plus command and ability change speeds. Possesses average velocity and repeats ¾ delivery, but may struggle to get strikeouts at upper levels with below average SL. Arm action is stiff, but hasn't affected stamina.

Watt, Michael — SP — Los Angeles (N)

Thrws: L Age 19
2007 (2) HS (CA)

EXP MLB DEBUT: 2012 POTENTIAL: #4 starter **8E**

Year	Lev	Team	W	L	Sv	IP	K	ERA	WHIP	BF/G	OBA	H%	S%	xERA	Ctl	Dom	Cmd	hr/9	BPV
84-89 FB ++																			
73-75 CB +++																			
76-78 CU ++	2007	Rk	GCL Dodgers	0	0	0	21	18	3.00	1.14	8.3	233	30	71	2.31	2.6	7.7	3.0	0.0	118

Athletic/physical pitcher with quick arm action that generates solid movement to pitches. Velocity will project with maturity and CB has tight rotation that nets strikeouts. Commands plate well, but will need to disguise CU and possibly elongate motion in back.

Weathers, Casey — RP — Colorado

Thrws: R Age 23
2007 (1) Vanderbilt

EXP MLB DEBUT: 2008 POTENTIAL: Setup reliever/closer **9D**

Year	Lev	Team	W	L	Sv	IP	K	ERA	WHIP	BF/G	OBA	H%	S%	xERA	Ctl	Dom	Cmd	hr/9	BPV
90-97 FB ++++																			
84-88 SL ++++	2007	A-	Asheville	0	1	2	13	19	4.77	0.98	3.9	139	18	55	2.07	4.8	13.0	2.7	1.4	121
CU +	2007	A+	Modesto	0	0	0	1	2	0.00	2.00	4.8	0	0	100	2.09	18.0	18.0	1.0	0.0	184

Aggressive college closer with plus velocity and a SL that generates swings and misses. Tall/athletic frame and good arm action provide him with movement and durability. Command can be inconsistent and CU is ineffective which need to improve if he's to close in Majors.

Welker, Duke — SP — Pittsburgh

Thrws: R Age 22
2007 (2) Arkansas

EXP MLB DEBUT: 2009 POTENTIAL: #4 starter **7D**

Year	Lev	Team	W	L	Sv	IP	K	ERA	WHIP	BF/G	OBA	H%	S%	xERA	Ctl	Dom	Cmd	hr/9	BPV
88-94 FB ++++																			
76-79 SL +++																			
71-74 CB ++	2007	A-	State College	2	2	0	30	27	2.38	1.29	17.7	254	32	84	3.51	3.0	8.0	2.7	0.6	91

Tall projectable pitcher with history of injuries (labrum-05 and elbow-07). Overpowers hitters with FB and SL from a repetitive delivery. Uses CB as off-speed pitch, but it can get loose in its rotation. Throws strikes, but needs to pitch more aggressively and not nibble at strike zone.

West, Sean — SP — Florida

Thrws: L Age 22
2005 (1-S) HS (LA)

EXP MLB DEBUT: 2010 POTENTIAL: #3 starter **8E**

Year	Lev	Team	W	L	Sv	IP	K	ERA	WHIP	BF/G	OBA	H%	S%	xERA	Ctl	Dom	Cmd	hr/9	BPV
88-94 FB ++++	2005	Rk	GCL Marlins	2	3	0	38	40	2.36	1.05	16.4	235	31	79	2.52	1.7	9.4	5.7	0.5	171
74-78 CB +++	2005	A-	Jamestown	0	2	0	11	14	5.73	2.00	17.7	354	48	71	7.03	4.1	11.5	2.8	0.8	87
CU +	2006	A-	Greensboro	8	5	0	120	102	3.75	1.29	23.5	253	30	71	3.86	3.0	7.6	2.6	1.0	74
	2007																		

Missed 2007 season with shoulder surgery. Projectable arm and height creates solid downward plane. FB and CB are above average offerings and repeats delivery well for size, which aids in command. Will need to regain feel for CU and prove that his shoulder is sound.

Whelan, Kevin — SP — New York (A)

Thrws: R Age 24
2005 (4) Texas A&M

EXP MLB DEBUT: 2008 POTENTIAL: Setup reliever/closer **8C**

Year	Lev	Team	W	L	Sv	IP	K	ERA	WHIP	BF/G	OBA	H%	S%	xERA	Ctl	Dom	Cmd	hr/9	BPV
88-94 FB ++++	2005	A-	W. Michigan	0	0	11	12	22	0.74	0.50	2.9	105	25	83	0.00	1.5	16.4	11.0	0.0	363
85-87 SL ++++	2005	A-	Oneonta	1	1	4	12	19	2.25	0.67	3.8	56	6	71	0.00	4.5	14.3	3.2	0.8	173
77-82 SP ++++	2006	A+	Lakeland	4	1	27	53	68	2.72	1.17	4.2	181	28	75	1.88	4.9	11.5	2.3	0.2	132
	2007	A+	Tampa	2	0	0	28	28	1.93	0.82	14.6	122	15	81	0.86	3.9	9.0	2.3	0.6	114
	2007	AA	Trenton	4	2	4	54	68	2.99	1.40	7.4	182	27	78	2.64	7.0	11.3	1.6	0.3	110

Moved him to rotation with solid results. Misses bats with a plus SPL and good velocity, and may have as much pitch movement as anyone in the organization. Highly aggressive, but pitches with effort and command is inconsistent. Despite success, he likely returns to bullpen.

Willems, Colton — SP — Washington

Thrws: R Age 19
2006 (1-C) HS (FL)

EXP MLB DEBUT: 2010 POTENTIAL: #2 starter **9E**

Year	Lev	Team	W	L	Sv	IP	K	ERA	WHIP	BF/G	OBA	H%	S%	xERA	Ctl	Dom	Cmd	hr/9	BPV
90-95 FB ++++																			
87-88 SL +++																			
71-76 CB +++	2006	Rk	GCL Nationals	0	1	0	16	8	3.38	1.63	14.2	338	37	80	5.63	1.7	4.5	2.7	0.6	54
78-81 CU +	2007	A-	Vermont	3	2	0	58	31	1.86	1.39	20.4	251	28	87	3.49	4.0	4.8	1.2	0.3	49

Tall/athletic pitcher with plus FB and three breaking pitches he can turn to. Stiff arm action makes it difficult to mask CU and command pitches, which ultimately affects ability to dominate. To his credit, he gets outs when he needs to and represents tons of upside.

Windsor, Jason — SP — Oakland

Thrws: R Age 25
2004 (3) Cal St Fullerton

EXP MLB DEBUT: 2006 POTENTIAL: #4 starter **7C**

Year	Lev	Team	W	L	Sv	IP	K	ERA	WHIP	BF/G	OBA	H%	S%	xERA	Ctl	Dom	Cmd	hr/9	BPV
85-90 FB +++	2005	AA	Midland	3	6	0	56	39	5.77	1.64	22.8	303	35	64	3.51	3.7	6.2	1.7	0.8	43
79-82 SL +++	2006	AA	Midland	4	1	0	33	35	2.99	1.12	21.7	224	30	74	2.63	2.7	9.5	3.5	0.5	124
70-72 CB +++	2006	AAA	Sacramento	13	1	0	118	123	3.73	1.35	24.6	276	36	72	3.89	2.4	9.4	3.8	0.5	121
80-83 CU ++++	2006	MLB	Oakland	0	1	0	13	6	6.82	1.97	15.8	361	38	67	7.66	3.4	4.1	1.2	1.4	-8
	2007	AAA	Sacramento	5	3	0	56	41	5.44	1.64	25.0	297	35	65	4.91	4.0	6.6	1.6	0.5	55

Decline in base skills/velocity attributed to sore shoulder which required an operation in July. Pitches to contact and shows plus command, throwing a plus CU and interchanging all four pitches to keep hitters off-balance. Deceptive with high ¾ delivery and likes to work quickly.

Withrow, Chris — SP — Los Angeles (N)

Thrws: R Age 19
2007 (1) HS (TX)

EXP MLB DEBUT: 2012 POTENTIAL: #2 starter **9E**

Year	Lev	Team	W	L	Sv	IP	K	ERA	WHIP	BF/G	OBA	H%	S%	xERA	Ctl	Dom	Cmd	hr/9	BPV
89-96 FB ++++																			
74-78 CB +++																			
79-81 CU +++	2007	Rk	GCL Dodgers	0	0	0	9	13	5.00	1.00	5.7	165	29	44	1.10	4.0	13.0	3.3	0.0	168

Athletic pitcher with plus velocity, command, and ability to dominate. Advanced for age, pitching like a veteran by mixing comps and pitching to hitters' weaknesses. May not project more velocity, but getting stronger could allow him to maintain it longer.

Wood, Blake — SP — Kansas City

Thrws: R Age 22
2006 (3) Georgia Tech

EXP MLB DEBUT: 2009 POTENTIAL: #5 starter **7C**

Year	Lev	Team	W	L	Sv	IP	K	ERA	WHIP	BF/G	OBA	H%	S%	xERA	Ctl	Dom	Cmd	hr/9	BPV
87-93 FB +++	2006	Rk	Idaho Falls	3	1	0	52	46	4.50	1.25	17.6	254	33	61	3.02	2.6	8.0	3.1	0.2	111
77-80 CB +++	2007	Rk	AZL Royals	0	0	0	9	15	0.00	0.98	8.7	258	45	100	2.15	0.0	14.7		0.0	92
79-81 CU ++	2007	A-	Burlington	2	1	0	35	26	3.07	1.31	20.8	244	28	79	3.59	3.6	6.6	1.9	0.8	62
	2007	A+	Wilmington	0	1	0	9	11	4.89	1.30	19.0	258	35	64	3.93	2.9	10.8	3.7	1.0	116

Tall/projectable pitcher missed part of 2007 with surgery to correct herniated disc. Overhauled mechanics, eliminating motion across body which left pitches elevated. Works primarily with FB and CB and will throw strikes, but needs better command within strike zone.

PITCHERS

Wood,Travis — SP — Cincinnati

EXP MLB DEBUT: 2009 | POTENTIAL: #3 starter/setup reliever | 8C

Thrws L Age 21
2005 (2) HS (AK)

Velo	Pitch	Grade
87-92	FB	++++
72-75	CB	++
78-80	CU	++++

Year	Lev	Team	W	L	Sv	IP	K	ERA	WHIP	BF/G	OBA	H%	S%	xERA	Ctl	Dom	Cmd	hr/9	BPV
2005	Rk	GCL Reds	0	0	0	24	45	0.75	0.83	11.0	161	36	90	0.60	2.6	16.9	6.4	0.0	259
2005	Rk	Billings	2	0	0	24	22	1.86	1.16	16.0	180	24	82	1.71	4.8	8.2	1.7	0.0	104
2006	A-	Dayton	10	5	0	140	133	3.54	1.16	20.7	213	26	72	2.95	3.6	8.6	2.4	0.9	87
2007	A+	Sarasota	3	2	0	46	54	4.88	1.65	17.2	274	36	73	5.20	5.3	10.5	2.0	1.2	70

Athletic pitcher with repeatable delivery and plus CU. FB is good enough to keep hitters honest and his quick arm provides enough movement for him to miss bats. CB needs a tighter rotation and does pitch with effort which was the source of his sore shoulder.

Worrell,Mark — RP — St. Louis

EXP MLB DEBUT: 2008 | POTENTIAL: Setup reliever | 6B

Thrws R Age 26
2004 (12) Florida Int.

Velo	Pitch	Grade
85-90	FB	+++
80-82	SL	+++
77-79	CU	+++

Year	Lev	Team	W	L	Sv	IP	K	ERA	WHIP	BF/G	OBA	H%	S%	xERA	Ctl	Dom	Cmd	hr/9	BPV
2004	A-	Peoria	0	2	6	14	20	4.44	1.06	4.6	184	26	62	2.64	3.8	12.7	3.3	1.3	126
2004	Rk	Johnson City	1	0	6	22	35	1.22	0.86	4.8	161	29	89	1.08	2.9	14.3	5.0	0.4	201
2005	A+	Palm Beach	2	3	35	56	53	2.25	1.02	4.1	194	23	84	2.42	3.1	8.5	2.8	1.0	97
2006	AA	Springfield	3	7	27	61	75	4.42	1.16	4.3	228	30	66	3.51	2.9	11.0	3.8	1.3	115
2007	AAA	Memphis	3	2	4	67	66	3.09	1.24	5.4	235	30	78	3.32	3.4	8.9	2.6	0.8	92

Successful reliever with an unorthodox delivery which sees him stepping towards first base dugout and will purposely change arm slots. Stuff in underwhelming on an individual basis, but commands plate, keeps ball low, and is able to generate strikeouts.

Wright,Chase — SP — New York (A)

EXP MLB DEBUT: 2007 | POTENTIAL: Middle reliever | 6A

Thrws R Age 25
2000 (2) Wake Forest

Velo	Pitch	Grade
85-90	FB	+++
72-78	CB	++
78-81	CU	+++

Year	Lev	Team	W	L	Sv	IP	K	ERA	WHIP	BF/G	OBA	H%	S%	xERA	Ctl	Dom	Cmd	hr/9	BPV
2005	A-	Charleston	10	4	0	144	110	3.75	1.37	24.1	240	28	73	3.56	4.3	6.9	1.6	0.6	63
2006	A+	Tampa	13	3	0	120	100	1.80	1.16	12.9	221	28	83	2.26	3.2	7.5	2.3	0.1	102
2007	AA	Trenton	5	2	0	59	41	3.65	1.28	24.3	248	27	76	4.01	3.2	6.2	2.0	1.2	47
2007	AAA	Scranton/WB	8	3	1	85	40	4.02	1.42	24.1	248	26	73	3.93	4.4	4.2	1.0	0.7	29
2007	MLB	New York (A)	2	0	0	10	8	7.20	1.80	15.4	299	26	77	9.11	5.4	7.2	1.3	4.5	-69

Keeps hitters off-balanced with deceptive ¾ delivery that features hesitation and ability to change speeds. Mixes pitches well, commands plate, and keeps ball low, while being very stingy with long ball. FB tends to be straight and performs better when he pitches backwards.

Wright,Steven — SP — Cleveland

EXP MLB DEBUT: 2009 | POTENTIAL: Setup reliever | 7D

Thrws R Age 23
2006 (2) Hawaii

Velo	Pitch	Grade
87-91	FB	+++
80-83	SL	++++
74-76	CB	++
	CU	+

Year	Lev	Team	W	L	Sv	IP	K	ERA	WHIP	BF/G	OBA	H%	S%	xERA	Ctl	Dom	Cmd	hr/9	BPV
2007	A-	Lake County	4	7	0	66	75	4.63	1.15	18.7	247	32	63	3.63	2.0	10.2	5.0	1.2	135
2007	A+	Kinston	3	2	0	48	39	7.13	1.79	17.0	321	39	58	5.74	4.1	7.3	1.8	0.6	55

Possesses plus SL and sinking action to FB that are tough on RH batters and nets him strikeouts. Pitches aggressively, which can get him in trouble, as he was victimized by the long ball. With a poor CU and tendency to short-arm ball, he may have more value as a reliever.

Yabuta,Yasuhiko — RP — Kansas City

EXP MLB DEBUT: 2008 | POTENTIAL: Setup reliever | 7B

Thrws R Age 35
2007 FA (Japan)

Velo	Pitch	Grade
88-92	FB	+++
	SL	++
	SP	++++
	CU	+++

Year	Lev	Team	W	L	Sv	IP	K	ERA	WHIP	BF/G	OBA	H%	S%	xERA	Ctl	Dom	Cmd	hr/9	BPV
2002	Int	Chiba Lotte	1	2	0	11	8	8.92	1.80	17.1	338	34	56	8.58	3.2	6.5	2.0	3.2	-29
2003	Int	Chiba Lotte	5	6	0	68	44	5.94	1.48	17.3	278	29	63	5.27	3.6	5.8	1.6	1.6	21
2004	Int	Chiba Lotte	3	4	2	77	71	2.80	1.25	4.7	222	28	78	2.86	4.0	8.3	2.1	0.5	90
2005	Int	Chiba Lotte	7	4	2	55	54	3.10	1.00	4.1	212	26	75	2.75	2.1	8.8	4.2	1.1	118
2006	Int	Chiba Lotte	4	2	1	55	48	2.62	1.25	4.8	217	27	80	2.85	4.3	7.9	1.8	0.5	83

Athletic reliever who relies on changing speeds, pinpoint command, and keeping hitters off-balance with deception. FB possesses average movement, but repeats delivery well for both CU and SPL. Strikeout rate may not translate to Majors, but supports a strong G/F ratio.

Yates,Kyle — SP — Toronto

EXP MLB DEBUT: 2007 | POTENTIAL: Setup reliever | 7C

Thrws R Age 25
2004 (13) Texas

Velo	Pitch	Grade
85-89	FB	++
78-80	CB	++++
77-81	CU	+++

Year	Lev	Team	W	L	Sv	IP	K	ERA	WHIP	BF/G	OBA	H%	S%	xERA	Ctl	Dom	Cmd	hr/9	BPV
2005	A-	Lansing	4	3	0	81	81	4.44	1.25	23.6	264	34	64	3.59	2.1	9.0	4.3	0.7	126
2005	A+	Dunedin	7	3	0	75	67	1.92	1.17	21.4	246	31	86	2.99	2.3	8.0	3.5	0.5	114
2006	A+	Dunedin	2	0	0	14	13	0.64	0.57	11.9	168	23	88	0.10	0.0	8.4		0.0	71
2006	AA	New Hamp.	6	9	1	127	102	3.75	1.23	18.4	248	30	71	3.38	2.7	7.2	2.7	0.7	84
2007	AA	New Hamp.	9	9	0	151	98	4.53	1.50	24.2	302	33	74	5.43	2.6	5.8	2.3	1.3	38

Possesses outstanding CB and changes speeds well, but doesn't miss a lot of bats due to subpar velocity. Command regressed slightly, but did a better job of not overusing CB. Pitches with effort and struggles multiple times through lineup, so may be better suited for relief work.

Zagurski,Michael — RP — Philadelphia

EXP MLB DEBUT: 2007 | POTENTIAL: Situational reliever | 6A

Thrws L Age 25
2005 (12) Kansas

Velo	Pitch	Grade
88-94	FB	++++
82-86	SL	+
81-83	CU	+++

Year	Lev	Team	W	L	Sv	IP	K	ERA	WHIP	BF/G	OBA	H%	S%	xERA	Ctl	Dom	Cmd	hr/9	BPV
2006	A-	Lakewood	4	4	1	56	75	3.51	1.21	5.4	225	36	84	5.66	3.5	12.0	3.4	3.5	48
2007	A+	Clearwater	0	0	5	16	30	1.10	0.62	4.6	117	29	70	0.67	2.2	16.8	7.5	1.1	256
2007	AA	Reading	0	0	0	7	8	1.29	0.57	4.0	92	23	68	0.53	2.6	10.3	4.0	1.3	144
2007	AAA	Ottawa	0	0	0	9	11	2.00	1.44	5.5	216	30	82	4.71	6.0	11.0	1.8	2.0	56
2007	MLB	Philadelphia	1	0	0	21	21	5.91	1.71	3.8	296	30	69	10.20	4.7	9.0	1.9	6.0	-89

Stocky reliever with overpowering FB from a low ¾ slot and ability to change speeds. Improved velocity with move to bullpen and works exclusively from stretch. SL is only effective to LH batters. Command is usually consistent and can be more than a situational reliever.

Zarate,Mauro — RP — San Diego

EXP MLB DEBUT: 2007 | POTENTIAL: Setup reliever | 6B

Thrws R Age 25
2001 FA (Venezuela)

Velo	Pitch	Grade
89-94	FB	++++
80-83	SL	+++
	CU	+

Year	Lev	Team	W	L	Sv	IP	K	ERA	WHIP	BF/G	OBA	H%	S%	xERA	Ctl	Dom	Cmd	hr/9	BPV
2006	A-	Greensboro	3	5	7	79	80	3.19	1.33	6.2	252	25	80	6.01	3.4	9.1	2.7	3.2	64
2007	A+	Jupiter	2	2	1	26	20	2.42	1.15	7.4	206	28	82	4.29	3.8	6.9	1.8	2.4	68
2007	AA	Carolina	0	1	1	25	32	1.40	0.91	5.5	165	30	74	2.23	3.2	11.4	3.6	1.4	122
2007	AAA	Albuqurque	2	0	0	34	23	2.38	1.21	5.5	232	32	84	4.71	3.2	6.1	1.9	2.4	66
2007	MLB	Florida	0	0	0	5	3	5.40	2.40	6.5	438	31	68	19.22	1.8	5.4	3.0	10.8	-161

Medium-framed reliever whose sinker/SL combination and deceptive low ¾ slot is devastating to RH batters. Induces tons of groundballs which lowers oppBA, and command is a strength. Ineffective CU will pigeon-hole him as a match-up reliever unless he improves pitch.

Ziegler,Brad — SP — Oakland

EXP MLB DEBUT: 2008 | POTENTIAL: Setup reliever | 6B

Thrws R Age 28
2003 (20) SW Missouri St

Velo	Pitch	Grade
85-90	FB	+++
75-79	SL	+++
73-78	CU	++

Year	Lev	Team	W	L	Sv	IP	K	ERA	WHIP	BF/G	OBA	H%	S%	xERA	Ctl	Dom	Cmd	hr/9	BPV
2005	A+	Stockton	9	7	0	141	144	4.66	1.32	24.3	295	38	65	4.37	1.3	9.2	7.2	0.8	178
2006	AA	Midland	9	6	0	141	88	3.44	1.33	25.5	275	30	78	4.39	2.4	5.6	2.4	1.1	51
2006	AAA	Sacramento	0	1	0	21	11	6.00	1.76	24.1	351	38	68	6.88	2.1	4.7	2.2	1.3	21
2007	AA	Midland	4	0	1	23	18	1.16	0.99	5.9	225	29	87	1.83	1.6	7.0	4.5	0.0	146
2007	AAA	Sacramento	8	3	1	54	44	2.99	1.11	6.1	231	30	70	2.20	2.3	7.3	3.1	0.0	119

Tall/thin pitcher resurrected career by dropping arm slot to low ¾ and pounding strike zone with his sinker/SL combo. Keeps ball down effectively, gets strikeouts, and commands both sides of plate. Improvement in new CU could expand role beyond a match-up reliever.

Zimmerman,Jordan — SP — Washington

EXP MLB DEBUT: 2009 | POTENTIAL: #3 starter | 9D

Thrws R Age 22
2007 (2) Wisc-Stevens Pt

Velo	Pitch	Grade
88-93	FB	++++
78-81	SL	+++
72-74	CU	++
79-82		+++

Year	Lev	Team	W	L	Sv	IP	K	ERA	WHIP	BF/G	OBA	H%	S%	xERA	Ctl	Dom	Cmd	hr/9	BPV
2007	A-	Vermont	5	2	0	53	71	2.38	1.19	16.0	228	29	79	2.88	3.1	12.1	3.9	0.3	114

Tall/projectable pitcher generates plus FB movement with quick arm action and leverage. Pitches aggressively with FB showing impressive command and strikeout ability. CB isn't better than SL at moment, but may be more conducive to arm slot and velocity differential.

Zincola,Zech — RP — Washington

EXP MLB DEBUT: 2009 | POTENTIAL: Setup reliever | 8D

Thrws R Age 23
2006 (6) Arizona St

Velo	Pitch	Grade
89-94	FB	++++
82-85	SL	++
	CU	++

Year	Lev	Team	W	L	Sv	IP	K	ERA	WHIP	BF/G	OBA	H%	S%	xERA	Ctl	Dom	Cmd	hr/9	BPV
2006	A-	Vermont	0	0	4	9	10	0.00	0.78	4.0	191	28	100	0.86	1.0	10.0	10.0	0.0	287
2006	A+	Potomac	3	0	3	13	13	2.05	1.06	5.7	228	31	79	2.03	2.0	8.9	4.3	0.0	154
2006	AA	Harrisburg	1	1	5	10	8	2.70	2.20	5.0	281	35	86	5.62	9.9	7.2	0.7	0.0	57
2007	AA	Harrisburg	0	4	6	57	45	5.46	1.56	6.0	247	33	81	8.72	5.7	7.1	1.3	0.5	46

Aggressive reliever struggled through season with command, which left him behind in the count and made him hittable. Smooth arm action provides sinking movement, but hasn't found consistency with comps. Needs to repeat delivery, which could alleviate problems.

MAJOR LEAGUE EQUIVALENTS

In his 1985 *Baseball Abstract*, Bill James introduced the concept of major league equivalencies. His assertion was that, with the proper adjustments, a minor leaguer's statistics could be converted to an equivalent major league level performance with a great deal of accuracy.

Because of wide variations in the level of play among different minor leagues, it is difficult to get a true reading on a player's potential. For instance, a .300 AVG achieved in the high-offense Pacific Coast League is not nearly as much of an accomplishment as a similar level in the Eastern League. MLEs normalize these types of variances, for all statistical categories.

The actual MLEs are not projections. They represent how a player's previous performance might look at the major league level. However, that MLE stat line can be used in forecasting future performance in just the same way as a major league stat line would.

The model we use contains a few minor variations to James' version and updates all of the minor league and ballpark factors. In addition, we have designed a module to convert pitching statistics, which is something James did not do.

Another of the enhancements we made is to include an adjustment for each player's age and relative level reached at that age. This serves to truly separate the prospects from the suspects. In other words, it might seem that Adam Boeve's 21 HR, .271 season looks worthy of a full-time shot in the majors, but a veteran 27-year-old facing young Double-A pitching is bound to put up good numbers. His MLE of 14 HRs, .209 shows the appropriate — albeit radical — adjustment facing potential big league pitchers, and diffuses any thought of him being able to help a major league club in any more than a platoon or reserve role.

Do MLEs really work?

Used correctly, MLEs are excellent indicators of potential. But, just like we cannot take traditional MLB stats at face value, the same goes for MLEs. The underlying measures of base skill — batting eye ratios, pitching command ratios, etc. — are far more accurate in evaluating future talent than raw home runs, batting averages or ERAs.

The charts here provide up to *five year's worth of data* for the players covered in the main section of the book. This provides the perspective of identifying players improving their skills, or struggling, as they rise through more difficult levels of competition.

Here are some things to look for as you scan these charts:

Target players who...

- spend full seasons at progressively higher levels. Those promoted more rapidly may reach the Majors sooner, but full seasons provide a better foundation for success.
- had consistent playing time from one year to the next
- maintained or improved their skills as they were promoted

Raise the warning flag for players who...

- were stuck at the same level for multiple years, or regressed
- displayed marked changes in playing time each year
- showed large drops in BPIs from one year to the next

Also keep an eye on each player's age. While minor leaguers over 26 have officially lost their "prospect" status, there are still some who will make it to the majors. Don't discount them completely or you might end up missing out on a player like Jack Cust.

Each player's actual AB and IP totals are used as the base for the conversion. However, it is more useful to compare performances using common levels, so rely on the ratios and sabermetric gauges. Complete explanations of these formulas appear in the glossary.

The MLE conversions work well at both the Triple-A and Double-A levels, but not at all at Single-A or below. As such, the only players included in this section are those who have accumulated at least 100 AB or 30 IP at the Double-A or Triple-A level in any of the past five seasons.

BATTER	YR	Age	Pos	Lev	Tm	AB	R	H	D	T	HR	RBI	BB	K	SB	CS	BA	OB	Slg	OPS	bb%	Ct%	Eye	PX	SX	RC/G	BPV
Anderson,Bryan	07	21	2	aa	STL	389	44	107	14	1	5	45	28	59	0	1	275	325	356	681	7%	85%	0.48	54	39	4.24	24
Anderson,Josh	05	23	8	aa	HOU	524	61	140	16	9	1	23	25	75	46	19	267	300	335	635	5%	86%	0.34	44	171	3.44	14
	06	24	8	aa	HOU	561	67	152	22	4	3	41	22	65	35	14	271	298	339	637	4%	88%	0.33	48	128	3.53	17
Andino,Robert	05	21	6	aa	FLA	516	56	127	28	0	4	42	34	103	19	8	246	293	324	616	6%	80%	0.33	60	86	3.32	13
	06	22	6	aaa	FLA	498	57	116	16	5	6	38	28	79	11	14	232	273	323	596	5%	84%	0.36	57	109	2.76	8
	07	23	6	aa	FLA	598	70	146	22	10	11	42	35	121	17	15	245	287	368	655	6%	80%	0.29	75	143	3.44	18
Arias,Joaquin	05	21	6	aa	TEX	499	52	147	22	6	5	45	14	36	16	12	295	314	393	707	3%	93%	0.39	65	114	4.23	33
	06	22	6	aaa	TEX	493	56	139	15	12	4	48	19	56	26	11	281	308	383	691	4%	89%	0.34	60	178	4.17	25
Aubrey,Michael	04	22	3	aa	CLE	134	11	31	7	0	4	18	12	16	0	0	231	295	373	668	8%	88%	0.75	92	13	3.87	30
	05	23	3	aa	CLE	106	15	26	5	1	3	16	6	16	1	0	247	286	393	680	5%	84%	0.35	91	97	4.00	27
	07	25	30	aa	CLE	207	17	42	10	0	5	27	9	34	0	0	204	238	330	568	4%	83%	0.26	83	22	2.60	7
Aviles,Mike	05	25	6	aa	KC	521	56	119	28	5	9	57	22	49	8	8	228	259	348	607	4%	91%	0.44	80	100	2.91	18
	06	26	6	aaa	KC	469	46	115	21	3	6	42	25	41	12	5	245	283	340	623	5%	91%	0.60	64	97	3.33	20
	07	27	654	aa	KC	538	58	129	23	4	11	57	23	56	3	5	239	270	362	632	4%	90%	0.40	78	79	3.25	20
Balentien,Wladimir	06	22	8	aa	SEA	444	72	96	22	1	21	77	69	139	13	7	216	322	412	734	13%	69%	0.50	119	91	4.60	31
	07	23	8	aa	SEA	477	65	122	22	2	19	71	48	100	13	5	256	324	433	757	9%	79%	0.48	108	93	5.03	39
Barton,Brian	06	24	8	aa	CLE	151	29	47	5	0	5	23	11	26	13	5	308	357	434	791	7%	83%	0.43	77	112	5.77	43
Barton,Daric	05	20	3	aa	OAK	212	32	62	19	1	4	30	28	23	1	1	292	376	451	826	12%	89%	1.24	114	62	6.48	69
	06	21	3	aaa	OAK	147	22	36	7	2	2	19	28	18	1	0	247	366	367	732	16%	88%	1.51	76	103	5.19	44
	07	22	3	aa	OAK	516	71	139	37	3	7	59	65	56	3	5	269	351	393	745	11%	89%	1.16	90	65	5.06	50
Bernadina,Rogearvin	07	23	8	a/a	WAS	413	56	96	16	2	5	33	40	81	35	16	232	300	317	617	9%	80%	0.49	57	129	3.24	11
Bixler,Brian	06	24	6	aa	PIT	226	32	64	13	1	3	16	14	53	6	2	283	324	386	710	6%	77%	0.26	73	99	4.61	30
	07	25	6	aa	PIT	475	62	116	22	7	4	41	42	115	23	5	244	305	342	647	8%	76%	0.36	65	161	3.84	16
Blanco,Gregor	05	22	8	aa	ATL	401	56	92	10	8	5	32	64	108	24	13	229	335	332	667	14%	73%	0.59	59	176	3.95	13
	06	23	8	a/a	ATL	520	84	146	27	3	0	27	93	107	30	16	281	390	344	734	15%	79%	0.87	51	110	5.20	32
	07	24	8	aaa	ATL	464	73	124	17	4	3	31	56	78	21	20	267	346	341	687	11%	83%	0.72	50	116	4.00	24
Boeve,Adam	05	25	8	aa	PIT	158	17	38	8	1	4	16	15	43	4	2	239	306	370	677	9%	73%	0.35	86	86	3.98	22
	06	26	8	a/a	PIT	454	50	115	25	2	7	52	39	119	23	6	254	312	365	677	8%	74%	0.33	77	108	4.16	23
	07	27	8	aa	PIT	413	48	86	12	2	14	42	44	124	17	7	209	285	350	635	10%	70%	0.35	83	101	3.37	11
Boggs,Brandon	07	25	8	aa	TEX	354	55	85	19	3	16	45	56	89	9	4	239	343	445	788	14%	75%	0.63	125	107	5.50	44
Bonifacio,Emilio	07	22	46	aa	ARI	551	70	147	20	4	2	34	32	86	34	15	267	307	328	636	5%	84%	0.37	44	129	3.54	15
Bowker,John	07	24	8	aa	SF	522	63	139	31	5	16	71	32	89	2	8	266	308	437	745	6%	83%	0.36	109	71	4.56	41
Brantley,Michael	07	20	8	aa	MIL	187	25	45	6	1	0	19	27	22	15	3	241	338	286	624	13%	88%	1.25	35	119	3.88	20
Brignac,Reid	06	21	6	aa	TAM	110	20	35	6	2	3	18	7	31	3	0	315	358	496	854	6%	71%	0.23	112	172	7.04	56
	07	22	6	aa	TAM	527	77	124	27	4	15	69	48	82	13	6	235	299	387	686	8%	84%	0.59	96	115	4.02	30
Bruce,Jay	07	20	8	a/a	CIN	253	36	81	20	2	15	39	22	54	3	3	322	376	600	976	8%	79%	0.41	171	83	8.45	86
Buscher,Brian	05	24	5	aa	SF	215	15	43	7	1	1	18	16	32	4	3	199	255	252	507	7%	85%	0.51	38	70	2.13	-8
	06	25	5	aa	SF	467	40	109	21	3	6	45	36	83	5	4	233	288	330	618	7%	82%	0.43	65	69	3.28	13
	07	26	50	a/a	MIN	379	47	98	23	1	11	48	33	42	3	2	259	319	408	727	8%	89%	0.79	99	58	4.67	43
Cannon,Chip	05	24	3	aa	TOR	166	15	42	14	1	7	21	10	58	2	0	251	293	467	760	6%	65%	0.17	141	73	4.87	45
	06	25	3	aa	TOR	475	70	111	25	1	26	62	46	160	0	2	234	301	452	753	9%	66%	0.29	131	44	4.70	38
	07	26	3	aa	TOR	394	42	79	20	1	14	40	40	143	1	0	201	274	359	633	9%	64%	0.28	100	50	3.37	14
Carroll,Brett	06	24	8	aa	FLA	251	28	52	13	3	8	29	18	68	4	1	208	261	375	636	7%	73%	0.26	104	119	3.32	17
	07	25	8	aa	FLA	417	56	110	29	5	17	67	26	84	0	7	264	307	481	788	6%	80%	0.30	136	78	4.92	50
Casto,Kory	06	25	5	aa	WAS	489	72	114	21	5	16	68	67	102	5	6	233	326	394	720	12%	79%	0.66	98	94	4.50	31
	07	26	58	aaa	WAS	408	50	91	18	2	9	50	48	98	4	4	223	304	342	646	10%	76%	0.48	77	74	3.62	16
Chavez,Angel	04	23	6	aa	SF	308	19	55	7	2	0	18	20	48	5	4	180	230	214	445	6%	84%	0.42	25	79	1.60	-21
	05	24	6	aaa	SF	334	32	79	15	2	7	45	12	41	4	1	237	263	356	619	3%	88%	0.29	77	84	3.22	17
	06	25	5	a/a	PHI	464	55	114	30	2	10	54	26	85	13	3	246	285	387	672	5%	82%	0.30	96	106	3.90	28
	07	26	546	aaa	NYY	430	55	114	23	1	10	58	23	76	5	3	266	304	393	696	5%	82%	0.31	85	74	4.22	30
Clement,Jeff	06	23	2	aaa	SEA	304	26	72	15	1	5	36	20	55	0	2	237	284	342	626	6%	82%	0.36	72	36	3.31	16
	07	24	20	aa	SEA	455	62	107	31	2	16	66	52	85	0	0	236	315	420	734	10%	81%	0.61	120	47	4.72	40
Clevlen,Brent	06	23	8	aa	DET	395	44	86	15	0	10	43	44	128	6	2	218	296	332	628	10%	68%	0.34	73	63	3.48	9
	07	24	8	aaa	DET	322	30	67	13	5	6	33	36	100	4	4	208	288	335	623	10%	69%	0.36	78	120	3.25	9
Colvin,Tyler	07	22	8	aa	CHC	247	29	67	10	2	8	26	4	46	6	1	271	283	425	708	2%	81%	0.09	93	112	4.29	31
Conrad,Brooks	04	25	4	aa	HOU	480	65	121	32	5	10	64	47	87	6	8	251	318	404	721	9%	82%	0.53	102	96	4.40	37
	05	26	4	a/a	HOU	491	77	110	24	3	17	53	52	103	16	3	224	299	389	688	10%	79%	0.51	102	125	4.16	27
	06	27	4	aaa	HOU	532	81	126	34	13	19	76	43	114	12	7	237	294	458	751	7%	78%	0.37	134	185	4.54	42
	07	28	4	aa	HOU	533	58	87	27	2	16	48	42	146	8	2	164	225	308	533	7%	73%	0.29	93	97	2.26	-1
Crabbe,Callix	05	23	4	aa	MIL	385	33	81	14	3	1	26	51	53	14	7	210	303	270	573	12%	86%	0.96	43	98	2.93	7
	06	24	4	aa	MIL	472	54	117	17	2	5	43	68	63	30	14	249	343	325	668	13%	87%	1.08	52	99	4.11	26
	07	25	48	aaa	MIL	457	74	122	22	7	8	33	62	64	15	16	267	355	398	753	12%	86%	0.97	83	131	4.84	43
Crowe,Trevor	06	23	8	aa	CLE	154	18	33	7	1	1	12	19	22	15	6	214	301	292	593	11%	86%	0.86	56	127	3.08	12
	07	24	8	aa	CLE	518	74	119	25	2	4	43	55	66	24	10	230	305	309	614	10%	87%	0.84	58	113	3.36	17
Cumberland,Shaun	07	23	8	aa	CIN	467	36	108	20	1	7	42	29	79	3	10	231	276	322	598	6%	83%	0.37	63	38	2.82	10
Cunningham,Aaron	07	21	8	aa	ARI	118	21	32	8	3	5	17	10	22	1	3	271	328	517	845	8%	81%	0.45	148	169	5.60	61
Curtis,Colin	07	23	8	aa	NYY	240	32	57	11	1	3	15	17	48	1	1	238	288	329	617	7%	80%	0.35	64	73	3.30	12
Delaney,Jason	07	25	38	aa	PIT	223	20	52	10	0	6	29	29	45	0	0	234	324	354	677	12%	80%	0.65	77	14	4.18	23
Desmond,Ian	06	21	6	aa	WAS	121	7	20	4	1	0	3	4	32	4	1	165	192	215	407	3%	74%	0.13	37	114	1.34	-27
Duncan,Eric	05	21	5	aa	NYY	448	55	101	14	2	18	56	51	114	8	3	225	305	384	689	10%	74%	0.45	93	86	4.13	22
	06	22	5	a/a	NYY	316	39	74	18	2	11	35	39	57	0	1	233	317	402	719	11%	82%	0.68	107	54	4.50	35
	07	23	30	aaa	NYY	411	44	98	25	1	11	59	45	71	2	2	238	313	381	694	10%	83%	0.63	96	49	4.22	31
Duncan,Shelley	05	26	3	aa	NYY	533	64	101	21	1	26	69	41	143	3	2	189	247	379	626	7%	73%	0.29	112	61	3.07	15
	06	27	8	a/a	NYY	394	39	81	20	0	17	53	30	97	3	1	205	262	382	644	7%	75%	0.32	110	46	3.38	20
	07	28	8	aaa	NYY	336	49	87	16	1	22	67	37	82	2	2	260	334	512	846	10%	76%	0.46	147	53	6.12	56
Duran,German	07	23	4	aa	TEX	480	67	132	30	4	19	69	28	65	9	2	275	315	475	790	6%	86%	0.43	125	109	5.44	52
Ellsbury,Jacoby	06	23	8	aa	BOS	198	25	57	11	2	3	16	21	23	14	9	289	358	407	765	10%	89%	0.94	79	119	5.06	48
	07	24	8	a/a	BOS	436	69	131	25	5	2	35	32	48	35	8	300	348	394	742	7%	89%	0.66	68	156	5.36	41
Escobar,Alcides	07	21	6	aa	MIL	226	24	62	5	3	1	25	11	31	3	3	274	306	339	646	4%	86%	0.33	40	108	3.62	15

BATTER	YR	Age	Pos	Lev	Tm	AB	R	H	D	T	HR	RBI	BB	K	SB	CS	BA	OB	Slg	OPS	bb%	Ct%	Eye	PX	SX	RC/G	BPV
Evans,Terry	06	25	8	aa	STL	263	42	66	11	1	11	29	14	58	10	9	249	288	430	718	5%	78%	0.25	109	112	3.89	33
	07	26	8	aa	LAA	475	58	126	34	3	12	61	21	120	20	9	265	296	423	718	4%	75%	0.17	107	117	4.28	36
Falu,Irving	07	24	64	aa	KC	476	37	102	11	5	1	23	29	38	12	10	214	258	263	521	6%	92%	0.75	33	101	2.21	-0
Fiorentino,Jeff	06	23	8	aa	BAL	385	59	99	13	0	13	58	51	56	9	3	257	345	388	733	12%	86%	0.92	80	74	4.99	37
	07	24	8	aa	BAL	436	54	106	15	2	12	52	36	76	7	5	244	302	373	674	8%	83%	0.48	79	80	3.90	23
Francisco,Ben	04	23	8	aa	CLE	497	60	113	27	2	12	60	42	77	18	6	227	288	362	650	8%	85%	0.55	89	105	3.62	23
	05	24	8	a/a	CLE	330	39	91	18	4	5	39	21	51	12	5	276	319	400	719	6%	85%	0.41	82	127	4.58	34
	06	25	8	aaa	CLE	515	76	134	32	3	14	56	44	70	24	5	260	318	416	734	8%	86%	0.63	102	125	4.86	41
	07	26	8	aaa	CLE	377	51	109	27	1	10	44	33	60	19	9	289	346	444	789	8%	84%	0.55	106	97	5.53	51
Gaetti,Joe	06	25	8	aa	COL	392	49	105	21	4	13	46	28	75	4	2	267	315	441	756	7%	81%	0.37	108	96	4.98	41
	07	26	8	aa	COL	421	48	93	22	4	15	45	33	121	4	5	220	277	398	675	7%	71%	0.27	109	88	3.61	24
Gardner,Brett	06	23	8	aa	NYY	217	39	55	4	2	0	13	24	40	26	5	255	330	291	620	10%	81%	0.60	24	166	3.93	7
	07	24	8	a/a	NYY	384	75	100	16	6	1	24	49	75	36	7	260	343	341	684	11%	80%	0.64	55	189	4.66	22
Giarratano,Tony	05	23	6	aa	DET	346	33	82	18	3	2	26	26	59	10	6	237	290	324	614	7%	83%	0.44	63	104	3.21	14
	06	24	6	aa	DET	269	32	72	16	6	0	17	20	43	15	4	267	318	371	690	7%	84%	0.47	73	177	4.36	29
Gil,Jerry	04	22	6	aaa	ARI	421	38	110	30	7	8	42	9	61	8	1	262	278	429	707	2%	86%	0.16	110	141	4.23	36
	05	23	6	aa	ARI	199	22	47	7	3	8	23	7	40	8	8	236	262	422	684	3%	80%	0.18	107	143	3.20	26
	06	24	6	a/a	ARI	493	64	120	28	5	24	74	15	103	6	7	243	266	467	732	3%	79%	0.15	135	109	4.01	40
Gold,Nate	06	26	3	aa	TEX	452	54	110	23	1	28	76	40	80	3	3	243	304	481	785	8%	82%	0.50	141	43	5.02	49
	07	27	3	aa	TEX	469	52	107	20	1	20	73	28	104	0	0	228	272	402	674	6%	78%	0.27	105	33	3.75	25
Gonzalez,Alberto	06	23	6	a/a	ARI	449	58	122	20	3	5	43	33	35	4	1	272	322	363	685	7%	92%	0.94	63	87	4.31	35
	07	24	6	a/a	NYY	493	58	120	28	8	1	48	31	63	12	6	244	289	338	627	6%	87%	0.49	67	139	3.38	19
Gonzalez,Carlos	07	22	8	aa	ARI	500	60	136	37	3	16	71	32	89	8	6	272	316	454	770	6%	82%	0.36	120	85	5.03	47
Gorneault,Nick	03	24	8	aa	LAA	110	16	33	6	3	2	16	7	22	2	0	302	342	458	800	6%	80%	0.30	96	171	6.03	46
	04	25	8	a/a	LAA	515	69	120	25	2	14	63	33	111	5	6	232	279	371	650	6%	79%	0.30	89	79	3.45	20
	05	26	8	aaa	LAA	484	74	116	21	6	17	76	39	89	5	8	240	297	417	714	7%	82%	0.44	106	111	4.11	32
	06	27	8	aaa	LAA	407	49	96	21	5	10	58	28	87	5	5	236	284	387	672	6%	79%	0.32	96	109	3.69	24
	07	28	8	aa	LAA	471	59	92	18	1	13	42	41	123	12	7	195	259	318	577	8%	74%	0.33	77	92	2.70	3
Guzman,Freddy	03	23	8	a/a	SD	187	27	45	4	1	1	10	22	31	36	8	241	321	289	609	11%	83%	0.71	32	154	3.76	8
	04	24	8	a/a	SD	402	59	105	15	5	2	22	39	63	56	11	261	327	338	665	9%	84%	0.62	52	177	4.38	21
	06	26	8	aaa	TEX	376	47	96	15	4	3	22	39	42	33	14	255	325	340	664	9%	89%	0.91	56	139	3.91	27
	07	27	8	aa	TEX	535	68	117	18	6	3	25	45	83	42	14	220	280	296	576	8%	85%	0.55	50	158	2.91	5
Guzman,Javier	05	21	6	aa	PIT	260	21	56	9	1	2	19	8	34	6	6	215	239	281	520	3%	87%	0.24	46	81	2.06	-5
	06	22	6	aa	PIT	485	52	125	23	4	6	37	23	58	11	9	258	291	359	650	5%	88%	0.40	68	99	3.51	22
	07	23	6	aa	PIT	171	16	49	13	0	2	20	4	18	6	0	284	300	391	691	2%	90%	0.22	83	78	4.42	33
Guzman,Jesus	05	21	5	aa	SEA	453	54	105	16	6	8	47	43	95	5	12	232	298	347	645	9%	79%	0.45	70	103	3.32	15
	06	22	5	aa	SEA	408	54	98	17	2	9	52	45	74	7	3	240	316	358	674	10%	82%	0.61	75	89	4.06	23
Guzman,Joel	04	20	6	aa	LA	182	25	51	11	2	9	35	13	37	1	2	278	327	508	835	7%	80%	0.35	139	95	5.81	57
	05	21	6	aa	LA	439	54	112	26	1	14	63	34	99	6	4	256	309	414	723	7%	77%	0.34	103	71	4.48	35
	06	22	5	aaa	TAM	405	44	107	20	2	12	56	26	70	8	7	263	309	413	721	6%	83%	0.38	94	79	4.37	34
	07	23	50	aaa	TAM	414	44	100	17	2	16	64	23	108	9	2	241	281	406	687	5%	74%	0.21	99	96	3.98	26
Haerther,Cody	05	22	8	aa	STL	208	22	53	9	1	7	27	7	33	0	1	255	279	409	688	3%	84%	0.21	95	50	3.89	28
	06	23	8	aa	STL	412	45	100	25	2	9	42	29	49	2	5	243	292	377	669	7%	88%	0.59	91	57	3.71	30
	07	24	8	aa	STL	142	17	34	10	0	4	22	12	26	0	0	241	302	395	696	8%	81%	0.47	107	29	4.23	34
Hamilton,Mark	07	23	3	aa	STL	248	25	52	13	0	5	32	19	45	1	1	211	268	321	589	7%	82%	0.43	75	43	2.92	10
Harper,Brett	04	23	3	aa	NYM	174	18	37	11	0	6	20	11	51	0	0	212	257	374	631	6%	71%	0.21	106	28	3.24	19
	05	24	3	aa	NYM	224	27	52	10	0	12	30	18	71	0	0	233	290	441	732	7%	69%	0.26	123	21	4.46	34
	07	26	38	aa	NYM	476	50	110	20	0	17	64	24	114	2	0	232	270	378	648	5%	76%	0.21	91	47	3.52	19
Heether,Adam	06	25	5	aa	MIL	244	19	48	6	0	1	16	25	53	1	1	195	269	230	498	9%	78%	0.47	27	36	2.16	-15
	07	26	5	aa	MIL	432	47	107	23	4	7	49	42	89	2	6	248	315	369	684	9%	79%	0.48	81	67	3.98	26
Hernandez,Anderson	04	22	6	aa	DET	394	56	97	16	3	4	25	21	75	15	7	246	284	332	617	5%	81%	0.28	58	131	3.24	12
	05	23	4	a/a	NYM	526	65	151	18	3	7	44	28	85	28	21	287	323	373	696	5%	84%	0.33	56	107	4.00	25
	06	24	6	aaa	NYM	414	43	100	11	3	0	22	20	67	15	5	242	276	283	559	5%	84%	0.30	30	117	2.75	-1
	07	25	64	aa	NYM	554	67	143	25	3	4	33	25	72	12	10	259	291	334	625	4%	87%	0.35	55	96	3.30	16
Hernandez,Diory	07	23	64	aa	ATL	433	43	121	23	1	6	50	24	63	18	22	280	318	379	697	5%	85%	0.39	70	76	3.70	30
Hernandez,Luis	05	21	6	aa	ATL	415	41	92	11	4	2	28	36	49	4	6	222	284	282	566	8%	88%	0.73	39	83	2.69	5
	06	22	6	a/a	ATL	453	40	112	15	3	2	33	20	52	4	5	247	279	307	586	4%	89%	0.38	42	72	2.89	7
	07	23	6	a/a	BAL	397	42	90	14	4	0	36	16	48	5	5	227	257	282	539	4%	88%	0.33	40	104	2.37	-1
Herrera,Jonathan	07	23	6	aa	COL	509	54	126	23	3	3	33	31	53	15	13	248	291	322	613	6%	90%	0.58	54	94	3.09	17
Hoffpauir,Jarrett	06	23	4	aa	STL	393	44	85	18	1	5	36	43	34	7	7	217	294	306	600	10%	91%	1.25	63	69	3.04	23
	07	24	4	aa	STL	393	39	106	22	0	9	45	44	34	4	5	271	344	392	735	10%	91%	1.30	83	37	4.87	50
Horwitz,Brian	06	24	8	a/a	SF	285	21	74	10	1	2	26	29	32	3	3	260	328	323	651	9%	89%	0.91	45	48	3.84	23
	07	25	8	aa	SF	400	39	111	24	2	2	25	27	27	3	1	278	323	361	684	6%	93%	0.97	64	65	4.31	39
House,J.R.	03	24	2	aa	PIT	63	11	19	6	0	2	10	5	9	0	0	308	357	493	850	7%	85%	0.52	129	39	6.75	66
	04	25	2	aaa	PIT	309	30	80	20	1	11	38	18	53	1	1	259	300	437	737	6%	83%	0.34	115	44	4.61	41
	06	27	2	a/a	HOU	493	64	140	31	2	12	81	31	56	2	2	285	327	425	752	6%	89%	0.55	95	59	5.08	45
	07	28	203	aaa	BAL	419	48	115	29	1	10	62	41	58	1	5	274	339	424	763	9%	86%	0.71	103	36	5.12	48
Huber,Justin	03	21	2	aa	NYM	193	13	44	11	0	5	29	15	45	0	2	228	284	363	646	7%	77%	0.33	91	15	3.42	20
	04	22	2	a/a	NYM	252	40	63	17	1	10	31	41	52	2	2	250	355	444	799	14%	79%	0.79	125	66	5.75	51
	05	23	3	a/a	KC	448	67	127	26	3	15	75	52	78	8	4	283	358	455	813	10%	83%	0.67	109	93	6.09	53
	06	24	3	aaa	KC	352	42	91	22	2	12	39	36	81	2	2	259	327	435	762	9%	77%	0.44	113	65	5.10	42
	07	25	83	aa	KC	286	30	65	12	1	13	52	16	44	1	0	227	268	406	674	5%	84%	0.36	107	49	3.73	27
Iribarren,Hernan	07	23	4	aa	MIL	479	61	132	21	10	4	44	39	102	16	17	275	330	385	714	7%	79%	0.38	70	153	4.19	28
Ishikawa,Travis	06	23	3	aa	SF	298	33	67	13	4	10	42	35	91	0	0	225	306	391	697	10%	70%	0.38	99	83	4.24	24
	07	24	3	aa	SF	173	13	31	3	1	2	13	13	41	1	0	181	240	242	481	7%	76%	0.32	36	65	1.97	-18
Janish,Paul	07	25	6	a/a	CIN	523	55	110	26	2	4	33	53	75	10	3	210	283	289	572	9%	86%	0.71	59	88	2.90	8
Jaramillo,Jason	06	24	2	a/a	PHI	328	32	77	23	1	6	37	28	53	0	1	234	294	364	658	8%	84%	0.54	93	38	3.73	27
	07	25	2	aaa	PHI	435	44	110	14	2	6	48	42	69	0	1	253	319	336	654	9%	84%	0.61	54	41	3.89	19
Jaso,John	07	24	20	aa	TAM	380	50	104	21	2	10	58	49	45	2	2	273	356	413	769	12%	88%	1.09	92	59	5.50	51

BATTER	YR	Age	Pos	Lev	Tm	AB	R	H	D	T	HR	RBI	BB	K	SB	CS	BA	OB	Slg	OPS	bb%	Ct%	Eye	PX	SX	RC/G	BPV
Jimerson,Charlton	04	25	8	aa	HOU	488	57	95	18	4	14	38	22	142	28	6	194	228	328	556	4%	71%	0.15	82	155	2.48	1
	05	26	8	a/a	HOU	444	50	95	21	3	12	34	21	139	22	10	213	248	351	599	4%	69%	0.15	87	132	2.77	10
	06	27	8	aaa	HOU	470	44	100	23	5	14	35	18	158	22	9	212	241	372	613	4%	66%	0.11	99	145	2.88	14
	07	28	8	aa	SEA	387	42	79	17	2	17	56	25	160	24	9	205	253	387	639	6%	59%	0.16	109	125	3.14	16
Johnson,Elliot	05	22	4	aa	TAM	260	26	62	8	5	2	17	11	56	12	6	238	269	331	600	4%	78%	0.20	56	167	2.94	7
	06	23	4	aa	TAM	494	72	138	21	10	15	52	40	130	21	18	279	333	453	787	7%	74%	0.31	103	172	5.01	42
	07	24	4	aaa	TAM	463	53	91	16	5	11	43	41	134	15	6	197	262	324	586	8%	71%	0.31	77	137	2.84	3
Johnson,Rob	06	23	2	aaa	SEA	337	24	69	8	2	3	28	11	66	12	8	205	230	267	497	3%	80%	0.17	40	99	1.89	-12
	07	24	20	aa	SEA	422	47	97	23	0	5	32	33	60	6	8	230	286	317	603	7%	86%	0.55	65	58	3.00	15
Jones,Brandon	06	23	8	aa	ATL	176	17	46	9	3	7	24	15	37	4	2	261	319	466	785	8%	79%	0.41	122	123	5.25	46
	07	24	8	a/a	ATL	535	75	149	32	5	17	89	54	109	15	8	279	345	452	797	9%	80%	0.50	110	113	5.65	48
Katin,Brendan	07	25	8	aa	MIL	450	59	102	22	0	20	77	35	155	3	2	226	282	407	689	7%	66%	0.23	112	55	3.93	26
Kottaras,George	06	23	2	a/a	SD	376	46	84	26	2	7	43	54	88	0	1	223	321	359	680	13%	77%	0.61	95	51	4.13	26
	07	24	2	aaa	BOS	294	29	70	24	0	8	35	28	64	1	1	238	304	401	706	9%	78%	0.44	114	34	4.29	35
Kroeger,Josh	03	21	8	aa	ARI	208	19	52	8	2	2	16	8	39	2	6	250	278	337	614	4%	81%	0.21	57	84	2.88	11
	04	22	8	a/a	ARI	453	52	136	49	3	14	62	27	67	3	3	300	340	514	854	6%	85%	0.40	149	68	6.42	70
	05	23	8	aaa	ARI	468	50	107	26	2	10	43	26	74	12	5	229	269	357	626	5%	84%	0.35	86	97	3.25	19
	06	24	8	aaa	PHI	441	41	103	26	4	10	41	22	100	6	3	234	270	379	649	5%	77%	0.22	95	98	3.46	22
	07	25	8	aa	CHC	400	51	111	18	2	17	62	35	69	6	5	277	335	459	794	8%	83%	0.51	110	73	5.52	48
Lambin,Chase	04	25	4	aa	NYM	410	47	80	18	2	7	47	34	93	3	2	195	257	301	558	8%	77%	0.37	70	78	2.60	1
	05	26	4	a/a	NYM	389	43	96	26	1	18	45	28	79	3	4	248	298	458	756	7%	80%	0.35	133	50	4.65	44
	06	27	6	a/a	NYM	403	48	80	19	2	7	43	47	99	4	3	199	282	307	589	10%	75%	0.48	73	78	2.96	6
	07	28	64	aa	FLA	434	44	90	22	4	10	40	33	126	2	6	206	262	343	605	7%	71%	0.26	88	85	2.89	10
LaRoche,Andy	05	22	5	aa	LA	223	33	53	10	0	7	34	24	44	2	2	238	312	377	688	10%	80%	0.55	88	58	4.11	27
	06	23	5	a/a	LA	432	66	122	24	1	17	69	55	57	8	6	282	363	461	824	11%	87%	0.96	112	70	6.16	60
	07	24	5	aa	LA	265	44	71	15	1	15	38	31	38	2	2	269	346	505	852	11%	86%	0.83	143	64	6.34	65
Lillibridge,Brent	07	24	6	a/a	ATL	525	67	135	20	4	11	50	34	111	36	13	257	302	371	673	6%	79%	0.30	72	135	3.94	22
Loadenthal,Carl	07	26	8	aa	ATL	476	57	121	14	4	0	24	49	80	32	18	253	323	299	621	9%	83%	0.61	33	120	3.37	10
Longoria,Evan	06	21	6	aa	TAM	105	15	27	5	0	6	20	1	21	2	1	257	264	476	740	1%	80%	0.05	131	79	4.22	41
	07	22	5	a/a	TAM	485	91	142	28	0	25	90	70	96	4	0	292	382	507	889	13%	80%	0.73	132	68	7.55	67
Lopez,Pedro	05	21	6	a/a	CHW	423	34	89	12	1	6	35	17	40	1	3	211	241	288	529	4%	91%	0.42	49	42	2.24	-1
	06	22	6	a/a	CHW	466	58	137	26	2	11	55	25	57	7	6	294	330	429	759	5%	88%	0.44	90	75	5.08	44
	07	23	6	aaa	CIN	285	36	76	12	1	3	25	25	34	4	3	267	326	347	673	8%	88%	0.74	57	73	4.09	27
Lowrie,Jed	07	23	6	a/a	BOS	497	71	143	51	5	10	60	66	78	4	4	288	371	471	842	12%	84%	0.85	131	88	6.57	67
Lubanski,Chris	06	22	8	aa	KC	524	72	131	32	8	10	54	56	84	9	8	250	322	399	721	10%	84%	0.67	97	125	4.48	37
	07	23	8	aa	KC	409	45	98	20	3	12	48	38	75	3	8	240	304	391	695	9%	82%	0.51	95	67	3.92	29
Maier,Mitch	05	23	8	aa	KC	322	40	68	17	4	5	35	11	35	7	4	211	236	334	571	3%	89%	0.30	82	137	2.53	10
	06	24	8	aa	KC	543	70	140	31	5	10	68	30	76	10	14	257	297	385	681	5%	86%	0.40	86	99	3.68	29
	07	25	8	aa	KC	544	58	127	26	4	10	48	26	82	5	2	233	268	349	617	5%	85%	0.32	76	91	3.22	16
Majewski,Val	04	23	8	aa	BAL	433	62	118	20	3	14	70	29	62	13	4	273	319	428	747	6%	86%	0.47	96	112	4.96	40
	06	25	8	aaa	BAL	323	44	80	15	4	4	39	39	71	7	8	248	329	356	684	11%	78%	0.55	71	114	4.01	23
	07	26	8	a/a	BAL	456	53	104	24	3	5	43	40	92	11	5	229	291	324	614	8%	80%	0.43	68	103	3.30	13
Manriquez,Salomon	06	24	2	aa	WAS	339	33	74	16	0	8	38	27	84	0	0	219	275	333	609	7%	75%	0.32	77	25	3.18	11
	07	25	20	aa	TEX	247	26	58	11	0	14	41	19	51	0	1	233	288	441	729	7%	79%	0.37	123	20	4.34	36
Mather,Joe	07	25	83	aa	STL	487	59	104	21	1	22	57	39	74	7	0	213	270	392	662	7%	85%	0.52	108	84	3.68	26
Mayberry,John	07	24	8	aa	TEX	245	29	53	10	0	13	31	16	53	6	1	218	267	412	679	6%	79%	0.31	115	74	3.77	26
McAnulty,Paul	05	25	3	a/a	SD	449	52	113	27	2	11	54	42	81	4	2	253	316	393	709	8%	82%	0.51	94	70	4.47	33
	06	26	3	aaa	SD	478	58	124	29	4	12	60	49	66	1	3	259	327	410	737	9%	86%	0.74	99	64	4.80	42
	07	27	8	aa	SD	233	19	48	9	1	3	24	23	51	0	2	205	276	295	571	9%	78%	0.45	59	39	2.74	2
McCutchen,Andrew	07	21	8	aa	PIT	513	68	133	25	2	9	47	42	74	19	5	260	316	373	688	8%	86%	0.57	76	107	4.30	29
Melillo,Kevin	05	23	4	aa	OAK	131	25	32	9	0	6	25	11	19	7	2	244	301	444	746	8%	86%	0.57	128	115	4.69	46
	06	24	4	aa	OAK	500	59	121	29	2	10	59	54	85	11	8	241	315	363	678	10%	83%	0.64	83	82	4.01	27
	07	25	4	aa	OAK	382	48	82	23	4	7	41	41	90	6	7	214	290	351	641	10%	76%	0.45	92	104	3.35	18
Miller,Jai	07	23	8	aa	FLA	406	46	96	24	2	12	49	50	115	10	6	236	320	394	714	11%	72%	0.43	102	86	4.41	30
Mitchell,Lee	06	24	5	aa	FLA	462	52	105	33	1	10	52	46	155	2	6	228	298	366	664	9%	67%	0.29	97	48	3.67	22
	07	25	5	aa	FLA	451	56	103	23	2	15	56	59	154	2	1	227	316	389	705	11%	66%	0.38	102	62	4.40	25
Moore,Scott	06	23	5	a/a	CHC	467	52	127	28	0	23	74	56	127	12	7	272	350	480	830	11%	73%	0.44	129	55	6.05	53
	07	24	5	aa	CHC	321	49	77	17	3	16	56	38	88	3	3	239	319	465	784	11%	73%	0.43	136	97	5.15	44
Morales,Jose	06	24	2	a/a	MIN	258	22	52	14	1	3	25	18	57	2	1	202	254	298	552	7%	78%	0.32	69	66	2.55	2
	07	25	2	aaa	MIN	376	41	114	24	1	2	37	28	45	1	4	303	351	388	740	7%	88%	0.62	67	40	5.04	41
Moran,Javon	06	24	8	aa	CIN	250	30	72	10	2	1	10	10	25	14	7	289	315	357	672	4%	90%	0.38	50	121	3.97	24
	07	25	8	a/a	PHI	425	62	102	17	3	2	17	35	72	23	15	239	297	306	604	8%	83%	0.49	48	127	3.01	10
Morgan,Nyjer	06	26	8	aa	PIT	219	31	56	5	3	1	8	12	29	17	10	254	294	322	615	5%	87%	0.42	41	168	3.00	10
	07	27	8	aa	PIT	164	22	39	3	1	0	7	10	28	18	7	238	282	268	550	6%	83%	0.36	22	142	2.64	-4
Morton,Colt	06	25	2	aa	SD	139	14	32	9	0	5	20	10	47	0	0	232	286	396	682	7%	66%	0.22	107	22	3.95	26
Moses,Matt	06	22	6	aa	MIN	474	44	113	15	2	14	68	32	111	2	2	238	287	367	654	6%	77%	0.29	77	53	3.64	17
	07	23	5	a/a	MIN	436	40	100	30	0	5	55	18	87	11	3	229	260	333	592	4%	80%	0.21	79	82	2.96	13
Moss,Brandon	05	22	8	aa	BOS	500	74	127	31	3	13	53	44	109	5	3	254	314	406	720	8%	78%	0.40	100	92	4.55	34
	06	23	8	aa	BOS	508	66	138	38	2	11	72	49	97	7	5	271	336	416	752	9%	81%	0.51	102	75	5.07	43
	07	24	8	aaa	BOS	493	59	136	46	1	13	70	54	133	3	5	276	347	452	800	10%	73%	0.41	125	47	5.68	52
Mulhern,Ryan	05	25	3	aa	CLE	242	33	66	17	2	11	37	23	61	3	2	271	334	499	832	9%	75%	0.37	142	88	5.98	57
	06	26	3	aa	CLE	452	54	101	23	2	11	58	34	129	1	0	223	278	354	632	7%	71%	0.27	86	65	3.42	15
	07	27	30	aaa	CLE	476	56	123	34	1	13	64	35	122	1	3	259	309	414	723	7%	74%	0.29	106	44	4.50	36
Murphy,David	05	24	8	aa	BOS	480	59	123	25	3	12	63	38	72	11	7	257	311	394	705	7%	85%	0.52	89	93	4.27	33
	06	25	8	a/a	BOS	490	59	127	43	4	10	61	49	74	6	5	259	327	422	749	9%	85%	0.67	115	86	4.91	47
	07	26	8	a/a	TEX	407	39	101	18	4	8	37	31	59	7	2	247	301	366	668	7%	86%	0.53	76	97	3.95	25
Navarro,Oswaldo	06	22	6	a/a	SEA	449	38	106	21	1	3	40	54	85	7	9	236	318	307	625	11%	81%	0.64	54	52	3.39	14
	07	23	64	aa	SEA	446	44	100	20	0	3	39	29	79	3	3	224	272	289	561	6%	82%	0.37	50	51	2.68	3

BATTER	YR	Age	Pos	Lev	Tm	AB	R	H	D	T	HR	RBI	BB	K	SB	CS	BA	OB	Slg	OPS	bb%	Ct%	Eye	PX	SX	RC/G	BPV
Nix,Jayson	04	22	4	aa	COL	456	50	96	17	1	15	50	33	81	12	3	211	264	351	615	7%	82%	0.41	86	91	3.16	14
	05	23	4	aa	COL	501	52	110	25	0	10	36	22	70	8	7	219	252	327	579	4%	86%	0.32	75	69	2.66	10
	06	24	4	aaa	COL	358	29	84	13	1	2	19	24	43	11	4	235	283	293	576	6%	88%	0.56	43	82	2.92	7
	07	25	4	aa	COL	439	59	111	29	2	9	43	23	68	18	8	252	290	387	677	5%	85%	0.35	93	114	3.83	29
Oeltjen,Trent	06	24	8	aa	MIN	401	55	112	16	8	3	40	32	59	21	12	278	332	377	709	7%	85%	0.54	63	164	4.41	29
	07	25	8	aaa	MIN	244	32	56	9	4	2	23	9	45	14	7	230	257	324	581	4%	82%	0.20	60	177	2.66	5
Palmisano,Lou	06	24	2	aa	MIL	332	35	73	16	1	4	33	45	67	2	0	220	313	309	622	12%	80%	0.66	63	58	3.55	13
	07	25	2	aa	MIL	351	38	75	19	1	9	50	47	80	6	2	213	305	349	654	12%	77%	0.59	90	73	3.80	20
Pascucci,Val	03	25	83	aaa	MON	459	60	114	28	1	12	64	73	98	2	2	248	352	392	744	14%	79%	0.74	96	48	5.11	37
	04	26	38	aaa	MON	392	62	107	33	1	20	69	56	71	7	2	273	364	513	877	13%	82%	0.80	154	78	7.01	70
	07	29	3	aa	FLA	447	64	92	20	1	22	67	49	140	6	1	206	284	404	688	10%	69%	0.35	119	86	3.98	25
Patterson,Eric	06	24	4	a/a	CHC	508	79	137	23	8	11	59	53	98	46	12	270	339	411	750	9%	81%	0.54	88	178	5.21	37
	07	24	48	aa	CHC	516	75	135	26	5	12	52	42	76	19	10	261	317	401	718	7%	85%	0.55	89	125	4.46	35
Patterson,Ryan	06	23	8	aa	TOR	187	17	47	15	1	6	18	12	49	2	0	249	293	431	724	6%	74%	0.24	122	70	4.50	38
	07	24	8	aa	TOR	446	42	105	24	0	15	53	18	89	1	5	234	264	390	654	4%	80%	0.20	100	28	3.35	23
Paul,Xavier	07	23	8	aa	LA	422	53	111	19	1	10	42	41	95	15	10	263	328	384	712	9%	77%	0.43	79	84	4.40	29
Pearce,Steven	07	24	3	aa	PIT	412	61	121	34	2	15	72	30	51	10	2	293	341	496	837	7%	88%	0.60	135	99	6.36	65
Perez,Fernando	07	24	8	aa	TAM	393	68	105	21	8	7	27	63	96	26	20	268	369	411	780	14%	76%	0.65	90	173	5.15	40
Perez,Yohannis	07	25	6	aa	MIL	190	15	32	4	2	0	13	13	52	2	3	170	224	210	434	7%	73%	0.26	27	98	1.48	-27
Peterson,Brock	07	24	30	aa	MIN	389	53	97	19	2	12	51	33	79	1	0	249	308	399	707	8%	80%	0.42	95	69	4.42	31
Petit,Gregorio	07	23	6	aa	OAK	503	45	135	25	0	5	50	34	75	8	6	268	315	348	663	6%	85%	0.45	59	53	3.89	23
Plouffe,Trevor	07	21	6	aa	MIN	497	62	122	34	1	7	41	29	76	10	8	245	287	360	647	6%	85%	0.38	84	84	3.47	24
Pope,Van	07	24	5	aa	ATL	421	41	85	21	3	5	37	30	71	9	6	203	256	302	558	7%	83%	0.42	69	98	2.53	4
Powell,Landon	07	26	2	aa	OAK	236	38	57	8	1	11	32	27	40	1	0	240	318	419	738	10%	83%	0.68	105	67	4.82	37
Prado,Martin	05	22	4	aa	ATL	143	15	37	6	1	1	10	15	15	3	3	259	329	336	665	9%	90%	1.00	54	79	3.88	29
	06	23	4	a/a	ATL	417	45	113	17	2	3	36	25	61	4	4	271	312	343	655	6%	85%	0.41	51	70	3.80	20
	07	24	4	aaa	ATL	395	55	119	22	2	4	37	30	38	5	4	301	351	397	748	7%	90%	0.79	69	79	5.20	45
Pridie,Jason	06	23	8	aa	TAM	460	40	102	11	4	5	35	31	102	16	5	221	271	293	564	6%	78%	0.30	44	116	2.77	-2
	07	24	8	a/a	TAM	525	80	149	30	10	13	59	33	85	23	11	284	326	453	779	6%	84%	0.39	106	170	5.22	46
Putnam,Danny	06	24	8	aa	OAK	225	27	48	11	1	7	29	18	32	2	1	211	270	359	629	7%	86%	0.57	94	73	3.28	21
	07	25	8	aa	OAK	223	17	44	15	1	2	24	16	40	3	5	198	252	299	551	7%	82%	0.41	77	65	2.34	6
Rasmus,Colby	07	21	8	aa	STL	472	76	113	32	2	22	59	58	87	15	4	239	323	456	778	11%	82%	0.67	136	108	5.27	49
Reimold,Nolan	07	24	8	aa	BAL	186	24	50	14	0	10	28	15	39	2	3	271	324	501	825	7%	79%	0.37	145	46	5.58	58
Riggans,Shawn	03	23	2	aa	TAM	62	7	16	6	0	1	10	4	13	0	0	250	294	391	686	6%	78%	0.29	107	30	4.08	33
	05	25	2	aa	TAM	310	30	77	16	0	5	40	19	66	1	2	250	293	354	647	6%	79%	0.29	73	35	3.60	19
	06	26	2	aaa	TAM	417	39	111	23	2	10	49	24	87	2	2	265	306	400	706	5%	79%	0.28	90	55	4.34	31
	07	27	2	aaa	TAM	121	10	30	9	1	4	14	4	31	0	3	251	274	432	706	3%	75%	0.12	118	62	3.65	35
Roberts,Brandon	07	23	8	aa	MIN	369	41	98	12	3	2	32	25	48	12	8	266	312	331	643	6%	87%	0.52	44	104	3.59	17
Robnett,Richie	07	24	8	aa	OAK	523	64	118	35	1	14	60	30	124	3	3	225	268	378	646	5%	76%	0.24	103	65	3.40	23
Rodriguez,Sean	07	22	6	aa	LAA	508	76	120	29	1	15	66	48	119	14	9	236	302	386	688	9%	77%	0.40	98	93	3.96	27
Rogowski,Casey	05	24	3	aa	CHW	501	62	125	29	4	8	58	44	94	15	13	250	310	370	680	8%	81%	0.47	82	104	3.84	27
	06	25	3	aaa	CHW	459	62	120	30	2	14	68	48	90	24	10	261	330	425	755	9%	80%	0.53	108	108	4.99	42
	07	26	38	aaa	CHW	453	54	103	25	0	15	48	55	102	15	5	227	311	379	690	11%	77%	0.54	99	78	4.19	27
Rottino,Vinny	05	25	5	a/a	MIL	494	49	124	19	4	6	40	32	62	2	2	250	296	338	634	6%	87%	0.52	59	69	3.54	18
	06	27	5	aaa	MIL	398	49	113	23	2	7	37	36	71	11	8	285	344	405	749	8%	82%	0.50	82	85	5.01	39
	07	27	28	aaa	MIL	377	49	96	15	2	10	45	32	56	12	10	255	313	388	701	8%	85%	0.58	83	94	4.10	31
Ruggiano,Justin	05	23	8	aa	LA	156	18	46	7	1	5	22	13	46	7	4	292	345	441	787	7%	70%	0.27	92	98	5.44	41
	06	24	8	aa	TAM	400	72	103	30	6	11	68	61	111	13	9	257	355	447	801	13%	72%	0.55	124	149	5.64	48
	07	25	8	aaa	TAM	482	73	141	27	2	19	69	51	148	25	12	292	360	472	832	10%	69%	0.35	113	106	6.19	51
Santos,Sergio	03	20	6	aa	ARI	137	11	34	6	1	2	13	6	17	0	0	245	278	353	631	4%	87%	0.37	71	46	3.43	18
	04	21	6	aa	ARI	347	38	89	18	4	8	38	19	64	2	2	256	295	401	696	5%	82%	0.30	92	92	4.12	29
	05	22	6	aaa	ARI	487	40	107	21	2	9	49	26	70	1	3	220	260	330	590	5%	86%	0.37	72	45	2.84	10
	06	23	6	aaa	TOR	481	44	100	25	1	5	34	22	89	1	3	208	243	295	538	4%	81%	0.25	64	49	2.33	1
	07	24	6	a/a	TOR	479	54	106	33	2	17	53	35	93	3	0	221	274	407	681	7%	81%	0.38	121	74	3.84	31
Schierholtz,Nate	06	23	8	aa	SF	470	56	127	26	7	14	55	27	81	8	3	270	310	445	755	5%	83%	0.33	108	127	4.93	41
	07	24	8	aa	SF	411	54	122	28	6	12	55	14	49	8	5	297	320	479	799	3%	88%	0.27	117	124	5.48	53
Schnurstein,Micah	06	22	5	aa	CHW	480	47	104	24	2	10	45	23	98	8	6	217	252	338	590	5%	80%	0.23	80	84	2.76	10
Sinisi,Vince	05	24	8	aa	TEX	248	21	58	9	0	4	22	12	32	3	5	235	269	317	586	4%	87%	0.36	55	47	2.73	8
	06	25	8	a/a	TEX	497	56	125	37	2	7	54	52	80	8	4	252	323	375	698	10%	84%	0.65	90	77	4.37	34
	07	26	8	aa	SD	303	36	77	16	1	7	30	16	43	5	3	252	290	383	674	5%	86%	0.37	87	77	3.85	27
Smith,David	06	26	8	aa	TOR	483	57	109	31	1	17	63	34	126	6	4	225	277	399	675	7%	74%	0.27	113	73	3.73	27
	07	27	80	aa	TOR	458	60	103	29	1	19	50	37	99	3	5	224	283	416	699	8%	78%	0.38	122	57	3.88	33
Smith,Seth	06	23	8	aa	COL	524	61	146	44	4	13	55	39	53	3	5	279	329	452	781	7%	90%	0.74	119	68	5.29	57
	07	24	8	aa	COL	451	50	124	28	5	14	61	30	63	5	3	275	320	447	767	6%	86%	0.47	110	93	5.16	47
Snyder,Brad	05	23	8	aa	CLE	301	46	73	19	2	12	46	21	88	4	3	242	292	435	727	7%	71%	0.24	123	103	4.32	36
	06	24	8	aa	CLE	523	75	124	27	3	14	63	56	157	17	2	236	310	380	690	10%	70%	0.36	92	123	4.33	24
	07	25	8	aaa	CLE	259	36	61	12	2	8	30	33	82	10	0	237	322	390	712	11%	68%	0.40	95	127	4.77	26
Soto,Geovany	04	22	2	aa	CHC	332	41	81	14	0	8	41	36	65	1	2	244	318	358	676	10%	80%	0.55	75	38	4.06	23
	05	23	2	aaa	CHC	288	24	66	13	0	3	32	40	58	0	1	230	323	306	630	12%	80%	0.69	56	18	3.61	13
	06	24	2	aaa	CHC	342	31	88	20	0	6	35	38	68	0	1	257	332	368	700	10%	80%	0.56	79	18	4.47	29
	07	25	23	aa	CHC	385	61	122	29	2	23	87	42	84	0	0	316	383	577	960	10%	78%	0.50	162	45	8.64	82
Span,Denard	05	22	8	aa	MIN	263	40	71	6	4	0	22	19	36	9	9	270	319	323	642	7%	86%	0.53	34	140	3.45	14
	06	23	8	aa	MIN	536	75	146	16	5	2	42	37	77	23	12	272	319	332	651	6%	86%	0.48	40	127	3.78	17
	07	24	8	aaa	MIN	487	58	127	20	6	3	54	37	92	25	14	261	313	345	658	7%	81%	0.40	57	137	3.72	18
Stansberry,Craig	05	24	4	aa	PIT	418	46	84	20	7	12	49	33	88	10	6	202	260	367	627	7%	79%	0.38	101	142	3.10	16
	06	25	4	a/a	PIT	457	70	105	28	4	12	50	59	93	16	6	229	318	384	702	11%	80%	0.64	101	127	4.35	31
	07	26	465	aa	SD	466	68	103	25	2	12	61	58	100	8	10	220	306	357	663	11%	79%	0.58	90	82	3.64	22
Stavinoha,Nick	06	24	8	aa	STL	417	43	106	24	2	9	57	22	69	2	1	255	292	383	675	5%	83%	0.31	86	63	3.95	27
	07	25	8	aa	STL	499	37	103	14	0	9	36	23	72	5	1	206	241	287	528	4%	86%	0.32	52	58	2.34	-4

BATTER	YR	Age	Pos	Lev	Tm	AB	R	H	D	T	HR	RBI	BB	K	SB	CS	BA	OB	Slg	OPS	bb%	Ct%	Eye	PX	SX	RC/G	BPV
Stewart,Caleb	07	25	8	aa	NYM	433	47	87	12	1	11	51	27	93	3	7	202	248	308	556	6%	78%	0.29	64	57	2.38	-0
Stewart,Ian	06	22	5	aa	COL	462	58	118	39	6	9	55	38	74	2	9	255	312	424	736	8%	84%	0.51	116	90	4.39	43
	07	22	5	aa	COL	414	60	121	22	2	13	54	42	72	9	2	292	357	449	807	9%	83%	0.58	100	93	6.15	50
Sweeney,Ryan	05	21	8	aa	CHW	426	54	120	21	2	1	39	29	41	4	7	281	327	348	675	6%	90%	0.72	52	69	4.00	29
	06	22	8	aaa	CHW	449	64	142	26	2	15	70	35	61	7	8	316	366	488	853	7%	86%	0.58	109	72	6.56	62
	07	23	8	aaa	CHW	397	47	107	17	1	12	45	47	62	7	5	270	347	405	752	11%	84%	0.76	85	64	5.13	40
Teagarden,Taylor	07	24	0	aa	TEX	102	16	27	3	0	6	14	8	33	0	0	266	318	466	784	7%	68%	0.24	114	32	5.37	40
Thomas,Clete	07	24	8	aa	DET	528	91	138	27	6	7	49	55	106	16	11	261	331	373	704	9%	80%	0.52	75	135	4.37	28
Timpner,Clay	06	23	8	a/a	SF	499	51	118	18	4	5	28	20	53	14	14	236	266	319	585	4%	89%	0.38	55	104	2.64	9
	07	24	8	aa	SF	392	40	103	10	3	5	30	29	59	7	12	262	312	337	649	7%	85%	0.48	47	76	3.41	16
Tolbert,Matt	06	24	6	aa	MIN	248	29	58	14	1	3	31	27	44	5	1	234	308	333	641	10%	82%	0.60	72	85	3.74	20
	07	25	4	aaa	MIN	417	63	118	23	6	6	51	34	58	11	3	283	336	408	744	7%	86%	0.58	83	141	5.14	40
Tuiasosopo,Matt	06	20	6	aa	SEA	216	16	39	4	0	1	9	21	60	2	1	180	253	214	466	9%	72%	0.35	46	46	1.87	-23
	07	21	5	aa	SEA	446	64	105	25	3	8	49	68	104	3	9	235	337	359	695	13%	77%	0.65	83	71	4.17	26
Valbuena,Luis	07	22	4	aa	SEA	444	47	95	21	2	9	38	43	76	9	7	214	283	331	614	9%	83%	0.57	77	82	3.14	14
Velez,Eugenio	07	25	84	aa	SF	394	45	97	14	6	1	19	21	62	41	18	247	284	322	606	5%	84%	0.33	50	176	2.99	10
Votto,Joey	06	23	3	aa	CIN	508	78	152	45	1	21	71	69	105	22	7	300	383	517	901	12%	79%	0.65	144	92	7.64	73
	07	24	38	aaa	CIN	496	66	138	20	1	22	82	62	98	15	11	278	358	456	814	11%	80%	0.63	106	70	5.85	49
Walker,Neil	07	22	5	aa	PIT	495	71	128	33	2	6	72	8	62	8	3	259	320	394	714	8%	85%	0.63	94	85	4.46	37
Webster,Anthony	06	24	8	a/a	TEX	458	60	129	24	6	8	34	28	53	17	10	282	323	413	736	6%	88%	0.53	85	131	4.67	40
	07	24	80	aa	TEX	411	53	102	23	3	7	31	17	47	24	11	247	277	365	643	4%	88%	0.36	80	133	3.33	23
Whitesell,Josh	06	24	3	aa	WAS	402	40	90	10	0	15	48	45	123	2	7	225	302	362	664	10%	69%	0.36	79	25	3.63	15
	07	25	30	aa	WAS	387	60	88	19	1	15	58	66	103	5	2	228	340	400	740	15%	73%	0.64	106	71	4.97	33
Wilson,Bobby	06	24	2	aa	LAA	374	32	89	22	0	7	38	23	36	1	8	239	283	353	636	6%	90%	0.65	81	26	3.18	26
	07	24	2	aa	LAA	313	33	78	20	1	8	42	26	42	5	3	249	306	392	697	8%	87%	0.61	97	68	4.20	35
Wimberly,Corey	07	24	4	aa	COL	365	50	91	14	1	3	26	16	41	29	10	250	280	316	597	4%	89%	0.38	48	131	3.09	10
Winfree,David	07	22	350	aa	MIN	460	47	110	24	3	9	42	20	91	0	0	239	271	363	634	4%	80%	0.22	82	56	3.40	18
Wood,Brandon	06	22	6	aa	LAA	453	55	107	37	2	18	61	39	110	14	4	236	297	446	743	8%	76%	0.35	138	103	4.61	43
	07	23	56	aa	LAA	437	66	111	25	1	20	70	40	109	9	1	254	317	453	770	8%	75%	0.37	124	94	5.23	43
Young,Delwyn	05	23	4	a/a	LA	526	54	133	29	0	15	55	24	86	1	4	253	285	394	679	4%	84%	0.28	93	30	3.82	28
	06	24	8	aaa	LA	532	58	124	35	0	14	75	32	82	2	5	233	277	378	654	6%	85%	0.39	99	40	3.48	26
	07	25	8	aa	LA	490	81	134	44	3	14	74	30	100	3	4	274	315	457	773	6%	80%	0.30	127	87	5.10	50

PITCHER	Yr	Age	Lev	Org	W	L	G	Sv	IP	H	ER	HR	BB	K	ERA	Br/IP	BF/G	OBA	bb/9	K/9	Cmd	HR/9	H%	S%	BPV
Abreu,Winston	04	27	a/a	ARI	3	3	45	3	77	98	76	25	60	61	8.87	2.05	8.5	303	7.0	7.1	1.0	3.0	32%	62%	-30
	05	28	aaa	ARI	2	3	27	2	33.1	43	28	6	15	35	7.60	1.75	5.7	308	4.1	9.6	2.3	1.8	39%	58%	48
	06	29	aaa	BAL	9	4	46	1	65.1	72	28	5	23	65	3.87	1.45	6.2	275	3.1	9.0	2.9	0.7	36%	75%	92
	07	30	aaa	WAS	3	0	37	5	52.1	31	10	2	23	62	1.73	1.04	5.6	170	4.0	10.7	2.7	0.4	25%	85%	130
Acosta,Manny	06	25	a/a	ATL	1	6	51	21	60	58	33	6	54	48	4.89	1.86	5.6	248	8.1	7.1	0.9	0.9	30%	75%	38
	07	26	aaa	ATL	9	3	40	12	59.2	56	19	0	38	47	2.82	1.58	6.7	244	5.8	7.1	1.2	0.0	32%	80%	74
Albaladejo,Jonathan	06	24	aa	PIT	1	2	18	1	36	51	22	5	5	22	5.41	1.55	8.9	325	1.3	5.6	4.3	1.3	36%	67%	76
	07	25	a/a	WAS	7	3	36	2	60.2	52	25	5	23	46	3.70	1.23	6.9	227	3.4	6.8	2.0	0.8	27%	72%	70
Alexander,Mark	06	26	a/a	LA	5	3	52	27	61.1	43	12	2	24	68	1.71	1.10	4.7	195	3.6	10.1	2.8	0.3	28%	85%	127
	07	27	aa	LA	5	1	48	5	79.1	91	69	15	62	73	7.85	1.93	8.0	282	7.1	8.3	1.2	1.7	34%	61%	22
Anderson,Brian	07	24	aa	SF	1	5	47	29	50.1	65	27	4	21	37	4.92	1.72	4.9	308	3.8	6.7	1.8	0.8	37%	72%	48
Andrade,Steve	05	28	aa	TOR	3	2	35	3	50.1	35	20	5	22	52	3.68	1.13	5.8	193	3.9	9.4	2.4	0.9	25%	70%	97
	06	29	aaa	SD	3	2	38	0	67.2	63	29	4	32	55	3.89	1.42	7.7	244	4.3	7.3	1.7	0.6	31%	73%	69
	07	30	aaa	TAM	3	2	38	0	59.1	70	45	5	37	40	6.86	1.82	7.4	290	5.7	6.1	1.1	0.8	34%	61%	31
Arredondo,Jose	06	23	aa	LAA	2	3	11	0	60.2	83	44	7	20	41	6.58	1.71	25.3	321	3.0	6.1	2.1	1.0	37%	61%	39
	07	24	aa	LAA	0	1	25	10	28	22	10	2	14	24	3.31	1.29	4.7	209	4.6	7.8	1.7	0.7	26%	76%	75
Ascanio,Jose	06	21	aa	ATL	4	2	24	0	38	46	25	2	19	33	5.92	1.71	7.3	293	4.5	7.8	1.7	0.5	37%	63%	66
	07	22	aa	ATL	2	2	44	10	78	77	28	1	19	61	3.23	1.23	7.4	253	2.2	7.0	3.2	0.1	32%	72%	111
Bailey,Homer	06	20	aa	CIN	7	1	13	0	68	57	15	1	28	68	2.02	1.25	21.8	223	3.7	9.0	2.5	0.1	31%	83%	113
	07	21	aaa	CIN	6	3	12	0	67.1	53	27	5	30	55	3.66	1.23	23.2	212	4.0	7.4	1.8	0.6	26%	71%	77
Balester,Collin	07	21	a/a	WAS	4	10	27	0	150.1	165	74	11	46	103	4.45	1.40	24.0	273	2.7	6.2	2.3	0.7	32%	68%	64
Banks,Josh	04	22	aa	TOR	6	6	18	0	91.1	112	75	22	31	66	7.41	1.57	22.7	296	3.1	6.5	2.1	2.2	32%	56%	14
	05	23	aa	TOR	8	12	27	0	162.1	209	107	27	12	124	5.95	1.37	25.7	307	0.7	6.9	10.0	1.5	35%	59%	201
	06	24	aaa	TOR	10	11	29	0	170.2	224	135	47	30	109	7.14	1.49	25.9	311	1.6	5.8	3.6	2.5	32%	57%	29
	07	25	aaa	TOR	12	10	27	0	169	227	112	28	25	85	5.97	1.49	27.6	315	1.3	4.5	3.4	1.5	34%	63%	45
Barone,Daniel	07	24	aa	FLA	8	3	23	0	136.1	151	73	14	35	79	4.80	1.36	25.3	275	2.3	5.2	2.3	0.9	31%	66%	52
Bazardo,Yorman	05	21	SEA	SEA	11	8	25	0	142	172	82	17	51	91	5.20	1.57	25.5	293	3.2	5.8	1.8	1.1	33%	68%	36
	06	22	aa	SEA	6	5	25	0	138.1	171	73	12	49	72	4.76	1.59	24.9	298	3.2	4.7	1.5	0.8	33%	71%	31
	07	23	aaa	DET	10	6	23	0	136.2	159	74	9	43	60	4.89	1.48	26.1	286	2.8	4.0	1.4	0.6	32%	66%	33
Begg,Chris	03	24	aa	SF	2	1	4	0	24.2	36	14	2	13	10	5.09	2.00	29.8	336	4.7	3.9	0.8	0.8	37%	75%	5
	04	25	a/a	SF	11	6	25	0	135.1	163	65	12	28	63	4.35	1.42	23.4	293	1.9	4.2	2.2	0.8	32%	70%	45
	05	26	aa	SF	8	7	23	0	138	185	64	9	26	64	4.20	1.53	26.7	315	1.7	4.1	2.4	0.6	35%	73%	49
	06	27	aa	SF	13	10	26	0	174.2	246	122	12	41	69	6.29	1.65	30.6	326	2.1	3.6	1.7	0.6	36%	60%	28
	07	28	aa	SF	14	5	27	0	166	283	110	24	33	57	5.96	1.90	29.6	368	1.8	3.1	1.7	1.3	39%	70%	-2
Bierd,Randor	07	24	aa	DET	3	2	27	1	45.2	39	24	1	10	44	4.72	1.09	6.7	229	2.1	8.7	4.2	0.2	31%	53%	144
Blackburn,Nick	05	24	a/a	MIN	2	4	10	0	63	63	22	3	13	30	3.14	1.21	26.0	255	1.9	4.3	2.3	0.4	29%	74%	65
	06	25	aa	MIN	7	8	30	0	132.1	181	94	15	43	66	6.38	1.70	20.3	319	2.9	4.5	1.5	1.0	35%	62%	20
	07	26	a/a	MIN	10	4	25	0	148.2	164	54	9	22	58	3.26	1.26	24.8	275	1.3	3.5	2.6	0.6	30%	75%	59
Blackley,Travis	03	21	aa	SEA	17	3	27	0	162.1	137	55	10	61	135	3.07	1.22	24.9	225	3.4	7.5	2.2	0.6	28%	76%	84
	04	22	aaa	SEA	8	6	19	0	110.1	99	47	12	42	81	3.86	1.28	24.3	236	3.4	6.7	1.9	1.0	28%	73%	60
	06	24	a/a	SEA	9	12	27	0	155	172	86	23	53	94	4.99	1.45	25.1	275	3.1	5.5	1.8	1.3	30%	69%	30
	07	25	aa	SF	10	8	28	0	162.1	186	105	22	71	98	5.84	1.58	26.1	282	3.9	5.4	1.4	1.2	31%	65%	23
Blevins,Jerry	07	24	aa	OAK	4	5	41	4	54	51	17	3	13	57	2.81	1.17	5.4	243	2.1	9.5	4.5	0.5	33%	77%	142
Broadway,Lance	06	23	a/a	CHW	8	8	26	0	160.1	202	68	15	44	100	3.82	1.54	27.4	302	2.5	5.6	2.3	0.8	35%	77%	51
	07	24	aaa	CHW	8	9	27	0	155	189	110	25	83	96	6.39	1.75	26.8	295	4.8	5.6	1.2	1.5	32%	66%	10
Brown,Brooks	07	22	aa	ARI	4	4	12	0	66.1	88	41	4	42	41	5.61	1.98	27.0	314	5.8	5.6	1.0	0.5	37%	70%	31
Buchholz,Clay	07	23	a/a	BOS	8	5	24	0	125.1	103	44	10	36	146	3.17	1.11	21.0	220	2.6	10.5	4.1	0.7	31%	74%	138
Buckner,Billy	06	23	aa	KC	5	3	13	0	75.2	87	43	6	36	53	5.18	1.63	26.3	283	4.3	6.4	1.5	0.7	34%	68%	46
	07	24	aa	KC	10	10	31	0	124	156	71	16	33	81	5.12	1.52	17.8	301	2.4	5.9	2.5	1.1	34%	68%	48
Bulger,Jason	05	27	aaa	ARI	3	6	56	4	56	56	24	3	26	49	3.81	1.45	4.4	254	4.1	7.8	1.9	0.5	32%	74%	76
	06	28	aaa	LAA	2	2	27	4	34.1	34	20	0	15	35	5.28	1.42	5.5	253	3.9	9.3	2.4	0.0	36%	59%	110
	07	29	aa	LAA	5	2	49	10	52.2	75	35	5	31	55	6.03	2.04	5.3	330	5.4	9.5	1.8	0.9	43%	70%	57
Campillo,Jorge	05	27	aaa	SEA	4	1	12	0	66.1	72	23	5	19	37	3.15	1.37	23.6	271	2.6	5.0	2.0	0.7	31%	79%	51
	07	29	aa	SEA	9	6	24	0	149.1	225	79	15	55	67	4.75	1.88	29.8	341	3.3	4.0	1.2	0.9	37%	76%	10
Carrasco,Carlos	07	21	aa	PHI	6	4	14	0	70.1	70	43	10	44	44	5.50	1.63	22.8	256	5.6	5.7	1.0	1.3	28%	69%	19
Carrillo,Cesar	05	21	SD	SD	4	0	5	0	30.2	25	12	2	7	32	3.58	1.06	24.0	221	2.1	9.5	4.6	0.6	30%	67%	146
	06	22	a/a	SD	1	3	10	0	53.1	51	21	4	18	39	3.56	1.30	22.4	248	3.1	6.6	2.2	0.7	30%	74%	70
Cassel,Jack	04	24	aa	SD	4	2	57	1	74.2	91	39	4	27	42	4.72	1.59	5.9	295	3.3	5.1	1.5	0.5	34%	69%	43
	05	25	a/a	SD	6	5	47	1	82	109	39	2	33	44	4.27	1.73	8.1	314	3.6	4.8	1.3	0.2	36%	74%	42
	06	26	aa	SD	9	8	30	0	155	196	91	14	51	95	5.29	1.59	23.3	302	3.0	5.5	1.8	0.8	35%	67%	41
	07	27	aa	SD	7	14	27	0	156.2	277	98	17	53	85	5.62	2.11	29.1	378	3.1	4.9	1.6	1.0	42%	74%	13
Chamberlain,Joba	07	22	a/a	NYY	5	2	11	0	48.1	45	20	5	17	70	3.74	1.29	18.4	243	3.2	13.1	4.1	0.9	38%	74%	143
Chavez,Jesse	05	22	aa	TEX	4	3	31	1	57	84	47	13	25	23	7.42	1.91	8.9	335	3.9	3.6	0.9	2.1	34%	65%	-33
	06	23	a/a	PIT	4	6	51	4	78	86	47	6	37	74	5.42	1.58	6.9	274	4.3	8.5	2.0	0.7	35%	65%	73
	07	24	aa	PIT	3	3	46	2	80.1	113	44	4	19	51	4.97	1.64	7.9	325	2.1	5.8	2.7	0.5	38%	69%	67
Cherry,Rocky	06	27	a/a	CHC	5	1	33	2	51.1	67	25	5	20	40	4.45	1.69	7.1	309	3.4	7.0	2.0	0.8	37%	75%	54
	07	28	aaa	CHC	2	0	43	7	51	73	41	8	24	38	7.28	1.89	5.7	327	4.2	6.6	1.6	1.3	38%	62%	23
Clippard,Tyler	06	22	aa	NYY	12	10	28	0	166.1	144	85	18	60	145	4.61	1.23	24.6	229	3.3	7.9	2.4	1.0	28%	64%	78
	07	23	a/a	NYY	6	5	20	0	96	126	65	15	50	70	6.09	1.83	22.8	310	4.7	6.6	1.4	1.4	36%	69%	20
Corcoran,Roy	03	23	a/a	MON	1	1	16	3	25.2	15	1	0	7	22	0.36	0.87	6.0	169	2.5	7.9	3.1	0.0	23%	95%	134
	04	24	aaa	MON	5	1	30	5	44.1	44	18	0	23	29	3.67	1.52	6.5	255	4.7	5.9	1.3	0.0	32%	73%	66
	05	25	aaa	WAS	4	4	51	3	67.2	70	36	6	32	47	4.87	1.52	5.8	262	4.3	6.2	1.4	0.8	31%	68%	46
	06	26	a/a	WAS	2	6	49	27	59.2	46	13	1	40	59	2.03	1.45	5.3	209	6.1	8.9	1.5	0.2	29%	86%	92
	07	27	aa	FLA	4	4	53	15	61	84	34	1	41	40	4.98	2.05	5.7	321	6.0	5.9	1.0	0.2	39%	74%	41

PITCHER	Yr	Age	Lev	Org	W	L	G	Sv	IP	H	ER	HR	BB	K	ERA	Br/IP	BF/G	OBA	bb/9	K/9	Cmd	HR/9	H%	S%	BPV
Cruceta,Francisco	03	22	aa	CLE	13	9	27	0	163.1	169	75	9	71	115	4.14	1.47	26.5	262	3.9	6.3	1.6	0.5	32%	71%	60
	04	23	a/a	CLE	10	13	29	0	171.2	182	90	16	70	91	4.73	1.47	25.9	267	3.7	4.8	1.3	0.8	30%	69%	32
	05	24	aaa	SEA	7	5	32	0	111.1	139	64	16	33	93	5.18	1.55	15.5	300	2.7	7.5	2.8	1.3	36%	69%	61
	06	25	aaa	SEA	13	9	28	0	160.1	170	91	27	79	164	5.11	1.55	25.6	266	4.4	9.2	2.1	1.5	33%	71%	55
	07	26	aa	TEX	3	0	25	1	65.2	52	33	3	46	52	4.60	1.50	11.5	214	6.3	7.2	1.1	0.5	27%	68%	65
Cueto,Johnny	07	22	a/a	CIN	8	4	14	0	83	83	31	10	12	88	3.41	1.15	24.1	255	1.3	9.6	7.1	1.0	33%	74%	180
Davidson,David	07	23	aa	PIT	4	1	45	2	67.1	60	37	3	33	52	4.98	1.38	6.4	234	4.4	7.0	1.6	0.4	29%	62%	71
Davis,Wade	07	22	aa	TAM	7	3	14	0	80	84	34	3	31	71	3.83	1.44	24.9	264	3.5	8.0	2.3	0.3	34%	72%	88
Day,Dewon	07	27	a/a	CHW	2	5	34	2	39.1	51	32	1	39	49	7.41	2.29	6.0	307	9.0	11.2	1.2	0.3	45%	65%	79
Deduno,Samuel	07	24	aa	COL	5	8	21	0	124	154	106	18	69	104	7.72	1.80	27.9	298	5.0	7.5	1.5	1.3	36%	57%	33
DeSalvo,Matt	06	26	a/a	NYY	6	10	27	0	116.2	168	121	14	111	61	9.38	2.40	22.9	331	8.6	4.7	0.6	1.1	37%	60%	-5
	07	27	aaa	NYY	9	5	20	0	113.1	115	46	5	61	81	3.69	1.55	25.3	258	4.9	6.4	1.3	0.4	31%	76%	57
Devine,Joey	07	24	a/a	ATL	5	4	50	20	57	49	15	2	21	65	2.44	1.23	4.7	229	3.3	10.3	3.2	0.3	33%	80%	127
Deza,Fredy	07	25	aa	BAL	7	8	36	0	124	157	77	25	43	84	5.58	1.61	15.6	302	3.1	6.1	1.9	1.8	33%	70%	17
Diamond,Thomas	05	22	aa	TEX	5	4	14	0	69	78	53	11	39	59	6.91	1.70	22.7	279	5.1	7.7	1.5	1.4	33%	60%	34
	06	24	aa	TEX	12	5	27	0	129.1	128	84	20	82	121	5.82	1.63	21.8	253	5.7	8.5	1.5	1.4	31%	66%	45
Doyne,Cory	05	24	aa	STL	2	1	48	19	55.1	40	13	4	35	45	2.06	1.36	4.9	199	5.7	7.3	1.3	0.7	24%	88%	65
	06	25	a/a	STL	1	7	56	6	71.1	61	32	1	47	67	4.00	1.52	5.6	227	6.0	8.4	1.4	0.1	31%	72%	86
	07	26	aaa	BAL	0	1	42	29	44.1	29	15	0	18	42	3.16	1.05	4.2	183	3.6	8.5	2.4	0.0	26%	67%	119
Duensing,Brian	06	24	aa	MIN	1	2	10	0	49.1	64	28	8	21	24	5.10	1.72	22.8	308	3.8	4.4	1.2	1.5	33%	74%	-1
	07	25	aa	MIN	15	6	28	0	167.1	198	76	18	41	98	4.11	1.43	26.0	289	2.2	5.3	2.4	1.0	33%	73%	51
Dumatrait,Phil	05	24	aa	CIN	4	12	24	0	127.2	129	51	4	69	81	3.57	1.56	23.8	258	4.9	5.7	1.2	0.3	31%	76%	53
	06	25	a/a	CIN	8	11	26	0	137.1	183	95	20	64	82	6.22	1.80	24.9	314	4.2	5.4	1.3	1.3	35%	67%	12
	07	26	aaa	CIN	10	6	22	0	125	139	66	13	53	63	4.75	1.53	25.3	276	3.8	4.5	1.2	1.0	30%	71%	23
Elbert,Scott	06	21	aa	LA	6	4	11	0	62.1	47	33	13	47	64	4.78	1.51	25.0	206	6.8	9.3	1.4	1.9	23%	75%	42
Estrada,Paul	06	24	aa	HOU	8	5	56	15	88.2	74	38	12	39	107	3.87	1.28	6.6	222	4.0	11.0	2.8	1.2	31%	74%	99
	07	25	aa	HOU	1	8	53	36	70.1	91	53	8	47	52	6.85	1.97	6.5	308	6.0	6.7	1.1	1.0	36%	65%	27
Fruto,Emiliano	04	20	aa	SEA	3	3	43	1	68.1	84	50	6	36	55	6.54	1.76	7.4	297	4.8	7.2	1.5	0.8	36%	62%	48
	05	21	a/a	SEA	3	5	48	12	76.2	70	38	7	31	71	4.50	1.34	6.8	241	3.7	8.4	2.3	0.8	31%	67%	82
	06	22	aaa	SEA	1	3	28	10	45.1	35	18	1	21	51	3.61	1.25	6.7	211	4.2	10.3	2.5	0.2	31%	69%	120
	07	23	a/a	ARI	3	10	24	0	98.1	96	63	7	66	72	5.78	1.65	18.7	251	6.1	6.6	1.1	0.6	30%	64%	48
Galarraga,Armando	05	24	aa	WAS	3	3	12	0	71.1	86	48	10	19	47	6.13	1.46	26.0	292	2.3	5.9	2.5	1.3	33%	59%	46
	06	25	aa	TEX	1	6	9	0	41	71	35	7	14	31	7.63	2.05	22.7	371	3.0	6.9	2.3	1.6	43%	64%	22
	07	26	aa	TEX	11	8	27	0	152.1	191	101	21	64	104	5.98	1.68	25.9	301	3.8	6.1	1.6	1.2	34%	66%	28
Gallagher,Sean	06	21	aa	CHC	7	5	15	0	86.1	94	41	6	62	84	4.28	1.81	27.2	273	6.5	8.8	1.4	0.6	36%	77%	64
	07	22	aa	CHC	10	3	19	0	101.2	101	44	5	38	76	3.91	1.37	22.9	255	3.4	6.8	2.0	0.4	31%	71%	73
Garcia,Harvey	07	24	aa	FLA	6	3	60	1	72.1	92	53	12	41	62	6.56	1.84	5.7	304	5.1	7.7	1.5	1.5	36%	67%	26
Garcia,Jaime	07	21	aa	STL	5	9	18	0	103.1	103	48	14	43	85	4.19	1.42	24.8	255	3.8	7.4	2.0	1.2	30%	74%	53
Garcia,Jose	06	22	aa	FLA	6	7	14	0	84.2	94	44	12	28	79	4.70	1.45	26.3	277	3.0	8.4	2.8	1.3	34%	71%	71
Green,Nick	06	28	aa	LAA	8	5	17	0	112.1	149	69	25	24	52	5.52	1.54	29.4	312	1.9	4.2	2.2	2.0	32%	70%	3
Gronkiewicz,Lee	04	26	a/a	CLE	1	4	53	20	66.1	79	27	6	23	52	3.63	1.55	5.6	290	3.2	7.1	2.2	0.8	35%	78%	64
	05	27	a/a	TOR	2	1	66	30	66.2	62	20	7	28	55	2.66	1.35	4.3	243	3.8	7.5	2.0	0.9	29%	85%	65
	06	28	aaa	TOR	2	3	41	17	44	61	24	5	10	27	4.84	1.61	4.9	323	2.0	5.5	2.8	1.1	37%	72%	49
	07	29	a/a	TOR	3	0	47	13	74.2	98	30	11	12	58	3.70	1.48	6.9	310	1.5	7.1	4.8	1.3	36%	80%	96
Guevara,Carlos	06	25	aa	CIN	2	3	49	1	77.1	94	45	8	29	71	5.28	1.60	7.1	294	3.4	8.3	2.4	1.0	37%	68%	67
	07	26	aa	CIN	1	2	51	16	62	66	22	6	26	67	3.23	1.47	5.3	266	3.7	9.7	2.6	0.8	36%	81%	90
Gutierrez,Juan	06	23	aa	HOU	8	4	20	0	103.2	111	43	11	35	87	3.78	1.42	22.4	270	3.1	7.6	2.5	1.0	33%	76%	69
	07	24	aa	HOU	5	10	26	0	156	184	91	21	66	86	5.22	1.61	27.2	288	3.8	5.0	1.3	1.2	32%	70%	18
Haeger,Charles	05	22	aa	CHW	6	3	13	0	85.2	94	42	1	44	41	4.44	1.62	29.8	274	4.6	4.3	0.9	0.1	33%	70%	43
	06	23	aaa	CHW	14	6	26	0	170	172	78	13	83	111	4.13	1.50	28.9	257	4.4	5.9	1.3	0.7	30%	73%	46
	07	24	aaa	CHW	5	16	24	0	147.2	168	92	24	71	112	5.63	1.62	27.9	281	4.3	6.8	1.6	1.5	32%	68%	29
Haigwood,Daniel	05	22	aa	CHW	6	1	11	0	67.1	44	15	0	30	65	2.01	1.10	24.5	183	4.0	8.7	2.2	0.0	26%	80%	116
	06	23	aa	TEX	3	7	27	0	146	174	86	16	93	123	5.30	1.83	25.7	290	5.7	7.6	1.3	1.0	35%	72%	41
	07	24	aa	BOS	3	5	17	0	69	80	56	12	51	60	7.26	1.90	19.6	285	6.6	7.8	1.2	1.6	34%	63%	22
Hammond,Steve	06	24	aa	MIL	5	6	13	0	73.2	82	36	9	29	49	4.40	1.52	25.0	278	3.6	6.1	1.7	1.2	32%	74%	36
	07	25	aa	MIL	7	9	29	1	142	211	103	24	51	89	6.55	1.85	23.3	337	3.2	5.6	1.7	1.5	37%	67%	12
Hansack,Devern	06	29	aa	BOS	8	7	31	1	132.1	184	81	21	46	86	5.54	1.74	19.9	323	3.2	5.9	1.9	1.4	36%	71%	22
	07	30	aaa	BOS	10	7	25	0	139.2	167	84	20	46	102	5.40	1.53	24.8	291	3.0	6.6	2.2	1.3	34%	67%	44
Harben,Adam	06	23	aa	MIN	4	9	29	1	122.2	148	76	6	77	61	5.62	1.85	20.1	294	5.7	4.5	0.8	0.5	33%	68%	26
Harrison,Matt	06	21	aa	ATL	3	4	13	0	77.1	102	44	7	19	48	5.14	1.57	26.6	312	2.2	5.6	2.5	0.8	36%	68%	55
	07	22	aa	ATL	5	7	20	0	116.2	138	56	7	35	67	4.34	1.49	25.6	289	2.7	5.2	1.9	0.5	33%	70%	52
Hart,Kevin	07	25	aa	CHC	12	6	27	0	158	192	93	25	54	105	5.28	1.55	26.2	293	3.1	6.0	1.9	1.4	33%	69%	30
Hawksworth,Blake	06	24	aa	STL	4	2	13	0	79.2	82	35	8	31	55	3.98	1.43	26.5	263	3.5	6.3	1.8	0.9	31%	75%	50
	07	25	aa	STL	4	13	25	0	129.2	174	91	24	41	74	6.31	1.66	23.7	315	2.9	5.2	1.8	1.7	34%	65%	10
Hedrick,Justin	07	25	aa	SF	4	6	41	1	71.1	69	22	4	40	56	2.81	1.53	7.7	249	5.1	7.1	1.4	0.6	31%	83%	60
Hernandez,Fernando	07	23	aa	CHW	1	3	60	9	85.1	92	41	6	26	73	4.36	1.38	6.1	270	2.7	7.7	2.8	0.7	34%	69%	87
Hochevar,Luke	07	24	a/a	KC	9	4	27	0	152	198	107	25	48	116	6.36	1.62	25.6	308	2.9	6.9	2.4	1.5	36%	63%	40
Hoey,James	07	25	a/a	BAL	3	0	40	16	45.2	34	5	1	14	58	1.03	1.07	4.5	205	2.9	11.6	4.0	0.2	32%	91%	162
Holliman,Mark	07	24	aa	CHC	10	11	27	0	161.1	193	84	20	62	86	4.70	1.58	26.9	291	3.5	4.8	1.4	1.1	32%	73%	21
Horne,Alan	07	25	aa	NYY	12	4	27	0	153.1	196	80	15	66	131	4.70	1.71	26.3	305	3.9	7.7	2.0	0.9	38%	74%	56
Hudgins,John	04	23	a/a	TEX	5	4	15	0	81	90	44	18	24	62	4.89	1.41	23.4	276	2.7	6.9	2.6	2.0	30%	73%	35
	05	24	a/a	TEX	4	9	22	0	120	166	93	16	45	74	6.96	1.76	25.5	321	3.4	5.5	1.6	1.2	36%	61%	21
	06	25	a/a	TEX	6	5	18	0	76.2	89	45	6	26	64	5.35	1.52	18.8	287	3.1	7.5	2.4	0.7	35%	64%	71
Hurley,Eric	06	21	aa	TEX	3	1	6	0	37	25	11	5	11	27	2.68	0.97	24.0	188	2.7	6.6	2.5	1.2	21%	81%	72
	07	22	aa	TEX	11	9	28	0	162	161	93	33	55	115	5.17	1.33	24.6	254	3.1	6.4	2.1	1.8	27%	67%	31
Ingram,Jesse	07	25	aa	TEX	3	1	56	26	62	57	42	14	31	54	6.13	1.42	4.8	238	4.5	7.8	1.7	2.1	26%	62%	28

PITCHER	Yr	Age	Lev	Org	W	L	G	Sv	IP	H	ER	HR	BB	K	ERA	Br/IP	BF/G	OBA	bb/9	K/9	Cmd	HR/9	H%	S%	BPV
Jackson,Zach	05	22	a/a	TOR	8	7	17	0	101.1	142	68	8	35	67	6.05	1.75	27.8	325	3.1	6.0	1.9	0.7	38%	64%	45
	06	23	aaa	MIL	4	6	18	0	107	126	65	14	47	52	5.47	1.62	27.0	287	4.0	4.4	1.1	1.2	31%	68%	12
	07	24	aaa	MIL	11	10	29	0	169.2	216	107	15	68	112	5.69	1.68	26.8	304	3.6	6.0	1.6	0.8	36%	66%	41
James,Brad	07	23	aa	HOU	1	5	9	0	47	62	33	2	21	18	6.32	1.75	24.4	311	3.9	3.5	0.9	0.4	34%	62%	21
Johnson,James	06	23	aa	BAL	13	6	27	0	156	207	109	18	61	108	6.30	1.72	26.8	313	3.5	6.2	1.8	1.0	36%	63%	37
	07	24	aaa	BAL	6	12	26	0	148	202	94	20	50	95	5.72	1.70	26.3	319	3.0	5.8	1.9	1.2	36%	68%	29
Jurrjens,Jair	06	21	aa	DET	4	3	12	0	67	81	31	8	21	48	4.22	1.52	24.8	293	2.8	6.5	2.3	1.0	34%	75%	53
	07	22	aa	DET	7	5	19	0	112.2	136	55	8	32	81	4.41	1.50	26.1	293	2.6	6.5	2.5	0.6	35%	71%	69
Kinney,Josh	03	25	aa	STL	2	1	29	2	39.2	24	4	2	14	42	0.97	0.97	5.3	175	3.1	9.6	3.1	0.5	24%	94%	127
	04	26	aa	STL	3	8	50	4	55.2	82	42	7	37	38	6.88	2.15	5.6	338	6.0	6.2	1.0	1.1	39%	68%	13
	05	26	a/a	STL	6	4	58	11	67.2	80	31	6	32	53	4.17	1.67	5.3	290	4.3	7.1	1.6	0.7	35%	76%	52
	06	28	aaa	STL	2	2	51	3	71	57	16	2	32	63	2.00	1.25	5.8	215	4.0	7.9	2.0	0.3	28%	84%	93
Komine,Shane	03	23	aa	OAK	4	6	19	0	103.1	118	48	6	30	64	4.19	1.44	23.6	282	2.6	5.6	2.1	0.5	33%	70%	61
	04	24	aa	OAK	4	5	17	0	94.1	118	59	11	29	53	5.62	1.56	24.8	300	2.8	5.1	1.8	1.1	33%	65%	32
	05	25	aa	OAK	2	1	5	0	31.1	31	13	5	7	27	3.66	1.22	25.7	252	2.1	7.7	3.6	1.5	29%	77%	81
	06	26	aaa	OAK	11	8	24	0	140	159	69	13	35	98	4.42	1.39	25.1	280	2.3	6.3	2.8	0.8	33%	69%	70
	07	27	aa	OAK	5	12	23	0	133	187	100	25	51	74	6.77	1.79	27.2	325	3.4	5.0	1.5	1.7	35%	65%	-1
Laffey,Aaron	06	21	aa	CLE	8	3	19	0	112.1	139	54	9	34	54	4.34	1.54	26.3	298	2.7	4.3	1.6	0.7	33%	73%	33
	07	22	a/a	CLE	13	4	22	0	131.1	135	51	7	31	90	3.50	1.27	24.9	261	2.1	6.2	2.9	0.5	31%	72%	86
Lambert,Chris	05	23	aa	STL	3	8	18	0	85	100	59	8	44	61	6.25	1.69	21.8	287	4.7	6.5	1.4	0.8	34%	63%	40
	06	24	a/a	STL	10	10	24	0	124.2	150	90	21	63	99	6.52	1.71	24.0	293	4.6	7.2	1.6	1.5	34%	64%	27
	07	25	a/a	DET	1	6	34	0	90	123	80	18	41	65	8.04	1.82	12.6	318	4.1	6.5	1.6	1.8	36%	57%	11
Lannan,John	07	23	a/a	WAS	6	3	13	0	74	70	24	3	27	33	2.92	1.31	24.1	245	3.3	4.0	1.2	0.4	28%	78%	45
Lerew,Anthony	05	23	a/a	ATL	10	6	27	0	148	153	75	17	55	102	4.56	1.41	23.7	261	3.3	6.2	1.9	1.0	30%	70%	48
	06	24	a/a	ATL	7	7	25	0	119.2	166	98	16	53	93	7.40	1.84	22.7	323	4.0	7.0	1.8	1.2	38%	60%	33
Lewis,Scott	07	24	aa	CLE	7	9	27	0	134.2	163	71	14	37	105	4.73	1.49	21.9	294	2.5	7.0	2.8	0.9	35%	69%	70
Liz,Radhames	06	23	aa	BAL	3	1	10	0	50.1	69	42	12	33	48	7.59	2.04	24.8	321	5.9	8.5	1.4	2.2	38%	67%	6
	07	24	aa	BAL	11	4	25	0	137	121	61	15	71	133	4.01	1.40	23.7	232	4.6	8.7	1.9	1.0	30%	74%	72
Lumsden,Tyler	06	23	aa	CHW	11	5	27	0	159	168	56	10	60	80	3.15	1.43	25.6	266	3.4	4.5	1.3	0.6	30%	79%	39
	07	24	aa	KC	9	6	25	0	119.1	172	102	12	61	62	7.72	1.95	23.2	330	4.6	4.7	1.0	0.9	37%	59%	12
Machi,Jean	06	24	aa	TAM	6	1	49	16	71.2	89	32	3	43	56	4.04	1.85	6.9	299	5.5	7.1	1.3	0.4	37%	78%	53
	07	25	aa	TOR	2	4	48	2	81.2	82	41	11	25	46	4.55	1.32	7.2	257	2.8	5.1	1.8	1.2	28%	68%	37
Martinez,Carlos	07	25	aa	FLA	2	1	23	0	23.2	30	11	2	7	17	4.31	1.58	4.5	307	2.6	6.6	2.6	0.9	37%	74%	61
Masterson,Justin	07	22	aa	BOS	4	3	10	0	58	66	40	5	21	43	6.21	1.50	25.6	280	3.3	6.6	2.0	0.7	34%	57%	59
Mateo,Juan	06	24	aa	CHC	7	4	18	0	92.2	107	49	10	32	60	4.83	1.51	22.7	285	3.1	5.9	1.9	1.0	33%	70%	43
	07	25	aa	CHC	2	3	8	0	40	61	24	11	12	23	5.45	1.82	23.7	343	2.6	5.1	2.0	2.4	36%	78%	-13
Mathieson,Scott	06	23	a/a	PHI	10	3	19	0	127	124	70	15	41	113	4.96	1.30	28.2	251	2.9	8.0	2.8	1.1	31%	63%	79
Matos,Osiris	07	23	aa	SF	5	0	35	4	56	59	22	3	22	36	3.48	1.44	7.0	264	3.5	5.8	1.7	0.5	31%	76%	57
McBeth,Marcus	06	26	a/a	OAK	3	3	51	25	61.2	61	30	8	28	56	4.41	1.45	5.2	255	4.1	8.2	2.0	1.1	31%	73%	61
	07	27	a/a	CIN	2	1	38	17	41.2	54	16	6	11	26	3.52	1.59	4.9	310	2.5	5.7	2.3	1.3	35%	83%	37
McCutchen,Daniel	07	25	aa	NYY	3	2	7	0	41	41	18	3	14	27	3.90	1.36	25.0	256	3.2	5.9	1.9	0.7	30%	72%	57
McDonald,James	07	23	aa	LA	7	2	10	0	52.2	46	10	6	16	56	1.72	1.19	21.4	232	2.8	9.7	3.5	1.0	30%	93%	109
Meyer,Dan	04	23	a/a	ATL	9	6	26	0	126.1	130	43	8	36	126	3.07	1.32	20.5	261	2.6	9.0	3.5	0.6	35%	78%	113
	05	24	aaa	OAK	2	8	19	0	89	108	56	15	41	54	5.66	1.67	21.5	294	4.1	5.5	1.3	1.5	32%	69%	11
	06	25	aaa	OAK	3	3	10	0	49.2	69	30	10	19	25	5.54	1.79	23.2	323	3.5	4.5	1.3	1.8	34%	74%	-11
	07	26	aa	OAK	8	2	22	0	119.1	141	62	17	61	79	4.69	1.70	25.0	289	4.6	6.0	1.3	1.3	33%	76%	21
Mijares,Jose	07	23	a/a	MIN	5	4	51	9	69.2	58	39	11	57	66	5.07	1.66	6.2	223	7.4	8.6	1.2	1.4	27%	73%	43
Miller,Adam	06	22	a/a	CLE	15	6	27	0	158.1	147	60	9	46	150	3.42	1.22	24.2	241	2.6	8.5	3.3	0.5	32%	72%	112
	07	23	aaa	CLE	5	4	19	0	65.1	73	40	4	20	65	5.53	1.43	14.9	278	2.8	9.0	3.3	0.5	37%	60%	106
Miller,Greg	06	22	a/a	LA	4	0	44	1	59.2	48	22	1	44	49	3.33	1.54	6.0	216	6.7	7.5	1.1	0.1	28%	77%	76
	07	23	aa	LA	2	3	34	1	76.2	73	58	3	89	85	6.85	2.13	11.3	247	10.5	10.0	1.0	0.4	35%	65%	75
Miller,Jim	06	24	aa	COL	0	3	45	12	44.1	62	26	14	14	33	5.37	1.72	4.5	325	2.8	6.8	2.4	2.8	35%	80%	-2
	07	25	a/a	BAL	3	5	52	7	66.1	63	34	4	43	66	4.59	1.61	5.8	247	5.9	8.9	1.5	0.6	33%	71%	74
Misch,Pat	04	23	aa	SF	7	6	26	0	159	165	69	12	36	101	3.91	1.26	25.6	262	2.0	5.7	2.8	0.7	31%	70%	75
	05	24	aa	SF	7	11	28	0	163.1	219	105	22	45	92	5.80	1.62	26.4	315	2.5	5.1	2.0	1.2	35%	66%	29
	06	25	a/a	SF	9	6	28	0	168.2	208	74	16	37	110	3.94	1.46	26.3	298	2.0	5.9	3.0	0.8	35%	75%	68
	07	26	aa	SF	2	5	34	1	66.2	70	30	5	22	55	4.06	1.39	8.4	266	3.0	7.5	2.5	0.6	33%	71%	80
Mock,Garrett	06	23	aa	WAS	4	12	27	0	147.2	209	120	21	61	104	7.31	1.83	25.9	327	3.7	6.3	1.7	1.3	38%	60%	26
	07	24	aa	WAS	1	5	11	0	51.1	78	40	5	29	32	7.05	2.10	23.3	343	5.2	5.7	1.1	0.9	39%	66%	16
Morales,Alexis	07	25	a/a	WAS	4	3	28	2	38	32	24	2	44	42	5.62	2.01	6.7	224	10.5	9.9	0.9	0.5	31%	71%	75
Morales,Franklin	07	22	aa	COL	5	4	20	0	112.2	118	60	12	58	83	4.81	1.57	25.2	265	4.7	6.7	1.4	1.0	31%	71%	43
Morillo,Juan	06	23	aa	COL	12	8	27	0	140.1	151	93	17	77	113	5.97	1.63	23.6	270	4.9	7.3	1.5	1.1	32%	64%	43
	07	24	aa	COL	6	5	53	0	67	64	27	3	32	61	3.60	1.43	5.5	246	4.3	8.2	1.9	0.4	32%	74%	83
Morton,Charlie	07	24	aa	ATL	4	6	41	0	79.2	96	49	3	40	55	5.62	1.72	9.0	293	4.6	6.3	1.4	0.4	36%	65%	52
Mullins,Ryan	07	24	a/a	MIN	4	6	18	0	101	136	73	8	30	64	6.50	1.64	25.6	316	2.7	5.7	2.1	0.7	37%	59%	50
Munoz,Arnaldo	03	21	aaa	CHW	4	3	49	6	55	56	35	8	25	63	5.65	1.49	4.9	260	4.2	10.3	2.5	1.3	34%	64%	76
	04	22	CHW	9	8	26	0	144	155	77	14	53	112	4.81	1.44	24.2	269	3.3	7.0	2.1	0.9	32%	68%	61
	05	23	aaa	CHW	8	13	39	1	126.2	156	69	20	58	91	4.92	1.70	14.9	297	4.1	6.5	1.6	1.4	34%	75%	25
	06	24	a/a	CHW	2	5	33	2	52.1	61	41	7	24	44	7.12	1.62	7.2	286	4.1	7.5	1.8	1.2	34%	56%	44
	07	25	aaa	WAS	3	1	54	0	52.2	54	19	5	18	39	3.31	1.37	4.2	260	3.1	6.7	2.1	0.9	31%	79%	61
Nestor,Scott	07	23	aa	FLA	2	4	58	1	75	75	44	5	43	77	5.32	1.58	5.8	256	5.2	9.2	1.8	0.6	34%	65%	78
Niemann,Jeff	06	24	aa	TAM	5	5	14	0	77.1	73	35	8	34	70	4.09	1.39	23.7	245	4.0	8.2	2.1	1.0	31%	73%	69
	07	25	aaa	TAM	10	7	26	0	131	175	79	16	50	108	5.43	1.72	24.3	314	3.4	7.4	2.2	1.1	38%	70%	49
Ohlendorf,Ross	06	24	a/a	ARI	10	8	28	0	182.2	226	88	16	30	111	4.33	1.40	28.1	298	1.5	5.5	3.7	0.8	34%	70%	81
	07	25	aaa	NYY	3	4	22	0	68.1	106	51	9	25	41	6.67	1.93	15.0	348	3.3	5.4	1.6	1.2	39%	66%	15
Olson,Garrett	06	23	aa	BAL	6	5	14	0	84.1	95	44	6	32	76	4.71	1.51	26.6	279	3.4	8.1	2.4	0.6	36%	69%	79
	07	24	aaa	BAL	9	7	22	0	128	117	63	17	40	105	4.43	1.23	24.1	238	2.8	7.4	2.6	1.2	28%	67%	71

PITCHER	Yr	Age	Lev	Org	W	L	G	Sv	IP	H	ER	HR	BB	K	ERA	Br/IP	BF/G	OBA	bb/9	K/9	Cmd	HR/9	H%	S%	BPV
Orenduff,Justin	05	22	aa	LA	5	1	13	0	61.1	54	27	6	21	53	3.98	1.23	19.5	232	3.1	7.8	2.5	0.9	29%	70%	82
	06	23	aa	LA	4	2	10	0	50.1	48	26	5	21	45	4.63	1.38	21.5	249	3.7	8.0	2.2	0.9	31%	68%	71
	07	24	aa	LA	8	5	27	0	109	132	62	19	47	95	5.13	1.64	18.4	292	3.9	7.8	2.0	1.6	35%	73%	39
Oxspring,Chris	03	26	aa	SD	10	6	40	0	135.2	138	61	7	72	93	4.06	1.56	15.1	259	4.8	6.2	1.3	0.5	31%	73%	54
	04	27	aaa	SD	6	4	17	0	85.2	93	42	6	43	66	4.45	1.59	22.6	271	4.6	6.9	1.5	0.7	33%	72%	54
	05	28	aaa	SD	12	6	26	0	160.2	165	76	12	42	106	4.29	1.29	25.9	260	2.4	6.0	2.5	0.7	31%	67%	72
	07	30	aaa	MIL	7	5	18	0	96	118	53	12	51	86	5.00	1.76	25.0	296	4.8	8.1	1.7	1.1	36%	74%	46
Parisi,Michael	07	24	aa	STL	8	13	28	0	165	223	106	17	65	93	5.80	1.75	27.5	317	3.6	5.1	1.4	1.1	35%	68%	18
Parnell,Robert	07	23	aa	NYM	5	5	17	0	88.2	113	56	9	38	62	5.68	1.72	24.1	306	3.9	6.3	1.6	0.9	36%	67%	38
Patterson,Scott	06	27	aa	NYY	0	1	26	1	38.2	39	17	10	11	30	3.97	1.29	6.2	257	2.6	7.0	2.8	2.3	27%	82%	36
	07	28	a/a	NYY	4	2	44	2	77.1	65	14	1	19	65	1.65	1.08	7.0	223	2.2	7.6	3.5	0.1	29%	84%	125
Patton,Troy	06	21	aa	HOU	2	5	8	0	45.1	55	27	7	13	31	5.39	1.51	25.0	295	2.6	6.2	2.4	1.4	33%	67%	41
	07	22	aa	HOU	10	8	24	0	151.1	159	70	17	44	80	4.17	1.34	26.8	265	2.6	4.8	1.8	1.0	29%	72%	38
Pauley,David	05	22	aa	BOS	9	7	27	0	156	199	85	20	34	89	4.90	1.49	25.5	304	2.0	5.1	2.6	1.2	34%	69%	45
	06	23	a/a	BOS	3	6	19	0	110.2	139	65	20	36	63	5.31	1.59	26.1	302	2.9	5.1	1.8	1.6	32%	71%	13
	07	24	aaa	BOS	6	6	27	0	153.2	198	100	21	52	94	5.87	1.63	25.8	307	3.1	5.5	1.8	1.2	34%	66%	28
Paulino,Felipe	07	24	aa	HOU	4	5	22	0	112	121	56	7	51	90	4.47	1.53	22.6	269	4.1	7.2	1.8	0.6	33%	70%	65
Pelland,Tyler	06	23	aa	CIN	9	5	28	0	142	179	88	15	96	87	5.55	1.94	24.6	302	6.1	5.5	0.9	1.0	34%	72%	18
	07	24	a/a	CIN	6	5	54	2	89.2	94	47	9	40	84	4.74	1.50	7.3	265	4.0	8.5	2.1	0.9	34%	70%	70
Pereira,Nick	06	24	aaa	SF	4	3	15	0	79	94	57	9	45	51	6.49	1.76	24.6	290	5.1	5.8	1.1	1.0	33%	63%	25
	07	25	aaa	SF	9	9	26	0	143.1	157	71	17	71	95	4.47	1.59	24.8	273	4.5	5.9	1.3	1.1	31%	74%	33
Perez,Juan	03	23	aa	BOS	3	3	18	0	30.2	48	18	4	12	18	5.30	1.99	8.2	351	3.6	5.4	1.5	1.3	39%	76%	8
	04	24	aa	BOS	5	1	46	6	78.1	85	44	12	37	66	5.11	1.56	7.6	270	4.3	7.6	1.8	1.4	32%	71%	41
	05	25	aaa	BOS	4	5	40	1	62	68	35	7	28	63	5.08	1.55	6.9	273	4.1	9.1	2.3	1.0	35%	69%	72
	06	26	aaa	PIT	0	1	47	0	70	90	30	5	42	48	3.87	1.89	7.2	306	5.4	6.2	1.2	0.7	36%	81%	34
	07	27	aa	PIT	3	2	40	2	55.2	79	47	7	33	40	7.61	2.03	6.8	328	5.4	6.5	1.2	1.1	38%	62%	21
Perez,Oneli	07	24	aa	CHW	6	2	59	16	77	80	26	8	22	75	3.08	1.33	5.5	262	2.6	8.8	3.4	1.0	33%	81%	97
Pignatiello,Carmen	04	22	aa	CHC	9	7	27	0	148	189	89	18	41	123	5.41	1.55	24.5	304	2.5	7.5	3.0	1.1	37%	67%	69
	05	23	a/a	CHC	6	9	37	0	126	128	58	11	49	104	4.14	1.40	14.7	258	3.5	7.4	2.1	0.8	32%	72%	69
	06	24	a/a	CHC	3	1	46	0	67	77	31	4	25	67	4.15	1.52	6.5	283	3.3	9.0	2.7	0.6	37%	73%	92
	07	25	aa	CHC	2	0	50	4	55.2	54	21	7	21	38	3.44	1.37	4.7	252	3.4	6.2	1.8	1.1	29%	79%	46
Plummer,Jarod	07	24	aa	KC	5	6	46	11	82	84	41	15	19	78	4.53	1.24	7.4	259	2.0	8.5	4.2	1.7	31%	70%	91
Pomeranz,Stuart	05	21	aa	STL	5	5	18	0	98.2	109	54	10	35	61	4.98	1.46	23.9	275	3.2	5.6	1.7	0.9	31%	67%	44
	06	22	aa	STL	7	4	18	0	98.1	119	55	13	29	55	5.05	1.51	24.1	293	2.7	5.0	1.9	1.2	32%	69%	31
Purcey,David	05	23	aa	TOR	4	3	8	0	43	42	22	3	29	39	4.53	1.65	24.6	252	6.0	8.1	1.3	0.6	32%	73%	62
	06	24	a/a	TOR	6	12	28	0	140	191	125	23	93	106	8.02	2.03	24.7	318	6.0	6.8	1.1	1.5	37%	61%	12
	07	25	aa	TOR	3	5	11	0	62	86	51	6	18	42	7.42	1.67	25.9	321	2.6	6.1	2.4	0.8	38%	53%	53
Ramirez,Edwar	07	27	a/a	NYY	4	0	34	0	56.2	36	8	1	27	77	1.25	1.11	6.7	178	4.3	12.3	2.9	0.2	30%	89%	148
Ramos,Cesar	07	23	aa	SD	13	9	27	0	163.2	178	76	16	46	77	4.21	1.38	26.0	272	2.6	4.2	1.7	0.9	30%	71%	33
Register,Steven	06	23	aa	COL	4	10	27	0	155	231	129	34	53	64	7.48	1.83	27.3	338	3.1	3.7	1.2	2.0	35%	62%	-24
	07	24	aa	COL	1	3	61	37	58	81	38	4	17	41	5.88	1.69	4.4	324	2.6	6.3	2.4	0.7	39%	64%	60
Reineke,Chad	06	25	aa	HOU	1	3	15	0	44.1	40	19	3	27	36	3.87	1.53	13.1	237	5.6	7.4	1.3	0.6	29%	75%	60
	07	25	aa	HOU	5	5	32	0	100	124	69	9	58	72	6.20	1.82	14.8	299	5.2	6.5	1.2	0.8	35%	65%	36
Robertson,Connor	06	25	aa	OAK	7	2	55	6	83.2	91	33	1	23	75	3.61	1.38	6.5	273	2.5	8.1	3.2	0.1	36%	72%	113
	07	26	aa	OAK	4	1	31	2	39.1	56	26	3	23	30	6.09	2.03	6.2	330	5.3	6.8	1.3	0.8	40%	70%	33
Rohrbaugh,Robert	06	23	aa	SEA	5	5	14	0	85.2	103	47	11	29	57	4.96	1.55	27.2	293	3.1	6.0	2.0	1.2	33%	70%	39
	07	24	aa	SEA	13	8	28	0	170.1	194	71	16	51	97	3.76	1.44	26.5	281	2.7	5.1	1.9	0.9	32%	76%	44
Romero,Ricky	07	23	aa	TOR	3	6	18	0	88.1	113	59	11	52	68	6.03	1.87	23.5	305	5.3	6.9	1.3	1.1	36%	69%	29
Roquet,Rocky	07	25	aa	CHC	4	0	28	7	39.2	39	21	5	20	33	4.83	1.50	6.2	254	4.6	7.6	1.7	1.2	30%	71%	49
Rosa,Carlos	07	23	aa	KC	6	6	21	1	97	121	60	8	43	60	5.55	1.69	21.3	299	4.0	5.6	1.4	0.8	34%	67%	35
Russell,Adam	06	23	aa	CHW	3	3	10	0	55	75	43	8	22	39	7.09	1.76	25.8	319	3.5	6.3	1.8	1.3	37%	60%	26
	07	24	aa	CHW	9	11	38	1	138.2	204	107	13	65	81	6.99	1.95	17.7	336	4.3	5.3	1.2	0.8	38%	63%	21
Sadler,Billy	04	23	aa	SF	0	3	17	0	30.1	26	16	3	19	19	4.93	1.47	7.8	227	5.5	5.8	1.0	0.9	26%	68%	39
	05	24	aa	SF	6	5	46	5	82.1	76	39	4	33	63	4.27	1.32	7.6	240	3.6	6.9	1.9	0.5	30%	67%	75
	06	25	a/a	SF	6	3	51	21	55.2	35	20	2	33	65	3.26	1.22	4.5	177	5.3	10.5	2.0	0.3	26%	73%	114
	07	26	aa	SF	3	2	49	7	54.2	51	40	7	46	57	6.68	1.78	5.2	242	7.6	9.5	1.2	1.1	31%	63%	56
Salas,Marino	06	26	aa	BAL	2	6	44	19	49.1	52	24	4	19	37	4.48	1.45	4.9	267	3.5	6.8	2.0	0.8	32%	70%	59
	07	27	a/a	MIL	0	1	51	17	61.2	68	27	11	26	44	3.92	1.53	5.3	275	3.8	6.5	1.7	1.6	31%	81%	26
Sanchez,Humberto	05	22	aa	DET	3	5	14	0	62	75	43	9	24	53	6.24	1.60	20.0	293	3.5	7.7	2.2	1.3	35%	62%	50
	06	23	a/a	DET	10	6	20	0	123	116	47	5	48	111	3.44	1.33	26.2	244	3.5	8.1	2.3	0.4	32%	74%	92
Sarfate,Dennis	04	24	aa	MIL	7	12	28	0	129	164	86	18	88	93	5.97	1.95	22.4	303	6.1	6.5	1.1	1.2	35%	71%	19
	05	24	a/a	MIL	9	10	26	0	142	141	66	14	63	102	4.18	1.44	23.8	254	4.0	6.5	1.6	0.9	30%	73%	49
	06	26	aaa	MIL	10	7	34	0	125	151	68	9	85	103	4.87	1.88	17.7	292	6.1	7.4	1.2	0.7	36%	74%	47
	07	26	aaa	MIL	2	7	45	4	61.2	74	41	7	52	60	6.06	2.06	6.8	293	7.6	8.8	1.2	1.1	37%	71%	42
Scherzer,Max	07	23	aa	ARI	4	4	14	0	73.2	77	42	4	41	65	5.20	1.62	23.7	266	5.1	8.0	1.6	0.5	34%	67%	68
Schultz,Mike	05	85	aa	ARI	4	6	63	6	65.1	96	38	5	48	53	5.20	2.22	5.3	337	6.7	7.3	1.1	0.7	41%	76%	35
	06	27	a/a	ARI	3	4	58	7	65.1	81	33	1	26	38	4.61	1.64	5.1	299	3.5	5.2	1.5	0.2	35%	69%	53
	07	28	aa	ARI	4	5	54	6	77	118	52	6	42	37	6.06	2.08	7.1	344	4.9	4.3	0.9	0.7	38%	70%	9
Shafer,David	05	24	aa	CIN	1	6	34	6	39.2	34	20	3	24	33	4.50	1.47	5.1	229	5.4	7.6	1.4	0.7	29%	70%	63
	06	25	aa	CIN	1	2	44	26	49.2	47	19	3	18	42	3.47	1.33	4.7	248	3.3	7.6	2.3	0.6	31%	75%	83
	07	26	aa	OAK	1	1	51	8	58.1	71	48	11	34	34	7.40	1.82	5.4	295	5.3	5.3	1.0	1.7	32%	61%	-3
Sharpless,Josh	06	26	a/a	PIT	3	1	37	9	54	52	16	1	26	48	2.63	1.44	6.4	246	4.4	8.1	1.8	0.2	33%	81%	88
	07	27	aa	PIT	1	5	43	3	64.1	80	44	11	44	50	6.13	1.94	7.2	301	6.1	7.1	1.2	1.6	35%	71%	13
Shearn,Tom	04	27	a/a	CIN	6	5	48	5	79	85	47	14	38	57	5.37	1.56	7.4	269	4.3	6.5	1.5	1.6	30%	69%	25
	05	28	aaa	CIN	4	4	43	1	92	96	51	13	45	73	4.94	1.53	9.5	263	4.4	7.1	1.6	1.3	31%	71%	41
	06	29	a/a	CIN	9	4	33	0	98.2	129	49	16	55	57	4.47	1.88	14.3	311	5.0	5.2	1.0	1.5	34%	80%	3
	07	30	aaa	CIN	7	10	26	0	143.2	202	98	13	59	84	6.15	1.82	26.1	326	3.7	5.3	1.4	0.8	37%	66%	26
Sipp,Tony	06	23	aa	CLE	4	2	29	3	60.1	53	27	2	23	69	4.01	1.25	8.6	231	3.4	10.3	3.0	0.3	33%	66%	125

PITCHER	Yr	Age	Lev	Org	W	L	G	Sv	IP	H	ER	HR	BB	K	ERA	Br/IP	BF/G	OBA	bb/9	K/9	Cmd	HR/9	H%	S%	BPV
Slocum,Brian	05	24	aa	CLE	7	5	21	0	102.1	117	62	9	39	79	5.47	1.53	21.6	282	3.4	7.0	2.0	0.8	34%	64%	58
	06	26	aaa	CLE	6	3	27	1	94	93	45	5	39	80	4.35	1.41	15.1	253	3.8	7.7	2.0	0.5	32%	68%	79
Smith,Brett	07	24	aa	NYY	7	4	17	0	91	80	45	11	55	64	4.48	1.48	23.6	231	5.4	6.3	1.2	1.0	26%	72%	40
Smith,Dan	06	31	aa	ATL	3	6	28	0	60.1	60	35	5	41	65	5.29	1.68	9.9	255	6.2	9.7	1.6	0.7	35%	68%	74
	07	24	a/a	ATL	7	7	23	0	109	115	61	8	64	66	5.02	1.65	21.6	266	5.3	5.4	1.0	0.7	31%	69%	36
Smith,Sean	06	23	aa	CLE	10	5	25	0	144	161	76	10	46	84	4.75	1.44	25.1	277	2.9	5.3	1.8	0.6	32%	66%	51
	07	24	aaa	CLE	9	7	24	0	133.1	148	76	16	59	82	5.14	1.56	24.8	276	4.0	5.5	1.4	1.1	31%	69%	30
Sosa,Oswaldo	07	22	aa	MIN	1	4	9	0	48	51	28	4	23	28	5.25	1.54	23.8	267	4.3	5.3	1.2	0.8	30%	66%	36
Speier,Ryan	04	25	COL		3	1	62	37	62.1	47	23	6	30	53	3.38	1.23	4.2	205	4.3	7.7	1.8	0.8	25%	75%	73
	05	26	aaa	COL	2	2	44	6	51.1	75	31	2	16	36	5.45	1.80	5.5	335	2.9	6.3	2.2	0.4	40%	68%	61
	07	28	COL		1	4	50	33	49.1	71	41	5	29	29	7.56	2.04	4.9	332	5.3	5.3	1.0	0.9	38%	62%	14
Swarzak,Anthony	07	22	aa	MIN	5	4	15	0	86.1	88	37	6	24	62	3.87	1.30	24.2	259	2.5	6.5	2.6	0.6	31%	71%	77
Talbot,Mitch	06	23	aa	TAM	10	7	28	1	156.2	168	59	7	48	133	3.40	1.38	24.0	269	2.8	7.7	2.8	0.4	34%	75%	93
	07	24	aaa	TAM	13	9	29	0	161	205	110	16	64	109	6.15	1.67	25.5	304	3.6	6.1	1.7	0.9	35%	63%	40
Tata,Jordan	06	25	aaa	DET	10	6	21	0	122	140	69	13	51	73	5.07	1.56	26.1	283	3.7	5.4	1.5	1.0	32%	69%	32
	07	26	aaa	DET	4	5	14	0	82.2	81	37	9	29	42	4.06	1.34	25.0	253	3.2	4.6	1.4	1.0	28%	72%	32
Thatcher,Joe	07	26	a/a	SD	4	1	46	1	46.2	46	8	0	11	53	1.64	1.23	4.2	256	2.1	10.4	5.1	0.0	38%	85%	172
Thomas,Justin	07	24	aa	SEA	4	9	24	0	119.1	170	88	11	66	87	6.62	1.98	24.3	328	5.0	6.6	1.3	0.9	39%	66%	31
Thompson,Sean	05	25	aa	SD	4	5	20	0	113.2	144	66	8	56	82	5.27	1.77	26.5	304	4.4	6.5	1.5	0.7	36%	70%	44
	06	24	aa	SD	6	10	27	0	154	177	86	18	51	114	5.00	1.48	25.1	283	3.0	6.7	2.3	1.0	33%	68%	55
	07	25	aa	COL	9	8	27	0	133.2	161	79	16	61	68	5.33	1.67	22.6	293	4.1	4.6	1.1	1.1	32%	69%	16
Trahern,Dallas	07	22	a/a	DET	13	6	27	0	169	207	90	13	52	85	4.82	1.53	27.9	295	2.8	4.5	1.6	0.7	33%	69%	36
Troncoso,Ramon	07	25	aa	LA	7	3	35	7	52	61	22	3	19	32	3.83	1.54	6.6	287	3.3	5.6	1.7	0.5	34%	75%	51
Van Buren,Jermaine	04	24	a/a	CHC	3	2	54	22	57.1	29	13	3	25	60	2.11	0.94	4.1	148	3.9	9.5	2.4	0.5	20%	80%	119
	05	25	aaa	CHC	2	3	52	25	54.2	36	13	5	22	56	2.18	1.08	4.2	187	3.7	9.4	2.5	0.8	25%	85%	102
	06	26	aaa	BOS	4	0	33	16	45.1	47	22	3	20	39	4.32	1.49	6.0	265	3.9	7.7	2.0	0.6	33%	71%	72
	07	27	a/a	OAK	1	3	47	3	64	72	36	10	34	44	5.01	1.67	6.3	279	4.8	6.1	1.3	1.5	31%	74%	19
Vasquez,Esmerling	07	24	aa	ARI	10	6	29	0	165.1	151	72	14	62	129	3.93	1.29	23.9	238	3.4	7.0	2.1	0.8	29%	71%	70
Vasquez,Virgil	05	23	aa	DET	2	8	15	0	83.2	105	56	9	13	45	6.02	1.42	24.1	302	1.4	4.8	3.3	1.0	34%	58%	63
	06	24	aa	DET	7	12	27	0	173.2	219	101	25	54	105	5.25	1.57	28.8	302	2.8	5.5	2.0	1.3	34%	69%	29
Vasquez,Virgil	07	25	aaa	DET	12	5	25	0	155	167	79	20	33	109	4.57	1.29	26.1	269	1.9	6.3	3.3	1.2	31%	67%	73
Veras,Jose	03	23	a/a	TAM	6	9	30	0	135.2	140	73	15	58	103	4.86	1.46	19.8	262	3.9	6.9	1.8	1.0	31%	68%	51
	04	24	a/a	TAM	7	6	33	0	94.1	129	70	11	42	60	6.70	1.82	13.5	319	4.0	5.7	1.4	1.1	36%	63%	24
	05	25	aaa	TEX	3	5	57	24	61.2	69	29	4	31	62	4.26	1.63	4.9	279	4.6	9.1	2.0	0.6	37%	74%	78
	06	26	aaa	NYY	5	3	50	21	59.2	58	20	4	20	55	3.07	1.31	5.0	250	3.1	8.4	2.7	0.6	32%	78%	95
Warden,Jim Ed	06	27	aa	CLE	5	2	55	11	59	48	28	4	36	35	4.23	1.43	4.7	219	5.5	5.3	1.0	0.6	25%	70%	47
	07	28	a/a	CLE	5	5	56	6	74.2	119	49	7	34	53	5.99	2.06	6.6	354	4.1	6.4	1.5	0.9	42%	71%	29
Whelan,Kevin	07	24	aa	NYY	4	2	31	4	54.1	43	27	3	47	55	4.46	1.68	8.0	215	7.9	9.2	1.2	0.5	29%	73%	76
Windsor,Jason	05	23	aa	OAK	3	6	11	0	56.2	76	39	5	23	32	6.27	1.76	23.9	317	3.6	5.1	1.4	0.8	36%	64%	27
	06	24	a/a	OAK	17	2	26	0	151.1	175	70	9	41	131	4.18	1.43	25.3	284	2.5	7.8	3.2	0.6	36%	71%	95
	07	25	aa	OAK	5	3	10	0	56.2	84	46	3	27	32	7.30	1.98	27.5	340	4.3	5.0	1.2	0.5	39%	61%	26
Worrell,Mark	06	24	aa	STL	3	7	57	27	61.2	60	37	10	20	63	5.46	1.30	4.5	251	2.9	9.3	3.2	1.5	31%	61%	83
	07	25	aa	STL	3	2	49	4	67	67	27	6	25	55	3.68	1.38	5.4	256	3.4	7.4	2.2	0.8	31%	76%	69
Wright,Chase	07	25	a/a	NYY	13	5	25	1	145	168	88	20	70	66	5.44	1.64	26.5	284	4.4	4.1	0.9	1.2	30%	69%	6
Yates,Kyle	06	24	aa	TOR	6	9	28	1	127.1	152	78	14	43	85	5.55	1.53	20.2	290	3.1	6.0	2.0	1.0	33%	65%	44
	07	25	aa	TOR	9	9	27	0	151	223	99	28	46	80	5.90	1.78	26.3	336	2.8	4.8	1.7	1.7	36%	71%	2
Zarate,Mauro	07	25	aa	FLA	2	1	42	1	59.2	51	16	4	23	48	2.40	1.24	5.9	226	3.5	7.2	2.1	0.6	28%	83%	77
Ziegler,Brad	06	27	a/a	OAK	9	7	27	0	162.2	231	86	23	46	74	4.78	1.71	27.8	328	2.6	4.1	1.6	1.3	35%	75%	10
	07	28	aa	OAK	12	3	50	2	78.1	89	30	0	20	44	3.47	1.40	6.8	281	2.4	5.1	2.1	0.0	34%	73%	74

THE MEGA-LISTS

This section of the book may be the smallest as far as word count is concerned, but may be the most important, as this is where players' skills and potential are tied together and ranked against their peers. The rankings that follow are divided into long-term potential in the Major Leagues and fantasy value.

TOP 100: Lists the top 100 minor league prospects in terms of long-range potential in the Major Leagues.

ORGANIZATIONAL: Lists the top 15 minor league prospects within each organization in terms of long-range potential in the Major Leagues.

POSITIONAL: Lists the top 15 minor league prospects, by position, in terms of long-range potential in the Major League.

TOP POWER: Lists the top 30 prospects that have the potential to hit for power in the Major Leagues, combining raw power, plate discipline, and at the ability to make their power game-usable.

TOP BA: Lists the top 30 prospects that have the potential to hit for high batting average in the Major Leagues, combining contact ability, plate discipline, hitting mechanics, and strength.

TOP SPEED: Lists the top 30 prospects that have the potential to steal bases in the Major Leagues, combining raw speed and base-running instincts.

TOP 100 FANTASY PROSPECTS: Lists the top 100 minor league prospects that will have the most value to their respective fantasy teams in 2008.

TOP 100 ARCHIVE: Takes a look back at the top 100 lists from the past six years.

FINAL NOTE: The rankings in this book are the creation of the minor league department at Baseball HQ. While several baseball personnel contributed player information to the book, no opinions were solicited or received in comparing players.

1. Jay Bruce (OF, CIN)
2. Evan Longoria (3B, TAM)
3. Clay Buchholz (RHP, BOS)
4. Clayton Kershaw (LHP, LAD)
5. Joba Chamberlain (RHP, NYY)
6. Colby Rasmus (OF, STL)
7. Cameron Maybin (OF, FLA)
8. Homer Bailey (RHP, CIN)
9. David Price (LHP, TAM)
10. Andrew McCutchen (OF, PIT)

11. Brandon Wood (3B/SS, LAA)
12. Matt Wieters (C, BAL)
13. Jacoby Ellsbury (OF, BOS)
14. Travis Snider (OF, TOR)
15. Reid Brignac (SS, TAM)
16. Jacob McGee (LHP, TAM)
17. Wade Davis (RHP, TAM)
18. Adam Miller (RHP, CLE)
19. Rick Porcello (RHP, DET)
20. Franklin Morales (LHP, COL)

21. Carlos Triunfel (SS, SEA)
22. Andy LaRoche (3B/OF, LAD)
23. Jordan Schafer (OF, ATL)
24. Kosuke Fukodome (OF, CHC)
25. Jose Tabata (OF, NYY)
26. Carlos Gonzalez (OF, OAK)
27. Joey Votto (1B/OF, CIN)
28. Daric Barton (1B, OAK)
29. Angel Villalona (3B, SF)
30. Eric Hurley (RHP, TEX)

31. Nick Adenhart (RHP, LAA)
32. Fernando Martinez (OF, NYM)
33. Ross Detwiler (LHP, WAS)
34. Johnny Cueto (RHP, CIN)
35. Chris Marrero (OF, WAS)
36. Jason Heyward (OF, ATL)
37. Mike Moustakas (SS, KC)
38. Elvis Andrus (SS, TEX)
39. Taylor Teagarden (C, TEX)
40. Ian Kennedy (RHP, NYY)

41. Kasey Kiker (LHP, TEX)
42. Scott Elbert (LHP, LAD)
43. Justin Masterson (RHP, BOS)
44. Max Scherzer (RHP, ARI)
45. Brandon Jones (OF, ATL)
46. Josh Vitters (3B, CHC)
47. Jarrod Parker (RHP, ARI)
48. Matt Antonelli (2B, SD)
49. Gio Gonzalez (LHP, CHW)
50. Ian Stewart (3B, COL)

51. Chase Headley (3B, SD)
52. Anthony Swarzak (RHP, MIN)
53. Jair Jurrjens (RHP, DET)
54. Billy Rowell (3B, BAL)
55. Jeff Clement (C, SEA)
56. Tyler Colvin (OF, CHC)
57. Neil Walker (3B, PIT)
58. Geovany Soto (C/1B, CHC)
59. Steven Pearce (1B/OF, PIT)
60. Fautino de los Santos (RHP, CHW)

61. Manny Parra (LHP, MIL)
62. Matt LaPorta (OF, MIL)
63. Austin Jackson (OF, NYY)
64. Carlos Carrasco (RHP, PHI)
65. Jed Lowrie (SS/2B, BOS)
66. Deolis Guerra (RHP, NYM)
67. Jonathon Meloan (RHP, LAD)
68. Chin-Lung Hu (SS, LAD)
69. Blake Beaven (RHP, TEX)
70. Michael Main (RHP, TEX)

71. Gorkys Hernandez (OF, ATL)
72. Jeff Niemann (RHP, TAM)
73. Desmond Jennings (OF, TAM)
74. Radhames Liz (RHP, BAL)
75. Chuck Lofgren (LHP, CLE)
76. Luke Hochevar (RHP, KC)
77. Brent Lillibridge (SS, ATL)
78. Jaime Garcia (LHP, STL)
79. Bryan Anderson (C, STL)
80. Troy Patton (LHP, BAL)

81. Nolan Reimold (OF, BAL)
82. Matt Latos (RHP, SD)
83. Tommy Hanson (RHP, ATL)
84. Aaron Poreda (LHP, CHW)
85. Cole Rohrbough (LHP, ATL)
86. Lars Anderson (1B, BOS)
87. Chris Volstad (RHP, FLA)
88. Henry Sosa (RHP, SF)
89. Madison Baumgarner (LHP, SF)
90. Michael Bowden (RHP, BOS)

91. Hank Conger (C, LAA)
92. JR Towles (C, HOU)
93. Greg Reynolds (RHP, COL)
94. Adrian Cardenas (2B/SS, PHI)
95. Chris Nelson (SS, COL)
96. Ryan Kalish (OF, BOS)
97. Dexter Fowler (OF, COL)
98. James McDonald (RHP, LAD)
99. Beau Mills (3B/1B, CLE)
100. Michael Burgess (OF, WAS)

AMERICAN LEAGUE EAST

BALTIMORE
1. **Matt Wieters** (C)
2. **Bill Rowell** (3B)
3. **Radhames Liz** (RHP)
4. **Troy Patton** (LHP)
5. **Nolan Reimold** (OF)
6. **Jake Arrieta** (RHP)
7. **Garrett Olson** (LHP)
8. **Chorye Spoone** (RHP)
9. **Brandon Erbe** (RHP)
10. **James Hoey** (RHP)
11. **Pedro Beato** (RHP)
12. **Brandon Snyder** (C)
13. **David Hernandez** (RHP)
14. **Mike Costanzo** (3B)
15. **Bob McCrory** (RHP)

BOSTON
1. **Clay Buchholz** (RHP)
2. **Jacoby Ellsbury** (OF)
3. **Justin Masterson** (RHP)
4. **Jed Lowrie** (SS/2B)
5. **Lars Anderson** (1B)
6. **Michael Bowden** (RHP)
7. **Ryan Kalish** (OF)
8. **Nick Hagadone** (LHP)
9. **Oscar Tejeda** (SS)
10. **Brandon Moss** (OF)
11. **Chris Carter** (1B)
12. **Josh Reddick** (OF)
13. **Will Middlebrooks** (3B)
14. **Ryan Dent** (2B/SS)
15. **Carlos Fernandez-Oliva** (OF)

YANKEES
1. **Joba Chamberlain** (RHP)
2. **Jose Tabata** (OF)
3. **Ian Kennedy** (RHP)
4. **Austin Jackson** (OF)
5. **Alan Horne** (RHP)
6. **Andrew Brackman** (RHP)
7. **Dellin Betances** (RHP)
8. **Jesus Montero** (1B/C)
9. **Humberto Sanchez** (RHP)
10. **Jeff Marquez** (RHP)
11. **Kevin Whelan** (RHP)
12. **George Kontos** (RHP)
13. **Ross Ohlendorf** (RHP)
14. **Shelly Duncan** (OF/1B)
15. **Kelvin DeLeon** (OF)

TAMPA BAY
1. **Evan Longoria** (3B)
2. **David Price** (LHP)
3. **Reid Brignac** (SS)
4. **Jacob McGee** (LHP)
5. **Wade Davis** (RHP)
6. **Jeff Neimann** (RHP)
7. **Desmond Jennings** (OF)
8. **Jeremy Hellickson** (RHP)
9. **Eduardo Morlan** (RHP)
10. **Glenn Gibson** (LHP)
11. **John Jaso** (C/1B)
12. **Ryan Royster** (OF)
13. **Mitch Talbot** (RHP)
14. **Chris Mason** (RHP)
15. **Sergio Pedroza** (OF/C)

TORONTO
1. **Travis Snider** (OF)
2. **Brett Cecil** (LHP)
3. **Kevin Ahrens** (3B/SS)
4. **John Tolisano** (2B)
5. **Eric Eiland** (OF)
6. **Yohermyn Chavez** (OF)
7. **JP Arencibia** (C/1B)
8. **Trystan Magnuson** (RHP)
9. **Ricky Romero** (LHP)
10. **Kyle Ginley** (RHP)
11. **Ryan Patterson** (OF)
12. **David Purcey** (LHP)
13. **Balbino Fuenmayor** (3B)
14. **Justin Jackson** (SS)
15. **Marc Rzepczynski** (LHP)

AMERICAN LEAGUE CENTRAL

CHICAGO
1. **Gio Gonzalez** (LHP)
2. **Fautino de los Santos** (RHP)
3. **Aaron Poreda** (RHP)
4. **Ryan Sweeney** (OF)
5. **Jose Martinez** (OF)
6. **Jack Egbert** (RHP)
7. **Lance Broadway** (RHP)
8. **John Shelby** (2B)
9. **Sergio Miranda** (SS)
10. **Oneli Perez** (RHP)
11. **Kyle McCulloch** (RHP)
12. **Micah Schnurstein** (1B/3B)
13. **John Ely** (RHP)
14. **Charles Haeger** (RHP)
15. **Nevin Griffith** (RHP)

CLEVELAND
1. **Adam Miller** (RHP)
2. **Chuck Lofgren** (LHP)
3. **Beau Mills** (3B/1B)
4. **Aaron Laffey** (LHP)
5. **Nick Weglarz** (OF/1B)
6. **Wes Hodges** (3B)
7. **Josh Rodriguez** (SS)
8. **Jordan Brown** (OF/1B)
9. **Trevor Crowe** (OF)
10. **David Huff** (LHP)
11. **John Drennen** (OF)
12. **Matt McBride** (C)
13. **Jared Goedert** (3B/2B)
14. **Scott Lewis** (LHP)
15. **Ben Francisco** (OF)

DETROIT
1. **Rick Porcello** (RHP)
2. **Brandon Hamilton** (RHP)
3. **Michael Holliman** (2B/SS)
4. **Scott Sizemore** (2B/SS)
5. **Jeff Larish** (1B)
6. **Danny Worth** (SS)
7. **Yorman Bazardo** (RHP)
8. **Cale Iorg** (SS)
9. **Virgil Vasquez** (RHP)
10. **Matt Joyce** (OF)
11. **Charlie Furbush** (LHP)
12. **Casey Crosby** (LHP)
13. **Jordan Tata** (RHP)
14. **James Skelton** (C)
15. **Freddy Guzman** (OF)

KANSAS CITY
1. **Mike Moustakas** (SS)
2. **Luke Hochevar** (RHP)
3. **Daniel Cortes** (RHP)
4. **Danny Duffy** (LHP)
5. **Julio Pimentel** (RHP)
6. **Blake Wood** (RHP)
7. **Chris Lubanski** (OF)
8. **Carlos Rosa** (RHP)
9. **Jeff Bianchi** (SS)
10. **Sam Runion** (RHP)
11. **Justin Huber** (1B/OF)
12. **Joe Dickerson** (OF)
13. **Mitch Maier** (OF)
14. **Blake Johnson** (RHP)
15. **Jarod Plummer** (RHP)

MINNESOTA
1. **Anthony Swarzak** (RHP)
2. **Ben Revere** (OF)
3. **Tyler Robertson** (LHP)
4. **Jeff Manship** (RHP)
5. **Chris Parmelee** (OF/1B)
6. **Jason Pridie** (OF)
7. **Brian Duensing** (LHP)
8. **Trevor Plouffe** (SS)
9. **David Bromberg** (RHP)
10. **Nick Blackburn** (RHP)
11. **Oswaldo Sosa** (RHP)
12. **Joe Benson** (OF)
13. **Mike McCardell** (RHP)
14. **Yohan Pino** (RHP)
15. **Danny Valencia** (3B/1B)

AMERICAN LEAGUE WEST

LOS ANGELES
1. **Brandon Wood** (SS)
2. **Nick Adenhart** (RHP)
3. **Hank Conger** (C)
4. **Jordan Walden** (RHP)
5. **Sean Rodriguez** (SS)
6. **Sean O'Sullivan** (RHP)
7. **Matt Sweeney** (3B)
8. **Chris Pettit** (OF)
9. **Terry Evans** (OF)
10. **Jose Arredondo** (RHP)
11. **Peter Bourjos** (OF)
12. **Jonathon Bachanov** (RHP)
13. **Thomas Mendoza** (RHP)
14. **Mason Tobin** (RHP)
15. **PJ Phillips** (SS)

OAKLAND
1. **Carlos Gonzalez** (OF)
2. **Daric Barton** (1B)
3. **Brett Anderson** (LHP)
4. **Trevor Cahill** (RHP)
5. **James Simmons** (RHP)
6. **Aaron Cunningham** (OF)
7. **Andrew Bailey** (RHP)
8. **Corey Brown** (OF)
9. **Sean Doolittle** (1B)
10. **Henry Rodriguez** (RHP)
11. **Chris Carter** (1B)
12. **Cliff Pennington** (SS)
13. **Javier Herrera** (OF)
14. **Jermaine Mitchell** (OF)
15. **Sam Demel** (RHP)

SEATTLE
1. **Carlos Triunfel** (SS)
2. **Jeff Clement** (C)
3. **Tony Butler** (LHP)
4. **Chris Tillman** (RHP)
5. **Wladimir Balentien** (OF)
6. **Phillippe Aumont** (RHP)
7. **Juan Ramirez** (OF)
8. **Greg Halman** (OF)
9. **Kam Mickolio** (RHP)
10. **Matt Mangini** (3B)
11. **Ryan Rowland-Smith** (LHP)
12. **Michael Saunders** (OF)
13. **Anthony Varvaro** (RHP)
14. **Matt Tuiasosopo** (3B)
15. **Mario Martinez** (SS/3B)

TEXAS
1. **Eric Hurley** (RHP)
2. **Elvis Andrus** (SS)
3. **Taylor Teagarden** (C)
4. **Kasey Kiker** (LHP)
5. **Blake Beaven** (RHP)
6. **Michael Main** (RHP)
7. **Matt Harrison** (LHP)
8. **Chris Davis** (3B)
9. **Johnny Whittleman** (3B)
10. **German Duran** (2B)
11. **Neftali Feliz** (RHP)
12. **Julio Borbon** (OF)
13. **John Mayberry, Jr.** (OF)
14. **Omar Poveda** (RHP)
15. **Fabio Castillo** (RHP)

NATIONAL LEAGUE EAST

ATLANTA
1. **Jordan Schafer** (OF)
2. **Jason Heyward** (OF)
3. **Jair Jurrjens** (RHP)
4. **Brandon Jones** (OF)
5. **Gorkys Hernandez** (OF)
6. **Brent Lillibridge** (SS)
7. **Tommy Hanson** (RHP)
8. **Cole Rohrbough** (LHP)
9. **Jeff Locke** (LHP)
10. **Joey Devine** (RHP)
11. **Cody Johnson** (OF)
12. **Josh Anderson** (OF)
13. **Jon Gilmore** (3B)
14. **Julio Teheran** (RHP)
15. **Steven Evarts** (LHP)

FLORIDA
1. **Cameron Maybin** (OF)
2. **Chris Volstad** (RHP)
3. **Matt Dominguez** (3B)
4. **Chris Coghlan** (2B)
5. **Brett Sinkbeil** (RHP)
6. **Eulogio de la Cruz** (RHP)
7. **Gaby Hernandez** (RHP)
8. **Ryan Tucker** (RHP)
9. **Aaron Thompson** (LHP)
10. **Dallas Trahern** (RHP)
11. **Harvey Garcia** (RHP)
12. **Carlos Martinez** (RHP)
13. **Robert Andino** (SS)
14. **Jai Miller** (OF)
15. **Gaby Sanchez** (1B/C/3B)

NEW YORK
1. Fernando Martinez (OF)
2. Deolis Guerra (RHP)
3. Phil Humber (RHP)
4. Jonathon Niese (LHP)
5. Kevin Mulvey (RHP)
6. Ruben Tejada (SS)
7. Scott Moviel (RHP)
8. Nate Vineyard (LHP)
9. Robert Parnell (RHP)
10. Brant Rustich (RHP)
11. Eddie Kunz (RHP)
12. Mike Carp (1B)
13. Nick Evans (1B)
14. Hector Pellot (2B)
15. Anderson Hernandez (SS/2B)

PHILADELPHIA
1. Carlos Carrasco (RHP)
2. Adrian Cardenas (2B)
3. Joe Savery (LHP)
4. JA Happ (LHP)
5. Kyle Drabek (RHP)
6. Travis Mattair (3B/SS)
7. Josh Outman (LHP)
8. Drew Carpenter (RHP)
9. Jason Donald (SS)
10. Dominic Brown (OF)
11. Lou Marson (C)
12. Edgar Garcia (RHP)
13. Greg Golson (OF)
14. Michael Zagurski (LHP)
15. Travis d'Arnaud (C)

WASHINGTON
1. Ross Detwiler (LHP)
2. Chris Marrero (OF)
3. Michael Burgess (OF)
4. Josh Smoker (LHP)
5. Jordan Zimmerman (RHP)
6. Collin Balester (RHP)
7. Jack McGeary (LHP)
8. Justin Maxwell (OF)
9. Esmailyn Gonzalez (SS)
10. Colton Willems (RHP)
11. Tyler Clippard (RHP)
12. John Lannan (LHP)
13. Adam Carr (RHP)
14. Jake Smolinski (OF)
15. Matt Whitney (1B)

NATIONAL LEAGUE CENTRAL

CHICAGO
1. Kosuke Fukodome (OF)
2. Josh Vitters (3B)
3. Tyler Colvin (OF)
4. Geovany Soto (C/1B)
5. Jeff Samardzija (RHP)
6. Sean Gallagher (RHP)
7. Jose Ceda (RHP)
8. Eric Patterson (2B)
9. Donald Veal (LHP)
10. Josh Donaldson (C)
11. Jose Ascanio (RHP)
12. Darwin Barney (SS)
13. Chris Huseby (RHP)
14. Tony Thomas (2B)
15. Kevin Hart (RHP)

CINCINNATI
1. Jay Bruce (OF)
2. Homer Bailey (RHP)
3. Joey Votto (1B)
4. Johnny Cueto (RHP)
5. Drew Stubbs (OF)
6. Todd Frazier (SS)
7. Travis Wood (LHP)
8. Devin Mesoraco (C)
9. Juan Francisco (3B)
10. Matt Maloney (LHP)
11. Chris Valaika (SS)
12. Josh Roenicke (RHP)
13. Daniel Dorn (OF)
14. Sam LeCure (RHP)
15. Daryl Thompson (RHP)

HOUSTON
1. JR Towles (C)
2. Felipe Paulino (RHP)
3. Jordan Parraz (OF)
4. Bud Norris (RHP)
5. Brad James (RHP)
6. Max Sapp (C)
7. Brian Bogusevic (LHP)
8. Mitch Einertson (OF)
9. Eli Iorg (OF)
10. Chad Reineke (RHP)
11. Tommy Manzella (SS)
12. Sergio Perez (RHP)
13. Sam Gervacio (RHP)
14. Paul Estrada (RHP)
15. Josh Flores (OF)

MILWAUKEE
1. Manny Parra (LHP)
2. Matt LaPorta (OF)
3. Jeremy Jeffress (RHP)
4. Angel Salome (C)
5. Brent Brewer (SS)
6. Mat Gamel (3B)
7. Alcides Escobar (SS)
8. Cole Gillespie (OF)
9. Taylor Green (3B)
10. Michael Brantley (OF/1B)
11. Darren Ford (OF)
12. Jon Lucroy (C)
13. Zach Braddock (LHP)
14. Lorenzo Cain (OF)
15. Hernan Iribarren (2B)

PITTSBURGH
1. Andrew McCutchen (OF)
2. Neil Walker (3B)
3. Steve Pearce (1B/OF)
4. Brad Lincoln (RHP)
5. Daniel Moskos (LHP)
6. Todd Redmond (RHP)
7. Jamie Romak (OF)
8. Brian Bixler (SS)
9. Shelby Ford (2B)
10. Nyjer Morgan (OF)
11. Jason Delaney (1B)
12. James Boone (OF)
13. Duke Welker (RHP)
14. Brian Friday (SS)
15. Brian Bullington (RHP)

ST. LOUIS
1. Colby Rasmus (OF)
2. Jaime Garcia (LHP)
3. Bryan Anderson (C)
4. Chris Perez (RHP)
5. Peter Kozma (SS)
6. Clayton Mortensen (RHP)
7. Brian Barton (OF)
8. Adam Ottavino (RHP)
9. Tyler Herron (RHP)
10. Mark Hamilton (1B)
11. Jose Martinez (2B/SS)
12. John Jay (OF)
13. David Freese (3B)
14. Blake Hawksworth (RHP)
15. Joe Mather (1B/OF)

NATIONAL LEAGUE WEST

ARIZONA
1. Max Scherzer (RHP)
2. Jarrod Parker (RHP)
3. Gerardo Parra (OF)
4. Wes Roemer (RHP)
5. Brooks Brown (RHP)
6. Juan Gutierrez (RHP)
7. Ed Easley (C)
8. Billy Buckner (RHP)
9. Emilio Bonafacio (2B)
10. Barry Enright (RHP)
11. Cyle Hankerd (OF)
12. Reynaldo Navarro (SS)
13. Hector Ambriz (RHP)
14. Esmerling Vasquez (RHP)
15. Jamie D'Antona (1B/C/3B)

COLORADO
1. Franklin Morales (LHP)
2. Ian Stewart (3B)
3. Greg Reynolds (RHP)
4. Chris Nelson (SS)
5. Dexter Fowler (OF)
6. Casey Weathers (RHP)
7. Juan Morillo (RHP)
8. Seth Smith (OF)
9. Chaz Roe (RHP)
10. Brandon Hynick (RHP)
11. Aneury Rodriguez (RHP)
12. Pedro Strop (RHP)
13. Jayson Nix (2B)
14. Hector Gomez (SS)
15. Joe Koshansky (1B)

LOS ANGELES
1. Clayton Kershaw (LHP)
2. Andy LaRoche (3B)
3. Scott Elbert (LHP)
4. Jonathon Meloan (RHP)
5. Chin-Lung Hu (SS)
6. James McDonald (RHP)
7. Hiroki Kuroda (RHP)
8. Chris Withrow (RHP)
9. Andrew Lambo (OF/1B)
10. Pedro Baez (3B)
11. Blake DeWitt (2B)
12. Delwyn Young (OF)
13. James Adkins (LHP)
14. Ivan DeJesus (SS)
15. Josh Bell (3B)

SAN DIEGO
1. **Matt Antonelli** (3B)
2. **Chase Headley** (3B)
3. **Matt Latos** (RHP)
4. **Will Inman** (RHP)
5. **Cedric Hunter** (OF)
6. **Kyle Blanks** (1B)
7. **Kellen Kulbacki** (OF)
8. **Chad Huffman** (OF)
9. **Corey Luebke** (LHP)
10. **Wade LeBlanc** (LHP)
11. **Mitch Canham** (C)
12. **Drew Miller** (RHP)
13. **Drew Cumberland** (SS)
14. **Cesar Carrillo** (RHP)
15. **Will Venable** (OF)

SAN FRANCISCO
1. **Angel Villanoa** (3B)
2. **Henry Sosa** (RHP)
3. **Madison Baumgarner** (LHP)
4. **Nick Noonan** (2B/SS)
5. **Tim Alderson** (RHP)
6. **Nate Schierholtz** (OF)
7. **Eugenio Velez** (OF/2B)
8. **Emmanuel Burris** (SS)
9. **Clayton Tanner** (LHP)
10. **Billy Sadler** (RHP)
11. **Eddy Martinez-Esteve** (OF)
12. **Marcus Sanders** (2B/SS)
13. **Osiris Matos** (RHP)
14. **John Bowker** (OF)
15. **Nick Pereira** (RHP)

TOP PROSPECTS BY POSITION

CATCHER
1. Matt Wieters (BAL)
2. Taylor Teagarden (TEX)
3. Jeff Clement (SEA)
4. Geovany Soto (CHC)
5. Bryan Anderson (STL)
6. Hank Conger (LAA)
7. JR Towles (HOU)
8. Angel Salome (MIL)
9. Devin Mesoraco (CIN)
10. Josh Donaldson (CHC)
11. Ed Easley (ARI)
12. John Jaso (TAM)
13. Lou Marson (PHI)
14. Mitch Canham (SD)
15. JP Arencibia (TOR)

FIRST BASE
1. Joey Votto (CIN)
2. Daric Barton (OAK)
3. Lars Anderson (BOS)
4. Jesus Montero (NYY)
5. Kyle Blanks (SD)
6. Chris Carter (BOS)
7. Sean Doolittle (OAK)
8. Chris Carter (OAK)
9. Brandon Snyder (BAL)
10. Mark Hamilton (STL)
11. Joel Guzman (TAM)
12. Jeff Larish (DET)
13. Kyle Orr (LAD)
14. Joe Koshansky (COL)
15. Michael Aubrey (CLE)

SECOND BASE
1. Matt Antonelli (SD)
2. Adrian Cardenas (PHI)
3. Nick Noonan (SF)
4. Chris Coghlan (FLA)
5. German Duran (TEX)
6. John Tolisano (TOR)
7. Eric Patterson (CHC)
8. Scott Sizemore (DET)
9. Tony Thomas (CHC)
10. Ryan Dent (BOS)
11. Eugenio Velez (SF)
12. Emilio Bonafacio (ARI)
13. Eric Sogard (SD)
14. Hernan Iribarren (MIL)
15. Jose Martinez (STL)

THIRD BASE
1. Evan Longoria (TAM)
2. Brandon Wood (LAA)
3. Andy LaRoche (LAD)
4. Angel Villlalona (SF)
5. Ian Stewart (COL)
6. Josh Vitters (CHC)
7. Chase Headley (SD)
8. Billy Rowell (BAL)
9. Neil Walker (PIT)

10. Beau Mills (CLE)
11. Chris Davis (TEX)
12. Johnny Whittleman (TEX)
13. Kevin Ahrens (TOR)
14. Wes Hodges (CLE)
15. Pedro Baez (LAD)

SHORTSTOP
1. Reid Brignac (TAM)
2. Carlos Triunfel (SEA)
3. Mike Moustakas (KC)
4. Elvis Andrus (TEX)
5. Chin-Lung Hu (LAD)
6. Brent Lillibridge (ATL)
7. Jed Lowrie (BOS)
8. Chris Nelson (COL)
9. Peter Kozma (STL)
10. Sean Rodriguez (LAA)
11. Todd Frazier (CIN)
12. Esmailyn Gonzalez (WAS)
13. Oscar Tejeda (BOS)
14. Darwin Barney (CHC)
15. Hector Gomez (COL)

OUTFIELD
1. Jay Bruce (CIN)
2. Colby Rasmus (STL)
3. Cameron Maybin (FLA)
4. Andrew McCutchen (PIT)
5. Jacoby Ellsbury (BOS)
6. Travis Snider (TOR)
7. Jordan Schafer (ATL)
8. Kosuke Fukodome (CHC)
9. Jose Tabata (NYY)
10. Carlos Gonzalez (OAK)
11. Fernando Martinez (NYM)
12. Chris Marrero (WAS)
13. Justin Heyward (ATL)
14. Brandon Jones (ATL)
15. Tyler Colvin (CHC)
16. Steven Pearce (PIT)
17. Matt LaPorta (MIL)
18. Austin Jackson (NYY)
19. Gorkys Hernandez (ATL)
20. Desmond Jennings (TAM)
21. Nolan Reimold (BAL)
22. Gerardo Parra (ARI)
23. Ryan Sweeney (CHW)
24. Ryan Kalish (BOS)
25. Michael Burgess (WAS)
26. Wladimir Balentien (SEA)
27. Drew Stubbs (CIN)
28. Dexter Fowler (COL)
29. Cedric Hughes (SD)
30. Aaron Cunningham (OAK)
31. Ben Revere (MIN)
32. Brian Barton (STL)
33. Justin Maxwell (WAS)
34. Andrew Lambo (LAD)
35. Kellen Kulbacki (SD)
36. Chad Huffman (SD)

OUTFIELD (cont'd)
37. Nick Weglarz (CLE)
38. Ryan Sweeney (CHW)
39. Jordan Brown (CLE)
40. Corey Brown (OAK)
41. Chris Pettit (LAA)
42. Josh Reddick (BOS)
43. Trevor Crowe (CLE)
44. Jose Martinez (CHW)
45. John Drennen (CLE)

STARTING PITCHER
1. Clay Buchholz (RHP, BOS)
2. Clayton Kershaw (LHP, LAD)
3. Joba Chamberlain (RHP, NYY)
4. Homer Bailey (RHP, CIN)
5. David Price (LHP, TAM)
6. Jacob McGee (LHP, TAM)
7. Wade Davis (RHP, TAM)
8. Adam Miller (RHP, CLE)
9. Rick Porcello (RHP, DET)
10. Franklin Morales (LHP, COL)
11. Eric Hurley (RHP, TEX)
12. Nick Adenhart (RHP, LAA)
13. Ross Detwiler (LHP, WAS)
14. Ian Kennedy (RHP, NYY)
15. Kasey Kiker (LHP, TEX)
16. Johnny Cueto (RHP, CIN)
17. Scott Elbert (LHP, LAD)
18. Justin Masterson (RHP, BOS)
19. Max Scherzer (RHP, ARI)
20. Jarrod Parker (RHP, ARI)
21. Gio Gonzalez (LHP, CHW)
22. Anthony Swarzak (RHP, MIN)
23. Jair Jurrjens (RHP, ATL)
24. Fautino de los Santos (RHP, CHW)
25. Manny Parra (LHP, MIL)
26. Carlos Carrasco (RHP, PHI)
27. Deolis Guerra (RHP, NYM)
28. Blake Beaven (RHP, TEX)
29. Michael Main (RHP, TEX)
30. Jeff Niemann (RHP, TAM)
31. Radhames Liz (RHP, BAL)
32. Chuck Lofgren (LHP, CLE)
33. Luke Hochevar (RHP, KC)
34. Jaime Garcia (LHP, STL)
35. Troy Patton (LHP, BAL)
36. Matt Latos (RHP, SD)
37. Tommy Hanson (LHP, ATL)
38. Aaron Poreda (RHP, CHW)
39. Cole Rohrbough (LHP, ATL)
40. Chris Volstad (RHP, FLA)

41. Henry Sosa (RHP, SF)
42. Madison Baumgarner (LHP, SF)
43. Michael Bowden (RHP, BOS)
44. Greg Reynolds (RHP, COL)
45. James McDonald (RHP, LAD)
46. Aaron Laffey (LHP, CLE)
47. Jeremy Hellickson (RHP, TAM)
48. Jordan Walden (RHP, LAA)
49. Hiroki Kuroda (RHP, LAD)
50. Brett Anderson (LHP, OAK)
51. Alan Horne (RHP, NYY)
52. Matt Harrison (LHP, TEX)
53. Jake Arrieta (RHP, BAL)
54. Will Inman (RHP, SD)
55. Tony Butler (LHP, SEA)
56. Trevor Cahill (RHP, OAK)
57. James Simmons (RHP, OAK)
58. Clayton Mortensen (RHP, STL)
59. Tim Alderson (RHP, SF)
60. Tyler Robertson (LHP, MIN)
61. Garrett Olson (LHP, BAL)
62. Joe Savery (LHP, PHI)
63. Chris Tillman (RHP, SEA)
64. Felipe Paulino (RHP, HOU)
65. Chorye Spoone (RHP, BAL)
66. Chris Withrow (RHP, LAD)
67. Andrew Brackman (RHP, NYY)
68. Dellin Betances (RHP, NYY)
69. Jeff Samardzija (RHP, CHC)
70. Sean Gallagher (RHP, CHC)
71. Brandon Erbe (RHP, BAL)
72. Sean O'Sullivan (RHP, LAA)
73. David Huff (LHP, CLE)
74. Eulogio de la Cruz (RHP, FLA)
75. Phil Humber (RHP, NYM)

RELIEF PITCHER
1. Jonathon Meloan (LAD)
2. Chris Perez (STL)
3. James Hoey (RHP, BAL)
4. Joey Devine (RHP, ATL)
5. Casey Weathers (RHP, COL)
6. Edurado Morlan (RHP, TAM)
7. Juan Morillo (RHP, COL)
8. Wes Roemer (RHP, ARI)
9. Masahide Kobayashi (RHP, CLE)
10. Jose Ascanio (RHP, CHC)
11. Kam Mickolio (RHP, SEA)
12. Billy Sadler (RHP, SF)
13. Bob McCrory (RHP, BAL)
14. Josh Roenicke (RHP, CIN)
15. Jose Arredondo (RHP, LAA)

Brandon Wood (SS, LAA)
Jay Bruce (OF, CIN)
Evan Longoria (3B, TAM)
Travis Snider (OF, TOR)
Carlos Gonzalez (OF, OAK)
Justin Heyward (OF, ATL)
Matt LaPorta (OF, MIL)
Matt Wieters (C, BAL)
Michael Burgess (OF, WAS)
Chris Marrero (OF/1B, WAS)
Ian Stewart (3B, COL)
Wladimir Balentien (OF, SEA)
Jeff Clement (C, SEA)
Billy Rowell (3B, BAL)
Andy LaRoche (3B, LAD)
Beau Mills (3B, CLE)
Lars Anderson (1B, BOS)
Chris Davis (3B, TEX)
Mike Moustakas (SS, KC)
Josh Vitters (3B, CHC)
Kyle Blanks (1B, SD)
Nolan Reimold (OF, BAL)
Cameron Maybin (OF, FLA)
Colby Rasmus (OF, STL)
Nick Weglarz (OF/1B, CLE)
Shelley Duncan (OF/1B, NYY)
Cody Johnson (OF, ATL)
Joe Koshansky (1B, COL)
Jesus Montero (C/1B, NYY)
Hank Conger (C, LAA)

Daric Barton (1B, OAK)
Jacoby Ellsbury (OF, BOS)
Colby Rasmus (OF, STL)
Delwyn Young (OF, LAD)
Mike Moustakas (SS, KC)
Evan Longoria (3B, TAM)
Matt Wieters (C, BAL)
Chase Headley (3B, SD)
Andrew McCutchen (OF, PIT)
Cameron Maybin (OF, FLA)
Carlos Triunfel (SS, SEA)
Esmailyn Gonzalez (SS, WAS)
Gorkys Hernandez (OF, ATL)
Nick Noonan (2B/SS, SF)
Matt Antonelli (2B, SD)
Ben Revere (OF, MIN)
Jordan Schafer (OF, ATL)
Desmond Jennings (OF, TAM)
Jay Bruce (OF, CIN)
Angel Villalona (3B, SF)
Joey Votto (1B/OF, CIN)
Neil Walker (3B, PIT)
Brian Anderson (C, STL)
Peter Kozma (SS, STL)
Jed Lowrie (SS/2B, BOS)
Chad Huffman (OF, SD)
Adrian Cardenas (2B, PHI)
Chris Coghlan (2B, FLA)
Sean Doolittle (1B, OAK)
Josh Horton (SS, OAK)

TOP 100 FANTASY PROSPECTS

Andrew McCutchen (OF, PIT)
Jacoby Ellsbury (OF, BOS)
Desmond Jennings (OF, TAM)
Gorkys Hernandez (OF, ATL)
Cameron Maybin (OF, FLA)
Ben Revere (OF, MIN)
Eric Patterson (2B/OF, CHC)
Darren Ford (OF, MIL)
Eugenio Velez (2B/OF, SF)
Nyjer Morgan (OF, PIT)
Fernando Perez (OF, TAM)
Dexter Fowler (OF, COL)
Josh Anderson (OF, ATL)
Jordan Schafer (OF, ATL)
Emmanuel Burriss (SS, SF)
Drew Stubbs (OF, CIN)
Chris Nelson (SS, COL)
Julio Borbon (OF, TEX)
Eric Eiland (OF, TOR)
Eric Young (2B, COL)
Brett Gardner (OF, NYY)
Wendell Fairley (OF, SF)
Corey Wimberly (2B, COL)
Elvis Andrus (SS, ATL)
Cedric Hunter (OF, SD)
Freddy Guzman (OF, DET)
Emiliano Bonifacio (2B, ARI)
Greg Golson (OF, PHI)
Brad Chalk (OF, SD)
Hernan Iribarren (2B, MIL)

1. Clay Buchholz (RHP, BOS)
2. Joba Chamberlain (RHP, NYY)
3. Evan Longoria (3B, TAM)
4. Jacoby Ellsbury (OF, BOS)
5. Kosuke Fukodome (OF, LAD)
6. Joey Votto (1B/OF, CIN)
7. Daric Barton (1B, OAK)
8. Geovany Soto (C/1B, CHC)
9. Franklin Morales (LHP, COL)
10. Homer Bailey (RHP, CIN)

11. Colby Rasmus (OF, STL)
12. Cameron Maybin (OF, FLA)
13. Ian Kennedy (RHP, NYY)
14. Stephen Pearce (OF/1B, PIT)
15. Aaron Laffey (LHP, CLE)
16. Brandon Jones (OF, ATL)
17. Nate Schierholtz (OF, SF)
18. Ian Stewart (3B, COL)
19. Brandon Wood (3B/SS, LAA)
20. Manny Parra (LHP, MIL)

21. Jay Bruce (OF, CIN)
22. JR Towles (C, HOU)
23. Brian Barton (OF, STL)
24. Jair Jurrjens (RHP, ATL)
25. Luke Hochevar (RHP, KC)
26. Gio Gonzalez (LHP, CHW)
27. Josh Anderson (OF, ATL)
28. Andy LaRoche (3B/OF, LAD)
29. Jonathon Meloan (RHP, LAD)
30. Garrett Olson (LHP, BAL)

31. Adam Miller (RHP, CLE)
32. Eric Hurley (RHP, TEX)
33. James Hoey (RHP, BAL)
34. Jason Pridie (OF, MIN)
35. Eugenio Velez (2B/OF, SF)
36. Shelley Duncan (OF/1B, NYY)
37. Felipe Paulino (RHP, HOU)
38. Lance Broadway (RHP, CHW)
39. Alexei Ramirez (OF/SS, CHW)
40. Ryan Rowland-Smith (LHP, SEA)

41. Joey Devine (RHP, ATL)
42. Chase Headley (3B/OF, SD)
43. Ross Olendorf (RHP, NYY)
44. Andrew McCutchen (OF, PIT)
45. Juan Morillo (RHP, COL)
46. David Murphy (OF, TEX)
47. Radhames Liz (RHP, BAL)
48. Billy Buckner (RHP, ARI)
49. Phil Humber (RHP, NYM)
50. Richard Thompson (RHP, LAA)

51. Sean Gallagher (RHP, CHC)
52. Troy Patton (LHP, BAL)
53. Johnny Cueto (RHP, CIN)
54. Edwar Ramirez (RHP, NYY)
55. Ryan Sweeney (OF, CHW)
56. Taylor Teagarden (C, TEX)
57. Kevin Hart (RHP, CHC)
58. Wade Davis (RHP, TAM)
59. Anthony Swarzak (RHP, MIN)
60. Billy Sadler (RHP, SF)

61. Chris Perez (RHP, STL)
62. Juan Gutierrez (RHP, ARI)
63. Delwyn Young (OF, LAD)
64. Chin-Lung Hu (SS, LAD)
65. Neil Walker (3B, PIT)
66. Terry Evans (OF, LAA)
67. David Price (LHP, TAM)
68. Jacob McGee (LHP, TAM)
69. Eulogio de la Cruz (RHP, FLA)
70. Brian Buscher (3B, MIN)

71. Seth Smith (OF, COL)
72. Yorman Bazardo (RHP, DET)
73. Jarod Plummer (RHP, KC)
74. Jed Lowrie (SS/2B, BOS)
75. Matt Antonelli (2B, SD)
76. Jeff Neimann (RHP, TAM)
77. Max Scherzer (RHP, ARI)
78. Oneli Perez (RHP, CHW)
79. Tyler Clippard (RHP, WAS)
80. John Lannan (LHP, WAS)

81. Ben Francisco (OF, CLE)
82. Eric Patterson (2B/OF, CHC)
83. Luis Pena (LHP, MIL)
84. Brett Gardner (OF, NYY)
85. Chris Lubanski (OF, KC)
86. Brandon Moss (OF, BOS)
87. Wladimir Balentien (OF, SEA)
88. Jose Morales (C, MIN)
89. Nick Hundley (C, SD)
90. Anderson Hernandez (SS/2B, NYM)

91. Nyjer Morgan (OF, PIT)
92. German Duran (2B, TEX)
93. Ross Detwiler (LHP, WAS)
94. Jaime Garcia (LHP, STL)
95. Nick Blackburn (RHP, MIN)
96. Kam Mickolio (RHP, SEA)
97. Jayson Nix (2B, COL)
98. Brent Lillibridge (SS, ATL)
99. Jeff Clement (C, SEA)
100. Carlos Carrasco (RHP, PHI)

2007

1. Delmon Young (OF, TAM)
2. Alex Gordon (3B, KC)
3. Daisuke Matsuzaka (RHP, BOS)
4. Justin Upton (OF, ARI)
5. Homer Bailey (RHP, CIN)
6. Philip Hughes (RHP, NYY)
7. Brandon Wood (SS, LAA)
8. Jay Bruce (OF, CIN)
9. Billy Butler (OF, KC)
10. Cameron Maybin (OF, DET)

11. Andrew McCutchen (OF, PIT)
12. Troy Tulowitzki (SS, COL)
13. Evan Longoria (3B, TAM)
14. Jose Tabata (OF, NYY)
15. Reid Brignac (SS, TAM)
16. Chris Young (OF, ARI)
17. Adam Miller (RHP, CLE)
18. Mike Pelfrey (RHP, NYM)
19. Carlos Gonzalez (OF, ARI)
20. Tim Lincecum (RHP, SF)

21. Andy LaRoche (3B, LAD)
22. Fernando Martinez (OF, NYM)
23. Yovani Gallardo (RHP, MIL)
24. Colby Rasmus (OF, STL)
25. Ryan Braun (3B, MIL)
26. Scott Elbert (LHP, LAD)
27. Nick Adenhart (RHP, LAA)
28. Andrew Miller (LHP, DET)
29. Billy Rowell (3B, BAL)
30. John Danks (LHP, CHW)

31. Luke Hochevar (RHP, KC)
32. Erick Aybar (SS, LAA)
33. Jacoby Ellsbury (OF, BOS)
34. Eric Hurley (RHP, TEX)
35. Ian Stewart (3B, COL)
36. Clay Buchholz (RHP, BOS)
37. Elvis Andrus (SS, ATL)
38. Jason Hirsh (RHP, COL)
39. Hunter Pence (OF, HOU)
40. Franklin Morales (LHP, COL)

41. Adam Lind (OF, TOR)
42. Travis Snider (OF, TOR)
43. Jeff Niemann (RHP, TAM)
44. Clayton Kershaw (LHP, LAD)
45. James Loney (1B, LAD)
46. Chris Iannetta (C, COL)
47. Elijah Dukes (OF, TAM)
48. Chuck Lofgren (LHP, CLE)
49. Joey Votto (1B, CIN)
50. Jacob McGee (LHP, TAM)

51. Adam Jones (OF, SEA)
52. Brad Lincoln (RHP, PIT)
53. Brian Barton (OF, CLE)
54. Will Inman (RHP, MIL)
55. Wade Davis (RHP, TAM)
56. Donald Veal (LHP, CHC)
57. Michael Bowden (RHP, BOS)
58. Ryan Sweeney (OF, CHW)
59. Josh Fields (3B, CHW)
60. Jarrod Saltalamacchia (C, ATL)

61. Felix Pie (OF, CHC)
62. Brandon Erbe (RHP, BAL)
63. Giovanny Gonzalez (LHP, CHW)
64. Trevor Crowe (OF, CLE)
65. Travis Buck (OF, OAK)
66. Daric Barton (1B, OAK)

67. Kevin Kouzmanoff (3B, SD)
68. Jeff Clement (C, SEA)
69. Neil Walker (C, PIT)
70. Troy Patton (LHP, HOU)

71. Brandon Morrow (RHP, SEA)
72. Dustin Pedroia (2B, BOS)
73. Blake DeWitt (2B, LAD)
74. Carlos Carrasco (RHP, PHI)
75. Jonathon Meloan (RHP, LAD)
76. Hank Conger (C, LAA)
77. Sean Rodriguez (SS, LAA)
78. Humberto Sanchez (RHP, NYY)
79. Phil Humber /b> (RHP, NYM)
80. Edinson Volquez (RHP, TEX)

81. Dustin Nippert (RHP, ARI)
82. Anthony Swarzak (RHP, MIN)
83. Chris Parmalee (OF/1B, MIN)
84. Ubaldo Jimenez (RHP, COL)
85. Dexter Fowler (OF, COL)
86. Drew Stubbs (OF, CIN)
87. Miguel Montero (C, ARI)
88. Carlos Gomez (OF, NYM)
89. Kevin Slowey (RHP, MIN)
90. Nolan Reimold (OF, BAL)

91. Daniel Bard (RHP, BOS)
92. Chris Nelson (SS, COL)
93. Cedric Hunter (OF, SD)
94. Angel Villanoa (3B, SF)
95. Jamie Garcia (LHP, STL)
96. Travis Wood (LHP, CIN)
97. Cesar Carillo (RHP, SD)
98. Pedro Beato (RHP, BAL)
99. Joba Chamberlain (RHP, NYY)
100. Kei Igawa (LHP, NYY)

2006

1. Delmon Young (OF, TAM)
2. Justin Upton (OF/SS, ARI)
3. Brandon Wood (SS, LAA)
4. Ian Stewart (3B, COL)
5. Prince Fielder (1B, MIL)
6. Jeremy Hermida (OF, FLA)
7. Chad Billingsley (RHP, LAD)
8. Stephen Drew (SS, ARI)
9. Andy Marte (3B, BOS)
10. Francisco Liriano (LHP, MIN)

11. Alex Gordon (3B, KC)
12. Jarrod Saltalamacchia (C, ATL)
13. Carlos Quentin (OF, ARI)
14. Lastings Milledge (OF, NYM)
15. Conor Jackson (1B, ARI)
16. Joel Guzman (SS, LAD)
17. Nick Markakis (OF, BAL)
18. Adam Miller (RHP, CLE)
19. Matt Cain (RHP, SF)
20. Erick Aybar (SS, LAA)

21. Billy Butler (OF, KC)
22. Justin Verlander (RHP, DET)
23. Howie Kendrick (2B, LAA)
24. Andy LaRoche (3B, LAD)
25. Troy Tulowitski (SS, COL)
26. Jered Weaver (RHP, LAA)
27. Ryan Zimmerman (3B, WAS)
28. Chris Young (OF, ARI)
29. Elvis Andrus (SS, ATL)
30. Daric Barton (1B, OAK)
31. Scott Olson (LHP, FLA)
32. Jon Lester (LHP, BOS)

33. Cole Hamels (LHP, PHI)
34. Anthony Reyes (RHP, STL)
35. Mike Pelfrey (RHP, NYM)
36. Andrew McCutchen (OF, PIT)
37. Ryan Braun (3B, MIL)
38. Chris Nelson (SS, COL)
39. Kendry Morales (1B/OF, LAA)
40. Anibal Sanchez (RHP, FLA)

41. Hanley Ramirez (SS, FLA)
42. John Danks (LHP, TEX)
43. Edison Volquez (RHP, TEX)
44. Russell Martin (C, LAD)
45. Dustin Nippert (RHP, ARI)
46. Jon Papelbon (RHP, BOS)
47. Carlos Gonzales (OF, ARI)
48. Felix Pie (OF, CHC)
49. Yusmeiro Petit (RHP, FLA)
50. Dustin Pedroia (2B, BOS)

51. Joel Zumaya (RHP, DET)
52. Gio Gonzalez (LHP, PHI)
53. Hayden Penn (RHP, BAL)
54. Nolan Reimold (OF, BAL)
55. Homer Bailey (RHP, CIN)
56. Mark Pawelek (LHP, CHC)
57. Neil Walker (C, PIT)
58. Philip Hughes (RHP, NYY)
59. Jonathon Broxton (RHP, LAD)
60. Dustin McGowan (RHP, TOR)

61. Cameron Maybin (OF, DET)
62. Scott Elbert (LHP, LAD)
63. Andrew Lerew (RHP, ATL)
64. Yuniel Escobar (SS, ATL)
65. Jose Tabata (OF, NYY)
66. Craig Hansen (RHP, BOS)
67. Javier Herrera (OF, OAK)
68. James Loney (1B, LAD)
69. Matt Kemp (OF, LAD)
70. Jairo Garcia (RHP, OAK)

71. Ryan Sweeney (OF, CHW)
72. Thomas Diamond (RHP, TEX)
73. Cesar Carillo (RHP, SD)
74. Adam Loewen (LHP, BAL)
75. Chuck Tiffany (LHP, LAD)
76. Brian Anderson (OF, CHW)
77. Jeremy Sowers (LHP, CLE)
78. Matt Moses (3B, MIN)
79. Angel Guzman (RHP, CHC)
80. Jeff Clement (C, SEA)

81. Kenji Jojima (C, SEA)
82. Fernando Nieve (RHP, HOU)
83. Corey Hart (OF/3B, MIL)
84. Eric Duncan (3B, NYY)
85. Justin Huber (1B, KC)
86. Jeff Niemann (RHP, TAM)
87. Cliff Pennington (SS, OAK)
88. Jeff Mathis (C, LAA)
89. Troy Patton (LHP, HOU)
90. Jay Bruce (OF, CIN)

91. Colby Rasmus (OF, STL)
92. Jeff Bianchi (SS, KC)
93. Joaquin Arias (SS, TEX)
94. Eddy Martinez-Esteve (OF, SF)
95. Jason Kubel (OF, MIN)
96. Adam Jones (OF, SEA)
97. Ian Kinsler (2B, TEX)
98. Eric Hurley (RHP, TEX)
99. Anthony Swarzak (RHP, MIN)
100. Josh Barfield (2B, SD)

2005

1. Delmon Young (OF, TAM)
2. Casey Kotchman (1B, ANA)
3. Felix Hernandez (RHP, SEA)
4. Ian Stewart (3B, COL)
5. Andy Marte (3B, ATL)
6. Rickie Weeks (2B, MIL)
7. Adam Miller (RHP, CLE)
8. Prince Fielder (1B, MIL)
9. Scott Kazmir (LHP, TAM)
10. Dallas McPherson (3B, ANA)

11. Jeff Francis (LHP, COL)
12. Jeff Francouer (OF, ATL)
13. Chris Nelson (SS, COL)
14. Hanley Ramirez (SS, BOS)
15. Matt Cain (RHP, SF)
16. Edwin Jackson (RHP, LA)
17. Joel Guzman (SS, LA)
18. JJ Hardy (SS, MIL)
19. Carlos Quentin (OF, ARI)
20. Lastings Milledge (OF, NYM)

21. Jeremy Hermida (OF, FLA)
22. Daric Barton (C/1B, OAK)
23. James Loney (1B, LA)
24. Chad Billingsley (RHP, LA)
25. John Danks (LHP, TEX)
26. Josh Barfield (2B, SD)
27. Ervin Santana (RHP, ANA)
28. Ryan Sweeney (OF, CHW)
29. Kendry Morales (1B/OF, ANA)
30. Erick Aybar (SS, ANA)
31. Conor Jackson (OF, ARI)
32. Yuresimo Petit (RHP, NYM)
33. Anthony Reyes (RHP, STL)
34. Joe Blanton (RHP, OAK)
35. Michael Aubrey (1B, CLE)
36. Nick Swisher (OF, OAK)
37. Jason Kubel (OF, MIN)
38. Michael Hinckley (LHP, WAS)
39. Gavin Floyd (RHP, PHI)
40. Jose Capellan (RHP, MIL)

41. Dan Meyer (LHP, OAK)
42. Eric Duncan (3B, NYY)
43. Cole Hamels (LHP, PHI)
44. Jeremy Reed (OF, SEA)
45. Jesse Crain (RHP, MIN)
46. Franklin Gutierrez (OF, CLE)
47. Shin Soo Choo (OF, SEA)
48. Guillermo Quiroz (C, TOR)
49. Jeff Mathis (C, ANA)
50. Jeff Niemann (RHP, TAM)

51. JD Durbin (RHP, MIN)
52. Dustin McGowan (RHP, TOR)
53. Scott Olsen (LHP, FLA)
54. Francisco Rosario (RHP, TOR)
55. Aaron Hill (SS, TOR)
56. Jason Bartlett (SS, MIN)
57. Brian Anderson (OF, CHW)
58. Sergio Santos (SS, ARI)
59. Jered Weaver (RHP, ANA)
60. Justin Verlander (RHP, DET)

61. Russ Adams (SS, TOR)
62. Brandon League (RHP, TOR)
63. Brandon McCarthy (RHP, CHW)
64. Juan Dominguez (RHP, TEX)
65. Huston Street (RHP, OAK)
66. Jairo Garcia (RHP, OAK)
67. John Maine (RHP, BAL)

68. Javier Herrera (OF, OAK)
69. Chuck Tiffany (LHP, LA)
70. Angel Guzman (RHP, CHC)

71. Felix Pie (OF, CHC)
72. Josh Fields (3B, CHW)
73. Fernando Nieve (RHP, HOU)
74. Chris Burke (2B, HOU)
75. Ian Kinsler (SS, TEX)
76. Brian Dopirak (1B, CHC)
77. John VanBenscoten (RHP, PIT)
78. Zach Duke (LHP, PIT)
79. Greg Miller (LHP, LA)
80. Ryan Howard (1B, PHI)

81. Dan Johnson (1B, OAK)
82. Andy LaRoche (3B, LA)
83. Merkin Valdez (RHP, SF)
84. Homer Bailey (RHP, CIN)
85. Nick Marakis (OF, BAL)
86. Ubaldo Jimenez (RHP, COL)
87. Phil Humber (RHP, NYM)
88. Edwin Encarnacion (3B, CIN)
89. Kyle Davies (RHP, ATL)
90. Vince Sinisi (OF, TEX)

91. Thomas Diamond (RHP, TEX)
92. Stephen Drew (SS, ARI)
93. Denny Bautista (RHP, KC)
94. Matt Moses (3B, MIN)
95. Chris Snyder (C, ARI)
96. Billy Butler (3B, KC)
97. Brian McCann (C, ATL)
98. Mark Teahen (3B, KC)
99. Corey Hart (OF, MIL)
100. Matt Bush (SS, SD)

2004

1. Joe Mauer (C, MIN)
2. BJ Upton (SS, TAM)
3. Zach Greinke (RHP, KC)
4. Andy Marte (3B, ATL)
5. Casey Kotchman (1B, ANA)
6. Edwin Jackson (RHP, LA)
7. Justin Morneau (1B, MIN)
8. Scott Kazmir (LHP, NYM)
9. Cole Hamels (LHP, PHI)
10. Alexis Rios (OF, TOR)

11. JJ Hardy (SS, MIL)
12. Rickie Weeks (2B, MIL)
13. Delmon Young (OF, TAM)
14. Prince Fielder (1B, MIL)
15. Bobby Crosby (SS, OAK)
16. Greg Miller (LHP, LA)
17. David Wright (3B, NYM)
18. Dustin McGowan (RHP, TOR)
19. Jeremy Reed (OF, CHW)
20. Khalil Greene (SS, SD)

21. Josh Barfield (2B, SD)
22. Gavin Floyd (RHP, PHI)
23. Chin-hui Tsao (RHP, COL)
24. Jeff Mathis (C, ANA)
25. Grady Sizemore (OF, CLE)
26. Ervin Santana (RHP, ANA)
27. Joe Blanton (RHP, OAK)
28. Hanley Ramirez (SS, BOS)
29. Jeff Francouer (OF, ATL)
30. Scott Hairston (2B, ARI)
31. Jeremy Hermida (OF, FLA)
32. Angel Guzman (RHP, CHC)

33. John VanBenschoten (RHP, PIT)
34. Gabe Gross(OF, TOR)
35. Guillermo Quiroz (C, TOR)
36. Dallas McPherson (3B, ANA)
37. Merkin Valdez (RHP, SF)
38. Clint Nageotte (RHP, SEA)
39. Adam Wainwright (RHP, STL)
40. Joel Hanrahan (RHP, LA)

41. James Loney (1B, LA)
42. Franklin Gutierrez (OF, CLE)
43. Juan Dominguez (RHP, TEX)
44. Ian Stewart (3B, COL)
45. Adrian Gonzalez (1B, TEX)
46. Andy Sisco (LHP, CHC)
47. Chris Snelling (OF, SEA)
48. Ryan Harvey (OF, CHC)
49. Justin Jones (LHP, CHC)
50. Sergio Santos (SS, ARI)

51. Sean Burnett (LHP, PIT)
52. Kris Honel (RHP, CHW)
53. Francisco Cruceta (RHP, CLE)
54. Bobby Jenks (RHP, ANA)
55. Adam Loewen (LHP, BAL)
56. Brandon Claussen(LHP, CIN)
57. Ryan Wagner (RHP, CIN)
58. Dioner Navarro (C, NYY)
59. Neal Cotts (LHP, CHW)
60. Jeff Allison (RHP, FLA)

61. Brian Bullington (RHP, PIT)
62. Jason Bay (OF, PIT)
63. Taylor Buchholz (RHP, HOU)
64. Felix Pie (OF, CHC)
65. John Maine (RHP, BAL)
66. Blake Hawksworth (RHP, STL)
67. Clint Everts (RHP, MON)
68. Matt Moses (3B/SS, MIN)
69. Conor Jackson (OF, ARI)
70. Jeff Francis (LHP, COL)

71. Brad Nelson (OF/1B, MIL)
72. Jose Lopez (SS/2B, SEA)
73. Michael Aubrey (1B, CLE)
74. Macay McBride (LHP, ATL)
75. Manny Parra (RHP, MIL)
76. Boof Bonser (RHP, MIN)
77. JD Durbin (RHP, MIN)
78. Aaron Hill (SS, TOR)
79. John Danks (LHP, TEX)
80. Ryan Sweeney (OF, CHW)

81. Chris Lubanski (OF, KC)
82. Jesse Crain (RHP, MIN)
83. Jason Stokes (1B, FLA)
84. Matt Cain (RHP, SF)
85. Rett Johnson (RHP, SEA)
86. Russ Adams (SS, TOR)
87. Scott Olsen (LHP, FLA)
88. David Bush (RHP, TOR)
89. Mike Jones (RHP, MIL)
90. Corey Hart (3B/1B, MIL)

91. Dan Meyer (LHP, ATL)
92. Kyle Sleeth (RHP, DET)
93. Travis Blackley (LHP, SEA)
94. Ramon Nivar (OF, TEX)
95. Shin-Soo Choo (OF, SEA)
96. Jason Bartlett (SS, MIN)
97. Adam LaRoche (1B, ATL)
98. Denny Bautista (RHP, BAL)
99. Jason Arnold (RHP, TOR)
100. Kazuhito Tadano (RHP, CLE)

2003

1. Mark Teixeira (3B, TEX)
2. Brandon Phillips (SS/2B, CLE)
3. Jose Reyes (SS, NYM)
4. Joe Borchard (OF, CHW)
5. Jesse Foppert (RHP, SF)
6. Joe Mauer (C, MIN)
7. Michael Cuddyer (OF, MIN)
8. Victor Martinez (C, CLE)
9. Hee Seop Choi (1B, CHC)
10. Josh Hamilton (OF, TAM)

11. Justin Morneau (1B, MIN)
12. Rocco Baldelli (OF, TAM)
13. Francisco Rodriguez (RHP, ANA)
14. Casey Kotchman (1B, ANA)
15. Wilson Betemit (SS, ATL)
16. Kurt Ainsworth (RHP, SF)
17. Jerome Williams (RHP, SF)
18. Chris Snelling (OF, SEA)
19. Adam Wainwright (RHP, ATL)
20. Miguel Cabrera (3B, FLA)

21. Gavin Floyd (RHP, PHI)
22. Marlon Byrd (OF, PHI)
23. Cliff Lee (LHP, CLE)
24. Jeremy Bonderman (RHP, DET)
25. Scott Kazmir (LHP, NYM)
26. Rafael Soriano (RHP, SEA)
27. Khalil Greene (SS, SD)
28. Rich Harden (RHP, OAK)
29. Colby Lewis (RHP, TEX)
30. Laynce Nix (OF, TEX)
31. Gabe Gross (OF, TOR)
32. Shin Soo Choo (OF, SEA)
33. John Patterson (RHP, ARI)
34. Scott Hairston (2B, ARI)
35. Adrian Gonzalez (1B, FLA)
36. Hanley Ramirez (SS, BOS)
37. Jeff Francouer (OF, ATL)
38. Clint Nageotte (RHP, SEA)
39. Aaron Heilman (RHP, NYM)
40. Dewon Brazelton (RHP, TAM)

41. Andy Sisco (LHP, CHC)
42. Jason Stokes (1B, FLA)
43. Jeff Mathis (C, ANA)
44. Boof Bonser (RHP, SF)
45. Andy Marte (3B, ATL)
46. James Loney (1B, LA)
47. Brad Nelson (1B/OF, MIL)
48. Michael Restovich (OF, MIN)
49. Jason Arnold (RHP, TOR)
50. Bobby Jenks (RHP, ANA)

51. Todd Linden (OF, SF)
52. Taggert Bozied (1B, SD)
53. Mark Phillips (LHP, NYY)
54. John Buck (C, HOU)
55. Grady Sizemore (OF, CLE)
56. Travis Hafner (1B, CLE)
57. Ben Kozlowski (LHP, TEX)
58. Kris Honel (RHP, CHW)
59. Juan Rivera (OF, NYY)
60. Jon Rauch (RHP, CHW)

61. Matt Belisle (RHP, ATL)
62. Kelly Johnson (SS, ATL)
63. Macay McBride (LHP, ATL)
64. Miguel Olivo (C, CHW)
65. Jonathon Figueroa (LHP, LA)
66. Chin-hui Tsao (RHP, COL)
67. John Van Benschoten (RHP, PIT)
68. Corey Hart (3B/1B, MIL)
69. Jose Castillo (SS, PIT)
70. Taylor Buchholz (RHP, PHI)

71. Franklyn German (RHP, DET)
73. Bobby Crosby (SS, OAK)
74. Russ Adams (SS, TOR)
74. Aaron Cook (RHP, COL)
75. Jack Cust (OF, BAL)
76. Jimmy Gobble (LHP, KC)
77. Francisco Cruceta (RHP, CLE)
78. Mike Gosling (LHP, ARI)
79. Dustin McGowan (RHP, TOR)
80. Joel Hanrahan (RHP, LA)

81. Dustin Moseley (RHP, CIN)
82. Ryan Ludwick (OF, TEX)
83. Brad Lidge (RHP, HOU)
84. Bobby Basham (RHP, CIN)
85. Seung Song (RHP, MON)
86. Dontrelle Willis (LHP, FLA)
87. Lyle Overbay (1B, ARI)
88. Antonio Perez (2B/SS, TAM)
89. BJ Upton (SS, TAM)
90. Justin Huber (C, NYM)

91. Drew Henson (3B, NYY)
92. Dan Haren (RHP, STL)
93. Billy Traber (LHP, CLE)
94. David Wright (3B, NYM)
95. Josh Karp (RHP, MON)
96. John-Ford Griffin (OF, TOR)
97. Kenny Nelson (RHP, ATL)
98. Jose Lopez (SS, SEA)
99. Joe Thurston (2B, LA)
100. Alex Escobar (OF, CLE)

2002

1. Josh Beckett (RHP, FLA)
2. Hank Blalock (3B, TEX)
3. Sean Burroughs (3B, SD)
4. Austin Kearns (OF, CIN)
5. Carlos Pena (1B, OAK)
6. Josh Hamilton (OF, TAM)
7. Joe Borchard (OF, CHW)
8. Wilson Betemit (SS, ATL)
9. Nick Neugebauer (RHP, MIL)
10. Mark Prior (RHP, CHC)

11. Nick Johnson (1B, NYY)
12. Drew Henson (3B, NYY)
13. Jacob Peavy (RHP, SD)
14. Juan Cruz (RHP, CHC)
15. Brandon Phillips (SS, MON)
16. Michael Cuddyer (3B/OF, MIN)
17. Mark Teixeira (3B, TEX)
18. Carl Crawford (OF, TAM)
19. Dennis Tankersley (RHP, SD)
20. Ryan Anderson (LHP, SEA)

21. Antonio Perez (SS, SEA)
22. Hee Seop Choi (1B, CHC)
23. Chris Snelling (OF, SEA)
24. Joe Crede (3B, CHW)
25. Jon Rauch (RHP, CHW)
26. Brett Myers (RHP, PHI)
27. Angel Berroa (SS, KC)
28. Brandon Claussen (LHP, NYY)
29. Kevin Mench (OF, TEX)
30. Shin-Soo Choo (OF, SEA)

31. Marlon Byrd (OF, PHI)
32. Joe Mauer (C, MIN)
33. Gabe Gross (OF, TOR)
34. Justin Morneau (1B, MIN)
35. Ty Howington (LHP, CIN)
36. Boof Bonser (RHP, SF)
37. Matt Belisle (RHP, ATL)
38. Kurt Ainsworth (RHP, SF)
39. Jerome Williams (RHP, SF)
40. Casey Kotchman (1B, ANA)

41. Miguel Cabrera (SS, FLA)
42. Adrian Gonzalez (1B, FLA)
43. Xavier Nady (1B, SD)
44. Sueng Song (RHP, BOS)
45. Chris Bootcheck (RHP, ANA)
46. Adam Johnson (RHP, MIN)
47. Ben Christianson (RHP, CHC)
48. Adam Wainwright (RHP, ATL)
49. Bobby Hill (2B/SS, CHC)
50. Brett Evert (RHP, ATL)

51. Kelly Johnson (SS, ATL)
52. Chin Feng Chen (OF, LA)
53. Brad Wilkerson (OF, MON)
54. Ryan Ludwick (OF, TEX)
55. Corwin Malone (LHP, CHW)
56. Alex Escobar (OF, CLE)
57. Rafael Soriano (RHP, SEA)
58. Tony Blanco (3B, BOS)
59. Jack Cust (OF, COL)
60. Eric Hinske (3B, TOR)

61. Carlos Hernandez (LHP, HOU)
62. Jeff Heaverlo (RHP, SEA)
63. Ryan Christiansen (C, SEA)
64. John Buck (C, HOU)
65. JR House (C/1B, PIT)
66. Jose Reyes (SS, NYM)
67. Jim Journall (RHP, STL)
68. Colby Lewis (RHP, TEX)
69. Carlos Zambrano (RHP, CHC)
70. Mark Phillips (LHP, SD)

71. Aaron Heilman (RHP, NYM)
72. Ben Broussard (1B, CIN)
73. Jason Romano (2B/OF, TEX)
74. Denny Bautista (RHP, FLA)
75. Abraham Nunez (OF, FLA)
76. Luis Montanez (SS, CHC)
77. Dewon Brazelton (RHP, TAM)
78. Rich Stahl (LHP, BAL)
79. Juan Pena (LHP, OAK)
80. Chris Burke (SS, HOU)

81. Ramon Santiago (SS, DET)
82. Wily Mo Pena (OF, CIN)
83. David Espinosa (SS, CIN)
84. Michael Restovich (OF, MIN)
85. Erik Bedard (LHP, BAL)
86. Deivi Mendez (SS, NYY)
87. David Kelton (3B, CHC)
88. Juan Rivera (OF, NYY)
89. Hong-Chih Kuo (LHP, LA)
90. John Patterson (RHP, ARI)

91. Chris Narveson (LHP, STL)
92. Ryan Dittfurth (RHP, TEX)
93. Jason Botts (OF/1B, TEX)
94. Eric Munson (1B, DET)
95. Jason Jennings (RHP, COL)
96. Nate Cornejo (RHP, DET)
97. Francisco Rodriguez (RHP, ANA)
98. Kenny Baugh (RHP, DET)
99. Chin-Hui Tsao (RHP, COL)
100. Roscoe Crosby (OF, KC)

GLOSSARY

AVG: Batting Average (see also BA)

BA: Batting Average (see also AVG)

Base Performance Indicator (BPI): A statistical formula that measures an isolated aspect of a player's situation-independent raw skill or a gauge that helps capture the effects of random chance has on a skill. Although there are many such formulas, there are only a few that we are referring to when the term is used in this book. For pitchers, our BPI's are control (bb%), dominance (k/9), command (k/bb), opposition on base average (OOB), ground/line/fly ratios (G/L/F), and expected ERA (xERA). Random chance is measured witih the hit rate (H%) and strand rate (S%).

Base Performance Value (BPV): A single value that describes a pitcher's overall raw skill level. This is more useful than any traditional statistical gauge to track performance trends and project future statistical output. The actual BPV formula combines and weights several BPI's:

(Dominance Rate x 6) + (Command ratio x 21) – Opposition HR Rate x 30) – ((Opp. Batting Average - .275) x 200)

The formula combines the individual raw skills of power, command, the ability to keep batters from reaching base, and the ability to prevent long hits, all characteristics that are unaffected by most external team factors. In tandem with a pitcher's strand rate, it provides a complete picture of the elements that contribute to a pitcher's ERA, and therefore serves as an accurate tool to project likely changes in ERA. **BENCHMARKS:** We generally consider a BPV of 50 to be the minimum level required for long-term success. The elite of bullpen aces will have BPV's in the excess of 100 and it is rare for these stoppers to enjoy long-term success with consistent levels under 75.

Batters Faced per Game *(Craig Wright)*

((IP x 2.82) + H + BB) / G

A measure of pitcher usage and one of the leading indicators for potential pitcher burnout.

Batting Average (BA, or AVG)

(H/AB)

Ratio of hits to at-bats, though it is a poor evaluative measure of hitting performance. It neglects the offensive value of the base on balls and assumes that all hits are created equal.

Batting Eye (Eye)

(Walks / Strikeouts)

A measure of a player's strike zone judgment, the raw ability to distinguish between balls and strikes. **BENCHMARKS:** The best hitters have eye ratios over 1.00 (indicating more walks than strikeouts) and are the most likely to be among a league's .300 hitters. At the other end of the scale are ratios less than 0.50, which represent batters who likely also have lower BA's.

bb%: Walk rate (hitters)

bb/9: Opposition Walks per 9 IP

BF/Gm: Batters Faced Per Game

BPI (Base Performance Indicator)

BPV (Base Performance Value)

Cmd: Command ratio

Command Ratio (Cmd)

(Strikeouts / Walks)

This is a measure of a pitcher's raw ability to get the ball over the plate. There is no more fundamental a skill than this, and so it is accurately used as a leading indicator to project future rises and falls in other gauges, such as ERA. Command is one of the best gauges to use to evaluate minor league performance. It is a prime component of a pitcher's base performance value. **BENCHMARKS:** Baseball's upper echelon of command pitchers will have ratios in excess of 3.0. Pitchers with ratios under 1.0 — indicating that they walk more batters than they strike out — have virtually no potential for long term success. If you make no other changes in your approach to drafting a pitching staff, limiting your focus to only pitchers with a command ratio of 2.0 or better will substantially improve your odds of success.

Contact Rate (ct%)

((AB - K) / AB)

Measures a batter's ability to get wood on the ball and hit it into the field of play. **BENCHMARK:** Those batters with the best contact skill will have levels of 90% or better. The hackers of society will have levels of 75% or less.

Control Rate (bb/9), or Opposition Walks per Game

BB Allowed x 9 / IP

Measures how many walks a pitcher allows per game equivalent. **BENCHMARK:** The best pitchers will have bb/9 levels of 3.0 or less.

Ct%: Contact rate

Ctl: Control Rate

Dom: Dominance Rate

Dominance Rate (k/9), or Opposition Strikeouts per Game

(K Allowed x 9 / IP)

Measures how many strikeouts a pitcher allows per game equivalent. **BENCHMARK:** The best pitchers will have k/9 levels of 6.0 or higher.

Expected Earned Run Average *(Gill and Reeve)*

(.575 x H [per 9 IP]) + (.94 x HR [per 9 IP]) + (.28 x BB [per 9 IP]) - (.01 x K [per 9 IP]) - Normalizing Factor

"xERA represents the expected ERA of the pitcher based on a normal distribution of his statistics. It is not influenced by situation-dependent factors." xERA erases the inequity between starters' and relievers' ERA's, eliminating the effect that a pitcher's success or failure has on another pitcher's ERA.

Similar to other gauges, the accuracy of this formula changes with the level of competition from one season to the next. The normalizing factor allows us to better approximate a pitcher's actual ERA. This value is usually somewhere around 2.77 and varies by league and year. **BENCHMARKS:** In general, xERA's should approximate a pitcher's ERA fairly closely. However, those pitchers who have large variances between the two gauges are candidates for further analysis.

Extra-Base Hit Rate (X/H)

(2B + 3B + HR)/Hits

X/H is a measure of power and can be used along with a player's slugging percentage and isolated power to gauge a player's ability to drive the ball. **BENCHMARKS:** Players with above average power will post X/H of greater than 38% and players with moderate power will post X/H of 30% or greater. Weak hitters with below aveage power will have a X/H level of less than 20%.

Eye: Batting Eye

H%: Hit rate (batters) or Hits Allowed per Balls in Play (pitchers)

Hit Rate (H%)

(H—HR) / (AB – HR - K)

The percent of balls hit into the field of play that fall for hits.

hr/9: Opposition Home Runs per 9 IP

ISO: Isolated Power

Isolated Power (ISO)

(Slugging Percentage-Batting Average)

Isolated Power is a measurement of power skill. Subtracting a player's BA from his SLG, we are essentially pulling out all the singles and single bases from the formula. What remains are the extra-base hits. ISO is not an absolute measurement as it assumes that two doubles is worth one home run, which certainly is not the case, but is another statistic that is a good measurement of raw power. **BENCHMARKS:** The game's top sluggers will tend to have ISO levels over .200. Weak hitters will be under .100.

k/9: Dominance rate (opposition strikeouts per 9 IP)

Major League Equivalency *(Bill James):* A formula that converts a player's minor or foreign league statistics into a comparable performance in the major leagues. These are not projections, but conversions of current performance. Contains adjustments for the level of play in individual leagues and teams, and the player's age as compared to that level. Works best with Triple-A stats, not quite as well with Double-A stats, and hardly at all with the lower levels. Foreign conversions are still a work in process. James' formula only addressed batting. Our research has devised conversion formulas for pitchers, however, their best use comes when looking at BPI's, not traditional stats.

MLE: Major League Equivalency

OBP: On Base Percentage (batters)

OBA: Opposition Batting Average (pitchers)

On Base Percentage (OBP)

(H + BB) / (AB + BB)

Addressing one of the two deficiencies in BA, OBP gives value to those events that get batters on base, but are not hits. By adding walks (and often, hit batsmen) into the basic batting average formula, we have a better gauge of a batter's ability to reach base safely. An OBP of .350 can be read as "this batter gets on base 35% of the time."

Why this is a more important gauge than batting average... When a run is scored, no distinction is made as to how that runner reached base. So, two thirds of the time — about how often a batter comes to the plate with the bases empty — a walk really is as good as a hit. **BENCHMARKS:** We all know what a .300 hitter is, but what represents "good" for OBP? That comparable level would likely be .400, with .275 representing the level of futility.

On Base Plus Slugging Percentage (OPS): A simple sum of the two gauges, it is considered as one of the better evaluators of overall performance. OPS combines the two basic elements of offensive production — the ability to get on base (OBP) and the ability to advance baserunners (SLG). **BENCHMARKS:** The game's top batters will have OPS levels over .900. The worst batters will have levels under .600.

Opposition Batting Average (OBA)

(Hits Allowed / ((IP x 2.82) + Hits Allowed))

A close approximation of the batting average achieved by opposing batters against a particular pitcher. **BENCHMARKS:** The converse of the benchmark for batters, the best pitchers will have levels under .250; the worst pitchers levels over .300.

Opposition Home Runs per Game (hr/9)

(HR Allowed x 9 / IP)

Measures how many home runs a pitcher allows per game equivalent. **BENCHMARK:** The best pitchers will have hr/9 levels of under 1.0.

Opposition On Base Average (OOB)

(Hits Allowed + BB) / ((IP x 2.82) + H + BB)

A close approximation of the on base average achieved by opposing batters against a particular pitcher. **BENCHMARK:** The best pitchers will have levels under .300; the worst pitchers levels over .375.

Opposition Strikeouts per Game: See Dominance Rate.

Opposition Walks per Game: See Control Rate.

OPS: On Base Plus Slugging Percentage

RC: Runs Created

RC/G: Runs Created Per Game

Runs Created *(Bill James)*

(H + BB - CS) x (Total bases + (.55 x SB)) / (AB + BB)

A formula that converts all offensive events into a total of runs scored. As calculated for individual teams, the result approximates a club's actual run total with great accuracy.

Runs Created Per Game *(Bill James)*

Runs Created / ((AB - H + CS) / 25.5)

RC expressed on a per-game basis might be considered the hypothetical ERA compiled against a particular batter. **BENCHMARKS:** Few players surpass the level of a 10.00 RC/G in any given season, but any level over 7.50 can still be considered very good. At the bottom are levels below 3.00.

S%: Strand Rate

Save: There are six events that need to occur in order for a pitcher to post a single save...

1. The starting pitcher and middle relievers must pitch well.

2. The offense must score enough runs.

3. It must be a reasonably close game.

4. The manager must choose to put the pitcher in for a save opportunity.

5. The pitcher must pitch well and hold the lead.

6. The manager must let him finish the game.

Of these six events, only one is within the control of the relief pitcher. As such, projecting saves for a reliever has little to do with skill and a lot to do with opportunity. However, pitchers with excellent skills sets may create opportunity for themselves.

Situation Independent: Describing a statistical gauge that measures performance apart from the context of team, ballpark, or other outside variables. Strikeouts and Walks, inasmuch as they are unaffected by the performance of a batter's surrounding team, are considered situation independent stats.

Conversely, RBI's are situation dependent because individual performance varies greatly by the performance of other batters on the team (you can't drive in runs if there is nobody on base). Similarly, pitching wins are as much a measure of the success of a pitcher as they are a measure of the success of the offense and defense performing behind that pitcher, and are therefore a poor measure of pitching performance alone.

Situation independent gauges are important for us to be able to separate a player's contribution to his team and isolate his performance so that we may judge it on its own merits.

SLG: Slugging Percentage

Slugging Percentage (SLG)

(Singles + (2 x Doubles) + (3 x Triples) + (4 x HR)) / AB

A measure of the total number of bases accumulated per at bat. It is a misnomer; it is not a true measure of a batter's slugging ability because it includes singles. SLG also assumes that each type of hit has proportionately increasing value (i.e. a double is twice as valuable as a single, etc.) which is not true. **BENCHMARKS**: The top batters will have levels over .500. The bottom batters will have levels under .300.

Strand Rate (S%)

(H + BB - ER) / (H + BB - HR)

Measures the percentage of allowed runners a pitcher strands, which incorporates both individual pitcher skill and bullpen effectiveness. **BENCHMARKS**: The most adept at stranding runners will have S% levels over 75%. Once a pitcher's S% starts dropping down below 65%, he's going to have problems with his ERA. Those pitchers with strand rates over 80% will have artificially low ERAs, which will be prone to relapse.

Strikeouts per Game: See Opposition Strikeouts per game.

Walks + Hits per Innings Pitched (WHIP): The number of baserunners a pitcher allows per inning. **BENCHMARKS:** Usually, a WHIP of under 1.20 is considered top level and over 1.50 is indicative of poor performance. Levels under 1.00 — allowing fewer runners than IP — represent extraordinary performance and are rarely maintained over time.

Walk rate (bb%)

(BB / (AB + BB))

A measure of a batter's eye and plate patience. **BENCHMARKS:** The best batters will have levels of over 10%. Those with the least plate patience will have levels of 5% or less.

Walks per Game: See Opposition Walks per Game.

WHIP: Walks + Hits per Innings Pitched

Wins: There are five events that need to occur in order for a pitcher to post a single win...

1. He must pitch well, allowing few runs.

2. The offense must score enough runs.

3. The defense must successfully field all batted balls.

4. The bullpen must hold the lead.

5. The manager must leave the pitcher in for 5 innings, and not remove him if the team is still behind.

X/H: Extra-base Hit Rate

xERA: Expected ERA

TEAM AFFILIATIONS

TEAM	ORG	LEAGUE	CLASS	TEAM	ORG	LEAGUE	CLASS
Aberdeen	BAL	New York-Penn League	A	GCL Mets	NYM	Gulf Coast League	Rk
Akron	CLE	Eastern League	AA	GCL Nationals	WAS	Gulf Coast League	Rk
Albuquerque	FLA	Pacific Coast League	AAA	GCL Phillies	PHI	Gulf Coast League	Rk
Altoona	PIT	Eastern League	AA	GCL Pirates	PIT	Gulf Coast League	Rk
Arkansas	LAA	Texas League	AA	GCL Red Sox	BOS	Gulf Coast League	Rk
Asheville	COL	South Atlantic League	A-	GCL Reds	CIN	Gulf Coast League	Rk
Auburn	TOR	New York-Penn League	A	GCL Tigers	DET	Gulf Coast League	Rk
Augusta	SF	South Atlantic League	A-	GCL Twins	MIN	Gulf Coast League	Rk
AZL Angles	LAA	Arizona League	Rk	GCL Yankees	NYY	Gulf Coast League	Rk
AZL Athletics	OAK	Arizona League	Rk	Hagerstown	WAS	South Atlantic League	A-
AZL Brewers	MIL	Arizona League	Rk	Harrisburg	WAS	Eastern League	AA
AZL Cubs	CHC	Arizona League	Rk	Helena	MIL	Pioneer League	Rk
AZL Giants	SF	Arizona League	Rk	Hickory	PIT	South Atlantic League	A-
AZL Mariners	SEA	Arizona League	Rk	High Desert	SEA	California League	A+
AZL Padres	SD	Arizona League	Rk	Hudson Valley	TAM	New York-Penn League	A
AZL Rangers	TEX	Arizona League	Rk	Huntsville	MIL	Southern League	AA
AZL Royals	KC	Arizona League	Rk	Idaho Falls	KC	Pioneer League	Rk
Bakersfield	TEX	California League	A+	Indianapolis	PIT	International League	AAA
Batavia	STL	New York-Penn League	A	Inland Empire	LAD	California League	A+
Beloit	MIN	Midwest League	A-	Iowa	CHC	Pacific Coast League	AAA
Billings	CIN	Pioneer League	Rk	Jamestown	FLA	New York-Penn League	A
Binghamton	NYM	Eastern League	AA	Jacksonville	LAD	Southern League	AA
Birmingham	CHW	Southern League	AA	Johnson City	STL	Appalachian League	Rk
Bluefield	BAL	Appalachian League	Rk	Jupiter	FLA	Florida State League	A+
Boise	CHC	Northwest League	A	Kane County	OAK	Midwest League	A-
Bowie	BAL	Eastern League	AA	Kannapolis	CHW	South Atlantic League	A-
Brevard County	MIL	Florida State League	A+	Kingsport	NYM	Appalachian League	Rk
Bristol	CHW	Appalachian League	Rk	Kinston	CLE	Carolina League	A+
Brooklyn	NYM	New York-Penn League	A	Lake County	CLE	South Atlantic League	A-
Buffalo	CLE	International League	AAA	Lake Elsinore	SD	California League	A+
Burlington	KC	Midwest League	A-	Lakeland	DET	Florida State League	A+
Burlington	CLE	Appalachian League	Rk	Lakewood	PHI	South Atlantic League	A-
Carolina	FLA	Southern League	AA	Lancaster	BOS	California League	A+
Casper	COL	Pioneer League	Rk	Lansing	TOR	Midwest League	A-
Cedar Rapids	LAA	Midwest League	A-	Las Vegas	LAD	Pacific Coast League	AAA
Charleston	NYY	South Atlantic League	A-	Lexington	HOU	South Atlantic League	A-
Charlotte	CHW	International League	AAA	Louisville	CIN	International League	AAA
Chattanooga	CIN	Southern League	AA	Lowell	BOS	New York-Penn League	A
Clearwater	PHI	Florida State League	A+	Lynchburg	PIT	Carolina League	A+
Clinton	TEX	Midwest League	A-	Mahoning Vall	CLE	New York-Penn League	A
Colorado Spgs	COL	Pacific Coast League	AAA	Memphis	STL	Pacific Coast League	AAA
Columbus, GA	TAM	South Atlantic League	A-	Midland	OAK	Texas League	AA
Columbus, OH	WAS	International League	AAA	Mississippi	ATL	Southern League	AA
Connecticut	SF	Eastern League	AA	Missoula	ARI	Pioneer League	Rk
Corpus Christi	HOU	Texas League	AA	Mobile	ARI	Southern League	AA
Danville	ATL	Appalachian League	Rk	Modesto	COL	California League	A+
Dayton	CIN	Midwest League	A-	Montgomery	TAM	Southern League	AA
Daytona	CHC	Florida State League	A+	Myrtle Beach	ATL	Carolina League	A+
Delmarva	BAL	South Atlantic League	A-	Nashville	MIL	Pacific Coast League	AAA
Dunedin	TOR	Florida State League	A+	New Britain	MIN	Eastern League	AA
Durham	TAM	International League	AAA	New Hampshire	TOR	Eastern League	AA
Elizabethton	MIN	Appalachian League	Rk	New Orleans	NYM	Pacific Coast League	AAA
Erie	DET	Eastern League	AA	Norfolk	BAL	International League	AAA
Eugene	SD	Northwest League	A	Ogden	LAD	Pioneer League	Rk
Everett	SEA	Northwest League	A	Oklahoma	TEX	Pacific Coast League	AAA
Frederick	BAL	Carolina League	A+	Omaha	KC	Pacific Coast League	AAA
Fresno	SF	Pacific Coast League	AAA	Oneonta	DET	New York-Penn League	A
Frisco	TEX	Texas League	AA	Orem	LAA	Pioneer League	Rk
Ft. Myers	MIN	Florida State League	A+	Ottawa	PHI	International League	AAA
Ft. Wayne	SD	Midwest League	A-	Palm Beach	STL	Florida State League	A+
Great Falls	CHW	Pioneer League	Rk	Pawtucket	BOS	International League	AAA
Greensboro	FLA	South Atlantic League	A-	Peoria	CHC	Midwest League	A-
Greeneville	HOU	Appalachian League	Rk	Portland, ME	BOS	Eastern League	AA
Greenville	BOS	South Atlantic League	A-	Portland, OR	SD	Pacific Coast League	AAA
GCL Braves	ATL	Gulf Coast League	Rk	Potomac	WAS	Carolina League	A+
GCL Dodgers	LAD	Gulf Coast League	Rk	Princeton	TAM	Appalachian League	Rk
GCL Indians	CLE	Gulf Coast League	Rk	Pulaski	TOR	Appalachian League	Rk
GCL Marlins	FLA	Gulf Coast League	Rk	Quad Cities	STL	Midwest League	A-

TEAM	ORG	LEAGUE	CLASS		LEAGUE	ABBREVIATION
Rancho					International League	IL
Cucamonga	LAA	California League	A+		Pacific Coast League	PCL
Reading	PHI	Eastern League	AA		Eastern League	EL
Richmond	ATL	International League	AAA		Southern League	SL
Rochester	MIN	International League	AAA		Texas League	TL
Rome	ATL	South Atlantic League	A-		California League	CAL
Round Rock	HOU	Pacific Coast League	AAA		Carolina League	CAR
Sacramento	OAK	Pacific Coast League	AAA		Florida State League	FSL
Salem	HOU	Carolina League	A+		Midwest League	MWL
Salem-Keizer	SF	Northwest League	A		South Atlantic League	SAL
Salt Lake	LAA	Pacific Coast League	AAA		New York-Penn League	NY-P
San Antonio	SD	Texas League	AA		Northwest League	NWL
San Jose	SF	California League	A+		Pioneer League	PIO
Sarasota	CIN	Florida State League	A+		Appalachian League	APPY
Savannah	NYM	South Atlantic League	A-		Arizona League	AZL
Scranton/					Gulf Coast League	GCL
Wilkes-Barre	NYY	International League	AAA			
South Bend	ARI	Midwest League	A-			
Southwest						
Michigan	TAM	Midwest League	A-			
Springfield	STL	Texas League	AA			
Spokane	TEX	Northwest League	A			
State College	PIT	New York-Penn League	A			
Staten Island	NYY	New York-Penn League	A			
St. Lucie	NYM	Florida State League	A+			
Stockton	OAK	California League	A+			
Syracuse	TOR	International League	AAA			
Tacoma	SEA	Pacific Coast League	AAA			
Tampa	NYY	Florida State League	A+			
Tennessee	CHC	Southern League	AA			
Toledo	DET	International League	AAA			
Trenton	NYY	Eastern League	AA			
Tri-City	HOU	New York-Penn League	A			
Tri-City	COL	Northwest League	A			
Tucson	ARI	Pacific Coast League	AAA			
Tulsa	COL	Texas League	AA			
Vancouver	OAK	Northwest League	A			
Vermont	WAS	New York-Penn League	A			
Vero Beach	TAM	Florida State League	A+			
Visalia	ARI	Midwest League	A-			
West Michigan	DET	Midwest League	A-			
W.Tennessee	SEA	Southern League	AA			
West Virginia	MIL	South Atlantic League	A-			
Wichita	KC	Texas League	AA			
Williamsport	PHI	New York-Penn League	A			
Wilmington	BOS	Carolina League	A+			
Winston-Salem	CHW	Carolina League	A+			
Wisconsin	SEA	Midwest League	A-			
Yakima	ARI	Northwest League	A			

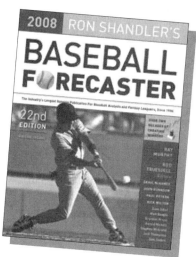